MASS CULTURE

MASS CULTURE

THE POPULAR ARTS IN AMERICA

EDITED BY *Bernard Rosenberg*

AND *David Manning White*

THE FREE PRESS
GLENCOE, ILLINOIS

&

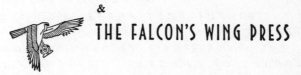 THE FALCON'S WING PRESS

Third Printing, 1958

COPYRIGHT 1957
BY THE FREE PRESS, A CORPORATION
PRINTED IN THE UNITED STATES OF AMERICA
DESIGNED BY SIDNEY SOLOMON
LIBRARY OF CONGRESS CATALOG CARD NO. 57-6749

Preface

THIS BOOK is the result of a need for such a collection which both editors personally experienced in trying to teach courses where no traditional source books were available. Although mass culture was destined to play a pervasive role in American social life from the moment the printing presses were turned by steam early in the nineteenth century, it is only in recent years that scholars have paid substantial attention to the interplay between the mass media and society.

The editors of this Reader come from different fields of academic learning. Yet although one has a background in literary history and journalism, while the other's major interests are in sociology and anthropology, both have a common concern about the cultural implications of the mass media. That we should represent, as it were, different disciplines is not in itself cause for surprise. For the mass media are being examined and analyzed in similar fashion by scholars in the humanities, English and American literature, American civilization, journalism, the communications arts of radio, television and cinema, as well as in sociology, psychology, economics and anthropology.

It seems to us that this area of study cuts across the artificial academic boundaries that so often serve as a barrier keeping scholars of like interests from speaking to each other. We hope that this Reader will be a step in the creation of an interdisciplinary focus on problems common to everyone who takes a serious interest in what is happening to this aspect of modern civilization. Although the book was compiled essentially for students of popular culture in university communities, we trust that it will be read by many other interested observers, particularly those within the media professions themselves.

The contributors include literary critics, social scientists, journalists and art critics, most of whose work in this area has been scattered in relatively inaccessible scholarly journals and the "little magazines." In this volume we have drawn together the insights of fifty-one observers commonly concerned with the social effects of the media on American life. It would be patently absurd on our part to claim that this book encapsulates all that might or should be said about mass culture. It will be discerned, however, that we have attempted to present the viewpoints of both those who look with optimism at the media and those who scrutinize them with great anxiety. It has not been our desire to prove any individual point of view the "right" one, but rather to examine the phenomena as fully as possible. That there have been far more excoriators of mass culture than defenders became readily apparent to us as we sought representative selections for both points of view.

(vi)

We wish to express our appreciation to many colleagues and other friends who helped us by their suggestions. To untwist a cliché, they bear considerable responsibility for the finished volume. Where we have disdained good advice regarding the inclusion of one author to the exclusion of another, the results (for good or ill) rest squarely on our shoulders.

This volume has no senior editor and junior editor; we are equally responsible for the book's contents, and have simply listed our names on the title page in alphabetical order. (The need for such an explanation reflects the power of mass culture in America, where even academic life is penetrated by the ethos of Hollywood's "star system.")

We owe a debt of long standing to two of our former professors, to whom in a large sense this volume is dedicated. They are Dr. Wilbur L. Schramm of Stanford University, whose contributions (both theoretical and substantive) to the field of mass communications study are many, and Dr. Ernest van den Haag, whose course at the New School for Social Research was one of the first systematic attempts to analyze the impact of what is variously called popular or mass culture.

Our sincere thanks again to the contributing authors, who not only graciously allowed us to reprint their work but in several cases revised their essays especially for this volume. To those who provided original papers to fill various lacunae in the available published material we are especially indebted. Dr. Arthur J. Brodbeck made valuable suggestions for the bibliography.

We are greatly obliged to Miss Elizabeth Merrylees, whose interest in the book provided her with the stamina to type a great many manuscripts, as well as to render skillful assistance in editing them. Without her help in co-ordinating a myriad of details the task of compiling this book would have been immeasurably more difficult. Mrs. Joan Bolen and Miss Elaine Elton also assisted in typing various portions of the manuscript.

To our wives, who gave sagacious words of encouragement at all stages of the venture and who cheerfully read page proofs, our grateful thanks.

Finally, we wish to state our gratitude to Ned Polsky and Jeremiah Kaplan of the Free Press, for their enthusiastic support of the idea underlying this book and their cogent suggestions throughout its compilation.

DAVID MANNING WHITE
BERNARD ROSENBERG

Boston University
City College of New York
August, 1956

CONTENTS

5. TELEVISION AND RADIO

6. DIVERTISSEMENT

7. ADVERTISING

8. THE OVERVIEW

1
The Issues Joined

Mass Culture in America

By BERNARD ROSENBERG

THE LATE MORRIS RAPHAEL COHEN, an extraordinarily gifted teacher, was perhaps best known in and out of the classroom as a superb critic of other philosophers. From time to time students would grumble about his negativism; Cohen tore down whole systems of philosophy without offering an alternative world-view of his own. On one such occasion he is said to have answered this charge as follows: "My first name is an Anglicization from the Hebrew for Moses, and like Moses, I can lead you through the wilderness without bringing you to the Promised Land." The editors of this anthology, whose subject matter is not the universe but only an increasingly significant part of it, feel much as Cohen must have felt when he found himself unable to formulate sweeping answers to every question. Mass culture is not only a wilderness—with oases here and there, to be sure—it is largely uncharted. Indeed, whole parts of it remain to be explored.

Moreover, at the end of this *terra incognita,* even if we wander over its surface for forty years, there may be no Promised Land. One can only have hunches—and of these there is a plethora. But any calculation of what lies before us is premature, especially if it proceeds by extrapolating the imperfectly understood situation that we face today. Our purpose in assembling this formidable selection of readings is rather to present the reader with a guide through what is now known, or thought to be known, about extremely problematic matters. Mass culture has reached into the Academy both by its pervasive influence and as a subject of serious study. The former, with such spectacular phenomena as audio-visual education, has been more striking than the latter. But, gradually, academicians and detached intellectuals are being drawn into the vortex by a suction force none can resist. They are beginning to ask themselves whether the quality of life has not been decisively altered by mass-circulation magazines, "comic" books, detective fiction, movies, radio, television—with all their meretricious and/or meritorious accompaniments.

Some thoughtful persons are pleased with machine civilization; many more are alarmed by its destructive force. We wish to suggest that this basic division—those who applaud and those who wring their hands over our technological apparatus—explains why there is such a range of differences in the assessment of mass culture. It tells even more than political position, which is also a fairly reliable index. The political lines that have crystallized are approximately these: radicals (Dwight Macdonald, Clement Greenberg, Irving Howe) who, like the arch-conservatives (Ortega y Gasset, T. S. Eliot, Bernard Iddings Bell), although for opposite reasons, are repelled by what they commonly regard as vulgar and exploitative, and the liberals

(Gilbert Seldes, David Riesman, Max Lerner) who take a predictable position in the middle. The parallel between left, right, and center in politics
and in the "popular arts" is virtually perfect.

Why, then, something still more fundamental? Because, in the mid-
twentieth century, political stances and cultural choices are part of a
much larger whole. In none of the archeological ages has human society
been so thoroughly revolutionary as at present. Consider that man, for the
million years since his origin as a distinct species, has had to struggle like
every other beast (and like the postgraduate ape he was) for the means
of subsistence. Only now, with mechanized agriculture, artificial photosyn-
thesis, use of algae and other foods from the sea, is it possible to speak of
a *well-fed* world population much larger than ours. That everyone could
enjoy an adequate diet, with relatively little physical exertion to secure it,
would have been unimaginable in any earlier age.

As Toynbee's Great West Wind blows all over the world, which quickly
gets urbanized and industrialized, as the birth rate declines and the population soars, a certain sameness develops everywhere. Clement Greenberg
can meaningfully speak of a universal mass culture (surely something new
under the sun) which unites a resident of Johannesburg with his neighbors
in San Juan, Hong Kong, Moscow, Paris, Bogota, Sydney and New York.
African aborigines, such as those recently described by Richard Wright,
leap out of their primitive past—straight into the movie house where, it is
feared, they may be mesmerized like the rest of us. First besieged with
commodities, postmodern man himself becomes an interchangeable part in
the whole cultural process. When he is momentarily freed from his own
kitsch, the Soviet citizen seems to be as titillated as his American counterpart by Tin Pan Alley's products. In our time, the basis for an international
sodality of man at his lowest level, as some would say, appears to have
been formed.

All this comes at a time when the species' dependence upon nature for
a steady food supply has virtually disappeared. Simultaneously, the curse
of Adam is being lifted. Frank Lloyd Wright half seriously suggests that
we will soon develop a paralysis of all our limbs except the pushbutton
finger by whose sweat, rather than the brow's, man may soon live. Utopian
philosophers used to speculate about who, in their good society, would do
the dirty work. That *someone* had to do it was as clearly an immutable fact
as the mortality of man. Now our answer, with imminent automation, and
not for the world of fancy but for that of reality, is, "Nobody." Manual
labor is becoming obsolete.

We can do no more than assimilate a fragment of the change before
it leads to another innovation whose significance is likewise imponderable.
Of this much one can be certain beforehand: no IBM machine, nor yet a
Univac, will tell us whether the latest development is for good or ill. Ambiguity is its key characteristic. If men are freed from manual labor and from

the struggle with nature, what will they do? Cultivate their minds? Improve their sensibilities? Heighten their understanding? Deepen and broaden themselves? Possibly. The precondition for transfiguring *Homo sapiens* into a higher species begins to exist. When our physical environment has been subdued we may become hypersentient beings. Drudgery, monotony, inanition and brutishness can then be dispelled along with the animal existence we used to lead.

That such a step in human evolution could take place is what makes the likelihood so much more tragic. Before man can transcend himself he is being dehumanized. Before he can elevate his mind, it is being deadened. Freedom is placed before him and snatched away. The rich and varied life he might lead is standardized. This breeds anxiety, and the vicious circle begins anew, for as we are objects of manipulation, our anxiety is exploitable. The mass grows; we are more alike than ever; and feel a deeper sense of entrapment and loneliness. And even if the incubus of hydrogen war could be lifted, these specters would still hover over us.

In short, the postmodern world offers man everything or nothing. Any rational consideration of the probabilities leads to a fear that he will be overtaken by the social furies that already beset him.

There can be no doubt that the mass media present a major threat to man's autonomy. To know that they might also contain some small seeds of freedom only makes a bad situation nearly desperate. No art form, no body of knowledge, no system of ethics is strong enough to withstand vulgarization. A kind of cultural alchemy transforms them all into the same soft currency. Never before have the sacred and the profane, the genuine and the specious, the exalted and the debased, been so thoroughly mixed that they are all but indistinguishable. Who can sort one from the other when they are built into a single slushy compost? Is there anything beyond a debased remnant of theology *or* of psychiatry left in the mind that has been encased in "peace" and whose soul has been similarly laid to rest? But what Norman Vincent Peale, Joshua Liebman and Bishop Sheen do for religion is qualitatively no different from what a horde of popularizers do in absolutely every domain. Nothing remains untouched.

Ernest van den Haag has suggested that there are two assumptions underlying all mass culture: (1) everything is understandable, and (2) everything is remediable. We might add a corollary to the first assumption: "Everything had better be made understandable." The more arcane a subject the less effort it should require for easy absorption. If education and cultivation are gradual, progressive, orderly processes, then popular education is its opposite. For what makes mass culture so tantalizing is the implication of effortlessness. Shakespeare is dumped on the market along with Mickey Spillane, and publishers are rightly confident that their audience will not feel obliged to make any greater preparation for the master of world literature than for its latest lickspittle.

II

This general phenomenon, although it frightens some and leaves others relatively undisturbed, has seldom been placed at the center of our attention. Now and then an important nineteenth-century figure such as Nietzsche or Tocqueville would express some sense of what lay in store for us. However, it remained for a novelist, Gustave Flaubert, to set the case before his readers in boldest outline. If this were a two-volume selection of readings on mass culture, *Madame Bovary,* saved from the vultures of condensation, would have to be presented in its entirety as a prolegomenon to the understanding of our subject. For Emma and her husband did not simply spring out of Flaubert's mind; they also sprang out of his times. And his times, as he understood them, were a prefiguration of our own.

As they are revealed to us in the novel, Emma's husband, Charles, suffers from an underdeveloped imagination, Emma from an overheated imagination, and neither of them was born or predestined to be that way. Charles is the familiar type of professional man who scarcely "has time to keep up with his medical journals." He has been given a narrow occupational training, and while this vehicle of his social ascent detaches him from the folk, it does not awaken his sensibilities. Charles, like his father, holds culture in small esteem. It cannot be otherwise: this is what his "embourgeoisement" means.

Emma's origins are as humble as her husband's. Her life slides off-center for the same reason, i.e., external forces impinge upon it, as they were soon to impinge upon and engulf the whole Western world. Charles goes to medical school and Emma to finishing school. Charles learns his lessons but remains otherwise unresponsive. Emma, to her mother-in-law's horror, studies dancing, geography, drawing, embroidery and the piano. With sovereign skill Flaubert spells out for us how Emma's mind was debauched, how her emotions were inflamed.

"For six months, Emma, when she was fifteen, battened on the garbage of those out of date 'Libraries of Choice Fiction.' Later on she came to read Walter Scott [This is a prime target of Flaubert's. Still later Emma is thrown into raptures at a production of *Lucie de Lammermoor* which she witnesses with husband and lover.] and got enthusiastic about historical things, forever dreaming of coffers, guardrooms and minstrels." Again, "In the music class, the songs she had to learn were all about little angels with golden pinions, madonnas, lagoons, gondoliers, compositions in which silly words and shoddy music could not conceal the attractive phantasmagoria of their sentimental substratum."

This is the stuff out of which Flaubert forms Emma's character; without it there is no adequate motivation for the behavior he wishes to describe. More, that background, rather than, or set in relief from, the rural milieu, lends a powerful element of inevitability to the drama. Emma, the little villager with her psyche on fire goes quixotically in search of the joy, passion, and intoxication "which had looked so fine to her in books." These are the first drippings of an osmotic process that has only in our day come into its own as full-blown mass culture. Once bathed in them and their deliquescent values, Emma can only be bored to death. She must seek satisfaction in adultery, and failing, seek it again. Any worldly man on the make can have her. She has learned what our mentors in Hollywood now teach us with even greater proficiency, namely, that love is something which

must come suddenly with a great display of thunder and lightning, descending on one's life like a tempest from above, turning it topsy-turvy, whirling away one's resolutions like leaves and bearing one onward, heart and soul toward the abyss.

Denis de Rougemont, a historian of romantic love, while tracing its medieval lineage, finds the aberration, as Flaubert did, a particularly virulent one in our day. The romantic complex thrives on inaccessibility in any prototypic representation of the past. Thus Tristan and Iseult or Romeo and Juliet. Consummation, prompted by boredom, brings more of the same in its wake. Emma might have been able to endure her lot if she had only flirted with Léon or merely dreamed of sleeping with Rodolphe. Wish fulfillment intensifies the original discomfort and renders it incurable. Illusions cannot persist when faced with the reality test of actual contact, and as they crumble there is nothing left to sustain their victim. Hence, one lover is discarded for another around whom the same false aura is soon spun. Emma, who could even romanticize Charles—from a distance—is still better at this game with Léon and Rodolphe, only to have each spell broken by prolonged *contact de deux épidermes*.

And in such a crisis, what does the deracinated woman do? "By moonlight in the garden she recited all the love poetry she knew and sighed and sang of love's sweet melancholy. But afterwards she found herself not a whit more calm, and Charles not a whit more amorous or emotional."

Nothing goes more directly to the core of mass culture than this. Any indictment of sleazy fiction, trashy films, and bathetic soap operas, in all their maddening forms, must come to rest finally on Flaubert's prescient insight. Far from dispelling unrest, all the (admittedly slim) evidence now on hand suggests that mass culture exacerbates it. Once understood, this fact cuts the ground from under those who justify organized distraction by claiming that it satisfies a fundamental need. Dwight Macdonald comes much closer to the point when he says that it *exploits* that need.

Contemporary man commonly finds that his life has been emptied of meaning, that it has been trivialized. He is alienated from his past, from his work, from his community, and possibly from himself—although this "self" is hard to locate. At the same time he has an unprecedented amount of time on his hands which, as van den Haag has pointed out, he must kill lest it kill him. Society abhors a vacuum, and quickly fills this one with diversion. Brutes and mimes achieve an apotheosis in these secular surroundings that they seldom enjoyed even in the late Roman Empire which, after all, had its more ethereal gods. All this is accepted—and celebrated by a certain percentage of the intelligentsia not altogether unrepresented in our anthology—as a highly desirable kind of public stupefaction. It is widely assumed that the anxiety generated by industrial civilization can be allayed, as the nerves are narcotized, by "historical" novels, radio or television programs, and all the other ooze of our mass media.

It is to be expected that someone will discover hidden virtue in the kind of pin-up magazine catalogued by Goeffrey Wagner, a collector of cultural curiosa. The titles tell us enough: *Cover Girls, Paris Models, Whirl, Laff, Keyhole, Zip, Wham, Stag, Brief, Bare, Eye, Rave, Wink, Titter, Eyeful, Flirt,* etc., etc. Harold Orlans writes, as a contributor to *Dissent* in the winter of 1954, of a situation that has since worsened:

> The postwar flood of pornography shows no signs of abating and, for once, it seems, the dim congressmen, stern churchmen, and stiff-laced ladies are complaining about something real and reckonable. . . . Its recent invasion of the public domain is unmistakable. The most obvious sign is that the two-bit monthlies "glorifying the American girl" which used to be confined to the newsstands around the tracks now overflow the back shelves of the racks in neighborhood drug and candy stores. Six years ago they could not be bought in a dry Southern village, although they were imported from the nearby city to the barber shop, poolroom, and bar. Today they will be found on all the newsstands in a quiet Quaker town—or they were there until a mother, the local editor, and several ministers pounced upon the hapless police chief. They will be back again the day after tomorrow. The magazines are all the same: bosoms and butts, high heels, opera hose, leopard skins, manacles, whips and wrestling ladies. In the back pages, ads for "art photos" sent in plain envelopes via railway express. Was it for this that Peter Zenger stood trial? . . . The bomb is not getting smaller. We have bread. (When do our children die?) On with the circus!

So frightful a juxtaposition of words as "war comics" and "horror comics" may be found in our new lexicon. There is a genre of popular literature—without the written word—that specializes in the representation of lesbians dressed in riding attire with spurs and whips, mercilessly flogging their victims. Yet none of this strikes such terror in the heart as an advertisement Wagner reports having seen for the past few years in *U. S. Camera* side by side with an offer of lewd photographs. This one announces sets of Nazi German atrocity pictures at thirty for two dollars.

Sometimes it seems as if we are overtaking and passing 1984, all unawares. The total obliteration of our privacy is, if not an accomplished fact, one technically easy to accomplish. Here is an illustrative item from *Newsweek* magazine, October 24, 1955:

> The Calbest Engineering and Electronics Co. announced that by the end of the year it would have perfected a cheatproof device for polling television without the set owners' cooperation or knowledge. Called the "Poll-o-meter," it is a compact portable unit with a directional antenna fitted at the end of a gun-type barrel. The operator drives down a residential street, aims his gadget at

passing TV aerials, and pulls a trigger. A sensitive electronic detector picks up each station's characteristic frequency signal and automatically records it.

At its worst, mass culture threatens not merely to cretinize our taste, but to brutalize our senses while paving the way to totalitarianism. And the interlocking media all conspire to that end. Wagner: "So Chop-Chop exclaims, as he wrenches a commie's head off in a *Blackhawk* [comic] book, 'Me study wrestling from television set.' "

But Emma Bovary resorts to the garbage on which she had battened as a girl and feels not a whit more calm—and neither do the rest of us when we follow her example. One feels bad because his life seems to be pointless; he is invited to divert himself, and gladly accepts, only to feel still worse afterwards.

Apart from its ghastliness, which is a matter of taste, mass culture must be indicted for this failure. In an anxious age mass culture builds the tension that it is usually credited with relieving. Meanwhile the electronic wonderworld and the rulers thereof, with a large number of collaborators from every entertainment industry, manage to debar the mass man they have created from any really satisfying experience. A genuine esthetic (or religious or love) experience becomes difficult, if not impossible, whenever *kitsch* pervades the atmosphere. And only the genuine experience, as Flaubert realized, can satisfy us. It presupposes effortful participation. In the arts this may mean no more than a willing suspension of disbelief, an *act* of the imagination which projects the reader or the audience into a state of empathy from which man's fate can be viewed with great understanding. Not everyone can achieve such a state today, and it will be argued that for those who cannot, experiences at a lower level may suffice. But surely those who know there are greater delectations than cultural pap and gruel, which cannot be concocted or appreciated without working at them, should say so.

All this applies with equal force to the pursuit of knowledge. Quite often the most "popular" teachers in our universities are those who simplify their material, make it look simple, and thereby foster the illusion that a challenging body of knowledge can be easily assimilated. This is catch-phrase pedagogy: Plato was an Idealist, Aristotle a Realist, Kant a Dialectician. All you need is a label, and every field has its Will Durant who will retail it for you. No discipline, however exacting, is insusceptible to this treatment. So, though we never really come to grips with philosophy this way, the dangerous belief that we have fully embraced it nevertheless persists. A true teacher will say, "No, there is so much more within your reach—only you must stretch yourself to find it." Such an attitude is frequently dismissed as snobbery, an egghead affectation, an expression of contempt for the ordinary man. It may be just the opposite, if we say to the *l'homme moyen sensuel,* "Here is what many of you could do. Why settle for so much less? What you consume now may please you for the moment; sub-art and pseudo-knowledge is shoveled down your open mouth; in another moment it will

leave you ravenous and restless once again." As *kitsch* is institutionalized
and we are robbed of our spontaneity, the likelihood of satisfaction, of
tension followed by distension, gets to be more and more remote. Culturally,
we become hungrier than ever—and our diet, though habit-forming, contains
less nourishment than ever.

Success is still the bitch-goddess of American society. The purveyors of
mass culture allege that it too can be achieved by passive absorption. Simple
rules are set forth in every sphere of activity. This is the significance of
what Dwight Macdonald has called "how-to-ism." Surely any of our ancestors would have been bewildered by the library of contemporary books
devoted to telling people how they should consummate the sex act—
successfully. The *New York Times Magazine* (January 22, 1956) runs a
large advertisement for The Salesmen's Book Club of Englewood Cliffs,
New Jersey. The club offers trial members a book for 99 cents ("Take
This $4.95 Value") called *The Power of Creative Selling* by Earl Prevette
which will do the following things for salesmen who read it attentively. It
will tell you:

How to plant YOUR ideas in the prospect's mind.
How to gain the complete attention and interest of every prospect.
How to anticipate your prospect's questions.
How to look behind a prospect's questions.
How to look behind an objection and learn what the prospect is really trying to
    tell you.
How to use the Law of Repetition.
How to use the Law of Averages.
How to use the Rule of Adaptation.
How to turn your "hunches" into sales—why your instinct is often wiser than
    your judgment.
How to use "key words" that move your prospect's mind toward a decision to buy.
How to train your imagination to originate a new selling idea, or improve an
    old one.
How to draw upon an "inner power" to make sales.

All for ninety-nine cents. Here the wedding with Marshall McLuhan's
Mechanical Bride is complete. Advertising officiates at the ceremonies, while
human engineers, sociologists, public relations executives, and psychologists
provide incidental trappings. C. Wright Mills has said that we are all, in
some sense, salesmen, and America is an enormous salesroom devoted to
the fetishism of commodities. (See *White Collar.*) Some of us are ad-
monished to join the ranks of full-fledged manipulators and achieve success in battering what remains of the American consciousness.

In 1934 three sociologists, George Lundberg, Mirra Komarovsky, and
Mary Alice McInerny reported the results of a valuable pioneer study in
their book, *Leisure.* It was already obvious to them that, "There are, un-
happily, many reasons why mere freedom from vigorous physical toil and
long hours of labor will not in itself insure men against heavy and unhappy
lives." They used a few random illustrations which have a figurative, as well

as a literal, significance: the enforced leisure of the physically handicapped, the blind, the deaf and the convalescent who are usually wretched in their idleness although they may not have economic worries; prisoners whose misery is increased by light work or no work; and millions of the unemployed who find "leisure more burdensome than work ever was"; the many people who "retire" in good health, and find only a debilitating vacuum to replace the old occupation. The authors remind us of Mahatma Ghandi's fear that modern machinery would leave India's millions with "too much leisure."

Twenty-five years ago, Professor L. P. Jacks asked the key (rhetorical) question about people with unprecedented leisure on their hands.

Will they take as the model for their leisure the sort of life now most favored by the "idle rich" and get as much of that sort of thing as their means enable them to procure—display, luxurious feeding, sex excitement, gambling, bridge, golf, globe-trotting and the rest? Or will they spend it in the way the idle poor—by whom I mean the unemployed—are now spending the leisure forced on them by the industrial crisis, which consists for the most part in just stagnating, physically, mentally and morally? Or will it be a mixture of the two— stagnation relieved by whatever doses of external excitement people may have the cash to purchase?

What "they" or "we" will do remains an open question, but one that seems to many of us, and to the majority of "highbrows" represented in this reader, to be closing very rapidly. Maybe not. Any judgment based upon necessarily faulty and partial perception can have only a limited validity. However, a few things do appear to be clear. For instance:

It is necessary to take as holistic a view as possible. No effort to comprehend and evaluate mass culture can start anywhere else than in a large sociocultural context. From such a standpoint we may clear the air of certain obviously erroneous assumptions:

1. *Capitalism is responsible for mass culture.* Not at all. It flourishes wherever the appropriate technological apparatus emerges, whether slowly or suddenly, and nowhere more so than in Soviet Russia which, whatever else it is, cannot be considered capitalist. A strong case could be made for pinpointing the most malignant features of mass culture where music, art, and ideas are publicly expressed only if they conform with a dictator's infantile conception of music, art, and ideas. In this realm, capitalist America has lost its leadership to the communist world. We are no longer the pacesetters. The view that we are is parochial. A cross-mass-cultural survey would dispel it.

2. *America is responsible for mass culture.* Hardly, and for the same reasons. There is nothing in our national character that makes us peculiarly vulnerable to a condition that is sweeping the earth.

3. *Democracy is responsible for mass culture.* Tocqueville was perhaps the first to make this common mistake. It was shared by democrats who thought that vulgarity through leveling was the price that had to be paid

for an otherwise beneficial system, and antidemocrats who thought the price too high.

If one can hazard a single positive formulation (in the form of a hypothesis) it would be that modern technology is the necessary and sufficient cause of mass culture. Neither national character nor the economic arrangement nor the political system has any final bearing on this question. All that really matters is the most recent industrial revolution.

The tentative technological determinism implicit in this formulation may be valid only for the present. *Today,* wherever modern tools are introduced and superimposed on any culture, the mixture seems to be deadly. Differences between backward and advanced countries become attenuated. They meet at the same low level. Maybe at a higher stage of development, society will be "ready" for industrialization, with consequences very different from those we see all around us in the here and now. Meanwhile, change, followed by barbarous accommodation proceeds at an accelerated tempo.

Mass Culture in America: Another Point of View

By DAVID MANNING WHITE

A NOTED COMMENTATOR was speaking. His intent audience nodded their heads in assent as he made one point after another that struck home. "Our youth," he said, "now love luxury. They have bad manners, contempt for authority. They show disrespect for elders and love chatter in place of exercise. They contradict their parents, chatter before company, gobble up their food and tyrannize their teachers."

The impassioned speaker was not a Dr. Wertham frightening the wits out of the Parent-Teachers Association of Scarsdale with his oversimplified message that comic books are turning American children into psychological cripples.[1] Although the speaker's words were as timely as many of the criticisms of mass culture in America, he had never visited this country. In fact he had never left his native Greece. For our speaker, as you now may have guessed, was Socrates, and the period was the Fifth Century, B.C.

The critics of mass culture take an exceedingly dim view of contemporary American society. If they do not exactly see Orwell's Big Brother glaring at them through their television screens it is only a matter of time. Besides, they reason, no individual who has inner resources would ever want to look at television.

Mass-circulation magazines, cinema, radio, television, *et al.,* are indeed pervasive influences in our American cultural life. But let us examine whether the castigators of mass culture are justified in their shrill pronunciamentos which damn the mass media as all black. Is it not true that the culture-Cassandras always catalogue the worst examples of the mass media's efforts and consequently generalize that Doomsday is surely near, otherwise how could the mass of people ingest such *kitsch* and be deluded into thinking it nourishment?

Such reasoning implies that if it weren't for these new devils, the media, the level of our artistic life would be high indeed. Our artists would not be tempted into debasing themselves in the fleshpots of Hollywood, Radio City, or the lesser talent mills. Without the gleam of gold blinding him, every writer who dissipates his genius writing banal slop for the soap operas and slick magazines could fulfill his destiny of becoming another Dostoevski. Without the mechanical bride of the media to narcotize them, the great majority of Americans could develop their artistic sensibilities to a point that would make the Renaissance seem insignificant by comparison. In the recuperative, selective memories of such critics, other countries and other ages are always remembered in a way that makes art and life synonymous.[2]

This line of reasoning seems to beg the question of history. There never

This essay is an expanded version of "What's Happening to Mass Culture?" originally published in *Saturday Review,* Vol. 39 (1956), pp. 11-13. Reprinted by permission of the publisher. (Copyright, 1956, by Saturday Review, Inc.)

was a country in which the great thoughts of mankind, the noblest works of art, literature and music were accepted by all segments of the population. Is it realistic to posit that the general level of culture—even in that cradle of culture, Europe—was so far advanced in the sixteenth or eighteenth centuries over our current American pattern? Would Brueghel's merry peasants even have been allowed to see their portrayed selves in the museums (non-existent), and, more important, would they have had the slightest desire to?

The xenophilic critics who discuss American culture as if they were holding a dead vermin in their hands seem to imply that in some other, better age the bulk of people were fair copies of Leonardo Da Vinci. No critic shudders more audibly when discussing the vulgarities of American life than T. S. Eliot. Yet it is only realistic to note that in the England which became Eliot's haven one of the most popular of diversions for nearly 700 years was bear-baiting. I do not cite this to demean the contributions to our world culture of a Chaucer, a Reynolds, a Thomas Tallis, or any English artist who added to the world's treasury, but only to draw the point that art was no more important to the mass of the people of their day than the goings-on at Paris Garden in Southwerk, the chief bear-garden in London.

When the Londoners got tired of seeing chained bears torn to pieces by the dogs they had other diversions. A nobleman of Elizabeth's Golden Age went to see a pony baited that had an ape tied to its back. As he so graphically put it, "to see the animal kicking amongst the dogs, with the screaming of the age, beholding the curs hanging from the ears and neck of the pony, is very laughable." We are told that good Queen Bess herself was not averse to the sport and that for a special baiting she attended in 1575 no less than thirteen bears were provided.

Apparently Sunday was the favorite day for this pastime, which Parliament finally outlawed in 1835. Yet, I daresay, most of the critics who develop such a frenzy over the stereotyped activity of the Lone Ranger as he shoots a couple of bad hombres on a Sunday's afternoon do not care to remember the sadistic pastimes at all the Paris Gardens of the past.

For my own part, although I deplore the pathological quality of some of the comic books (indeed a phenomena of our time), I cannot recall any that surpass the sight of half a dozen men armed with whips surrounding a blind bear and whipping him until they drew blood. How the crowd must have roared out its approval as the bear defended himself, striking the whips out of the hands of his tormentors, perhaps even clawing the men themselves. It is such remembrance of things past that leads me to take *cum grano salis* the bitter recriminations of our critics of mass culture.

There can be no defense (either on esthetic or moral grounds) for certain aspects of our mass culture which are banal, dehumanizing and downright ugly, both in form and content. Yet if we understand that every period of civilization has had its share of men who preyed upon the ignorance and insecurities of the largest part of the populace, we need not be so shocked that such men exist today.[3] The same Rome that found a Juvenal proclaiming *Mens sana in corpore sano* could also watch an Emperor Trajan celebrate his victory over Decebalus of Dacia in 106 A.D. with no fewer than 5,000 pairs of gladiators matched to the death. And this in the name of amusement!

II

Is it really true that the media have transformed the greatest part of the American population into this nebulous "mass mind" one reads about so often? Do the media contrive with all their cunning, Madison Avenue, grey-flanneled wit to keep Mencken's *booboisie* on the thirteen-year-old level? Many serious and earnest critics of the American scene imply this is so. In his book, *The Power Elite,* the noted sociologist C. Wright Mills decries what appears to him our inevitable trend to a mass society for which the mass media must be held to account. At the end of this road, on which we are travelling so precariously, Mills sees totalitarianism, as in Nazi Germany.

But, was the Germany of 1932 a "mass society" when it *voted* Hitler's party into power? To be sure, a dictator will grasp to his own use whatever mass media are available, but this is not the same as saying the mass media so weakened the people of Germany that they were helpless puppets in the hands of Goebbels.[4] This is the country which had more symphony orchestras per capita, published more books, pioneered and developed a cinema industry whose productions were of first quality, etc. From the eighteenth century its lead in the world of music had never been challenged—from Bach through titanic Beethoven to the serene Brahms. In its vaunted gymnasia what German youth could not cite or recite innumerable portions of such giants of the literary world as Goethe, Schiller or Lessing? Yet with all this great cultural buttress its best seller of all time was *Mein Kampf,* with its 10 million copies.

I am not suggesting that Hitlerism with its psychotic misanthropy was in any sense correlated with the high level of German culture. But is this any more illogical than the arguments of those who see us heading directly for an Orwellian 1984 (or worse) because of our mass media?

There was nothing to preclude an Ilse Koch from listening to the 2nd Brandenburg Concerto on her gramophone (as Eliot so nicely puts it, "When lovely woman stoops to folly. . . .") while she practiced her hobby of tanning the human skin of some unfortunate Jew who was placed in Belsen. We are told that she made lamp shades from some of the skins, or perhaps book covers to rebind her collected works of Nietzsche. The thread of psyche that spread between Attila and Adolf apparently was not weakened *or* strengthened by the cultural growth of the German people. Misanthropy and race hatred can be the common heritage of a musical genius like Wagner and a political demagogue like Senator Bilbo. No one could applaud the exquisite work of the Ballet at the Bolshoi Theater louder and longer than Comrade Stalin, but his appreciation of the arts did not stand in the way of the most utter ruthlessness. To equate sane and beneficent government with *haut culture* is to open a magic casement upon a scene that has no real basis in man's experience.

III

To imply that there is some kind of mysterious compact on the part of the executives of our television networks, large book publishers, cinema studios, *et al.,* to mongrelize the sensibilities of the mass of Americans, is not only a canard but logically untrue. Admittedly, the media are Big Business, and they must show profits at the end of the fiscal year in order to stay in business. Yet the facts are in plain view that on March 11, 1956, the National Broadcasting Company invested $500,000 to present a three-hour-long première of Sir Laurence Olivier's *Richard III.* This production, which drama critics have extolled in highest terms, was viewed by the largest daytime audience in television's history. Trendex surveys indicated that more than 50 million people watched some part of what is surely not one of Shakespeare's better-known plays. Conservative estimates place the number of viewers who stayed with the intrigues of the last of the Plantagenets throughout the three plot-laden hours at 20 to 25 million. The reassuring success of the venture will probably encourage the network to offer more entertainment of this caliber.

Television is capable of contributing its share to the best in our popular arts, as seen clearly in the Academy-Award-winning movie, *Marty,* originally a television play. That its author, Paddy Chayevsky, should go from television to the legitimate theater of New York, where his successful drama was staged by Joshua Logan, is but another example of the mobility of an artist who has something worth-while to say, no matter the medium.

Surely there is a great deal that is mediocre, repetitious and patronizing in television, or the movies. Yet in closing their eyes to the significant contributions of the mass media, the detractors encourage the very banality they purport to despise. For example, it is not difficult for them to look down their noses at the phenomenally successful *Life,* with its emphasis on photo-journalism. But not to take heed when *Life* presents a superb series, such as *The World We Live In,* or when it gives its several million readers the initial publication of Hemingway's *Old Man and The Sea,* is to invite the media to lose respect for the good things they themselves try to do. To lionize Tennessee Williams when the *Rose Tattoo* is available to the relatively few who attend its stage presentations but ignore it when he writes the same story into a movie of rich comic force, is to invite the cinema industry to cater to the lowest elements within itself rather than the best.

In the grim Orwellian world of 1984 which the critics of the mass society prophesy for us (if we continue to opiate ourselves with the mass media) there will be little reading done. By then we shall have gone through 3-D television, smellevision and on to Huxley's feelevision. Yet an interested party on the side of good reading, Bennett Cerf, the publisher of Random House, recently had this to say:

Television apparently has not been the destructive ogre that publishers feared so short a time ago. But then publishers always have been expecting *something* to end the practice of reading in America. Fifty years ago, believe it or not, a publisher seriously announced that so many devil-may-care citizens were risking life and limb on *interurban trolley cars* that they had no more time to peruse a book! Then came the menace of the tandem bicycle, followed in turn, by cheap automobiles, the movies, and radio. The fact is, of course, that nothing can replace a really good book.

Very well, the book publishing business has never had a better year than 1955, but what about the youngsters who spend innumerable hours watching television? Dr. Robert Goldenson, a psychology professor at Hunter College reports:

Instead of the adverse effect they feared, librarians and teachers report that the cultural values communicated by children's television programs are responsible for much wider exploration of the world of books by children than in pre-television days.

In 1955 youngsters set a record for borrowing books from public libraries, and much of this is due to their desire to delve more and more into literature dealing with exploration, general science, space travel and life in other countries. Professor Goldenson adds "the youngsters are often far ahead of many producers who think all that children want is blood and thunder." Children will, of course, watch what the programmers give them. But if every program of violence (and let the behavioral scientist define what is deleterious) were taken off the air tomorrow, there wouldn't be enough protest to give an agency man a heartburn.

In the minds of certain critics of mass culture the people will invariably choose the mediocre and the meretricious. This mixture of noblesse oblige and polite contempt for anyone outside of university circles, or avant-garde literary groups, seems to me just as authoritarian as the anti-intellectualism that the "masses" direct against the scholastics.

One gets the impression that those who find the mass media anathema would feel more secure if we could go back to a period that had no radios or television sets, no motion pictures, an era in which books were the possessions of the few and the newspapers were priced beyond the means of all but the élite whose class interests were catered to. Short of going back to this pre-media era, which is palpably impossible, they would remove from the "average" man's leisure anything that didn't meet their self-styled standards of high culture. If the "average" man is not quite ready to accept the best that art and literature have to offer him (and again I ask, in what period has he?) these critics turn their anger on the media.

Yet it is just these mass media that hold out the greatest promise to the "average" man that a cultural richness no previous age could give him is at hand. If television (or the other media) provided only a diet of the tried and true stereotyped programs, that is, allowed the majority taste to mandate every choice, then I would agree with these critics in their fear for the future. But the variety and quality of what is available to *national* audiences show this is not the case.

Take, for example, the offerings of the television networks on Sunday, March 18, 1956, a Sunday which I chose at random. The televiewer would have been able to see on this day a discussion of the times and works of Toulouse-Lautrec by three prominent art critics; an inspiring interview with Dr. Paul Tillich, the noted theologian; a sensitive adaptation of Walter von Tilburg Clark's "Hook," a story of a hawk's life; a powerful documentary on mental illness with Orson Welles and Dr. William Menninger; an interview with the Secretary of Health, Welfare and Education; an interview with the Governor of Minnesota on the eve of the primary elections in his state; an hour and a half performance of *Taming of the Shrew* in color with Maurice Evans and Lilli Palmer.

While the above may not be of the same cultural status as the works of Kant or the music of Bartok, it's a pretty substantial diet—certainly not pap. Very well, reply the detractors, so there is a modicum of cultural programs avaliable on Sunday. How do you know that people look at them? This can be answered in two ways: (1) Most of these programs are in a series, some sponsored and other maintained year after year by the networks. If they were not being watched they would have been replaced. (2) This is not a fair question. Nobody can force anyone to watch anything that does not interest him, except in a totalitarian state in which one watches or else! The important thing is that the networks *offer* these programs for those who do wish to watch. It is not the network's or anyone else's duty, to create the publics who will watch these programs.

To be sure, the editing and abridgment of Shakespeare's *Taming of the Shrew* to the hour-and-a-half period might be considered a watered down version of the sacred text by some. But Shakespeare himself was a player who had as good an eye on the house as on posterity. The skillful elimination of some of the tedious subplots by Mr. Evans (surely one of the great modern interpreters of Shakespeare) not only increased the pace of the play but made it more understandable.

There are dedicated groups of people in this country who instead of damning the media blanketly do something about improving what they dislike. Typical of such groups is the National Citizens' Committee for Educational Television, who have done more than cry about the low level of American culture. It is significant to note that by the end of 1956 there will be twenty-six educational television stations on the air. The eighteen stations now in operation are programming 340 hours weekly to a potential audience of 40 million. The new stations will bring an additional seven million viewers within the educational TV orbit. According to a recent survey by the Committee, 57 per cent of the programs were live and locally produced, the remainder were kinescopes and film. Through this medium many courses are being offered, the most popular of which are history and languages, with music appreciation high on the list.

An outstanding example of an educational television station in operation is WQED in Pittsburgh, which is on the air sixty-seven and a half hours a week. Recently one of its programs, the "Children's Corner," was signed for a three-year National Broadcasting contract. The commercial networks are watching the efforts of their educational confreres with more and more interest. It was also from WQED that Dr. Benjamin Spock, the well-known children's specialist, went to a network show on the National Broadcasting Company. As educational television networks develop throughout the states there will be few communities in America where the audiences do not have their choice any evening between Berle or Bach, Godfrey or Goya, the *$64,000 Question* or a discussion of Thucydides' historical method.

But to get back to books. As Clifton Fadiman pointed out recently, we are in the midst of a reprint revolution that may be the greatest boon since Gutenberg. This revolution, which started in 1939 when Pocket Books experimented with twenty-five cent reprints, saw 300 million paperbound books printed last year! Since 1939 we've consumed about two billion copies.

The encouraging aspect of the paperbound books is that the quality of the titles is constantly improving. Whereas a few years ago the first association that came to one's mind was Mickey Spillane, today one thinks of the very successful *Anchor* books published by Doubleday, Harcourt Brace's *Harvest* books, Knopf's *Vintage* books, the Beacon Press paperbacks, Penguin books, to mention only a few. There appears to be a very substantial public for these modestly priced reprints of works by Tocqueville, Ernst Cassirer, Stendhal. Take, for example, Saul Bellow's novel *Augie March*. Although it won the National Book Award in 1954, its trade edition sold only a moderate number of copies. In its paperbound edition, Bellow's novel has sold more than a million copies.

One further area we might look into before we call America a cultural wasteland is serious music. In the special fiftieth anniversary edition of *Variety,* which might appear to some as a most unlikely publication to present facts and figures about "longhair" art, Arthur Bronson has compiled some extremely significant data. In the fifty-year period covered by *Variety's* life serious musical expression has made extraordinary progress. Where in 1905 opera was the province of the few, today the listening audience of the Metropolitan Opera's Saturday afternoon broadcast alone is 15 million. To contrast with the half-dozen major symphony orchestras of a half-century ago, today we have thirty-two American symphonies. Ballet, which virtually was unknown in this country fifty years ago, now has three major American companies.

But, rejoins the detractor of American mass culture, what about the small cities? True, there may be four radio stations in Boston that broadcast a combined thirty to thirty-five hours *daily* of the finest classical music, but what about the hinterland? The answer to that is partly to be found in the fact that in 1940 there were 1,000 towns in this country offering concert series. Today there are some 2,500. As the sale of recordings of serious music by our symphony orchestras and noted artists have continued to grow, almost in direct correlation we have seen a growth in concert series. The two events are not without a causal relationship.

Since 1920 more than 20 million recordings of Arturo Toscanini alone have been sold, nor is it without significance that since 1903 when the first recordings were made of Mozart's work, more than 60 million records of his music have been sold.

Where 1916 saw the renowned Diaghilev ballet with Nijinsky come to America and cost its backers about $400,000, by 1954 the Sadler's Wells company of London arrived here and in twenty weeks of a national tour earned more than $2,500,000. More noteworthy, perhaps, is that the National Broadcasting Company on December 12, 1955, presented the Sadler's Wells ballet with Margot Fonteyn in an hour-and-a-half performance of Tchaikovsky's *Sleeping Beauty*. With the kind of courage that puts the lie to the adage that the giants of the mass media are afraid to buck the stereotype of the "thirteen-year-old mind," Producers' Showcase matched Fonteyn and company against CBS' Burns and Allen, Arthur Godfrey and *I Love Lucy* on the intensely competitive Monday night hours.

Millions of Americans were introduced to ballet for the first time that evening, but to me the significant factor is that they were provided with the opportunity to choose between Godfrey and the Sadler's Wells. If, as was the case, Godfrey's Talent Scouts program retained a higher audience rating, this is no cause to despair and decry the low tastes of the American people. Rather, such programs as Richard III, the Sadler's Wells ballet, Omnibus and scores more give me confidence that the media, as they, too, grow in stature and understanding, will offer more and more substantial fare.

Perhaps it is an invidious comparison to point out that in 1955 about 35 million people paid to attend classical music events as against the 15 million who attended baseball games. But it is no *non sequitur* to note that the 1955 attendance at serious music events is about double that of 1940.

That the performance of symphonic music is not restricted to larger cities may be seen when in the last dozen years orchestras have sprung up in such places as Phoenix, Arizona, San Jose, California, Great Falls, Montana, and even the atomic town of Oak Ridge, Tennessee. The 200 symphony orchestras in this country (80 per cent more than fifteen years ago and ten times as many as in the etarly 1920's) indicate a musical awareness such as we have never known.

Surely no one will claim that all (if any) of our small-town symphonies have the musicianship of a Boston, Philadelphia or St. Louis orchestra, but the members of these groups are donating their musical services free for the most part. In the city of Peoria, Illinois, for example, where I once lived, it was stimulating to be part of an orchestra where one colleague in the string section was a prominent attorney, another a chemistry professor and perhaps a third the owner of a small but profitable dry goods store. The strains of the Franck *D minor* symphony were meaningful to each of the citizen-musicians.

IV

Mass culture in America. If I have presented a hopeful picture of our future as we go into the era of extended leisure that Americans will share in the next decade or two, it is because I see substantial amelioration in the uses of our mass media. There has been such a rehearsal of all that is ugly and bathetic in our popular arts by critics whose sincerity cannot be questioned that it is time that the other side of the coin be examined.

Notes

1. This is not to say that I find anything of merit in the comic books. Yet to make of them the Dragon (whose slaying by this modern St. George will eliminate children's tensions, juvenile delinquency, etc.) is neither scientifically defensible or reasonable. I am aware that from time to time (in a population of roughly 47 million children fourteen years old and under) one unhappy child takes his own life with a horror comic book at his feet. By the same logic, what are we to do about the religious hysterics or paranoids who commit suicide with a Bible in their hands? Would the Dr. have attacked and obliterated the medieval Church in which a nun, Christine Ebner (1277-1356), cut the name of Jesus on her chest with a knife, and, because the scars did not last permanently, burnt them in with a candle? According to G. R. Taylor in his remarkable study, *Sex in History,* she was canonized in 1920. Masochism, sadism, sexual fantasies, etc., are as old as recorded history. Potiphar's wife lusted after the young Joseph sans benefit of comic books, soap operas, Bernarr Macfadden's *True Love Confessions,* or rock and roll. Serious students of disturbed youngsters, such as the Gluecks, have found no basis for comic-book reading as a cause of juvenile delinquency.

2. Freud in his *Moses and Monotheism* expresses this point very succinctly when he states: "Remote times have a great attraction—sometimes mysteriously so—for the imagination. As often as mankind is dissatisfied with its present—and that happens often enough—it harks back to the past and hopes at last to win belief in the never forgotten dreams of a Golden Age."

3. For example, Norman St. John-Stevas points out that an extensive trade in pornographic snuff boxes flourished in the early decades of the nineteenth century in England. Legal action to stop the trade came about in September, 1816, when a hawker of these wares was apprehended and confessed that he was in the habit of exposing these boxes to sale at Ladies' boarding schools and of disposing many of them to the young girls.

4. I realize that Eilhard Erich Pauls' study *Der Beginn der Buergerlichen Zeit* indicates that Germany was exposed to "mass culture" early in the nineteenth century.

2

Perspectives
of Mass Culture

*Whether one terms it "popular" or "mass culture" or the "public arts,"
there has been no dearth of spirited discussions and debates about what
Americans should do with their leisure hours. One debate that never took
place (since there is no reason to suspect the two gentlemen ever met) would
have been worth recording, whether by kinescope, tape, or merely the quill
pens of their day.*

*Much that has been said since by ideological devotees of the Comte de
Tocqueville and Walt Whitman might have emerged if such a debate had
ever come to pass. Although there are times when it appears that Tocqueville and Whitman were not so far apart, there is a basic point of view that
separates them. Both could say, for example, "The inhabitants of the United
States have at present, properly speaking, no literature." This certainly was
true in the 1830's when our literary endeavors consisted mainly of imitating
various English writers. Yet forty years later when Whitman wrote his
"Democratic Vistas" he too could say, "America has yet morally and artistically originated nothing. She seems singularly unaware that the models of
persons, books, manners, etc., appropriate for former conditions and for
European lands, are but exiles and exotics here." But here the similarity
ended. For where Tocqueville held little hope for a democracy to produce
great art or to provide a fertile environment for artists, Whitman could say
with characteristic vigor, "Literature, strictly considered, has never recognized the People, and, whatever may be said, does not today . . . Do you
term that perpetual, pistareen, paste-pot work, American art, American
drama, taste, verse? I think I hear, echoed as from some mountaintop afar
in the west, the scornful laugh of the Genius of these States."*

*In Tocqueville's eyes, America was destined to become the creator and
mass-acceptor of what later critics of American artistic life so pungently
term "kitsch." The cogency of Tocqueville's argument makes his critique
of American life as forceful and thought-provoking as if his visit to this
country had occurred yesterday instead of 125 years ago.*

*Whitman's "Democratic Vistas" written shortly after a tragic fratricidal
war, is no mere chauvinistic chant of a gifted, albeit uneven, personality. It
demands to be heard with Tocqueville's indictment of America's equalitari-
anism. For the Jacksonian democracy that so ruffled the sensibility of the
Frenchman was at the same time the source of Whitman's inspiration.*

*Ortega y Gasset, in the selection presented here, puts forward his now-
famous thesis that the central problem of our time concerns the rise to power
of the "mass man." The problem, for Ortega, is that the mass no longer
respects the values of the culture-bearing élite but supplants these values
with its own, commonplace, values.*

In the essay by Lowenthal the author shows that the central problem of the relationship of culture to leisure has perplexed such thinkers as Montaigne, Pascal and Nietzsche long before the mass media began to play their dominant roles. Lowenthal pleads for a historical and philosophical frame of reference, so that popular culture can be studied as a social phenomena.

Dwight Macdonald argues that mass culture constitutes a grave, unremitting threat to High Culture, as well as Folk Art. He sees mass culture as imposed from above, finally reaching out to engulf even the lords of "kitsch."

If Macdonald adheres (with a vengeance) to an argument that would have seemed plausible to Tocqueville, Gilbert Seldes would seem much closer in spirit to Whitman. Not that Seldes defends the popular arts uncritically; but he takes issue with those who blanketly damn them.

The final essay in this introductory section, by Clement Greenberg, sees "kitsch" as the product of the industrial revolution which urbanized the masses of western Europe and America and "established what is called universal literacy." Like Macdonald, he deplores the vicarious experiences which "kitsch" provides for the insensitive mass mind.

In What Spirit the Americans Cultivate the Arts

By ALEXIS DE TOCQUEVILLE

IT WOULD BE TO WASTE the time of my readers and my own, if I strove to demonstrate how the general mediocrity of fortunes, the absence of super-fluous wealth, the universal desire for comfort, and the constant efforts by which everyone attempts to procure it, make the taste for the useful pre-dominate over the love of the beautiful in the heart of man. Democratic nations, among whom all these things exist, will therefore cultivate the arts which serve to render life easy, in preference to those whose object is to adorn it. They will habitually prefer the useful to the beautiful, and they will require that the beautiful should be useful.

But I propose to go further; and, after having pointed out this first feature, to sketch several others.

It commonly happens that, in the age of privilege, the practice of almost all the arts becomes a privilege, and that every profession is a separate domain into which it is not allowable for everyone to enter. Even when productive industry is free, the fixed character which belongs to aristocratic nations gradually segregates all the persons who practice the same art till they form a distinct class, always composed of the same families, whose members are all known to each other, and among whom a public opinion of their own and a species of corporate pride soon spring up. In a class or guild of this kind each artisan has not only his fortune to make, but his reputation to preserve. He is not exclusively swayed by his own interest or even by that of his customer, but by that of the body to which he belongs; and the interest of that body is that each artisan should produce the best possible workmanship. In aristocratic ages the object of the arts is therefore to manufacture as well as possible, not with the greatest dispatch or at the lowest rate.

When, on the contrary, every profession is open to all, when a multitude of persons are constantly embracing and abandoning it, and when its several members are strangers, indifferent to, and because of their numbers hardly seen by, each other, the social tie is destroyed, and each workman, standing alone, endeavors simply to gain the most money at the least cost. The will of the customer is then his only limit. But at the same time a corresponding change takes place in the customer also. In countries in which riches, as well as power, are concentrated and retained in the hands of a few, the use of the greater part of this world's goods belongs to a small number of indi-viduals, who are always the same. Necessity, public opinion, or moderate desires exclude all others from the enjoyment of them. As this aristocratic

---

Reprinted from *Democracy in America* (1835). Adapted from the Henry Reeve translation.

class remains fixed at the pinnacle of greatness on which it stands, without diminution or increase, it is always acted upon by the same wants and affected by them in the same manner. The men of whom it is composed naturally derive from their superior and hereditary position a taste for what is extremely well made and lasting. This affects the general way of thinking of the nation in relation to the arts. It often occurs, among such a people, that even the peasant will rather go without the objects he covets than procure them in a state of imperfection. In artistocracies, then, the handicraftsmen work for only a limited number of fastidious customers; the profit they hope to make depends principally on the perfection of their workmanship.

Such is no longer the case when, all privileges being abolished, ranks are intermingled and men are forever rising or sinking upon the social scale. Among a democratic people a number of citizens always exist whose patrimony is divided and decreasing. They have contracted, under more prosperous circumstances, certain wants, which remain after the means of satisfying such wants are gone; and they are anxiously looking out for some surreptitious method of providing for them. On the other hand, there are always in democracies a large number of men whose fortune is on the increase, but whose desires grow much faster than their fortunes, and who gloat upon the gifts of wealth in anticipation, long before they have means to obtain them. Such men are eager to find some short cut to these gratifications, already almost within their reach. From the combination of these two causes the result is that in democracies there is always a multitude of persons whose wants are above their means, and who are very willing to take up with imperfect satisfaction rather than abandon the object of their desires altogether.

The artisan readily understands these passions, for he himself partakes in them. In an aristocracy he would seek to sell his workmanship at a high price to the few; he now conceives that the more expeditious way of getting rich is to sell them at a low price to all. But there are only two ways of lowering the price of commodities. The first is to discover some better, shorter, and more ingenious method of producing them; the second is to manufacture a larger quantity of goods, nearly similar, but of less value. Among a democratic population all the intellectual faculties of the workman are directed to these two objects: he strives to invent methods which may enable him not only to work better, but quicker and cheaper; or, if he cannot succeed in that, to diminish the intrinsic quality of the thing he makes, without rendering it wholly unfit for the use for which it is intended. When none but the wealthy had watches, they were almost all very good ones; few are now made which are worth much, but everybody has one in his pocket. Thus the democratic principle not only tends to direct the human mind to the useful arts, but it induces the artisan to produce with great rapidity many imperfect commodities, and the consumer to content himself with these commodities.

Not that, in democracies, the arts are incapable, in case of need, of producing wonders. This may occasionally be the case, if customers appear who are ready to pay for time and trouble. In this rivalry of every kind of industry, in the midst of this immense competition and these countless experiments, some excellent workmen are formed who reach the utmost limits of their craft. But they rarely have an opportunity of showing what they can do; they are scrupulously sparing of their powers; they remain in a state of accomplished mediocrity, which judges itself, and, though well able to shoot beyond the mark before it, aims only at what it hits. In aristocracies, on the contrary, workmen always do all they can; and when they stop, it is because they have reached the limit of their art.

When I arrive in a country where I find some of the finest productions of the arts, I learn from this fact nothing of the social condition or of the political constitution of the country. But if I perceive that the productions of the arts are generally of an inferior quality, very abundant, and very cheap, I am convinced that, among the people where this occurs, privilege is on the decline, and that ranks are beginning to intermingle and will soon be confounded together.

The handicraftsmen of democratic ages endeavor not only to bring their useful productions within the reach of the whole community, but strive to give to all their commodities attractive qualities that they do not in reality possess. In the confusion of all ranks, everyone hopes to appear what he is not, and makes great exertions to succeed in this object. This sentiment, indeed, which is but too natural to the heart of man, does not originate in the democratic principle; but that principle applies it to material objects. The hypocrisy of virtue is of every age, but the hypocrisy of luxury belongs more particularly to the ages of democracy.

To satisfy these new cravings of human vanity, the arts have recourse to every species of imposture; and these devices sometimes go so far as to defeat their own purpose. Imitation diamonds are now made which may be easily mistaken for real ones; as soon as the art of fabricating false diamonds shall become so perfect that they cannot be distinguished from real ones, it is probable that both will be abandoned, and become mere pebbles again.

This leads me to speak of those arts which are called, by way of distinction, the fine arts. I do not believe that it is a necessary effect of a democratic social condition and of democratic institutions to diminish the number of those who cultivate the fine arts; but these causes exert a powerful influence on the manner in which these arts are cultivated. Many of those who had already contracted a taste for the fine arts are impoverished; on the other hand, many of those who are not yet rich begin to conceive that taste, at least by imitation; the number of consumers increases, but opulent and fastidious consumers become more scarce. Something analogous to what I have already pointed out in the useful arts then takes place in the fine arts; the productions of artists are more numerous, but the merit of each production is diminished. No longer able to soar to what is great, they cultivate what is pretty and elegant, and appearance is more attended to than reality.

In aristocracies a few great pictures are produced; in democratic countries a vast number of insignificant ones. In the former, statues are raised of bronze; in the latter, they are modeled in plaster.

When I arrived for the first time at New York, by that part of the Atlantic Ocean which is called the East River, I was surprised to perceive along the shore, at some distance from the city, a number of little palaces of white marble, several of which were of classic architecture. When I went the next day to inspect more closely one which had particularly attracted my notice, I found that its walls were of whitewashed brick, and its columns of painted wood. All the edifices which I had admired the night before were of the same kind.

The social condition and the institutions of democracy impart, moreover, certain peculiar tendencies to all the imitative arts, which it is easy to point out. They frequently withdraw them from the delineation of the soul to fix them exclusively on that of the body, and they substitute the representation of motion and sensation for that of sentiment and thought; in a word, they put the Real in the place of the Ideal.

I doubt whether Raphael studied the minute intricacies of the mechanism of the human body as thoroughly as the draftsmen of our time. He did not attach the same importance as they do to rigorous accuracy on this point, because he aspired to surpass nature. He sought to make of man something which should be superior to man, and to embellish beauty itself. David and his scholars were, on the contrary, as good anatomists as they were painters. They wonderfully depicted the models which they had before their eyes, but they rarely imagined anything beyond them; they followed nature with fidelity, while Raphael sought for something better than nature. They have left us an exact portraiture of man, but he discloses in his works a glimpse of the Divinity.

This remark as to the manner of treating a subject is no less applicable to the choice of it. The painters of the Renaissance generally sought far above themselves, and away from their own time, for mighty subjects, which left to their imagination an unbounded range. Our painters often employ their talents in the exact imitation of the details of private life, which they have always before their eyes; and they are forever copying trivial objects, the originals of which are only too abundant in nature.

LITERARY CHARACTERISTICS OF DEMOCRATIC TIMES

The inhabitants of the United States have . . . at present, properly speaking, no literature. The only authors whom I acknowledge as American are the journalists. They indeed are not great writers, but they speak the language of their country and make themselves heard. Other authors are aliens; they are to the Americans what the imitators of the Greeks and Romans were to us at the revival of learning, an object of curiosity, not of general sympathy. They amuse the mind, but they do not act upon the manners of the people.

I have already said that this state of things is far from originating in democracy alone, and that the cause of it must be sought for in several peculiar circumstances independent of the democratic principle. If the Americans, retaining the same laws and social condition, had had a different origin, and had been transported into another country, I do not question that they would have had a literature. Even as they are, I am convinced that they will ultimately have one; but its character will be different from that which marks the American literary productions of our time, and that character will be peculiarly its own. Nor is it impossible to trace this character beforehand.

Let us picture an aristocratic people amongst whom letters are cultivated; the labor of the mind, as well as the affairs of state, are conducted there by a ruling class in society. The literary as well as the political career is almost entirely confined to this class, or to those nearest to it in rank. These premises suffice for a key to all the rest.

When a small number of the same men are engaged at the same time upon the same objects, they easily concert with one another and agree upon certain leading rules that are to govern them each and all. If the object which attracts the attention of these men is literature, the productions of the mind will soon be subjected by them to precise canons, from which it will no longer be allowable to depart. If these men occupy a hereditary position in the country, they will be naturally inclined, not only to adopt a certain number of fixed rules for themselves, but to follow those which their forefathers laid down for their own guidance; their code will be at once strict and traditional. As they are not necessarily engrossed by the cares of daily life—as they have never been so, any more than their fathers were before them—they have learned to take an interest, for several generations back, in the labors of the mind. They have learned to understand literature as an art, to love it in the end for its own sake, and to feel a scholar-like satisfaction in seeing men conform to its rules. Nor is this all: the men of whom I speak began and will end their lives in easy or affluent circumstances; hence they have naturally conceived a taste for choice gratifications and a love of refined and delicate pleasures. Nay, more: a kind of softness of mind and heart, which they frequently contract in the midst of this long and peaceful enjoyment of so much welfare, leads them to put aside, even from their pleasures, whatever might be too startling or too acute. They had rather be amused than intensely excited; they wish to be interested, but not to be carried away.

Now let us fancy a great number of literary performances executed by the men, or for the men, whom I have just described, and we shall readily conceive a style of literature in which everything will be regular and prearranged. The slightest work will be carefully finished in its least details; art and labor will be conspicuous in everything; each kind of writing will have rules of its own, from which it will not be allowed to swerve, and which distinguish it from all others. Style will be thought of almost as much importance as thought, and the form will be no less considered than the matter; the diction will be polished, measured, and uniform. The tone of the mind will be always dignified, seldom very animated; and writers will care more to perfect what they produce than to multiply their productions. It will sometimes happen that the members of the literary class, always living among themselves, and writing for themselves alone, will entirely lose sight of the rest of the world, which will infect them with a false and labored style; they will lay down minute literary rules for their exclusive use, which will insensibly lead them to deviate from common sense and finally to transgress the bounds of nature. By dint of striving after a mode of parlance different from the common, they will arrive at a sort of aristocratic jargon which is hardly less remote from pure language than is the coarse dialect of the people. Such are the natural perils of literature among aristocracies. Every aristocracy that keeps itself entirely aloof from the people becomes impotent, a fact which is as true in literature as it is in politics.[1]

Let us now turn the picture and consider the other side of it: let us transport ourselves into the midst of a democracy not unprepared by ancient traditions and present culture to partake in the pleasures of mind. Ranks are there intermingled and confounded; knowledge and power are both infinitely subdivided and, if I may use the expression, scattered on every side. Here, then, is a motley multitude whose intellectual wants are to be supplied. These new votaries of the pleasures of mind have not all received the same education; they do not resemble their fathers—nay, they perpetually differ from themselves, for they live in a state of incessant change of place, feelings, and fortunes. The mind of each is therefore unattached to that of his fellows by tradition or common habits; and they have never had the power, the inclination, or the time to concert together. It is, however, from the bosom of this heterogeneous and agitated mass that authors spring; and from the same source their profits and their fame are distributed.

I can without difficulty understand that, under these circumstances, I must expect to meet in the literature of such a people with but few of those strict conventional rules which are admitted by readers and writers in aristocratic times. If it should happen that the men of some one period were agreed upon any such rules, that would prove nothing for the following period; for, among democratic nations, each new generation is a new people. Among such nations, then, literature will not easily be subjected to strict rules, and it is impossible that any such rules should ever be permanent.

In democracies, it is by no means the case that all who cultivate literature have received a literary education; and most of those who have some tinge of belles-lettres are engaged either in politics or in a profession which only allows them to taste occasionally and by stealth the pleasures of mind. These pleasures, therefore, do not constitute the principal charm of their lives, but they are considered as a transient and necessary recreation amidst the serious labors of life. Such men can never acquire a sufficiently intimate knowledge of the art of literature to appreciate its more delicate beauties; and the minor shades of expression must escape them. As the time they can devote to letters is very short, they seek to make the best use of the whole of it. They prefer books which may be easily procured, quickly read, and which require no learned researches to be understood. They ask for beauties self-proffered and easily enjoyed; above all, they must have what is unexpected and new. Accustomed to the struggle, the crosses, and the monotony of practical life, they require strong and rapid emotions, startling passages, truths or errors brilliant enough to rouse them up and to plunge them at once, as if by violence, into the midst of the subject.

Why should I say more? or who does not understand what is about to follow, before I have expressed it? Taken as a whole, literature in democratic ages can never present, as it does in the periods of aristocracy, an aspect of order, regularity, science, and art; its form will, on the contrary, ordinarily be slighted, sometimes despised. Style will frequently be fantastic, incorrect, overburdened, and loose, almost always vehement and bold. Authors will aim at rapidity of execution, more than at perfection of detail. Small productions will be more common than bulky books; there will be more wit than erudition, more imagination than profundity; and literary performances will bear marks of an untutored and rude vigor of thought, frequently of great variety and singular fecundity. The object of authors will be to astonish rather than to please, and to stir the passions more than to charm the taste.

Here and there, indeed writers will doubtless occur who will choose a different track and who will, if they are gifted with superior abilities, succeed in finding readers, in spite of their defects or their better qualities; but these exceptions will be rare; and even the authors who shall so depart from the received practice in the main subject of their works, will always relapse into it in some lesser details.

I have just depicted two extreme conditions: the transition by which a nation passes from the former to the latter is not sudden, but gradual, and marked with shades of very various intensity. In the passage which conducts a letter people from the one to the other, there is almost always a moment at which the literary genius of democratic nations has its confluence with that of aristocracies, and both seek to establish their joint sway over the human mind. Such epochs are transient, but very brilliant; they are fertile without exuberance, and animated without confusion. The French literature of the eighteenth century may serve as an example.

I should say more than I mean if I were to assert that the literature of a nation is always subordinate to its social state and its political constitution. I am aware that, independently of these causes, there are several others which confer certain characteristics on literary productions; but these appear to me to be the chief. The relations that exist between the social and political condition of a people and the genius of its authors are always numerous; whoever knows the one is never completely ignorant of the other.

Democracy not only infuses a taste for letters among the trading classes, but introduces a trading spirit into literature.

In aristocracies, readers are fastidious and few in number; in democracies, they are far more numerous and far less difficult to please. The consequence is that among aristocratic nations no one can hope to succeed without great exertion, and this exertion may earn great fame, but can never procure much money; while among democratic nations a writer may flatter himself that he will obtain at a cheap rate a moderate reputation and a large fortune. For this purpose he need not be admired, it is enough that he is liked.

The ever increasing crowd of readers, and their continual craving for something new, insures the sale of books which nobody much esteems.

In democratic times, the public frequently treat authors as kings do their courtiers; they enrich and despise them. What more is needed by the venal souls who are born in courts or are worthy to live there?

Democratic literature is always infested with a tribe of writers who look upon letters as a mere trade; and for some few great authors who adorn it, you may reckon thousands of idea-mongers.

Note

1. All this is especially true of the aristocratic countries that have been long and peacefully subject to a monarchical government. When liberty prevails in an aristocracy, the higher ranks are constantly obliged to make use of the lower classes; and when they use, they approach them. This frequently introduces something of a democratic spirit into an aristocratic community. There springs up, moreover, in a governing privileged body, an energy and habitually bold policy, a taste for stir and excitement, which must infallibly affect all literary performances.

From "Democratic Vistas"

By WALT WHITMAN

THE UNITED STATES are destined either to surmount the gorgeous history of feudalism, or else prove the most tremendous failure of time. Not the least doubtful am I on any prospects of their material success. The triumphant future of their business, geographic and productive department, on larger scales and in more varieties than ever, is certain. In those respects the republic must soon (if she does not already) outstrip all examples hitherto afforded, and dominate the world.

Admitting all this, with the priceless value of our political institutions, general suffrage (and fully acknowledging the latest, widest opening of the doors), I say that, far deeper than these, what finally and only is to make of our Western world a nationality superior to any hither known, and outtopping the past, must be vigorous, yet unsuspected Literatures, perfect personalities and sociologies, original, transcendental, and expressing (what, in highest sense, are not yet expressed at all) democracy and the modern.

I say that democracy can never prove itself beyond cavil, until it founds and luxuriantly grows its own forms of art, poems, schools, theology, displacing all that exists, or that has been produced anywhere in the past, under opposite influences. It is curious to me that while so many voices, pens, minds, in the press, lecture rooms, in our Congress, etc., are discussing intellectual topics, pecuniary dangers, legislative problems, the suffrage, tariff and labor questions, and the various business and benevolent needs of America, with propositions, remedies, often worth deep attention, there is one need, a hiatus the profoundest, that no eye seems to perceive, no voice to state. Our fundamental want today in the United States, with closest amplest reference to present conditions, and to the future, is of a class, and the clear idea of a class, of native authors, literatures, far different, far higher in grade, than any yet known, sacerdotal, modern, fit to cope with our occasions, lands, permeating the whole mass of American mentality, taste, belief, breathing into it a new breath of life, giving it decision, affecting politics far more than the popular superficial suffrage, with results inside and underneath the elections of Presidents or Congresses—radiating, begetting appropriate teachers, schools, manners, and, as its grandest result, accomplishing (what neither the schools nor the churches and their clergy have hitherto accomplished, and without which this nation will no more stand, permanently, soundly, than a house will stand without a sub-stratum), a religious and moral character beneath the political and productive and

Reprinted from *Democratic Vistas*, 1871.

intellectual bases of the States. For know you not, dear, earnest reader, that the people of our land may all read and write, and may all possess the right to vote—and yet the main things may be entirely lacking?—(and this to suggest them).

It may be claimed (and I admit the weight of the claim) that common and general worldly prosperity, and a populace well-to-do, and with all life's material comforts, is the main thing, and is enough. It may be argued that our republic is, in performance, really enacting today the grandest arts, poems, etc., by beating up the wilderness into fertile farms, and in her railroads, ships, machinery, etc. And it may be asked, Are these not better, indeed, for America, than any utterances even of greatest rhapsode, artist, or literatus?

I too hail those achievements with pride and joy; then answer that the soul of man will not with such only—nay, not with such at all—be finally satisfied; but needs what (standing on these and on all things, as the feet stand on the ground) is addressed to the loftiest, to itself alone.

Out of such considerations, such truths, arises for treatment in these Vistas the important question of character, of an American stock-personality, with literatures and arts for outlets and return-expressions, and, of course, to correspond, within outlines common to all. To these, the main affair, the thinkers of the United States, in general so acute, have either given feeblest attention, or have remained, and remain, in a state of somnolence.

The People! Like our huge earth itself, which, to ordinary scansion, is full of vulgar contradictions and offense, man, viewed in the lump, displeases, and is a constant puzzle and affront to the merely educated classes. The rare, cosmical, artist-mind, lit with the Infinite, alone confronts his manifold and oceanic qualities—but taste, intelligence and culture (so-called), have been against the masses, and remain so. There is plenty of glamour about the most damnable crimes and hoggish meannesses, special and general, of the feudal and dynastic world over there, with its *personnel* of lords and queens and courts, so well dressed and so handsome. But the People are ungrammatical, untidy, and their sins gaunt and ill bred.

Literature, strictly considered, has never recognized the People, and, whatever may be said, does not today. Speaking generally, the tendencies of literature, as hitherto pursued, have been to make mostly critical and querulous men. It seems as if, so far, there were some natural repugnance between a literary and professional life, and the rude rank spirit of the democracies. There is, in later literature, a treatment of benevolence, a charity business, rife enough it is true; but I know nothing more rare, even in this country, than a fit scientific estimate and reverent appreciation of the People—of their measureless wealth of latent power and capacity, their vast, artistic contrasts of lights and shades—with, in America, their entire reliability in emergencies, and a certain breadth of historic grandeur, of peace or war, far surpassing all the vaunted samples of book-heroes, or any *haut ton* coteries, in all the records of the world.

The great poems, Shakespeare included, are poisonous to the idea of the pride and dignity of the common people, the life-blood of democracy. The models of our literature, as we get it from other lands, ultramarine, have had their birth in courts, and basked and grown in castle sunshine; all smells of princes' favors. Of workers of a certain sort, we have, indeed, plenty, contributing after their kind; many elegant, many learned, all complacent. But touched by the national test, or tried by the standards of democratic personality, they wither to ashes. I say I have not seen a single writer, artist, lecturer, or what not, that has confronted the voiceless but ever erect and active, pervading, underlying will and typic aspiration of the land, in a spirit kindred to itself. Do you call those genteel little creatures American poets? Do you term that perpetual, pistareen, paste-pot work, American art, American drama, taste, verse? I think I hear, echoed as from some mountaintop afar in the west, the scornful laugh of the Genius of these States.

America has yet morally and artistically originated nothing. She seems singularly unaware that the models of persons, books, manners, etc., appropriate for former conditions and for European lands, are but exiles and exotics here. No current of her life, as shown on the surfaces of what is authoritatively called her society, accepts or runs into social or aesthetic democracy; but all the currents set squarely against it. Never, in the Old World, was thoroughly upholstered exterior appearance and show, mental and other, built entirely on the idea of caste, and on the sufficiency of mere outside acquisition—never were glibness, verbal intellect more the test, the emulation—more loftily elevated as head and sample—than they are on the surface of our republican States this day. The writers of a time hint the mottoes of its gods. The word of the modern, say these voices, is the word Culture.

We find ourselves abruptly in close quarters with the enemy. This word Culture, or what it has come to represent, involves, by contrast, our whole theme, and has been, indeed, the spur, urging us to engagement. Certain questions arise. As now taught, accepted and carried out, are not the processes of culture rapidly creating a class of supercilious infidels, who believe in nothing? Shall a man lose himself in countless masses of adjustments, and be so shaped with reference to this, that, and the other, that the simply good and healthy and brave parts of him are reduced and clipped away, like the bordering of box in a garden? You can cultivate corn and roses and orchards—but who shall cultivate the mountain peaks, the ocean, and the tumbling gorgeousness of the clouds? Lastly—is the readily given reply that culture only seeks to help, systematize, and put in attitude, the elements of fertility and power, a conclusive reply?

I do not so much object to the name, or word, but I should certainly insist, for the purposes of these States, on a radical change of category, in the distribution of precedence. I should demand a program of culture, drawn out, not for a single class alone, or for the parlors or lecture rooms, but with an eye to practical life, the west, the workingmen, the facts of farms and jack-planes and engineers, and of the broad range of the women also of the middle and working strata, and with reference to the perfect equality of women, and of a grand and powerful motherhood. I should demand of this program or theory a scope generous enough to include the widest human area. It must have for its spinal meaning the formation of a typical personality of character, eligible to the uses of the high average of men—and *not* restricted by conditions ineligible to the masses. The best culture will always be that of the manly and courageous instincts, and loving perceptions, and of self-respect—aiming to form, over this continent, an idiocrasy of universalism, which, true child of America, will bring joy to its mother, returning to her in her own spirit, recruiting myriads of off-spring, able, natural, perceptive, tolerant, devout believers in her, America, and with some definite instinct why and for what she has arisen, most vast, most formidable of historic births, and is, now and here, with wonderful step, journeying through Time.

What, however, do we more definitely mean by New World literature? Are we not doing well enough here already? Are not the United States this day busily using, working, more printer's type, more presses, than any other country? uttering and absorbing more publications than any other? Do not our publishers fatten quicker and deeper? (helping themselves, under shelter of a delusive and sneaking law, or rather absence of law, to most of their forage, poetical, pictorial, historical, romantic, even comic, without money and without price—and fiercely resisting the timidest proposal to pay for it.) Many will come under this delusion—but my purpose is to dispel it. I say that a nation may hold and circulate rivers and oceans of very readable print, journals, magazines, novels, library books, "poetry," etc.—such as the States today possess and circulate—of unquestionable aid and value—hundreds of new volumes annually composed and brought out here, respectable enough, indeed unsurpassed in smartness and erudition —with further hundreds, or rather millions (as by free forage or theft aforementioned), also thrown into the market—and yet, all the while, the said nation, land, strictly speaking, may possess no literature at all.

Repeating our inquiry, what, then, do we mean by real literature? especially the democratic literature of the future? Hard questions to meet. The clues are inferential, and turn us to the past. At best, we can only offer suggestions, comparisons, circuits.

It must still be reiterated, as, for the purpose of these memoranda, the deep lesson of history and time, that all else in the contributions of a nation or age, through its politics, materials, heroic personalities, military *éclat,* etc., remains crude, and defers, in any close and thoroughgoing estimate, until vitalized by national, original archetypes in literature. They only put the nation in form, finally tell anything—prove, complete anything—perpetuate anything. Without doubt, some of the richest and most powerful and populous communities of the antique world, and some of the grandest personalities and events, have, to after and present times, left themselves entirely unbequeathed. Doubtless, greater than any that have come down to us, were among those lands, heroisms, persons, that have not come down to us at all, even by name, date, or location. Others have arrived safely, as from voyages over wide, century-stretching seas. The little ships, the miracles that have buoyed them, and by incredible chances safely conveyed them (or the best of them, their meaning and essence) over long wastes, darkness, lethargy, ignorance, etc., have been a few inscriptions— a few immortal compositions, small in size, yet compassing what measureless values of reminiscence, contemporary portaitures, manners, idioms and beliefs, with deepest inference, hint and thought, to tie and touch forever the old, new body, and the old, new soul! These! and still these! bearing the freight so dear—dearer than pride—dearer than love. All the best experience of humanity, folded, saved, freighted to us here. Some of these tiny ships we call Old and New Testament, Homer, Aeschylus, Plato, Juvenal, etc. Precious minims! I think, if we were forced to choose, rather than have you, and the likes of you, and what belongs to, and has grown of you, blotted out and gone, we could better afford, appalling as that would be, to lose all actual ships, this day fastened by wharf, or floating on wave, and see them, with all their cargoes, scuttled and sent to the bottom.

Compared with the past, our modern science soars, and our journals serve—but ideal and even ordinary romantic literature, does not, I think, substantially advance. Behold the prolific brood of the contemporary novel, magazine tale, theatre play, etc. The same endless thread of tangled and superlative love story, inherited, apparently from the Amadises and Palmerins of the thirteenth, fourteenth and fifteenth centuries over there in Europe. The costumes and associations brought down to date, the seasoning hotter and more varied, the dragons and ogres left out—but the *thing,* I should say, has not advanced—is just as sensational, just as strained—remains about the same, nor more, nor less.

What is the reason our time, our lands, that we see no fresh local courage, sanity, of our own—the Mississippi, stalwart Western men, real mental and physical facts, Southerners, etc., in the body of our literature? especially the poetic part of it. But always, instead, a parcel of dandies and ennuyees, dapper little gentlemen from abroad, who flood us with their thin sentiment of parlors, parasols, piano songs, tinkling rhymes, the five-hundredth importation—or whimpering and crying about something, chasing one aborted conceit after another, and forever occupied in dyspeptic amours with dyspeptic women. While, current and novel, the grandest events and revolutions, and stormiest passions of history are crossing today with unparalleled rapidity and magnificence over the stages of our own and all the continents, offering new materials, opening new vistas, with largest needs, inviting the daring launching forth of conceptions in literature, inspired by them, soaring in highest regions, serving art in its highest (which is only the other name for serving God, and serving humanity), where is the man of letters, where is the book, with any nobler aim than to follow in the old track, repeat what has been said before—and, as its utmost triumph, sell well, and be erudite or elegant?

In the prophetic literature of these States (the reader of my speculations will miss their principal stress unless he allows well for the point that a new Literature, perhaps a new Metaphysics, certainly a new Poetry, are to be, in my opinion, the only sure and worthy supports and expressions of the American Democracy), Nature, true Nature, and the true idea of Nature, long absent, must, above all, become fully restored, enlarged, and must furnish the pervading atmosphere to poems, and the test of all high literary and aesthetic compositions. I do not mean the smooth walks, trimmed hedges, posys and nightingales of the English poets, but the whole orb, with its geologic history, the cosmos, carrying fire and snow, that rolls through the illimitable areas, light as a feather, though weighing billions of tons. Furthermore, as by what we now partially call Nature is intended, at most, only what is entertainable by the physical conscience, the sense of matter, and of good animal health—on these it must be distinctly accumulated, incorporated, that man, comprehending these, has, in towering superaddition, the moral and spiritual consciences, indicating his destination beyond the ostensible, the mortal.

We see our land, America, her literature, aesthetics, etc., as, substantially, the getting in form, or effusement and statement, of deepest basic elements and loftiest final meanings, of history and man—and the portrayal (under the eternal laws and conditions of beauty) of our own physiognomy, the subjective tie and expression of the objective, as from our own combination, continuation, and points of view—and the deposit and record of the national mentality, character, appeals, heroism, wars, and even liberties —where these, and all, culminate in native literary and artistic formulation, to be perpetuated; and not having which native, first-class formulation, she will flounder about, and her other, however imposing, eminent greatness, prove merely a passing gleam; but truly having which, she will understand herself, live nobly, nobly contribute, emanate, and, swinging, poised safely on herself, illumined and illuming, become a full-formed world, and divine Mother not only of material but spiritual worlds, in ceaseless succession through time—the main thing being the average, the bodily, the concrete, the democratic, the popular, on which all the superstructures of the future are to permanently rest.

The Coming of the Masses

By JOSÉ ORTEGA Y GASSET

THERE IS ONE FACT which, whether for good or ill, is of utmost importance in public life at the present moment. This fact is the accession of the masses to complete social power. As the masses, by definition, neither should nor can direct their own personal existence, and still less rule society in general, this fact means that actually Europe is suffering from the greatest crisis that can afflict peoples, nations, and civilization. Such a crisis has occurred more than once in history. Its characteristics and its consequences are well known. So also is its name. It is called the rebellion of the masses. In order to understand this formidable fact, it is important from the start to avoid giving to the words "rebellion," "masses," and "social power" a meaning exclusively or primarily political. Public life is not solely political, but equally, and even primarily, intellectual, moral, economic, religious; it comprises all our collective habits, including our fashions both of dress and of amusement.

Perhaps the best line of approach to this historical phenomenon may be found by turning our attention to a visual experience, stressing one aspect of our epoch which is plain to our very eyes. This fact is quite simple to enunciate, though not so to analyze. I shall call it the fact of agglomeration, of "plenitude." Towns are full of people, houses full of tenants, hotels full of guests, trains full of travellers, cafés full of customers, parks full of promenaders, consulting rooms of famous doctors full of patients, theatres full of spectators, and beaches full of bathers. What previously was, in general, no problem, now begins to be an everyday one, namely, to find room.

That is all. Can there be any fact simpler, more patent, more constant in actual life? Let us now pierce the plain surface of this observation and we shall be surprised to see how there wells forth an unexpected spring in which the white light of day, of our actual day, is broken up into its rich chromatic content. What is it that we see, and the sight of which causes us so much surprise? We see the multitude, as such, in possession of the places and the instruments created by civilization. The slightest reflection will then make us surprised at our own surprise. What about it? Is this not the ideal state of things? The theatre has seats to be occupied—in other words, so that the house may be full—and now they are overflowing; people anxious to use them are left standing outside. Though the fact be quite logical and natural, we cannot but recognize that this did not happen before and that now it does; consequently, there has been a change, an innovation, which justifies, at least for the first moment, our surprise.

Reprinted from *The Revolt of the Masses* (1932), pp. 11-19, by permission of the publisher. (Copyright 1932, by W. W. Norton and Company, Inc.)

To be surprised, to wonder, is to begin to understand. This is the sport, the luxury, special to the intellectual man. The gesture characteristic of his tribe consists in looking at the world with eyes wide open in wonder. Everything in the world is strange and marvellous to well-open eyes. This faculty of wonder is the delight refused to your football "fan," and, on the other hand, is the one which leads the intellectual man through life in the perpetual ecstasy of the visionary. His special attribute is the wonder of the eyes. Hence it was that the ancients gave Minerva her owl, the bird with ever dazzled eyes.

Agglomeration, fullness, was not frequent before. Why then is it now? The components of the multitudes around us have not sprung from nothing. Approximately the same number of people existed fifteen years ago. Indeed, after the war it might seem natural that their number should be less. Nevertheless, it is here we come up against the first important point. The individuals who make up these multitudes existed, but not *qua* multitude. Scattered about the world in small groups, or solitary, they lived a life, to all appearances, divergent, dissociate, apart. Each individual or small group occupied a place, its own, in country, village, town, or quarter of the great city. Now, suddenly, they appear as an agglomeration, and looking in any direction our eyes meet with the multitudes. Not only in any direction, but precisely in the best places, the relatively refined creation of human culture, previously reserved to lesser groups, in a word, to minorities. The multitude has suddenly become visible, installing itself in the preferential positions in society. Before, if it existed, it passed unnoticed, occupying the background of the social stage; now it has advanced to the footlgihts and is the principal character. There are no longer protagonists; there is only the chorus.

The concept of the multitude is quantitative and visual. Without changing its nature, let us translate it into terms of sociology. We then meet with the notion of the "social mass." Society is always a dynamic unity of two component factors: minorities and masses. The minorities are individuals or groups of individuals which are specially qualified. The mass is the assemblage of persons not specially qualified. By masses, then, is not to be understood, solely or mainly, "the working masses." The mass is the average man. In this way what was mere quantity—the multitude—is converted into a qualitative determination: it becomes the common social quality, man as undifferentiated from other men, but as repeating in himself a generic type. What have we gained by this conversion of quantity into quality? Simply this: by means of the latter we understand the genesis of the former. It is evident to the verge of platitude that the normal formation of a multitude implies the coincidence of desires, ideas, ways of life, in the individuals who constitute it. It will be objected that this is just what happens with every social group, however select it may strive to be. This is true; but there is an essential difference. In those groups which are characterized by not being multitude and mass, the effective coincidence of its members is based on some desire, idea, or ideal, which of itself excludes the great number. To form a minority, of whatever kind, it is necessary beforehand that each member separate himself from the multitude for *special,* relatively personal, reasons. Their coincidence with the others who form the minority is, then, secondary, posterior to their having each adopted an attitude of singularity, and is consequently, to a large extent, a coincidence in not coinciding. There are cases in which this singularizing character of the group appears in the light of day: those English groups, which style themselves "nonconformists," where we have the grouping together of those who agree only in their disagreement in regard to the limitless multitude. This coming together of the minority precisely in order to separate themselves from the majority is a necessary ingredient in the formation of every minority. Speaking of the limited public which listened to a musician of refinement, Mallarmé wittily says that this public by its presence in small numbers stressed the absence of the multitude.

Strictly speaking, the mass, as a psychological fact, can be defined without waiting for individuals to appear in mass formation. In the presence of one individual we can decide whether he is "mass" or not. The mass is all that which sets no value on itself—good or ill—based on specific grounds, but which feels itself "just like everybody," and nevertheless is not concerned about it; is, in fact, quite happy to feel itself as one with everybody else. Imagine a humble-minded man who, having tried to estimate his worth on specific grounds—asking himself if he has any talent for this or that, if he excels in any direction—realizes that he possesses no quality of excellence. Such a man will feel that he is mediocre and commonplace, ill-gifted, but will not feel himself "mass."

When one speaks of "select minorities" it is usual for the evil-minded to twist the sense of this expression, pretending to be unaware that the select man is not the petulant person who thinks himself superior to the rest, but the man who demands more of himself than the rest, even though he may not fulfill in his person those higher exigencies. For there is no doubt that the most radical division that it is possible to make of humanity is that which splits it into two classes of creatures: those who make great demands on themselves, piling up difficulties and duties; and those who demand nothing special of themselves, but for whom to live is to be every moment what they already are, without imposing on themselves any effort towards perfection; mere buoys that float on the waves. This reminds me that orthodox Buddhism is composed of two distinct religions: one, more rigorous and difficult, the other easier and more trivial: the Mahayana— "great vehicle" or "great path"—and the Hinayana—"lesser vehicle" or "lesser path." The decisive matter is whether we attach our life to one or the other vehicle, to a maximum or a minimum of demands upon ourselves.

The division of society into masses and select minorities is, then, not a division into social classes, but into classes of men, and cannot coincide with the hierarchic separation of "upper" and "lower" classes. It is, of course, plain that in these "upper" classes, when and as long as they really are so, there is much more likelihood of finding men who adopt the "great vehicle," whereas the "lower" classes normally comprise individuals of minus quality. But, strictly speaking, within both these social classes, there are found mass and genuine minority. As we shall see, a characteristic of our times is the predominance, even in groups traditionally selective, of the mass and the vulgar. Thus, in the intellectual life, which of its essence requires and presupposes qualification, one can note the progressive triumph of the pseudo-intellectual, unqualified, unqualifiable, and, by their very mental texture, disqualified. Similarly, in the surviving groups of the "nobility," male and female. On the other hand, it is not rare to find today amongst working men, who before might be taken as the best example of what we are calling "mass," nobly disciplined minds.

There exist, then, in society, operations, activities, and functions of the most diverse order, which are of their very nature special, and which consequently cannot be properly carried out without special gifts. For example: certain pleasures of an artistic and refined character, or again the functions of government and of political judgment in public affairs. Previously these special activities were exercised by qualified minorities, or at least by those who claimed such qualification. The mass asserted no right to intervene in them; they realized that if they wished to intervene they would necessarily have to acquire those special qualities and cease being mere mass. They recognized their place in a healthy, dynamic social system.

If we now revert to the facts indicated at the start, they will appear clearly as the heralds of a changed attitude in the mass. They all indicate that the mass has decided to advance to the foreground of social life, to occupy the places, to use the instruments and to enjoy the pleasures hitherto reserved to the few. It is evident, for example, that the places were never intended for the multitude, for their dimensions are too limited, and the crowd is continuously overflowing; thus manifesting to our eyes and in the clearest manner the new phenomenon: the mass, without ceasing to be mass, is supplanting the minorities.

No one, I believe, will regret that people are today enjoying themselves in greater measure and numbers than before, since they have now both the desire and the means of satisfying it. The evil lies in the fact that this decision taken by the masses to assume the activities proper to the minorities is not, and cannot be, manifested solely in the domain of pleasure, but that it is a general feature of our time. Thus—to anticipate what we shall see later—I believe that the political innovations of recent times signify nothing less than the political domination of the masses. The old democracy was tempered by a generous dose of liberalism and of enthusiasm for law. By serving these principles the individual bound himself to maintain a severe discipline over himself. Under the shelter of liberal principles and the rule of law, minorities could live and act. Democracy and law—life in common under the law—were synonymous. Today we are witnessing the triumphs of a hyperdemocracy in which the mass acts directly, outside the law, imposing its aspirations and its desires by means of material pressure. It is a false interpretation of the new situation to say that the mass has grown tired of politics and handed over the exercise of it to specialized persons. Quite the contrary. That was what happened previously; that was democracy. The mass took it for granted that after all, in spite of their defects and weaknesses, the minorities understood a little more of public problems than it did itself. Now, on the other hand, the mass believes that it has the right to impose and to give force of law to notions born in the café. I doubt whether there have been other periods of history in which the multitude has come to govern more directly than in our own. That is why I speak of hyperdemocracy.

The same thing is happening in other orders, particularly in the intellectual. I may be mistaken, but the present-day writer, when he takes his pen in hand to treat a subject which he has studied deeply, has to bear in mind that the average reader, who has never concerned himself with this subject, if he reads does so with the view, not of learning something from the writer, but rather, of pronouncing judgment on him when he is not in agreement with the commonplaces that the said reader carries in his head. If the individuals who make up the mass believed themselves specially qualified, it would be a case merely of personal error, not a sociological subversion. *The characteristic of the hour is that the commonplace mind, knowing itself to be commonplace, has the assurance to proclaim the rights of the commonplace and to impose them wherever it will.* As they say in the United States: "to be different is to be indecent." The mass crushes beneath it everything that is different, everything that is excellent, individual, qualified and select. Anybody who is not like everybody, who does not think like everybody, runs the risk of being eliminated. And it is clear, of course, that this "everybody" is not "everybody." "Everybody" was normally the complex unity of the mass and the divergent, specialized minorities. Nowadays, "everybody" is the mass alone. Here we have the formidable fact of our times, described without any concealment of the brutality of its features.

Historical Perspectives of Popular Culture

By LEO LOWENTHAL

THIS PAPER was written to be provocative, by one who has been engaged in empirical research for a considerable number of years and who has recently been charged with the administration of a large-scale research program. The author has taken it upon himself to act as the spokesman for an approach to popular culture which some will call "social theory" and others "obsolete, abstract criticism." Specifically, the paper deals with aspects of the historical and theoretical frame of reference which seem to me to be a basic requirement for the study of mass communications and yet a blind spot in contemporary social science. I know of no better statement with which to highlight this blind spot in contemporary analyses of mass phenomena than de Tocqueville's remarks on the fact-finding obsession of the American mind a century ago:

> The practice of Americans leads their minds to fixing the standard of their judgment in themselves alone. As they perceive that they succeed in resolving without assistance all the little difficulties which their practical life presents, they readily conclude that everything in the world may be explained, and that nothing in it transcends the limits of the understanding. Thus they fall to denying what they cannot comprehend; which leaves them but little faith for whatever is extraordinary and an almost insurmountable distaste for whatever is supernatural. As it is on their own testimony that they are accustomed to rely, they like to discern the object which engages their attention with extreme clearness; they therefore strip off as much as possible all that covers it; they rid themselves of whatever separates them from it, they remove whatever conceals it from sight, in order to view it more closely and in the broad light of day. This disposition of mind soon leads them to condemn forms, which they regard as useless and inconvenient veils placed between them and the truth.[1]

My plea on behalf of these "veils" takes the form of five rather unsystematic groups of observations: (1) I shall indicate that the discussion of popular culture has a century-old tradition in modern history; (2) the historical locus of popular culture today will be fixed; (3) an attempt will be made to evaluate the over-all approach of empirical research to the social function of contemporary popular culture; (4) the current philosophical, qualitative, nonresearch analysis of popular culture will be summarized briefly; and (5) some programmatic notes will be offered on the relationship between social criticism and social research.

1. POPULAR CULTURE—AN OLD DILEMMA

In a survey recently undertaken of radio-listening habits in a foreign country, one of the respondents remarked:

Reprinted from *The American Journal of Sociology*, Vol. 55 (1950), pp. 323-32, by permission of the author and the publisher. (Copyright, 1950, by The University of Chicago Press.)

Radio is the companion of the lonely. It has made gigantic strides for almost half a century. Women in particular, especially those with small pensions and without other resources, who are completely isolated, are now in touch with the whole world thanks to the radio. They have undergone a regular transformation; they have found a kind of second youth. They are up-to-date and they know the stars of the headlines, of the theatre, the movies, the world of sports, etc. I have heard village people, discussing the merits of Mozart and Chopin, refer to what the radio had said.

In quite the opposite vein another woman revealed that she did not have a radio set in her home. Asked to explain why, she answered:

Because once there is a set in the house, one cannot resist. Everybody listens idiotically, the kids and the others too. When we stay with my friend G., my husband plays with the radio all the time.

Her view was supported by a male respondent, who also refuses to permit a radio in the house. He believes that studies, conversation, and activity around the house provide enough interest, that the indiscriminate outpouring of music and talk over the radio lowers everyone's intellectual level.

These spontaneous remarks reveal two leitmotifs which have run continuously through the modern era: on the one hand, a positive attitude toward all instrumentalities for the socialization of the individual; on the other hand, a deep concern about the inner fate of the individual under the impact of the leveling powers of institutional and other organized forms of leisure activity. This basic dilemma concerning man's existence beyond the requirements of biological and material survival, the vital question of how to live out that stretch of life which is neither sleep nor work, can be said to have found its classic intellectual expression in a philosophical dialogue that never took place. Montaigne in the sixteenth century took stock of the situation of the individual after the breakdown of medieval culture. He was particularly struck by the phenomenon of loneliness in a world without faith, in which tremendous pressures were being exerted on everyone under the conditions of a postfuedal society. To escape destruction by these pressures, to avoid becoming lost in the horrors of isolation, Montaigne suggested distraction as a way out:

Variety always solaces, dissolves, and scatters. If I cannot combat it, I run away from it; and in running away I double and change my direction. By changing place, occupation, company, I escape into the crowd of other thoughts and diversions, where it loses my trace, and leaves me safe. . . .

Is it reasonable that even the arts should take advantage of and profit by our natural stupidity and feebleness of mind? The barrister, says Rhetoric, in that farce they call pleading, will be moved by the sound of his own voice and his feigned emotion, and will suffer himself to be cozened by the passion he is acting. He will affect a real and substantial grief in this mummery he is playing, to transmit it to the jury who are still less concerned in the matter than he. Like those men who are hired at funerals to assist in the ceremonial of mourning, who sell their tears and grief by weight and measure; for, although they are stirred by borrowed emotions, it is certain that, through the habit of settling their countenance to suit the occasion, they are often quite carried away and affected with genuine melancholy.[2]

It is significant that quite a few basic concepts which we have been accustomed to regard as very modern emerge as early as the sixteenth century: escape, distraction, entertainment, and, last but not least, vicarious living.

The reply to Montaigne came a century later. Commercial culture had developed in the meantime, and the waning influence of religion, pre- or post-Reformation, had made itself felt much more strongly in the average way of life. Restlessness, the search for relief everywhere and anywhere, had become a major social phenomenon. It was then that Pascal spoke up against the complete surrender of man to self-destroying restlessness:

> Men are entrusted from infancy with the care of their honor, their property, their friends, and even with the property and the honor of their friends. They are overwhelmed with business, with the study of languages, and with physical exercise; and they are made to understand that they cannot be happy unless their health, their honor, their fortune and that of their good friends be in good condition, and that a single thing wanting will make them unhappy. Thus they are given cares and business which make them bustle about from break of day.— It is, you will exclaim, a strange way to make them happy! What more could be done to make them miserable?—Indeed! what could be done? We should only have to relieve them from all these cares; for then they would see themselves: they would reflect on what they are, whence they came, whither they go, and thus we cannot employ and divert them too much. And this is why, after having given them so much business, we advise them, if they have some time for relaxation, to employ it in amusement, in play, and to be always fully occupied.
> How hollow and full of ribaldry is the heart of man![3]

Again and again he warned against what he called "diversion" as a way of life which could lead only to permanent unhappiness:

> When I have occasionally set myself to consider the different distractions of men, the pains and perils to which they expose themselves at court or in war, whence arise so many quarrels, passions, bold and often bad ventures, etc., I have discovered that *all the unhappiness of men arises from one single fact, that they cannot stay quietly in their own chamber.*
> . . . They have a secret instinct which impels them to seek amusement and occupation abroad, and which arises from the sense of their constant unhappiness.[4]

Thus the attitude toward leisure which, for Montaigne, guarantees survival means self-destruction to Pascal. And the controversy is still going on. Each side has its partisans on all intellectual levels in everyday life, as illustrated in the study on radio as well as in learned treatises. On one side there is the benevolent analyst of a mass medium who seems to say that, while everything is not yet wonderful, it is getting better every day:

> For in the old days the artists and writers and craftsmen were not writing at the behest of the people, but to please small powerful groups, the kings and lords and chieftains, who drew the talent of the time inward towards them and kept it

circumscribed within the bounds of their castles and baronies. Much of the fine art of today remains alive only through a similar connection.

Yet, taking civilizaton as a whole, this ancient process is now in reverse. There is an outward movement. Pictures, entertainment, fun, are beginning to be seen as the rightful possession of all, and the comics join in and reflect this spreading democratization. And if the people's standards are at present lower than those which were set by workers around the seats of the mighty, the people's artists will have the satisfaction of knowing that they are identified with a vast and forward movement, which is giving to everyday folks their right to laugh and flourish under the sun.[5]

On the other hand, we find the nonconformist social critic who connects the loneliness of modern man with his interest in mass media as a setup of utter frustration:

The conditions of earning one's bread in this society create the lonely modern man.

Such conditions help explain the need, sometimes feverish, for an entertainment that so repetitively presents the same reveries, the same daydreams, the same childish fables of success and happiness. So much of the inner life of men is dried up that they tend to become filled with yearnings and to need the consolation of these reveries about people who are happy, healthy, and always successful. . . .

Hence, parallel to the retrogression of consciousness in, say, the Hollywood writer, there is a more widespread and also more pernicious retrogression of consciousness in the motion-picture audience. Social and economic conditions have established the basis for this; the motion picture further enforces it.[6]

The differences in the verbalization of the dilemma are obvious. The language of the sixteenth- and seventeenth-century philosophers is still deeply steeped in religious terminology; that of the modern writers in sociological terms; that of the nonprofessional radio listeners or nonlisteners in the ordinary words of everyday life. But beneath these differences in nomenclature the dilemma remains the same: perhaps it could be called a conflict between the psychological and the moral approaches to popular culture.

2. THE HISTORICAL LOCUS OF POPULAR CULTURE

This section of my discussion will be somewhat dogmatic in character, partly for the sake of brevity but also because it ought to be permissible to pause from time to time in our sociological routine and to speculate about the secular trend in which we, together with our objects of research, find ourselves.

The counterconcept to popular culture is art. Today artistic products are losing the character of spontaneity more and more and are being replaced by the phenomena of popular culture, which are nothing but a manipulated reproduction of reality as it is; and, in so doing, popular culture sanctions and glorifies whatever it finds worth echoing. Schopenhauer remarked that music is "the world once more." This philosophical aphorism throws light on the unbridgeable difference between art and popular culture: it is the difference between an increase in insight through a medium possessing self-sustaining means and mere repetition of given facts with the use of borrowed tools.

A superficial inventory of the contents and motivations in the products of the entertainment and publishing worlds in our Western civilization will include such themes as the nation, the family, religion, free enterprise, individual initiative; and in the Eastern orbit, higher production achievements, national cultures, the moral corruption of the West. The topical differences are not very decisive and, in any case, considerably smaller than the political differences which keep these two worlds apart. Saint-Simon, the great French pre-Marxian socialist philosopher, whose life extended from the *ancien régime* through the Revolution and the Napoleonic era into the days of the reactionary Bourbon restoration, once remarked that, while he had experienced the most contradictory political systems, he realized that consistent, deeply rooted social tendencies which were completely impervious to political change made themselves felt in those decades. The very concept of society rests in this insight. Rigidly and consistently different as political systems are from one another today, there is also a complete inconsistency in the content of popular culture within a given political system—and popular culture is an element of society of the first order. The yardstick is expediency, within the total social situation, of course, and particularly the distribution of power.

Nietzsche, who may be called the discoverer and matchless critical analyst of modern popular culture, has formulated its relativism with respect to content:

Modern counterfeit practices in the arts: regarded as necessary—that is to say, as fully in keeping with the needs most proper to the modern soul. . . .
Artists harangue the dark instincts of the dissatisfied, the ambitious, and the self-deceivers of a democratic age: the importance of poses. . . . The procedures of one art are transferred to the realm of another; the object of art is confounded with that of science, with that of the Church, or with that of the interests of the race (nationalism), or with that of philosophy—a man rings all bells at once, and awakens the vague suspicion that he is a god. . . .
Artists flatter women, sufferers, and indignant folk. Narcotics and opiates are made to preponderate in art. The fancy of cultured people, and of readers of poetry and ancient history, is tickled.[7]

What Nietzsche expressed in the general terms of the philosopher of culture has its spokesmen today. In an analysis of cartoon films a modern writer has pointed to the criterion of social expediency in the selection of their materials:

It is just Disney's distinguishing characteristic that he is uncritical of what he reflects. He is quite artless. If the values by which the society lives are still serving, if the prevailing outlook is relatively brightfaced and aggressive, he will improvise from that—and give us Mickey Mouse. If the time is one of crisis, and these values will no longer serve but are in conflict and in question, if the prevailing state of mind is a deep bewilderment, he will improvise with equal lack of inhibition. His particular talent is that he does not embarrass himself. This makes his dreams sometimes monstrous. But it gives them a wide reference.[8]

It may be noted in passing that in the present postwar period disillusionment over the lack of definitive cultural and moral solutions has become prevalent. It finds expression in an artificial permeation of entertainment products with religion. In the average movie the pursuit of love almost invariably means the appearance of the clergyman. Nietzsche had already commented on the artificial respiration administered to religion in an era of decadence and nihilism. When he said, "God is dead," he meant that the frenzied activities of modern life produce popular culture in an attempt to fill a vacuum which cannot be filled. Nietzsche linked the precarious role of religion, the pressure of civilization, and its neuroticizing influence on people:

> *In the Neighborhood of Insanity.*—The sum of sensations, knowledge and experiences, the whole burden of culture, therefore, has become so great that an overstraining of nerves and powers of thought is a common danger, indeed the cultivated classes of European countries are throughout neurotic, and almost every one of their great families is on the verge of insanity in one of their branches. True, health is now sought in every possible way; but in the main a diminution of that tension of feeling, of that oppressive burden of culture, is needful, which, even though it might be bought at a heavy sacrifice, would at least give us room for the great hope of a *new Renaissance.*[9]

With this quotation we return to the differences between popular culture and art, between spurious gratification and a genuine experience as a step to greater individual fulfilment (this is the meaning of Aristotle's *catharsis*). Art lives on the threshold of action. Men free themselves truly from the mythical relation to things by stepping back, so to speak, from that which they once worshiped and which they now discover as the Beautiful. To experience beauty is to be liberated from the overpowering domination of nature over men. In popular culture, men free themselves from mythical powers by discarding everything, even reverence for the Beautiful. They deny anything that transcends the given reality.[10] This is exactly what de Tocqueville meant, I think, in our opening quotation. From the realm of beauty man walks into the realm of entertainment, which is, in turn, integrated with the necessities of society and denies the right to individual fulfilment:

> Under the absolute sway of one man the body was attacked in order to subdue the soul; but the soul escaped the blows which were directed against it and rose proudly superior. Such is not the course adopted by tyranny in democratic republics; there the body is left free, and the soul is enslaved. The master no longer says: "You shall think as I do or you shall die"; but he says: "You are free to think differently from me and to retain your life, your property, and all that you possess; but you are henceforth a stranger among your people. You may retain your civil rights, but they will be useless to you, for you will never be chosen by your fellow citizens if you solicit their votes; and they will affect to scorn you if you ask for their esteem. You will remain among men, but you will

be deprived of the rights of mankind. Your fellow creatures will shun you like
an impure being; and even those who believe in your innocence will abandon
you, lest they should be shunned in their turn. Go in peace! I have given you
your life, but it is an existence worse than death."[11]

Men no longer surrender to illusions.

3. SOCIAL RESEARCH AND POPULAR CULTURE

The problem is whether, and to what extent, modern social science is
equipped to deal with modern social culture. The instruments of research
have been brought to a high degree of refinement. But is this enough? Empirical social science has become a kind of applied asceticism. It stands
clear of any entanglements with foreign powers and thrives in an atmosphere
of rigidly enforced neutrality. It refuses to enter the sphere of meaning. A
study of television, for instance, will go to great heights in analyzing data
on the influence of television on family life, but it will leave to poets and
dreamers the question of the actual human values of this new institution.
Social research takes the phenomena of modern life, including the mass
media, at face value. It rejects the task of placing them in a historical and
moral context. In the beginning of the modern era, social theory had theology as its model, but today the natural sciences have replaced theology.
This change in models has far-reaching implications. Theology aims at salvation, natural science at manipulation; the one leads to heaven and hell,
the other to technology and machinery. Social science is today defined as
an analysis of painstakingly circumscribed, more or less artificially isolated,
social sectors. It imagines that such horizontal segments constitute its research laboratory, and it seems to forget that the only social research
laboratories that are properly admissible are historical situations.

This has not always been the case. Popular culture, particularly as represented by the newspapers, has been a subject of discussion for about a
hundred and fifty years. Before the naturalistic phase of social science set
in, the phenomena of popular culture were treated as a social and historical
whole. This holds true for religious, philosophical, and political discussions
from the time of Napoleon to Hitler. Our contemporary social science
literature seems completely void of any knowledge of, or at least of any
application and reference to, the voluminous writings produced on both
the left and the right wings of the political and cultural fronts in the nineteenth century. It seems to ignore Catholic social philosophy as well as
Socialist polemics, Nietzsche as well as the great, but completely unknown,
Austrian critic Karl Kraus, who tried to validate the notion of the crisis
of modern culture by a critique of popular culture. Kraus focused attention
on the analysis of language. The common denominator of his essays is
his thesis that it is in the hollowing out of language that we can see the
disintegration, and even the disappearance, of the concept and existence
of the autonomous individual, of the personality in its classical sense.

Studies of the role of the press, even of such specialized problems as readership figures, would do well to go back to the nineteenth- and early twentieth-century analyses of the press in Germany. There they would find, in the different political and philosophical camps, illustrations of the fruit-fulness of studying social phenomena in context—in the case of the press, the relationship of the modern newspaper to the history of the economic, social, and political emancipation of the middle classes. A study of the modern newspaper is meaningless, in the very exact sense of the word, if it is not aware of the historical framework, which is composed of both critical materials like those of Karl Kraus, writing at the end of an epoch, and optimistic attitudes like the following, from the work of the German publicist, Joseph Goerres, at the beginning of the nineteenth century:

What everybody desires and wants shall be expressed in the newspapers; what is depressing and troubling everybody may not remain unexpressed; there must be somebody who is obliged to speak the truth, candid, without reservation, and unfettered. For, under a good constitution the right of freedom of expression is not merely tolerated but is a basic requirement; the speaker shall be looked upon as a holy person until he forfeits his right by his own fault and lies. Those who work against such freedom leave themselves open to the charge that the consciousness of their own great faults weighs heavily upon them; those who act justly do not shun free speech—it can in the end lead only to "honor be to whom honor is due"; but those who are dependent on dirt and darkness certainly like secretiveness.[12]

This is not to say that the whole field of sociology has been given over to historical asceticism. Quite a number of leading scholars in social theory and social history have kept alive the conscience of a historical civilization. It is worth our while to read again the following remarks by Robert E. Park:

In fact, the reason we have newspapers at all, in the modern sense of the term, is because about one hundred years ago, in 1835 to be exact, a few newspaper publishers in New York City and in London discovered (1) that most human beings, if they could read at all, found it easier to read news than editorial opinion and (2) that the common man would rather be entertained than edified. This, in its way, had the character and importance of a real discovery. It was like the discovery, made later in Hollywood, that gentlemen prefer blonds. At any rate, it is to the consistent application of the principle involved that the modern newspaper owes not merely its present character but its survival as a species.[13]

His point of view finds confirmation in an excellent study in the history of mass culture by Louis B. Wright:

If it is desirable to trace the pedigree of the popular culture of modern America, it is possible to find most of its ideology implicit in the middle-class thought of Elizabethan England. The historian of American culture must look back to the Renaissance and read widely in the forgotten literature of tradesmen.[14]

One of the difficulties which have occasionally arisen in intellectual inter-course between people of American and European backgrounds is perhaps due to the antihistorical allergy of the former and the historical over-sensitivity of the latter. I can illustrate this point by a very recent example.

When I received the first two volumes of the outstanding work by Samuel A. Stouffer and his staff, *The American Soldier,* I was curious to learn how the authors would place their research within the context of the social theories about the soldier that have been developed from Plato on. To my amazement, I could find no historical reference beyond a solitary quotation from Tolstoi, who wrote in one place in *War and Peace*: "In warfare the force of armies is a product of the mass multiplied by something else, an unknown x." The authors added the following comment: "Thus for perhaps the first time in military history it is possible to present statistical evidence relating to the factor x described in the quotation from Tolstoi's *War and Peace* at the beginning of this chapter."[15] They seem to have been fascinated by the mathematical symbolism of Tolstoi's sentence, but they successfully resisted the temptation to compare the social situation of armies in the time of Napoleon with modern conditions. In the face of such heroic restraint, it seems appropriate to quote the following flippant remark of a fellow-sociologist: "In this respect I speak of the failure of modern psychology. I firmly believe that one can learn more about the *ordre du coeur* from La Rochefoucauld and Pascal (who was the author of this term) than from the most up-to-date textbook on psychology or ethics."[16]

It seems to me that the splendid isolation of the social researcher is likely to reinforce a common suspicion, namely, that social research is, in the final analysis, nothing but market research, an instrument of expedient manipulation, a tool with which to prepare reluctant customers for enthusiastic spending. Only twenty years ago, social scientists were well aware of the dangers in the mass media, and they did not consider it beyond their duty to concern themselves with the negative, as well as the positive, potentialities of these mass media. In the pioneering article on "The Agencies of Communication," Malcolm M. Willey and Stuart A. Rice wrote:

> The effects produced may now be quite unpremeditated, although the machinery opens the way for mass impression in keeping with special ends, private or public. The individual, the figures show, increasingly utilizes these media and they inevitably modify his attitudes and behavior. What these modifications are to be depends entirely upon those who control the agencies. Greater possibilities for social manipulation, for ends that are selfish or socially desirable, have never existed. The major problem is to protect the interests and welfare of the individual citizen.[17]

Today, manipulation is taken for granted as an end of social science. A publisher can now dare to praise an outstanding sociological work with the following blurb on the jacket of the book:

> For the first time on such a scale an attempt was made to direct human behavior on a basis of scientific evidence, and the results suggest the opening of a new epoch in social studies and in social management.
> It is the editor's hope that the value to social science will prove to be as great as to the military, for whom the original research was undertaken. . . .
> The problems were Army problems, for the most part peculiar to wartime. But the implications are universal.[18]

Expediency and the lack of a historical or philosophical frame of reference make a sorry marriage of convenience.

4. SOCIAL CRITICISM OF POPULAR CULTURE TODAY

No systematic body of theories is available. The situation has been characterized very aptly by Frederick Laws:

> It will hardly be denied that the *condition of criticism today is chaotic*, especially when it is applied to the products of these immense distributing machines, *the new media*. Much reviewing is unselective in its enthusiasm and can with difficulty be distinguished from advertising copy. . . . *There is a lack of clearly expressed and generally recognized standards of value.* We believe that this confusion is partly due to a failure to realize or accept the fact that *the social framework in which works of art are produced and judged has changed fundamentally.* It is nonsense to suppose that the means of distribution or the size of social origin of the audience wholly determine the quality of art or entertainment, but it is stupid to pretend that they do not affect it. . . .[19]

There is a literature on popular culture today which is thoroughly critical. I shall try to summarize the findings of this body of writings in a few brief generalizations.[20] Some direct their critique against the product, but many turn it against the system on which the product depends. In special analyses, as in studies of a purely philosophical and sociological character, most authors concur in their final characterization of the products of popular culture.

The decline of the individual in the mechanized working processes of modern civilization brings about the emergence of mass culture, which replaces folk art or "high" art. A product of popular culture has none of the features of genuine art, but in all its media popular culture proves to have its own genuine characteristics: standardization, stereotypy, conservatism, mendacity, manipulated consumer goods.

There is an interdependence between what the public wants and what the powers of control enforce upon the public in order to remain in power. Most students are of the opinion that the habit of advertisement is the main motivating force in creating receptivity to popular culture and that the products themselves eventually take on the character of advertising.

There is no consensus on the taste of the populace. Whereas some have confidence in the people's instinct for the good, the prevailing view seems to be that only the bad and the vulgar are the yardsticks of their aesthetic pleasure.

There is considerable agreement that all media are estranged from values and offer nothing but entertainment and distraction—that, ultimately, they expedite flight from an unbearable reality. Wherever revolutionary tendencies show a timid head, they are mitigated and cut short by a false fulfilment of wish dreams, like wealth, adventure, passionate love, power, and sensationalism in general.

Prescriptions for improvement run the gamut from naïve proposals to

offer aesthetically better merchandise, in order to create in the masses a
taste for the valuable in life, to the theory that within the present setup of
social power there is no hope whatsoever for improvement and that better
popular culture presupposes a better society.

Finally, there is considerable speculation about the relations between
the product of mass culture and real life. The radio, the movies, the newspapers, and the best sellers are, at the same time, models for the way of
life of the masses and an expression of their actual way of life.

5. SOME THESES ON CRITICAL THEORY AND EMPIRICAL RESEARCH

In this section, I shall present some of the theoretical motivations which
underlie contemporary philosophical speculation about mass media. They
comprise some of the ideas which the staff of the Institute of Social Research,
under the leadership of Max Horkheimer, has tried to apply in a number
of writings during the last fifteen years.[21]

(*a*) The starting point is not market data. Empirical research, it is
argued, is laboring under the false hypothesis that the consumers' choice is
the decisive social phenomenon from which one should begin further analysis. We first ask: What are the functions of cultural communication within
the total process of a society? Then we ask such specific questions as these:
What passes the censorship of the socially powerful agencies? How are
things produced under the dicta of formal and informal censorship?

(*b*) We do not conceive such studies to be psychological in the narrow
sense. They aim rather at finding out how the objective elements of a
social whole are produced and reproduced in the mass media. Thus we
would not accept the taste of the masses as a basic category but would
insist on finding out how taste is fed to the consumers as a specific out-
growth of the technological, political, and economic conditions and interests of the masters in the sphere of production. We would want to investigate
what "likes" or "dislikes" really mean in social terms. While it is true,
for example, that people today behave as if there were a large free area of
selection according to taste and while they tend to vote fanatically for or
against a specific presentation of popular culture, the question remains as
to how such behavior is compatible with the actual elimination of free choice
and the institutionalized repetition characteristic of all media. This is probably the theoretical area in which one would have to examine the replacement of taste—a concept of liberalism—by the quest for information.

(*c*) We would question certain more or less tacit assumptions of empirical research, as, for example, the differentiation into "serious" and "nonserious" written, visual, or auditory communications. We would say that
the problem of whether we are faced with serious or nonserious literature
is two-dimensional. One would first have to furnish an aesthetic analysis
of qualities and then investigate whether the aesthetic qualities are not
subject to change under the conditions of mass reproduction. We would
challenge the assumption that a higher increase in so-called "serious" pro-

grams or products automatically means "progress" in educational and social responsibility, in the understanding of art, and so on. We would say that it is erroneous to assume that one cannot decide what is right and what is wrong in aesthetic matters. A good example of the establishment of aesthetic criteria will be found in the works of Benedetto Croce, who tries to show concretely that works of art have immanent laws which permit decisions about their "validity." It is neither necessary nor sufficient to supplement a study of the reaction of respondents by a study of the intentions of art producers in order to find out the nature and quality of the artistic products, or vice versa.

(*d*) We are disturbed by the acceptance at face value of such concepts as "standardization." We want to know what standardization means in industry, in behavior patterns, and in popular culture. We think that the specifically psychological and anthropological character of popular culture is a key to the interpretation of the function of standardization in modern man.

(*e*) In connection with the latter point, we are particularly interested in the phenomenon of psychological regression. We wish to know whether the consummation of popular culture really presupposes a human being with preadult traits or whether modern man has a split personality: half mutilated child and half standardized adult. We want to know the mechanisms of interdependence between the pressures of professional life and the freedom from intellectual and aesthetic tension in which popular culture seems to indulge.

(*f*) As for the problem of the stimulus and its nature, here the connection with European philosophical heritage is particularly noticeable. Our thinking has its roots in the concept of understanding (*Verstehen*) as it was established philosophically and historically by Dilthey and sociologically by Simmel. We are inclined to think that empirical research conceives the stimulus to be as devoid of content as a color stimulus in a psychological laboratory. We hold that the stimulus in popular culture is itself a historical phenomenon and that the relation between stimulus and response is preformed and pre-structured by the historical and social fate of the stimulus as well as of the respondent.

Notes

1. Alexis de Tocqueville, *Democracy in America* (New York: Knopf, 1945), p. 4.
2. E. J. Trechmann (trans.), *The Essays of Montaigne* (New York: Oxford University Press, 1935), II, 291 ff.
3. Blaise Pascal, *Pensées* (London and New York: Everyman's Library, 1931), p. 44.
4. *Ibid.*, pp. 39-42.
5. Coulton Waugh, *The Comics* (New York: Macmillan Co., 1947), p. 354.

6. James T. Farrell, *The League of Frightened Philistines* (New York: Vanguard Press, n.d.), pp. 176-77.

7. Friedrich Nietzsche, *The Will to Power* (*Complete Works* [London, 1910], II, 265-66).

8. Barbara Deming, "The Artlessness of Walt Disney," *Partisan Review*, Spring, 1945, p. 226.

9. Friedrich Nietzsche, *Human All-Too-Human: A Book for Free Spirits* (*Complete Works*, VII, 227).

10. For a comprehensive theory on myth and art see Max Horkheimer and Theodor W. Adorno, *Dialektik der Aufklärung* (Amsterdam: Querido Verlag, 1947), passim.

11. Tocqueville, *op. cit.*, I, 264.

12. Joseph Goerres, *Rheinischer Merker*, July 1 and 3, 1814.

13. Introduction to *News and the Human Interest Story*, by Helen MacGill Hughes (Chicago: University of Chicago Press, 1940), pp. xii-xiii.

14. *Middle-Class Culture in Elizabethan England* (Chapel Hill: University of North Carolina Press, 1935), pp. 659-69.

15. Samuel A. Stouffer and others, *The American Soldier: Adjustment during Army Life* (Princeton: Princeton University Press, 1949), I, 8.

16. J. P. Mayer, *Sociology of Film* (London: Faber & Faber, 1945), p. 273.

17. *Recent Social Trends in the United States*, I (New York and London: McGraw-Hill Book Co., 1933), 215.

18. Jacket of Vols. I and II of Samuel A. Stouffer and others, *op. cit.*

19. Introduction to *Made for Millions: A Critical Study of the New Media of Information and Entertainment* (London: Contact Publishers, 1947), p. xvii.

20. I am preparing a study of the more philosophical and theoretical aspects of the literature on mass communications under the auspices of the Bureau of Applied Social Research, Columbia University.

21. E.g., Max Horkheimer, "Art and Mass Culture," *Studies in Philosophy and Social Science*, Vol. IX (1941); T. W. Adorno, "On Popular Music," *Studies in Philosophy and Social Science*, Vol. IX; Leo Lowenthal, "Biographies in Popular Magazines," *Radio Research, 1942-43*, ed. Paul F. Lazarsfeld and Frank Stanton (New York, 1944).

A Theory of Mass Culture

By DWIGHT MACDONALD

FOR ABOUT A CENTURY, Western culture has really been two cultures: the traditional kind—let us call it "High Culture"—that is chronicled in the textbooks, and a "Mass Culture" manufactured wholesale for the market. In the old art forms, the artisans of Mass Culture have long been at work: in the novel, the line stretches from Eugène Sue to Lloyd C. Douglas; in music, from Offenbach to Tin-Pan Alley; in art from the chromo to Maxfield Parrish and Norman Rockwell; in architecture, from Victorian Gothic to suburban Tudor. Mass Culture has also developed new media of its own, into which the serious artist rarely ventures: radio, the movies, comic books, detective stories, science fiction, television.

It is sometimes called "Popular Culture,"[1] but I think "Mass Culture" a more accurate term, since its distinctive mark is that it is solely and directly an article for mass consumption, like chewing gum. A work of High Culture is occasionally popular, after all, though this is increasingly rare. Thus Dickens was even more popular than his contemporary, G. A. Henty, the difference being that he was an artist, communicating his individual vision to other individuals, while Henty was an impersonal manufacturer of an impersonal commodity for the masses.

THE NATURE OF MASS CULTURE

The historical reasons for the growth of Mass Culture since the early 1800's are well known. Political democracy and popular education broke down the old upper-class monopoly of culture. Business enterprise found a profitable market in the cultural demands of the newly awakened masses, and the advance of technology made possible the cheap production of books, periodicals, pictures, music, and furniture, in sufficient quantities to satisfy this market. Modern technology also created new media such as the movies and television which are specially well adapted to mass manufacture and distribution.

The phenomenon is thus peculiar to modern times and differs radically from what was hitherto known as art or culture. It is true that Mass Culture began as, and to some extent still is, a parasitic, a cancerous growth on High Culture. As Clement Greenberg pointed out in "Avant-Garde and *Kitsch*" (*Partisan Review,* Fall, 1939): "The precondition of *kitsch* (a German term for 'Mass Culture') is the availability close at hand of a fully matured cultural tradition, whose discoveries, acquisitions, and per-

Reprinted from *Diogenes*, No. 3, Summer, 1953, pp. 1-17, by permission of the author and the publisher. (Copyright, 1953, by Intercultural Publications, Inc.)

fected self-conscious *kitsch* can take advantage of for its own ends." The connection, however, is not that of the leaf and the branch but rather that of the caterpillar and the leaf. *Kitsch* "mines" High Culture the way improvident frontiersmen mine the soil, extracting its riches and putting nothing back. Also, as *kitsch* develops, it begins to draw on its own past, and some of it evolves so far away from High Culture as to appear quite disconnected from it.

It is also true that Mass Culture is to some extent a continuation of the old Folk Art which until the Industrial Revolution was the culture of the common people, but here, too, the differences are more striking than the similarities. Folk Art grew from below. It was a spontaneous, autochthonous expression of the people, shaped by themselves, pretty much without the benefit of High Culture, to suit their own needs. Mass Culture is imposed from above. It is fabricated by technicians hired by businessmen; its audiences are passive consumers, their participation limited to the choice between buying and not buying. The Lords of *kitsch,* in short, exploit the cultural needs of the masses in order to make a profit and/or to maintain their class rule—in Communist countries, only the second purpose obtains. (It is very different to *satisfy* popular tastes, as Robert Burns' poetry did, and to *exploit* them, as Hollywood does.) Folk Art was the people's own institution, their private little garden walled off from the great formal park of their masters' High Culture. But Mass Culture breaks down the wall, integrating the masses into a debased form of High Culture and thus becoming an instrument of political domination. If one had no other data to go on, the nature of Mass Culture would reveal capitalism to be an exploitative class society and not the harmonious commonwealth it is sometimes alleged to be. The same goes even more strongly for Soviet Communism and *its* special kind of Mass Culture.

MASS CULTURE: U.S.S.R.

"Everybody" knows that America is a land of Mass Culture, but it is not so generally recognized that so is the Soviet Union. Certainly not by the Communist leaders, one of whom has contemptuously observed that the American people need not fear the peace-loving Soviet state which has absolutely no desire to deprive them of their Coca-Cola and comic books. Yet the fact is that the U.S.S.R. is even more a land of Mass Culture than is the U.S.A. This is less easily recognizable because their Mass Culture is *in form* just the opposite of ours, being one of propaganda and pedagogy rather than of entertainment. None the less, it has the essential quality of Mass, as against High or Folk, Culture: it is manufactured for mass consumption by technicians employed by the ruling class and is not an expression of either the individual artist or the common people themselves. Like our own, it exploits rather than satisfies the cultural needs of the masses, though for political rather than commercial reasons. Its quality is even lower: our Supreme Court building is tasteless and pompous, but not to the lunatic degree of the proposed new Palace of the Soviets—a huge wedding cake of columns mounting up to an eighty-foot statue of Lenin; Soviet movies are so much duller and cruder than our own that even the American comrades shun them; the childish level of *serious* Soviet magazines devoted to matters of art or philosophy has to be read to be believed, and as for the popular press, it is as if Colonel McCormick ran every periodical in America.

GRESHAM'S LAW IN CULTURE

The separation of Folk Art and High Culture in fairly watertight compartments corresponded to the sharp line once drawn between the common people and the aristocracy. The eruption of the masses onto the political stage has broken down this compartmentation, with disastrous cultural results. Whereas Folk Art had its own special quality, Mass Culture is at best a vulgarized reflection of High Culture. And whereas High Culture could formerly ignore the mob and seek to please only the *cognoscenti,* it must now compete with Mass Culture or be merged into it.

The problem is acute in the United States and not just because a prolific Mass Culture exists here. If there were a clearly defined cultural *élite,* then the masses could have their *kitsch* and the *élite* could have its High Culture, with everybody happy. But the boundary line is blurred. A statistically significant part of the population, I venture to guess, is chronically confronted with a choice between going to the movies or to a concert, between reading Tolstoy or a detective story, between looking at old masters or at a TV show; i.e., the pattern of their cultural lives is "open" to the point of being porous. Good art competes with *kitsch,* serious ideas compete with commercialized formulae—and the advantage lies all on one side. There seems to be a Gresham's Law in cultural as well as monetary circulation: bad stuff drives out the good, since it is more easily understood and enjoyed. It is this facility of access which at once sells *kitsch* on a wide market and also prevents it from achieving quality.[2] Clement Greenberg writes that the special aesthetic quality of *kitsch* is that it "predigests art for the spectator and spares him effort, provides him with a shortcut to the pleasures of art that detours what is necessarily difficult in genuine art" because it includes the spectator's reactions in the work of art itself instead of forcing him to make his own responses. Thus "Eddie Guest and the Indian Love Lyrics are more 'poetic' than T. S. Eliot and Shakespeare." And so, too, our "collegiate Gothic" such as the Harkness Quadrangle at Yale is more picturesquely Gothic than Chartres, and a pinup girl smoothly airbrushed by Petty is more sexy than a real naked woman.

When to this ease of consumption is added *kitsch's* ease of production because of its standardized nature, its prolific growth is easy to understand. It threatens High Culture by its sheer pervasiveness, its brutal, overwhelming *quantity.* The upper classes, who begin by using it to make money from the crude tastes of the masses and to dominate them politically, end by finding their own culture attacked and even threatened with destruction by the instrument they have thoughtlessly employed. (The same irony may be observed in modern politics, where most swords seem to have two edges; thus Nazism began as a tool of the big bourgeoisie and the army *Junkers* but ended by using *them* as *its* tools.)

HOMOGENIZED CULTURE

Like nineteenth-century capitalism, Mass Culture is a dynamic, revolutionary force, breaking down the old barriers of class, tradition, taste, and dissolving all cultural distinctions. It mixes and scrambles everything together, producing what might be called homogenized culture, after another American achievement, the homogenization process that distributes the globules of cream evenly throughout the milk instead of allowing them to float separately on top. It thus destroys all values, since value judgments imply discrimination. Mass Culture is very, very democratic: it absolutely refuses to discriminate against, or between, anything or anybody. All is grist to its mill, and all comes out finely ground indeed.

Consider *Life,* a typical homogenized mass-circulation magazine. It appears on the mahogany library tables of the rich, the glass end-tables of the middle-class and the oilcloth-covered kitchen tables of the poor. Its contents are as thoroughly homogenized as its circulation. The same issue will contain a serious exposition of atomic theory alongside a disquisition on Rita Hayworth's love life; photos of starving Korean children picking garbage from the ruins of Pusan and of sleek models wearing adhesive brassieres; an editorial hailing Bertrand Russell on his eightieth birthday ("A GREAT MIND IS STILL ANNOYING AND ADORNING OUR AGE") across from a full-page photo of a housewife arguing with an umpire at a baseball game ("MOM GETS THUMB"); a cover announcing in the same size type "A NEW FOREIGN POLICY, BY JOHN FOSTER DULLES" and "KERIMA: HER MARATHON KISS IS A MOVIE SENSATION"; nine color pages of Renoirs plus a memoir by his son, followed by a full-page picture of a roller-skating horse. The advertisements, of course, provide even more scope for the editor's homogenizing talents, as when a full-page photo of a ragged Bolivian peon grinningly drunk on coca leaves (which Mr. Luce's conscientious reporters tell us he chews to narcotize his chronic hunger pains) appears opposite an ad of a pretty smiling, well-dressed American mother with her two pretty, smiling, well-dressed children (a boy and a girl, of course—children are always homogenized in American ads) looking raptly at a clown on a TV set ("RCA VICTOR BRINGS YOU A NEW KIND OF TELEVISION—SUPER SETS WITH 'PICTURE POWER' "). The peon would doubtless find the juxtaposition piquant if he could afford a copy of *Life* which, fortunately for the Good Neighbor Policy, he cannot.

ACADEMICISM AND AVANTGARDISM

Until about 1930, High Culture tried to defend itself against the encroachments of Mass Culture in two opposite ways: Academicism, or an attempt to compete by imitation; and Avantgardism, or a withdrawal from competition.

Academicism is *kitsch* for the *élite*: spurious High Culture that is outwardly the real thing but actually as much a manufactured article as the cheaper cultural goods produced for the masses. It is recognized at the time for what it is only by the Avantgardists. A generation or two later, its real nature is understood by everyone and it quietly drops into the same oblivion as its franker sister-under-the-skin. Examples are painters such as Bougereau and Rosa Bonheur, critics such as Edmund Clarence Stedman and Edmund Gosse, the Beaux Arts school of architecture, composers such as the late Sir Edward Elgar, poets such as Stephen Phillips, and novelists such as Alphonse Daudet, Arnold Bennett, James Branch Cabell and Somerset Maugham.

The significance of the Avantgarde movement (by which I mean poets such as Rimbaud, novelists such as Joyce, composers such as Stravinsky, and painters such as Picasso) is that it simply refused to compete. Rejecting Academicism—and thus, at a second remove, also Mass Culture—it made a desperate attempt to fence off some area where the serious artist could still function. It created a new compartmentation of culture, on the basis of an intellectual rather than a social *élite*. The attempt was remarkably successful: to it we owe almost everything that is living in the art of the last fifty or so years. In fact, the High Culture of our times is pretty much identical with Avantgardism. The movement came at a time (1890-1930) when bourgeois values were being challenged both culturally and politically. (In this country, the cultural challenge did not come until World War I, so that our Avantgarde flourished only in the twenties.) In the thirties the two streams mingled briefly, after each had spent its real force, under the aegis of the Communists, only to sink together at the end of the decade into the sands of the wasteland we still live in. The rise of Nazism and the revelation in the Moscow Trials of the real nature of the new society in Russia inaugurated the present period, when men cling to the evils they know rather than risk possibly greater ones by pressing forward. Nor has the chronic state of war, hot or cold, that the world has been in since 1939 encouraged rebellion or experiment in either art or politics.

A MERGER HAS BEEN ARRANGED

In this new period, the competitors, as often happens in the business world, are merging. Mass Culture takes on the color of both varieties of the old High Culture, Academic and Avantgarde, while these latter are increasingly watered down with Mass elements. There is slowly emerging a tepid, flaccid Middlebrow Culture that threatens to engulf everything in its spreading ooze. Bauhaus modernism has at last trickled down, in a debased form of course, into our furniture, cafeterias, movie theatres, electric toasters, office buildings, drug stores, and railroad trains. Psychoanalysis is expounded sympathetically and superficially in popular magazines, and the psychoanalyst replaces the eccentric millionaire as the *deus ex machina* in many a movie. T. S. Eliot writes *The Cocktail Party* and it becomes a Broadway hit. (Though in some ways excellent, it is surely inferior to his *Murder in the Cathedral,* which in the unmerged thirties had to depend on WPA to get produced at all.)

The typical creator of *kitsch* today, at least in the old media, is an indeterminate specimen. There are no widely influential critics so completely terrible as, say, the late William Lyon Phelps was. Instead we have such gray creatures as Clifton Fadiman and Henry Seidel Canby. The artless numbers of an Eddie Guest are drowned out by the more sophisticated though equally commonplace strains of Benet's *John Brown's Body.* Maxfield Parrish yields to Rockwell Kent, Arthur Brisbane to Walter Lippman, Theda Bara to Ingrid Bergman. We even have what might be called *l'avant-garde pompier* (or, in American, "phoney Avantgardism"), as in the buildings of Raymond Hood and the later poetry of Archibald MacLeish, as there is also an academic Avantgardism in *belles lettres* so that now the "little" as well as the big magazines have their hack writers.

All this is not a raising of the level of Mass Culture, as might appear at first, but rather a corruption of High Culture. There is nothing more vulgar than sophisticated *kitsch.* Compare Conan Doyle's workmanlike and unpretentious Sherlock Holmes stories with the bogus "intellectuality" of Dorothy M. Sayers, who, like many contemporary detective-story writers, is a novelist *manquée* who ruins her stuff with literary attitudinizing. Or consider the relationship of Hollywood and Broadway. In the twenties, the two were sharply differentiated, movies being produced for the masses of the hinterland, theatre for an upper-class New York audience. The theatre was High Culture, mostly of the Academic variety (Theatre Guild) but with some spark of Avantgarde fire (the "little" or "experimental" theatre movement). The movies were definitely Mass Culture, mostly very bad but with some leaven of Avantgardism (Griffith, Stroheim) and Folk Art (Chaplin and other comedians). With the sound film, Broadway and Hollywood drew closer together. Plays are now produced mainly to sell the movie rights, with many being directly financed by the film companies. The merger has standardized the theatre to such an extent that even the early Theatre Guild seems vital in retrospect, while hardly a trace of the "experimental" theatre is left. And what have the movies gained? They are more sophisticated, the acting is subtler, the sets in better taste. But they too have become standardized: they are never as awful as they often were in the old days, but they are never as good either. They are better entertainment and worse art. The cinema of the twenties occasionally gave us the fresh charm of Folk Art or the imaginative intensity of Avantgardism. The coming of sound, and with it Broadway, degraded the camera to a recording instrument for an alien art form, the spoken play. The silent film had at least the *theoretical possibility,* even within the limits of Mass Culture, of being artistically significant. The sound film, within those limits, does not.

DIVISION OF LABOR

The whole field could be approached from the standpoint of the division of labor. The more advanced technologically, the greater the division. Cf. the great Blackett-Semple-Hummert factory—the word is accurate—for the mass production of radio "soap operas." Or the fact that in Hollywood a composer for the movies is not *permitted* to make his own orchestrations any more than a director can do his own cutting. Or the "editorial formula" which every big-circulation magazine tailors its fiction and articles to fit, much as automobile parts are machined in Detroit. *Time* and *Newsweek* have carried specialization to its extreme: their writers don't even sign their work, which in fact is not properly theirs, since the gathering of data is done by a specialized corps of researchers and correspondents and the final article is often as much the result of the editor's blue-pencilling and rewriting as of the original author's efforts. The *"New Yorker* short story" is a definite genre—smooth, minor-key, casual, suggesting drama and sentiment without ever being crude enough to actually create it—which the editors have established by years of patient, skilful selection the same way a gardener develops a new kind of rose. They have, indeed, done their work all too well: would-be contributors now deluge them with lifeless imitations, and they have begun to beg writers not to follow the formula *quite* so closely.

Such art workers are as alienated from their brainwork as the industrial worker is from his handwork. The results are as bad qualitatively as they are impressive quantitatively. The only great films to come out of Hollywood, for example, were made before industrial elephantiasis had reduced the director to one of a number of technicians all operating at about the same level of authority. Our two greatest directors, Griffith and Stroheim, were artists, not specialists; they did everything themselves, dominated everything personally: the scenario, the actors, the comera work, and above all the cutting (or *montage*). Unity is essential in art; it cannot be achieved by a production line of specialists, however competent. There have been successful collective creations (Greek temples, Gothic churches, perhaps the *Illiad*) but their creators were part of a tradition which was strong enough to impose unity on their work. We have no such tradition today, and so art —as against *kitsch*—will result only when a single brain and sensibility is in full command. In the movies, only the director can even theoretically be in such a position; he was so in the pre-1930 cinema of this country, Germany, and the Soviet Union.

Griffith and Stroheim were both terrific egoists—crude, naïve, and not without charlatanry—who survived until the industry became highly enough organized to resist their vigorous personalities. By about 1925, both were outside looking in; the manufacture of commodities so costly to make and so profitable to sell was too serious a matter to be entrusted to artists.

"One word of advice, Von," Griffith said to Stroheim, who had been his assistant on *Intolerance,* when Stroheim came to him with the news that he had a chance to make a picture himself. "Make your pictures in your own way. Put your mark on them. Take a stand and stick to your guns. You'll make some enemies, but you'll make good pictures." Could that have been only thirty years ago?

ADULTIZED CHILDREN AND INFANTILE ADULTS

The homogenizing effects of *kitsch* also blurs age lines. It would be interesting to know how many adults read the comics. We do know that comic books are by far the favorite reading matter of our soldiers and sailors, that some forty million comic books are sold a month, and that some seventy million people (most of whom must be adults, there just aren't that many kids) are estimated to read the newspaper comic strips every day. We also know that movie Westerns and radio and TV programs such as "The Lone Ranger" and "Captain Video" are by no means enjoyed only by children. On the other hand, children have access to such grown-up media as the movies, radio and TV. (Note that these newer arts are the ones which blur age lines because of the extremely modest demands they make on the audience's cultural equipment; thus there are many children's books but few children's movies.)

This merging of the child and grown-up audience means: (1) infantile regression of the latter, who, unable to cope with the strains and complexities of modern life, escape via *kitsch* (which in turn, confirms and enhances their infantilism); (2) "overstimulation" of the former, who grow up too fast. Or, as Max Horkheimer well puts it: "Development has ceased to exist. The child is grown up as soon as he can walk, and the grown-up in principle always remains the same." Also note (a) our cult of youth, which makes 18-22 the most admired and desired period of life, and (b) the sentimental worship of Mother ("Momism") as if we couldn't bear to grow up and be on our own. Peter Pan might be a better symbol of America than Uncle Sam.

IDOLS OF CONSUMPTION

Too little attention has been paid to the connection of our Mass Culture with the historical evolution of American Society. In *Radio Research, 1942-43* (Paul F. Lazarsfeld, ed.), Leo Lowenthal compared the biographical articles in *Collier's* and *The Saturday Evening Post* for 1901 and 1940-41 and found that in the forty-year interval the proportion of articles about business and professional men and political leaders had declined while those about entertainers had gone up 50 per cent. Furthermore, the 1901 entertainers are mostly serious artists—opera singers, sculptors, pianists, etc.—while those of 1941 are *all* movie stars, baseball players, and such;

and even the "serious" heroes in 1941 aren't so very serious after all: the businessmen and politicians are freaks, oddities, not the really powerful leaders as in 1901. The 1901 *Satevepost* heroes he calls "idols of production," those of today "idols of consumption."

Lowenthal notes that the modern *Satevepost* biographee is successful not because of his own personal abilities so much as because he "got the breaks." The whole competitive struggle is presented as a lottery in which a few winners, no more talented or energetic than any one else, drew the lucky tickets. The effect on the mass reader is at once consoling (it might have been me) and deadening to effort, ambition (there are no rules, so why struggle?). It is striking how closely this evolution parallels the country's economic development. Lowenthal observes that the "idols of production" maintained their dominance right through the twenties. The turning point was the 1929 depression when the problem became how to consume goods rather than how to produce them, and also when the arbitrariness and chaos of capitalism was forcefully brought home to the mass man. So he turned to "idols of consumption," or rather these were now offered him by the manufacturers of Mass Culture, and he accepted them. "They seem to lead to a dream world of the masses," observes Lowenthal, "who are no longer capable or willing to conceive of biographies primarily as a means of orientation and education. . . . He, the American mass man, as reflected in his 'idols of consumption' appears no longer as a center of outwardly directed energies and actions on whose work and efficiency might depend mankind's progress. Instead of the 'givers' we are faced with the 'takers'. . . . They seem to stand for a phantasmagoria of world-wide social security —an attitude which asks for no more than to be served with the things needed for reproduction and recreation, an attitude which has lost every primary interest in how to invent, shape, or apply the tools leading to such purposes of mass satisfaction."

SHERLOCK HOLMES TO MIKE HAMMER

The role of science in Mass Culture has similarly changed from the rational and the purposive to the passive, accidental, even the catastrophic. Consider the evolution of the detective story, a genre which can be traced back to the memoirs of Vidocq, the master-detective of the Napoleonic era. Poe, who was peculiarly fascinated by scientific method, wrote the first and still best detective stories: *The Purloined Letter, The Gold Bug, The Mystery of Marie Roget, The Murders in the Rue Morgue.* Conan Doyle created the great folk hero, Sherlock Holmes, like Poe's Dupin a sage whose wizard's wand was scientific deduction (Poe's "ratiocination"). Such stories could only appeal to—in fact, only be *comprehensible* to—an audience accustomed to think in scientific terms: to survey the data, set up a hypothesis, test it by seeing whether it caught the murderer. The very idea of an art genre cast in the form of a problem to be solved by purely intellectual means could only have arisen in a scientific age. This kind of detective fiction, which might be called the "classic" style, is still widely practiced (well by Agatha Christie and John Dickson Carr, badly by the more popular Erle Stanley Gardiner) but of late it has been overshadowed by the rank, noxious growth of works in the "sensational" style. This was inaugurated by Dashiel Hammett (whom André Gide was foolish enough to admire) and has recently been enormously stepped up in voltage by Mickey Spillane, whose six books to date have sold thirteen million copies. The sensationalists use what for the classicists was the point—the uncovering of the criminal—as a mere excuse for the minute description of scenes of bloodshed, brutality, lust, and alcoholism. The cool, astute, subtle Dupin-Holmes is replaced by the crude man of action whose prowess is measured not by intellectual mastery but by his capacity for liquor, women, and mayhem (he can "take it" as well as "dish it out"—Hammett's *The Glass Key* is largely a chronicle of the epic beatings absorbed by the hero before he finally staggers to the solution). Mike Hammer, Spillane's aptly named hero, is such a monumental blunderer that even Dr. Watson would have seen through him. According to Richard W. Johnston (*Life,* June 23, 1952), "Mike has one bizarre and memorable characteristic that sets him apart from all other fictional detectives: sheer incompetence. In the five Hammer cases, 48 people have been killed, and there is reason to believe that if Mike had kept out of the way, 34 of them—all innocent of the original crime—would have survived." A decade ago, the late George Orwell, apropos a "sensationalist" detective story of the time, *No Orchids for Miss Blandish,* showed how the brutalization of this genre mirrors the general degeneration in ethics from nineteenth-century standards. What he would have written had Mickey Spillane's works been then in existence I find it hard to imagine.

FRANKENSTEIN TO HIROSHIMA

The real heirs of the "classic" detective story today, so far as the exploitation of science is concerned, are the writers of science fiction, where the marvels and horrors of the future must always be "scientifically possible"— just as Sherlock Holmes drew on no supernatural powers. This is the approach of the bourgeoisie, who think of science as their familiar instrument. The masses are less confident, more awed in their approach to science, and there are vast lower strata of science fiction where the marvellous is untrammeled by the limits of knowledge. To the masses, science is the modern *arcanum arcanorum,* at once the supreme mystery and the philosopher's stone that explains the mystery. The latter concept appears in comic strips such as "Superman" and in the charlatan-science exploited by "health fakers" and "nature fakers." Taken this way, science gives man mastery over his environment and is beneficent. But science itself is not understood, therefore not mastered, therefore terrifying because of its very power. Taken *this* way, as the supreme mystery, science becomes the stock in trade of the "horror" pulp magazines and comics and movies. It has got to the point, indeed, that if one sees a laboratory in a movie, one shudders, and the white coat of the scientist is as blood-chilling a sight as Count Dracula's black cloak. These "horror" films have apparently an indestructible popularity: *Frankenstein* is still shown, after twenty-one years, and the current revival of *King Kong* is expected to gross over 2 million dollars.

If the scientist's laboratory has acquired in Mass Culture a ghastly atmosphere, is this perhaps not one of those deep popular intuitions? From Frankenstein's laboratory to Maidenek and Hiroshima is not a long journey. Was there a popular suspicion, perhaps only half conscious, that the nineteenth-century trust in science, like the nineteenth-century trust in popular education, was mistaken, that science can as easily be used for antihuman as for prohuman ends, perhaps even more easily? For Mrs. Shelley's Frankenstein, the experimenter who brought disaster by pushing his science too far, is a scientific folk hero older than and still as famous as Mr. Doyle's successful and beneficent Sherlock Holmes.

THE PROBLEM OF THE MASSES

Conservatives such as Ortega y Gasset and T. S. Eliot argue that since "the revolt of the masses" has led to the horrors of totalitarianism (and of California roadside architecture), the only hope is to rebuild the old class walls and bring the masses once more under aristocratic control. They think of the popular as synonymous with cheap and vulgar. Marxian radicals and liberals, on the other hand, see the masses as intrinsically healthy but as the dupes and victims of cultural exploitation by the Lords of *kitsch*—in the style of Rousseau's "noble savage" idea. If only the masses were offered good stuff instead of *kitsch,* how they would eat it up! How the level of Mass Culture would rise! Both these diagnoses seem to me fallacious: they assume that Mass Culture is (in the conservative view) or could be (in the liberal view) an expression of *people,* like Folk Art, whereas actually it is an expression of *masses,* a very different thing.

There are theoretical reasons why Mass Culture is not and can never be any good. I take it as axiomatic that culture can only be produced by and for human beings. But in so far as people are organized (more strictly, disorganized) as masses, they lose their human identity and quality. For the masses are in historical time what a crowd is in space: a large quantity of people unable to express themselves as human beings because they are related to one another neither as individuals nor as members of communities—indeed, they are not related *to each other* at all, but only to something distant, abstract, nonhuman: a football game or bargain sale in the case of a crowd, a system of industrial production, a party or a State in the case of the masses. The mass man is a solitary atom, uniform with and undifferentiated from thousands and millions of other atoms who go to make up "the lonely crowd," as David Riesman well calls American society. A folk or a people, however, is a community, i.e., a group of individuals linked to each other by common interests, work, traditions, values, and sentiments; something like a family, each of whose members has a special place and function as an individual while at the same time sharing the group's interests (family budget) sentiments (family quarrels), and culture (family jokes). The scale is small enough so that it "makes a difference" what the individual does, a first condition for human—as against mass-existence. He is at once more important as an individual than in mass society and at the same time more closely integrated into the community, his creativity nourished by a rich combination of individualism and communalism. (The great culture-bearing *élites* of the past have been communities of this kind.) In contrast, a mass society, like a crowd, is so undifferentiated and loosely structured that its atoms, in so far as human values go, tend to cohere only along the line of the least common denominator; its morality sinks to that of its most brutal and primitive members, its taste to that of the least sensitive and most ignorant. And in addition to everything else, the scale is simply too big, there are just *too many people*.

Yet ths collective monstrosity, "the masses," "the public," is taken as a human norm by the scientific and artistic technicians of our Mass Culture. They at once degraded the public by treating it as an object, to be handled with the lack of ceremony and the objectivity of medical students dissecting a corpse, and at the same time flatter it, pander to its level of taste and ideas by taking these as the criterion of reality (in the case of questionnaire-sociologists and other "social scientists") or of art (in the case of the Lords of *kitsch*). When one hears a questionnaire-sociologist talk about how he will "set up" an investigation, one feels he regards people as a herd of dumb animals, as mere congeries of conditioned reflexes, his calculation being which reflex will be stimulated by which question. At the same time, of necessity, he sees the statistical majority as the great Reality, the secret of life he is trying to find out; like the *kitsch* Lords, he is wholly without values, willing to accept any idiocy if it is held by many people. The aristocrat and the democrat both criticize and argue with popular taste, the one with hostility, the other in friendship, for both attitudes proceed from a set of values. This is less degrading to the masses than the "objective" approach of Hollywood and the questionnaire-sociologists, just as it is less degrading to a man to be shouted at in anger than to be quietly assumed to be part of a machine. But the *plebs* have their dialectical revenge: complete indifference to their human *quality* means complete prostration before their statistical *quantity*, so that a movie magnate who cynically "gives the public what it wants"— i.e., assumes it wants trash—sweats with terror if box-office returns drop 10 per cent.

THE FUTURE OF HIGH CULTURE: DARK

The conservative proposal to save culture by restoring the old class lines has a more solid historical base than the Marxian hope for a new democratic, classless culture, for, with the possible (and important) exception of Periclean Athens, all the great cultures of the past were *élite* cultures. Politically, however, it is without meaning in a world dominated by the two great mass nations, U.S.A. and U.S.S.R. and becoming more industrialized, more massified all the time. The only practical thing along those lines would be to revive the *cultural élite* which the Avantgarde created. As I have already noted, the Avantgarde is now dying, partly from internal causes, partly suffocated by the competing Mass Culture, where it is not being absorbed into it. Of course this process has not reached 100 per cent, and doubtless never will unless the country goes either Fascist or Communist. There are still islands above the flood for those determined enough to reach them, and to stay on them: as Faulkner has shown, a writer can even use Hollywood instead of being used by it, if his purpose is firm enough. But the homogenization of High and Mass Culture has gone far and is going farther all the time, and there seems little reason to expect a revival of Avantgardism, that is, of a successful countermovement to Mass Culture. Particularly not in this country, where the blurring of class lines, the absence of a stable cultural tradition, and the greater facilities for manufacturing and marketing *kitsch* all work in the other direction. The result is that our intelligentsia is remarkably small, weak, and disintegrated. One of the odd things about the American cultural scene is how many brainworkers there are and how few intellectuals, defining the former as specialists whose thinking is pretty much confined to their limited "fields" and the latter as persons who take all culture for their province. Not only are there few intellectuals, but they don't hang together, they have very little *esprit de corps,* very little sense of belonging to a community; they are so isolated from each other they don't even bother to quarrel—there hasn't been a really good fight among them since the Moscow Trials.

THE FUTURE OF MASS CULTURE: DARKER

If the conservative proposal to save our culture via the aristocratic Avantgarde seems historically unlikely, what of the democratic-liberal proposal? Is there a reasonable prospect of raising the level of Mass Culture? In his recent book, *The Great Audience,* Gilbert Seldes argues there is. He blames the present sad state of our Mass Culture on the stupidity of the Lords of *kitsch,* who underestimate the mental age of the public; the arrogance of the intellectuals, who make the same mistake and so snobbishly refuse to work for such mass media as radio, TV and movies; and the passivity of the public itself, which doesn't insist on better Mass Cultural products. This diagnosis seems to me superficial in that it blames everything on subjective, moral factors: stupidity, perversity, failure of will. My own feeling is that, as in the case of the alleged responsibility of the German (or Russian) people for the horrors of Nazism (or Soviet Communism), it is unjust to blame social groups for this result. Human beings have been caught up in the inexorable workings of a mechanism that forces them, with a pressure only heroes can resist (and one cannot *demand* that anybody be a hero, though one can *hope* for it), into its own pattern. I see Mass Culture as a reciprocating engine, and who is to say, once it has been set in motion, whether the stroke or the counterstroke is "responsible" for its continued action?

The Lords of *kitsch* sell culture to the masses. It is a debased, trivial culture that voids both the deep realities (sex, death, failure, tragedy) and also the simple, spontaneous pleasures, since the realities would be too real and the pleasures too *lively* to induce what Mr. Seldes calls "the mood of consent," i.e., a narcotized acceptance of Mass Culture and of the commodities it sells as a substitute for the unsettling and unpredictable (hence unsalable) joy, tragedy, wit, change, originality and beauty of real life. The masses, debauched by several generations of this sort of thing, in turn come to demand trivial and comfortable cultural products. Which came first, the chicken or the egg, the mass demand or its satisfaction (and further stimulation) is a question as academic as it is unanswerable. The engine is reciprocating and shows no signs of running down.

Indeed, far from Mass Culture getting better, we will be lucky if it doesn't get worse. When shall we see another popular humorist like Sholem Aleichem, whose books are still being translated from the Yiddish and for whose funeral in 1916 a hundred thousand inhabitants of the Bronx turned out? Or Finlay Peter Dunne, whose Mr. Dooley commented on the American scene with such wit that Henry Adams was a faithful reader and Henry James, on his famous return to his native land, wanted to meet only one American author, Dunne? Since Mass Culture is not an art form but a manufactured commodity, it tends always downward, toward cheapness—and so standardization—of production. Thus, T. W. Adorno has noted, in his brilliant essay "On Popular Music" (*Studies in Philosophy and Social Science,* New York, No. 1, 1941) that the chorus of every popular song *without* exception has the same number of bars, while Mr. Seldes remarks that Hollywood movies are cut in a uniformly rapid tempo, a shot rarely being held more than forty-five seconds, which gives them a standardized effect in contrast to the varied tempo of European film cutting. This sort of standardization means that what may have begun as something fresh and original is repeated until it becomes a nerveless routine—*vide* what happened to Fred Allen as a radio comedian. The only time Mass Culture is good is at the very beginning, before the "formula" has hardened, before the money boys and efficiency experts and audience-reaction analysts have moved in. Then for a while it may have the quality of real Folk Art. But the Folk artist today lacks the cultural roots and the intellectual toughness (both of which the Avantgarde artist has relatively more of) to resist for long the pressures of Mass Culture. His taste can easily be corrupted, his sense of his own special talent and limitations obscured, as in what happened to Disney between the gay, inventive early Mickey Mouse and Silly Symphony cartoons and the vulgar pretentiousness of *Fantasia* and heavy-handed sentimentality of *Snow White,* or to Westbrook Pegler who has regressed from an excellent sports writer, with a sure sense of form and a mastery of colloquial satire, into the rambling, course-grained, garrulous political pundit of today. Whatever virtues the Folk artist has, and they are many, staying power is not one of them. And staying power is the essential virtue of one who would hold his own against the spreading ooze of Mass Culture.

Notes

1. As I did myself in "A Theory of Popular Culture" (*Politics,* February, 1944) parts of which have been used or adapted in the present article.

2. The success of *Reader's Digest* illustrates the law. Here is a magazine that has achieved a fantastic circulation—some fifteen millions, much of which is accounted for by its foreign editions, thus showing that *kitsch* by no means appeals only to Americans—simply by reducing to even lower terms the already superficial formulae of other periodicals. By treating a theme in two pages which they treat in six, the *Digest* becomes three times as "readable" and three times as superficial.

The People and the Arts

By GILBERT SELDES

THE STANDARD OF LIVING

SPORTS and the cultural enterprises which do not saturate the mass give us perspective on the popular arts. Certainly the mass media are more interesting than sport, and their exceptional products are prophetic of greatness; the danger in them is that the bulk of their product has none of the range of the popularizers. The tendency is to approach the lower end of the scale of values, to exclude the exceptional. The result is that the popular arts not only convey a flat and limited picture of life, they actually encourage people to limit the range of their emotions and interests. Our standard of living is still considered the highest on earth, but the standard of life is going down. We begin to accept completely the teenage standard. Nothing in our daily lives must interfere with our having a good time; everything must be attractive to the adolescent. We gain by this a vast improvement in the appearance of our kitchens and living rooms, but the life of charm and leisure (as it appears in advertisements for washing machines) escapes us. Dr. Margaret Mead has suggested that even the young and successful housewife feels this; "she chose wifehood and motherhood, but she did not necessarily choose to 'keep house.' " Perhaps it is because the picture in her mind, as she got it from the movies and radio and from ads in the magazines is not "keeping house" but "playing house." The reluctance to take on the responsibilities of parenthood is in part a refusal to sacrifice the irresponsibility of adolescence and in part a fear that children will interfere with adult pleasures. Marriage itself is not a boundary line between youth and maturity, but having children is; and nothing in the representation of life by the popular arts suggests the intense, complex, and rewarding life of parents; instead we have child worship, which has nothing to do with parenthood, and idolatry for the old mother, which has nothing to do with childhood.

The realities of adult life arrive as a series of shocks. Our psychological systems are unprepared for them, and they are resented because they do not correspond to the promises made to us. Because we reject them, these experiences cannot enrich our emotional life, and we cling to the sensations of youth. We have evolved devices to put off the appearance of maturity and gadgets to entertain us, and we do not feel that our lives lack in variety, that we may become impoverished in our feelings as we become superficial in our thoughts; the gadgets are the most intricate in the world, and they

Reprinted from *The Great Audience* (1951), pp. 250-84, by permission of the author and the Viking Press. (Copyright, 1950, by Gilbert Seldes.)

prevent us from facing actuality. But "the contemplation of things as they are, without superstition or imposture, is in itself worth more than a whole harvest of inventions."

It is the function of the popular arts to divert, but not to deceive. When they become the only arts of great numbers of people, they can be held to account for what they do.

Moralists from Plato on down have condemned all the arts because they represent something less than the literal truth; and artists have replied, with some arrogance, that they alone penetrate to the essence of truth below the deceptive surface of facts and figures. To avoid the swampy ground of aesthetic dispute, we can find a reasonable place for the popular arts by putting theories aside and fixing our minds on what these arts actually do to people. Not what their exceptional efforts do, but what they do in bulk, what they are compelled to do by the conditions they have imposed on themselves. If they represent a view of life so false that it is dangerous to us, if they prevent the community from raising mature and responsible citizens, their function as entertainment is not fulfilled, and the good they do must be balanced against their failures while we try to discover whether they can change direction without losing their vigor and attractiveness.

So long as the popular arts do not blank out the great arts, comparison between them is useless. When they do, it is worth while examining the qualities ascribed to the great arts to see whether any of them apply to the others. In general it has been assumed that the great arts have these functions:

They give form and meaning to life, which might otherwise seem shapeless and without sense.
They give us a deeper understanding of our own lives and the lives of others.
They express the spirit of an age or people.
By all these things they create a certain unity of feeling.
They provide diversion from the cares of the day and satisfy desires unfulfilled in our common life.

The great arts and the folk arts have in different ways accomplished some or all of these purposes for a great many people. I will presently put down my reasons for not accepting the assertion that the fine arts alone represent all that is worth remembering in the life of a nation and for believing that the popular arts have a useful function outside of the one they now perform, which is the last on the list above. As background, I propose to examine some theories about the popular arts and some very practical uses to which they have been put outside of the United States.

"THE TREASON OF THE INTELLECTUALS"

The popular arts have always worried the moralist and the aesthete.

The true Puritan condemns the pleasures of the people because they are not uplifting, they do not contribute to the glory of God; the aesthete condemns the popular arts because they are vulgar parodies of the great. In the United States the intellectual has reflected both of these attitudes, and, perhaps without knowing it, he has reflected also the complex social situation created by the immigrant and the pioneer. During the early days the culture and a great part of the wealth of the country was managed by the Anglo-Saxons on the Eastern seaboard, while the land was taken over by westward-moving seekers for security who were presently reinforced by people of various European stocks. Even before the Revolution, New England divines denounced the democratic mob, and the struggle between the coast, the tidewaters, and the hinterland was on. The strain of radicalism is one of the few constants in our history, a bright red thread to follow from the time of Nathaniel Bacon, through Shays and Jackson, down to our own time. In the great century of expansion, Eastern bankers financed the railroads that opened the West, but they also took mortgages on farms and controlled the price of money, so that the wheat grower and the herder felt that they had to pay back twice as much, in the hard terms of their product, as they had borrowed in currency. In the 1880's the Populists concentrated fifty years of dissatisfaction into a movement which colored American political life for generations, as their useful proposals and their evangelical tone were taken over by Bryan, Theodore Roosevelt, Wilson, and the New Deal.

There have always been a few writers of radical temperament, but in the formative century of our growth from a coastal fringe to a continental nation, the major intellectual movement was transcendental or communistic or both, and was fatally divorced from the aspirations of the traditional American radical, whose chief ambition has always been to correct the unequal distribution of land or money or power; the average voter, Jacksonian or Populist, Progressive or New Dealer, never turned against private wealth: he wanted more people to enjoy it. The hapless Alcott who could not run a farm, the "cranks" who attended reform conventions, the phalansteries and communities whose sawmills always burned down, did not impress the westward-moving settler. The intellectuals wanted to make toil agreeable and to share a common wealth; the average man, radical or not, was accustomed to long hours of labor and wanted only a chance to earn as comfortable a living as his neighbor; he did not want to divide his earnings with others. He was not surprised to hear that Charles Fourier, who inspired so many utopian communities, had predicted that the waters of the seven seas would turn into oceans of lemonade; everything the Fourierites suggested seemed equally probable, and nothing they did was any more helpful to the victims of our first era of expansion. Not for the first time or the last, the common man was suspicious of those who loved him.

The writers and the painters longed for European recognition, and many of them went to Europe; the gap between the intellectual and the people widened. The thin and sentimental novels, the stiff pretty paintings, had nothing to say to men who may have been, as Lewis Mumford has said, brutalized by their "rape of a continent"; the men left the arts to the women, and another American tradition took root—that the intellectual life of a community was women's affair. It was an unfortunate division of interest, reducing the area of sympathy between men and women, encouraging men to keep their active life away from their women and women to keep the life of the mind and the spirit away from their husbands; encouraging also the artist to address himself chiefly to women, to be precious and flattering and dandified. Not only did the Hartford Wits and the minor poets of New York divorce themselves from the common life; when the horrors of the degraded mills of Massachusetts were first exposed, and a New England philosopher was asked to help the miserable workers, he answered, "Are they my poor?" Emerson looked back on the era that began scientific studies at the colleges, a time that brought a host of practical inventions as well as the beginnings of a strong labor movement, and coldly remarked that there had not been "a book, a speech, a conversation, or an idea" in the state of Massachusetts. On the day after Lincoln's call for volunteers, the poet-prophet of the common man wrote: "I have this day, this hour, resolved to inaugurate for myself a pure, perfect, sweet, clean-blooded, robust body, by ignoring all drinks but water and pure milk, and all fat meats, late suppers—a great body, a purged, cleansed, spiritualized, invigorated body." Whitman's fellow countrymen ("I utter the word Democracy, the word En Masse") were about to undergo a less dainty regime.

The artists of mid-nineteenth century America set the tradition of escaping to Europe or staying at home and forming coteries of contempt. "Our country is deficient in materials of society most pertinent to the purposes of the novelist," wrote Cooper, and a minor artist like Freneau asked, "How can a poet hope for success in a city where there are not three persons possessed of elegant ideas?" Before he discovered the dense intellectual life that actually surrounded our writers, Van Wyck Brooks accepted this tradition and said that "a vast unconscious conspiracy actuated all America against the creative arts"; at the same time he told us that the world of Longfellow was "a German picture book," that Hawthorne "modeled in mist," that Poe was "sterile and inhuman," and the heroes and heroines of fiction in their time "lived in a world of moan and moonlight . . . irreparable farewells, dungeons, assassinations, premature burials, hidden treasure . . . gothic castles."

"When one views the nineteenth century in perspective," says Bertrand Russell, "it is clear that Science is its only claim to distinction. Its literary men were second-rate, its philosophers sentimental, its artists inferior to those of other times. Science ruthlessly forced novelties upon it, while men of 'culture' tried to preserve the old picturesque follies by wrapping them in a mist of muddled romanticism." This is the judgment not of a philistine but of a philosopher who is an artist in his own right. If Russell is right, the men who were too busy conquering a wilderness to pay much attention to the arts were less to blame for the isolation of the intellectuals than the intellectuals themselves.

The tradition that America had no place for the artists who alone could express its inmost soul continued well into our own time. "Suppose I am the national genius," Ludwig Lewisohn suggested in the 1920's "Dreiser and Mencken and Francis Hackett and I." And Ernest Hemingway wrote that "a country, finally, erodes and the dust blows away, the people die and none of them were of any importance except those who practiced the arts." I cannot accept this elevation of a host of second-and third-rate men for the sake of the merest handful of great artists in any country at any given era; nor do I know any system of values in which the roadbuilder and the research scientist, the saint and the average sinful man who leads a decent life, become of no importance—and along with them Lincoln and Marx, Edison and Freud and Mr. Hemingway's own Belmonte, James J. Hill, Joseph Goldberger and John Humphrey Noyes, in a single universal relegation to non-importance. The idea that only the writer-painter-composer expresses the genius of a nation comes naturally to writers and painters and poets, and a tiny fragment of their work does resist the ravages of time and fashion. But the soul of man manifests itself also in the Declaration of Independence and in a tariff bill, in the song of a stevedore and in the laughter at a clown in the circus.

Both Lewisohn and Hemingway lived for considerable time in Europe during the time of the second great expatriation of American artists. It was natural for those who had a high regard for their sacred mission to go where they thought they would be appreciated, and it was also a little irritating for them to discover that part, at least, of the avant-garde abroad was enchanted by the very rudeness and bad taste and bumptiousness from which the Americans had fled. The self-exiles and the debunkers denounced America, shrilly or humorously, their books were bought by the American people, but their total effect on our national culture was not great. They contributed to some refinement of manners, but they did not rescue the country from materialism and they probably helped to bring into existence the anti-intellectual superpatriot who dominated the last years of the 1940's.

It is not an edifying story, and the intellectual can take as little pride in it as the philistine. From the time of James Fenimore Cooper to the day of Sinclair Lewis, writers have found some way to attack the average American, not in loving correction but in contempt. In all that time perhaps two dozen men and women have been artists so great that they were misunderstood; the rest were good, but not good enough to separate themselves from their fellow men; they made little effort to understand what was happening in America, were incapable of helping or guiding or comforting. The theory that the artist was respected by Americans because he disclosed the emptiness of their lives is only half true; the other half is that the artist had little to give Americans, little that was relevant to their time and situation in the world. "The American intelligentsia," says Eric Bentley, "consists of people isolated from their communities." The isolation is partly self-exile.

Perspective on this long separation between the artist and the people is helpful in understanding the present relation between them. The "mis-understood" artist of the past has given way to the artist who no longer cares whether he is understood or not, since he is not trying to communicate anything in the traditional sense of the word. "All modern art," says Ortega y Gasset, "is unpopular, and it is not so accidentally and by chance, but essentially and by fate." Popular taste has always demanded the recogniz-able object in a painting, the melody that can be hummed, the order of words that is easy to follow; and the great masters of our time have not been willing to satisfy these demands—nor, indeed, to be romantic or sentimental or particularly moral. Like Stendhal, they are making appointments with posterity.

FOLK AND "THE FOLKS"

It is natural that other forms of expression should spring up to serve those whom the lofty arts leave behind. When we meet these forms in the past, we call them folk art; we have been taught to respect them. The ballads of the Scottish border, Negro spirituals, old English songs kept alive in the Appalachians, are among these; they are anonymous, they come down to us changed by generations of singers from their lost original form. As an enemy of "the people," H. L. Mencken vigorously refutes the theory of spontaneous creation, assuming that there must have been an individual who composed a melody or wrote the words, even if nothing was put on paper; but this is political more than aesthetic argument. It is certain that besides the work of professional artists there have been songs and crude drawings and (as in our West) tall tales which gave pleasure to people and were adaptable, so that they ran through many changes and persisted for generations. (The smutty story is a modern example; I do not know of an authoritative study of its origins and transmutations.)

In spite of their obvious differences, folk art and popular art have much in common; they are easy to understand, they are romantic, patriotic, con-ventionally moral, and they are held in deep affection by those who are suspicious of the great arts. Popular artists can be serious, like Frederic Remington, or trivial, like Charles Dana Gibson; they can be men of genius like Chaplin or men of talent like Harold Lloyd; they can be as universal as Dickens or as parochial as E. P. Roe; one thing common to all of them is the power to communicate directly with everyone.

ART AND POLITICS

As I am concerned with the practical effects of the popular arts, I am not too interested in theories of their origin. But as most modern theories on the subject are actually extensions of political argument, and as politics may decide whether the popular arts are to continue free, I have made notes on a few interesting points of view, some of them totally opposed to my own. T. S. Eliot's conviction that all culture must be aristocratic and re-ligious reflects his admiration for a churchly and highly classified society;

romantic rebels against tradition exalt the primitive, the naive artists; the demagogue sneers at the intellectual minority and calls its art anti-American; and the noncommunist Marxian holds that the popular arts are commercialized and corrupted versions of the arts of the people.

The theory that assigns the most important position to the popular arts is held in Moscow; the Soviet Union is the only place in the world where a movie, a comic strip, a comedy, a magazine illustration, must be considered primarily for its effect on the people, and the only place where symphonic composers are rebuked by the government for deviation from true principles. If we are shocked by a composer's unmanly haste to repent, we must remember that even a reprimand from the Politburo is such recognition of the power of the artist as he could never find elsewhere. The principle that the artist must serve the state, following an official aesthetic, is foreign to us, and I am not sure that the reports we have of the merit of Soviet art are altogether unprejudiced.

But if the details of Soviet practice seem ludicrous to us, the basic approach to the arts has to be reckoned with. The artist is believed to have a profound influence, he is as important as the educator, the police spy, or the statesman in the united effort to establish the socialist state and create a new man. With this approach all entertainment must fall under the direction of the state. In the United States the influence of government, whether federal or local, is limited to those artists who voluntarily accept work from the state, and the entertainment arts are, officially, untouched by the hand of authority. The function of the artist is not defined, his activities are not restricted except by the specific laws covering obscenity, slander, and other misdemeanors which he may commit as a citizen. Our general attitude toward the artist is one of tolerant skepticism if he is difficult; it ranges from deep affection to idolatry if he is simple; but he has no position as a revolutionary power; except in wartime he is not an instrument of policy.

It would be remarkable if these two diametrically opposite principles should, in practice, produce identical results. They often do.

The analysis of the entertainment arts offered by noncommunist radicals shows how. These critics are enemies of the all-powerful state and of uninhibited capitalism; they are consequently in the traditional line of American radical thought. They differ from Mencken and his followers because they earnestly want the artist to speak to the people; they want him to be aware of his creative power; they want him to reflect in his work the issues of our time. They are, moreover, emancipated from the genteel tradition and do not scorn the comic strip or film or radio, although they are not always successful in using these instruments. Among them, James T. Farrell and Dwight Macdonald are particularly clear in their statements.

"In America," says Mr. Farrell, "a tremendous commercial culture has developed as a kind of substitute for a genuinely popular, a genuinely democratic culture." By his definition, a democratic culture "would re-create and thus communicate how the mass of the people live, how they feel about working, loving, enjoying, suffering, and dying." But, "owing to basic economic causes, something of the most profound significance has happened in American culture: it has been invaded by finance capital. American commercial culture is owned and operated by finance capital." Finance capital is responsible for the conditions of American life which "create alienated and truncated personalities. . . . The conditions of earning one's bread in this society create the lonely modern man." Mr. Farrell sees the movies answering a desperate want of companionship, presenting again and again "the same reveries, the same daydreams, the same childish fables of success and happiness. So much of the inner life of men is dried up that they tend to become filled with yearnings and to need . . . consolation. Tastes are thus conditioned."

The movies serve the finance-capitalistic state because most of them "distract the masses of the people from becoming more clearly aware of their real needs; . . . they distract people from the real and most important problems of life." They do this by the perpetuation of certain myths. "The values generally emphasized are those of rugged individualism. . . . The dominant characteristics . . . are those of the pioneer. The past is re-created in accents of weak nostalgia; the present glorified. The future is promised as no different. . . . What characterizes almost all Hollywood pictures is their inner emptiness. A culture . . . should help to create those states of consciousness, of awareness of one's self, of others, and of the state of the world, which aid in making people better, and in preparing them to make the world better." (Substitute "citizens of the Soviet state" for "people" and the categorical imperative would be accepted in Moscow.) "Hollywood films usually have precisely the opposite effect; most of them make people less aware, or else falsely aware. This, to me, is the sense in which Hollywood films fail to fulfill the real cultural needs of the masses."

Mr. Farrell is a candid moralist; in other passages his contempt for the film as entertainment is made clear. "What serious person in the whole history of mankind has ever argued that in order to bring light to a darkened world . . . it is necessary to entertain?" he asks, discussing war propaganda films and Hollywood's insistence that films with serious messages must be successful at the box office. "Did Jesus Christ and the Twelve Apostles believe that in order to spread the Gospel they had to do so with entertainment? . . . When you really teach, you do not need to entertain. . . ." This is an attitude with which I do not sympathize, but I can respect Mr. Farrell's position; in hundreds of films he has seen every element of intelligence, of human reason, of individual character, degraded in the sacred name of entertainment; he feels that when people are entertained by low devices, their status as human beings deteriorates; so he turns against entertainment.

Dwight Macdonald's position strikes me as being somewhat less doctrinaire; T. S. Eliot has said that it is the only position opposed to his own for which he has much respect. In an essay on "High and Popular Culture,"

Macdonald has developed these points: The old upper-class monopoly of culture has been broken down by political democracy and mass education, and capitalism has found a market for mass-culture products; in order to sell their movies, phonograph records, reprint books, and the like, the dealers in these products manipulate the cultural needs of the people; they do not satisfy popular taste (as Robert Burns did)—they exploit it. On one side, popular culture is a continuation of folk art, but it is also a vulgarized reflection of high culture, and the pressure on artists has become so great that they now must compete with the merchants of popular art—because bad stuff, following Gresham's law, drives out good. A generation or so ago the avant-garde did not compete, the theater had not degraded itself into being a feeder for the movies, and the movies themselves had a small coterie of artists, including Griffith and Chaplin. Now the theater and the movies are at the same level, and the movies, though better entertainment, are worse art. Since the popular arts feed foolish myths to the people and at the same time draw down the level of the great arts, the exploitation of popular taste becomes a serious threat to democracy.

I have always found the Marxists' analysis of the past more persuasive than their prophetic vision; and these two non-Stalinist dissections of the present state of popular culture seem to me impressive because they deal with a possible situation: the creation of a democratic art. They also imply the alternative: the development of a popular art which will end with the robotization of humanity. Mr. Eliot's position is irrelevant to my interests because I neither foresee (nor desire to experience) the creation of a highly stratified aristocratic and hierarchic state in America. His own early poetry indicates that he once was influenced by, and perhaps even took pleasure in, one of the popular arts, in his use of the rhythms of jazz to contrast with the stately phrases of the past. But I feel that he is not a useful guide to the politics of democratic culture precisely because he has turned his back on the reasonably possible future.

In the sections devoted to the separate entertainment arts I have tried to sketch the economic background of each and have accepted, as normal and natural, that the popular arts in a capitalist society reflect the ethics and practices and mythology of capitalism. My major ground of criticism has been that we are also in a democratic society which is not totally capitalist, and that the popular arts do not sufficiently reflect the ethics and the aspirations of a democracy; holding no grudge against entertainment, I feel that the failure of the popular arts rises from the low value placed on them by the exploiters who are willing to provide entertainment for a mass minority; they neglect the profit and honor they could win if they cultivated the entire field instead of plowing and harrowing the same lower forty over and over again. I differ from Mr. Farrell because I do not believe as devoutly as he does in the mission of the arts, great or small; I see a place even for entertainment that distracts and limits, provided it does not monopolize the field, provided even those who care for the cheapest kind of diversion are exposed at intervals to other types of entertainment.

My difference with Mr. Macdonald is largely one of approach. He seems to feel that the big battalions cannot be on the side of God and that mass entertainment under capitalism is condemned to operate on a quick turnover of the cheapest and shoddiest goods. Neither he nor Mr. Farrell allows sufficiently for the particular arrangements of the movie industry—for instance, the system of distribution which dominates the methods of production and which is not the only system capable of operating with profit; they seem to assume that the present combinations are not only typically capitalist but unchangeable. They may be right, but I do not believe they are. The manipulators of public taste will change their methods under pressure and give us new kinds of pictures and programs if that is the only way for them to make a profit.

I differ with Mr. Macdonald also in his dark diagnosis of the ills of the superior artist who is compelled to compromise with his inferiors. He appears to believe that expanding capitalism drove between the artist and the people, forcing them apart, and compelled the artist to work for a small, appreciative fringe group; but, as I have noted in the preceding section, it seems equally fair to say that the artist in America took the initiative, rejecting the woes and passions of the average man, and then complained that he was not appreciated.

It is a misfortune that this tradition of hostility between the artist and the people should persist in the age of mass entertainment. As each new medium comes into being, the intellectual shies away. In fifty years of movies, many first-rate novels and plays have been adapted, but few writers of the first order have tried to master the movies as a craft, as a new mode of expression for themselves. In radio's brief span, one American poet, Archibald MacLeish, has been conspicuously represented by a work expressly written to be broadcast; there have been one or two others who halfheartedly tried their hands at the job, without troubling too much to learn the capacities and the limitations of the instrument; I know of no attempt made by broadcasters to enlist poets. The only complete reconciliation between the American artist-intellectual and the average man came between Pearl Harbor and the death of President Roosevelt; we have reverted since to an armed truce, with serious threats of open conflict. The congressional ferret is only a symptom of a sustained effort to make all intellectual activity appear disloyal; modern painting, progressive education, serious fiction, purely theoretical approaches to sexual problems, have been as viciously attacked in Congress or in the press as the Mendelian law in the Soviet Union. We are still able to fight back at encroachments on our civil liberties, but the atmosphere of free activity in which the speculative mind lives is being polluted. The attack is so determined, and the defense so splintered, that Huey Long's prediction of a dictatorship may come true in the realm of the intellect long before our actual political liberty is jeopardized; and as Long suggested, it will be 100 per cent American.

THE COMMON OAF

I have emphasized the estrangement between the artists and the audience because a revolutionary change of attitude is urgent. It may even be too late. The manufacturers of commercial entertainment have done their work well, and the audience is conditioned to suspect or despise the thinking man. But it is not too late for the average intelligent man to become aware of the new situation and to do something drastic about it.

The new situation, as I see it, is a persistent, unremitting, successful attack on the reasonable man of intelligence, the balanced man of thought and feeling, the individual who has so far escaped the contagion of mass thinking.

In an extreme and obvious form, this anti-intellectualism appears in both radio and the movies as an attack on education; not only on progressive methods (which would reflect the social attitude of twenty years ago) but on all education, and this goes against the essential American tradition. At a time when the school system of the entire country is woefully understaffed and teachers are forced to menial occupations in order to eke out their substandard salaries, both radio and the movies consistently present two images: the angular spinster and the absent-minded professor, the former without sympathy, the latter without respect. Perhaps there have been some favorable presentations of the teacher, but in years of listening at random and in something like eighteen months of scrupulous observation, I have noted not one comedy program in which a teacher was not made into a figure of fun. Then, too, all the programs about adolescents are in the same vein: the sympathetic character is the one that, in a group of semi-intelligent people, knows less than they do. The studious child, the adolescent who reads a book, the young professional man able to discuss his own work, are all foils for the triumphant ape.

The movie version is necessarily drenched in romance. The wise elderly character-actor-professor occasionally appears, and the research laboratory, which is highly pictorial, is used as a setting. The typical figure remains the youngish scholar so engrossed in his work that he forgets about love and is brought down by an adolescent chit. Her wisdom is greater than his. The movies' great tribute to the intellect is in the figure of Mr. Belvedere, a man of vast erudition, possessed of an elaborate vocabulary and a studied rudeness. A novelist working as a baby-sitter, he develops the attributes of the Admirable Crichton, coping with all domestic emergencies, notably disposing of an unruly child by plastering its face with porridge. The novelty of an intellectual who could deal with practical affairs was a nine-days' wonder; on the tenth Belvedere was cut down to size and became a figure in a movie series, the old stereotype standing on its head for a change, a loquacious marionette.

The stereotype was invented in the days when the man of learning was rare, a remote and cloistered figure, and even primary education was limited to the few. Since the principle of universal education has been accepted, since heavy industry is founded on scientific research, since higher education is becoming more and more a requirement for good jobs, the attack on the trained mind is a mean anachronism. It flatters and exploits the victims of our educational system, those who have failed to benefit by it, and it calls in question the basic premise of the American political system.

THE AGE OF CONSENT

The motives for using stock figures to belittle the intelligence are mixed. In general, stock figures possess certain advantages: they are ready-made, requiring no brainwork or imagination to launch them into action; they are familiar to the audience; they correspond to the myths being told. But there are other motives. Radio, perhaps unconsciously, pokes fun at the average intelligent person because he does not fit into the climate of passive acceptance which commercial broadcasting has to induce; the intelligent man is to an extent critical; he asks questions, he is curious. These aspects of his nature are not necessary to the success of broadcasting, which concentrates on the average man's weariness after a day's work as it does on the daydreams of women when husband and children have left them to do the housework alone. A mixture of laughter, excitement, and sentimentality is indicated; the audience must be receptive, as nearly passive as possible; as a service to his clients, the broadcaster must paralyze the critical, questioning faculties of the human mind. The commercial message will be delivered smoothly or peremptorily, it will appeal to the customer's ambitions, offer him a way to success in life and a solution to personal problems, or it will hammer hammer hammer (in the triple rhythm of repeated assertions, with three double-barreled adjectives) and the audience must never sense the exaggeration, never ask for proof. This is "the engineering of consent" carried to a high pitch, for it not only induces a mood of friendliness, it blankets and suffocates all those faculties which interfere with the creation of the empty mind.

Radio has a supreme advantage over the movies because its fundamental rhythm is natural, it is based on the rising and the setting of the sun, the division of time into days; and this is fortified by the common rhythm of the working day, the rhythm of the recurrent days of rest. Five days a week we come home at 6:16 and are through dinner at 7:30 and go to bed at 10; into that routine the radio fits admirably. The rhythm of a new picture every Thursday and Monday is artificial, and each offering must be advertised as a powerful attraction because going to the movies is a break in routine for grownups, not a habit. The movies, with nothing to sell but the entertainment they offer, with no obligation to a commercial sponsor, might be freer to induce the mood of contemplation or the mood of criticism in the audience; they have not done so because they have chosen to work for a minority audience, profiting by the habit of movie-going before the years of maturity. Radio has a wider range and a narrrower objective. It must make more and more people more and more suggestible. It does this not only by the quality of its entertainment but by its mass. What one station cannot attract, another will; there is always something on the air; more abundant and more accessible than any other diversion known to man, its grand objective is to make man want diversion of no other kind or quality.

In *The Mature Mind,* Dr. Harry Overstreet has analyzed this aspect of broadcasting and noted that "from the advertiser's point of view" it is not good business to put on programs "that raise any basic issue about the economic structure within which advertising operates." This is true in practice, and it is not surprising; it points, however, to a remarkable psychological effect: the revolutionary new medium of communication is almost entirely in the service of the past. By a sort of internal pun, radio has succumbed to its first enemy: it has become static.

A review of the salient characteristics of broadcasting will demonstrate this. The repetitive beat is in itself an argument against change; it is an invitation to do the same thing at the same time, without end. The immortality of the daytime serial is only an extreme form of the permanence of radio types; the characters created by comedians are almost equally static—they may be old for the sake of a gag, but they do not age. Dramatic productions are drawn from the past or from the current movies glorifying the attitude of the past, using characters which became stereotypes in the past. The resistance to change is reflected in the popularity of program types and of individuals: The ten highest-ranking programs of last year were the ten favorites of 1940, with only a slight shift in the order of popularity, and the programs were fundamentally unchanged in material and techniques. We are getting prewar entertainment in the postwar world.

Our present political temper is a reassertion of the American past against the Communist future; in this atmosphere radio does not need to be illiberal in order to slow down the tempo of change. It is enough to sentimentalize or glorify the past, and radio does this not only by using history and by reviving stock figures of the past, but, more subtly, by implying that the future will be based not so much on the present as on the past. "The same thing but more of it" is the essence of radio's promise. It requires no effort, the receptive listener at home need neither think nor act. He is being kept comfortable, he is being entertained, in an America gone static.

The fundamental American tradition is that we came away from the fixed world of Europe to create a dynamic country, with freedom to move, to change, to work; with opportunity to learn; with a chance to rise in the world; with a duty to keep the free spirit of the country free. Even the concentration of power in relatively few hands and the full development of vast industrial operations has not entirely checked the flow of Americans from job to job, from place to place, from the south to the north, from farms

to cities to suburbs, from everywhere to California; and this persistence of
change reflects the one emotion all Americans hold in common, that the
future is theirs to create. It is a confession that the present is not perfect
and an assertion that nothing in the present can prevent us from changing
for the better.

OTHER PEOPLE, OTHER SYSTEMS

The creation of a social apparatus for controlling the effects of our
mass media will have to come from ourselves, but we can learn something
from observing the machinery used elsewhere. In the Soviet Union the popular arts are in the service of the state and are recognized as creative forces;
they condition people to be good by the Soviet standard of goodness. We
maintain that this results in slavery, which is approximately what they think
of our system. The grain of truth we can get from the Soviet critics is important: they see that our mass media do have a creative effect on our lives.
That they do not like the effect is of small consequence.

In the British system of broadcasting, which came into being long before the Labour government, a corporation created by the state is allowed
to function independently, subject to criticism and review. The listener contributes to the cost of broadcasting through an annual tax on receivers, and
this probably tends to limit the distribution of radio sets; compared to one
set for every two inhabitants in the United States, Britain has one for hardly
every family. The listener has a choice of stations, and in addition to the
erudite Third Program, popular and highbrow entertainments are balanced
on the regular schedules. Although the BBC is licensed by the state, it has
not been seriously accused of following a party line under the present government or its Conservative predecessor. It has been notably successful in
dramatic experiments and, like our radio, has created popular personalities
in the field of comedy. One of its signal achievements was the magnificent
pioneer work done in television; by 1939 British TV programs were as far
advanced as ours were ten years later.

The purpose of the BBC is to give the listener a great deal of what he
wants and to give him a chance to want other things as well. The British
fall below our standards of showmanship, especially in serious programs;
on the other hand, the prestige of such programs is high, they are offered
at hours of peak listening, not apologetically. Like the controlled radio of
the Soviet Union, the responsible radio of Britain is engaged in the business
of making good citizens; unlike the Soviet radio, the BBC holds with us
that the citizen is all the better for exercising the right to choose what he
shall hear; and, unlike ourselves, the British offer not only different programs, but programs of different kinds, reflecting many levels of experience,
and offers them with equal enthusiasm. The "mixed economy" of British
radio has not been entirely satisfactory to all the listeners, some of whom
express admiration for the livelier air of America and tune in to the Continental stations, which carry commercials and are more competitive. The

British system has been held up as a model to Americans, but no one has persuaded the American people that they can entrust any part of their entertainment to a government corporation which might become partisan or highbrow and take from us the double challenge of freedom to offer and freedom to choose.

Both the Soviet and the British systems confront us with the same problem: can we afford a completely free market in entertainment, particularly in those entertainments which are also means of communication?

The alternative to the free market is some sort of official control. Although the freedom of the market is only relative and real power tends to become concentrated in fewer hands, we are not yet in the hands of monopoly, and the regulation of the big entertainment business may still be possible without calling in Big Government. The number of broadcasting stations (AM, FM, and TV) has risen to over three thousand, and while few of the influential ones are really independent, the opportunity for individual action remains; the hold of the big studios on the big theaters has been relaxed. We are actually in a swing of the pendulum away from bureaucratic control, and only monumental follies committed by the exploiters of our mass media will persuade the average man, or the average congressman, that the movies should operate under federal license or television be policed for good taste by the FCC.

THE "BOOK" BUSINESS

In one associated field the folly has been monumental enough, and although the action taken has been on a limited and local scale, the failure of law that is not backed by public opinion is clear. That is in the case of the comic books. In several respects these books resemble the other media I have discussed; they are pervasive, with some seven hundred million of them printed each year; they are readily accessible; they exist at a single intellectual level; and their mass coupled with the velocity of their circulation makes it difficult for printed material at other levels to overtake them. At post exchanges during the war they sold ten times as many copies as *Life, The Reader's Digest,* and *The Saturday Evening Post* combined. Unlike the other mass media, comic books have almost no aesthetic interest.

They provide, on the other hand, the best example of the paralysis of public power, and it is primarily in that respect that I am considering them here. The reader knows that the comic books are a lineal descendant of the newspaper comic strip, which has itself undergone many changes in recent years. The self-contained strip of a generation ago, with a joke of sorts in the final picture, has been almost entirely displaced by continued stories, many of them of domestic life, and the Chicago school of comic artists responsible for this realism is also responsible for the most conspicuous use of the comic strip for fairly open political propaganda; on the other hand, the spirit of true fantasy which vanished when George Herrimann, the creator of Krazy Kat, died, has reappeared to a degree in the work of the gifted Al Capp. Like the comic books, strips are popular among adults.

After a number of strips had been collected and printed in book form, the potential popularity of the new form was shown when one book was offered as a premium by a radio advertiser; but the true comic book, a work created expressly for monthly publication, did not impress the public until "Superman" appeared in the June 1938 issue of *Action Comics*. When it became clear that the success of *Action Comics* was largely due to the "Superman" section, the hero achieved a remarkable eminence; he appeared in a quarterly, all by himself (he was also in a newspaper strip, on the air, and for a brief time in the movies—the wild laughter of the movie audiences may have frightened the producers). Dozens of imitators appeared, and some established themselves. Eventually a practical psychologist, deciding that America was becoming a matriarchy, created a superwoman. The preoccupation with crime foreshadowed by an earlier book, *Detective Comics,* did not diminish, and these books are, in fact, the ones that have brought down the fury of parents, police powers, and psychiatrists. As the business grew, other types appeared: the comic book has its economic background in the pulp-magazine business, and romantic stories, true confessions, and the other staples of the pulps have been adapted to the new medium.

Several of the publishing houses have provided themselves with distinguished advisory boards, including psychiatrists who defend the comic books on the ground that they stir the imagination of children, present life in the only terms the children understand, and give the young a sense of security. Neither they nor their opponents can isolate the effect of the comic books from the effect of the movies and radio, from the headlines and the pictures in tabloids, from conversations in the street and the particular tensions which a child absorbs from his surroundings. The defenders concede the occasional appearance of a sadistic panel, but they assert that the bulk of the comic books is essentially serviceable to society. In the few instances where crime has been traced to the reading of this literature, the defenders say that the connection is loose, that a predisposition to delinquency must have existed, and that normal children must not be denied their rights because of the slight danger that a few may be badly affected.

The attack takes several forms. Attempts have been made to compete in the market, notably by Parent-Teacher groups who have encouraged the publication of historical or scientific books similar in appearance to the horrors;[1] small boycotts have been threatened; bills forbidding the sale of comic books to children under a specific age have been introduced in state legislatures; and in extreme cases summary action has been taken. In Los Angeles County, in 1948, an ordinance was passed to prevent the sale of any publications depicting "the commission or attempted commission of the crimes of arson, assault with caustic chemicals, assault with a deadly weapon, burglary, kidnapping, mayhem, murder, rape, robbery, theft, or voluntary manslaughter." Before the law had gone into effect, the sheriff of the County learned from a fourteen-year-old boy that a recipe for poison in a comic book had given him the idea of poisoning an old woman, and a hanging and a burglary were also traced to the inspiration of comic books. In half a dozen other communities, within the space of a few months, similar cases were reported. Agitation flared up, the Association of Comic Magazine Publishers, representing only a limited number of important houses in the field, announced a code of minimum editorial standards which emphasized indecency as much as violence; the bathing suit was accepted as the norm for nudity, and "sexy, wanton comics" were banned. The presentation of crime was accepted, but a warning was issued against throwing sympathy against law and justice, and comics were urged not to show details and methods of crime (when committed by young people); sadistic torture was not to be shown, and "divorce should not be treated humorously"—a hint that the Production Code of the movies had been remembered. Two years later juvenile crimes were still being traced to comic books, laws were still being proposed, and parents were raging helplessly. An early tabulation based on a hundred comic books to which had been added a thousand comic strips, gave the following figures; major crimes depicted, 218; minor crimes, 313; physical assaults, 531; sadistic acts, 87; physical monstrosities, 165.

One comic book of 1948 examined by Albert Deutsch "demonstrates to the child reader now to gouge eyes with the thumb, choke off the windpipe, kick an opponent in the stomach . . . flatten his arch with the heel, bite his ears, kick him in the liver area, punch him in the spine . . . all this under the protective title 'self-defense' with the explanation that this is the way T-men render their enemies *hors de combat.*" The late George Orwell, who had a fine eye for popular iconography, connected American comics with the dollar shortage. "Are we actually using dollars to pay for this pernicious rubbish?" he inquired, and proceeded to describe: ". . . a beautiful creature called The Hangman, who has a green face, and, like so many characters in American strips, can fly. . . . A picture of . . . an ape-like lunatic, or an actual ape dressed up as a man, strangling a woman so realistically that her tongue is sticking four inches out of her mouth. . . . A python looping itself around a man's neck and then hanging him by suspending itself over a balustrade: . . . a man jumping out of a skyscraper window and hitting the pavement with a splash. There is much else of the same kind." The testimony continues: Sterling North noted "women strapped while sleeping, women thrown to their deaths from skyscraper windows, men shot in the back . . . children being tortured, specifically named poison being slipped into drinks. . . ." G. Legman, analyzing the comics in *Neurotica,* says, "With rare exceptions every child in America who was six years old in 1938 has by now (1948) absorbed an absolute minimum of eighteen thousand pictorial beatings, shootings, stranglings, blood-puddles, and torturings-to-death from comic (ha-ha) books. . . ."

The Queensboro Federation of Mothers Clubs find "manifestations of brutality, cruelty, and violence, . . . sexy portrayals and abominable English. . . ."

I have quoted the testimony of others because my own list is limited and because most of these outcries represent the attitude of parents searching for a way to cope with a powerful business enterprise which they consider positively evil. Even if they are exaggerating, even if the effect of the comic books on their children is not corrupting, the basic situation is still that parents have not been able to impose their will upon the publishers. Not enough parents are concerned, and those who are have not yet found the way to make their pressure felt. In that respect they are an ominous example; for the urgent need of the moment is precisely to discover new modes of applying pressure, to persuade a sufficient number of people that their own immunity from any ill is only an illusion, to persuade them to observe the facts and to act. The occasional flurry of good resolutions that follows even partial action against the comic books is a good sign; but, like the code of the broadcasters, the lofty promises of the publishers flourish on violations. Year after year Dr. Fredric Wertham brings forth panels showing new ugliness and sadistic atrocities; year after year his testimony is brushed aside as extravagant and out of date. The paralysis of the parent is almost complete.

The economic situation is a simple one. The newsstand receipts for comic books totals seventy-two million dollars a year; the wholesale distributors of these books count on them for a third of their total magazine sale; the spending money of the young runs to seventy million a week, and this vast sum (about three billion dollars a year) must be absorbed; the drug and candy sales (of sodas, fountain pens, mouth organs, and ukuleles), and the books must be carried to attract the trade. The field is dominated by a half-dozen houses each of which publishes a wide range of books: Western, romance, "scientific," murder, and so on. Like the movies, they have developed a system of block-booking which prevents the retailer from exercising any discretion: if he wants the best seller, he must take the others as well; he cannot eliminate those which bring disrepute.

The comic book is often compared to the dime novel of fifty years ago, chiefly by friends of the publishers and by independent admirers of gore for the little ones; it is not altogether a safe comparison for them to make. The dime novel was a printed text, sparsely illustrated, if at all, and therefore had to be read; the number of different ones available to the average child was small compared to a selection of dozens of comic books at every stand, out of a total of over two hundred and fifty published each month; and the dime novel was severely criticized precisely because it was different in tone from everything else the child could enjoy; there were neither serial movies, nor murder-and-suspense programs on the radio to reinforce the lessons in violence. Present-day sentimentality over the Nick Carter stories is, finally, a throwback to youth; and the comic book, as we know, does

not give up its hold as youth passes. It appears to be the most satisfactory
kind of reading matter when one cannot go to the movies or listen to the
radio.

We have here perhaps the real reason for the paralysis of the parents.
In a Midwest city nearly two-thirds of the comic-book readers are adults;
in the low-income groups, nearly one-third of all adults are readers. It is
possible that some of these enthusiasts will keep their favorite reading from
their children, but not probable. The parents who wish to keep the comic
books from their children are nonreaders; they may outnumber the fans in
a specific community, but they cannot take effective action unless they bring
to their side the childless who dislike the comic books and the parents whose
children have grown up—they have to convince that part of the general
public which has no immediate personal interest in the matter, the same
public that must learn the truth about all the popular arts: you cannot, by
avoiding them, escape their effect. But the citizen who thinks himself untouched because he excludes any influence of the mass media from his life
is harder to reach, unless, perhaps, his protected child is attacked by a
gang of boys who have not been protected. He believes that some things
are bad for people, but he thinks of "people" as "other people." There are,
to be sure, private vices which by common consent are tolerated—such as
gluttony. There are offenses against custom which are punished privately,
as divorcees are ostracized at Court; an extensive local option is invoked to
protect a township or a county where the variety of opinion in an entire
state prevents a general law; and by a wise tradition federal laws are limited
to such actions as no smaller body can cope with. Of all crimes against the
person, only kidnaping is punishable under a federal statute; murder and
reckless driving are local affairs. But recognizable danger eventually brings
the appropiate defense into play; no appeal to State Rights will stop the
government from acting against a plague, and the citizen seeing contagion
spread across his boundary line will demand action at the highest level,
by-passing local authority, if panic sets in.

Crime is the spectacular feature of the comic books, and since I am
interested in public reaction, I have used it to illustrate a point. But it would
not be entirely honorable if I did not note that after some ten years of unavailing public protest the emphasis has shifted; in the first half of 1950
dozens of crime, Western, and other comic books became "love books,"
comparable in material to the confession and romance pulp magazines. I
cannot say with certainty that this change was caused by objections to the
horror magazines, of which an ample number remain in the field; I do know
that parents have begun to object as seriously to the tone of these books as
they did to the others. Those I have seen appear to range from the innocuous
to the vulgar, but I am not yet familiar enough with them to say whether
they will do anything more than repeat the conventional love patterns of
the other mass media.

CORDON SANITAIRE

The good and the evil of the communications arts have often been assessed; their special quality, which on the bad side can be called contagion, is not fully understood. If we become suddenly aware of it, if demagogues exaggerate the evil for their own purpose, we can get a hysterical cry for the government to step in. We can avoid the disaster if we know precisely how great the danger is and find the means to contain it, moving deliberately to isolate the danger spots; we can do it only if we know there is no immunity for ourselves, there is no place to hide.

Although the comic book in itself is not as spectacular as other media, it is an excellent proving ground for all the forms of pressure and control. The dispute between psychiatrists and the conflicting testimony of other authorities can be resolved, and the serious charge that psychiatrists are paid to defend the comic books can be impartially examined. A body of fact is ascertainable, the potential evil can be estimated. If the facts warrant, action can be taken step by step, without permanent damage to any civilian right, because any law that limits the circulation of comic books can eventually be brought to the Supreme Court. Local ordinances are naturally directed against the seller. As many states have a law against the publication and/or sale of indecent and lewd books, the courts can be called on to determine whether the ordinances are legal. Some of the fifty communities which have taken this first step have tried to ban comic books entirely or to forbid their sale to children under eighteen. In California and New York attempts have been made to pass a state law against the sale, not the publication, of offensive literature. One law, vetoed by Governor Dewey, required a seal of approval from a state agency, which would have meant, in effect, that the state was exercising a censorship in advance of publication. Local boards, operating as various state boards of censorship do for the movies, have been set up to sift the acceptable comic books from the objectionable, giving the seller immunity from prosecution if he handles only those that are approved. In all cases of action based on local or state law, two possibilities arise: the law invoked locally may head off any appeal to higher authority or—the reverse—the acceptance of a local law may be only the entering wedge for state or eventually federal action.

The slightest appeal to law brings up thorny questions, the first of which is whether any community can forbid the sale of any printed matter to minors alone without violating the First Amendment; the appeal to law also reflects the feeling that no other power can be completely effective. In Hammond, Indiana, the newsdealers eliminated thirty-eight books against which religious and civic leaders had protested—a threat of total boycott went with the protest. It was pointed out that children could still get what they wanted by taking a five-minute bicycle ride to adjoining Calumet City. It was also pointed out, in connection with using the code as a form of

protection, that only 30 per cent of the industry subscribed to it; the publishers of some of the best and of all of the worst are not members of the
Association.

The sudden spurt of anger, the quick decision to do something, accomplish limited objectives. They prove that public opinion can be massed and
that pressure can be effective at isolated points. The opponents of legal
action invoke the principle of clear and present danger; when an ordinance
is passed or other summary action is taken after an overt act, the danger is
presumed to exist, but the spasmodic action is usually temporary and local,
and we have something like the Eighteenth Amendment on a small scale with
bootlegging not far behind. The publishers are untouched because fundamentally the public is untouched; the problem of eliminating a social danger
without destroying the right to publish has not been met because the danger
is still considered a private one.

THE LAW OF THE LAWLESS

I have omitted adjacent but vitally significant problems of the comic
book because I wanted to concentrate on the one aspect that can lead to
intelligent action, the connection with crime. I have not even assumed that
the connection is proved; a spokesman for part of the industry has entered
a blanket denial. I assume only that proof or disproof can be found, and
if the connection is established attention will be focused on the inadequacy
of our present social apparatus to deal with it.

To that weakness the other aspects of the comic book contribute, by
creating an atmosphere favorable to their prosperity. It is an atmosphere
of violence, of contempt for the processes of law; not only is the criminal
central to action, but the hero is himself lawless; he beats up villains, he
kills enemies, without benefit of trial by jury. He parlays hero worship into
Führer worship, and in this he is enormously aided by the figures who defy
the laws of gravitation and smash the lightning with their fists, destroying
malefactors and monsters, annihilating, on their way, "the armies of un-
alterable law." Children have always doted on the impossible, but at the
same time they erect a logic of their own by which to judge what they
hear. They accept the conditional mode of the old fairy tale where everything is given to the hero provided he does not forget to touch a certain
flower or to say a specific word; they accept penalties and forfeits, which
reflect something perilous in the adventures of life. The comic-book "heroes"
are outside all conditions. "At the rate I'm going," says Superman, speed-
ing to prevent a bomb explosion on a train, "we're sure to be on the scene
of the disaster wherever it happens." This is more than omnipresence: it is
a super-Einsteinian binding of time and space. This world of supernatural
power in which beings constantly fight, but never work or think, is contrasted with the world of men, and the men come off badly; Superman has
a human alter ego, Clark Kent; Kent is not very interesting.

In this world of scientific marvels, the scientist is either "mad" or works for the general good, and obviously in a world where science is in itself sane enough, but has been put to the uses of mass destruction, the comic book version is reassuring. Science is reduced to the fabrication of gadgets which reverse the laws of science—in this the sane and the mad do not differ—and on the side of society or against it, science is used to do what human law, and civilization based on law, cannot do. It is a complete surrender to the philosophy of power. That is the sum of the comic book report on society; about the individual it tells us that the criminal is a monster, which justifies any atrocity practiced upon him.

As Mr. Legman has pointed out, in his "Psychopathology of the Comics," the punishment that followed the escapades of the Katzenjammer Kids is no longer required; their butt was a human being, Der Captain, and justice was done at the end of each series; when a monstrous menace was substituted for a human being, no punishment, but rather reward or honor, follows the most violent brutality. I should note that Mr. Legman believes that the aggression enjoyed vicariously by children is actually hostility against their fathers. In "The Three Little Pigs" (comic-strip version) "the wolf is papa, tricked out in animal false-face so he can be righteously beaten to death"; and on the basis of this analysis he raises an interesting question: "The admission . . . that children need these aggressive outlets in fantasy against their parents, teachers, policemen, and total social environment is an admission that this social environment does not have a place for the child. The necessity for the same escape by adults then means that the social environment has no place in it for adults. For whom has the social environment a place?" It is a serious question, and it suggests another: is the comic book less an outlet for aggression than an instigation? In a society that respects neither the laws of nature nor of nature's God, that transfers all dignity and power to anti-Man whom it calls Superman, and that is built on the certainty that all encounters must be hostile and end in violence, we are confirmed in our fears and encouraged only to seek power from the unnatural, which is called the supernatural.

In that world who can care what happens to children? Who can care what will happen to the world the children will inhabit?

There are, no doubt, dozens of steps parents can take to counteract the influence of the comic books, and the fact that appeal to law is futile makes personal action all the more imperative. I have overemphasized the weakness of social action deliberately, using the comic books as the best illustration of a dilemma that occurs in the other popular arts as well: the liberal-minded citizen dislikes coercive action, tries to escape from corruption privately, and discovers that he cannot escape if his neighbors, his community, are infected. The same problem has become acute in relation to the hours spent watching television by high-school students—about as many as they spend in school, it appears. When the facts became known,

Jack Gould, radio critic of the New York *Times,* said that the broadcasters cannot escape their responsibility; while John Crosby, of the *Herald Tribune,* offered what he called "an old-fashioned" opinion that "the parents have no one but themselves to blame." There is, at present, no satisfactory social apparatus for compelling the networks to bring more useful programs to the children, and no one dreams of asking them to stay off the air at stated hours.[2] On the other hand, parents who limit the TV hours of their children will see those children grow up into a world of the half-educated, possibly into a world managed by the half-educated, if millions of other parents do not do the same. In self-defense, parents may move to areas of bad reception, but that is a Maginot Line, dangerous because they will think themselves secure and will not work out the necessary controls. The other danger was marked when the chairman of the FCC, Wayne Coy, warned telecasters to keep their programs clean of scatalogical jokes under threats of public protest and ultimately federal interference.

There is a sad footnote to this story of the comic books. "I remember," writes John Houseman, "the time when Disney and his less successful imitators concerned themselves with the frolicsome habits of bees, birds, and the minor furry animals. *Joie de vivre* was the keynote. Sex and parenthood played an important and constructive role, illustrated by such cheerful fertility symbols as storks, Easter eggs, bunnies, et cetera. Now all this is changed. The fantasies which our children greet with howls of joy run red with horrible savagery. Today the animated cartoon has become a bloody battlefield through which savage and remorseless creatures, with single-track minds, pursue one another, then rend, gouge, twist, tear, and mutilate each other with sadistic ferocity." This indictment is too harsh; the shorter Disneys often preserve the tenderness of his early work, even if the surface is violent; but the induction of fear or horror has become a deliberate purpose of his major pieces. As the imaginative powers have dwindled, excitement has been pumped up; too often, when he is not exciting, Disney falls into a depressing area of sentimentality. What was once a unique bedazzlement of the senses has become routine and stale. The shorts, even *The Three Little Pigs* and great masterpieces like *The Band Concert,* did not pay well, distribution of shorts being controlled by major studios interested primarily in their features; Disney elaborated his techniques, built a huge studio, and drew in the kind of investment that finances the major companies. He was compelled to go into quantity production, into making long features; he also found himself involved in a strike he could not understand ("Why, they all call me 'Walt,'" he said, honestly bewildered), and the sweetness and the lightness went out of his work. The conviction was gone too; he made pictures with human beings, he did nothing after the war that reflected the brilliant techniques of his military work. In 1950 he released a picture he was destined to make, *Cinderella,* which was an affirmation of an old faith but without the miracle the old faith had worked. How much Disney was affected by the change in children's tastes and how much they were affected by the comic books are matters of surmise. We only know that the one powerful countervailing force to the ugliness and the brutality of the comic book has retained a superficial prettiness without growing in range of imagination and warmth of heart.

Notes

1. Commercial houses have also experimented. In a comic-book version of *Macbeth*, the witches and murders and battles are faithfully exploited; the poetry is adapted to the style of the drawings. Thoughtful readers, however, will note that Shakespeare is corrected, his speech and his grammar being considered improper for the young. "Lay on, MacDuff" is acceptable; the rest of the exhortation has been changed to read: "and cursed be him who first cries 'Hold, enough.' "

2. Mr. Gould's stinging rebuke to a network for permitting a horror drama to appear in the midst of several programs for children was promptly effective. The offense was rank, the criticism exceptionally harsh and direct. Mr. Gould deserves the gratitude not only of parents, but of the entire community, for the demonstration he has given of the power of protest.

Avant-Garde and Kitsch

By CLEMENT GREENBERG

ONE AND THE SAME CIVILIZATION produces simultaneously two such different things as a poem by T. S. Eliot and a Tin Pan Alley song, or a painting by Braque and a *Saturday Evening Post* cover. All four are on the order of culture, and ostensibly, parts of the same culture and products of the same society. Here, however, their connection seems to end. A poem by Eliot and a poem by Eddie Guest—what perspective of culture is large enough to enable us to situate them in an enlightening relation to each other? Does the fact that a disparity such as this within the frame of a single cultural tradition, is and has been taken for granted—does this fact indicate that the disparity is a part of the natural order of things? Or is it something entirely new, and particular to our age?

The answer involves more than an investigation in aesthetics. It appears to me that it is necessary to examine more closely and with more originality than hitherto the relationship between aesthetic experience as met by the specific—not generalized—individual, and the social and historical contexts in which that experience takes place. What is brought to light will answer, in addition to the question posed above, other and perhaps more important ones.

1

A society, as it becomes less and less able, in the course of its development, to justify the inevitability of its particular forms, breaks up the accepted notions upon which artists and writers must depend in large part for communication with their audiences. It becomes difficult to assume anything. All the verities involved by religion, authority, tradition, style, are thrown into question, and the writer or artist is no longer able to estimate the response of his audience to the symbols and references with which he works. In the past such a state of affairs has usually resolved itself into a motionless Alexandrianism, an academicism in which the really important issues are left untouched because they involve controversy, and in which creative activity dwindles to virtuosity in the small details of form, all larger questions being decided by the precedent of the old masters. The same themes are mechanically varied in a hundred different works, and yet nothing new is produced: Statius, mandarin verse, Roman sculpture, Beaux Arts painting, neo-republican architecture.

It is among the hopeful signs in the midst of the decay of our present society that we—some of us—have been unwilling to accept this last phase

Reprinted from *The Partisan Reader* (1946), pp. 378-89, by permission of the author and the publisher. (Copyright, 1946, by The Dial Press.)

for our own culture. In seeking to go beyond Alexandrianism, a part of Western bourgeois society has produced something unheard of heretofore: avant-garde culture. A superior consciousness of history—more precisely, the appearance of a new kind of criticism of society, an historical criticism—made this possible. This criticism has not confronted our present society with timeless utopias, but has soberly examined in the terms of history and of cause and effect the antecedents, justifications, and functions of the forms that lie at the heart of every society. Thus our present bourgeois social order was shown to be, not an eternal, "natural" condition of life, but simply the latest term in a succession of social orders. New perspectives of this kind, becoming a part of the advanced intellectual conscience of the fifth and sixth decades of the nineteenth century, soon were absorbed by artists and poets, even if unconsciously for the most part. It was no accident, therefore, that the birth of the avant-garde coincided chronologically—and geographically too—with the first bold development of scientific revolutionary thought in Europe.

True, the first settlers of bohemia—which was then identical with the avant-garde—turned out soon to be demonstratively uninterested in politics. Nevertheless, without the circulation of revolutionary ideas in the air about them, they would never have been able to isolate their concept of the "bourgeois" in order to define what they were *not*. Nor, without the moral aid of revolutionary political attitudes would they have had the courage to assert themselves as aggressively as they did against the prevailing standards of society. Courage indeed was needed for this, because the avant-garde's emigration from bourgeois society to bohemia meant also an emigration from the markets of capitalism, upon which artists and writers had been thrown by the falling away of aristocratic patronage. (Ostensibly, at least, it meant this—meant starving in a garret—although, as will be shown later, the avant-garde remained attached to bourgeois society precisely because it needed its money.)

Yet it is true that once the avant-garde had succeeded in "detaching" itself from society, it proceeded to turn around and repudiate revolutionary as well as bourgeois politics. The revolution was left inside society, a part of that welter of ideological struggle which art and poetry find so unpropitious as soon as it begins to involve those "precious," axiomatic beliefs upon which culture thus far has had to rest. Hence it was developed that the true and most important function of the avant-garde was not to "experiment," but to find a path along which it would be possible to keep culture *moving* in the midst of ideological confusion and violence. Retiring from public altogether, the avant-garde poet or artist sought to maintain the high level of his art by both narrowing and raising it to the expression of an absolute in which all relativities and contradictions would be either resolved or beside the point: "Art for art's sake" and "pure poetry" appear, and subject matter or content becomes something to be avoided like a plague.

It has been in search of the absolute that the avant-garde has arrived at "abstract" or "nonobjective" art—and poetry, too. The avant-garde poet or artist tries in effect to imitate God by creating something valid solely on its own terms in the way nature itself is valid, in the way a landscape—not its picture—is aesthetically valid; something *given,* increate, independent of meanings, similars, or originals. Content is to be dissolved so completely into form that the work of art or literature cannot be reduced in whole or in part to anything not itself.

But the absolute is absolute, and the poet or artist, being what he is, cherishes certain relative values more than others. The very values in the name of which he invokes the absolute are relative values, the values of aesthetics. And so he turns out to be imitating, not God—and here I use "imitate" in its Aristotelian sense—but the disciplines and processes of art and literature themselves. This is the genesis of the "abstract."[1] In turning his attention away from subject matter of common experience, the poet or artist turns it in upon the medium of his own craft. The nonrepresentational or "abstract," if it is to have aesthetic validity, cannot be arbitrary and accidental, but must stem from obedience to some worthy constraint or original. This constraint, once the world of common, extraverted experience has been renounced, can only be found in the very processes or disciplines by which art and literature have already imitated the former. These themselves become the subject matter of art and literature. If, to continue with Aristotle, all art and literature are imitation, then what we have here is the imitation of imita*ting.* To quote Yeats:

> "Nor is there singing school but studying
> Monuments of its own magnificence."

Picasso, Braque, Mondrian, Miro, Kandinsky, Brancusi, even Klee, Matisse, and Cézanne, derive their chief inspiration from the medium they work in.[2] The excitement of their art seems to lie most of all in its pure preoccupation with the invention and arrangement of spaces, surfaces, shapes, colors, etc., to the exclusion of whatever is not necessarily implicated in these factors. The attention of poets like Rimbaud, Mallarmé, Valéry, Eluard, Pound, Hart Crane, Stevens, even Rilke and Yeats, appears to be centered on the effort to create poetry and on the "moments" themselves of poetic conversion rather than on experience to be converted into poetry. Of course, this cannot exclude other preoccupations in their work, for poetry must deal with words, and words must communicate. Certain poets, such as Mallarmé and Valéry,[3] are more radical in this respect than others—leaving aside those poets who have tried to compose poetry in pure sound alone. However, if it were easier to define poetry, modern poetry would be much more "pure" and "abstract." . . . As for the other fields of literature—the definition of avant-garde aesthetics advanced here is no Procrustean bed. But aside from the fact that most of our best contemporary novelists have gone to school with the avant-garde, it is significant that Gide's most ambitious book is a novel about the writing of a novel, and that Joyce's *Ulysses* and *Finnegans Wake* seem to be above all, as one French critic says, the reduction of experience to expression for the sake of expression, the expression mattering more than what is being expressed.

That avant-garde culture is the imitation of imitat*ing*—the fact itself—calls for neither approval nor disapproval. It is true that this culture contains within itself some of the very Alexandrianism it seeks to overcome. The lines quoted from Yeats above referred to Byzantium, which is very close to Alexandria; and in a sense this imitation of imitat*ing* is a superior sort of Alexandrianism. But there is one most important difference: the avant-garde moves, while Alexandrianism stands still. And this, precisely, is what justifies the avant-garde's methods and makes them necessary. The necessity lies in the fact that by no other means is it possible today to create art and literature of a high order. To quarrel with necessity by throwing about terms like "formalism," "purism," "ivory tower," and so forth is either dull or dishonest. This is not to say, however, that it is to the *social* advantage of the avant-garde that it is what it is. Quite the opposite.

The avant-garde's specialization of itself, the fact that its best artists are artists' artists, its best poets, poets' poets, has estranged a great many of those who were capable formerly of enjoying and appreciating ambitious art and literature, but who are now unwilling or unable to acquire an initiation into their craft secrets. The masses have always remained more or less indifferent to culture in the process of development. But today such culture is being abandoned by those to whom it actually belongs—our ruling class. For it is to the latter that the avant-garde belongs. No culture can develop without a social basis, without a source of stable income. And in the case of the avant-garde this was provided by an élite among the ruling class of that society from which it assumed itself to be cut off, but to which it has always remained attached by an umbilical cord of gold. The paradox is real. And now this élite is rapidly shrinking. Since the avant-garde forms the only living culture we now have, the survival in the near future of culture in general is thus threatened.

We must not be deceived by superficial phenomena and local successes. Picasso's shows still draw crowds, and T. S. Eliot is taught in the universities; the dealers in modernist art are still in business, and the publishers still publish some "difficult" poetry. But the avant-garde itself, already sensing the danger, is becoming more and more timid every day that passes. Academicism and commercialism are appearing in the strangest places. This can mean only one thing: that the avant-garde is becoming unsure of the audience it depends on—the rich and the cultivated.

Is it the nature itself of avant-garde culture that is alone responsible for the danger it finds itself in? Or is that only a dangerous liability? Are there other, and perhaps more important, factors involved?

2

Where there is an avant-garde, generally we also find a rear-guard. True enough—simultaneously with the entrance of the avant-garde, a second new cultural phenomenon appeared in the industrial West: that thing to which the Germans gave the wonderful name of *Kitsch*: popular, commercial art and literature with their chromeotypes, magazine covers, illustrations, ads, slick and pulp fiction, comics, Tin Pan Alley music, tap dancing, Hollywood movies, etc., etc. For some reason this gigantic apparition has always been taken for granted. It is time we looked into its whys and wherefores.

Kitsch is a product of the industrial revolution which urbanized the masses of western Europe and America and established what is called universal literacy.

Previous to this the only market for formal culture, as distinguished from folk culture, had been among those who in addition to being able to read and write could command the leisure and comfort that always goes hand in hand with cultivation of some sort. This until then had been inextricably associated with literacy. But with the introduction of universal literarcy, the ability to read and write became almost a minor skill like driving a car, and 'it no longer served to distinguish an individual's cultural inclinations, since it was no longer the exclusive concomitant of refined tastes. The peasants who settled in the cities as proletariat and petty bourgeois learned to read and write for the sake of efficiency, but they did not win the leisure and comfort necessary for the enjoyment of the city's traditional culture. Losing, nevertheless, their taste for the folk culture whose background was the countryside, and discovering a new capacity for boredom at the same time, the new urban masses set up a pressure on society to provide them with a kind of culture fit for their own consumption. To fill the demand of the new market a new commodity was devised: ersatz culture, kitsch, destined for those who, insensible to the values of genuine culture, are hungry nevertheless for the diversion that only culture of some sort can provide.

Kitsch, using for raw material the debased and academicized simulacra of genuine culture, welcomes and cultivates this insensibility. It is the source of its profits. Kitsch is mechanical and operates by formulas. Kitsch is vicarious experience and faked sensations. Kitsch changes according to style, but remains always the same. Kitsch is the epitome of all that is spurious in the life of our times. Kitsch pretends to demand nothing of its customers except their money—not even their time.

The precondition for kitsch, a condition without which kitsch would be impossible, is the availability close at hand of a fully matured cultural tradition, whose discoveries, acquisitions, and perfected self-consciousness kitsch can take advantage of for its own ends. It borrows from it devices, tricks, stratagems, rules of thumb, themes, converts them into a system, and discards the rest. It draws its life blood, so to speak, from this reservoir of accumulated experience. This is what is really meant when it is said that the popular art and literature of today were once the daring, esoteric art and literature of yesterday. Of course, no such thing is true. What is meant is that when enough time has elapsed the new is looted for new "twists," which are then watered down and served up as kitsch. Self-evidently, all kitsch is academic, and conversely, all that's academic is kitsch. For what is called the academic as such no longer has an independent existence, but has become the stuffed-shirt "front" for kitsch. The methods of industrialism displace the handicrafts.

Because it can be turned out mechanically, kitsch has become an integral part of our productive system in a way in which true culture could never be except accidentally. It has been capitalized at a tremendous investment which must show commensurate returns; it is compelled to extend as well as to keep its markets. While it is essentially its own salesman, a great sales apparatus has nevertheless been created for it, which brings pressure to bear on every member of society. Traps are laid even in those areas, so to speak, that are the preserves of genuine culture. It is not enough today, in a country like ours, to have an inclination toward the latter; one must have a true passion for it that will give him the power to resist the faked article that surrounds and presses in on him from the moment he is old enough to look at the funny papers. Kitsch is deceptive. It has many different levels, and some of them are high enough to be dangerous to the naïve seeker of true light. A magazine such as the *New Yorker,* which is fundamentally high-class kitsch for the luxury trade, converts and waters down a great deal of avant-garde material for its own uses. Nor is every single item of kitsch altogether worthless. Now and then it produces something of merit, something that has an authentic folk flavor; and these accidental and isolated instances have fooled people who should know better.

Kitsch's enormous profits are a source of temptation to the avant-garde itself, and its members have not always resisted this temptation. Ambitious writers and artists will modify their work under the pressure of kitsch, if they do not succumb to it entirely. And then those puzzling borderline cases appear, such as the popular novelist, Simenon, in France, and Steinbeck in this country. The net result is always to the detriment of true culture, in any case.

Kitsch has nas not been confined to the cities in which it was born, but has flowed out over the countryside, wiping out folk culture. Nor has it shown any regard for geographical and national-cultural boundaries. Another mass product of Western industrialism, it has gone on a triumphal tour of the world, crowding out and defacing native cultures in one colonial country after another, so that it is now by way of becoming a universal culture, the first universal culture ever beheld. Today the Chinaman, no less than the South American Indian, the Hindu, no less than the Polynesian, have come to prefer to the products of their native art, magazine covers, rotogravure sections, and calendar girls. How is this virulence of kitsch, this irresistible attractiveness, to be explained? Naturally, machine-made kitsch can undersell the native hand-made article, and the prestige of the West also helps, but why is kitsch a so much more profitable export article than Rembrandt? One, after all, can be reproduced as cheaply as the other.

In his article on the Soviet cinema in the *Partisan Review*, Dwight Mac-donald points out that kitsch has in the last ten years become the dominant culture in Soviet Russia. For this he blames the political régime—not only for the fact that kitsch is the official culture, but also that it is actually the dominant, most popular culture; and he quotes the following from Kurt London's *The Seven Soviet Arts*: ". . . the attitude of the masses both to the old and new art styles probably remains essentially dependent on the nature of the education afforded them by their respective states." Macdonald goes on to say: "Why after all should ignorant peasants prefer Repin (a leading exponent of Russian academic kitsch in painting) to Picasso, whose abstract technique is at least as relevant to their own primitive folk art as is the former's realistic style? No, if the masses crowd into the Tretyakov (Moscow's museum of contemporary Russian art: kitsch) it is largely because they have been conditioned to shun 'formalism' and to admire 'socialist realism.' "

In the first place it is not a question of a choice between merely the old and merely the new, as London seems to think—but of a choice between the bad, up-to-date old and the genuinely new. The alternative to Picasso is not Michelangelo, but kitsch. In the second place, neither in backward Russia nor in the advanced West do the masses prefer kitsch simply because their governments condition them toward it. Where state educational systems take the trouble to mention art, we are told to respect the old masters, not kitsch; and yet we go and hang Maxfield Parrish or his equivalent on our walls, instead of Rembrandt and Michelangelo. Moreover, as Macdonald himself points out, around 1925 when the Soviet régime was encouraging avant-garde cinema, the Russian masses continued to prefer Hollywood movies. No, "conditioning" does not explain the potency of kitsch. . . .

All values are human values, relative values, in art as well as elsewhere. Yet there does seem to have been more or less of a general agreement among the cultivated of mankind over the ages as to what is good art and what bad. Taste has varied, but not beyond certain limits: contemporary connoisseurs agree with eighteenth-century Japanese that Hokusai was one of the greatest artists of his time; we even agree with the ancient Egyptians that Third and Fourth Dynasty art was the most worthy of being selected as their paragon by those who came after. We may have come to prefer Giotto to Raphael, but we still do not deny that Raphael was one of the best painters of his *time*. There has been an agreement then, and this agreement rests, I believe, on a fairly constant distinction made between those values only to be found in art and the values which can be found elsewhere. Kitsch, by virtue of rationalized technique that draws on science and industry, has erased this distinction in practice.

Let us see for example what happens when an ignorant Russian peasant such as Macdonald mentions stands with hypothetical freedom of choice before two paintings, one by Picasso, the other by Repin. In the first he sees, let us say, a play of lines, colors, and spaces that represent a woman. The abstract technique— to accept Macdonald's supposition, which I am inclined to doubt—reminds him somewhat of the icons he has left behind him in the village, and he feels the attraction of the familiar. We will even suppose that he faintly surmises some of the great art values the cultivated find in Picasso. He turns next to Repin's picture and sees a battle scene. The technique is not so familiar—as technique. But that weighs very little with the peasant, for he suddenly discovers values in Repin's picture which seem far superior to the values he has been accustomed to finding in icon art; and the unfamiliar techique itself is one of the sources of those values: the values of the vividly recognizable, the miraculous, and the sympathetic. In Repin's picture the peasant recognizes and sees things in the way in which he recognizes and sees things outside of pictures—there is no discontinuity between art and life, no need to accept a convention and say to oneself, that icon represents Jesus because it intends to represent Jesus, even if it does not remind me very much of a man. That Repin can paint so realistically that identifications are self-evident immediately and without any effort on the part of the spectator—that is miraculous. The peasant is also pleased by the wealth of self-evident meanings which he finds in the picture: "it tells a story." Picasso and the icons are so austere and barren in comparison. What is more, Repin heightens reality and makes it dramatic: sunset, exploding shells, running and falling men. There is no longer any question of Picasso or icons. Repin is what the peasant wants, and nothing else but Repin. It is lucky, however, for Repin that the peasant is protected from the products of American capitalism, for he would not stand a chance next to a *Saturday Evening Post* cover by Norman Rockwell.

Ultimately, it can be said that the cultivated spectator derives the same values from Picasso that the peasant gets from Repin, since what the latter enjoys in Repin is somehow art too, on however low a scale, and he is sent to look at pictures by the same instincts that send the cultivated spectator. But the ultimate values which the cultivated specator derives from Picasso are derived at a second remove, as the result of reflection upon the immediate impression left by the plastic values. It is only then that the recognizable, the miraculous, and the sympathetic enter. They are not immediately or externally present in Picasso's painting, but must be projected into it by the spectator sensitive enough to react sufficiently to plastic qualities. They belong to the "reflected" effect. In Repin, on the other hand, the "reflected" effect has already been included in the picture, ready for the spectator's unreflective enjoyment.[4] Where Picasso paints cause, Repin paints effect. Repin pre-digests art for the spectator and spares him effort, provides him with a short cut to the pleasure of art that detours what is necessarily difficult in genuine art. Repin, or kitsch, is synthetic art.

The same point can be made with respect to kitsch literature: it provides vicarious experience for the insensitive with far greater immediacy than serious fiction can hope to do. And Eddie Guest and the *Indian Love Lyrics* are more poetic than T. S. Eliot and Shakespeare.

3

If the avant-garde imitates the processes of art, kitsch, we now see, imitates its effects. The neatness of this antithesis is more than contrived; it corresponds to and defines the tremendous interval that separates from each other two such simultaneous cultural phenomena as the avant-garde and kitsch. This interval, too great to be closed by all the infinite gradations of popularized "modernism" and "modernistic" kitsch, corresponds in turn to a social interval, a social interval that has always existed in formal culture as elsewhere in civilized society, and whose two termini converge and diverge in fixed relation to the increasing or decreasing stability of the given society. There has always been on one side the minority of the powerful—and therefore the cultivated—and on the other the great mass of the exploited and poor—and therefore the ignorant. Formal culture has always belonged to the first, while the last have had to content themselves with folk or rudimentary culture, or kitsch.

In a stable society which functions well enough to hold in solution the contradictions between its classes the cultural dichotomy becomes somewhat blurred. The axioms of the few are shared by the many; the latter believe superstitiously what the former believe soberly. And at such moments in history the masses are able to feel wonder and admiration for the culture, on no matter how high a plane, of its masters. This applies at least to plastic culture, which is accessible to all.

In the Middle Ages the plastic artist paid lip service at least to the lowest common denominators of experience. This even remained true to some extent until the seventeenth century. There was available for imitation a universally valid conceptual reality, whose order the artist could not tamper with. The subject matter of art was prescribed by those who commissioned works of art, which were not created, as in bourgeois society, on speculation. Precisely because his content was determined in advance, the artist was free to concentrate on his medium. He needed not to be philosopher, or visionary, but simply artificer. As long as there was general agreement as to what were the worthiest subjects for art, the artist was relieved of the necessity to be original and inventive in his "matter" and could devote all his energy to formal problems. For him the medium became, privately, professionally, the content of his art, even as today his medium is the public content of the abstract painter's art—with that difference, however, that the medieval artist had to suppress his professional preoccupation in public—had always to suppress and subordinate the personal and professional in the finished, official work of art. If, as an ordinary member of the Christian community, he felt some personal emotion about his subject matter, this only contributed to the enrichment of the work's public meaning. Only with the Renaissance do the inflections of the personal become legitimate, still to be kept, however, within the limits of the simply and universally recognizable. And only with Rembrandt do "lonely" artists began to appear, lonely in their art.

But even during the Renaissance, and as long as Western art was endeavoring to perfect its technique, victories in this realm could only be signalized by success in realistic imitation, since there was no other objective criterion at hand. Thus the masses could still find in the art of their masters objects of admiration and wonder. Even the bird who pecked at the fruit in Zeuxis' picture could applaud.

It is a platitude that art becomes caviar to the general when the reality it imitates no longer corresponds even roughly to the reality recognized by the general. Even then, however, the resentment the common man may feel is silenced by the awe in which he stands of the patrons of this art. Only when he becomes dissatisfied with the social order they administer does he begin to criticize their culture. Then the plebian finds courage for the first time to voice his opinions openly. Every man, from the Tammany alderman to the Austrian house-painter, finds that he is entitled to his opinion. Most often this resentment toward culture is to be found where the dissatisfaction with society is a reactionary dissatisfaction which expresses itself in revivalism and puritanism, and latest of all, in fascism. Here revolvers and torches begin to be mentioned in the same breath as culture. In the name of godliness or the blood's health, in the name of simple ways and solid virtues, the statue-smashing commences.

Notes

1. The example of music, which has long been an abstract art, and which avant-garde poetry has tried so much to emulate, is interesting. Music, Aristotle said curiously enough, is the most imitative and vivid of all arts because it imitates its original—the state of the soul—with the greatest immediacy. Today this strikes us as the exact opposite of the truth, because no art seems to us to have less reference to something outside itself than music. However, aside from the fact that in a sense Aristotle may still be right, it must be explained that ancient Greek music was closely associated with poetry, and depended upon its character as an accessory to verse to make its imitative meaning clear. Plato, speaking of music, says: "For when there are no words, it is very difficult to recognize the meaning of the harmony and rhythm, or to see that any worthy object is imitated by them." As far as we know, all music originally served such an accessory function. Once, however, it was abandoned, music was forced to withdraw into itself to find a constraint or original. This is found in the various means of its own composition and performance.

2. I owe this formulation to a remark made by Hans Hofmann, the art teacher, in one of his lectures. From the point of view of this formulation surrealism in plastic art is a reactionary tendency which is attempting to restore "outside" subject matter. The chief concern of a painter such as Dali is to represent the processes and concepts of his consciousness, not the processes of his medium.

3. See Valéry's remarks about his own poetry.

4. T. S. Eliot said something to the same effect in accounting for the shortcomings of English Romantic poetry. Indeed, the Romantics can be considered the original sinners whose guilt kitsch inherited. They showed kitsch how. What does Keats write about mainly, if not the effect of poetry upon himself?

FURTHER READING

Angoff, Charles. "Culture at Cut Rates," *New Republic,* Vol. 133, 1955, pp. 18-19.

Barzun, Jacques. *God's Country and Mine.* Boston: Little, Brown, 1954.

Bell, Bernard Iddings. *Crowd Culture.* New York: Harper, 1952.

Bell, Daniel. "The Theory of Mass Society," *Commentary,* Vol. 22, 1956, pp. 75-83.

Benjamin, Walter. "L'ouvre d'art à l'époque de sa reproduction mécanisée," *Zeitschrift für Sozialforschung,* Vol. V, 1936, pp. 45 ff.

Berger, John. "The Cultural Snob: There Is No Highbrow Art," *Nation,* Vol. 181, 1955, pp. 380-82.

Bogan, Louise. "Some Notes on Popular and Unpopular Art," *Partisan Review,* Vol. 10, 1943, pp. 391-401.

Brogan, D. W. *The American Character.* New York: Alfred Knopf, 1945.

Brogan, D. W. "The Problem of High Culture and Mass Culture," *Diogenes,* No. 5, 1954, pp. 1-13.

Brown, Spencer. "Beepage: the Language of Popularization," *Commentary,* Vol. 14, 1952, pp. 372-75.

Commanger, Henry Steele. *The American Mind.* New Haven: Yale University Press, 1950.

Dulles, Foster Rhea. *America Learns to Play.* New York: Appleton-Century-Crofts, 1940.

Freidson, Eliot. "Communication Research and the Concept of the Mass," *American Sociological Review,* Vol. 18, 1953, pp. 313-17.

Freidson, Eliot. "Consumption of Mass Media by Polish-American Children," *Quarterly of Film, Radio and Television,* Vol. 9, 1954, pp. 92-101.

Friedrich, Carl J. *The New Belief in the Common Man.* Boston: Little, Brown, 1942.

Friedrich, Carl J. *The New Image of the Common Man.* Boston: Beacon Press, 1950.

Gorer, Geoffrey. *The American People.* New York: Norton, 1948.

Greenberg, Clement. "Work and Leisure Under Industrialization," *Commentary,* in two parts, Vol. 15, 1953, pp. 559-66, and Vol. 16, 1954, pp. 54-62.

Gurko, Leo. *Heroes, Highbrows, and the Popular Mind.* Indianapolis: Bobbs-Merrill, 1953.

Henry, Nelson B. (ed.). *Mass Media and Education.* Chicago: University of Chicago Press, 1954.

Horkheimer, Max. "Art and Mass Culture," *Studies in Philosophy and Social Science,* Vol. 9, 1941.

Hovland, Carl I. "Effects of the Mass Media of Communications," *Handbook of Social Psychology,* Vol. II; Lindzey, G., (ed.). Cambridge: Addison-Wesley, 1954, pp. 1062-1103.

Johnson, Alvin. "The Nouveau Riche and Culture," *Commentary,* Vol. 16, 1953, pp. 343-46.

Katz, Elihu, and Lazarsfeld, Paul F. *Personal Influence.* Glencoe: Free Press, 1956.

Kerr, Walter. "Art and the Box Office," *Commonweal,* Vol. 62, 1955, pp. 80-82.

Klapp, Orrin E. "The Creation of Popular Heroes," *American Journal of Sociology,* Vol. 54, 1948, pp. 135-41.

Klapper, Joseph. "Mass Media and the Engineering of Consent," *American Scholar,* Vol. 17, 1948, pp. 419-30.

Klonsky, Milton. "Along the Midway of Mass Culture," *Partisan Review,* Vol. 16, 1949, pp. 348-65.

Kronenberger, Louis. *Company Manners.* New York: Bobbs-Merrill, 1951.

Krutch, Joseph, and others. *Is the Common Man Too Common?* Norman, Okla.: University of Oklahoma Press, 1954.

Laski, Harold J. *The American Democracy.* New York: Viking, 1948.

Laws, F. (ed.). *Made for the Millions: A Critical Study of the Media of Information and Entertainment.* London: Contact Publications, 1947.

Lundberg, G. A.; Komarovsky, M.; and McInerny, Mary A. *Leisure: A Suburban Study.* New York: Columbia University Press, 1934.

Lynes, Russell. *The Taste-makers.* New York: Harper, 1954.

Lyness, Paul. "Patterns in the Mass Communications Taste of the Young Audience," *Journal of Educational Psychology,* Vol. 42, 1951, pp. 449-67.

Lyness, Paul. "The Place of Mass Media in the Lives of Boys and Girls," *Journalism Quarterly,* Vol. 29, 1952, pp. 3-14.

Malraux, André. "Art, Popular Art, and the Illusion of the Folk," *Partisan Review,* Vol. 18, 1951, pp. 487-95.

Miller, Perry. "What Drove Me Crazy in Europe," *Atlantic,* Vol. 187, 1951, p. 41-46.

Mills, C. Wright. *The Power Elite.* New York: Oxford University Press, 1956.

Mills, C. Wright. *White Collar: The American Middle Classes.* New York: Oxford University Press, 1951.

Neumeyer, Martin H., and Neumayer, Esther S. *Leisure and Recreation.* New York: A. S. Barnes, 1949.

"Our Country and Our Culture," a symposium, *Partisan Review,* Vol. 19, 1952, pp. 282-326, 420-50, 562-97.

"The People's Tastes in Movies, Books, Radio," *Fortune,* March, 1949, pp. 39-44.

Peters, H. F. "American Culture and the State Department," *American Scholar,* Vol. 21, 1952, pp. 265-74.

Rice, Elmer. "Entertainment in the Age of McCarthy," *New Republic,* Vol. 128, 1953, pp. 14-18.

Riesman, David, and Denney, Reuel. "Leisure in Urbanized America," *Reader in Urban Sociology,* Hatt, Paul K., and Reiss, Albert J., Jr., eds. Glencoe: Free Press, 1951, pp. 469-80.

Riesman, David, and Denney, Reuel. "Leisure in an Industrial Civilization," *Creating an Industrial Civilization: A Report on the Corning Conference,* Staley, Eugene, ed., New York: Harper, 1952.

Riesman, David; Denney, Reuel; and Glazer, Nathan. *The Lonely Crowd: A Study of the Changing American Character.* New Haven: Yale University Press, 1950.

Riesman, David. "Some Observations on Changes in Leisure Attitudes," *Antioch Review,* Vol. 12, 1952, pp. 417-36.

Riley, Matilda W., and Riley, John W., Jr. "A Sociological Approach to Communications Research," *Public Opinion Quarterly,* Vol. 15, 1951, pp. 445-60.

Rosenberg, Bernard. *The Values of Veblen.* Washington: Public Affairs Press, 1956.

Rourke, Constance. *American Humor, a Study of the National Character.* New York: Harcourt, Brace, 1931.

Saroyan, William. "Art for Man's Sake: a Minority View," *Nation,* Vol. 180, 1955, pp. 364-66.

Schwartz, Delmore. "The Grapes of Crisis," *Partisan Review,* Vol. 18, 1951, pp. 7-15.

Schwartz, Delmore. "Survey of Our National Phenomena," *New York Times Magazine,* April 15, 1956, pp. 28-29.

Sherif, Muzafer, and Stansfeld, Sargents. "Ego-Involvement and the Mass Media," *Journal of Social Issues,* Vol. 16, 1947, pp. 8-16.

Steiner, Jesse. *Americans at Play.* New York: McGraw-Hill, 1933.

Veblen, Thorstein. *The Theory of the Leisure Class.* New York: The Modern Library, 1931.

Wagner, Geoffrey. *Parade of Pleasure: a Study of Popular Iconography in the U.S.A.* New York: Library Publishers, 1955.

Waples, Douglas (ed.). *Print, Radio and Film in a Democracy.* Chicago: University of Chicago Press, 1942.

Warshow, Robert. "The Legacy of the 30's: Middle-Class Culture and the Intellectual's Problem," *Commentary,* Vol. 4, 1947, pp. 538-45.

Warner, W. Lloyd. "Mass Media: A Social and Psychological Analysis," *American Life.* Chicago: University of Chicago Press, 1953.

3
Mass Literature

BOOKS

There is an obvious symbolism in the fact that Winston Smith and Julia tryst (and are ultimately betrayed) above an all-but-deserted book store, in George Orwell's phantasy of 1984. That Orwell was implying the mass media of today will lead us to the doublethink world of tomorrow seems quite obvious. Whether 1984 will prove to be a prophetic analysis of contemporary trends or not no one can foresee. But as of 1956 the book business in America appears to many to be far from moribund. With the advent of the corner drug store as an important outlet for the "paperbacks," a given book (including such as Orwell's 1984) sells into the hundreds of thousands. Thirty years ago there were no book clubs in the United States. Today, according to Dr. Charles Lee, there are about ninety. Although a few of them (including the enormously successful Book-of-the-Month Club, which alone has sent more than 125 million books into American homes) distribute general trade titles, most of the clubs specialize in such classifications as history, biography, drama, art, religion and economics—not to mention detective fiction. Together the book clubs have accounted for more than 500 million books (both good and bad) in American homes during the last three decades.

In examining the nature of book reading in our contemporary scene, Frank Luther Mott discusses the nature of the "best seller" formula. He concludes that there is such a variety of forms, qualities, appeals and characteristics, that there is no sure-fire way of predicting a best seller.

Bernard Berelson summarizes lengthy research in the area of who reads books and why. His outlook for reading as a leisure activity is optimistic.

On the other hand, Alan Dutscher views the book business in America with considerable pessimism. Through his analysis of the economic factors involved in publishing books, he concludes that the American book industry has never faced a deeper crisis than the present one.

Cecil Hemley (himself a publisher) deals with the problems of the paperbacks. His criticism of them is that although they frequently disseminate the best from the past they also print the most mediocre from the present. This, to his mind, puts the new writer of quality in jeopardy, since, for contemporary writings, the publishers increasingly fall back on genres (such as the mystery or the western) which have vast, ready-made audiences waiting for them.

Is There a Best Seller Formula?

By FRANK LUTHER MOTT

WHAT makes a best seller? This is the sixty-four dollar question. It can be answered, though largely by guess and surmise, and never satisfactorily to the inquirer, who always wants a formula. There is no formula which may be depended upon to produce a best seller.

There are too many impalpable considerations, too many chances and accidents, too complex a combination of conditions affecting the writing, publication, and selling of a book to make the attainment of the top rank by even the most promising candidate a certainty. The creation of a best seller does not follow an exact pattern, or patterns, any more than does the making of a successful man; there are too many intangibles, too many un-measurable human values, too many vicissitudes of fortune involved. More-over, since there is not just one best seller audience, no single formula could be expected to provide books for a buying public which is, thank God, pretty heterogeneous after all.

But just as the biographer, the psychologist, or the sociologist may cor-relate cases in order to study the roots of human success, so may the student of best sellers analyze and classify his materials to learn more about what seems to have made books succeed. Many lines of investigation immediately present themselves, but only a few of the more obvious conclusions of such a study will be presented here. One cannot escape the almost constant appearance in all periods of our best seller history of certain elements of popular appeal—as religion, sensationalism, information and guidance, ad-venture, democracy, humor, characterization, juvenile suitability, timeliness, and so on.

The religious appeal is strong from one end of the list to the other. Of the first twenty best sellers, thirteen were definitely books of religious teach-ing, and that element was strong in four others. This was not remarkable in view of the prominence of religion in the life of early Colonial years; but it is more striking to find that of the 279 best sellers up to 1915,[1] eighty-seven (or almost one-third) contained a strong religious element. Though the average is much lower for the thirty years following 1915, the extraordinary records of *The Robe* and of other books which did not quite reach the top rank (like *The Song of Bernadette*) make us realize that religion is still a strong factor in popular reading. Many of the topmost best sellers have abounded in religious teaching, as *Uncle Tom's Cabin, The Wide, Wide World, Ben-Hur, In His Steps,* and the novels of E. P. Roe and Harold

Bell Wright. Almost 15 per cent of our best sellers have been written by clergymen.

Sensationalism, as the word is employed here, must not be understood to mean anything necessarily morbid, but rather an emotional excitement produced by extreme means, such as a definite emphasis on horrors, murder, extreme violence, irregular sex relations, or extraordinary adventures. Such things may be morbid and unwholesome in their effects, or they may stir one's deepest and finest feelings, according to the degree of art in presentation and the capabilities of the reader. They are inescapable in literature high and low; they are found in *Oedipus Rex* and *King Lear* and in Mrs. Southworth's *Ishmael*. They appear in remarkable quantity throughout the best seller list. Evaluation of such elements in a given book depends, of course, upon anyone's critical judgment; in that of the present writer, one or more of these sensational factors is strongly emphasized in just a little over half the books of our list. To give an idea of the range of this element in imaginative literature on the best seller level we need only mention *The History of Dr. Faustus* in the eighteenth century, the stories of Indian captivities, the devious intrigues of Quasimodo in Hugo's *Notre-Dame* or Sikes in Dickens' *Oliver Twist,* the whipping to death of Uncle Tom, the melodrama of Lippard and Southworth, the dime novels, the weird adventures of Rider Haggard's characters, the novels about courtesans, and the murder stories of the last period. This element is by no means limited to fiction; we find it in poetry, history, religion, and other categories. Indeed, it is very common in early religious books. The pictures of hell in *The Day of Doom* and *The Practice of Piety* and the tortures of Protestants in Fox's *Book of Martyrs* are extremely sensational, and Maria Monk's *Awful Disclosures* was part of a religious controversy.

The self-improvement motive may be founded on a desire for prestige, or a hope to get ahead, or simply upon the need for deeply personal satisfactions. But whatever its basis, its impulsions to education and training are about the same. The fields of literature into which it sends a reader are varied indeed. Such books on our list as Shakespeare's plays and Emerson's essays have been commonly read for the sake of self-improvement. An advertisement of the Classics Club recently contained this paragraph:

> It is not necessary to have a "higher education" to appreciate these books; and, after you have read and know them, you will have acquired a broader and more liberal education than most of your business and professional acquaintances. You will have lost any personal concern about an "inferiority complex" and any fear about not being equal of others whose formal education is greater than your own.

Somewhat the same drive operates as soon as any book begins to lead the weekly best seller lists; the reader who wishes to be well informed feels that he must read it at once. But in the years before the world of readers was best-seller-conscious there was rather less reading for this by-product of vainglory; certainly in both earlier and later times a sincere desire for real self-improvement has been a major compelling force in readership. Not only the classics in belles-lettres, but history, biography, and all informative and personal-guidance books have been regarded as "improving."

Ten historical works appear on the best seller list, and eight biographies. Designation of historical novels is not easy, because there is no rule about how far back the "contemporary scene" reaches before it becomes history; but our count yields forty-nine historical romances, distributed rather evenly through the decades from *Thaddeus of Warsaw* to *The Black Rose.* Biographies make a poor showing in this list of the topmost best sellers. There is no life of Lincoln, though fiction introduces him more than once. A witticism in the book trade runs like this: Since books about Lincoln are always best sellers, and so are books about doctors and books about dogs, why doesn't someone write a sure-fire book about Lincoln's doctor's dog? The "gag" was not based on a list of overall best sellers, but presumably upon such successes as Sandburg's *Lincoln,* Heiser's *An American Doctor's Odyssey,* and Eric Knight's *Lassie Come Home.*

But the self-improvement books devoted to personal precept and guidance make an impressive catalogue by themselves. They include most of the religious books, to begin with, and then there are ten or a dozen behavior books which emphasize rules of living; many novels, from *Pamela* to *Pollyanna,* which teach somewhat less by precept than by example; and books of advice from Chesterfield to Dale Carnegie. Nearly half the books on our list contain a large element of didacticism. Scores of guides in the Little Blue Books series told their readers *How to Improve Your Conversation, How to Play Golf, How to Write Advertising,* and so on; and each sold in the hundreds of thousands.

Another important element in best sellers is that of personal adventure. We find it in the narratives of Indian captivity, in *Pilgrim's Progress,* and in *Robinson Crusoe,* for the Colonial Period; but it was not until Scott and Cooper showed what thrills the adventure story held that American readers made vicarious derring-do a favorite diversion. Since then tales of action and courage have been evenly distributed through the decades, whether in historical romance, dime novels, Zenda stories, "westerns," mysteries, or what-not.

Many readers think of adventure as being a chief ingredient in "a good story," and so it often is. Another factor is strong characterization and though not a few novels on our best seller list get along with typed characters, a survey of the entire roll shows almost two-thirds of them placing strong emphasis on characters. That mythical person whom we adumbrate as "the general reader" likes people—and particularly strong, individualistic human beings. Dorothy Canfield Fisher, a member of the Book-of-the-Month Club board of selection, declares, "By and large, what readers seem to like to find in a book is contact with living, vital personalities."

The quality of vividness also ranks high. We find superior vividness—in portrayal of scenes, action, persons—in about half the books on our list. Force (to use the rhetoricians' old term) falls much lower in the scale.

Sentiment, verging commonly into sentimentality, is hard to evaluate; but it seems to characterize about half the books between 1775 and 1915, while it is less apparent in the earlier and later periods.

So far as literary style in general is concerned, it would be absurd to generalize in the face of so much variety. There are, of course, those books which have become best sellers largely because they are classics; and there are others of much literary skill and power, from *The Practice of Piety* to *Mrs. Miniver*. On the other hand, there is much bad writing. In what we may call the lower third of the heap, it is easy to pick out nearly a hundred books that are ill-written and quite devoid of any of the literacy graces. They make it clear that a vast reading public is not concerned with niceties of style. These are the books that critics often call "typical best sellers" simply because their immense popularity seems, to a reader sufficiently irked by sloppy writing, to be their only quality worth considering. But this is a double mistake. In the first place, there is no such thing as a "typical best seller"; and in the second place, it is not bad writing that has made them popular, and they all have their qualities. They usually have body and abundance of materials, they are commonly teeming with rather vital stuff, and more often than not they are well organized. Walter Hines Page published a discriminating essay in 1905 in which he pointed out "Why Bad Novels Succeed": he was convinced that "literary quality" made little difference in sales, but "substance" and construction met a popular demand.[2] Certainly a book does not have to be well written to become a best seller.

Democracy is another element of popular appeal that should not be neglected. The word is perhaps too big. What is intended to be designated is emphasis on the lives and aspirations of the common people, whether in fiction or nonfiction. It is in the very atmosphere and mood of *The Vicar of Wakefield,* the poems of Robert Burns, all the Dickens novels, *David Harum, The Egg and I;* and it marks four-tenths of all our best sellers.

Timeliness, or topical interest, has made many popular books, but few best sellers of the first rank. The thirty-nine which have some topical interest are an intervening group, however. *Common Sense* and *M'Fingal* belong to the Revolution, with *The Federalist* coming a little later. Hannah F. Lee's *Three Experiments of Living* was a hard-times story of 1837. *Uncle Tom's Cabin, Ten Nights in a Bar-Room, Progress and Poverty,* and *Black Beauty* reflect popular crusades. *Parson Brownlow's Book* was a Civil War product. *Coin's Financial School* and *In His Steps* were definitely topical and timely —and so on, down to best sellers like *The Grapes of Wrath* and *One World.* Timing a book is often important, and taking fortune at the flood has sometimes resulted in a first-class best seller, especially in these later years of quick sales. Philip Van Doren Stern has pointed out that if the publication dates of Margaret Halsey's anti-British *With Malice Toward Some* (1938) and Jan Struther's pro-British *Mrs. Miniver* (1940) had been exchanged, probably neither would have been very successful.

The element of humor is marked in a little less than one-fourth of the books, though only seventeen may be said to be primarily or very largely humorous. Of these, only two—the Knickerbocker *History of New York* and the *Pickwick Papers*—were published before the 1870's, while seven of the seventeen belong to the last twenty-five years. Dickens did much to bring up the average of humor in the middle of the nineteenth century. He was the greatest of best sellers, and his popularity was built largely upon his humor: he could make his readers cry two or three times in a novel, but he made them laugh much oftener than that.

Fantasy is a notable characteristic of one-eighth of the best sellers. Fairytale motifs and sleight-of-hand with the semi-mystical have an appeal for many readers, though one finds such things chiefly in poetry and juveniles. Our judgment of this element of literary art as a lure to the general reader and a maker of best sellers is complicated by the fact that it is always closely integrated with other qualities and techniques which may have been more effective causes of popularity. To take a modern example of fantasy, Thorne Smith's *Topper* probably would not have been a winner without its sex appeal and the picture of slightly adorned feminine pulchritude on the cover of the Pocket Books edition.

Which suggests a word about pictures as a selling aid before we take up the matter of sex appeal. Of course, pictures on covers and jackets are advertising rather than contents, but many best sellers have owed much of their popularity to pictures which were integral with the text. This is true of such older books as *Pilgrim's Progress,* Fox's *Book of Martyrs,* and *Aesop's Fables,* and of such diverse and more modern offerings as *Innocents Abroad, Trilby,* and Ripley's *Believe It or Not.* Illustration was important in many of the editions of Dickens and Thackeray, and of the *Rubaiyat,* James Whitcomb Riley's poems, *The Virginian,* and many other books. Motion picture editions of best sellers, adorned by "stills" from the films, have usually supplied a few hundred thousand copies to movie-goers. And of course, juveniles have always sold largely on the basis of their pictorial illustration.

As to the old S. A., which one writer of best sellers called "It," authors and publishers have in this element of life and literature a two-edged sword. Emphasis on sex may attract a large body of readers, and it may make the book a kind of bawdy joke. Being banned in Boston has its desirable features from the publishers' point of view, but it is probably not, on the whole, an experience to be invited. Though we find books of strong sex appeal scattered through all periods of our publishing history (varying from a tenth to a fifth of the best sellers), fashions in such things do change, and a big splurge by a book like *The Sheik* is likely to be followed by imitators and then by a reaction. Not long after the publication of *Forever Amber,* which undoubtedly was intended as a serious historical romance, a publisher advertised a new offering to booksellers in the *Publishers' Weekly* as "the boldest and bawdiest" yet; some months later *Amber's* publishers, presenting a new historical novel, were insisting that there was not a bedroom scene in it.

About one-eighth of our best sellers employ exotic settings. By no means all foreign settings are exotic, and perhaps we have to split hairs too much. The Paris of *Trilby* was exotic to its readers, while that of *The Razor's Edge* was not. At any rate, the exotic has had an appeal to the popular audiences from the time of *The Oeconomy of Human Life* (1751) to *The Black Rose* (1945), and about one-eighth of our best sellers have used it to a marked degree.

And finally, a word about juveniles. Since our best seller list is confined to "general reading," juveniles would be excluded were it not for the fact that it is quite impossible to draw a line between books for children and those for adults. Most readers have agreed with what Theodore Roosevelt once wrote in a *Bookman* article: "A thoroughly good book for young people is almost invariably one of the best books that grown people can read." Probably half of the best sellers which we classify as having juvenile appeal were actually written mainly for adults, as *Robinson Crusoe, Gulliver's Travels,* and so on. A little over a fifth of our books have that appeal. It was especially strong in the Colonial Period, when ten out of the thirty best sellers were used for the instruction and entertainment of children, and in the one before the First World War, which included the stories of Gene Stratton-Porter and her compeers.

And so, after all, where are we with regard to the formula for best sellers? It is lost in the variety of forms, qualities, appeals, characteristics. The study of successful books may be rewarding to both writer and publisher, as well as to sociologists and historians, but it will not point out to anyone an easy way to produce a sure-fire best seller.

Notes

1. It is convenient to divide the history of American publishing into six periods, as follows: 1638-1775, 1776-1840, 1841-1870, 1871-1895, 1896-1915, and 1916-1945.

2. *A Publisher's Confession* (New York, 1905—anonymous until Page's death), chapter entitled "Why 'Bad' Novels Succeed and 'Good' Ones Fall."

Who Reads What Books and Why?

By BERNARD BERELSON

WHO reads what books and why?

The answer to this general question is by no means easy to give. The state of popular reading is complex and changing: different kinds of people are reading different amounts of books for different reasons. Mrs. Jones down the street is reading light fiction "to pass the time" and books on child-rearing because she wants to do well by her children and to hold her own with other mothers. Her husband reads an occasional mystery story and a technical book on his occupation. The people next door don't read books at all because "they don't have time," although they manage to spend four hours a day with radio and television. The people on the other side read classical novels, modern poetry, and the latest serious books on political affairs. And so it goes; the variety is so extensive that any reasonable ordering of the data is bound to violate some aspects of the overall picture.

And yet some ordering is necessary if we are to secure a systematic answer to the question. In recent years, with the development of communication research in industry and in the universities, a body of data has been assembled which presents a reasonably coherent picture of the state of book reading in this country today. We can by no means answer all—or even very many—of the questions we would like to ask about book reading, but we can answer some. Unfortunately, definite answers cannot be given without a great deal of careful (and costly) research, much of which has not yet been done. In some cases technical problems have not been solved. In this connection we know a good deal more about magazine reading and radio listening than about book reading. At the same time, however, the studies done to date, utilizing social-science techniques for collecting and analyzing empirical data, have provided valid and reliable data on questions which previously were largely subject to literary impression, historical speculation, or commercial preference. Conclusions based upon these methods have not infrequently mistaken the particular for the general, the familiar for the typical, the dramatic for the general, or the preferred for the actual. The business of the social scientist, if I may say so, is to see book reading steadily and to see it whole—and, while he cannot claim to have done the job, it is fair to say that he has made a start.

What, then, is the state of adult (nonspecialized) book reading today? Let us review the major facts (or best guesses) by organizing them around

Reprinted from *Saturday Review of Literature*, May 12, 1951, pp. 7-8, 30-31, by permission of the author and publisher. (Copyright, 1951, by the Saturday Review Associates, Inc.)

some assumptions held by various people and encountered here and there, explicitly or implicitly, in popular writing on the subject.

Assumption: that "the American people" read many books or, alternately, that they don't read them. This assumption comes both ways, depending upon whether the writer is in a mood to praise or blame—or perhaps depending upon the point he wants to make at the time. Many librarians, especially when writing their annual reports, like to think that people do read books; many critics stress the latter part of the assumption, especially when writing for the "little" magazines. Actually, of course, the statement is so undifferentiated that, like many statements about "the American public" or "the people of this country" or "we," it doesn't make sense anyway. The obvious fact is that some Americans read books frequently, some read them occasionally, some seldom, and some not at all.

If by "book reader" we mean anyone who reads at least one book every six months, then about half the adult population would qualify. If the definition requires the reading of at least one book a month—the usual definition in the field—the figure becomes 25 to 30 per cent; and if it requires at least one book a week then only 6 to 8 per cent of the adult population are "book readers." By a reasonable definition, then, only from one quarter to one third of the adults qualify as "book readers." This makes the actual audience for books the smallest among the major media of communication; radio-television, newspapers, magazines, and motion pictures all attract much larger numbers than books. Although the evidence on this point is not definitive, there are some data which suggest that there is less book reading in the United States than in such countries as Britain, Denmark, Sweden, Norway, and Holland.

More than that: the so-called concentration of the audience is higher for book reading than for the other media. About 10 per cent of the adult population does 70 per cent of the book reading. Within the book-reading group itself (as defined) 20 per cent of the readers do 70 per cent of the reading. Thus a relatively small group of people accounts for a large share of the reading. Nor does the tremendous sale of quarter books contradict this point: 10 per cent of the buyers are responsible for 80 per cent of the sales. The reading of books is certainly not evenly distributed throughout society.

Assumption: that the book reading public is representative of the total population. Not only does the frequency of book reading vary markedly; it is also unevenly distributed among the constituent groups of the community. For a variety of reasons some kinds of people read a great deal and some not much. The major factor which differentiates readers from nonreaders in research to date is education—in the limited sense of number of years of formal schooling. The more years of schooling the individual has, the more likely he is to read books. In one national survey only 12 per cent of the college-educated had not read a book in the preceding year as against 75 per cent of those with only some grammar-school education or less.

Now, this might mean several things. It might mean that additional schooling has improved the individual's basic reading skills, or that it has developed his reading habits, or that it has produced in him the types of interests which are ordinarily satisfied by books, or even that the people who go on to further schooling already have a reading disposition which formal education only reinforces. Research has not yet settled the matter, any more than it can say now why *some* college graduates do not read or why *some* people with little schooling read not only a great deal but well. There are numerous hypothesis but few data. But research *has* demonstrated the high relationship between formal education and the practice of book reading, and it seems quite likely that the schools have progressively developed book readers.

Other personal characteristics also affect the amount of book reading. Contrary to the popular conception, men read just about as much as women, although they tend to read differently. Young adults read more than their elders, but that is directly traceable to their greater degree of formal education; among people on the same educational level the older people more than hold their own. The sharpest and most dramatic drop in book reading comes at the school-leaving age—whatever that may imply about the educational system. Wealthier people read more than poorer people, again largely —though apparently not exclusively—because of their greater education. This means that the "higher" occupations provide more book readers than the "lower"; there are relatively fewer readers among the working class. Finally, because of the availability of sources (and again the educational level) urban residents read more than rural ones do.

In sum, then, college-educated, better-off, middle-aged people living in the city are most likely to be book readers in this country today. And people combining the opposite characteristics are the least likely. Thus it is clear that book readers as a group are far from representative of the total population. They live differently from the population as a whole, they have different attitudes and interests, they have different tastes. In short, projecting the book readers as "America" is apt to be just plain wrong.

Assumption: that the amount and/or the quality of book reading in this country has fallen off in recent years. It is not hard to find writers who are alarmed about the Deplorable State of popular reading. In 1949 Clifton Fadiman, regretting "the decline of attention," concluded that the "main stream [of our culture] is composed largely of men and women whose faculty of attention is in process either of decay or displacement." Another writer at about the same time asserted that "never before have there been so few good readers—so few who have retained anything or profited from what they read." Fadiman himself quoted Cyril Connolly to the effect that "we must accustom ourselves to a reading public which is both too slothful and too restless to read until a sense of values is restored to it." And, what is more, he noted that Henry James had done the same job of deploring fifty years earlier and Wadsworth a century before that—without drawing therefrom what seems to be an obvious inference.

The point is that this kind of Viewing with Alarm the state of popular culture is by no means limited to our day; it is characteristic of the intellectuals of every period since popular education began to create what might be called a mass audience. Today they hearken back to the good old days of a century ago when "the people" were reading *Walden*. A century ago, however, Hawthorne was fulminating against the "mob of scribbling women. . . . I should have no chance of success while the public taste is occupied with their trash."

In this sense the good old days probably never did exist; that is, there probably never was a *mass* audience for good books. Almost certainly there are more book readers today than ever before. It may be that the average quality of all the book reading done today is lower than the average quality decades or a few centuries ago—although this is far from certain. We tend to forget the poorer books of 1850 that were widely read (for example, *The Lamplighter*) and remember only the better ones that were not, then or since (except in the schools). At best all we can do is to compare the book reading of a highly selected group totaling less than 5 per cent of the population with a public five or six times larger today. Despite the general and pervasive impact of mass culture today, it is altogether likely that there is just as large and hard a core of serious readers today as there ever was. I personally believe it is larger and that it will grow with increases in popular education.

Assumption: that the competition of the mass media of communication is crowding out the book. Now that the book business has survived price cutting, book clubs, quarter books, and high manufacturing costs, the new menace is television. A generation ago it was radio. Here again the broad assumption is too gross to fit the facts. In some ways the different media are in competition, in other ways not. In the first place book readers are more active users of the other media (except perhaps radio-television) than the nonreaders. They read more newspapers, they see more films, they read more magazines. Secondly, the kind of person who is attracted to serious reading is not ordinarily the kind distracted by the nature of much of the mass media content. Third, there is a considerable amount of intermedia stimulation—some people read the book after they have seen the film adapted from it or have read a magazine condensation. Fourth, in general, intermedia relations show a supplementary rather than complementary pattern; people who read books about, say, politics are also likely to listen to discussions of politics on the air and read about it in magazines and newspapers. Or again: the readers of better books are likely to be listeners to serious radio. Finally, there is a sort of reverse competition in operation, in that book readers are found relatively often among the critics of the other media. They are more likely than nonreaders to be dissatisfied with the radio or with the movies or with their newspapers. Not only is their better education responsible for this tendency; their book reading probably helps to sustain their critical faculties against the flood.

A word on the effect of TV. It is too early, in my judgment, to say anything definitive about the impact of television on book reading. Most studies to date to show that television owners read fewer books than non-owners. It is not completely clear, however, that this is altogether due to television itself; they may have read less or differently before. More important, it is not clear yet just how book reading will be affected over a long period by the kind of television content that is now available. Once the novelty wears off, assuming that the content remains at the present level, television may affect book reading as little as radio does. And, of course, we do not yet know what will happen to the book reading of a generation raised on television. If television content improves considerably it may affect book reading rather more. So far it does seem to have cut down the gross amount of book reading, though probably it will not affect the reading of quality books.

Assumption: that "the American public" reads poor books or, alternately, that it reads good books. This assumption also comes both ways. For example, at the same time Henry Seidel Canby was claiming to have discovered that "the intelligent interest of the American public had been grossly underestimated by publishers and advertisers," Edmund Wilson concluded that the popularity of Lloyd Douglas "is something to give pause to anyone who may have supposed that the generation of Mencken had lifted the taste of the American public above the level of Gene Stratton Porter and Harold Bell Wright." Again, it is necessary to point out that the substance of both these observations may be true for different groups of readers or even for the same people at different times, although neither statement is correct as it stands. At the risk of being tiresome one must insist upon differentiating within "the American public," upon recognizing the complexity of the actual reading picture.

This particular question is further complicated by lack of agreement upon the standards by which quality is to be judged. If by "poor books" we mean light fiction of the adventure, Western, romance, and mystery type, then at least 60 per cent of adult book reading qualifies as "poor" (although the data on this are not too clear). If by "good books" we mean recognized classics and highly regarded contemporary writing of a serious sort, then perhaps 10 to 15 per cent of book reading is "good." A couple of years ago a well-known librarian claimed for the ALA's list of "Notable Books" that it was "representative of what people the country over are reading." The list included such titles as Bush's *Modern Arms and Free Men,* Bemis' *John Quincy Adams and the Foundation of American Foreign Policy,* Kluckhohn's *Mirror for Man,* and Welty's *Golden Apples;* the best sellers for that year included such titles as Douglas's *The Big Fisherman,* Waltari's *The Egyptian,* Keyes' *Dinner at Antoine's,* a Costain, a Yerby, and the Zoo and Canasta books.

Put it this way: book reading in this country varies in quality as widely as do the books themselves. Much of the reading involves books whose quality does not justify any particular consideration just because the pages are bound inside a hard cover. More fiction is read than nonfiction (especially by women) and more "light" fiction than "heavy." There is a substantial core of "good readers." And the more formal education, the more likely one is to be a good reader.

Assumption: that people read what interests them. Of course subject interest is a major factor in the selection of reading matter, especially if other things are equal. However, they are not always equal or not often, so, and thus other influences come into play. Notable among them is the factor of accessibility, which determines some of what all of us read (the *National Geographic* in the dentist's waiting room) and a great deal of what some people read. Books that are handy are read more frequently than those even a little hard to get, especially for that large group of people who "just want something interesting." Books that are delivered to the house, for example, have a better chance to be read than books that have to be brought from the library or the bookstore. People who live close to a public library read more books than people who live some blocks away. Books that are easily accessible within a library—for example, on the "interesting books" shelf—are read more than books not so easily accessible —for example, on the bottom shelf of a dark stack. Books the public or rental librarian "pushes" are read more than others.

Another factor is readability. Experts tell us that for many people there simply are no readable books on subjects of interest to them. Then there is the great effect of social pressure, felt even when not articulated. People read what other people around them are reading; in a sense they are "forced" to read certain books in order to be up to date in bookish conversations. If everybody around you is reading *The Disenchanted* or *The Far Side of Paradise* you don't have to be particularly interested in F. Scott Fitzgerald to read them too—you "have to" read them as a matter of self-protection, if nothing else. Sometimes the social pressure generates interest, but even when it does not it can stimulate the reading of particular titles. In any case the motives for reading are extremely complex and in many instances interest is not the determining factor.

There are other assumptions commonly made about book reading, particularly about their effects upon individuals and the society, but we cannot go into them here. For example, there is the assumption that "reading maketh the full man"—which is probably true only for a very few readers, since the rest read rather narrowly in terms of subject or form. Or there is the assumption that book reading makes people into good citizens by informing them about current affairs—which is probably true only for a minority of the readers of political books, since most readers are deliberately reinforcing their own political viewpoints. Or there is the assumption that books have had great effects directly upon large classes of readers, as in Mark Twain's charge that the state of the South was attributable to the reading of Walter Scott or in Archibald MacLeish's assertion that the "distrustful" state of mind of a whole generation could be laid at the door of the World War I novelists. Actually "the books that changed our minds" (of the Freud-Marx-Darwin variety) have their major effects in an indirect and remote fashion upon people who have never read them and often hardly heard of them.

The general moral of this tale, then, is that the state of popular reading is complicated, uneven, shifting, sometimes obscure. The broad generalizations in terms of which the subject is usually discussed are simply not appropriate to a serious, realistic view of it. Although it is more fun that way, it is more correct to pay some respect to the accumulated evidence, such as it is, and hence to take account of the actual differentiation which characterizes the state of popular reading today.

The Book Business in America

By ALAN DUTSCHER

THE AMERICAN BOOK INDUSTRY is facing a crisis. This is nothing new for a business which produces one of the most negligible commodities sold in the Land of the Beautiful. The only new element in the situation is the generally acknowledged fact that as a result of the extremity it has become virtually impossible to publish a quality trade book.

The book has always been a marginal product in America largely because insofar as America does read it is pre-eminently the home of the cheap newspaper and magazine. Books, historically, have never been the profitable element for the army of manufacturers, publishers, writers, illustrators, wholesalers, and retailers economically involved in their existence in the United States. Rather they have figured either as an unremunerative sideline, or, conversely, they have been supported by other more lucrative activities engaged in by the adjutants of the aforementioned army. Thus American publishers prior to the twentieth century were able to put out books only because their revenues from the financially more important "ephemeral" material enabled them to do so; in recent years when the divarification of serial and book publishing has been established[1] the latter has become absolutely dependent for its continued existence upon subsidiary markets (book clubs, reprints, serial pre- or republication, rentals, the cinema).

Unlike his European counterparts, the American bookman has struck no roots in the national soil. This alienation is reflected in many ways: "A Gallup poll published in February, 1950, reports: 'Despite our mass education and high degree of literacy, the United States has the lowest proportion of book readers of any major democracy, judging by the results of an international survey in six nations. England ranked highest in the study, with well over half of her adult population reading some book or novel at the time the survey was conducted. Norway came next, then Canada, then Australia, and Sweden, and the United States brought up the rear, with only one adult in five reading books.' "[2] Other reading studies have been conducted, which substantially demonstrate the functional illiteracy of Americans insofar as books are concerned. The most comprehensive survey of all those made on the subject concluded that not more than 25 per cent of the population read books; magazines were read by 50 per cent, and newspapers by 90 per cent. It was the author's circumspect conviction that only one-half of the adults residing in the United States had sufficient skill to read and understand the books published for them.[3]

Reprinted from *Contemporary Issues*, Vol. 5, April-May, 1954, pp. 38-58, by permission of the author and the publisher. (Copyright, 1954, by Contemporary Press.)

Both as cause and effect of the paucity of book readers, satisfactory distribution of books is drastically delimited, geographically. While it was normally customary to have a well-stocked bookstore in almost every European township of any consequence, this has never been the case in America. One competent observer reported on the state of the ordinary bookstore in 1931, in these terms: "The stocks of books are inadequate at almost every point except New York. . . . The distribution system of the industry, as represented by its outlets is unsystematized, undeveloped, inffective, unprofitable and static. . . . Two-thirds of the counties of the United States and nearly one-half of the urban places between 5,000-100,000 population are without a book outlet worthy of the name. . . . Over 33,000,000 people are without access to an adequate book outlet. . . . Over fifty per cent of the people living in places from 10,000 to 25,000 are not served by such an outlet in their own communities, and constitute over fifty per cent in some of the best book states. . . . The degree of over-concentration is even higher in larger cities—the forty-one cities of over 200,000 population having twenty-four per cent of the population and thirty per cent of the book outlets—and the highest degree of concentration being in the first three cities."[4] These figures have, to some extent, been brought up to date: in a regional breakdown of the percentage of twenty publishers' 1946 direct sales as correlated with the percentage of U.S. population estimated for the same year, it was demonstrated that 40.6 per cent of the population (living in the Southeastern and West Central regions) have only 22.3 per cent of sales (to bookstores and individuals, and not including wholesalers). At the same time 26.5 per cent of the population (living in the Northeastern region) have 42.4 per cent of sales.[5] This enormous disproportion is perhaps more clearly shown by other regional figures reported for 1944, once again reflecting sales made to retailers and readers only: 22.2 per cent of total national sales were in New York State alone, while seventeen out of the remaining forty-seven states accounted for less than 4 per cent of the total books sold.[6]

As important as such figures are for indicting the poor condition of the book industry, they are perhaps even more important as an index to the cultural level of the nation which now assumes the "mantle of world leadership." Such phenomena as a country's unwillingness or inability to support cultural products are never simply "accidental"—they are among the surest signs of that nation's lack of maturity and civilizatory progress. America's cultural barbarism is but a symptom of the general barbarism implicit (and becoming increasingly explicit) in her structure. Nor is the impact of these figures mitigated by the extent of public library development in the United States. For as Lehmann-Haupt has ingeniously suggested, the traditional cultural backwardness which has always found it so difficult to maintain the book industry on an economic basis, itself must account in large measure for the phenomenal growth of the tax-supported library, which was, therefore, less an expression of educational yearning (the customary assumption) than of its direct opposite. That is, the real significance of the public library development in the United States is to be seen in the fact that America had to subsidize book outlets at a loss, at a time when the population of every other advanced nation in the world could profitably support them.

The central points this article will attempt to establish are: first, the wretched condition of the book industry, and second, the effects of these circumstances on the books themselves. In addressing ourselves to the former consideration it is possible to start at any step in the procedure, or any industry involved in the making or marketing of books. However, let us begin with publishing: "Despite nearly record sales the book industry is facing a crisis. Greatly increased costs for material and labor since the end of the war have virtually wiped out profit margins for publication of original trade books. According to an analysis appearing in the most recent statistical report (1947-1948): (A) Seven companies with annual volume in excess of two-and-a-half million [dollars—A.D.]showed operating profits before taxes averaging five per cent; (B) Five companies with gross sales between one and two-and-a-half million dollars had an average operating loss of three per cent before taxes; (C) Six companies, whose volume ranged from $250,000 to $1,000,000 for the year, showed an average operating loss before taxes of 3.4 per cent; (D) Nine companies with volume ranging from $250,000 to $10,000,000 showed an average operating loss before taxes averaging 20.1 per cent. These figures do not include 'other income' from subsidiary rights."[7] All but the last group made a small profit when income from subsidiary rights was included. Our source correctly adds therefore: "Thus we clearly see the serious situation facing the trade book publisher today as he is compelled to depend for his profits, if any, on the special income that comes to him from book-club adoptions, royalties from reprint houses and revenue from the sale of other subsidiary rights."[8] The consequence of this dependence will be considered later.

The common plaint of publishers is that costs have risen enormously, e.g., the average increase of linotype composition between the years 1942-1947 was 77 per cent, and of antique as well as coated paper, in the same period, 45 per cent. It is generally recognized by the industry that the prices of books cannot be raised proportionately, though they have definitely increased, because the commodity sold, being so peripheral, can easily price itself out of the market entirely. There are, on the other hand, easily discernible limits to every single method but one of lowering the cost of production, and only the "one way out" renders any efforts in this direction of appreciable value; for most books are already published in technically inferior bindings, with cheap paper, little or no margins (the libraries with their multiple circulation of books, and special rebinding problems are the first to suffer from these), inferior print, dearth of illustrative material, and considerably diminished in size.

The "one way out" is volume production; the publication of big editions and the concomitant discontinuance of publications likely to appeal to limited numbers of readers. That this is connected with the publishers' dependence on subsidiary markets which alone can effect the large-scale distribution that makes volume production possible, should be obvious. Two well-known statements on this matter bear repetition: "The pricing policy which a majority of the leading trade book publishers seem to be following will be unsound unless they can maintain volume, avoid small printings which cost much more than large ones, keep to a minimum the number of unprofitable books. . . . What perhaps is most disturbing about the present situation is that it lessens the chances of really promising young writers to get a hearing and is likely to limit seriously the publication of important and useful books, books of cultural value . . . books that are unlikely to have large sales."[9] The same year another authority wrote: ". . . the break-even point for a publisher used to be 2,500 to 4,000 copies [of any new book printed —A.D.]; now it is 10,000."[10] Note, the writer speaks of the break-even point, not of profit.

Having thus briefly indicated the problems of the publisher, let us next appraise those of the bookstore. The difference is somewhat akin to that between a localized and a metastasized cancer. Cheney reported the profits for an average bookstore with under a $60,000 annual volume of business (in this category were—and are—subsumed the overwhelming number of such outlets) in the "posperity year" 1929 to be minus 0.1 per cent, while the relatively poor store in the same classification made minus 6.9 per cent profit and the relatively good store had a profit of 5.9 per cent. He concluded that: "At least half the bookstores of the country are losing even in the best years, and the others are making too low a return for their efforts and hazards."[11]

It is important to understand that all "solutions" to the problems of the industry that are confined by the limits generally imposed, can, in fact, only aggravate the chronic malaise. Even the extremity of vertical monopolization, long a unique feature of the house of Doubleday, raises new problems. The fact that the firm is in possession of its own manufacturing plant means that it is confronted with yet another enormously expensive overhead charge which renders it imperative that the presses be kept running continuously if the business is to remain profitable. However, with the market for books as limited as it is in America, the condition of saturation is soon reached (as it has already for several kinds of "literature," e.g., juveniles, reprints). When that condition is attained the surplus is either remaindered at fantastically low prices by special dealers (who are thereby competing with the publishers' list price items, and with the vulnerable bookseller in the bargain) or it may be pulped at tremendous losses (this is just one step removed from burning the books, nonpolitically inspired examples of which process we may someday be privileged to see). Doubleday has been able to use yet another expedient: the control of many book clubs which it exercises enables the firm to get rid of its excess as "bonus" books and "dividends" to club members. However it requires no great imagination to see that this practice too has its limits.[12]

The consequences and conditions of volume will be seen if two subsidiary sources of publishers' income are examined in detail—the book clubs and the reprinters. There are about eighty book clubs in existence (the number is constantly changing), but of these perhaps three have developed "mass" markets.[13] The biggest is—or was—the Literary Guild, closely followed by the Book Of The Month Club and the Dollar Book Club (the first and third are among many controlled by Doubleday). Because of its highly developed mail order business the large book club is able to guarantee both author and publisher[14] a minimum sale of several hundred thousand copies of the book chosen. This may mean that the publisher will make $100,000 or more (a big sum for a small business!) if only one title is selected by a club. Because of the enormous volume in which the book clubs deal they are the first segment of the industry under discussion which do show handsome profits.[15] Bound writes: ". . . properly run, the book-club business can be extremely profitable. According to a prospectus of the Book Of The Month dated 20th March, 1947, in connection with the sale of capital stock, the company showed, in round numbers, for the years ending 31st December, 1944, 1945, and 1946, gross sales (less returns) respectively of $12,796,000, $13,551,000 and $18,190,000 with net profit after taxes for these years of $758,000, $759,000 and $1,346,000. . . . Figures given in confidence, which therefore cannot be revealed, show that other book clubs have done as well or better in 1947 and 1948. Totalling some of these figures we find a combined gross sale of $10,000,000 produced a net profit before taxes in excess of $2,500,000."

The publishers make money, the book clubs make money—on the surface everything (forgetting the bookseller and the kind of book sold) seems to be lovely. Nevertheless a few troublesome reflections irritate even the denizens of this fair elysium: Publishers complain that though the club sells a few books in great numbers, those selected constitute only an infinitesimal proportion of all titles issued—and here is the rub—while the remaining and greatest portion of the publishers' list (the part sold by him directly and hence the part from which he obtains a greater percentage of profit per book sold than the club can give him) must suffer in consequence. For all the blare of publicity and the grease of promotion is used up on the book club selections, from the sales of which the bulk of the publisher's revenue is not derived. An added feature of the same difficulty is the fact that the publishers must compete wildly for the chance to have a book or books of theirs so chosen. Hence they all try to turn out the same kind of best-seller trash, and this lack of variety produces great masses of books which duplicate each other and more easily become drugs on the market. More importantly, the publishers' dependence upon the book clubs and other subsidiaries forces them to issue ever greater number of books on the chance that the more titles they put out the better the opportunity to have a club selection among them—though conversely, also the better the chance to make a loss on the total annual business. As the title volume swells it works against each individual title by "A. Cutting down its share of available publishing attention. B. Reducing its share of promotion effort. C. Reducing its share of selling effort by publishers, traveler, bookseller, and clerk. D. Crowding dealer's stocks. E. Reducing the effectiveness of criticism. F. Increasing production costs. G. Increasing the hazards and losses for every branch of the industry."[16] The bookseller too, who, we should remember, never had a membership card to Elysium, complains that as practically all publicity is given to club selections (only the clubs are rich enough to spend the really big sums required for effective advertising campaigns, and naturally they will spend such money on their own books), the only kind of books that people know about and ask for are these same items, which the bookstore is hardly in a decent competitive position to sell inasmuch as they can be offered at far cheaper rates by the clubs.

The latter retort that they benefit the whole industry because they have introduced the habit of reading books to large numbers of new people and further because, given the enormous turnover in club membership, it is not too much to assume that ex-clubbers constitute a potential new market for books which offers great possibilities to both publishers and booksellers. Despite the noble pronunciamentos of these "educators," regional statistical breakdowns of book-club membership refute the first claim by revealing the usual disproportions: book-club membership in the Northeastern area is extremely high while membership in the Southeastern and West Central region is much lower. It is easily seen, therefore, that the book clubs are really gaining members among people who already have the facilities for the purchase, loan, or rental of such works. Upon analysis the "introduction to reading" argument turns out to be simply a smoke-screen for the destruction of the retail book business. As for the potential market of ex-members, Miller writes that the largest group of such fortunate people is assumed by persons in the trade to be composed of those unable any longer to afford four books a year, irrespective of the number of others offered free.

The only sense in which the reprint business differs from the book-club *geschäft* is that the books chosen by the former are, if this is at all conceivable, generally even more inferior.[17] Again the secret of "success" is volume. The average print order for a reprint is 250,000 copies . . . it is uneconomical to print less than 150,000 and it often takes more to break even. The reprint business basically constitutes an attempt to capture the more lucrative magazine market for books by using magazine methods and magazine "literature." Distribution is effected through periodical wholesalers who in turn load drug, candy, chain, stationery and other stores with the books. Discounting and pricing is similar to that of magazines. This happy scene is interpunctuated by occasional views of the mortal struggle between hard-cover reprinters and their soft-cover counterparts. While the latter are definitely winning, life is by no means so rosy, even for them: In 1946 overproduction of this trash reached such heights that 15,000,000 pocket books had to be called in. On the other side, original publishers, who are so dependent on their reprint subsidiaries, are slowly being strangled to death by their competition. It has come to a point where reprinters are selling originals and original publishers are selling "reprints."[18] The same process of strangulation is taking place in the area of bookselling, since the ordinary book outlet must now compete with everything from delicatessens to whore houses. As a by-product of this development the outlet becomes increasingly less bookstore and more of a five-and-dime affair for the sale of notions, toys, greeting cards and, perhaps, as the bookmen awaken to wider and wider possibilities, suppositories and condoms. Correspondingly, as less and less attention is devoted to the selling of books in these places, less and less books will be sold, and there will be fewer bookstores, as the term is usually understood.

To confirm the thesis that subsidiary publishing constitutes no economic salvation, it should be made clear that the subsidiaries bring pressure to bear for the creation of not merely more and more books, but—even in the case of reprinters—for new titles. The Brobdingnagian proportions of such an output must crush its producers underfoot. The reprinters, like the book clubs, contribute to the demand for more books, the principle of their distribution system being continual replacement of slow-sellers. This must be so as the profit per item is extremely low.[19] In addition the obligatory policy of full credit for unsold copies (obligatory, because that is the only way in which a drug store can be induced to give up valuable space to so valueless a commodity as a book) is an omnipresent worry; and finally, the reprinters are faced with the virtual impossibility of raising prices, because their books are competing in price not with other books but with newspapers, aspirins, cigarettes, laxatives, etc. This, perpetual replacement necessitates perpetual production, and it comes as no surprise that perhaps 20 per cent of the reprinters' lists are not reprints—but originals. What the continuation of this trend must eventually mean to publishers' subsidiary rights, to the quality of books in general, considering the kind of literature marketed by reprinters, and to publishers once more, in terms of direct competition in the issuance of originals, is obvious.

So far we have considered the conditions and consequent effects of the present situation on the economics of the book industry. We will now examine the effect of these same circumstances on the books themselves. It requires little documentation to establish the low quality of contemporary literature. There are innumerable pet theories which attempt to establish the reasons for this state, and practically all partake, in some measure, of the truth. In a word, it is true that the critics are to blame, as are the authors, the publishers, the booksellers, *ad infinitum*. The only thing to be added to the unerring collective consciousness that something is wong with the books put out today is the conviction that the rottenness permeates *every* area of the book field and is the necessary result of the overall system. To explain the phenomenon thoroughly would involve a cultural history of our era. This much, however, can be said, generally: ideology (a category which includes all literature) insofar as it is great can only reflect reality, insofar as it is inferior can only distort it. However, the reflection of reality, which is truth, is impossible under a system a precondition for whose existence is precisely the distortion of truth. When capitalism was still, qualitatively considered, progressive it could afford to be honest with and about itself; when it exhausted its progressive possibilities and in fact became retrogressive the truth became not merely a luxury, but the greatest menace to the system, and lying or evasion (which is a form of lying) became the only legitimate forms for literature. Thus, inferiority of production is not an abnormality of contemporary literature but is its function, and lies, evasions, and inconsequentiality are not the contingent results of this same literature but are rather what is required of it under the division of labor.

So we find that 100 years ago the works of Dickens, Thackeray, Cooper, the Bröntes, etc., were among the best sellers in America. Today the situation has been reversed with a vengeance. In fact literature has sunk so low in the last decade that it is now the fashion of a considerable section of the literati to look back with nostalgic longing upon the 1930's as a "golden age" of American art and thought. That the latter period was superior to our own we will not argue; however, as a reflection of what the present period must be like if the 1930's are to be called a golden age in comparison, we reproduce a list of the best sellers in the United States in the "golden age."[20]

1931 BUCK, PEARL: *The Good Earth.*
1931 QUEEN, ELLERY: *The Dutch Shoe Mystery.*
1932 QUEEN, ELLERY: *The Egyptian Cross Mystery.*
1933 ALLEN, HERVEY: *Anthony Adverse.*
1933 GARDNER, ERLE STANLEY: *The Case of the Sulky Girl.* (All Gardner's books are mysteries.)
1933 HILTON, JAMES: *Lost Horizon.*
1934 GARDNER, ERLE STANLEY: *The Case of the Curious Bride.*
1934 QUEEN, ELLERY: *The Chinese Orange Mystery.*
1935 GARDNER, ERLE STANLEY: *The Case of the Counterfeit Eye.*
1936 CARNEGIE, DALE: *How to Win Friends and Influence People.*
1936 GARDNER, ERLE STANLEY: *The Case of the Stuttering Bishop.*
1936 MITCHELL, MARGARET: *Gone With the Wind.*
1937 GARDNER, ERLE STANLEY: *The Case of the Dangerous Dowager.*
1937 GARDNER, ERLE STANLEY: *The Case of the Lame Canary.*
1938 BRAND, MAX: *Singing Guns.*
1938 GARDNER, ERLE STANLEY: *The Case of the Substitute Face.*
1938 PAGE, MARCO: *Fast Company.* (Mystery.)
1938 RUNYON, DAMON: *The Best of Damon Runyon.*
1939 STEINBECK, JOHN: *The Grapes of Wrath.*

To prove the contention that rottenness permeates every area of book production and renders bad work inevitable it is necessary to examine, in some detail, each major agent involved in the fabrication and diffusion of literature. Accordingly, we begin with the writer. And to guide us we have one of the professional breed.[21] Our quotation is taken from a discussion he gave before other men economically involved in literary production, and is thus characterized by a certain degree of frankness. Mr. Davis speaks of the professional author, and in particular of the case ". . . which unfortunately is far too common in this country . . . that of the man who has something to say, but not much. He says it, he acquires a certain degree of renown, or at least notoriety; he may even make some money out of it; if he has a fairly sustained capacity for production he becomes a professional writer—and all at once he discovers that he has nothing more to say, that he said it all in his first two or three books; but he is still a professional writer, with a family which has to be supported somehow, and which can perhaps be more easily and comfortably supported by the tricks which the professional writer has mastered than in any other way. This all too common situation has had a serious effect on the content and quality of American writing." Mr. Davis speaks now of the author's connection with the magazine industry, but since virtually the same conditions obtain, in this regard, for the book industry it is valuable to quote him: "At any rate starvation in a garret is no longer a problem for any writer who can meet the somewhat peculiar but not too rigidly specialized standards of the magazine market . . . and . . . magazine editors are expecting him to produce at the same old rate. For what the magazine editor wants is something that will build up, or keep up, the circulation; and well-known names, well known to the readers of that magazine as well as to the general public, are the thing that is most likely to do it. Accordingly, if you sell any given magazine ten stories in a year, you will get more for each story than if you sold them only three stories a year. It may well be that three stories, three good stories, are all you have in you that year; but if your production falls off your price is likely, sooner or later, to fall off, too. So you write your three good stories; and then you use the tricks of the trade that you have learned and your knowledge of the tastes of the editors of that particular magazine to knock off seven more stories that are good enough—good enough to sell with the advantage of a name well known to the magazine's readers, even though they might be sent back if they came up from Joe Blotz of Podunk Corners."

Still further on Mr. Davis touches upon the same problem from a somewhat different angle. He speaks of ". . . the problem of the promoted book . . . sometimes the publisher has the idea, sometimes the agent . . . [a particular publisher—A. D.] in the discussion . . . already cited, observes that a really successful author *seldom* [italics ours—A.D.] has time to write a book he wants to write, for the chances are that he is already under contract to write two or three books that his agent has thought of and wants him to write. . . ."

If it were only a question of the agent and publisher dictating the content of books, perhaps even so, the modern literary sense would not be as arid as it is. However, there are others as well. Direct and indirect coercion are exercised by the subsidiaries upon authors and publishers. Of the direct variety we have already seen one instance, that of the reprinters who have their trash pre-issued by original publishers for prestige and advertising reasons.

Indirect coercion, however, has even greater weight, and this results from the fact that original houses have to rely on subsidiary publishers for part of their profit, which compels them often to issue the kind of book that has a chance to compete for subsidiary rights. What kind of book does the club want? Miller quotes from the formula developed by one big book club (People's Book Club, which advertised the following statement on the back of the Sears & Roebuck—the owners of this club—1948 Spring and Summer Catalogue): "The standards by which our editors and critics judge literature contain this one very vital *must*: The books must be readable by every member of the family. They must be *family books* . . . So, if you like to read without blushing, without tearing pages out before passing the books on to younger members of your household, we invite you . . . to read about the advantages you will enjoy as a member of the People's Book Club."

The Book of the Month Club, on the other hand, prides itself on the fact that the tomes it offers are selected by a board of prominent literary critics and writers, and hence are, presumably, the cream of the country's authorial output. Nonetheless when one of these Solons was asked by an outside source to name the books published that year which she considered the best, or liked the most, only one of the seventeen titles she had chosen for the BOMC appeared on her tally; in the case of another of the judges not a single one of his BOMC selections were so listed.[22]

Having glimpsed something of the obstacles that stand in the author's way, should he wish to produce a good book, let us make the (increasingly metaphysical) assumption that somehow such a book does get written and reaches the publisher's desk. What kind of man is the publisher? Is he able to recognize good literature? Will he make personal, dare we say monetary, sacrifices to see that the book is issued? Banker Bound gives us this encouraging answer: "In the past it was customary for the publishing house to be dominated by an individual who was primarily interested in the literary aspects of the business . . . today the trend is towards including in top management experienced business men. . . . Frequently these are individuals with accounting or financial background." To be sure, this is just the sort of person needed to improve the quality of American literature.

Considering our obstinate fondness for metaphysical speculation, perhaps we will be indulged yet another fancy, namely, that despite current literary and publishing infelicity, an excellent work has been written and actually published. What then? The "life expectancy" of the average book is measured in terms of a few short weeks. That an early death is desirable for most books published today is not to be questioned. Unfortunately, this matter of "getting lost in the shuffle" affects the occasional good book as well. Works that do not quickly "catch on" are quickly replaced, and are soon permitted to go out of print. The business of "catching on" may be likened to an osmotic movement—it is a question of absorption through innumerable cells of public opinion, and the better the book is the longer it takes for it to find its audience, for the simple reason that the audience for good books is an extremely limited one at this time. From this standpoint the central importance of the literary critic, who constitutes the first and most important agent of the molecular process, and who is the winnower of a huge, amorphous mass of literary material, must be adjudged. Given the enormous, unending flow of bad and indifferent books it is practically impossible for the ordinary person to find decent reading material and it may therefore almost be said that the chief function of modern criticism should be to discover and lend a helping hand to the worthwhile book. Criticism goes much further in this direction, however, for it is endowed with the charity of sweet Jesus himself. Put another way the statement would read: the literary critics are indistinguishable from the writers of advertising copy. That this is more than a superficial impression has been proven on at least two separate occasions: in a compilation of reviews appearing in some 50 metropolitan newspapers and literary periodicals in one year, a writer found that 137 novels had, during that time, been hailed as "the best novel of the year," while 27 biographies were similarly endorsed.[23] In the second case 1,733 books were criticized in 8,086 reviews appearing in 67 publications. Of this total of 1,733 books reviewed, 787 received definite and unqualified reactions, as follows: 726 were favorably and only 31 were unfavorably reviewed.[24] That is the exact measure of modern criticism—only 31 books out of 1,733 were unfavorably reviewed.[25]

If the initial step in the circulation process is so disappointing can anything be said for the final step—the book outlet itself? With great expectations we shall first examine that outlet which, while not of major importance, is ordinarily thought of as the most favorable for quality books —the public library. The first question is: What are the libraries' book selection policies? Miller answers this when he writes of ". . . the libraries' . . . tendency to buy and circulate the most popular books. Best sellers, whether purchased from local dealers, wholesalers, or publishers, have usually been most in demand by adult and adolescent card holders and most generously supplied by the libraries. *Indeed, many public libraries select their adult books from best seller lists or from advertisements and reviews featuring candidates for such lists"* (italics ours).

Libraries however, are not the major agents for the dissemination of books. This function falls to the lot of the varied retail outlets. There can be no doubt that insofar as the latter are concerned, the quality publication has, if anything, less of a chance of being selected, or if that should by chance occur, of remaining in stock, than it would have in the libraries, and this for a number of reasons: First because of the already sufficiently delineated pickle which these shops are in. Quick sale or no sale, the traditional policy of the drug-store type of outlet, and of the department store, has perforce become the nostrum for all outlets. Needless to say excellent books, like most distinctive things, require some time to establish themselves—for the aforementioned molecular process to take effect. Under the present conditions it is highly improbable that they can do so. Secondly, because of the "star system" of book promotion which centers all advertising, critical attention, and salesmanship on book-club selections and their ilk. (That *all* elements in the book business will co-operate is assured, because all, in one way or another, are dependent on publishers' profits which in turn are contingent upon the sale of big-volume books.) Third, it is hardly to be expected that drug and department store clerks are themselves interested in books, not to mention good books, and would therefore attempt to sell the latter. Even the clerks in the traditional bookstore are most often merely salesmen on a commission, who have little or no idea of the nature of the wares they purvey. The same is true of the owners, for whom the only distinction between books is in their rate of sale. For a comparison we may revert to the example of the German book stores which customarily employed clerks conversant not only with business organization but with books as well.[26] In addition the book business there was (we are speaking of prewar conditions) sufficiently stabilized so that the store need not have been concerned with the sale of dime-store novelties to ensure its further existence.

To elaborate briefly on the quick sale or no sale policy. This principle guides not only distributors but producers as well. The non-selling title, for which appellative the serious work need never strive, is not simply removed from the bookstore's racks; it is remaindered and/or pulped. The publisher cannot afford to store these books, for under the present crowded conditions space has become as valuable as the objects that occupy it. Plates may even be thrown out or re-used—the latter particularly in periods when there is a shortage of metal, e.g., in time of war.

For that rare good book which survives this whole process a special fate is reserved—it simply gets lost. In Europe the second-hand book trade is a highly organized institution which has flourished since time immemorial. Not so in America, where virtually the entire industry is situated in a few city blocks along Fourth Avenue in Manhattan. American capitalism is distinguished, among other things, by the continuous and relentless pressure of new commodities. So that whether it is a pair of shoes that only last three months, or of women's stockings that wear for three days, or new books which enjoy a vogue for three weeks, the emphasis is always on the new, never on the durable. It is, on the one hand, a question of America rarely producing an item that can and will last, and, on the other hand, of the system's absolute dependence for its existence upon a shoddiness of production which necessitates continual replacement, that account for this phenomenon, and, incidentally, for the insignificance of the second-hand book trade. The ordinary retail outlet will not carry such books; neither the profit to be made on them nor the demand for them warrants it—and, in any case, patrons might soil their hands touching old books. The run of the mill outlets continually emphasize newness—it being the irrationality of capitalism, and particularly of its American variety, that newness in and of itself is a positive attribute. Thus, the useful function of preserving serious literature on the market can only devolve upon the narrow shoulders of the second-hand book trade, whose inconsequentiality, in America, is its chief distinction.

The description of the quality book's cycle of life and death is completed. Most manuscripts, of course, die long before they are remaindered, lost or pulped; in fact it can be categorically stated that the great majority of good literature that might be published never gets into print in the first place—is stillborn.

It has been stated by some people in and out of the book industry that even if trade publishing were to become 100 per cent best-seller purveying, this would not necessarily mean the end of serious literature in the United States because the university presses are able to fill the breach. This opinion is predicated upon the desideratum that the university press is ostensibly a nonprofit organization.[27] However when the directors of these presses were queried as to what their greatest problem was, in the words of the interrogator: "This inquiry provoked a 100 per cent response"[28]—the problem, as might be imagined, was financial. Kerr quotes one director as saying: "Although the absence of profits does not bother us, we must worry about losses. A university press is in business to break even on the publication of scholarship. Most presses have the advantage of some help from their universities, but once given this help they are expected to hold their own. And they have to do it by selling, in a fiercely competitive market, a product that was never designed for a large sale. If one book loses money, another must make it up. Thus if we publish some of Professor So and So's books at a considerable loss, we should like to have a chance at one or two of the others which might bring in a little profit." The nub of the matter is that even the break-even point in publishing involves best-sellerism. In the light of this the fact that the number of popularizations by these presses has almost doubled in twenty years (1927-1947)[29] assumes large significance. That this is more than one man's opinion is substantiated by William Miller's remark on the same point: "Yet more and more university presses have begun to use trade-book 'pyrotechnics' for money with which to meet current bills for 'salesless wonders.'" The extent of this development is indicated in an article that Miller quotes, which was prepared by Henry M. Silver for the Spring, 1949, issue of the *American Scholar*. Silver compared the number of university press books reviewed in the *Sunday New York Times Book Review* (the bulk of the books reviewed therein are trashy): ". . . during the first six months of 1938 with the same period of 1948"; he found 33 books in the first period and 63 in the second. "In the earlier period only one press had six titles or more covered, in the latter, five. The 33 books of 1938 came from 12 presses; those of 1948 from 16."

There is a terrible significance in the degeneration of the book industry, and this is discovered in the observation that books alone of all the mass media of communication remained, until recently, a possible outlet for genius and free expression. American newspapers and magazines have, for decades, exhibited the characteristically totalitarian monolithicism of thought, concentration of control, and artistic as well as ideational vacua, that declared their former progressive heritage, such as it was, to be forfeit. The cinema, radio and television, born into a world in retrogression, manifested from the very first, and in pure outline, the quantification and moronization which have marked their development ever since; thus they have hardly ever fought censorship, from whatever quarters it may have proceeded— rather it was always a question of which pressure to succumb to first—nor have they developed an artistic or intellectual tradition.[30]

It was the very insignificance and weakness of the book industry, the fact that large aggregations of capital were neither attracted to nor absolutely necessary for it which served to cushion the business from monopolization, and left it an arena for individuality and self-expression. However the same puissant economic trend which forces the consolidation of all industry and crushes, in particular, the consumer goods trades has fastened itself on the book business at last, with disastrous results whose effects on the personnel of publishing are of significance only insofar as they signal the death of free expression in America.

Notes

1. There has been more than one important instance of their monopolistic redintegration recently, and this may indicate a future trend.

2. Quoted from *The Book in America: A History of the Making and Selling of Books in the United States*, by Hellmut Lehmann-Haupt, in collaboration with Lawrence C. Wroth and Rollo G. Silver, 2nd edition, N. Y., Bowker, 1951.

3. *The Geography of Reading: A Study of the Distribution and Status of Libraries in the United States*, by Louis Round Wilson, Chicago, American Library Association and University of Chicago Press, 1938.

4. *Economic Survey of the Book Industry*, 1930-1931, by O. H. Cheney; with *1947-1948 Statistical Report*, N. Y., Bowker, 1931, reprinted 1949.

5. *The Book Industry (A Report of the Public Library Inquiry)*, by William Miller, N. Y., Columbia University Press, 1949.

6. *A Banker Looks at Book Publishing*, by Charles F. Bound, N. Y., Bowker, 1950.

7. Bound, *op. cit.*

8. *Ibid.*

9. "The Crisis in Book Publishing," by Alfred McIntyre, in *The Atlantic Monthly*, October, 1947.

10. "Trade Winds," by Bennett Cerf, in the *Saturday Review of Literature*, July 12, 1947.

11. Cheney, *op. cit.*

12. That ingenious bookmen may not arrive at "more and better" answers cannot be categorically stated in advance. Accordingly, an extremely beneficial use to which many of the surplus literary masterpieces of our time were put was in the development of "shooters."

To make a "shooter" one simply cuts a big hole out of the center of the book and inserts a coiled spring therein. When the unwary literateur opens his favorite *chef d'oeuvre* imagine his delight as the spring hits him on his scholarly snout. And for all we can tell the jack-in-the-box is the source of less pain than the book would have been.

13. It is not commonly realized that despite innumerable "free offers," advertisements, "bargains," premiums and the miserable quality of titles sold—which is supposed to be an advantage—the entire "mass" market of the book club has probably never exceeded three million.

14. It is worth noting that while most publishers' royalties to authors vary from 10 to 15 per cent of the retail price on the first 2500 to 5000 copies of a book sold, and are slightly pro-rated with increased sales, when a book is selected by a club receipts from the latter are equally divided between author and publisher. With some percentage variation this situation obtains for all subsidiary rights; hence publishers need hardly coerce authors into writing the kind of trash chosen by subsidiaries.

15. It should be clear that only the leading ones are meant. It is probably fair to say that three-quarters of all book clubs are marginal outfits, not much better off than the average publisher.

16. Cheney, *op. cit.*

17. In 1945 over 50 per cent of all reprint titles were "mystery stories." As if to testify to the intellectual growth taking place in America, three years later only about 25 per cent were mysteries, while proudly seated on the curve of litrary ascendance were "westerns" and "sex."

18. That is, the idiotic books manufactured for reprinters are submitted by them to regular houses for original publication in order to give such books the necessary veneer of respectability and prestige that comes with hard-cover publication. The publishers are forced to agree to this arrangment, otherwise they forfeit subsidiary royalties.

19. Bound's estimates for 25 cent reprints are as follows: The outlet pays 19 cents to the wholesaler, who returns 15½ cents to the publisher. However, the cost of production per copy is 10½ to 12½ cents and what remains to the publisher is between 2½ and 5 cents per copy, to cover cost of distribution, for reserves against returns—a very serious problem indeed—and for net profit.

20. Taken from *Golden Multitudes: the Story of Best Sellers in the United States,* by Frank Luther Mott, N. Y., Macmillan, 1947. Prof. Mott classifies as best sellers those books believed to have a total sale equal to one per cent of the population of the continental United States for the decade in which they were published. The required sale for the period 1930-1939 was 1,200,000.

21. *Some Aspects of the Economics of Authorship,* by Elmer Davis. The Bowker Lectures on Book Publishing; Second Series, N. Y., The Typophiles, 1945.

22. Miller, *op. cit.* BOMC pays its judges on a profit-sharing basis, thereby "possibly" inducing them to forego whatever standards they may have in order to select books of best-seller "quality."

23. "A Critique of Criticism," by Louis Bromfield, in *The Mirrors of the Year,* N. Y., Stokes, 1928.

24. Cheney, *op. cit.*

25. As for the books unfavorably reviewed: where personal clashes were not involved it can be said that this is the "pet plug" principle in operation once again. For, given the limitations of the market and the overproduction of books, at least some must be panned so that the others may sell.

26. Lehmann-Haupt, *op. cit.*

27. Considering the tenuous, often illusory, nature of the category profit for the book industry in general, differentiation on this basis partakes of the mythical.

28. *A Report on American University Presses,* by Chester Kerr. Association of American University Presses, 1949.

29. *Ibid.*

	1927	1947
1. (Books) Primarily addressed to Scholars	1119	1096
2. Textbooks (college and advanced)	471	337
3. Popularizations	302	521
	1892	1954

30. Of this the only thing that can be said is that the later the media developed, the more imbecile its content. Each succeeding medium compounds and itself reproduces solely the evils of its predecessors. So while the American cinema could, in its formative period, produce at least one genius—Chaplin—radio was never able to do so, and television is so nauseating that it makes even radio appear like a haven of intellectualism.

The Problem of the Paperbacks

By CECIL HEMLEY

IF CULTURE IS, as Matthew Arnold wrote, "the best that has been thought and said," then the paper reprints have made culture available to America. And, judging by the enormous sales of Shakespeare, Plato, the Bible, etc., in pocket book editions, the country is only too happy to be cultivated. Yet no one seriously believes that much has been accomplished. If anything, the prevailing mood is one of pessimism; in literary and intellectual circles there is much more talk of decadence than of renaissance.

The truth is that Arnold's definition is both priggish and false. "The best that has been thought and said" is only culture for the student and the historian of culture. A civilization which is vitally concerned with art and literature is above all interested in the art and literature it, itself, is producing. This inevitably will be of much less value than the output of all past ages; but it will be its own, its way or ways of seeing the world, and as such it will revitalize all which has preceded it.

I am, of course, not suggesting that the past be left unread. I am merely stating that it is fatal for a society to be enamored of the works of the past. And here is where paperbacked publishing is most open to criticism.

The tendency of paperbacked publishing has been to disseminate the best from the past and the most mediocre from the present. There have been obvious reasons for this. The reprinters must sell enormous editions to make their enterprise profitable, and therefore, when they consider works of high quality, they must be sure that these works have wide acceptance before they dare publish them. When it comes to Aristotle or Dante, they can be certain that the schools and colleges will, as a matter of routine, do sufficient publicity to produce the broad market that is necessary. However, the educational system cannot be relied upon to create a market for contemporary authors.

When it comes to contemporary writing the reprinter must perforce follow fashion—and not coterie fashion, it should be remembered, but large popular currents of taste. He must seek to reprint books that have demonstrated their appeal by selling widely in more expensive editions. Or, when this is not so, he must fall back on genres, such as the mystery or the western, which have wide, ready-made audiences waiting for them.

Since his motive is primarily economic, the reprinter is quite right in doing this. To survive he must sell; nor can he wait twenty years until the reputation of some current writer is sufficiently established for him to get

Reprinted from *The Commonweal*, Vol. 61 (1954), pp. 95-7, by permission of the author and the publisher. (Copyright, 1954, by The Commonweal Publishing Co.)

rid of his edition. And so inevitably he keeps away from the controversial and the extraordinary.

Should he drop his editions from one hundred thousand to twenty thousand and raise the price of his books (as Anchor and Vintage have done) he has more latitude, but not a great deal more. Now he does not do Dante and Shakespeare; he gambles on Mann, Gide or James.

The mere mention of these names is enough to make the point. All of these writers are world-famous; each has had a substantial vogue; each is on endless lists of supplementary reading. When books by less well-known authors are published by firms like Anchor or Vintage, it is because their academic reputation is high. But should a new G. M. Young or a new Basil Willey, let alone a new Mann or Kierkegaard, be somewhere writing his masterpiece, it is not likely that it will appear under the Anchor or Vintage imprint next year.

Nor should it. It has not been easy for fine writers to win recognition in the past. It will not be easy for them in the future. We must remember that a host of very great writers were forced to pay for the publication of their work. And this was in the era of the "cheap" hard book, when it was still profitable to print a very small edition. That day is long since past. If the printer and the binder are to live well, then it becomes economically unfeasible to do the novel that will sell only twenty-five hundred copies and the book of verse which will, perhaps, if the reviews are very good, sell three or four hundred.

As a matter of fact, novels in hard-back editions very often sell less than twenty-five hundred. And what publisher in his right mind will do a book of poems by an unknown? Here is where the impact of the paper reprints has been felt.

Not only has the publisher of hard books found himself forced by rising prices to do larger editions and to sell them at higher prices, but he has found himself in ruinous competition with the mass-production book. If one can buy Dante, Shakespeare, Lawrence, Huxley, *et al.,* at thirty-five to fifty cents, and Mann, Kierkegaard, James, etc., at eighty-five to ninety-five cents, why pay three-fifty or four dollars for a work of possibly inferior quality? No one, after all, can read all of even the great books of the world.

I know there are those who will dispute these conclusions. Their argument is that the cheap reprint has opened up a new market.

If this is so, what has happened to those who once did buy fiction in hard covers? It is surely odd that, with the advent of the paper reprint, sales of novels in hard covers have dropped off. The cry now is that the publisher of more expensive editions must concentrate on nonfiction. Should sales of nonfiction in expensive editions decline within the next few years, the conclusion will be obvious.

That the new writer of quality is in jeopardy, the reprinters themselves confess. It is for this reason, we are told, that such magazines as *New World Writing* and *Discovery* have been founded. The appearance of these magazines is certainly a good thing, but to think that it will solve the problem seems to me naive.

Writers are not developed through the publication of occasional short pieces in mass-distributed anthologies—at any rate not writers who work best in long forms. If we are to have new novelists of merit, they will have to come to maturity through the writing of novels, not through the random creation of short stories or fragments of novels. And the novels that they write will inevitably not all be masterpieces, and someone will have to foot the bill for the failures.

In the old days a publisher would every now and again take a chance on a writer of promise. Now, before he signs a contract, he wants to know what the subsidiary rights are, and, if neither the reprinters nor the motion pictures will buy, he cannot afford to publish.

If the picture that I am painting is a gloomy one, it must be remembered that actually it is only a little worse than it has always been. As I have said, there has been no time when it was not difficult for writers of merit to get published. Nor is it likely that any system will be devised to make it otherwise. Can we find an infallible test to distinguish capable editors from poor ones? Can we make it mandatory that all those who have sufficient capital to found a publishing house be persons of judgment and taste?

It is clear that in the future, as in the past, there will be in the publishing world much mediocrity mingled with some brilliance. As in the past, great writers will often find the doors of editors locked against them, and they will watch bad writers enter on their way to financial success and transitory glory. These are the normal hazards of being a fine writer. The abnormal ones arise because of technological and sociological changes. Through mass production one can produce cheaply, but one must sell widely.

It is for this reason that publishing by small, noncommercial presses, so-called fugitive presses, has become so difficult in this era. And it must be remembered that it was through fugitive publishing that many of our best writers became known. Fugitive publishing has been the corrective to mediocre commercial publishing.

But, in the era of the paper reprint, with the printing presses making available the innumerable masterpieces of the past at absurdly low prices, how can the new compete? Everything favors the old. It has been tried by time, is cheap, and is distributed everywhere. It is quite otherwise with the new. No critic has as yet discovered its merits; editors are dubious about it, and cannot recommend that money be risked on it—and so it must be produced shoddily, stamped with the stigma of the "vanity press," and distributed in a few large cities where sympathetic bookstore owners will, perhaps, take it on consignment.

And yet if there is to be a new, this is very likely the way it will arrive. Recently the reprinters have begun to issue and commission originals, but the same wariness operates here as in their other endeavors. If they want a book on art, they go to the world-famous art authorities. A book on literature? It is the same thing. So far the record of the reprinters has been to make the famous more famous.

It may be that American publishing is going through an enormous transition, and that at the end we will publish in the French manner, with the majority of books appearing in soft covers. If this is so, I will be the last to mourn; so far as I am concerned, in hard or soft covers, a book is a book. What I am principally concerned with is the nourishment of the best that is being thought and said at the moment. I cannot see that the dissemination of Shakespeare and Dante in cheap editions furthers this. I have no quarrel with either Dante or Shakespeare, and I am happy to see their posthumous fame growing larger each year. But it is a trifle ironic that competition from them should make it more difficult for the unnamed ones of the present, who—let us confess—will probably be only footnotes in literature, but who are, after all, our very own.

It will be difficult for them, but not impossible, let me add; for, although I have no good reasons for being optimistic, I have enough faith in chance to believe that we will, as always, stumble through to a partial solution. That is, now and again, by some miracle a fine writer will appear and become a vogue—and this whether books have soft or hard covers.

FURTHER READING

Asheim, Lester. "From Book to Film," *Reader in Public Opinion and Communication,* Berelson, Barnard, and Janowitz, Morris (eds.). Glencoe: Free Press, 1953.

Asheim, Lester. "Portrait of the Book Reader as Depicted in Current Research," *Mass Communications.* Urbana: University of Illinois Press, 1949, pp. 424-29.

Barrett, William. "American Fiction and American Values," *Partisan Review,* Vol. 18, 1951, pp. 681-90.

"The Battle for the Book," a symposium, *Saturday Review,* Vol. 39, 1956, pp. 5-9.

Benjamin, Curtis G. "How Bad Is the Big Book Business?," *Saturday Review,* October 9, 1954, pp. 11 and 32.

Bradbury, Ray. "Day After Tomorrow: Why Science Fiction?," *Nation,* Vol. 176, 1953, pp. 364-67.

Carruth, Hayden. "The Phenomenon of the Paperback," *Perspectives USA,* Vol. 15, 1956, pp. 192-204.

Cooley, Hazel. "Readers Still Read: Old Habits Survive TV," *Nation,* Vol. 181, 1955, pp. 378-79.

Cooney, Thomas. "Good News on Paper-backs," *Saturday Review,* June 11, 1955, pp. 20 and 36-37.

Dempsey, David. "The Revolution in Books," *Atlantic,* Vol. 191, 1953, pp. 75-79.

DeVoto, Bernard. "Culture at Two Bits," *Harper's,* Vol. 209, October, 1954, pp. 8-13.

DeVoto, Bernard. "Western Fiction," *Harper's,* Vol. 209, December 1954, pp. 10-14.

Fadiman, Clifton. "The Decline of Attention," *Saturday Review Reader.* New York: Bantam Books, 1951, pp. 23-36.

Farrar, John. "Publishing: Industry and Profession," *American Scholar,* Vol. 19, 1950, pp. 31-39.

Frase, R. W. "Books and the Mass Media," *New Republic,* Vol. 133, 1955, pp. 30-31.

"The Future of Books in America," *American Scholar,* Vol. 23, 1954, pp. 197-215.

Harvey, John. "The Content Characteristics of Best-Selling Books," *Public Opinion Quarterly,* Vol. 17, 1953, pp. 91-112.

Kappel, Joseph W. "Book Clubs and the Evaluation of Books," *Public Opinion Quarterly,* Vol. 12, 1948, pp. 243-53.

Krim, Seymour. "The Real World of Science Fiction," *Commonweal,* Vol. 5, 1953, pp. 252-54.

Krim, Seymour. "The Success of the Highbrow Paper-Backs," *New Republic,* Vol. 131, 1954, pp. 17-18.

Leavis, Q. D. *Fiction and the Reading Public.* London: Chatto and Windus, 1932.

Legman, Gershon. *Love and Death.* New York: Breaking Point Press, 1949.

Lehmann-Haupt, Hellmut; Wroth, Lawrence C.; and Silver, Rollo G. *The Book in America: A History of the Making and Selling of Books in the United States,* 2nd edition. New York: Bowker, 1951.

Levin, Meyer: "The East Side Gangsters of the Paperbacks," *Commentary,* Vol. 16, 1953, pp. 334-42.

Lowenthal, Leo. "Biographies in Popular Magazines," *Radio Research,* 1942-43, Lazarsfeld, Paul F., and Stanton, Frank K. (eds.). New York: Duell, Sloane, and Pearce, 1943.

McIntyre, Alfred. "The Crisis in Book Publishing," *Atlantic Monthly,* Vol. 180, 1947, pp. 107-11.

Miller, William. *The Book Industry: A Report of the Public Library Inquiry.* New York: Columbia University Press, 1949.

Rider, Alex. "Monsignor and Madame: the World of Paperbacks," *Nation,* Vol. 181, 1955, pp. 176-77.

Swados, Harvey. "Pompey's Head and the Middle-Class Hero," *Dissent,* Vol. 2, 1955, p. 379.

Voorhees, R. R. "What is Television Doing to Public Libraries?" *Library Journal,* Vol. 76, 1951, pp. 567-73.

Waples, Douglas; Berelson, Bernard; and Bradshaw, F. R. *What Reading Does to People.* Chicago: University of Chicago Press, 1940.

DETECTIVE FICTION

That he was to influence mass literature in a very perceptible way would have been the furthest thought from the mind of Francois Vidocq when he published his Memoires in 1829. Yet, the autobiography of this famous detective inspired Edgar Allen Poe and later Emile Gaboriau to write their pioneer works in detective fiction. Poe's Murders in the Rue Morgue is generally considered the first modern detective story, and in turn Gaboriau was to write the first detective novels. Today this genre has readers reaching into the millions in the United States. But the form of detective fiction has changed considerably since the time when Wilkie Collins could produce The Moonstone, or even since Conan Doyle created Sherlock Holmes. Although masters of the pure detective form, such as Agatha Christie, Dorothy Sayers, and Ellery Queen, have many devotees, the last two decades have seen an increasing emphasis on killing per se.

In his provocative book, Love and Death, Gershon Legman sees the popularity of detective fiction as part of the revolt against the frustrations of twentieth-century life with its antisexual morality. His ironic conclusion is that an author who thinks up new ways in which people can be murdered may become rich and famous in our culture, while any author who describes the physical act of love may find himself in jail for violating the obscenity laws.

Edmund Wilson, whose acerbic essay "Who Cares Who Killed Roger Ackroyd?" initiates the following section, speculates on why detective fiction has retained its popularity. To him, "the world during those years [i.e., the two decades between the great wars] was ridden by an all-pervasive feeling of guilt and by a fear of impending disaster which it seemed hopeless to try to avert because it never seemed conclusively possible to pin down the responsibility." In such a world nobody seems guiltless and nobody is safe. And finally when the murderer is spotted, "relief!—he is not, after all, a person like you or me. He is a villain—known to the trade as George Gruesome—and he has been caught by an infallible Power, the supercilious and omniscient detective, who knows exactly where to fix the guilt."

George Orwell draws the contrast between the moral atmosphere in which a Raffles can become one of the best known characters in modern popular fiction and that of No Orchids for Miss Blandish. Orwell's incisive critique of the two novels leads him to a consideration of mass culture in general.

To Charles Rolo, the detective story is modern man's Passion Play. Even Mike Hammer emerges as a Flaming Sword, a messenger of Jehovah, albeit a sadistic one. Since Spillane's hero is personally involved by the "initial murder" he becomes more graphically a part of the solution of the Evil, a

Superman who provides a compensatory daydream in which apparently millions of people can vicariously fight the Evil Forces of their lives.

Christopher La Farge, on the other hand, sees in Mike Hammer and his popularity the same forces that made McCarthyism a shadow over the entire nation. To Mr. La Farge it is a pity "that Mike Hammer and Mr. McCarthy cannot appear on the same television program and swap reminiscences during the Children's Hour!"

Who Cares Who Killed Roger Ackroyd?

By EDMUND WILSON

THREE MONTHS AGO I wrote an article on some recent detective stories. I had not read any fiction of this kind since the days of Sherlock Holmes, and, since I constantly heard animated discussions of the merits of the mystery writers, I was curious to see what they were like today. The specimens I tried I found disappointing, and I made some rather derogatory remarks in connection with my impressions of the genre in general. To my surprise, this brought me letters of protest in a volume and of a passionate earnestness which had hardly been elicited even by my occasional criticisms of the Soviet Union. Of the thirty-nine letters that have reached me, only seven approve my strictures. The writers of almost all the others seem deeply offended and shocked, and they all say almost exactly the same thing: that I had simply not read the right novels and that I would surely have a different opinion if I would only try this or that author recommended by the correspondent. In many of these letters there was a note of asperity, and one lady went so far as to declare that she would never read my articles again unless I were prepared to reconsider my position. In the meantime, furthermore, a number of other writers have published articles defending the detective story: Jacques Barzun, Joseph Wood Krutch, Raymond Chandler and Somerset Maugham have all had something to say on the subject— nor has the umbrageous Bernard De Voto failed to raise his voice.

Overwhelmed by so much insistence, I at last wrote my correspondents that I would try to correct any injustice by undertaking to read some of the authors that had received the most recommendations and taking the whole matter up again. The preferences of these readers, however, when I had a tabulation of them made, turned out to be extremely divergent. They ranged over fifty-two writers and sixty-seven books, most of which got only one or two votes each. The only writers who got as many as five or over were Dorothy L. Sayers, Margery Allingham, Ngaio Marsh, Michael Innes, Raymond Chandler and the author who writes under the names of Carter Dickson and John Dickson Carr.

The writer that my correspondents were most nearly unanimous in putting at the top was Miss Dorothy L. Sayers, who was pressed upon me by eighteen people, and the book of hers that eight of them were sure I could not fail to enjoy was a story called *The Nine Tailors*. Well, I set out to read *The Nine Tailors* in the hope of tasting some novel excitement, and I declare that it seems to me one of the dullest books I have ever encountered

Reprinted from *Classics and Commercials* (1950), pp. 257-65, by permission of the author and the publisher. (Copyright, 1950, by Edmund Wilson.)

(149)

in any field. The first part of it is all about bell-ringing as it is practiced in English churches and contains a lot of information of the kind that you might expect to find in an encyclopedia article on campanology. I skipped a good deal of this, and found myself skipping, also, a large section of the conversations between conventional English village characters: "Oh, here's Hinkins with the aspidistras. People may say what they like about aspidistras, but they do go on all the year round and make a background," etc. There was also a dreadful stock English nobleman of the casual and debonair kind, with the embarrassing name of Lord Peter Wimsey, and although he was the focal character in the novel, being Miss Dorothy Sayer's version of the inevitable Sherlock Holmes detective, I had to skip a good deal of him, too. In the meantime, I was losing the story, which had not got a firm grip on my attention, but I went back and picked it up and steadfastly pushed through to the end, and there I discovered that the whole point was that if a man was shut up in a belfry while a heavy peel of chimes was being rung, the vibrations of the bells might kill him. Not a bad idea for a murder, and Conan Doyle would have known how to dramatize it in an entertaining tale of thirty pages, but Miss Sayers had not hesitated to pad it out to a book of three hundred and fifty, contriving one of those hackeneyed cock-and-bull stories about a woman who commits bigamy without knowing it, and larding the whole thing with details of church architecture, bits of quaint lore from books about bell-ringing and the awful whimsical patter of Lord Peter.

I had often heard people say that Dorothy Sayers wrote well, and I felt that my correspondents had been playing her as their literary ace. But, really, she does not write very well: it is simply that she is more consciously literary than most of the other detective-story writers and that she thus attracts attention in a field which is mostly on a subliterary level. In any serious department of fiction, her writing would not appear to have any distinction at all. Yet, commonplace in this respect though she is, she gives an impression of brilliant talent if we put her beside Miss Ngaio Marsh, whose *Overture to Death* was also suggested by several correspondents. Mr. De Voto has put himself on record as believing that Miss Marsh, as well as Miss Sayers and Miss Allingham, writes her novels in "excellent prose," and this throws for me a good deal of light on Mr. De Voto's opinions as a critic. I hadn't quite realized before, though I had noted his own rather messy style, to what degree he was insensitive to writing. I do not see how it is possible for anyone with a feeling for words to describe the unappetizing sawdust which Miss Marsh has poured into her pages as "excellent prose" or as prose at all except in the sense that distinguishes prose from verse. And here again the book is mostly padding. There is the notion that you could commit a murder by rigging up a gun in a piano in such a way that the victim will shoot himself when he presses down the pedal, but this is embedded in the dialogue and doings of a lot of faked-up English country people who are even more tedious than those of *The Nine Tailors*.

The enthusiastic reader of detective stories will indignantly object at this point that I am reading for the wrong things: that I ought not to be expecting good writing, characterization, human interest or even atmosphere. He is right, of course, though I was not fully aware of it till I attempted *Flowers for the Judge,* considered by connoisseurs one of the best books of one of the masters of this school, Miss Margery Allingham. This tale I found completely unreadable. The story and the writing both showed a surface so wooden and dead that I could not keep my mind on the page. How can you care who committed a murder which has never really been made to take place, because the writer hasn't any ability of even the most ordinary kind to persuade you to see it or feel it? How can you probe the possibilities of guilt among characters who all seem alike, because they are all simply names on the page? It was then that I understood that a true connoisseur of this fiction must be able to suspend the demands of his imagination and literary taste and take the thing as an intellectual problem. But how do you arrive at that state of mind is what I do not understand.

In the light of this revelation, I feel that it is probably irrelevant to mention that I enjoyed *The Burning Court,* by John Dickson Carr, more than the novels of any of these ladies. There is a tinge of black magic that gives it a little of the interest of a horror story, and the author has a virtuosity at playing with alternative hypotheses that makes this trick of detective fiction more amusing than it usually is.

I want, however, to take up certain points made by the writers of the above-mentioned articles.

Mr. Barzun informs the non-expert that the detective novel is a kind of game in which the reader of a given story, in order to play properly his hand, should be familiar with all the devices that have already been used in other stories. These devices, it seems, are now barred: the reader must challenge the writer to solve his problem in some novel way, and the writer puts it up to the reader to guess the new solution. This may be true, but I shall never qualify. I would rather play Twenty Questions, which at least does not involve the consumption of hundreds of ill-written books.

A point made by three of these writers, Mr. Maugham, Mr. De Voto and Mr. Krutch, is that the novel has become so philosophical, so psychological and so symbolic that the public have had to take to the detective story as the only department of fiction where pure story-telling survives.

This seems to me to involve two fallacies. On the one hand, it is surely not true that "the serious novelists of today"—to quote Mr. Maugham's assertion—"have often," in contrast to the novelists of the past, "little or no story to tell," that "they have allowed themselves to be persuaded that to tell a story is a negligible form of art." It is true, of course, that Joyce and Proust—who, I suppose, must be accounted the heaviest going—have their various modern ways of boring and playing tricks on the reader. But how about the dreadful bogs and obstacles that one has to get over in Scott? the interpolated essays in Hugo? the leaking tap of Thackeray's reflections on life, in which the story is always trickling away? Is there anything in first-rate modern fiction quite so gratuitous as these *longueurs?* Even Proust and Joyce and Virginia Woolf do certainly have stories to tell, and they have organized their books with an intensity which has been relatively rare in the novel and which, to my mind, more than makes up for the occasional viscosity of their narrative.

On the other hand, it seems to me—for reasons suggested above—a fantastic misrepresentation to say that the average detective novel is an example of good story-telling. The gift for telling stories is uncommon, like other artistic gifts, and the only one of this group of writers—the writers my correspondents have praised—who seems to me to possess it to any degree is Mr. Raymond Chandler. His *Farewell, My Lovely* is the only one of these books that I have read all of and read with enjoyment. But Chandler, though in his recent article he seems to claim Hammett as his master, does not really belong to this school of the old-fashioned detective novel. What he writes is a novel of adventure which has less in common with Hammett than with Alfred Hitchcock and Graham Greene—the modern spy story which has substituted the jitters of the Gestapo and the G.P.U. for the luxury world of E. Phillips Oppenheim. It is not simply a question here of a puzzle which has been put together, but of a malaise conveyed to the reader, the horror of a hidden conspiracy that is continually turning up in the most varied and unlikely forms. To write such a novel successfully you must be able to invent character and incident and to generate atmosphere, and all this Mr. Chandler can do, though he is a long way below Graham Greene. It was only when I got to the end that I felt my old crime-story depression descending upon me again—because here again, as is so often the case, the explanation of the mysteries, when it comes, is neither interesting nor plausible enough. It fails to justify the excitement produced by the elaborate build-up of picturesque and sinister happenings, and one cannot help feeling cheated.

My experience with this second batch of novels has, therefore, been even more disillusioning than my experience with the first, and my final conclusion is that the reading of detective stories is simply a kind of vice that, for silliness and minor harmfulness, ranks somewhere between smoking and crossword puzzles. This conclusion seems borne out by the violence of the letters I have been receiving. Detective-story readers feel guilty, they are habitually on the defensive, and all their talk about "well-written" mysteries is simply an excuse for their vice, like the reasons that the alcoholic can always produce for a drink. One of the letters I have had shows the addict in his frankest and most shameless phase. This lady begins by pretending, like the others, to guide me in my choice, but she breaks down and tells the whole dreadful truth. Though she has read, she says, hundreds of detective stories, "it is surprising," she finally confesses, "how few I would recommend to another. However, a poor detective story is better than none at all. Try again. With a little better luck, you'll find one you admire and enjoy. Then you, too, may be

A MYSTERY FIEND."

This letter has made my blood run cold: so the opium smoker tells the novice not to mind if the first pipe makes him sick; and I fall back for reassurance on the valiant little band of my readers who sympathize with my views on the subject. One of these tells me that I have underestimated both the badness of detective stories themselves and the lax mental habits of those who enjoy them. The worst of it is, he says, that the true addict, half the time, never even finds out who has committed the murder. The addict reads not to find anything out but merely to get the mild stimulation of the succession of unexpected incidents and of the suspense itself of *looking forward* to learning a sensational secret. That this secret is nothing at all and does not really account for the incidents does not matter to such a reader. He has learned from his long indulgence how to connive with the author in the swindle: he does not pay any real attention when the disappointing dénouement occurs, he does not think back and check the events, he simply shuts the book and starts another.

To detective-story addicts, then, I say: Please do not write me any more letters telling me that I have not read the right books. And to the seven correspondents who are with me and who in some cases have thanked me for helping them to liberate themselves from a habit which they recognized as wasteful of time and degrading to the intellect but into which they had been bullied by convention and the portentously invoked examples of Woodrow Wilson and André Gide—to these staunch and pure spirits I say: Friends, we represent a minority, but Literature is on our side. With so many fine books to be read, so much to be studied and known, there is no need to bore ourselves with this rubbish. And with the paper shortage pressing on all publication and many first-rate writers forced out of print, we shall do well to discourage the squandering of this paper that might be put to better use.

Raffles and Miss Blandish

By GEORGE ORWELL

NEARLY HALF A CENTURY after his first appearance, Raffles, "the amateur cracksman," is still one of the best-known characters in English fiction. Very few people would need telling that he played cricket for England, had bachelor chambers in the Albany and burgled the Mayfair houses which he also entered as a guest. Just for that reason he and his exploits make a suitable background against which to examine a more modern crime story such as *No Orchids for Miss Blandish*. Any such choice is necessarily arbitrary—I might equally well have chosen *Arsene Lupin,* for instance—but at any rate *No Orchids* and the Raffles books[1] have the common quality of being crime stories which play the limelight on the criminal rather than the policeman. For sociological purposes they can be compared. *No Orchids* is the 1939 version of glamorised crime, *Raffles* the 1900 version. What I am concerned with here is the immense difference in moral atmosphere between the two books, and the change in the popular attitude that this probably implies.

At this date, the charm of Raffles is partly in the period atmosphere and partly in the technical excellence of the stories. Hornung was a very conscientious and on his level a very able writer. Anyone who cares for sheer efficiency must admire his work. However, the truly dramatic thing about Raffles, the thing that makes him a sort of byword even to this day (only a few weeks ago, in a burglary case, a magistrate referred to the prisoner as "a Raffles in real life"), is the fact that he is a *gentleman*. Raffles is presented to us—and this is rubbed home in countless scraps of dialogue and casual remarks—not as an honest man who has gone astray. His remorse, when he feels any, is almost purely social; he has disgraced "the old school," he has lost his right to enter "decent society," he has forfeited his amateur status and become a cad. Neither Raffles nor Bunny appears to feel at all strongly that stealing is wrong in itself, though Raffles does once justify himself by the casual remark that "the distribution of property is all wrong anyway." They think of themselves not as sinners but as renegades, or simply as outcasts. And the moral code of most of us is still so close to Raffles' own that we do feel his situation to be an especially ironical one. A West End club man who is really a burglar! That is almost a story in itself, is it not? But how if it were a plumber or a greengrocer who was really a burglar? Would there be anything inherently dramatic in

---

Reprinted from *Dickens, Dali and Others* (1946), pp. 202-21, by permission of the publisher. (Copyright, 1946, by Reynall and Co.)

that? No—although the theme of the "double life," of respectability cover-ing crime, is still there. Even Charles Peace in his clergyman's dog-collar seems somewhat less of a hypocrite than Raffles in his Zingari blazer.

Raffles, of course, is good at all games, but it is peculiarly fitting that his chosen game should be cricket. This allows not only of endless analogies between his cunning as a slow bowler and his cunning as a burglar, but also helps to define the exact nature of his crime. Cricket is not in reality a very popular game in England—it is nowhere near so popular as foot-ball, for instance—but it gives expression to a well-marked trait in the English character, the tendency to value "form" or "style" more highly than success. In the eyes of any true cricket-lover it is possible for an innings of ten runs to be "better" (i.e., more elegant) than an innings of a hundred runs: cricket is also one of the very few games in which the amateur can excel the professional. It is a game full of forlorn hopes and sudden dramatic changes of fortune, and its rules are so ill-defined that their interpretation is partly an ethical business. When Larwood, for in-stance, practised body line bowling in Australia he was not actually break-ing any rule: he was merely doing something that was "not cricket." Since cricket takes up a lot of time and is rather an expensive game to play, it is predominantly an upper-class game, but for the whole nation it is bound up with such concepts as "good form," "playing the game," etc., and it has declined in popularity just as the tradition of "don't hit a man when he's down" has declined. It is not a twentieth-century game, and nearly all modern-minded people dislike it. The Nazis, for instance, were at pains to discourage cricket, which had gained a certain footing in Germany before and after the last war. In making Raffles a cricketer as well as a burglar, Hornung was not merely providing him with a plausible disguise; he was also drawing the sharpest moral contrast that he was able to imagine.

Raffles, no less than *Great Expectations* or *Le Rouge et le Noir,* is a story of snobbery, and it gains a great deal from the precariousness of Raf-fles's social position. A cruder writer would have made the "gentleman burglar" a member of the peerage, or at least a baronet. Raffles, however, is of upper-middle-class origin and is only accepted by the aristocracy be-cause of his personal charm. "We were in Society but not of it," he says to Bunny towards the end of the book; and "I was asked about for my cricket." Both he and Bunny accept the values of "Society" unquestionably, and would settle down in it for good if only they could get away with a big enough haul. The ruin that constantly threatens them is all the blacker because they only doubtfully "belong." A duke who has served a prison sentence is still a duke, whereas a mere man about town, if once disgraced, ceases to be "about town" for evermore. The closing chapters of the book, when Raffles has been exposed and is living under an assumed name, have a twilight of the gods feeling, a mental atmosphere rather similar to that of Kipling's poem "Gentleman Rankers":

> "Yes, a trooper of the forces—
> Who has run his own six horses!" etc.

Raffles now belongs irrevocably to the "cohorts of the damned." He can still commit successful burglaries, but there is no way back into Paradise, which means Piccadilly and the M.C.C. According to the public-school code there is only one means of rehabilitation: death in battle. Raffles dies fighting against the Boers (a practised reader would foresee this from the start), and in the eyes of both Bunny and his creator this cancels his crimes.

Both Raffles and Bunny, of course, are devoid of religious belief, and they have no real ethical code, merely certain rules of behaviour which they observe semi-instinctively. But it is just here that the deep moral difference between *Raffles* and *No Orchids* becomes apparent. Raffles and Bunny, after all, are gentlemen, and such standards as they do have are not to be violated. Certain things are "not done," and the idea of doing them hardly arises. Raffles will not, for example, abuse hospitality. He will commit a burglary in a house where he is staying as a guest, but the victim must be a fellow-guest and not the host. He will not commit murder,[2] and he avoids violence wherever possible and prefers to carry out his robberies unarmed. He regards friendship as sacred, and is chivalrous though not moral in his relations with women. He will take extra risks in the name of "sportsmanship," and sometimes even for aesthetic reasons. And above all, he is intensely patriotic. He celebrates the Diamond Jubilee ("For sixty years, Bunny, we've been ruled over by absolutely the finest sovereign the world has ever seen") by despatching to the Queen, through the post, an antique gold cup which he has stolen from the British Museum. He steals, from partly political motives, a pearl which the German Emperor is sending to one of the enemies of Britain, and when the Boer War begins to go badly his one thought is to find his way into the fighting line. At the front he unmasks a spy at the cost of revealing his own identity, and then dies gloriously by a Boer bullet. In this combination of crime and patriotism he resembles his near-contemporary Arsene Lupin, who also scores off the German Emperor and wipes out his very dirty past by enlisting in the Foreign Legion.

It is important to note that by modern standards Raffles' crimes are very petty ones. Four hundred pounds' worth of jewellery seems to him an excellent haul. And though the stories are convincing in their physical detail, they contain very little sensationalism—very few corpses, hardly any blood, no sex crimes, no sadism, no perversions of any kind. It seems to be the case that the crime story, at any rate on its higher levels, has greatly increased in blood-thirstiness during the past twenty years. Some of the early detective stories do not even contain a murder. The Sherlock Holmes stories, for instance, are not all murders, and some of them do not even deal with an indictable crime. So also with the John Thorndyke stories, while of the Max Carrados stories only a minority are murders. Since 1918, however, a detective story not containing a murder has been a great rarity, and the most disgusting details of dismemberment and exhumation are commonly exploited. Some of the Peter Wimsey stories, for instance, display an extremely morbid interest in corpses. The Raffles stories, written from the angle of the criminal, are much less anti-social than many modern stories written from the angle of the detective. The main impression that they leave behind is of boyishness. They belong to a time when people had standards, though they happened to be foolish standards. Their key-phrase is "not done." The line that they draw between good and evil is as senseless as a Polynesian taboo, but at least, like the taboo, it has the advantage that everyone accepts it.

So much for *Raffles*. Now for a header into the cesspool. *No Orchids for Miss Blandish,* by James Hadley Chase, was published in 1939, but seems to have enjoyed its greatest popularity in 1940, during the Battle of Britain and the blitz. In its main outlines its story is this:

Miss Blandish, the daughter of a millionaire, is kidnapped by some gangsters who are almost immediately surprised and killed off by a larger and better organised gang. They hold her to ransom and extract half a million dollars from her father. Their original plan had been to kill her as soon as the ransom-money was received, but a chance keeps her alive. One of the gang is a young man named Slim, whose sole pleasure in life consists in driving knives into other people's bellies. In childhood he has graduated by cutting up living animals with a pair of rusty scissors. Slim is sexually impotent, but takes a kind of fancy to Miss Blandish. Slim's mother, who is the real brains of the gang, sees in this the chance of curing Slim's impotence, and decides to keep Miss Blandish in custody till Slim shall have succeeded in raping her. After many efforts and much persuasion, including the flogging of Miss Blandish with a length of rubber hosepipe, the rape is achieved. Meanwhile Miss Blandish's father has hired a private detective, and by means of bribery and torture the detective and the police manage to round up and exterminate the whole gang. Slim escapes with Miss Blandish and is killed after a final rape, and the detective prepares to restore Miss Blandish to her family. By this time, however, she has developed such a taste for Slim's caresses[3] that she feels unable to live without him, and she jumps out of the window of a sky-scraper.

Several other points need noticing before one can grasp the full implications of this book. To begin with, its central story bears a marked resemblance to William Faulkner's novel, *Sanctuary*. Secondly, it is not, as one might expect, the product of an illiterate hack, but a brilliant piece of writing, with hardly a wasted word or a jarring note anywhere. Thirdly, the whole book, *récit* as well as dialogue, is written in the American language; the author, an Englishman who has (I believe) never been in the United States, seems to have made a complete mental transference to the American underworld. Fourthly, the book sold, according to its publishers, no less than half a million copies.

I have already outlined the plot, but the subject-matter is much more sordid and brutal than this suggests. The book contains eight full-dress murders, an unassessable number of casual killings and woundings, an exhumation (with a careful reminder of the stench), the flogging of Miss Blandish, the torture of another woman with red-hot cigarette-ends, a strip-tease act, a third-degree scene of unheard-of cruelty and much else of the same kind. It assumes great sexual sophistication in its readers (there is a scene, for instance, in which a gangster, presumably of masochistic tendency, has an orgasm in the moment of being knifed), and it takes for granted the most complete corruption and self-seeking as the norm of human behaviour. The detective, for instance, is almost as great a rogue as the gangsters, and actuated by nearly the same motives. Like them, he is in pursuit of "five hundred grand." It is necessary to the machinery of the story that Mr. Blandish should be anxious to get his daughter back, but apart from this, such things as affection, friendship, good nature or even ordinary politeness simply do not enter. Nor, to any great extent, does normal sexuality. Ultimately only one motive is at work throughout the whole story: the pursuit of power.

It should be noticed that the book is not in the ordinary sense pornography. Unlike most books that deal in sexual sadism, it lays the emphasis on the cruelty and not on the pleasure. Slim, the ravisher of Miss Blandish, has "wet, slobbering lips": this is disgusting, and it is meant to be disgusting. But the scenes describing cruelty to women are comparatively perfunctory. The real high-spots of the book are cruelties committed by men upon other men: above all, the third-degreeing of the gangster, Eddie Schultz, who is lashed into a chair and flogged on the windpipe with truncheons, his arms broken by fresh blows as he breaks loose. In another of Mr. Chase's books, *He Won't Need It Now,* the hero, who is intended to be a sympathetic and perhaps even noble character, is described as stamping on somebody's face, and then, having crushed the man's mouth in, grinding his heel round and round in it. Even when physical incidents of this kind are not occurring, the mental atmosphere of these books is always the same. Their whole theme is the struggle for power and the triumph of the strong over the weak. The big gangsters wipe out the little ones as mercilessly as a pike gobbling up the little fish in a pond; the police kill off the criminals as cruelly as the angler kills the pike. If ultimately one sides with the police against the gangsters, it is merely because they are better organised and more powerful, because, in fact, the law is a bigger racket than crime. Might is right: *vae victis.*

As I have mentioned already, *No Orchids* enjoyed its greatest vogue in 1940, though it was successfully running as a play till some time later. It was, in fact, one of the things that helped to console people for the boredom of being bombed. Early in the war the *New Yorker* had a picture of a little man approaching a newsstall littered with papers with such headlines as "Great Tank Battles in Northern France," "Big Naval Battle in the North Sea," "Huge Air Battles over the Channel," etc. etc. The little man is saying, *"Action Stories,* please." That little man stood for all the drugged millions to whom the world of the gangsters and the prize-ring is more "real," more "tough," than such things as wars, revolutions, earthquakes, famines and pestilences. From the point of view of a reader of *Action Stories,* a description of the London blitz, or of the struggles of the European underground parties, would be "sissy stuff." On the other hand, some puny gun-battle in Chicago, resulting in perhaps half a dozen deaths, would seem genuinely "tough." This habit of mind is now extremely widespread. A soldier sprawls in a muddy trench, with the machine-gun bullets crackling a foot or two overhead, and whiles away his intolerable boredom by reading an American gangster story. And what is it that makes that story so exciting? Precisely the fact that people are shooting at each other with machine-guns! Neither the soldier nor anyone else sees anything curious in this. It is taken for granted that an imaginary bullet is more thrilling than a real one.

The obvious explanation is that in real life one is usually a passive victim, whereas in the adventure story one can think of oneself as being at the centre of events. But there is more to it than that. Here it is necessary to refer again to the curious fact of *No Orchids* being written—with technical errors, perhaps, but certainly with considerable skill—in the American language.

There exists in America an enormous literature of more or less the same stamp as *No Orchids.* Quite apart from books, there is the huge array of "pulp magazines," graded so as to cater to different kinds of fantasy, but nearly all having much the same mental atmosphere. A few of them go in for straight pornography, but the great majority are quite plainly aimed at sadists and masochists. Sold at threepence a copy under the title of Yank Mags,[4] these things used to enjoy considerable popularity in England, but when the supply dried up owing to the war, no satisfactory substitute was forthcoming. English imitations of the "pulp magazine" do now exist, but they are poor things compared with the original. English crook films, again, never approach the American crook film in brutality. And yet the career of Mr. Chase shows how deep the American influence has already gone. Not only is he himself living a continuous fantasy-life in the Chicago underworld, but he can count on hundreds of thousands of readers who know what is meant by a "clipshop" or the "hotsquat," do not have to do mental arithmetic when confronted by "fifty grand," and understand at sight a sentence like "Johnnie was a rummy and only two jumps ahead of the nut-factory." Evidently there are great numbers of English people who are partly Americanised in language and, one ought to add, in moral outlook. For there was no popular protest against *No Orchids.* In the end it was withdrawn, but only retrospectively, when a later work, *Miss Callaghan Comes to Grief,* brought Mr. Chase's books to the attention of the authorities. Judging by casual conversations at the time, ordinary readers got a mild thrill out of the obscenities of *No Orchids,* but saw nothing undesirable in the book as a whole. Many people, incidentally, were under the impression that it was an American book reissued in England.

The thing that the ordinary reader *ought* to have objected to—almost certainly would have objected to, a few decades earlier—was the equivocal attitude towards crime. It is implied throughout *No Orchids* that being a criminal is only reprehensible in the sense that it does not pay. Being a policeman pays better, but there is no moral difference, since the police use essentially criminal methods. In a book like *He Won't Need It Now* the distinction between crime and crime-prevention practically disappears. This is a new departure for English sensational fiction, in which till recently there has always been a sharp distinction between right and wrong and a general agreement that virtue must triumph in the last chapter. English books glorifying crime (modern crime, that is—pirates and highwaymen are different) are very rare. Even a book like *Raffles,* as I have pointed out, is governed by powerful taboos, and it is clearly understood that Raffles' crimes must be expiated sooner or later. In America, both in life and fiction, the tendency to tolerate crime, even to admire the criminal so long as he is successful, is very much more marked. It is, indeed, ultimately this attitude that has made it possible for crime to flourish upon so huge a scale. Books have been written about Al Capone that are hardly different in tone from the books written about Henry Ford, Stalin, Lord Northcliffe and all the rest of the "log cabin to White House" brigade. And switching back eighty years, one finds Mark Twain adopting much the same attitude towards the disgusting bandit Slade, hero of twenty-eight murders, and towards the Western desperadoes generally. They were successful, they "made good," therefore he admired them.

In a book like *No Orchids* one is not, as in the old-style crime story, simply escaping from dull reality into an imaginary world of action. One's escape is essentially into cruelty and sexual perversion. *No Orchids* is aimed at the power-instinct, which *Raffles* or the Sherlock Holmes stories are not. At the same time the English attitude towards crime is not so superior to the American as I may have seemed to imply. It too is mixed up with power-worship, and has become more noticeably so in the last twenty years. A writer who is worth examining is Edgar Wallace, especially in such typical books as *The Orator* and the Mr. J. G. Reeder stories. Wallace was one of the first crime-story writers to break away from the old tradition of the private detective and make his central figure a Scotland Yard official. Sherlock Holmes is an amateur, solving his problems without the help and even, in the earlier stories, against the opposition of the police. Moreover, like Lupin, he is essentially an intellectual, even a scientist. He reasons logically from observed fact, and his intellectuality is constantly contrasted with the routine methods of the police. Wallace objected strongly to this slur, as he considered it, on Scotland Yard, and in several newspaper articles he went out of his way to denounce Holmes by name. His own ideal was the detective inspector who catches criminals not because he is intellectually brilliant but because he is part of an all-powerful organization. Hence the curious fact that in Wallace's most characteristic stories the "clue" and the "deduction" play no part. The criminal is always defeated either by an incredible coincidence, or because in some unexplained manner the police know all about the crime beforehand. The tone of the stories makes it quite clear that Wallace's admiration for the police is pure bully-worship. A Scotland Yard detective is the most powerful kind of being that he can imagine, while the criminal figures in his mind as an outlaw against whom anything is permissible, like the condemned slaves in the Roman arena. His policemen behave much more brutally than British policemen do in real life—they hit people without provocation, fire revolvers past their ears to terrify them and so on—and some of the stories exhibit a fearful intellectual sadism. (For instance, Wallace likes to arrange things so that the villain is hanged on the same day as the heroine is married.) But it is sadism after the British fashion: that is to say, it is unconscious, there is not overtly any sex in it, and it keeps within the bounds of the law. The British public tolerates a harsh criminal law and gets a kick out of monstrously unfair murder trials: but still this is better, on any count, than tolerating or admiring crime. If one must worship a bully, it is better that he should be a policeman than a gangster. Wallace is still governed to some extent by the concept of "not done." In *No Orchids* anything is "done" so long as it leads on to power. All the barriers are down, all the motives are out in the open. Chase is a worse symptom than Wallace, to the extent that all-in wrestling is worse than boxing, or Fascism is worse than capitalist democracy.

In borrowing from William Faulkner's *Sanctuary,* Chase only took the plot; the mental atmosphere of the two books is not similar. Chase really derives from other sources, and this particular bit of borrowing is only symbolic. What it symbolises is the vulgarization of ideas which is constantly happening, and which probably happens faster in an age of print. Chase has been described as "Faulkner for the masses," but it would be more accurate to describe him as Carlyle for the masses. He is a popular writer—there are many such in America, but they are still rarities in England—who has caught up with what it is now fashionable to call "realism," meaning the doctrine that might is right. The growth of "realism" has been the great feature of the intellectual history of our own age. Why this should be so is a complicated question. The interconnection between sadism, masochism, success-worship, power-worship, nationalism and totalitarianism is a huge subject whose edges have barely been scratched, and even to mention it is considered somewhat indelicate. To take merely the first example that comes to mind, I believe no one has ever pointed out the sadistic and masochistic element in Bernard Shaw's work, still less suggested that this probably has some connection with Shaw's admiration for dictators. Fascism is often loosely equated with sadism, but nearly always by people who see nothing wrong in the most slavish worship of Stalin. The truth is, of course, that the countless English intellectuals who kiss the arse of Stalin are not different from the many who give their allegiance to Hitler or Mussolini, nor from the efficiency experts who preached "punch," "drive," "personality" and "learn to be a Tiger man" in the nineteen-twenties, nor from the older generation of intellectuals, Carlyle, Creasey and the rest of them, who bowed down before German militarism. All of them are worshipping power and successful cruelty. It is important to notice that the cult of power tends to be mixed up with a love of cruelty and wickedness *for their own sakes*. A tyrant is all the more admired if he happens to be a bloodstained crook as well, and "the end justifies the means" often becomes, in effect, "the means justify themselves provided they are dirty enough." This idea colours the outlook of all sympathizers with totalitarianism, and accounts, for instance, for the positive delight with which many English intellectuals greeted the Nazi-Soviet pact. It was a step only doubtfully useful to the U.S.S.R., but it was entirely unmoral, and for that reason to be admired; the explanations of it, which were numerous and self-contradictory, could come afterwards.

Until recently the characteristic adventure stories of the English-speaking peoples have been stories in which the hero fiights *against odds*. This is true all the way from Robin Hood to Popeye the Sailor. Perhaps the basic myth of the Western world is Jack the Giant-killer, but to be brought up to date this should be renamed Jack the Dwarf-killer, and there already exists considerable literature which teaches, either overtly or implicity, that one should side with the big man against the little man. Most of what is now written about foreign policy is simply an embroidery on this theme, and for several decades such phrases as "Play the game," "Don't hit a man when he's down" and "It's not cricket" have never failed to draw a snigger from anyone of intellectual pretensions. What is comparatively new is to find the accepted pattern according to which (a) right is right and wrong is wrong, whoever wins, and (b) weakness must be respected, disappearing from popular literature as well. When I first read D. H. Lawrence's novels, at the age of about twenty, I was puzzled by the fact that there did not seem to be any classification of the characters into "good" and "bad." Lawrence seemed to sympathize with all of them about equally and this was so unusual as to give me the feeling of having lost my bearings. To-day no one would think of looking for heroes and villains in a serious novel, but in lowbrow fiction one still expects to find a sharp distinction between right and wrong and between legality and illegality. The common people, on the whole, are still living in the world of absolute good and evil from which the intellectuals have long since escaped. But the popularity of *No Orchids* and the American books and magazines to which it is akin shows how rapidly the doctrine of "realism" is gaining ground.

Several people, after reading *No Orchids,* have remarked to me, "It's pure Fascism." This is a correct description, although the book has not the smallest connection with politics and very little with social or economic problems. It has merely the same relation to Fascism as, say, Trollope's novels have to nineteenth-century capitalism. It is a day dream appropriate to a totalitarian age. In his imagined world of gangsters Chase is presenting, as it were, a distilled version of the modern political scene, in which such things as mass bombing of civilians, the use of hostages, torture to obtain confessions, secret prison, execution without trial, floggings with rubber truncheons, drowning in cesspools, systematic falsification of records and statistics, treachery, bribery and quislingism are normal and morally neutral, even admirable when they are done in a large and bold way. The average man is not directly interested in politics, and when he reads, he wants the current struggles of the world to be translated into a simple story about individuals. He can take an interest in Slim and Fenner as he could not in the G.P.U. and the Gestapo. People worship power in the form in which they are able to understand it. A twelve-year-old boy worships Jack Dempsey. An adolescent in a Glasgow slum worships Al Capone. An aspiring pupil at a business college worships Lord Nuffield. A *New Statesman* reader worships Stalin. There is a difference in intellectual maturity, but none in moral outlook. Thirty years ago the heroes of popular fiction had nothing in common with Mr. Chase's gangsters and detectives, and the idols of the English liberal intelligentsia were also comparatively sympathetic figures. Between Holmes and Fenner on the one hand, and between Abraham Lincoln and Stalin on the other, there is a similar gulf.

One ought not to infer too much from the success of Mr. Chase's books. It is possible that it is an isolated phenomenon, brought about by the mingled boredom and brutality of war. But if such books should definitely acclimatize themselves in England, instead of being merely a half-understood import from America, there would be good grounds for dismay. In choosing *Raffles* as a background for *No Orchids* I deliberately chose a book which by the standards of its time was morally equivocal. Raffles, as I have pointed out, has no real moral code, no religion, certainly no social consciousness. All he has is a set of reflexes—the nervous system, as it were, of a gentleman. Give him a sharp tap on this reflex or that (they are called "sport," "pal," "woman," "king and country" and so forth), and you get a predictable reaction. In Mr. Chase's books there are no gentlemen and no taboos. Emancipation is complete, Freud and Machiavelli have reached the outer suburbs. Comparing the schoolboy atmosphere of the one book with the cruelty and corruption of the other, one is driven to feel that snobbishness, like hypocrisy, is a check upon behaviour whose value from a social point of view has been underrated.

Notes

1. *Raffles, A Thief in the Night* and *Mr. Justice Raffles,* by E. W. Hornung. The third of these is definitely a failure, and only the first has the true Raffles atmosphere. Hornung wrote a number of crime stories, usually with a tendency to take the side of the criminal. A successful book in rather the same vein as *Raffles* is *Stingaree.*

2. 1945. Actually Raffles does kill one man and is more or less consciously responsible for the death of two others. But all three of them are foreigners and have behaved in a very reprehensible manner. He also, on one occasion, contemplates murdering a black-mailer. It is, however, a fairly well-established convention in crime stories that murdering a blackmailer "doesn't count."

3. 1945. Another reading of the final episode is possible. It may mean merely that Miss Blandish is pregnant. But the interpretation I have given above seems more in keeping with the general brutality of the book.

4. They are said to have been imported into this country as ballast, which accounted for their low price and crumpled appearance. Since the war the ships have been ballasted with something more useful, probably gravel.

Simenon and Spillane:
The Metaphysics of Murder for the Millions

By CHARLES J. ROLO

IN APRIL, 1841, the world's first mass-circulation magazine, *Graham's,* published a story which connoisseurs of the whodunit regard as the first detective story—"The Murders in the Rue Morgue" by Edgar Allan Poe. The new form caught on fairly rapidly, and for a century its popularity has steadily increased. Last year, one out of every four works of fiction newly published and reprinted in the United States was a murder mystery. The total sale of mysteries was around 66,000,000 copies.

Even *aficionados* of murder fiction will concede, in a moment of honesty, that except in the hands of a few writers it has been a subliterary product— characters unreal, dialogue artificial, plots highly improbable. Raymond Chandler, who writes classy shockers of the hard-boiled school but prefers to read the old-fashioned, jig-saw puzzle kind, has indicted his preferred reading in two lethal phrases: "They fail to come off intellectually as problems, and they do not come off artistically as fiction." A critic impervious to the seductions of the whodunit, Mr. Edmund Wilson has said that reading detective fiction is rather like having "to unpack large crates by swallowing the excelsior in order to find at the bottom a few bent and rusty nails."

And yet, as mystery fans love to point out, the detective story, besides delighting millions, has regaled great men and great minds—chiefs of state (F.D.R. and Woodrow Wilson); men of letters revered by the highbrows (Gide, Eliot, Yeats); college presidents, renowned generals and scientific geniuses. There have been maestros of the detective story who, like Jimmy Durante, could lay claim to being "duh toast of duh intellectuals." What charms has this unreal, mechanical brand of fiction which soothes the troubled breast of lowbrow, highbrow and middlebrow? What do we find in its corpse-strewn cosmos that makes an escape there so refreshing?

These are solemn questions worthy of being explored with the ant-like industry of aspirants to a Ph.D. But alas, no such scholarly excavations have been made, presumably on the theory that nothing of consequence is buried beneath the frivolous facade of the murder mystery. This theory, as I hope to demonstrate, if only in strictly amateur fashion, is grievously in error. As a start, let's take a look at the main explanations advanced for the detective story's popularity.

The common-sense explanation is that most people enjoy trying to solve a puzzle and derive a peculiarly intense satisfaction from seeing it solved.

Reprinted from *New World Writing,* No. 1 (1952), pp. 234-45, by permission of the author and the publisher. (Copyright, 1952, by The New American Library.)

The mystery story draws us into a suspenseful game, in which we can't lose. If we figure out the answer, we feel devilishly smart; if we don't, we enjoy a juicy surprise. There are at least three clues, however, which suggest that this view doesn't close the case: (1) A number of confirmed addicts frequently cheat—as soon as the puzzle has taken shape they look up the solution—and still they are able to go back and read through the book with considerable enjoyment. (2) Several whodunit fiends have confessed to me that they don't care a hoot who killed Sir Archibald; don't bother to master the ground plan of Footledowne Manor; and never notice half of the clues. (3) The mystery writers of the hardboiled school have actually junked the jigsaw-puzzle formula—to follow their plot line with comfort sometimes calls for a mind at home with differential calculus. Their books nonetheless sell in vast quantities.

Mr. Somerset Maugham has suggested that a great many people have been turning to the detective story because it is the only department of fiction where pure story-telling survives; the serious novelist, says Mr. Maugham, has gotten "namby-pamby" on the story level—too philosophical, too psychiatric, too symbolic. Any self-respecting highbrow would either disagree with Maugham that, say, Proust and Faulkner don't tell a good story, or would reject his emphasis on story-telling as immaterial. As for the other categories of reader, they can find plenty of popular fiction which is yarn-spinning and nothing else.

Thirdly, there's the psychiatric explanation, which claims that in murder mysteries we are able to "act out," guiltlessly, the aggressive fantasies buried in the unconscious: we kill with the killer and we gratify the hunting instinct as the killer is tracked down, a kind of heads-I-win-tails-you-lose psychological deal. If this were the whole story, one would expect the success of detective fiction to be bound up with the quantity of mayhem between the covers—and this just isn't so: some of the most famous whodunits have contained but a single tidy murder. It's true that there's a trend toward more corpses and blatant sadism in the murder mystery, but the form has done nicely in the past with all hands, except for one part, behaving in the most genteel manner.

The preceding explanations probably contain varying degrees of truth, but none of them fits all of the facts. The solution to the mystery of the murder mystery's appeal must apply to all types and all times. It must be something very basic to explain an appeal that has proved so enduring, so potent, and so widespread. This something, I suspect, has little to do with the concatenation of clues or the accumulation of corpses, and a great deal to do with the largest of all fictional themes—an accounting of man's destiny. My hypothesis is that the murder mystery is, in essence, a metaphysical success story.

To examine, as light-heartedly as possible, the relationship between murder and metaphysics I am going to look into the work of two writers who stand at opposite poles—Mickey Spillane and Georges Simenon—but who have one arresting thing in common. Mickey Spillane is the author of super-tough whodunits which belong, intellectually, to approximately the same world as the comic strip. Georges Simenon, who has published a raft of detective novels featuring Inspector Maigret and also a great deal of serious fiction, has been mentioned as a candidate for the Nobel Prize. The common denominator between Spillane and Simenon is that both are phenomenally popular. Spillane, during the past three years, has become the fastest-selling writer in America; Simenon, over the past twenty years, has been probably the fastest-selling writer in Europe.

Spillane's first novel, *I, The Jury,* has to date sold over 2,000,000 copies in its hard-cover and reprint editions; his next three—*My Gun Is Quick, Vengeance Is Mine, One Lonely Night*—have all passed the million mark. The New American Library, which publishes the 25-cent edition of Spillane's books, launched his fourth title, *The Big Kill,* with a record-breaking first printing of 2,500,000 copies. When Spillane's latest, *The Long Wait,* is released for the mass market, there will be well over 10,000,000 copies of his books in print.

In a crude way, Mickey Spillane is something of an innovator. He has hopped up the hard-boiled murder mystery into a shocker which combines features of the western, the animated film strip, the pulp sex story, William Steig's "Dreams of Glory" cartoons, and the sermons of Savonarola. His setting is the world of organized crime—the kind of world we glimpsed in the hearings of the Kefauver Committee—and his hero, private detective Mike Hammer, is what Joe Doakes might see himself as in a daydream that compensates his most acute frustrations: a Superman who goes crashing through life beating the hell out of the bad men and getting lustfully played by females who are Sex Appeal personified—smooth, impossibly beautiful sirens who are killers, and dames who are just impossibly beautiful; a Superman who, in many respects is a very ordinary Joe.

Mike Hammer is a New Yorker. He owns two suits (one custom-built to conceal his underarm artillery). He smokes Luckies incessantly, and downs a fair amount of liquor, but he is no boozehound. His favorite dishes are steak, fried chicken and pie. He drives an old automobile, "the heap," whose engine has been souped up for professional reasons. He is sentimental about children, and he has a fixation about plunging necklines and the female bosom in general. Intellectually (though we are told he has a "huge" mind), he is a smutty-minded primitive. His ignorance of world affairs is such that he is amazed and driven beserk when he stumbles upon the fact that the Communists are up to no good right here in the U.S.A.

Hammer is on fairly good terms with the police and respects them— Pat Chambers, Captain of Homicide, is an old and loyal friend, But the police, Hammer feels, are tied down by rules and regulations. Often dirty politics prevent a clean cop from doing a clean job; often it's a hard thing to prove murder in a court of law. And this has made Mike Hammer God's

Angry Man: he has appointed himself detective, judge, jury and executioner. To Chambers he says: "Tell me I'm interfering in police work, and I'll tell you how sick I am of what goes on in this town. I live here, see? I got a damn good right to keep it clean even if I have to kill a few bastards to do it."

A six-footer weighing 190 pounds, Hammer is unquestionably the toughest, most sadistic detective in the annals of murder fiction. "I do my own leg work," he says, "and there are a lot of guys will tell me what I want to know because they know what I'll do to them if they don't." Here's a sample of the Hammer treatment: "I brought my knee up and smashed his nose to a pulp and when he screamed he choked on his own blood. I . . . yanked him up and held him against the car, then used my fist on his face." Here's another: "He came right at me with his head down and I took my own damn time about kicking him in the face. . . . He smashed into the door and lay there bubbling. For laughs I gave him a taste of his own sap on the back of his hand, and felt the bones go into splinters."

Mike can dodge a bullet fired at point-blank range, and his hand travels faster than the eye to the .45 under his jacket. Occasionally—with a gun in his ribs, another in his back, and a gloating voice saying that in ten seconds he'll be dead—Hammer *does* become a trifle anxious. But the bad men get careless for a second, and he blasts them from here to eternity.

Where women are concerned, Hammer might be described as an *homme fatal* in every sense of the phrase—he slays the girls with his rugged virility, and the girls around him are apt to get slaughtered for keeping him company. He can't so much as hand his coat to a hat-check girl without getting propositioned, and no sooner is a female alone with him than she whips off her clothes and strikes an inviting pose in the nude. Hammer, I'm sorry to say, is a terrible *voyeur*: he looks the lady over, lecherously, then usually goes off after the killer. But unlike most fictional detectives, he does, occasionally, succumb—two or three times in each story, to be Kinsey-ish about his private life.

In spite of his boudoir-hopping, Hammer is quite a romantic and an idealist about marriage. His great dream is to marry his stunningly beautiful secretary Velda, who, naturally, is madly in love with him. Aside from a rare kiss and smutty wisecrack, he is the parfit gentil knight where Velda is concerned, though she, too, parades before him in a transparent nightgown. A couple of books back, Hammer gave Velda an engagement ring. But in the sequel their engagement was still "an engagement to be engaged," and Mike was getting himself seduced all over the place.

Spillane has, incontestably, a remarkable talent for keeping the action moving fast and furiously; and his climaxes (until you get to know his plotting) are packed with suspense and surprise—melodramatic beyond belief. But his imagination, though it dreams up sensational stuff, is pretty limited in range—in book after book, he uses the same scenes, the same gimmicks, the same overall formula. A friend of Hammer's is killed or

Mike is at hand when a murder is committed. The trail takes him to night clubs for the sucker trade, gambling joints, call-girl establishments and brothels. He finds himself tangling with a big-time racketeer and his hoods. Bullets miss him by inches, blackjacks come crashing on his skull; and he, in turn, dishes out terrific punishment. The people who help him or offer "leads" get murdered one by one, and Hammer goes crazy with "kill-lust." No writer of whodunits has given the customers so much mayhem and murder as Spillane. According to my count, there are (as Mr. Hemingway would put it) fifty-eight "deads" in his six novels, and the signs are that Spillane is caught in an inflationary spiral—the last three books contained almost twice as many "deads" as the first three.

As Hammer closes in, he uncovers a big-time network trafficking in narcotics, or prostitution, or blackmail based on compromising photographs. When the professionals in the outfit have been liquidated or exposed —the high-powered racketeer with connections, the torpedoes, the middlemen—there remains, still, the master mind to be unmasked. In one story, after knocking off part of the opposition, Hammer compares his mission to eating "a turkey dinner"—the killer's outfit is the meal, "the killer the dessert." In each case the "dessert" turns out to be a person whom Hammer has been closely involved with—a woman who has bewitched him with her admiration and her glamour, or a man whom he has deeply respected.

Spillane's books have been described by Mr. Max Lerner as "really prolonged literary lynchings, strip-teases and rapes," which pander to "our sick cravings." There is, I'm sure, a good deal of truth in this, but I don't think that the supercharge of sex and sadism is the decisive factor behind Spillane's unique popularity—those ingredients are being used by plenty of other whodunit writers without anything like the same box-office results. While the Spillane books may be bliss to the peeping tom and a delight to respectable folk who like their fictional murder laced with rough stuff, the Hammer stories also answer an altogether different, primitively moralistic set of cravings. I suspect this is the crucial underlying factor in their phenomenal appeal.

During the past two decades, monstrous evils—total war, political purges, the systematic sadism of the Gestapo—have become part of our everyday consciousness. And lately, Americans have been made more sharply aware that, here in the United States, there flourish crime networks organized on the lines of big business and well-barbered racketeers who have found answers even to the income tax. The signs are that more and more people feel personally steamed up about all this, and, at the same time, have a frustrated feeling that the individual can't do much about it. Perhaps the acutest frustration of our time is this sense that the individual has been reduced to impotence in a world where the principle of large-scale organization has spread so far into human affairs, legitimate and nefarious.

This moral indignation and this frustration in the face of large-scale evil (and neither can properly be called "sick") are reproduced more intensely in the Hammer books than in any other murder mysteries. Hammer, unlike most fictional detectives, is personally touched by the initial murder, much as we, nowadays, are touched by aggression wherever it occurs; and he is enraged (as we are angered) that smooth deadly criminals should go unpunished and even prosper mightily. Now begins the compensatory daydream in which the Superman fights our fight against the forces of evil. Hammer is not just any superman—he has The Call. Hammer is Jehovah's messenger; he is the avenging hand of the Jehovah of *Proverbs,* who ordains that "destruction shall be to the workers of iniquity." When Hammer, in the apocalyptic dénouements, pumps a bullet into the killer, he kills a part of himself—love or respect. His mission is to be the Flaming Sword.

In Spillane's books we see, as through a magnifying glass, the drama inherent in the formula of the detective story. Every murder mystery poses symbolically (in the form of the initial murder) the problem of Evil—and resolves it; every detective story therefore meets a deep metaphysical need. Some reflect more sharply than others the needs of a particular time and a particular place.

The detective story began to flourish in an age in which science was beginning to undermine the traditional teachings of religion, notably the belief that man's life was ordered by a Divine Providence. Science offered, as a consolation prize, the doctrine of inevitable progress, which affirmed that man would eventually solve all his problems by applying to them the methods of Science. This is the credo enshrined in the classic detective story. Sherlock Holmes, with his microscope-like eye, his tireless pursuit of clues, the flawlessly empirical march of his logic, is—and has often been called—"the scientific detective." Holmes himself, of course, is a uniquely inspired figure, but he was preceded and has been followed by detectives galore who are prophets of the Scientific Method.

The nineteenth century's optimistic rationalism was reflected in another classic type of detective, first cousin to the "scientific detective"—the Thinking Machine. He did not bother much with footprints and bits of fluff, but put the "little gray cells' to work. He was the prophet of Pure Intellect (the forerunner of today's theoretical physicist who finds the key to the universe by messing around with mathematical equations).

The promise of science began to lose its sheen in the disillusionment that set in after World War I; and rationalism in general lost face as Freud's theories spread the idea that reason was outmaneuvered and outgunned by the irrational forces of the unconscious. These changes were followed, after a certain time-lag, by noticeable changes in the murder mystery. To be sure, the scientific detective is still with us and also the Thinking Machine. But they are decidedly less in evidence (especially in America, which has always had more faith in men of action than in intellectuals). Generally speaking, there is less sifting of clues in the contemporary whodunit and more banging around with guns and blackjacks; the trend is away from the puzzle story toward the action story.

Out of the turbulent thirties and forties came a new kind of detective fiction—the hard-boiled murder mystery, pioneered by Dashiell Hammett. The old-fashioned puzzle whodunit—with its slow, stuffy plot, its detective of exquisite gentility and impossible deductive powers, its sexless romantic heroine and pat unraveling of the tangled skein of crime—was well suited to the genteel nineteenth-century book-buyer, to whom killing was not (as it has since become) an ugly commonplace, but a piquant eccentricity; and who, anyhow, didn't like to face the seamy side of life. Dashiell Hammett, Raymond Chandler and other gifted practitioners of the hard-boiled school have tried to get the murder mystery closer to contemporary realities. They have taken murder fiction away from the upper classes, the week-end house party and the vicar's rose garden and have turned it over to the people who are good at it, the pros; they have placed it in a setting—the glossy underworld—where crime is part and parcel of everyday reality.

The hero who marches down these mean streets is, at his finest embodiment, Raymond Chandler's Philip Marlowe, private dick. He is *the man who gets things done*—a tough hombre behind whose rude wit and cynicism there lies the *chevalier sans peur et sans reproche;* a pistol-packin' knight errant who sallies forth on his trusty charge, a Chrysler convertible, to do battle with the dragons, the bad giants and the weavers of black spells that infest Los Angeles and surrounding California. Chandler's shamus—forever ploughing into the heart of trouble, a sucker, at heart, for a dame in distress —represents the wish-fulfillment of an ideal not yet quite dead. In Marlowe we see reincarnated, with a Democratic New-Look, ye olde champion of the Chivalric Code.

The moral fabric of any age, any society, is a tapestry in which there are strikingly different and even antithetical motifs. Our popular art forms show that the prevailing fashion in heroes runs to the extroverted he-man, the tough guy who saves the world with a terrific sock on the jaw of the transgressors, and the bang, bang of his pistol. But even this generation, so much exposed to philosophies of power, has its hankering for the light that comes from within; and in its folklore there appears, intermittently, a new kind of priest-hero—the psychoanalyst. He offers us a full-blown metaphysic in which the Fall has become the Trauma; in which man is redeemed from Guilt by wrestling with the Complex on the *via dolorosa* of the Couch. He tells us—and the notion has gained official acceptance to a limited degree —that crime is not so much willful sin as the product of sickness. He tells us that even he who murders is not Gruesome George but a fouled-up unfortunate whose parents didn't get him started right. This outlook has deeply colored the fiction of Georges Simenon.

Simenon was born in Liege, Belgium, in 1903. He published his first novel when he was seventeen; and in the next ten years, writing under a score of pseudonyms, he produced some two hundred potboilers which he regarded as an apprenticeship for more ambitious things to come. In the early 1930's, he launched his Inspector Maigret detective stories, which instantly achieved enormous popularity. A few years later, he also started writing "straight" psychological novels. To date, he has published (not counting his anonymous early works) thirty-nine Maigret books, seven whodunits without Maigret, and seventy-five serious novels (he writes a whodunit in a month, straight novel in three). His books have been translated into seventeen languages, and more than twenty of them have been made into movies. The two Simenon novels published in the United States since the war are climbing rapidly toward the million mark in their N.A.L. reprint editions.

In addition to pleasing the millions, Simenon has been highly praised by exacting judges—not merely as a superior confectioner of mysteries but as a literary artist. André Gide has described him as "the most novelistic novelist in French literature today"; and a leading British critic, Raymond Mortimer, says: "I suspect Simenon to be among the most gifted novelists now alive."

Simenon has said that thanks to mass communications—the press and radio, photography, the movies, and now television—the reader's horizon has been so enormously enlarged that elaborate documentation no longer has any place in the novel; the novelist should be able to suggest a setting, evoke an atmosphere, in a few swift strokes. The time has therefore come, Simenon believes, to try to write what he calls *"le roman pur"*—the quintessential novel—which should do for our time what was done by the tragedies of ancient Greece. Starting at the moment of decisive crisis, it should pose the problem of man's destiny; should give an accounting of a man's life. Simenon was attracted to the murder mystery because it offers a convenient way of doing just this in terms of the murderer, the detective serving as an explanatory prop akin to the Chorus in Greek tragedy.

In working his way toward the *roman pur* via detective fiction, Simenon brought a crucial innovation to the whodunit. He made it an exploration of personality—a quest whose goal is not so much punishment of the crime as understanding of the criminal; a mystery whose solution unravels not so much a tangled skein of events as a tangled skein of motives. In Simenon's hands, the whodunit is essentially a whydunit.

Though the detective story leaves no room for portraiture-in-depth, Simenon's sharply sketched characters are living, three-dimensional individuals. His décor, achieved with masterly economy, is marvelously authentic. His plots seldom contain anything far-fetched.

It is impossible to categorize the world of Maigret because it is the real world—Paris, the provincial towns of France, the Riviera—and the crimes in it are committed by ordinary people deranged by jealousy, or ambition, or greed, or to cover up some scandal which threatens them with ruin. Maigret himself, in his habits and appearance, is a typical French *bourgeois,* married to a *bonne bourgeoise* who tries, vainly, to make him cut down his incessant pipe-smoking, and who knows better than any chef how to prepare her husband's favorite dishes—creamed cod and *créme au citron*. Always clad in a black suit and a derby, Maigret is a quiet, unexcitable man, who detests hurry; a stolid, peaceable figure who might be a schoolmaster or a country doctor.

Maigret has little interest in fingerprints, footprints, alibis, how the murderer entered and how he got away, in most of the data which are the foundation of the conventional whodunit. Sometimes he doesn't even give the corpse itself more than a casual glance. In one sense, Maigret is the least realistic of Simenon's characters; he will hardly pass, under rigorous scrutiny, as an Inspector of the Paris Police Judiciare—he simply doesn't know his job. He is very real, however, as a man, a man of deep humanity, with a profound insight into people.

Maigret's compass is not the logic of events but the logic of passions. The clues he follows are looks, words, gestures. He works through his feelings, his intuition, his knowledge of men. He tries, and the reader tries with him, to grope his way toward the psychological crisis which provoked the murder. The disclosure of the truth, with its revelation of the dire pressures that shape human conduct, usually brings a measure of sympathy for the criminal, a kind of absolution. The leitmotif of Simenon's work is: "It is a difficult job to be a man."

This theme is treated with far greater complexity, finesse and depth in Simenon's serious novels, which are really psychological mystery stories. *The Snow Was Black* is the drama of an adolescent whose mother runs a flourishing brothel and who has never known his father. Out of a cold, defiant despair, Frank Friedmaier is trying to destroy, systematically, everything in him that is human. For no other reason than this, he kills; he engineers a revolting betrayal of the young girl who loves him; he robs and murders an old woman who cared for him in his infancy. While he is in jail, awaiting execution, there occurs an event which reconciles him both to life and death. We finally understand, completely, the source of Frank's terrible life-hatred, and our disgust is transmuted into compassion.

In *The Heart of a Man,* the mystery hinges on the savage unhappiness of an aging Parisian actor, "the great Maugin," who with the aid of *vin ordinaire* and a periodic shot of cognac is drinking himself across the river and into the trees. At the novel's opening, Maugin hears a specialist's verdict that at fifty-nine he has a seventy-five-year-old heart; and the story describes the last weeks of his life with flashbacks into his past. Interweaving past and present, Simenon tries to show precisely what has made Maugin the man he is—a tortured colossus, hounded by rage, irrational jealousy and self-disgust.

Simenon's latest novel, *The Girl in his Past,* is his most daring exploration of the role of sex in the inner drama of a man's life. Albert Bauche, after murdering his employer—a movie promoter, Serge Nicholas—surrenders himself to the police. He refused to plead that the murder was "a crime of passion," though he knew his wife to be Nicholas' mistress; and he insists that he is sane. His motive, he explains, was the discovery that he had been deceived into aiding and abetting an unscrupulous swindler. Eventually the police have him examined by a psychiatrist, and with remarkable subtlety and suspense we are led back into his hidden obsessions and frustrations until, in a moment of shattering awareness, he himself understands the *real* reason why he killed.

The answers in Simenon's books always penetrate to the deepest recesses of the unconscious and they are never glib or patly presented. Simenon is too much of "a natural"—a born story-teller and a magnificent creator of character—to write clinical case histories. A comment he made on the work of another writer admirably conveys the flavor of his own work: "There is no psychologizing, and yet every personage has a private life which is his own and his alone. There is no sound and fury, no striving for the picturesque, but always the people having the universe glued to their skin."

Like the psychoanalyst, Simenon does not condemn. Nothing shocks him, for he believes that between the cruelest murder and the most decent citizen there lies but the turn of a screw in the psyche. The catharsis his climaxes provide lies in the revelation that human beings are not evil but merely human. "It is a difficult job to be a man."

We have shown how, in different ways, the mystery story is involved with the problem of evil; how it provides us with a hero who answers deep-seated needs. It is time, now, to tidy up loose ends; to go straight to the root of the murder mystery's appeal. It is time to anatomize the underlying metaphysical pattern—*the detective story is modern man's Passion Play*.

In the beginning is the murder, and the world is sorely out of joint. There appears the detective-hero and his foil, the latter representing the blindness of ordinary mortals—Dr. Watson, or the police, or, if the hero is a policeman, his bumbling associates. The detective is a man like the rest of us, with his share of human failings—Nero Wolfe swills beer; Maigret is helpless without his pipe; Hammer goes in for venery. But this mortal has The Call—he is a Savior. In him is Grace, and we know that he will bring the Light.

The hero suspects everyone, for the murderer is Everyman; the murder is the symbol of the guilt, the imperfection, that is in all of us. In his search for the hidden truth, the hero is exposed to danger, thrashes about in darkness, sometimes suffers in the flesh, for it is by his travail that the Savior looses the world of its sins. In the detective's hour of triumph, the world is, for a moment, redeemed. Unconsciously we die a little when the murderer meets his fate, and thus we are purged of guilt. We rejoice in the reassurance that beyond the chaos of life there is order and meaning (the writer who leaves bits of chaos lying around condemns the reader to Purgatory). We exult that Truth has been made known and that Justice has prevailed. All this the lowly whodunit offers. And still that is not all.

By his personality, his deeds, his methods, the hero bears witness to a system of belief, a secular credo for a religious doctrine. He is the apostle of Science, like Holmes, or of Pure Reason, like Hercule Poirot. He may, like Maigret, believe that Understanding is the highest good and that its fruit is Compassion. He may, like Hammer, be the vessel of wrath which executes Jehovah's vengeance on those who plowed iniquity. There are other kinds of hero detectives, and they are true prophets all. For in the detective story, Paradise is always regained. And still this is not all.

If the reader—be he anything from Anabaptist to Zoroastrian—truly enters into the detective's quest, the hero's spirit lays its hands upon him. He becomes compassionate with Maigret and condemns no man; he waxes savage with Hammer and rejoices as the wicked become the dead. Whatever system of belief the hero acts out will, for the duration, infuse something of itself into the reader. He will find himself saving the world with a borrowed credo which is temporarily *his*. And herein lies the hidden seduction of the whodunit. Mystery stories are bloodstained fairy tales which enact the cycle, Paradise Lost—Paradise Sought For—Paradise Regained. *They allow us to play, vicariously, the role of different kinds of Savior.*

You pays your money, and you takes your choice.

Mickey Spillane and His Bloody Hammer

By CHRISTOPHER LA FARGE

MANY MILLION PEOPLE in the United States have bought, and presumably read, the books on the adventures of Mickey Spillane's creation, Mike Hammer, the Vigilante-Killer. I know that there have been at least six of these published since 1947; and that the one called *I, the Jury* had sold by August, 1953, 1,600,000 copies. As of June, 1954, 24,000,000 copies of Spillane's books had been published. One of these books, called *Kiss Me, Deadly,* even had the unusual record for a so-called murder mystery (Spillane's books have much murder and little mystery), of finding itself on the best-seller lists of the *New York Herald Tribune* and *The New York Times.*

This is a phenomenon that merits examination, although part of that examination has been made before. What is phenomenal about it is that a series of books can be written in what is supposed to be the form of fiction, but is not truly fiction, but rather a wholly unadmirable kind of wish-fulfilment on both an immature and a potentially destructive level, and be immediately successful on a scale far beyond average.

It would be a lot more fun (and a lot easier) to write a parody of these Mike Hammer books instead of an article, but the point to be made is a serious one, unfortunately, and the parody is limited in its application and has already been brilliantly done by Walt Kelly in his *Uncle Pogo So-So Stories* under the title of "The Bloody Drip by Muckey Spleen," about "Meat Hamburg, Private Eye, Ear, Nose, Throat, and Leg Man, in another Big Game of Corpse and Robbers."

I don't know what moved Spillane to write about Mike Hammer as he did. Certainly there is in none of the three books I have made myself read anything whatever to justify the assumption that the series was cynically begun merely as a way of creating a highly salable commodity; though the continuance of the series might be a cynical act on the part of both author and publishers. Cynicism implies a form of prior intelligence that is nowhere evident. Rather there is indicated clearly by these books something very like a necessity felt by the author to explain again and again, and to attempt to justify, the philosophy of the very central character of all of them, Mike Hammer, as though that philosophy were justifiable. Many an author has felt himself compelled to create a character who is evil, or sadistic, or immoral, or a combination of these (as is Mike Hammer), and has been equally compelled to attempt to make some facet of that character sympa-

Reprinted from *The Saturday Review*, November 6, 1954, pp. 11-12, 54-59, by permission of the author and the publisher. (Copyright, 1954, by the Saturday Review Associates, Inc.)

thetic or even attractive to his readers, either through a genuine compassion or an intellectual conception of the variations possible within one human being. But it has never been my experience before to read of a sadist whose sadism was held up as a justifiable means to an admirable end.

What troubles me about this manifestation is that Spillane seems to have succeeded in making the character of Mike Hammer acceptable to a huge public. In this I believe he but reflects (and profits by reflecting) an attitude already held by that public—an attitude which has grown to an extent that is at the least inimical to the basic principles on which our country has so far operated. Mike Hammer is the logical conclusion, almost a sort of brutal apotheosis, of McCarthyism: when things seem wrong, let one man cure the wrong by whatever means he, as a privileged savior, chooses.

There is nothing new in history about McCarthyism, which has occurred again and again since recorded time, and reflects nowadays the human impatience of men at the necessarily slow movements of a government of laws, not of men. There is equally nothing new about the essential skeleton of a character like Mike Hammer, who represents in himself a one-man army of Vengeance and Retribution. In essence (but only in essence) he belongs to the Robin Hood tradition: the man who operates on the side of the Good but outside of, or in conflict with, Constituted Authority; and who (for whatever reasons) decides entirely for himself what is the Good and what is the Bad. He has even two recent forerunners in Edgar Wallace's "Ringer" and Leslie Charteris' "Saint"; and Erle Stanley Gardner's "Perry Mason," a lawyer, breaks the laws so that Right may Triumph. Hammer shares with all of these a willingness to take the law into his own hands, to bring to trial, to judge, to condemn (but in his case even personally to execute) those who he singly decides to have been of the Bad; and there is given to him, as to them, always some motivation, some purpose, that is in part laudable or, at least, popular. With them too he operates, as has Senator McCarthy, on the final philosophy that the end can justify the means: in this Hammerism and McCarthyism are similar.

We hear a great deal nowadays about witch-hunting, and this reflects the disgust of all truly liberal minds with the continuance of an old and bloody tradition in our country. The witch-hunt is still practised because we continue to have within us a strong residue of fanaticism, which operates to force us toward the elimination, rather than the alteration, of anything we disapprove, regardless of any balanced judgment and in conflict with all liberality of being; and because we are still close to the frontier days when it seemed necessary for men to take the law into their own hands, there being no other apparent alternative. The existence of the Vigilantes seemed to frontiersmen necessary, and such a system fitted into their impatience with what they saw as wrongdoing and the remoteness of the law. That such a system should ultimately spread from the elimination of cattle rustlers and brigands to persons whose moral, racial, religious, or political outlook was disliked by the majority of a community was inevitable. Its children have been the persecutions and intolerances, the riots and the lynchings that mar so much of what is fine and good in our historical growth as a nation.

It is well, in thinking of this (as we must to understand Hammerism's popularity), to add to it another modern factor. This is the huge, impersonal groupings of an industrial civilization, creating (almost by opposites) a frontier of overpopulation instead of isolated dwellings of scattered humanity. No system of law-enforcement has yet been devised which can operate successfully within an industrial complex composed of a packed humanity of diverse and disparate backgrounds, desires, income, needs, and social habits that does not seem to such people cold and impersonal and essentially hostile. To many overcrowded city men, infected with the impatient fanaticism which colors our historical tradition (or the tradition they stem from in other lands), Hammerism must appear to be a comprehensible and justifiable method, one that the individual can grasp. It is the dream of justice, however imperfect, meted out without delay, with fierce and wonderfully satisfying immediacy? Those who, in their massed anonymity, feel their own individual helplessness and isolation tend to see in all the slow process of law the corruption of justice by the privileged. Hammerism, like McCarthyism, seems to cut through to that swiftness of retribution, regardless of privilege, that they themselves (the unprivileged) despair of. That this can spell the ultimate corruption of a republic of laws is not realized by such people. But I shall have more to say of this, in illustration, later on.

Mike Hammer, like the stories in which he appears, also derives from the recent work of other writers in America, the so-called Tough School of Fiction. Spillane has simply carried further—I believe to a point beyond which it will, happily, be impossible to go—the work of such great or truly gifted writers as Ernest Hemingway, William Faulkner, John Steinbeck, and more exactly, Dashiell Hammett, James M. Cain, and Raymond Chandler. The interesting and significant difference here is that all of these men write with brilliance and ability and their characters, however hard boiled, have reality and three full dimensions. Mr. Spillane's writing is frequently and painfully bad by any standard; and none of his characters, including Mike Hammer, has any true reality whatever.

I do not think one can explain, even partially, the popularity of Mr. Spillane's bloody murder stories by saying that there was so much killing done by so many Americans between 1941 and 1945 that millions of them became calloused to death by violence. History doesn't support that thesis. Some men were much toughened by combat but the huge majority of them came off from the experience with a desire to put that side of war—and the brutal methods self-preservation taught them—as far back in their minds as possible. The truly toughened man who has actually fought in combat is more often able to afford psychologically to be gentle than the untried or the untoughened. Judging entirely from the evidence of these three books, one would say that Spillane had never been in actual combat and might, indeed, be somewhat compensating for that in these stories. (Since writing this I have learned that Spillane was in the Army Air Forces during the last war, but was kept in the U.S. as an instructor; and that he volunteered for active duty in Korea, but was not accepted.)

What then, is the explanation for the great popularity of the stories about Mike Hammer? Perhaps it will be well to see what sort of man he is, as Spillane presents him to his enormous public.

Hammer is a large man, described as extremely powerful physically. His physical prowess of all sorts is in no way impaired by heavy drinking and smoking, of course; and this follows a usual stereotype. He is irresistible to all the women he meets, and his effect on all of them is identical: they want to have physical intercourse with him at once, and often do. This occurs with frequency in the three books I have read, with the two notable exceptions of Velda, his secretary and female counterpart, of whom I shall say more later; and Charlotte (in *I, the Jury*), whom he later murders by shooting her in the stomach while she is unarmed. To both these women he becomes (in different books) engaged and, with a stereotyped nobility of character nowhere else evident in him, he refuses to sleep with them before marriage, though both of them urge him passionately to do so. This nobility of soul is faintly clouded by the fact that he is well supplied with a succession of women toward whom he doesn't have to be noble at all; and isn't.

All the women are identical physically (with the single exception of Linda Holbright in *One Lonely Night,* who is described as having a face that is not pretty), being young and full-bosomed, wide shouldered, with perfect bodies and legs. Their only differences are the color of their eyes and hair; and Mike Hammer is so perceptive that he can foretell an un-bleached blonde from a photograph. They frequently wear nothing at all under their outer clothes (except for Velda, who packs a .32 automatic); these outer clothes are skin tight to show ALL; and they unzip these garments as soon as possible after meeting Mike Hammer. One can, perhaps, best form an estimate of the moral code of Mike Hammer both in relation to women and as a Reformer by his experience with the plain-faced (but not -bodied) Linda.

Linda is a member of the Communist Party. Hammer smiles at her at a Communist meeting. She gives him "the damndest look you ever saw." "Just for the hell of it" he gives her "one back with a punch to it. What she made of it stopped her breathing a second." Because of this soul-shattering experience, Linda follows the true Spillane pattern and arrives at Hammer's apartment, unbid, later that night; has a drink; is kissed; unzips her dress (which had nothing under it and "peeled off like paint") and offers herself —having never before (a) had a drink or (b) kissed a man or (c) had physical relations with a man. She simply asked of Hammer "nothing except to be shown how to be a woman." She was shown. She left then at once and most conveniently, wanting "to be part of the darkness and alone."

Poor Hammer feels so like a heel that he can't finish more than half of his drink until he comes to this comforting conclusion: "Then it occurred to me that now that she had a little taste of life maybe she'd go out and seek some different company for a change." He stops feeling like a heel, pours another drink and is able to finish it, and goes contentedly to bed. It is an interesting though conceivably ineffective way to reform Communists. And of course provided One not entirely Lonely Night.

Velda, the secretary, is the Lilith conception: every immature or adolescent male's dream. She is beautiful, attractive, young, available, faithful. She will wait for her man forever, and forever want him wholly when he comes back from whatever absence or adventure including a lot of other women. She is simply cross with her man when he forgets to wipe off the most recent other woman's lipstick. Velda has, by the end of the latest book I have read, *Kiss Me, Deadly,* killed two men herself. She can and does beat up and disfigure permanently any man who makes improper advances to her. Indeed, in these books the only persons who can safely make improper advances are women and to Hammer. Velda "could whip off a shoe and crack a skull before you could bat an eye." Whatever Mike Hammer says is so and true, that is so and true for Velda without further necessity of proof. It is for this that I have characterized her as Hammer's counterpart, because he needs no proof of anything beyond his own personal judgment. Whatever violence Hammer may commit is right in Velda's eyes because he committed it. She shares with him his entire moral outlook on life.

What is that moral outlook?

In each of the three books I have read there is a Vengeance to be executed on the exact basis of an eye for an eye, a tooth for a tooth. In *I, the Jury* it is to revenge the murder of a man who was Hammer's war buddy and an ex-cop. In *One Lonely Night* it is to revenge the murders and thefts of secret documents of a Communist ring. In *Kiss Me, Deadly* it is to revenge the murders and acts of drug-peddling members of the Mafia.

In each case Mike Hammer sets out to solve the problem of who is doing these things—not with the intention of bringing the guilty to justice or even to the electric chair, but that he may personally find, judge, condemn, and kill these persons before the police can get them. Not only that: but also that he may act as executioner of his victims in a manner precisely as brutal and violent as the brutality and violence he judges them to have practised. This intention he also publicly proclaims.

It would be strange enough if a man in fact could do this in the United States at this time of its history and still be allowed at large with a permit to carry a deadly weapon. It would be even stranger if the police co-operated with him, worked with him, fed him information, and protected him. Yet this happens in all three books. Mike Hammer's best and most loyal friend is Captain of Police Pat Chambers. Oh, Chambers warns him from time to time that what he is doing is sort of illegal, this business of going around by himself and killing people he has decided need to be killed; but that is all. Chambers sees, as Hammer does, that the end—the destruction of evil persons or at least of those that Hammer decides are evil—justifies the means to that end. It's quicker that way. Add it to the brutality of the methods of revenge in which Hammer is allowed to indulge to his own entire and declared satisfaction, and you begin to get the moral picture clear. An example from *Kiss Me, Deadly* may help.

Hammer, disarmed by the FBI, his license as a private investigator temporarily revoked, publicly hunts for two professional killers, Sugar Smallhouse and Charlie Max, off Broadway at night. Both the police and the FBI know that these two are at large and that Hammer has passed the word around that he will get them. He has been told they are out to get him. He finds them in a bar. He renders Smallhouse unconscious by a sort of jujitsu hold from behind, "like a kid snapping worms." He gets Charlie Max, as Max reaches for his gun, by kicking him in the face so that "the things that were in Charlie's face splashed all over the floor." He then breaks Max's arm by kicking that. As he reaches for the gun that Max dropped three members of the FBI stop him, search him, register extreme surprise that he is unarmed, and—let him go. Of this Hammer says, "There wasn't a damn thing they could do and they knew it, so I turned around, walked back outside, and started crosstown to the Astor." He gets there, too, unmolested. This was necessary to the story, of course, as he is going to meet a woman at the Astor who has fallen for him so hard that she is going to betray her half-brother to him. It gives one an odd impression of the limitations of legal law enforcement as well as family feeling.

In *One Lonely Night* the book begins with Hammer irrationally upset because a Judge has excoriated him publicly as a killer. The Judge's voice, which had been righteous, says Hammer, "changed into disgusted hatred because I was a licensed investigator who knocked off somebody who needed knocking off bad and he couldn't get to me."

This makes Hammer think, to the extent that that process is possible to him, and he thus describes himself: "That was me. I could have made it sound better if I'd said it. There in the muck and slime of the jungle, there in the stink that hung over the beaches rising from the bodies of the dead, there in the half-light of too many dusks and dawns laced together with the crisscrossed patterns of bullets, I had gotten a taste of death and found it palatable to the extent I could never again eat the fruits of a normal civilization." This is the police-licensed Private Investigator.

Velda's comment on the Judge's words was, "Let's get out of here, Mike. I hate people with little minds. . . . Mike . . . that judge was a bastard. You're an all-right guy."

Another quotation from a later passage in the same book sums up the philosophy of Hammerism throughout all three books. Hammer is answering the Judge in his own thoughts, in the italics which are Spillane's. He is referring to Communists who have stolen secret Government documents of extreme value, but it applies as well to his other acts of vengeance. It is interesting to note how closely his description of Communist methods matches his own.

My guts were all knotted up in a ball and my head felt like a machineshop was going on inside it. Here I had the whole lousy situation right in my hands and I had to keep it there.

Me, Mike Hammer. I was up in the big league now. No more plain and simple murders. I was playing with the big boys and they played rough. The end justified the means, that was their theory. Lie, steal, kill, do anything that was necessary to push a political philosophy that would enslave the world if we let it. Great!

Nice picture, Judge, a beautiful picture of a world in flames. You must be one of the normal people who get the trembles when they read the papers. A philosophy like that must give you the willies. What are you thinking now . . . how that same secret that was stolen might be the cause of your own death? And what would you say if you knew that I was the only one who might be able to stop it in time? Okay, Judge, sit your fanny in a chair and relax. I have a little philosophy of my own. Like you said, it's as bad as theirs. I don't give a damn for a human life any more, even my own. Want to hear that philosophy? It's simple enough. Go after the big boys. Oh, don't arrest them, don't treat them to the dignity of the democratic process of courts and law . . . do the same thing to them that they'd do to you! Treat 'em to the unglorious taste of sudden death. Get the big boys and show them the long road to nowhere and none of those stinking little people with little minds will want to get big. Death is funny, Judge, people are afraid of it. Kill 'em left and right, show 'em that we aren't so soft after all. Kill, kill, kill, kill! They'll keep away from us then!

For anything that tries to be so tough, the last six words sound remarkably like a frightened small boy.

But Mike Hammer doesn't confine the statement of his attitude to his private thoughts. He declares it to Captain of Police Pat Chambers at the outset of *I, the Jury*. Like this, after viewing the body of his murdered friend:

". . . by Christ, I'm not letting the killer go through the tedious process of the law. You know what happens, damn it. They get the best lawyer there is and screw up the whole thing and wind up a hero! . . . A jury is cold and impartial like they're supposed to be, while some snotty lawyer makes them pour tears as he tells how his client was insane at the moment or had to shoot in self-defense. Swell. The law is fine. But this time I'm the law and I'm not going to be cold and impartial. . . . You're a cop, Pat. You're tied down by rules and regulations. There's someone over you. I'm alone. . . . Some day, before long, I'm going to have my rod in my mitt and the killer in front of me. I'm going to watch the killer's face. I'm going to plunk one in his gut, and when he's dying on the floor I may kick his teeth out." (The killer turns out to be Charlotte and he does plunk one in her gut, but it doesn't say that he kicked her beautiful teeth out. Or in.)

So it goes in all three books. He shoots a lot of people in the gut and he kicks a lot of people's teeth out. It's all right because they are all Bad People and Deserve to Die Brutally. They are Bad because Hammer says so. It doesn't affect him at all (and in this he is also like Senator McCarthy) that he makes mistakes. In *One Lonely Night* he is being pursued by what believes to be Communists, chasing him at night in their car. He checks to be sure his .45 is free and ready and prepares to "haul the wheel right into them" as they begin to pass him. The car that is following goes off the road and rolls over in a field. It turns out later that its occupants were members of the FBI, ditched by some Communists following *them*. (Don't ask me how; it is all very obscure and badly written and improbable.) But that they were members of the FBI wouldn't have saved them from Hammer if they hadn't been ditched by the Communists. No, no, to *him* and *then* the FBI men were Communists. He takes the woman who was in the car with him to her country retreat (he had previously slept with her there) and tears her dress off and starts to beat her nakedness with his belt because he thinks she tipped off these men he thought were Communists to follow him; and the *real* Communists shoot her through the window. What she had tipped off was the FBI, thinking Hammer a Communist himself. Hammer the Infallible, the Judge, the Jury, the Executioner. But never forget that Communists are Very Bad People and the quickest and best thing to do to them (or members of the Mafia, or anyone you judge is ripe for it) is to shoot them in the gut, as a starter, of course.

Normally one would say that it was silly to write a critical article about a lot of books so very badly written, so essentially immature in their composition. That's what these books are. Their writing is turgid or grotesque or childish or simply the worst sort of lurid. Or it is plain revolting. A hunchbacked janitor from whom Hammer and his Velda rent a room (to go through it because it had been occupied by a suspect) offers them his own room because it is furnished with a bed and the other is not, and he misjudges their intentions. One can hardly blame him. Of this hunchback it is said: "He leered and looked somewhat dissatisfied because he wouldn't be able to sneak a look on something he probably never had himself." This comes from the mind of our hero, Hammer. One could multiply instances of mistakes in grammar and use of words ("they huddled in recessions of doorways"), inconsistencies (like the "cold, impartial jury" weeping) *ad nauseam*—and to no good end.

One can say that the readers of murder stories don't necessarily demand good English or even good writing, but simply what is usually described as "thrill-packed action." One can say that of the 24,000,000 persons who have bought or read Mr. Spillane's books many readers must be young and uncritical, and also that many must have got a vicarious satisfaction from the sexual passages reduced to such simple and unvarying animalism, either because their own lives provide no such satisfactions or because they'd like to think of themselves as having such physical prowess. One can say that in a tense world, full of hysterical shrillness, many, as I've attempted to suggest at the outset, isolated within the overlarge groupings of an industrial civilization, must derive from such writing a sort of satisfaction because the Bad get their come-uppance without need for the delays of lawful justice. If that were all it would not be very important. But it isn't all.

There is left the popularity of a Hero who, with such a character as has been described, mocks at and denies the efficacy of all law and decency, flouts all laws, statutory, ethical, and moral, delights in assault and murder that is brutally executed, sets his personal judgment always above that of all other men but in particular above that of those to whom government delegates law enforcement (which he thereby constantly derogates), and makes the words *soft* and *honorable* synonymous. This is the sort of philosophy, *mutatis mutandis,* that has permitted to Senator McCarthy his periods of extreme popularity throughout the nation: one man will, beyond the normal processes, unhampered by the normal and accepted restrains, bring the Bad to his own form of justice. Mike Hammer's Communists and members of the Mafia are, of course, all Very Bad. They are also described as soft, homosexual, stupid, gullible, childish, or easily tricked; but at the same time as the Most Dangerous Thing in the United States. *Any* means which will, with Hammer, lead to their extirpation and in particular their death by his hand are Good. With Senator McCarthy, any means that will expose Communists, including the derogation of all Public Servants, the telling of lies, the irreparable damaging of the innocent, the sensational and the unfounded charge, is justified so long as he thinks it is the right thing to do. Each, then, reflects the other, though McCarthyism kills but careers where Hammerism (perhaps in the end more mercifully) kills life itself.

When one has fought for years against the many forms and many evils of mistaken censorship one walks warily in asking the question, How much responsibility lies at the door of the publishers of Mickey Spillane? It cannot be possible to conceive of two firms as established as E. P. Dutton and Company and the New American Library of World Literature (which publishes Signet books) as being as naive as he makes himself appear by his writings. Was there in them at first but the wholly unanalyzed hope that this bloodier than the bloody, this tougher than the tough product would sell like hot cakes? Did they ever, as they continued to publish (but now with a full knowledge that they were exploiting a rarely excellent gold mine), stop to consider what they were doing in being the agents to disseminate books which would surely be read, and which would hold up to contempt almost every form of human decency in law and in life? Did they (incredibly) agree with the philosophy of Mike Hammer? Or did they decide that it was none of their business to pass a moral judgment on a man's books which had proved so financially profitable? Or did they perhaps generously plan to use the profits from the Spillane gold mine for the furtherance of the cause of true literature—even though that would be to accept the thesis that the end did justify the means? I do not know the answers to these questions.

If it were my responsibility now, I would neither censor nor ban the published works of Mickey Spillane; for the most worldly reason: to do so would be but to increase their sale. For another, a more difficult reason, it is hard always to establish that the reading of any such books is in itself a corrupting factor on any individual, no matter how young and callow and impressionable. But one must ask a larger and more difficult question than those concerning the responsibility of Spillane's publishers. What has come to our country that it can support and applaud these attitudes toward our common life as a country? Have we in fact become so impatient with due process of law, which is inevitably slow both in its creation, its interpretation, and its execution, that we are willing to abandon ourselves to the apparent quick curative of the Vigilante, the One Man in Power, for whom all laws with their checks and balances are ultimately suspended? Is this what the popularity of Hammerism and McCarthyism point to? If so, we had better realize it before their popularity is shared by a majority of our citizens, who can make valid their system of government by men. McCarthy is a fact. Mike Hammer is but fiction. Yet even as fiction his popularity, his acceptance point to something we would do well to reckon with, and soon. Eternal vigilance, goes the saying, is the price of liberty. It would be disastrous to change the word vigilance to vigilante.

What a pity it is that Mike Hammer and Mr. McCarthy cannot appear on the same television program and swap reminiscences during the Children's Hour!

FURTHER READING

Auden, W. H. "The Guilty Vicarage," *Harper's,* Vol. 196, May, 1948, pp. 406-12.

Bazelon, David. "Dashiell Hammett's 'Private Eye'," *Commentary,* Vol. 7, 1949, pp. 467-72.

Cowley, Malcolm. "Sex Murder Incorporated," *New Republic,* Vol. 126, 1952, pp. 17-18.

Ferkiss, Victor. "Cops, Robbers, and Citizens," *Commonweal,* Vol. 62, 1955, pp. 251-53.

Wilson, Edmund. "Why Do People Read Detective Stories?," *Classics and Commercials: A Literary Chronicle of the Forties.* New York: Farrar, Straus, 1950, pp. 231-37.

Although little research has been done regarding the effects of comic strips on their readers, it would seem apparent that popular strips, such as Blondie, Dick Tracy, Li'l Abner, and Orphan Annie, tell stories that are meaningful to the majority of Americans. Daily and Sunday strips are part of the reading habits of more than 100 million high-, middle-, and low-brows. Like hot dogs and popcorn, the comics are an American institution. The comic book (a genre which goes back to 1934 but attained its first great popularity with the Superman comics in 1939) is another matter. This flamboyant medium has raised many anxieties on the part of teachers, parents, psychiatrists and lawmakers.

Nevertheless, it is vastly popular, not only with impressionable children but with adults as well. For example, during World War II the sale of comic books at American military post exchanges was ten times greater than the combined sales of the two most popular weekly magazines published. No aspect of mass culture has been under more concerted attack than the comic books, whose existence has created censorship perils for other media.

In a pioneer study in the readership of comic strips, Leo Bogart found no evidence that readers whose interest in the comics is high have more reason or desire for escapist fantasy than those whose interest is low. The study substantiates the idea that comic strip readers "take roles" as they read, that they identify with the make-believe characters and invest them with a certain degree of independent reality.

The analysis of comic books by Robert Warshow reflects the doubts of one sensitive, broad-minded parent as he observes some of the reading matter of his eleven-year-old son. If he sees the strictures of Dr. Wertham as oversimplified, this does not mean that he likes or accepts the comic books. Yet by letting the boy, Paul, speak for himself, Warshow shows us that we can understand the problem better by assessing Paul's side of the story.

Llyle W. Shannon's content analysis of Little Orphan Annie reveals that this popular strip presents a middle- and upper-class view of American society. Annie's world is one in which the hard-working captains of industry struggle against a vicious and uncompromising underground in order to protect capitalism, earn large profits and thus assume their social responsibilities, i.e., be charitable to the needy.

Are comic strips sometimes more than mere vehicles of wish-fulfillment, the stuff that "dreams are made on"? In their analysis of Li'l Abner, Messrs.

Brodbeck and White indicate that this strip's real power lies in its masterful comic denial of certain painful aspects of American life. They show that the Dogpatchers act out many of the problems that have been previously described by such social scientists as Geoffrey Gorer in his provocative book The American People.

Comic Strips and Their Adult Readers

By LEO BOGART

THE POPULAR ARTS produced in our time by the mass media of communication command the attention of vast audiences. Four out of five Americans in towns over 2,500 read newspaper comic strips regularly or occasionally. Such a phenomenon deserves the study of social scientists, not merely because of its intrinsic interest, but because the steady increase in leisure time raises questions as to whether, and how, the popular arts will continue to fill this leisure. The present study sought to add an understanding of the popular arts by a detailed consideration of one of them, in relation to its audience.

The objectives of the study were: (1) To describe the nature of the comics reading experience in the lives of adult individuals and to examine the gratifications presented by this experience. (2) To consider the reasons why the comic strips were of more importance to some individuals than to others. (3) To describe the imagery of certain selected comics, as revealed in the strips themselves and as expressed in the recollections of their readers. (4) To analyze the reasons for variations in readers' tastes and preferences among the individual strips.

THEORETICAL CONSIDERATIONS

Through many centuries, aestheticians have provided extended description and discussion of the art experience. Their theories can not be applied to such a contemporary popular art form as the comic strips without considering first the distinctions between popular and traditional, élite art. We may distinguish popular art by such things as: (1) the huge size and heterogeneity of its audience; (2) the lack of direct, critical contact between artist and audience; (3) the adoption of wholly commercial criteria of success; (4) the use of simple, conservative themes, and of representational human elements with which the audience can readily "identify"; (5) the low level of attention or effort which it commands from its audience. Popular art may also be distinguished from the folk art of nonindustrial society.

Despite its use of such transcendental concepts as "beauty" which have little in common with the popular arts, aesthetic theory contributes a valuable notion, that of catharsis, which seems applicable in the present case. The weight of existing reflection on the subjects of art and play (under both of which headings the popular arts might be subsumed) sees them as means by which the individual divests himself of tension (which may be primarily "physical," "emotional" or "mental").

Published for the first time in this volume.

(189)

This concept suggests such propositions as these: (1) The comic strips are read because they provide some sort of satisfaction (some tension reduction) for the individual reader, either in a conscious, purposeful way, or in a mechanical, unconscious way. (2) Tensions may be reduced simply by a relief in monotony, by a break in accustomed activity, by the pure mechanics of variety, (all characteristic of play) or through dramatic catharsis (which is characteristic of art, and which is dependent on ideas and symbols). (3) Catharsis requires interest (mobilization and focussing of latent tension in the audience) and interest involves empathy or identification. (4) Identification may take place at the level of fantasy, or because of the direct similarity between the depicted situation and that of the audience. (5) Differences of taste reflect the capacity of different themes to reduce tensions for particular kinds of readers.

EXISTING STUDIES

Newspaper comic strips, the subject of this study, are not to be confused with comic books, although much of the existing literature lumps the two together. Most previous studies fall into two categories: (1) analyses of content, and (2) studies of the effect of the comics upon children. Content analysis of the comics (hitherto done on an overall basis, rather than for particular strips) shows the comics to contain a high degree of ethnocentrism, conservatism, violence, crime and sex. Studies of children's reading of the comics generally agree that comics satisfy normal emotional needs for fantasy. A survey of adult comics-reading habits has shown that readership declines with age and is highest in the lower-middle educational and socio-economic range. This survey (completed some time after the present work was undertaken) represents virtually the only existing research on the subject of adult reading of the comics, although the medium has a preponderantly adult audience.

METHOD OF THIS STUDY

To delimit the area of investigation, our study was confined to readers of two very similar tabloid newspapers in New York City, the *News* and the *Mirror*. (An analysis of the content of these two papers shows that they are generally comparable, and this fact is shown further by the high overlap of their readership). Extended interviews were conducted with 121 male workers of low social status, all but ten of whom live in the Lenox Hill slum neighborhood on Manhattan's upper east side. Selection of this particular group of readers focuses attention on the workings of the popular arts at a social level where they have little or no competition from élite art forms, where they constitute the only art experience.

Because of the difficulty of finding respondents in their homes, the sample was selected on a random basis, but its distribution corresponds well to available census data on the Lenox Hill neighborhood. One fourth of those interviewed are foreign-born, and the sample includes Irish, Czech, German and Italian ethnic strains which typify this community.

Virtually all questions used in the field interview were of the open-ended type, and answers were recorded in shorthand. Each interview included the following elements: (1) General questions on exposure to the mass media, especially newspapers. (2) Questions on comic strip reading, and on general experience with the medium. (3) Questions on attitudes toward the comic strips, requiring some evaluation of the medium and its influences on the reader. (4) Questions designed to reveal positive and negative preferences among individual strips. (5) Questions designed to reveal popular conceptions and imagery associated with particular strips and their characters. (6) Questions on the social characteristics of the readers. (7) Questions asked to indicate personality differences among the readers.

Cut-outs from some of the more popular comic strips were employed in the interview as a projective technique, with the respondents asked to explain what was happening in each scene, what the characters were saying, and what would happen next.

The interview data has been analyzed statistically insofar as possible, but the extensive nature of the interview transcripts also made possible considerable qualitative interpretation.

In addition to the field research, an intensive content analysis was made of four popular comic strips ("Dick Tracy," "Gasoline Alley," "Orphan Annie" and "Terry and the Pirates") over a six-month period. (Because the sample uncovered only a small group of readers who prefer the *Mirror* to the *News,* no detailed consideration is given to the *Mirror* strips and their readers, as was originally intended). This content analysis includes both a quantitative treatment and a more extensive interpretive discussion.

The content analysis has been used as a basis for setting up hypotheses with respect to the appeal and imagery aroused by particular strips in their readers, and these hypotheses have been considered in the light of the interview data.

PRINCIPAL FINDINGS: THE COMICS-READING EXPERIENCE

The comic strips are experienced as an integral part of the daily newspaper. They have a ritual aspect just as the paper does. They are one of many features which make the tabloid newspaper primarily a vehicle of entertainment rather than a vehicle of information. Without demanding too much effort or attention, these features relieve the monotony of existence. To lives which pursue much the same course from day to day they offer continual variety, and a sense of participation in a wider, more interesting society. They provide a means of occupation for people who have leisure time on their hands but who lack the resources for its more satisfactory use. For many readers, the newspaper represents an investment. The comics are read "because they're there," as part of the time-consuming process through which the entire contents of the paper are devoured and digested.

This does not mean that the comics have no significance for these readers. Precisely because they—like the rest of the paper—are an essential part of the daily routine, they may be most noticed when they are missed. At such times many readers seem to experience a vague discomfort, and they will often go out of the way to find out what they had been missing. Such interested readers are informed up to the minute on what the comics characters are doing, and they may open the paper immediately to a favorite strip if something especially interesting is about to occur.

Reading the comics has the characteristics of a habit. The characters are old friends whose adventures the reader has often followed since his childhood. As he matures his early interest in the comics wanes, but in most cases the thread of continuity is not lost. The comics are a link to the intimacies of the past. Therefore new comic strips find resistance on the part of adult readers; their characters are considered to be strangers. Curiously, the older a man is, and the longer he has been reading the comics (that is, the more habitual his reading has become), the less willing he is to admit the presence of habit (and the more necessary it appears to give his actions a functional, rational justification).

It appears that men begin to question the innocence of the comics only when they become fathers and are faced with the task of disciplining children whose interest in the comics parallels the interest they once felt.

Most of the strips (especially the popular ones) pursue a continuing course, with each day's episode left in a state of at least partial irresolution or suspense. The effect of each day's reading may therefore be to set up a small tension in the mind of the reader, to carry his interest on to the next episode. But these tensions are too petty to create any gnawing sense of irritation. The very fact that they are set up, that a small element of interest and variety has been added to the reader's day, makes for some dissipation of those greater, more deeply felt tensions which arise from boredom.

Therefore interest in the comic strips is independent of the reader's feeling that he knows how they are going to turn out. Certain elements—the essential characteristics of the strip's formula—remain fixed and predictable. The reader is impelled by curiosity over the means by which the expected equilibrium will be attained.

The comics act to reduce tension in their readers mainly by offering variety and a recurrent focus of interest. Their name implies that they also reduce tension through laughter. Actually, comic-strip humor, simple and stereotyped as much of it is, seems to produce a grim, unsmiling kind of amusement for the most part. Genuine, hearty laughs seem to be few and far between. Part of the reason for this may be that laughter is a social affair, and that the comics are usually read by single individuals. Since much of comic-strip humor pokes fun at everyday domestic occurrences, the strips alleviate some of the tensions which attend such occurrences in real life. But this is far from being a deep, cathartic kind of comic satisfaction.

Just as the comics are read "to pass the time," so they are talked about for the same reason. Men with above average education, who talk more about everything, also talk more about the comics. But such conversation is largely superficial banter; in groups where talk about politics or religion may be unwise, men may idly wonder about the next turn of events in a popular strip as they may idly talk about the weather. The comic-strip characters are universally known, and their traits or actions provide harmless satirical analogies for the small events of life. Such talk gives rise to no arguments. It is part of the endless chain of small things said and forgotten. Similarly, the comic strips seem to figure in individual reverie only as rare and disjointed fragments of thought: a stray comparison, the recollection of a pertinent joke.

However, comic-strip characters are part of the national lore. To children these characters appear to be real and alive. Even some adult readers invest these characters with a high degree of reality; they know, of course, that the characters do not exist, yet they cannot help speaking of them as though they in fact existed. It is just because the characters are so "real" that the authors remain anonymous even to the most constant readers. Awareness of the author would destroy the identity of his characters and reduce them to the level of mere artifice. When readers think of a strip's author, they often ascribe to him the traits of his principal character; the man who writes about "Dick Tracy" *is* Dick Tracy.

It might be thought that some readers are drawn to the comic strips because they identify directly with the characters or because the strips satirize familiar things, while other readers are out after pure escapist fantasy. Actually it is difficult to distinguish the "fantastic" characteristics of the strips from their "realistic" traits. Different readers derive different gratifications from the same strips.

PRINCIPAL FINDINGS: REASONS FOR VARIATIONS IN INTEREST

The interview data showed wide variation in the amount of interest which the comics generate. To examine this problem more closely, readers were separated into high, medium, and low interest groups on the basis of their answers to those questions which were considered indicative in this respect. Each of the following items counted for one point in computing an "Index of Comics Interest": (1) Usually reads at least one comic strip. (2) Mentions the comics as first or second most important element in the paper. (3) Regularly or occasionally turns to the comics before anything else in the paper. (4) Recalls the content of the morning's favorite strip. (5) Has gone out of his way to check up on comics he had missed. (6) Has talked about the comic strips. (7) Has daydreamed about the comic strips. (8) Says he would switch newspapers if the comic strips were changed.

As in other studies, it was found that the people who show the greatest interest in the comics are those who are in general most responsive to the mass media. The people whose interest in the comics is low are most apt to approach the newspaper as an organ of information, while those whose interest is high often seem to take the paper as entertainment—for "the features," of which the comics are one.

Interest in the comics is a matter of extent as well as intensity. The higher the general interest (that is, the more important one or a few comics appear to the reader), the more comics are read. But it is also true that some readers show high interest in just a few favorites, and ignore the others, while other readers regularly skim through all the comics, but have little interest in any or all of them.

Foreign-born persons show the least interest in the comics, which have not been part of their lives since childhood. The comics belong to their American-born children, and are often identified as "childish" things. But all persons, foreign- or native-born, seem to lose their interest in the comics as they grow older. This might be interpreted either as a sign of maturity, the sloughing off of a childhood survival, or else as a sign of intellectual constriction or atrophy, the loss of interest in outside stimuli. Persons with the least education show the least interest in the comics. (It would not, of course, follow that the most highly educated persons show the highest interest; a nationwide survey finds readership highest in the middle educational range.)

Apart from these few important considerations (and with sex and social status held constant, as they are in the sample used) comics interest appears to have no association with other individual variables, including personality variables. This would seem to support the notion that comics reading as a practice is widely shared in our culture, irrespective of individual traits.

There is not even a marked association between a man's interest in the comics and the kind of strip he likes best. Readers of different kinds of strips show an equivalent range of interest, from low to high. The explanation is that people do not read just one type of strip, either of the dramatic-adventure or the humorous kind. They read and like both types, for different reasons. This again points to the phenomenon of "readership by inertia"; the reader's eye wanders from strip to strip, irrespective of style or content. He is not looking for one particular kind of gratification; he takes the different types of offering which are presented to him. This does not mean that he has no favorites or pet peeves. But these preferences can only be understood in terms of the individual strips; they cannot be studied under the heading of strip types.

PRINCIPAL FINDINGS: ANALYSIS OF FOUR STRIPS AND THEIR READERS

In talking about the strips they liked and didn't like, the respondents gave frequent expressions of ambivalent feelings. In the analysis of the data, the most important thing seemed to be that a strip aroused some feeling, that it appeared to interest the reader. A negative attitude toward a particular comic strip appeared in many cases to be an inversion of its actual appeal for the reader; in such cases the strip's appeal appeared to hit the reader at a point on which he was personally sensitive. However, it is impossible to conclude that people who especially like a strip resemble those who dislike it more than they resemble the ones who are indifferent; the pattern was different for each of the strips studied in detail.

I. *"Dick Tracy"*

Analysis of the content of the "Dick Tracy" strip suggests that it might appeal to different kinds of readers for different reasons. It contains strong sensational components, which might satisfy sadistic or aggressive impulses. It provides the audience with a legitimate scapegoat, the criminal, who is relentlessly pursued. At the same time, it permits those readers who may identify themselves with the criminal vicariously to atone for their sins. The strips permit readers to fancy themselves in the role of the wise and powerful detective. It arouses a high degree of excitement, which remains bearable because the outcome is never in doubt.

Readers who single out this strip as a favorite give little emphasis to its aggressive or fantasy gratifications. They recognize these only in an occasional remark about the strip's possible effect upon children. They like it because of its continual suspense and mystery; they know that the detective will triumph over crime in the end, but they want to see how he does it. There is little outright identification with the hero, although secondary characters arouse a good deal of interest. Some readers try to explain away their interest in the strip by regarding it as a burlesque of itself. "Tracy" is highly popular and widely recognized. It is disliked by only a few readers. The strip appeals to those whose real-life gratifications are least, and who therefore are in greatest need of ready-made fantasy such as the strip provides.

II. *"Gasoline Alley"*

The content of "Gasoline Alley" has a dual appeal. Because it deals with everyday domestic scenes, it permits the readers to identify directly with the leading characters in their adventures, in their surmounting of obstacles. This identification is heightened because the characters have "aged" with the reader; in a sense they have shared experiences. The strip also lends itself to identification of the fantasy type, since the life it depicts may be more pleasant, easy-going and comfortable and perhaps at a higher social level than the reader's own.

The strip's "realism" is stated as a reason both by those who like and dislike it. Few admit that it expresses their own fantasies of a better life. However, "Gasoline Alley" has its greatest appeal to those readers who are young, single, and occupationally downward mobile (thus perhaps alive to the strip's strong social mobility theme, and to its setting of young married life). Those persons who dislike "Gasoline Alley" give some evidence of anxiety and of personal insecurity—they can't "take" the strip's optimistic, "All-American" aspect.

III. *"Orphan Annie"*

Analysis of the "Orphan Annie" strip suggests that it might have a strong appeal to persons who feel weak or frustrated. For them the strip provides wild fantasy, even magic. It permits regression to the happy days of childhood by introducing an all-powerful father-image who can always be counted upon to set things to rights. It offers hate objects, and objects of righteous superiority feelings. The strip has a strong political line which might intrigue some readers and antagonize others. It might be expected to antagonize those who identify themselves with characters portrayed unsympathetically, those whose own fantasies it expresses too sharply, or those who do not wish to be reminded of childhood.

It was found that those readers who liked the "Annie" strip often showed interest not in the heroine but in her "father" or his sinister associates. There was much reservation with respect to Annie's unchanging age, and this last point was the prime source of objection by the strip's critics. The strip was liked by persons of constricted reading habits, persons dissatisfied with their position in life, apparently with more than their share of aggressive feelings. It was disliked most by young men (perhaps insecure in their adult status or resentful of the "Annie" myth of fabulous wealth acquired through magic). Many who disliked the strip were occupationally downward mobile and economically insecure (the strip might therefore uncomfortably express their own yearnings for a quick magical solution to their problems).

IV. "Terry"

The hero of "Terry" is the "ideal" American male. The strip offers readers a thrilling identification with this hero in his adventures and romances. Through the symbol of flight and through its exotic settings, it offers freedom, power, escape from dull reality. It might be expected that the strip would appeal only to readers for whom this kind of vicarious adventure, or the identification with Terry, would not demand too much of a strain. Some persons might be antagonized because they would be reminded of their own age, weakness, or lack of achievement.

The respondents gave few statements of outright hostility to this strip; dislike was expressed as casual avoidance. The strip won its greatest approval among younger men; its fans showed a greater sense of personal potency and greater powers of imagination than those who are critical or indifferent.

On the whole, then, a fair degree of congruity was found between the content of each strip and the characteristics and reactions of the audience. (This would probably have been much more striking had the sample not been homogeneous.) The most important single variable influencing reactions to the strips was age. As men grow older they alter their conceptions of themselves, and this process is reflected in the degree to which they feel able to identify with particular comic-strip characters or to be inspired by particular comic-strip themes.

In studying preferences, few clear-cut distinctions were found, i.e., all the respondents with one set of social traits taking one point of view, and all those with the contrasting traits disagreeing. The same strip may be interpreted differently by various kinds of readers; we find some people liking strips for the "wrong" reasons. As might be expected, we often find differences between the justifications which readers provide for their own preferences and dislikes and the explanations suggested by statistical analysis.

The response to the cut-outs used in the projective question was sparse, dry, impersonal and unrevealing. This reflects the absence of imagination and the lack of verbal skills among the group studied. It also indicates that the comics are for the most part accepted at face value, that they are not invested with strong personal overtones. In general, the "projective" remarks follow closely the typical patterns of the strips themselves. The characters behave as they would in the strips, and act in the same kinds of situations. They remain themselves rather than surrogates of their readers. (The one notable exception to this is the frequent introduction of the theme of conflict between the sexes). Another indication that the characters remain themselves is the fact that the different categories of respondent make rather similar remarks about the same cut-outs. In every case, the people who especially like a strip give the fullest, most imaginative response to its cut-out.

There is little indication in this study that the comic strips stimulate much active fantasy in their adult readers. It is noteworthy that, throughout the interviews, there is a constant rejection of fantasy. What is disliked is described as "fantastic"; what is good is often "real"; the characters "grow." This fear and distrust of imagination is, of course, more typical of readers at this social level than at any other. The fantastic is the incomprehensible or the impossible; it presents a threat. Thus the comics gain acceptance so long as it is felt that they maintain some sort of connection with everyday life.

CONCLUSIONS

Discussion of the popular arts frequently assumes the form of a polarized argument, with one viewpoint that is essentially critical and another which is basically defensive. Both positions begin with a common assumption which may be stated as follows: The appeal of the popular arts stems from the fact that they express the fantasies, longings and suppressed impulses of people living in a chaotic world. To lives burdened by frustration and monotony they bring a momentary release. Their heroes and heroines do all the things which the reading, listening or viewing public would like to do.

The critical position then holds that this gratification is a dangerous and sinister thing: it caters to the lowest tastes of the audience and discourages both art and wholesome recreation; it turns the audience away from life's problems rather than to a realistic grappling with them, it titillates antisocial aggressive impulses which might otherwise be checked.

The defensive position maintains that the gratifications offered by the popular arts correspond accurately to the psychic needs of the audience, that they therefore serve a positive function for personal adjustment, that they provide a harmless outlet for impulses which would find expression in any case.

A third point of view, which does not figure much in the debate, is that which questions the strength of the compensatory gratifications offered by the popular arts, and which regards exposure to them as very often the result of chance, or the absence of alternative pastimes.

The present study offers some support to this last position. We have found the reading of comic strips to constitute a rather superficial experience. We have uncovered no evidence that those whose interest in the comics is high have more reason or desire for escapist fantasy than those whose interest is low. Furthermore, we have found a high overlap of readership between those strips which are quite fantastic and those which deal with fairly realistic themes.

We may consider the comics under both their recreational, "play" aspect and their ideational, "art" aspect. If we use the concept of "tension reduction," then the primary gratification afforded by the comics appears to be that they provide a break in the monotony of the day. The variety of their imagery seems of greater significance than the actual content of this imagery. Only to a limited extent, and only for certain readers, do the comics seem to serve a genuine cathartic function, through the fantasies which they arouse or express.

The comics do present their readers with fantasies of aggression, sex and achievement, and their appeal for particular groups of readers may be partly understood in these terms. But there is no evidence that the reader is drawn to the strips by a lust (either conscious or unconscious) for vicarious sensation; it seems rather that he brings his normal impulses to them as he does to other life experiences, and that the fantasies which they arouse, though based on these impulses, are brief and have a low emotional charge.

In fact it is noteworthy that these fantasy images are highly stereotyped —to the point of being impersonal. They do not express personal longings and strivings as much as a kind of collective imagery. The literal character of the whole experience is in keeping with the descriptions of other writers who have sought to differentiate between the popular and traditional arts.

Even though the reading of comics does not seem to be a highly important or emotionally charged thing, for most people, we have noted that varying preferences, within this medium, can to some extent be explained by differences in gratification, which arise in turn from the social and personality differences among groups and individuals.

The study substantiates the notion that comic strip readers "take roles" as they read, that they identify with the make-believe characters, and invest them with a certain degree of independent reality. But they seem able to alternate between roles which express their unconscious wishes and roles which remind them directly of themselves. Identification seems to make for a positive interest up to the point where it becomes uncomfortably sharp— where the reader feels his desires, traits or problems so accurately portrayed that he becomes uncomfortable, sometimes consciously so.

Within the limits of the small, homogeneous sample used in this study, group differences in identification and gratification appear small. The findings might be usefully compared in other situations and with other groups. In any case, it is impossible in the absence of further evidence to take conclusions which apply to the comics and extend them to other popular art media which use human actors and which require greater concentration on the part of the audience.

Paul, the Horror Comics, and Dr. Wertham

By ROBERT WARSHOW

MY SON, PAUL, who is eleven years old, belongs to the E.C. Fan-Addict Club, a synthetic organization set up as a promotional device by the Entertaining Comics Group, publishers of *Mad* ("Tales Calculated to Drive You MAD—Humor in a Jugular Vein"), *Panic* ("This is No Comic Book, This is a PANIC—Humor in a Varicose Vein"), *Tales from the Crypt, The Vault of Horror, Weird Science-Fantasy, Shock SuspenStories, Crime SuspenStories* ("Jolting Tales of Tension in the E.C. Tradition"), and, I imagine, various other such periodicals. For his twenty-five-cent membership fee (soon to be raised to fifty cents), the E.C. Fan-Addict receives a humorously phrased certificate of membership, a wallet-size "identification card," a pin and a shoulder-patch bearing the club emblem, and occasional mailings of the club bulletin, which publishes chitchat about the writers, artists, and editors, releases trial balloons on ideas for new comic books, lists members' requests for back numbers, and in general tries to foster in the membership a sense of identification with this particular publishing company and its staff. E.C. Fan-Addict Club Bulletin Number 2, March 1954, also suggests some practical activities for the members. "Everytime you pass your newsstand, fish out the E.C.'s from the bottom of the piles or racks and put 'em on top. . . . BUT PLEASE, YOU MONSTERS, DO IT NEATLY!"

Paul, I think, does not quite take this "club" with full seriousness, but it is clear that he does in some way value his membership in it, at least for the present. He has had the club shoulder-patch put on one of his jackets, and when his membership pin broke recently he took the trouble to send for a new one. He has recruited a few of his schoolmates into the organization. If left free to do so, he will buy any comic book which bears the E.C. trademark, and is usually quite satisfied with the purchase. This is not a matter of "loyalty," but seems to reflect some real standard of discrimination; he has occasionally sampled other comic books which imitate the E.C. group and finds them inferior.

It should be said that the E.C. comics do in fact display a certain imaginative flair. *Mad* and *Panic* are devoted to a wild, undisciplined machine-gun attack on American popular culture, creating an atmosphere of nagging hilarity something like the clowning of Jerry Lewis. They have come out with covers parodying the *Saturday Evening Post* and *Life,* and once with a vaguely "serious" cover in imitation of magazines like *Harper's*

Reprinted from *Commentary*, Vol. 17 (1954), pp. 596-604, by permission of the publisher. (Copyright, 1954, by The American Jewish Committee.)

or the *Atlantic*. ("Do you want to look like an idiot reading comic books all your life? Buy *Mad,* then you can look like an idiot reading high-class literature.") The current issue of *Mad* (dated August) has Leonardo's Mona Lisa on the cover, smiling as enigmatically as ever and cradling a copy of *Mad* in her arms. The tendency of the humor, in its insistent violence, is to reduce all culture to indiscriminate anarchy. These comic books are in a line of descent from the Marx Brothers, from the Three Stooges whose funniest business is to poke their fingers in each other's eyes, and from that comic orchestra which starts out playing "serious" music and ends up with all the instruments smashed. A very funny parody of the comic strip "Little Orphan Annie," in *Mad* or *Panic,* shows Annie cut into small pieces by a train because Daddy Warbucks' watch is slow and he has arrived just too late for the last minute; Annie's detached head complains: "It hurts when I laugh." The parody ends with the most obvious and most vulgar explanation of why Annie calls Daddy Warbucks "Daddy"; I had some difficulty in explaining that joke to Paul. One of the funnier stories in *Panic* tells of a man who finds himself on the television program "This Is Your Life"; as his old friends and neighbors appear one by one to fill in the story of his life, it becomes clear that nobody has seen his wife since 11:30 P.M. on the ninth of October 1943; shortly before that he had made some rather significant purchases: arsenic, a shovel, quicklime. Evidence piles up, including the actual bones of his wife (dug up by his old dog, Rover, who also appears on the program and will do nothing but growl at his former master). At the end of the program, of course, the man is arrested for murder; television's assault on privacy has reached its logical conclusion. I understand that *Mad* is rather popular among college students, and I have myself read it with a kind of irritated pleasure.

The straightforward crime and horror comics, such as *Shock SuspenStories, Crime SuspenStories,* or *The Vault of Horror,* exhibit the same undisciplined imaginativeness and volence without the leavening of humor. One of the more gruesome stories in *Crime Suspen-Stories* is simply a "serious" version of the story I have outlined from *Panic*: again a man murders his wife (this time with an ax) and buries her in the back yard, and again he is trapped on a television program. In another story, a girl some ten or eleven years old, unhappy in her home life, shoots her father, frames her mother and the mother's lover for the murder, and after their death in the electric chair ("Mommy went first. Then Steve.") is shown living happily with Aunt Kate, who can give her the emotional security she has lacked. The child winks at us from the last panel in appreciation of her own cleverness. Some of the stories, if one takes them simply in terms of their plots, are not unlike the stories of Poe or other writers of horror tales; the publishers of such comic books have not failed to point this out. But of course the bareness of the comic-book form makes an enormous difference. Both the humor and the horror in their utter lack of modulation yield too readily to the child's desire to receive his satisfactions immediately, thus tending to subvert one of the chief elements in the process of growing up, which is to learn to wait; a child's developing appreciation of the complexity of good literature is surely one of the things that contribute to his eventual acceptance of the complexity of life.

I do not suppose that Paul's enthusiasm for the products of this particular publisher will necessarily last very long. At various times in the past he has been a devotee of the Dell Publishing Company (*Gene Autry, Red Ryder, Tarzan, The Lone Ranger,* etc.), National Comics (*Superman, Action Comics, Batman,* etc.), *Captain Marvel, The Marvel Family, Zoo Funnies* (very briefly), *Sergeant Preston of the Yukon,* and, on a higher level, *Pogo Possum.* He has around a hundred and fifty comic books in his room, though he plans to weed out some of those which no longer interest him. He keeps closely aware of dates of publication and watches the newsstands from day to day and from corner to corner if possible; when a comic book he is concerned with is late in appearing, he is likely to get in touch with the publisher to find out what has caused the delay. During the *Pogo* period, indeed, he seemed to be in almost constant communication with Walt Kelly and the Post-Hall Syndicate, asking for original drawings (he has two of them), investigating delays in publication of the comic books (there are quarterly 15-cent comic books, published by Dell, in addition to the daily newspaper strip and the frequent paperbound volumes published at one dollar by Simon and Schuster), or tracking down rumors that a Pogo shirt or some other object was to be put on the market (the rumors were false; *Pogo* is being kept free of "commercialization"). During the 1952 presidential campaign, Pogo was put forward as a "candidate," and there were buttons saying "I Go Pogo"; Paul managed to acquire about a dozen of these, although, as he was told, they were intended primarily for distribution among college students. Even now he maintains a distant fondness for Pogo, but I am no longer required to buy the New York *Post* every day in order to save the daily strips for him. I think that Paul's desire to put himself directly in touch with the processes by which the comic books are produced may be the expression of a fundamental detachment which helps to protect him from them; the comic books are not a "universe" to him, but simply objects produced for his entertainment.

When Paul was home from school for his spring vacation this year, I took him and two of his classmates to visit the offices of the Entertaining Comics Group at 225 Lafayette Street. (I had been unable to find the company in the telephone book until I thought of looking it up as "Educational Comics"; I am told that this is one of five corporate names under which the firm operates.) As it turned out, there was nothing to be seen except a small anteroom containing a pretty receptionist and a rack of comic books; the editors were in conference and could not be disturbed. (Of course I knew there must be conferences, but this discovery that they actually occur at a particular time and place somehow struck me; I should have liked to know how the editors talked to each other.) In spite of our confinement to the anteroom, however, the children seemed to experience as great a sense of exaltation as if they had found themselves in the actual presence of, say, Gary Cooper.

One of Paul's two friends signed up there and then in the E. C. Fan-Addict Club (Paul had recruited the other one into the club earlier) and each boy bought seven or eight back numbers. When the receptionist obligingly went into the inner offices to see if she could collect a few autographs, the boys by crowding around the door as she opened it managed to catch a glimpse of one of the artists, Johnny Craig, whom Paul recognized from a drawing of him that had appeared in one of the comic books. In response to the boys' excitement, the door was finally opened wide so that for a few seconds they could look at Mr. Craig; he waved at them pleasantly from behind his drawing board and then the door was closed. Before we left, the publisher himself, William Gaines, passed through the anteroom, presumably on his way to the men's room. He too was recognized, shook hands with the boys, and gave them his autograph.

I am sure the children's enthusiasm contained some element of self-parody, or at any rate an effort to live up to the situation—after all, a child is often very uncertain about what is exciting, and how much. It is quite likely that the little sheets of paper bearing the precious autographs have all been misplaced by now. But there is no doubt that the excursion was a great success.

A few weeks later Mr. Gaines testified before a Congressional committee that is investigating the effects of comic books on children and their relation to juvenile delinquency. Mr. Gaines, as one would expect, was opposed to any suggestion that comic books be censored. In his opinion, he said, the only restrictions on the editors of comic books should be the ordinary restrictions of good taste. Senator Kefauver presented for his examination the cover of an issue of *Crime SuspenStories* (drawn by Johnny Craig) which shows a man holding by its long blond hair the severed head of a woman. In the man's other hand is the dripping ax with which he has just carried out the decapitation, and the lower part of the woman's body, with the skirt well up on the plump thighs, appears in the background. It was an illustration for the story I have described in which the murderer is finally trapped on a television program. Did Mr. Gaines think this cover in good taste? Yes, he did—for a horror comic. If the head had been held a little higher, so as to show blood dripping from the severed neck, that would have been bad taste. Mr. Gaines went on to say that he considers himself to be the originator of horror comics and is proud of it. He mentioned also that he is a graduate of the New York University School of Education, qualified to teach in the high schools.

I did not fail to clip the report of Mr. Gaines's testimony from the *Times* and send it to Paul, together with a note in which I said that while I was in some confusion about the comic-book question, at least I was sure I did not see what Mr. Gaines had to be so proud about. But Paul has learned a few things in the course of the running argument about comic books that has gone on between us. He thanked me for sending the clipping and declined to be drawn into a discussion. Such discussions have not proved very fruitful for him in the past.

They have not been very fruitful for me either. I know that I don't like the comics myself and that it makes me uncomfortable to see Paul reading them. But it's hard to explain to Paul why I feel this way, and somewhere along the line it seems to have been established that Paul is always entitled to an explanation: he is a child of our time.

I said once that the gross and continual violence of the comic books was objectionable.

He said: "What's so terrible about things being exciting?"

Well, nothing really; but there are books that are much more exciting, and the comics keep you from reading the books.

But I read books *too*. (He does, especially when there are no comics available.)

Why read the comics at all?

But you said yourself that *Mad* is pretty good. You gotta admit!

Yes, I know I did. But it's not that good. . . . Oh, the comics are just stupid, that's all, and I don't see why you should be wasting so much time with them.

Maybe they're stupid *sometimes*. But look at this one. This one is *really good*. Just read it! Why won't you just *read* it?

Usually I refuse to "just read it," but that puts me at once at a disadvantage. How can I condemn something without knowing what it is? And sometimes, when I do read it, I am forced to grant that maybe this particular story does have a certain minimal distinction, and then I'm lost. Didn't I say myself that *Mad* is pretty good?

I suppose this kind of discussion can be carried on better than I seem able to do, but it's a bad business getting into discussions anyway. If you're against comic books, then you say: no comic books. I understand there are parents who manage to do that. The best—or worst—that has happened to Paul was a limit on the number of comic books he was allowed to have in a week: I think it was three. But that was intolerable; there were special occasions, efforts to borrow against next week, negotiations for revision of the allotment; there was *always* a discussion.

The fundamental difficulty, in a way—the thing that leaves both Paul and me uncertain of our ground—is that the comics obviously do not constitute a serious problem in his life. He is in that Fan-Addict Club, all right, and he likes to make a big show of being interested in E.C. comics above all else that the world has to offer, but he and I both know that while he may be a fan, he is not an addict. His life at school is pretty busy (this has been his first year at school away from home) and comics are not encouraged, though they certainly do find their way in. Paul subscribes to *Mad* and, I think, *Pogo* (also to *Zoo Funnies* and *Atomic Mouse,* but he doesn't read those any more), and he is still inclined to haunt the news-stands when he is in New York; indeed, the first thing he wants to do when he gets off the train is buy a comic. In spite of all obstacles, I suppose he manages to read a hundred in a year, at worst perhaps even a hundred and fifty—that would take maybe seventy-five to a hundred hours. On the other hand, he doesn't see much television or listen much to the radio, and he does read books, draw, paint, play with toads, look at things through a miscroscope, write stories and poems, imitate Jerry Lewis, and in general do everything that one could reasonably want him to do, plus a few extras like skiing and riding. He seems to me a more alert, skillful, and self-possessed child than I or any of my friends were at eleven, if that's any measure.

Moreover, I can't see that his hundred or hundred and fifty comic books are having any very specific effects on him. The bloodiest of ax murders apparently does not disturb his sleep or increase the violence of his own impulses. *Mad* and *Panic* have helped to develop in him a style of humor which may occasionally be wearing but is in general pretty successful; and anyway, Jerry Jewis has had as much to do with this as the comics. Paul's writing is highly melodramatic, but that's only to be expected, and he is more likely to model himself on Erle Stanley Gardner or Wilkie Collins than on *Crime SuspenStories*. Sometimes the melodrama goes over the line into the gruesome, and in that the comic books no doubt play a role; but if there were no comic books, Paul would be reading things like "The Pit and the Pendulum" or *The Narrative of A. Gordon Pym*—which, to be sure, would be better. Now and then he has expressed a desire to be a comic-book artist when he grows up, or a television comedian. So far as I can judge, he has no inclination to accept as real the comic-book conception of human nature which sees everyone as a potential criminal and every criminal as an absolute criminal.[1]

As you see, I really don't have much reason to complain; that's why Paul wins the arguments. But of course I complain anyway. I don't like the comic books—not even *Mad,* whatever I may have unguardedly allowed myself to say—and I would prefer it if Paul did not read them. Like most middle-class parents, I devote a good deal of over-anxious attention to his education, to the "influences" that play on him and the "problems" that arise for him. Almost anything in his life is likely to seem important to me, and I find it hard to accept the idea that there should be one area of his experience, apparently of considerable importance to him, which will have no important consequences. One comic book a week or ten, they *must* have an effect. How can I be expected to believe that it will be a good one?

Testifying in opposition to Mr. Gaines at the Congressional hearing was Dr. Fredric Wertham, a psychiatrist who has specialized in work with prob-lem and delinquent children. Dr. Wertham has been studying and attacking the comic books for a number of years. His position on the question is now presented in full in his recently published book *Seduction of the Innocent.*

The most impressive part of the book is its illustrations: two dozen or so examples of comic-book art displaying the outer limits of that "good taste" which Mr. Gaines suggests might be a sufficient restraint upon the editors. There is a picture of a baseball game in which the ball is a man's head wth one eye dangling from its socket, the bat is a severed leg, the catcher wears a dismembered human torso as chest protector, the baselines are marked with stretched-out intestines, the bases are marked with the lungs, liver, and heart, the rosin-bag is the dead man's stomach, and the umpire dusts off home plate with the scalp. There is a close-up of a hanged man, tongue protruding, eyeballs turned back, the break in the neck clearly drawn. Another scene shows two men being dragged to death face down over a rocky road. "A couple more miles oughta do th' trick!" says the driver of the car. "It better," says his companion. "These ****!! GRAVEL ROADS are tough on tires!" "But you gotta admit," replies the driver, "there's nothing like 'em for ERASING FACES!" And so on. Dr. Wertham could surely have presented many more such examples if he had the space and could have obtained permission to reproduce them. From Paul's collection, I recall with special uneasiness a story in which a rotting corpse returns from the grave; in full color, the hues and contours of decay were something to see.

Among the recurrent motifs of the comic books, Dr. Wertham lists: hanging, flagellation, rape, torture of women, tying up of women, injury to the eye (one of the pictures he reproduces shows a horrifying close-up of a woman's eye about to be pierced by an ice-pick). If a child reads ten comics of this sort a week (a not unusual figure), he may absorb in the course of a year from fifteen hundred to two thousand stories emphasizing these themes (a comic book contains three or four stories). If he takes them with any seriousness at all—and it is difficult to believe that he will not—they surely cannot fail to affect his developing attitudes towards violence, sex, and social restraint.

What the effects will be, and how deep-seated, is not so easy to determine. And here Dr. Wertham is not very helpful. When he tells us of children who have been found hanging, with a comic-book nearby opened to a picture of a hanging, one can readily share his alarm. The fact that these children were probably seriously disturbed before they ever read a comic book, and the fact that fantasies of hanging are in any case common among children, does not relieve one of the feeling that comic books may have provided the immediate stimulus that led to these deaths. Even if there were no children who actually hanged themselves, is it conceivable that comic books which play so directly and so graphically on their deepest anxieties should be without evil consequences? On the other hand, when Dr. Wertham tells us of children who have injured themselves trying to fly because they have read *Superman* or *Captain Marvel,* one becomes skeptical. Children always want to fly and are always likely to try it. The elimination of *Superman* will not eliminate this sort of incident. Like many other children, I made my own attempt to fly after seeing *Peter Pan;* as I recall, I didn't really expect it to work, but I thought: who knows?

In general, Dr. Wertham pursues his argument with a humorless dedication that tends to put all phenomena and all evidence on the same level. Discussing *Superman,* he suggests that it wouldn't take much to change the "S" on that great chest to "S.S." With a straight face he tells us of a little boy who was asked what he wanted to be when he grew up and said, "I want to be a sex maniac!" He objects to advertisements for binoculars in comic books because a city child can have nothing to do with binoculars except to spy on the neighbors. He reports the case of a boy of twelve who had misbehaved with his sister and threatened to break her arm if she told anybody. "This is not the kind of thing that boys used to tell their little sisters," Dr. Wertham informs us. He quotes a sociologist who "analyzed" ten comic-book heroes of the Superman type and found that all of them "may well be designated as psychopathic deviates." As an indication that there are some children "who are influenced in the right direction by thoughtful parents," he tells us of the four-year-old son of one of his associates who was in the hospital with scarlet fever; when the nurses offered him some comic books, the worthy child refused them, "explaining . . . that his father had said they are not good for children." Dr. Wertham will take at face value anything a child tells him, either as evidence of the harmful effects of the comic books ("I think sex all boils down to anxiety," one boy told him; where could he have got such an idea except from the comics?) or as direct support for his own views: he quotes approvingly a letter by a thirteen-year-old boy taking solemn exception to the display of nudity in comic books, and a fourteen-year-old boy's analysis of the economic motives which lead psychiatrists to give their endorsements to comic books. I suspect it would be a dull child indeed who could go to Dr. Wertham's clinic and not discover very quickly that most of his problematical behavior can be explained in terms of the comic books.

The publishers complain with justice that Dr. Wertham makes no distinction between bad comic books and "good" ones. The Dell Publishing Company, for instance, the largest of the publishers, claims to have no objectionable comics on its list, which runs to titles like *Donald Duck* and *The Lone Ranger.* National Comics Publications (*Superman,* etc.), which runs second to Dell, likewise claims to avoid objectionable material and has an "editorial code" which specifically forbids the grosser forms of violence or any undue emphasis on sex. (If anything, this "code" is too puritanical, but mechanically fabricated culture can only be held in check by mechanical restrictions.) Dr. Wertham is largely able to ignore the distinction between "bad" and "good" because most of us find it hard to conceive of what a "good" comic book might be.[2]

Yet in terms of their effect on children, there must be a significant difference between *The Lone Ranger* or *Superman* or *Sergeant Preston of the Yukon* on the one hand and, say, the comic book from which Dr.

Wertham took that picture of a baseball game played with the disconnected parts of a human body. If *The Lone Ranger* and *Superman* are bad, they are bad in a different way and on a different level. They are crude, unimaginative, banal, vulgar, ultimately corrupting. They are also, as Dr. Wertham claims, violent—but always within certain limits. Perhaps the worst thing they do is to meet the juvenile imagination on its crudest level and offer it an immediate and stereotyped satisfaction. That may be bad enough, but very much the same things could be said of much of our radio and television entertainment and many of our mass-circulation magazines. The objection to the more unrestrained horror and crime comics must be a different one. It is even possible that these outrageous productions may be in one sense "better" than *The Lone Ranger* or *Sergeant Preston,* for in their absolute lack of restraint they tend to be somewhat livelier and more imaginative; certainly they are often less boring. But that does not make them any less objectionable as reading matter for children. Quite the contrary, in fact: *Superman* and *Donald Duck* and *The Lone Ranger* are stultifying; *Crime SuspenStories* and *The Vault of Horror* are stimulating.

A few years ago I heard Dr. Wertham debate with Al Capp on the radio. Mr. Capp at that time had introduced into *Li'l Abner* the story of the shmoos, agreeable little animals of 100 per cent utility who would fall down dead in an ecstasy of joy if one merely looked at them hungrily. All the parts of a shmoo's body, except the eyes, were edible, tasting variously like porterhouse steak, butter, turkey, probably even chocolate cake; and the eyes were useful as suspender buttons. Mr. Capp's fantasy was in this —as, I think, in most of his work—mechanical and rather tasteless. But Dr. Wertham was not content to say anything like that. For him, the story of the shmoos was an incitement to sadistic violence comparable to anything else he had discovered in his reading of comics. He was especially disturbed by the use of the shmoo's eyes as suspender buttons, something he took to be merely another repetition of that motif of injury to the eye which is exemplified in his present book by the picture of a woman about to be blinded with an ice-pick. In the violence of Dr. Wertham's discourse on this subject one got a glimpse of his limitations as an investigator of social phenomena.

For the fact is that Dr. Wertham's picture of society and human nature is one that a reader of comic books—at any rate, let us say, a reader of the "good" comic books—might not find entirely unfamiliar. Dr. Wertham's world, like the world of the comic books, is one where the logic of personal interest is inexorable, and *Seduction of the Innocent* is a kind of crime comic book for parents, as its lurid title alone would lead one to expect. There is the same simple conception of motives, the same sense of overhanging doom, the same melodramatic emphasis on pathology, the same direct and immediate relation between cause and effect. If a juvenile criminal is found in possession of comic books, the comic books produced the crime. If a publisher of comic books, alarmed by attacks on the industry, retains a psychiatrist to advise him on suitable content for his publications, it follows *necessarily* that the arrangement is a dishonest one. If a psychiatrist accepts a fee of perhaps $150 a month for carrying out such an assignment (to judge by what Dr. Wertham himself tells us, the fees are not particularly high), that psychiatrist has been "bought"; it is of no consequence to point out how easily a psychiatrist can make $150. It is therefore all right to appeal to the authority of a sociologist who has "analyzed" *Superman* "according to criteria worked out by the psychologist Gordon W. Allport" and has found him to be a "psychopathic deviate," but no authority whatever can be attached to the "bought" psychiatrist who has been professionally engaged in the problem of comic books. If no comic-book publisher has been prosecuted under the laws against contributing to the delinquency of minors, it cannot be because those laws may not be applicable; it must be because "no district attorney, no judge, no complainant, has ever had the courage to make a complaint."

Dr. Wertham also exhibits a moral confusion which, even if it does not correspond exactly to anything in the comic books, one can still hope will not gain a footing among children. Comic-book writers and artists working for the more irresponsible publishers have told Dr. Wertham of receiving instructions to put more violence, more blood, and more sex into their work, and of how reluctantly they have carried out these instructions. Dr. Wertham writes: "Crime-comic-book writers should not be blamed for comic books. They are not free men. They are told what to do and they do it— or else. They often are, I have found, very critical of comics. . . . But of course . . . they have to be afraid of the ruthless economic power of the comic-book industry. In every letter I have received from a writer, stress is laid on requests to keep his identity secret." What can Dr. Wertham mean by that ominous "or else" which explains everything and pardons everything? Will the recalcitrant writer be dragged face down over a rocky road? Surely not. What Dr. Wertham means is simply that the man might lose his job and be forced to find less lucrative employment. This economic motive is a sufficient excuse for the man who thought up that gruesome baseball game—I suppose because he is a "worker." But it is no excuse for a psychiatrist who advises the publishers of *Superman* and sees to it that no dismembered bodies are played with in that comic book. And of course it is no excuse for a publisher—he is "the industry." This monolithic concept of "the industry" is what makes it pointless to discover whether there is any difference between one publisher and another; it was not men who produced that baseball game—it was "the industry." Would Dr. Wertham suggest to the children who come to his clinic that they cannot be held responsible for anything they do so long as they are doing it to make a living? I am sure he would not. But he does quote with the greatest respect the words of that intelligent fourteen-year-old who was able to see so clearly that if a psychiatrist receives a fee, one can obviously not expect that he will continue to act honestly. And it is not too hard to surmise where this young student of society got the idea.

Apparently, also, when you are fighting a "ruthless industry" you are under no obligation to be invariably careful about what you say. Dr. Wertham very properly makes fun of the psychiatric defenders of comic books who consider it a sufficient justification of anything to say that it satisfies a "deep" need of a child. But on his side of the argument he is willing to put forward some equally questionable "deep" analysis of his own, most notably in his discussion of the supposedly equivocal relation between Batman and the young boy Robin; this particular analysis seems to me a piece of utter frivolity. He is also willing to create the impression that all comic books are on the level of the worst of them, and that psychiatrists have endorsed even such horrors as the piercing of women's eyes and the whimsical dismemberment of bodies. (In fact, the function performed by the reputable psychiatrists who have acted as advisers to the publishers has been to suggest what kind of comic books would be "healthy" reading for children. One can disagree with their idea of what is "healthy," as Dr. Wertham does, or one can be troubled, as I am, at the addition of this new element of fabrication to cultural objects already so mechanical; but there is no justification for implying that these psychiatrists have been acting dishonestly or irresponsibly.)

None of this, however, can entirely destroy Dr. Wertham's case. It remains true that there is something questionable in the tendency of psychiatrists to place such stress on the supposed psychological needs of children as to encourage the spread of material which is at best subversive of the same children's literacy, sensitivity, and general cultivation. *Superman* and *The Three Musketeers* may serve the same psychological needs, but it still matters whether a child reads one or the other. We are left also with the underworld of publishing which produced that baseball game, which I don't suppose I shall easily forget, and with Mr. Gaines' notions of good taste, with the children who have hanged themselves, and with the advertisements for switch-blade knives, pellet guns, and breast developers which accompany the sadistic and erotic stimulations of the worst comic books.[3] We are left above all with the fact that for many thousands of children comic books, whether "bad" or "good," represent virtually their only contact with culture. There are children in the schools of our large cities who carry knives and sometimes guns. There are children who reach the last year of high school without ever reading a single book. Even leaving aside the increase in juvenile crime, there seem to be larger numbers of children than ever before who, without going over the line into criminality, live almost entirely in a juvenile underground largely out of touch with the demands of social responsibility, culture, and personal refinement, and who grow up into an unhappy isolation where they are sustained by little else but the routine of the working day, the unceasing clamor of television and the juke boxes, and still, in their adult years, the comic books. This is a very fundamental problem; to blame the comic books, as Dr. Wertham does, is simple-minded. But to say that the comics do not contribute to the situation would be like denying the importance of the children's classics and the great English and European novels in the development of an educated man.

The problem of regulation or even suppression of the comic books, however, is a great deal more difficult than Dr. Wertham imagines. If the publication of comic books were forbidden, surely something on an equally low level would appear to take their place. Children do need some "sinful" world of their own to which they can retreat from the demands of the adult world; as we sweep away one juvenile dung heap, they will move on to another. The point is to see that the dung heap does not swallow them up, and to hope it may be one that will bring forth blossoms. But our power is limited; it is the children who have the initiative: they will choose what they want. In any case, it is not likely that the level of literacy and culture would be significantly raised if the children simply turned their attention more exclusively to television and the love, crime, and movie magazines. Dr. Wertham, to be sure, seems quite ready to carry his fight into these areas as well; ultimately, one suspects, he would like to see our culture entirely hygienic. I cannot agree with this tendency. I myself would not like to live surrounded by the kind of culture Dr. Wertham could thoroughly approve of, and what I would not like for myself I would hardly desire for Paul. The children must take their chances like the rest of us. But when Dr. Wertham is dealing with the worst of the comic books he is on strong ground; some kind of regulation seems necessary—indeed, the more respectable publishers of comic books might reasonably welcome it—and I think one must accept Dr. Wertham's contention that no real problem of "freedom of expression" is involved, except that it may be difficult to frame a law that would not open the way to a wider censorship.

All this has taken me a long way from Paul, who doesn't carry a switch-blade knife and has so far been dissuaded even from subscribing to Charles Atlas' body-building course. Paul only clutches at his chest now and then, says something like "arrgh," and drops dead; and he no longer does that very often. Perhaps even Dr. Wertham would not be greatly alarmed about Paul. But I would not say that Paul is not involved in the problem at all. Even if he "needs" *Superman,* I would prefer that he didn't read it. And what he does read is not even *Superman,* which is too juvenile for him; he reads some of the liveliest, bloodiest, and worst material that the "ruthless" comic-book industry has to offer—he is an E.C. Fan-Addict.

I think my position is that I would be happy if Senator Kefauver and Dr. Wertham could find some way to make it impossible for Paul to get *any* comic books. But I'd rather Paul didn't get the idea that I had anything to do with it.

Notes

1. The assumption that human beings will always follow out the logic of their character to the limit is one of the worst elements in the comic books, and is pretty widespread in them. If a man is a burglar, he will not hesitate to commit murder; and if he is going to commit murder, he is often as likely to think of boiling his victim in oil as of shooting him. In the radio serial "Mark Trail," a program no longer in existence which was based on the comic strip "Mark Trail," men engaged in such illegal activities as hunting beaver out of season would unhesitatingly shoot any game warden who came upon them. (The theme of the program was supposed to be conservation.) This kind of "logic" may seem very proper to children. When Paul was about four or five, a baby-sitter read him the story of Bluebeard. I was a little disturbed when he mentioned this to me the next morning and I tried to probe his reactions.

I said something like: "An exciting story, eh?"

"Oh, yes," said Paul.

"That Bluebeard was quite a nasty character, wasn't he?" I said.

"Oh, I don't know," said Paul.

"What do you mean you don't know? Didn't he try to murder his wife?"

"Well," said Paul, "he *told* her not to look in that closet."

2. I leave out of consideration a few comics like *Pogo Possum* and *Dennis the Menace* which I think could be called good without quotation marks, though it is possible Dr. Wertham might find grounds for objection to these also.

3. An advertisement on the back cover of recent issues of *Panic* and *Weird Science-Fantasy* strikes a loftier note:

BOYS, GIRLS, MEN, WOMEN!
The World Is On Fire
Serve The LORD
and You Can Have These PRIZES!

We will send you the wonderful prizes pictured on this page . . . all WITHOUT ONE PENNY OF COST. Crime, sin, graft, wars are the greatest they have ever been. Our leaders say a reawakening of Christianity is needed to save us. You can do your share by spreading the gospel into every house in your community. Merely show your friends and neighbors inspiring, beautiful Religious Wall Motto plaques. Many buy six or more . . . only 35c . . . sell on sight. . . . Serve the LORD and earn prizes you want.

The Opinions of Little Orphan Annie and Her Friends

By LYLE W. SHANNON

PUBLIC SPECULATION and a number of earlier articles on the effect of reading comic cartoon strips directed the author's attention to the problem of determining the social idealism expressed in such cartoon strips as Little Orphan Annie, Dick Tracy, Li'l Abner, Joe Palooka, Terry and the Pirates and others.[1] It has been said that Joseph Patterson guided his comics as cunningly as his anti-Roosevelt campaigns.[2] "By design or not, they all seem to be in harmony with the editorial views of the cartoonist's bosses, Capt. Joseph Patterson and Col. Robert McCormick."[3] It is the purpose of this article to present a detailed analysis of Little Orphan Annie, a strip, which has, unlike many others, a record of more adult than child readers.[4]

In August of 1944, Harold Gray sentenced Warbucks, his apotheosis of free enterprise, to a lingering death. Warbucks was a victim of the New Deal, a martyr to success in the twilight of rugged individualism. But, in August of 1945, Warbucks was resurrected against the protests of Mollie Slott, manager of the Chicago Tribune-New York News Syndicate. This was not the first time that Miss Slott had disagreed with Gray. "She guides and edits characters without trying to control their destinies. . . ."[5] Harold Gray has been her constant worry. When readers asked Gray why he had brought Warbucks back, they received this explanation: "The situation changed last April . . . Roosevelt died then."[6]

Little Orphan Annie has been accused of projecting a false concept of the OPA; social workers have objected to Annie's neat plan to evade the child-labor law; and the National Lawyers Guild has charged that the conspiracy of a judge, prosecuting attorney, and jury during Annie's trial for murder, "strikes at the roots of American faith in the judicial system."[7]

An earlier analysis of this cartoon strip for the period from January 1, 1946, through December 1947, enabled us to conclude that Little Orphan Annie and her friends support the status quo and in some respects would prefer to go back to the good old days. Orphan Annie approves the symbols which have traditionally represented good in our society and she condemns some of the well-known sins. Actually, she reflects the conservative social idealism of the middle class in our society. The strip emphasizes reliance on "providence," faith, hope and charity—but not too much charity. If people need help, let it be voluntary aid from their neighbors and associates, and not forced by the law. Orphan Annie is for the church, truth,

Reprinted from the *Public Opinion Quarterly*, Vol. 18, 1954, pp. 169-79, by permission of the author and the publisher. (Copyright, 1954, by Princeton University.)

hard work, and pressure when necessary in order to get what one wants. She opposes crooks, politicans, slowness in government, and foreigners who would like U. S. military secrets. An excerpt of conversation from Orphan Annie will give the reader some idea of the type of material which we shall attempt to classify more precisely later in this paper. When Annie, along with Professor and Mrs. Toggles, was held prisoner on a lonely island by Tidnab (backwards it is *Bandit*), a Japanese and a German, conversation dealt with the atom bomb. (January 13, 1946.)

Japanese: But Baron . . . is-sss it certain that Warbucks possesses the great secret?
German: Vell, if he does not possess it he can get it—Ya! and *he vill!*
Japanese: Yess . . . Warbucks is of the decadent soft American race . . . he is a sentimental fool. . . .
German: Ya! Not like der master race . . . for da brat he would do anything.
Japanese: Hee-hee! When Mr. Tidnab sends him one of the child's ears . . . what a surprise!
German: Ho-Ho! Dot iss a master stroke! How Himmler would have enjoyed dot vun!

METHODOLOGY

The Sunday comic section of Little Orphan Annie was collected for the period from April 18, 1948, through July 2, 1950, a period of some 110 weeks. In this analysis we shall define an *appearance* as the inclusion of a comic character in the cartoon section on the particular date referred to. The character may appear in the section one or more times on a particular date but we shall count an appearance on this date as *one* appearance regardless of the number of times that the artist shows the character. Thus, a character could have a maximum *appearance* of 110. The same approach has been used in measuring the relative importance of various goals in life suggested by Annie or her friends. Methods of reaching life's goals have likewise been enumerated in order to obtain some idea of the means most frequently suggested by Annie or her friends. Approved and condemned symbols are treated in the same fashion.

Each week's cartoon section of Little Orphan Annie was carefully read by two persons who answered the following questions in writing as they proceeded from week to week.

1. Which villains are pursuing Annie; which persons are in opposition to her?
2. What is the occupation, overt and covert, of the persons mentioned above?
3. Which opponents are killed or injured, how and by whom?
4. Who are Annie's friends?
5. What is the occupation, overt and covert, of the persons mentioned above?
6. Which friends of Annie are killed or injured, how and by whom?
7. What goals in life are approved by Annie and her friends?
8. What means or methods for reaching these goals are suggested by Annie and her friends?
9. What symbols are approved by Annie and her friends?
10. What symbols are condemned by Annie and her friends?

The author likewise read the entire series of Little Orphan Annie and collated the answer sheets of the other readers, thus arriving at a third set of answers which represented a consensus of three persons' answers to the questions listed above. These answers were further summarized in certain categories and will be presented later in the paper.

OBSERVATION OF THE DATA

But let us see what adventures Annie has had for this period of 110 weeks. It should not be too surprising to most readers to find that thirty-nine weeks were spent in conflict with foreign agents whose identities were thinly disguised and presumably Russian with such names as Ivan Ichalotski, Andrei and Alex. For another period of fifteen weeks Annie had numerous encounters with a gang of young hoodlums working the protection racket. Thus 50 per cent of Annie's time was devoted to conflict with specific persons and to definite causes, namely, preservation of capitalism in the struggle against Communism and aid to small, honest, decent businessmen having difficulty with young hoodlums engaged in the protection racket.

The other 50 per cent of Annie's time was devoted to helping the poor and unfortunate with money that she obtained either from the sale of her store or the vast treasure which she discovered with the aid of a magic whistle. As a result of her find Annie undertook construction of an entire community for orphans to live in and run in their own way. This project collapsed, however, when government men inadvertently toppled a mountain over the entrance to the treasure cave in their effort to retrieve and impound the treasure until the law was determined and taxes were computed.

The setting in which Annie's adventures took place change from time to time, and the people with whom she lived during this period of 110 weeks are listed below in chronological order:

27 weeks—Patrick and Mrs. Puddle, husband and wealthy millionaire who immigrated to U.S. as a boy and became great steel mill owner. (mansion)
29 weeks—Jeb and Flossie Jitters, poor n'er do well farmers, happily married but without children. (farm)
15 weeks—Rocky and Lena, rugged rolling-stone and girl whose wife-beating husband had left her. (barge)
16 weeks—Mr. and Mrs. Dan Drift and eight children, unemployed husband and sick, pregnant mother. (small house)
13 weeks—Daddy Warbucks, wealthy industrialist who uses his fortune to battle enemy countries in his own way. (estate)
10 weeks—on the road.

The above data indicate that Annie has an amazing ability to rub elbows with people in extreme walks of life, but it is rather noticeable that she has never lived with coal-miners, steel-workers, punch-press operators or laboring people in general. Annie's associates tend to be either the great captains of industry or the poor and unfortunate who lack initiative or are unwilling to work for a living. The latter usually benefit from their contact

with the ambitious and always energetic Orphan Annie. Her poor associates are not the great masses of people whose daily labors barely keep them
above the subsistence level, but instead are the poor whose personal disorganization clearly has no connection with the disorganization which exists
in our economic system. Thus we see that Annie is concerned with the
unfortunate, but the causes of their poverty are carefully shown to be of a
nonsocial nature.

Annie's opponents are polished off with a clock-like regularity which
must certainly secure the admiration of both our own F.B.I. and the Pied Piper
of yore. Foreign spies and their radical American counterparts are far and
away the wiliest opponents; their numbers are overwhelming as contrasted
to other opponents, such as hoodlums, young and old. In almost every
instance the criminals in this comic strip are the dirty-collar type of offender;
the white-collar criminal is seldom seen. The etiology of crime as presented
in this strip has all the authoritaranism of Ivan's pronouncements on the
class struggle, and less accuracy. The causes of juvenile delinquency are
likewise stated with the finality of holy writ.

We have already noted the frequent appearance of the needy, but we
may also observe that a large share of Annie's associations are with millionaire leaders of industry. Professional and middle-class people appear
as frequently as the wealthy, but most interesting is the appearance of tough
guys, largely in the employ of Daddy Warbucks, the benevolent millionaire.
Small business men appear often, but not as frequently as people in the
categories already mentioned.

Many of Annie's opponents are removed from the scene by the Pied
Piper-like schemes of Annie's friend Kansk while others disappear under
the magic cloak of Punjab, the giant Oriental. Annie's opponents are not
always removed with such convenience; others are drowned, shot, hanged
or their necks are broken. Some of Annie's adversaries receive rather bad
beatings and others are merely frightened away in one manner or another.
Annie is quite willing to use force when necessary.

Actually, Little Orphan Annie presents a picture of the world about
us as many see it, one in which the hard-working captains of industry
struggle against a vicious and uncompromising underground in order to
protect capitalism, earn large profits and thus assume their social responsibilities, i.e., be charitable to the needy. A much fuller elaboration of this
may be found in Max Weber, *The Protestant Ethic and the Spirit of
Capitalism.*

ANNIE'S LIFE GOALS

Let us consider the goals in life approved by Orphan Annie and her
friends and the methods which are proposed for their attainment. The goals
suggested in the strip do not appear to be greatly divergent from the goals
which people in our own society have. Making a large amount of money
was mentioned as a goal six times; doing charitable works appeared seven

times. We are told on three different occasions that the country should be kept free from the slavery of foreign lands. Being a law-abiding citizen is mentioned with the same frequency. At other times we are told that one should marry the rich and beautiful daughter of the boss, have a happy marriage, have a large happy family and bring up one's children to be good citizens. Money is both a means and an end in Annie's life. The methods suggested for reaching goals place considerable emphasis on the forceful techniques so eloquently condemned in the larger society. The use of force of one kind or another was mentioned nine times; hard work was mentioned five times; and wealth was mentioned on three other occasions. Annie's methodology is that of the Rockefellers, Carnegies and other captains of industry of the nineteenth century. How much of it is the methodology of mid-century government today is debatable. The most forceful speeches of Oliver Warbucks could well have come from the mouths of prominent leaders in either of the two major parties. The greatest divergence from today's ideology would probably occur in Warbucks' emphasis on doing things in his own way rather than appealing to the law. Other means of attaining goals mentioned are: thinking fast, outguessing the other boys, outtalking the other boys, using all the angles, taking chances, accepting poverty, providence, magic, and hope.

Orphans are approved five times and work is approved four times. Other symbols mentioned favorably are: honest merchants, smart business men, little business men, people with "class" whether they be rich or poor, honest-to-goodness people and the Horatio Alger type. In addition, Little Orphan Annie approves of honesty, brains, going straight, decency and fair dealing, curiosity, love of countrymen, Santa Claus, providence, school, peace, prosperity and equal opportunity.

On six occasions Annie vigorously condemns lazy, mean people who are unwilling to work. She refers to them as lazy, whining failures who sneer at success. Stupid radicals who do not know how well off they are, who follow the party line like sheep and who sell out their friends and country, are criticized four different times. On eleven occasions Annie condemns slave labor camps, truth treatments, fake confessions, the five-year plan, those who would make everybody equal to the lowest village idiot, and makes other similar references to conditions in the Soviet Union. Hitler and book-burning are condemned six times. Annie also disapproves of parents who do not take care of their children, the "bleeding hearts" who spend too much time worrying about the troubles of other people, the belief that wealth is a sin, people unwilling to pay the price for peace, and those who become too concerned with great causes and crackpot schemes.

Here again we see that the symbols approved or condemned are very similar to the symbols approved or condemned by the upper and middle classes in the United States. It is difficult to show the extent to which Gray leans in approving one set of symbols and totally ignoring others which are approved by a large section of the population, albeit by persons on a lower socio-economic level than many of the characters in Little Orphan Annie. The experience gained in our analysis of Little Orphan Annie suggests a larger project in which more refined techniques could be used in an analysis and comparison of the content of several comic strips.

Notes

1. The entire issue of the *Journal of Educational Sociology*, December, 1944, was devoted to a discussion of comic cartoon strips. A few but very inadequate articles have appeared on the effect of cartoon strips. The best empirical study to date is Katherine M. Wolf and Marjorie Fiske, "The Children Talk about Comics," in *Communications Research, 1948-49*, edited by Paul F. Lazarsfeld and Frank N. Stanton, Harpers, New York, 1949. Also see Norbert Muhlen, "Comic Books and Other Horrors," *Commentary*, 1948, pp. 80-87; Lauretta Bender and Reginald S. Lourie, "The Effect of Comic Books on the Ideology of Children," *The American Journal of Orthopsychiatry*, July, 1941, pp. 540-550; Fred L. Hadsel, "Propaganda in the Funnies," *Current History*, December 1941, Vol. 1, pp. 365-68.

2. *Time*, December 16, 1946, Vol. 48, pp. 77-78; January 13, 1947, Vol. 49, pp. 59-62.

3. *Newsweek*, August 6, 1945, Vol. 26, pp. 67-68.

4. Marion Harper, Jr. and V. M. Epes Harper, *4500 Newspaper Pictures and Their Significance for Advertisers*, McCann-Erickson Advertising Agency; *The Daily Oklahoman* reports for every 100 adult readers, Little Orphan Annie has 95 child readers as compared with Dick Tracy who has 161 child readers.

5. *Newsweek*, January 7, 1946, Vol. 27, p. 64.

6. *Newsweek*, August 6, 1945, Vol. 26, pp. 67-68.

7. *Newsweek*, July 23, 1945, Vol. 26, p. 76.

How to Read "Li'l Abner" Intelligently

By ARTHUR J. BRODBECK AND DAVID M. WHITE

IT IS A COMMON MISBELIEF that American comic strips consist of little more than "wish-fulfillment," slick attempts to provide 100 million readers with daily dreams of adventure and happiness, power and glory, the stuff of which dreams are made. Of course, "Li'l Abner," like other comic strips and popular art forms, *does* deal with wishes, for what are "wishes" but another name for "problems"? However, those who approach "Li'l Abner" as merely an excursion up the river toward the fulfillment of wishes will take back only a minor part of what it contains. For Al Capp's creation deals with some very painful parts of reality and, while it deals with wishes, it does not invariably fulfill them.

All art teaches us something—usually under conditions where we *think* we are being entertained. The secret of much art is that it tries to keep us off guard, subtly relaxing our shopworn critical senses, by *pretending* to be flattering our egos, while it nevertheless educates us. Art, whether in a play by Congreve or in the newer form utilized by a Harriman, a Walt Kelly or Capp, coaxes our minds to move out of their established conceptual grooves and liberates them for a fresh, creative look at reality. It tries to get us to practice a new kind of response to ourselves and the world. Yet all the while it keeps our fears down low enough by a certain amount of reassurance that things will all work out all right at the end.

"Li'l Abner" tries to do this. It may not always succeed, yet for more than two decades it has been telling millions of Americans each day something about the nature of our contemporary existence—and if we accept the "message" more easily because it is *only* a comic strip, that does not negate the artistic force of the strip.

We often go away from our daily visit to Dogpatch with renewed courage to tackle our own quarrels with urban living, deprivations to our social status and much else of the same kind. For "Li'l Abner" stresses how far from perfect we and our real world are. But through its art it enables us simultaneously to laugh at the discrepancy, to see our human condition humbly but bravely. The ability to laugh at ourselves always has an element of bravery in it.

Although "Li'l Abner" is concerned with a multitude of the facts of American culture, from a Liberace fad to our fantastic needs to "belong" (like the rejected member of the Gourmet Club), there is nonetheless one central problem on which it hinges: *the maternally overprotected boy,* the boy with an overpowering mother.

Published for the first time in this volume.

Some years ago a British anthropologist came over to view Americans as he might view a primitive tribe, reaching conclusions which were not too different from those of Al Capp about the central American problem. Geoffrey Gorer, in *The American People,* tried to compress in a short volume the structure of American culture, the problems and pains in it, as well as the satisfactions and joys it embodied.

His conclusions have been deeply resisted by Americans, since it is seldom pleasant to have to take a good frank look at ourselves. (The Irishman, for instance, who behaves exactly like Barry Fitzgerald is most likely to look upon him as "caricaturing" the Irish personality.) Yet, there are many who believe that Gorer was not too far from the truth about us, although still more remains to be said.

Gorer tried to show first that every "red-blooded" American boy is expected to be "better" than his parents; in fact, he's supposed to "outgrow" them. It is interesting that "Li'l Abner," when it first began in 1934, started off with Mammy and Pappy Yokum as tall as their son. But within a few months a curious thing happened. Mammy and Pappy began to shrink. It was a period of great conflict, perhaps second only to Li'l Abner's marriage. For the parents never remained "shrunken." They rose—first one, then the other—back to full initial stature again, or very near it, continuing to shrink and grow unpredictably. Finally, they were permanently "dwarfed" as they are now.

It was almost as if, as Al Capp made his way toward success (as every red-blooded American boy is supposed to do) he could "afford" to shrink the parent figures, to feel it was artistically right. In order to feel one's own sense of self-esteem, we Americans more frequently than not set, as a condition of that, some signs of tangible success—a better home, more money, wider acclaim, etc.—that "prove" we have risen "above" our parents. Change between generations is built into the structure of our society. And it is sometimes hard on us indeed. "Li'l Abner" symbolizes all of this wish for social mobility by a mere picture.

But this is to oversimplify what the strip tells us. For Mammy Yokum —small, wizened and masculinized as she is—is endowed with magical powers. She is par excellence the overprotecting mother. Or at least, she is her son's childlike conception of such a type of mother, the *way* in which he believes in her and imagines her to be. She can handle the "monsters" four times her size by "wrasslin' Dogpatch style"—which knowledge *she,* not Pappy, imparts to her son. She is the leader of her community, ready to impress by force if necessary her and her offspring's importance upon all others. When not using her "fisks," she divines truth by supernatural incantations and brings about justice in mysterious ways. Her famous duel with "Evil Eye" Fleegle (who symbolizes the "sinfulness" of city life), in which rays of "goodness" emerge from her eyes, casts Mammy Yokum in the heroic mold. Anything you can do she can do better. What woman could compare with her? The feminine Daisy Mae is weak and helpless. The city women are designing, shallow and seething with lust. (Basically, says the strip, all American women, unlike Mammy, are constantly trying to put a man's potency to test, when they are not engaged in distroying his independence and innocence through such devices as "Sadie Hawkins Days.") Beside Mammy, Li'l Abner's father is the merest caricature of a man— and to accentuate this feature, by a twist of Capp's special use of irony, Pappy is called "Lucifer," while Mammy is named "Pansy," which connotes inappropriately a shrinking, timid woman of delicate design and presents a denial of the masculinity and power of American mothers by the magic of words juxtaposed against what is so graphically otherwise.

As a matter of fact, what we are looking at is nothing but the American version of the Oedipus complex set in a mother-dominated family. To identify with Mother is to become a "Pansy"; yet, the source of strength lies nowhere else, since the protection and guidance of the son is all generated from the mother figure. Indeed, "Lucifer" is almost a cry of protest, comically contrived, against a father who is not there in any important sense.

In the early days of the strip, when Li'l Abner put on the wedding suit of his father, as he starts out to the big city and symbolically up the social ladder, the usual Oedipal feeling would demand that the suit be oversized. Instead, it is comically small and shrunken and leads the "sassiety" people into gales of laughter when they see it. Li'l Abner succeeds through his family connections on Mammy's side (her sister) and despite the inadequacy of Pappy's bequest to him.

But the Oedipus complex comes out fully and strongly in the traditional way—feelings of active possessiveness toward the mother and competitive feelings toward the father for her favors—as Abner moves among "high sassiety" people or aristocratic foreigners from the "old country." As Malinowski discovered, just as the uncle occupies the father's position in the Oedipus triangle among the Trobrianders, so the people above oneself in the social scale, as one moves out of the family, bring out one's true, not inverted, Oedipus feelings. One's masculinity is suddenly aroused as one moves up the social ladder. The "high sassiety" women are constantly acting out their sexual feelings toward Li'l Abner, and the "bosses" and the other male aristocrats of mass society vent their spleen on Li'l Abner, and sometimes compete with him for the favors of the women. A count who courts Li'l Abner's "high sassiety" aunt, and is continually frustrated in the courtship by Li'l Abner, finally delivers a blow (below the belt) to him, explaining that it's an "old custom" in his own land (the European land of patriarchy where the real Oedipus complex exists, instead of the American land of matriarchy where boys find their fathers nonentities). Dumpington Van Lump, a cruel, selfish and slobbish "high sassiety" creature, tries to wrench Daisy Mae away from Abner and to destroy all of Dogpatch—the primary ego—in the process.

Gorer has tried to show that it is the overprotective, all-powerful American mother who is the source of the strengths *and* weaknesses of American men. This contributes in subtle ways to their fears of being effeminate—since they identify with and get their source of strength and self-esteem from their mothers more than their fathers. It leads them to feel "guilty" about sex which is not "idealistic" and which doesn't partake of the noble and passive relationship the American male has had with his own Mother. But it makes him strong enough to be sympathetic and kind toward the weak, as Mother was. And it makes him able to endure stress, although sometimes complaining as one would to Mother, and to blind himself to the harm that others can (and sometimes do) cause him, because of the optimistic *weltanschauung* that mother bequeathed him.

Food, Gorer has pointed out, is the way in which American mothers and sons express their love for each other: the mother by filling the child with it and the child by passively allowing himself to be filled. Food themes abound everywhere in "Li'l Abner." At crucial moments in his life, moments of crisis and danger, Abner calls for his "Po'k chops." He is calling for Mother-Love, and attempting to assuage his anxiety by recalling the strength he has gotten from Mother. He is engaged in a magical act—and we laugh at the magic of it, the palpable absurdity—and yet, it is the type of magic that operates in both high and low places in the lives of American men. The "monsters" and "high sassiety" people often deprive Abner of his food indulgences. The world is not like the nursery, even though Abner frequently expects it to be bountiful in the food of Mother-Love.

There is a Henry James complexity to the strip. Each episode, depending on which character's eyes you see it from, takes on a slightly different meaning. In this way, Li'l Abner's personality is seen from a multitude of viewpoints that exist in American society, viewpoints that condemn the results of maternal overprotection and viewpoints which beam on it. In general, however, it is the problems which the overprotected boy causes for other people with whom he must constantly interact that is stressed. The complexity of the strip thus makes us see its most exaggerated consequences. And to repeat, it does this and makes us like it—whereas, when Geoffrey Gorer did it, we were repelled.

At no time does the strip allow us to examine the themes with complete pessimism or complete optimism. Li'l Abner's courage often seems incomprehensible and his pessimistic fears seem ridiculous. True, we always tend to feel that things will really work out for the best in the end, but never without a certain amount of "comic" pain and misery first. (Watch the way Li'l Abner "sweats" unremittingly on his way through life!) Nothing comes easy, except Mammy Yokum's strength and her willingness to use it for her son.

We can never be sure about endings in "Li'l Abner." All the shmoos were killed—and the shmoo was a sort of truncated symbol for the very concept of wish-fulfillment. And Truth, masquerading as the Bald Iggle, must be silenced in the end, even if it has to be by a female impersonator of Mother. And Abner does marry and so loses his boyish innocence.

No, "Li'l Abner" does not run away from reality, even when it is most fantastic; it doesn't hesitate to frustrate wishes, even when it ironically denies reality in ways in which many Americans deny it in their everyday lives. In fact, by *exaggerating* our own defenses against the painful parts of our American reality, especially those concerned with the pain in social mobility, it shows how absurd those defenses really are. It speaks in reverse English directly to our unconscious knowledge about ourselves and the world by overdoing the kind of flattery we treat ourselves to as we march through life. In his ironic "Did I say that?" type of artlessness, which is practiced as a high art, Capp gets us to see what hypocrites we are, and yet doesn't force us to hate ourselves for it. It is done so tactfully, so gently, as though we were all good friends. Indeed, there is a warmness for people in "Li'l Abner," an affectionate streak and a kind one, even though the sentiment is always firmly but fantastically married to realism. The eyes of the strip do not wear rose-colored glasses.

Even the style of the strip is completely American in its fierce "individualism," which it is constantly redefining. It never quite allows us to hate or love any one character or movement wholeheartedly. It sees imperfection everywhere. No one, not even Li'l Abner, is exempt from a savage honesty of appraisal, except again Mammy Yokum—and there have even been times when the strip, perhaps without knowing what it was doing, and getting carried away by its own style, took a fast-running, critical side-glance at her. The style permits of no whole-hearted sentimentalization of any person, idea or organization. Yet, though there is no *unqualified* love and adoration expressed toward anyone, there remains *warmth* and *compassion*. And is this not, truly, an American style of feeling, part of what we have come to mean by "individualism"? The very best we have in American Life? The very heart of the complexity of our spiritual quality existing among our technological and materialistic way of living?

Without plunging into the pros and cons of popular culture and mass society, let us not forget that Shakespeare was once an element in Elizabethan popular culture and that it took dozens of decades before the guardians of high literary standards allowed him to rise in respectability and permitted us to see his permanent worth. Any art, no matter how popular, which has the kind of complexity that is the substance of "Li'l Abner," and has learned to communicate the complexity to us so simply, so matter of factly, is bound to have a certain amount of lastingness, even though it is embodied in a particular time and place, even though it makes concessions to the "mass mind."

Does Capp altogether know what he is saying through his comic strip? Is it perhaps a case, more than with Shakespeare, of one person's unconscious speaking through a large circulation to millions of others? The answer is bound to be moot. Writers often learn an astonishing amount from their critics about what they have written. Since "Li'l Abner" depicts so much of the unconscious and unrecognized forces at work in American life, some of it is bound to well from Capp's own unconscious itself.

But reading "Li'l Abner" is much different than listening to the free associations of a single gifted exponent of American culture. These associations have become, through Capp's artistic talents, tranformed and universalized. He is not talking to an analyst, but he is communicating with twenty to thirty million fellow American citizens. The artistic transformation means that whatever is unique in one's associations must be communicated by more universal symbols or else it can not be shared. The artist need not be ashamed of the sources of his inspirations and we do not need to know what they are in order to judge the quality of his finished product.

It is often said that our "mass society" has produced a greater leisure than ever before for the general run of mankind; but the people have turned away from "the higher art" and "the better culture" to indulge themselves in the tawdry *kitsch* of the mass-media industry. Surely, the gulf between the higher and the popular arts is not quite so wide, and some of the elements of "good" art are present in Capp's comic-strip fantasies.

But may the public have turned away from the "higher art" because it is so full of pessimism and unhappy ending and no resolutions to the problems of life? It may be not so much that people want to be flattered, as they may want some *help* and *guidance* in finding solutions to the problems that confront them. The "higher art," many times, only reiterates the conflicts which they already feel and leaves them at the same, or even worse, impasse than that at which they were already. Hollywood takes over precisely because the most gifted and complex of artists share a grotesque form of pessimism about life's problems and present only masochistic reveries for people.

It is indeed fortunate that there is someone like Capp to fill the gap, until the "higher art" begins to offer solutions again to the woe-begotten state of life it depicts. If anything, Capp should not be criticized too much for the pleasantness of his comic reveries. Instead, like the "higher art," he frequently in his more recent work destroys hope and courage and becomes more devoid of solutions to the American dilemmas. One might wish him to be more optimistic, without losing his complexity. There never was a time when Americans, Mass or Elite, needed it more, if there are some realistic grounds on which it can be maintained.

FURTHER READING

Auster, Donald. "A Content Analysis of Little Orphan Annie," *Social Problems,* Vol. 2, 1954, pp. 26-33.

Bakwin, Ruth M. "The Comics," *Journal of Pediatrics,* Vol. 42, 1953, pp. 633-35.

Bender, L., and Lourie, R. S. "The Effects of Comic Books on the Ideology of Children," *American Journal of Orthopsychiatry,* Vol. 11, 1941, pp. 540-50.

Brown, Slater. "The Coming of Superman," *New Republic,* Vol. 103, 1940, p. 301.

Cummings, E. E. "Introduction," in George Herriman's *Krazy Kat,* unpaged [pp. 3, 5, 8-10]. New York: Holt, 1946.

Gruenberg, Sidonie M. "The Comics as a Social Force," *Journal of Educational Sociology,* Vol. 18, 1944, pp. 204-13.

Haggard, E. A. "A Projective Technique Using Comic Book Characters," *Character and Personality,* Vol. 10, 1942, pp. 289-95.

Hill, G. E. "Children's Interest in Comic Strips," *Educational Trends,* Vol. 1, 1939, March-April; also *Journal of Educational Research,* Vol. 34, 1940, pp. 30-36.

Kolaja, J. "American Magazine Cartoons and Social Control," *Journalism Quarterly,* Vol. 30, 1953, pp. 71-74

Kris, E. "Ego Development of the Comics," *International Journal of Psychoanalysis,* Vol. 19, 1938, pp. 1-10.

Lynes, Russell. "A Man Named Steinberg," *Harper's,* Vol. 209, August, 1954, pp. 45-52.

Muhlen, Norbert. "Comic Books and Other Horrors," *Commentary,* Vol. 7, 1949, pp. 80-88.

Murrell, W. *A History of American Graphic Humor.* New York: Macmillan, 1933.

Politzer, Heinz. "From Little Nemo to Li'l Abner," *Commentary,* Vol. 8, 1949, pp. 346-55.

Schwartz, Delmore. "Masterpieces as Cartoons," *Partisan Review,* Vol. 19, July-August, 1952.

Spiegelman, M.; Terwilliger, C.; and Fearing, F. "The Content of Comics: Goals and Means to Goals of Comic Strip Characters," *Journal of Social Psychology,* Vol. 37, 1953, pp. 189-203.

Strang, R. "Why Children Read Comics," *Elementary Schools Journal,* Vol. 43, 1942-43, pp. 336-42.

Thorndike, Robert L. "Words and the Comics," *Journal of Experimental Education,* 1941, pp. 110-13

Thrasher, Frederick M. "The Comics and Delinquency: Cause or Scapegoat," *Journal of Educational Sociology,* Vol. 23, 1949, pp. 195-205.

Warshow, Robert. "Krazy Kat," *Partisan Review,* Vol. 13, November-December, 1946.

Waugh, Coulton. *The Comics.* New York: Macmillan, 1947.

Wertham, Frederic. *Seduction of the Innocent.* New York: Rinehart, 1954.

Wolf, Katherine, and Fiske, Marjorie. "The Children Talk About Comics," *Communications Research,* 1948-49. New York: Harper, 1949, pp. 3-50.

MAGAZINES

If England "invented" the magazine, and Scotland the review, the United States stands indisputably as the greatest mass consumer of magazines of all types. The growth of this medium from Ben Franklin's attempt in 1741 to create a successful magazine until today has been gigantic. By mid-twentieth century there were nearly 7,000 magazines of every type (from avant-garde literary quarterlies to the monthly happenings of the Fraternal Order of Bisons). Approximately three and a half billion copies are distributed each year. More than forty magazines have achieved individual circulations of a million or more. With these vast circulations came rich prizes: twenty-eight magazines in 1952 carried 80 per cent of the 600 million dollars of advertising available to the entire field. One organization alone, Time, Inc., did a $156 million gross business that year.

Despite innumerable market surveys, which may tell the publishers of the magazines a good deal about the number of bathrooms in the median subscriber's home, we know relatively little about the way in which people read magazines or what they get from their reading. With all of the market research, statistical speculations and crystal ball gazing, the formula of the general circulation magazines is to give their readers that "something" which will entertain (and sometimes enlighten) them. At times it may appear that the often-described vicious circle is in operation, for the magazines will go to any length to repeat the pattern that has proved successful.

Thus, Drs. Johns-Heine and Gerth show that the magazine world offers only a limited range of models and themes at any given time. In the period immediately after World War I to the eve of World War II there was a decline of the classic "success" themes. This was paralleled by a rise in the idolization of the little man as the favored hero and the small town as the favored locale.

The Berelson-Salter study points out that our mass magazine fiction, although designed purely for entertainment and divertissement, contains a subtle discrimination against minorities and foreigners. Americans with names like Drew Bradford play the leading roles in most of the stories; they get more of the world's materials and occupy the superordinate roles in most of the human relationships.

Values in Mass Periodical Fiction, 1921-1940

By PATRICKE JOHNS-HEINE AND HANS H. GERTH

ANALYSIS of the content of mass periodical fiction rests not only on the assumption that magazines direct appeals to specialized audiences, but also that on the basis of those appeals we can infer certain social-psychological characteristics about the audience. The magazines in the following study were chosen precisely because each, in some measure, specialized its appeal and because each in a sense selected thematically a given aspect of the national inheritance for intensive treatment.

Psychologically, the gratification of the reader is obtained by identification with a hero, in his vicissitudes as well as in his final rewards. Since the reader identifies himself with a particular hero model, the fictional hero, together with his status, his qualities, and his achievements, becomes an important vehicle of social values. Heroes and heroines become the carriers of specific American values and traditions.

It is not our task to explore here that complex interaction between reader, writer, and publisher which results in the reader getting what he wants and wanting what he gets. Instead we shall focus on the typical clustering of stories about a few model themes: a clustering which suggests that the themes, once stabilized, express national traditions and values tacitly supported by all.[1]

Details of these traditions, however, become modified. There are critical cultural periods in which even the most enduring values do not remain unchallenged. What happens during these periods? Are the values forsaken or are they retained? If they are retained how are they reconciled with objective reality? Within the time span of our study the crisis of the thirties, with its depression and threat of war, may be contrasted with the golden age of the twenties. How the impact of these events affected the value system is reflected in periodical fiction published between 1921 and 1940. We shall discuss some of these effects below.

METHOD OF THE ANALYSIS

For purposes of content analysis a schedule was drawn up which included the following items: occupation, age, and personal characteristics of hero and heroine; setting of the story; and plot summary. We asked: Does the occupation of the hero correspond to that of those who read about him? What regions and locales become associated with specific hero types and to what extent do these become stereotyped? Is the hero successful or unsuccessful, and for what reasons? What moral qualities, if these are

---

Reprinted from *The Public Opinion Quarterly*, Vol. 13 (1949), pp. 105-113, by permission of the authors and the publisher. (Copyright, 1949, by Princeton University Press.)

embodied in the plot, are positively or negatively evaluated? What is the denouement, since "the happy end" reveals the final evaluation and reward of the hero?

Our sample of magazines was chosen so as to include representatives of various types which enjoyed large circulation. From the magazines of so-called general circulation we chose the *Saturday Evening Post,* from the household and women's group the *Ladies' Home Journal,* from the farm group the *Country Gentleman,* from the "class" magazines the *Atlantic,* and from magazines close to the pulp group, *True Story.* Maximum circulation for the magazines included was first reached in the period from 1928 to 1930, and after depression setbacks peak circulations were attained again in the years from 1937 to 1940.[2] Proportionate regional circulation of the magazines remained relatively stable, as did circulation in cities of different sizes.[3]

A random sample was taken of the issues from 1921 through 1940. The sample included four issues per year of each monthly and five issues per year of the weekly (the *Post*). From each issue two stories were randomly selected. The total stories by magazine were: *Atlantic,* 153; *Country Gentleman,* 151; *Ladies' Home Journal,* 160; *Saturday Evening Post,* 200; and *True Story,* 64.[4]

THE HEROES

Let us turn first to the occupational characteristic of the hero models. In Table 1 occupational data are summarized and we see that the general shift was away from the business model to the professional. This shift is the more impressive when the business category is broken down in such a way as to indicate that it is the business executive who becomes passé. Even *Country Gentleman,* with its increase from 18 per cent to 35 per cent for the whole business group (and a corresponding decrease in the farmer as hero model), follows the general trend of decreasing representation of the business executive. If we glance at the agricultural group of heroes we see first its notable decrease in the farm journal, paralleling a redirection of appeal to the small town as opposed to the strictly rural populace. In the

Table 1—Occupational Distribution of Heroes by Magazine and by Periods: (1) 1921-30, (2) 1931-40

Occupation	Ladies' Home Journal (1)	(2)	True Story (1)	(2)	Atlantic (1)	(2)	Saturday Evening Post (1)	(2)	Country Gentleman (1)	(2)
Business-Industry	32%	25%	42%	38%	23%	16%	38%	32%	18%	35%
Professional	24	22	42	40	24	21	18	29	11	15
Agricultural	5	6	—	6	10	19	9	9	35	18
Public Service	3	4	17	2	6	4	6	9	6	8
None Specified	25	32	—	6	24	29	19	10	14	15
All Other	12	10	—	8	13	10	9	10	16	9
Total number of heroes	76	77	12	50	70	70	99	97	71	79

Atlantic the increase in agricultural heroes is unique and is related to certain thematic emphases of this journal which will be mentioned below.

In general, both heroes and heroines tend to be younger than the reading audience and this youthfulness is, in most cases, even more emphasized in the second decade of our sample. Thus, *Post* heroes in their twenties increase from a representation of 38 per cent to 46 per cent by the second period; and a slight increase (36 per cent to 38 per cent) is found for heroes in their thirties.[5] These differentials are even more striking in the case of heroines and women readers, despite the fact that women readers generally tend to be younger than men readers. The audience which comes closest to corresponding to the age of the heroine it reads about is that of *True Story* (where it has been estimated that 41 per cent of the adult women readers are in the eighteen to twenty-four age group).[6] In *Ladies Home Journal,* where approximately 60 per cent of the heroines are in their twenties in both periods of our sample, an estimated 45 per cent of the women readers are thirty-five or over. Heroes and heroines in the *Atlantic* are considerably older; so in all probability are the readers of the *Atlantic.*[7]

THE SETTINGS

The most distinctive feature of the settings in which the stories occur is their nondescript character. By far the largest number of stories take place in an undesignated locale and in an unspecified region of the U.S. The metropolis is certainly the most frequently named locale, and is the favorite of the *Post.* The small town is least frequently given a name. The category "town" is the vaguest, being apparently an attempt to reach the "average American town," and it is found most often in the *Ladies' Home Journal.*

Hero models and themes tend in many instances to bear close relation to locale. A hero representing small town virtues is, of course, most frequently placed in the small town, just as the titan must be placed in the metropolis. Thus, when the hero model of the *Country Gentleman* changes, this development is paralleled by the decline of the farm locale to less than half its former representation. The slight shifts to rural and town locales in the *Post* also relate to modified themes.

THEMES IN THE WOMEN'S MAGAZINES

It is assumed that the most frequently appearing themes in each magazine reflect the salient type of appeal. Thus, for both the women's journals in our group and for both sample periods, the basic appeal is that of love. It appears as the major reward, the love relation presumably being the best and most worthy thing in life. On the one hand, this is to be understood in terms of the fact that the status of the housewife or the prospective housewife, her sense of fulfillment, and her personal happiness are directly bound together with the person she has chosen to love. On the other hand, it is a way of magnifying the importance of the woman's role. Exemplary of the latter is this: the classic success story is not an important theme in these journals. Successful marriage is, it is true, a constantly reiterated theme, but it is important to differentiate this from, say, a typical success story involving ascent through marriage (the Cinderella theme), stories which we found in our sample but only in insignificant proportions. Successful marriage, in this sense, is more commonly the sensible than the spectacular marriage. Practically, these stories admonish the woman to marry on the grounds of specific intrinsic qualities in her mate which she presumably can bring out by influence or by inspiration. Hence the role of the woman in creating the successful marriage or the happy home is given enormous

Table 2—Distribution of Locales by Magazine and by Periods:
  (1) 1921-30, (2) 1931-40

Locale	Ladies' Home Journal		True Story		Atlantic		Saturday Evening Post		Country Gentleman	
	(1)	(2)	(1)	(2)	(1)	(2)	(1)	(2)	(1)	(2)
Farm	4%	11%	8%	2%	9%	18%	6%	10%	46%	20%
Country	11	10	—	8	15	12	12	5	10	15
Small town	9	13	25	29	16	18	17	14	11	22
Town	56	42	25	44	12	26	26	31	16	16
Metropolis	9	16	42	10	16	8	30	31	3	9
Suburb	2	4	—	4	—	—	2	—	1	—
Indeterminate*	9	4	—	4	32	19	7	9	13	18
Total number of locales	80	79	12	52	75	74	100	100	71	80

* Includes settings on boats, on planes, in camps, in caves, and other.

importance and, presumably, it is the qualities which the woman brings to the relationship that are decisive.

One may impute that the function of such themes is the systematic magnification of the woman's traditional role precisely in contrast to her publicly changing role. Acclaim of the model lady, wife, and mother remains dominant in the face of current competing claims. It is significant in this regard to compare treatments of the "career woman." Unlike stories in the *Post,* for example, the heroine is never punished in the sense that she loses all she has struggled to achieve; but she is pictured as bearing extraordinary burdens. The heroine models may be eminently successful but they must suffer for that success, and of course they suffer in that sphere in which the housewife and mother is presumably most secure, namely, in love and affectional relationships. The partner and the loved one constitute the haven to which the heroine returns, and by the security of love is implied also a rootedness and a sense of belonging. Nostalgic love themes, in which "home" is where the loved one is, are common, and the sense of belonging ordinarily associated with home may be expressed simply as longing for love.

In the *Ladies' Home Journal* these models are defended and buttressed by simple middle-class virtues (such as loyalty, fidelity, unpretentiousness) and love is commonly the reward of virtue. In *True Story,* contravention of the moral code results in extraordinary suffering. In the one the positive symbols of safety and security predominate; in the other, negative and harshly punitive symbols. It is the difference between threatened loss of social position ("what people will think"), of such vast symbolic import for the middle-class reader, and threatened physical injury where not status but physical and moral integrity are imperiled. Symbolic controls operate at different levels, but the values remain the same.

CHANGING SUCCESS STORIES IN THE *Post*

Our analysis points to certain striking changes in hero models and themes. Let us take the success story, for example, and for our purposes here we may regard the *Post* as the vehicle of typical American success themes. We are still accustomed to think of the success story as a major career-achievement, but the transformations of success themes within the period studied resulted in a very different emphasis.

We differentiated success themes in terms of the reward. In the first period (1920's) the reward symbol is typically that of social ascent and its basis is a specific achievement. By the thirties, however, the predominant reward symbol is what we describe as recognition or deference from others. Its characteristic basis is moral virtue which is rewarded by love and esteem from others, sometimes even by a tangible reward; but never does it result in upward mobility marked by "wealth," "success," "status." The proportion of classic success themes does not change significantly in the total number of themes, but within the broadened success category it becomes secondary. For the *Post,* proportions are as follows:

Saurday Evening Post Success Themes

Reward	1921-30	1931-40
Ascent	17%	13%
via achievement	14	10
via marriage	3	1
via luck	—	2
Recognition	6	21

This change also represents a shift in emphasis away from the "titan" success theme, in which the hero is exalted for his own genius over and above other group values, to the "little man" success theme, in which the reward symbol is due the hero as the bearer of specific group virtues. The "local boy makes good" type is, of course, the other favorite. This theme, too, is contained in ascent stories and predominates in the first period. But again, unlike the little man stories in which the role and the virtues accompanying it are glorified, the hero transcends one or another role to attain greater things.

Just as the titan was invariably represented by the businessman in the first decade, so the favored little man models were the sailor or the farmer. Only by the second sample period do we even find a different model emerging: namely, the industrial worker. Salesmen, clerks, and "cops" are the subsidiary preferred types during this decade. In addition, the business-man who was the bearer of success values during the twenties is eclipsed by diverse professionals in the thirties (especially writers and reporters, engineers and professional entertainers), a fact which probably mirrors the objective social possibilities of ascent.

As for locale, there is no mistaking that the farm and with it the small town is exalted as representative of a whole way of life. It is significant that the typical conflict within the story is between the essential human goodness of small-town types as opposed to a metropolitan moneyed élite: unpretentiousness against pretentiousness, and littleness versus power. In short, those values lacking in the metropolis are the ones capitalized upon in the depiction of small-town or farm life, and the latter become personifications of good while the city remains the vessel of evil. We may assume that this is gratifying not only to those who live in towns and villages, but also to those persons who have recently migrated from farm or town to city and who have sentimental associations which find fulfillment here.

We may well reflect upon the passing of the titan, for he clearly belongs to another scene and another time. He is no longer the embodiment of mass longing and mass aspiration, but seems to have left the stage in favor of a more prosaic and traditional model representing the safe and the familiar. It is not simply that passing time and diminishing opportunity have made completely unreal the classic Dreiserian hero who used to have his counterpart in mass periodical fiction. Rather it is an attempt to perpetuate certain roots of American life, or the myth of them; and it is done by bringing the scope of fantasy in mass fiction into greater harmony with readers made constantly aware of the "closing of the frontiers." Hence it may be regarded as an attempt to give a compensating sense of independence and individual significance when power and prestige seem to have become firmly entrenched. The little man is, then, the familiar standard-bearer of democratic values. It is, perhaps, not accidental that this transformation began in the depression years, even if it did not end there. In those years traditional virtues were invoked with weary optimism; the "good heart" was supposed to replace the "big money."

THE SHIFT OF THE *Country Gentleman*

Just as new types of fictional appeals imply changing lines of gratification in a public which has not itself ostensibly changed in composition, so also content analysis reflects quite swiftly attempts at real circulation change. The *Country Gentleman* may be cited in this instance. We find between our sample periods a major shift in hero models and an increasing differentiation of hero types. And we find a corresponding shift in locale: a shift from farm to small town or village. It seems in fact to indicate that a new public is being deliberately sought in small towns and villages.[8]

The theme shift is clear. Beyond the specific values of farm work and farm life lie values which are transposed from the milieu and are expressed

Table 3—Distribution of Major Themes by Magazine and by Periods:
(1) 1921-30, (2) 1931-40*

Theme	Ladies' Home Journal		True Story		Atlantic		Saturday Evening Post		Country Gentleman	
	(1)	(2)	(1)	(2)	(1)	(2)	(1)	(2)	(1)	(2)
Success	10%	12%	14%	7%	5%	12%	24%	33%	13%	21%
Nostalgia	4	2	—	—	6	2	4	2	18	17
Virtue	17	17	29	24	17	16	16	20	30	32
Love	42	48	48	44	26	21	36	25	17	21
Religion	1	—	—	—	17	1	—	—	2	—
Crime	2	2	10	11	—	2	9	7	7	10
Personal Portrayals	6	3	5	4	8	21	4	1	—	—
All Other	18	15	—	8	20	25	7	11	12	9
Total number of themes	96	89	21	72	83	81	132	135	83	99

* Stories were classified in terms of major content, hence interlocking themes are classified as two distinct themes whenever a tangible reward, or rewards, was the outcome. The typical linkages are between love and success, love and virtue, or virtue and success.

† Includes adventure, animal, and "social issue" themes.

as national values. The carriers of these values were at first farmers; later they became small-town types of various occupations. It seems apparent that in the first period the *Country Gentleman* was still crusading against the shift away from the farm, and this accounts for the dominance of the nostalgic theme, a theme which consisted of the sentimentalization of the parental farm home and its associated values. By the second sample period that shift had already been accepted and the major concern remained the propagation of values which were at first transmitted exclusively as a part of rural living. But with the overwhelming growth of cities and in view of the great prestige of the metropolis, the policy of the magazine changed to focus upon the small town which, along with the farm, was to remain the "soul" of American life. We find the crucial shift expressed in decreased themes involving nostalgic return to the farm (there was a minor recrudescence of such themes during the depression) and the replacement of those themes by success stories which glorify the little man and his virtues.

TRENDS IN THE *Atlantic*

For the *Atlantic* perhaps the most apparent and consistent relationship exists between theme and age of readers. We find at one extreme several stories which are focused entirely upon the heroes' experience of growing old, anticipation of death, the experience of love late in life, and those also which point to the superior wisdom of older people. Similarly, the emphasis in the first period on religious themes seems to have been destined for older readers.

All of these associations are possible, but, of course, over-simplified. In relation to religious themes, for example, it may be mentioned that the 1920's were, after all, years in which general religious discussion dominated part of the intellectual scene. It was, presumably, a period during which basic religious values in America were reconsidered and religion became liberalized. It is in part this general discussion that we find reflected in *Atlantic* fiction themes.[9]

It would appear that by the second period interests were secularized, but again the treatment of such issues assumed a special character for this journal. Social issues are only rarely treated as such. Instead they are contained in the hero model and are translated into psychological portrayals of character types. Their emergence perhaps reflects a current "psychological" vogue, and its end seems to be the depiction of the unique and the eccentric (e.g., th peculiarities of "the monk," "the spinster") as well as what is simply different from one's own social position (the domestic servant or the workingman).

For the *Atlantic,* the professional is *the* hero model here in quite the same sense as the farmer is for the Country Gentleman, and when we find major shifts in models or themes we may ask what changes in the situation of the professional stratum may account for such shifts. Thus, farm locales and farmer heroes showed a unique rise in this journal in the second sample period. Farm life is depicted as intrinsic to American life. Here, particularly, the depiction is replete with historic associations and becomes the romantic vestige of the American frontier. But it may also be regarded as an appropriate refuge in the sense in which romanticization of the rural has always been dominant in the intellectual stream of America. The aspiration of the middle-class professional, who by that time was decisively cut off from his or his parents' place of origin, has not uncommonly been that of retiring to a farm or semi-rural milieu.

REFLECTIONS OF SOCIAL TRENDS

As our sample indicates, post-World War I expansiveness and optimism, long identified as archetypical of national characteristics, gave way in the thirties to more traditionalist values, presumably under the impact of economic depression on the one hand, and political pessimism on the other. These values were reflected by emphasis on the group-defined role and conventional virtues. Heroes and heroines, rather than transcending localized and conventional roles, became vehicles of long-established values—the good wife and mother of the women's journals and the little man who wins out for the *Country Gentleman* and the *Post.* Hence, too, the titan principle and with it the local-boy-makes-good theme, both of which point to self-realization over and above conventional group definitions, are passé. The decline and surpassing of these classic success themes is paralleled by a rise in the idolization of the little man as the favored hero and the small town as the favored locale. The fictional emphasis changes from the struggle for power of a self-made élite to these traditional symbols of democracy.

One may expect that such changes as these will be reflected in other mass entertainment media. The striking features of any given analysis of content lie less in any isolated significance they may have for the medium under study than in the fact that the models are constantly reiterated and reappear in other media. They become ubiquitous mass symbols; themes from popular periodical fiction are often transferred to movies and radio, and all popular culture with its quickly standardized and repetitive formulae assumes the aspect of mass advertisement.[10] It suggests that here as elsewhere in such a culture, mass media offer only a limited range of models and themes at any one time.

Notes

1. The authors are indebted to the Graduate School of the University of Wisconsin for the funds which made this study possible. It was completed in 1942.

2. See N. W. Ayer and Sons, *Directory of Newspapers and Periodicals,* Philadelphia.

3. The proportions were determined from data published by Standard Rate and Data Service, Chicago.

4. The *True Story* sample remains incomplete due to the difficulty of obtaining back issues. Sample adjustments were necessary for both *Country Gentleman* and *Atlantic* in the period 1921-24.

5. In a survey conducted by D. Starch for Macfadden Publications, the average age of adult male readers of the *Post* was computed as 36.8. From Basic Data Sheet E-7, Men-Women, *Magazine Effectiveness Report,* Division of Marketing and Research, Macfadden Publications, Inc., 1937.

6. *Ibid.*

7. We have no direct supporting data; but see Paul F. Lazarsfeld and R. Wyant, "Magazines in 90 Cities," *Public Opinion Quarterly,* Vol. 1, No. 4 (1937). The circulation of the *Atlantic* was found to be directly related to per cent of the population over forty-five in the cities examined.

8. Although not a totally new one, since many farmers retire to small villages and towns.

9. See H. Hart's "Changing Social Attitudes and Interests," in *Recent Social Trends* (Chap. 8), New York: McGraw-Hill, 1933. The Fundamentalist agitation brought a rise in the number of articles on religion from 1925-28; after this period there was a general decline in the number of such articles. The later interest is in spiritualism and psychical research, a trend likewise reflected in the *Atlantic.*

10. Cf. James T. Farrell, "The Fate of Writing in America," in *Literature and Morality,* New York: Vanguard, 1946.

Majority and Minority Americans:
An Analysis of Magazine Fiction

By BERNARD BERELSON AND PATRICIA J. SALTER

PREJUDICE against minority peoples in this country is widespread. It embraces a large number of groups: American Negroes and Jews are disapproved; Mexicans, Italian-Americans, Japanese-Americans are rejected as "out-group"; and even Irish-Americans are sometimes not accepted as "good Americans." Common to all these prejudices against minorities is the other side of the coin—prejudice in favor of the majority and approval of the "100 per cent Americans."

Discrimination based upon these prejudices is expressed in many ways. Negroes are often "the last to be hired and the first to be fired"; people of "pure American stock"—white, Protestant, Anglo-Saxons—often have the best chance at better jobs. The Epsteins and the Goldbergs are often barred from hotels which are glad to welcome the Smiths and the Joneses. The sons of South European or Oriental parents are less apt to be put up for Congress than their "100 per cent American" neighbors.

The fight against prejudice and discrimination is most likely to take place in areas where they are the most overt and intentional. But it is not only these overt and intentional areas of attack upon minority groups and support of "Americans" which serve as sources of such discrimination. Prejudice also finds its way into innocuous areas where people are exposed to them without consciousness that an ethnic problem is being raised at all.

This is a study of the latter kind of exposure to anti-minority and pro-majority discrimination: the treatment of majority and minority groups in the popular fiction appearing in mass magazines. How do people meet the various ethnic and religious groups of this country in this channel of communication, which reaches a large number of people in their relaxed, leisure hours? Are some groups presented as more important or more personable or wealthier than others? Do some groups in these stories get more of society's rewards, such as love or high position? What picture is presented of the relationships between different ethnic groups? In short, what kinds of people appear in typical magazine short stories in terms of their racial, religious, and national backgrounds, and how are they treated?

THE SAMPLE AND THE STORIES

The Sample: The object of analysis was a sample of 198 short stories

Reprinted from *Public Opinion Quarterly*, Vol. 10 (1946), pp. 168-97, by permission of the authors and the publisher. (Copyright, 1946, by Princeton University Press.)

published in eight of the country's most widely read magazines in 1937 and 1943: The magazines included in the study are the following:[2]

General Weeklies:	*Saturday Evening Post*
	Collier's
General Monthlies:	*American*
	Cosmopolitan
Women's:	*Woman's Home Companion*
	Ladies' Home Journal
Confessionals:	*True Story*
	True Confessions

The years 1937 and 1943 were selected in order to investigate the effect of World War II upon the fictional treatment of various groups. The standard analysis was done for a total of 185 stories—those with a United States locale or a "transferred" U. S. locale (i.e., the fifteen or so stories laid outside the United States but containing a predominantly American cast of characters). A special analysis was done for the thirteen stories in the sample which were laid in foreign countries and peopled with predominantly foreign characters. For each magazine for each year, four issues were selected at regular intervals (in order to avoid the possible bias of seasons or events), and the first, third, and fifth short stories were analyzed in each of the selected issues (in order to avoid the possible bias of placement in the magazine).[3] Serials and "short short stories" were omitted altogether.

The Stories: The majority of the analyzed stories were of the romantic love, boy-meets-girl type. Others dealt with family or domestic or marital problems, and there were some adventure and mystery stories. In the 1943 sample, several war-related stories appeared, but their plots were usually the standard romantic models with military personnel or settings appended, rather than treatments of wartime or military problems. On the whole, the stories were light-hearted in tone and were designed primarily if not solely for purposes of entertainment. They were chosen exclusively as a representative sample of the short stories appearing in such popular magazines and *not* with reference to their treatment of ethnic problems. Some representative plots:

A wealthy young society girl becomes infatuated with a handsome married man, although she is loved by a fine young man of her own set. She recognizes her foolishness when the wife appears, and returns to her young man.

A man who thinks he wants complete freedom discovers true happiness with the woman he loves and a place of his own.

A cab driver protects a beautiful woman who faces danger and death. Through his heroism he gets rid of her pursuers and wins her for himself.

The only son of an Irish family becomes involved in a murder as an accomplice. Through his mother's faith and the strong support of the family, he wins a new chance.

A shallow, dissipating girl who has led a glamorous New York life finds comfort, love, and peace of mind with a quiet Western rancher who sees what she is really like, underneath.

Almost all the stories (about 90 per cent) were laid in the contemporary world. Their locale strongly favors the East Coast, especially New York City, and discriminates against the South.[4]

THE METHOD

The Analysis Procedure: The central problem of the study was to investigate the existence and nature of differential treatment accorded various ethnic groups in magazine fiction. The procedures and techniques of the analysis can be described in the following stages, listed here in roughly chronological order.

1. On the basis of general knowledge of such stories, supplemented by the focused reading of a few of them, a set of hypotheses dealing with the problem at hand was formulated in terms of two major groups—the "Anglo-Saxons" and the "foreigners"—with the understanding that the actual analysis would establish empirically the ethnic composition of these two groups in the stories. The hypotheses dealt with the frequency of appearance of various groups, their characteristics, cultural contributions, relative status positions, and social interaction. In addition, hypotheses on time and locale differences were also formulated. From time to time during the study, some of the hypotheses were modified and a few were added.[5]

2. The conversion of the hypotheses into analytic operations took two forms, based upon two different units of analysis. The first unit was a character in the story and the second was the story as a whole.

The first called for the coding of eight characteristics for each of the speaking characters (or groups) in the story.[6] The eight characteristics for which data were secured whenever possible were the following: *Role* in the story (major, submajor, minor; hero, heroine, villain); *Sex; Status position* (occupation, economic status, educational level, "class"); *Social origin* (nationality, race, religion); *Personality traits; Goals or values* (the ends the characters were trying to realize, such as economic advancement, romantic love, settled marriage state, social position, etc.); *Plus-minus position* (the approval or disapproval of the character: sympathy-hostility, liking-disliking, desirability-undesirability, pleasantness-unpleasantness, etc.); *Summary identification* by ethnic groups (using both explicit and implicit indicators).

The analysts not only checked each of these categories for each speaking character, whenever applicable, but also documented their entry with a brief summary of or quotation from the appropriate story content, which were used to standardize the indices used by the analysts for certain categories.

The second form of analysis dealt with the story as a whole. The hypotheses not covered directly by the character analysis—e.g., the hypothesis that the stories do not *explicitly* deal with problems of ethnic relationships in American life—were listed, with five possible entries for each: confirmed;

refuted; both confirmed and refuted in the same story; indeterminate as between confirmation and refutation; not applicable. An entry for each hypothesis for each story was required, together with full documentation of the basis for decision.

3. After a period of instruction in the procedures of the study, the eight analysts (all graduate students in sociology) coded the same story. Differences in interpretation were discovered and minimized through redefinition of the disputed categories. In addition, the supervisor of the analysts checked a random sample of each analyst's work during the early stages of the study and standardized analytic procedures among the workers.

4. After the analysis of the story had been completed, codes were inductively constructed for the "open" categories in the character analysis, such as goals and traits. The codes were based upon a total of about a third of the analysis sheets; at about that point, additional analyses failed to yield additional categories for the code. The character analysis was coded for transfer to punch cards. The story analysis was hand-tallied because of the progressive redefinition of hypotheses in the course of the study and the necessity for standardization.

So much for the procedures. Now let us turn to the findings of the study. Did magazine short stories "prefer" some kinds of people to other kinds? If so, how did such preferential treatment operate? We shall present the results of our analysis in five main sections: the distribution of the characters; their role; their appearance; their status; and their goals.

DISTRIBUTION OF CHARACTERS

What was the composition of the fictional population? What groups of people appeared more and less frequently in the stories? The brief answer is that characters identifiable only as "Americans" more than filled the center of the stage.

The Americans and the Field: Of all the identifiable speaking characters, fully 84 per cent were presented just as Americans (Table 1). The others were about equally divided between the various American minorities on the one hand and various foreign groups on the other. The nearly 200 stories, containing nearly 900 identifiable characters, included only sixteen Negroes and only ten Jews. On the whole, this small number of minority and foreign characters is spread very thin throughout the stories. Very seldom did more than one of them appear in a single story. They typically filled isolated roles in order to provide background or "tone" or some other specialized function within the stories. The "Americans," on the other hand, appeared not only in almost every story, but also in whole aggregates of characters.

But what about the ethnic composition of the characters as compared to the ethnic composition of the people of the United States? Perhaps the distribution of the fictional characters simply reflected census statistics. Actually, however, census data only accentuate the differential treatment accorded "natives" and "minorities" in the stories. Although the "minorities"

Chart 1—There Are Many More Americans in the Stories than in the Population[8]

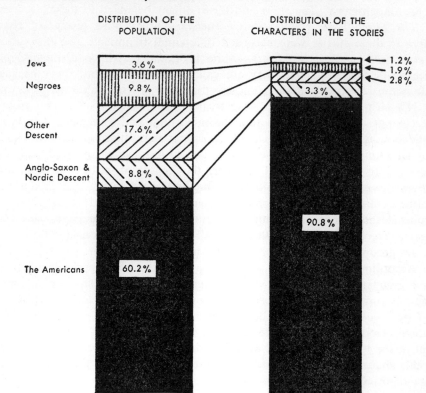

DISTRIBUTION OF THE POPULATION

DISTRIBUTION OF THE CHARACTERS IN THE STORIES

Jews — 3.6%
Negroes — 9.8%
Other Descent — 17.6%
Anglo-Saxon & Nordic Descent — 8.8%
The Americans — 60.2%

1.2%
1.9%
2.8%
3.3%
90.8%

(as here defined) make up 40 per cent of the population of the United States, they make up only 10 per cent of the population of the short stories (Chart 1). Every "minority" group appears less frequently in the stories than in the country. Only the "Americans" appear more frequently.

Thus we start with a fundamental conclusion: in popular-magazine short

Table 1—Minority and Foreign Groups in Magazine Short Stories Are Dwarfed by the "American" Giant[7]

"Americans"		84.0%
American Minorities		8.5
Anglo-Saxon and Nordic Hyphenates	3.0%	
Other Hyphenates	2.5	
Negroes	2.0—	
Jews	1.0+	
Foreigners		7.5
Anglo-Saxon and Nordic Groups	4.0	
Other Foreign Groups	3.5	
Total Number of Identifiable Characters (equalling 100%)		889

stories laid in the United States, minority and foreign groups were seldom represented. The American minorities appeared much less frequently in magazine fiction than in the population. Overwhelming attention was given to the "Americans." The stage and the spotlight belonged to them.

The Three Basic Groups of Characters: Three ethnic groups of characters in these stories were accorded differential treatment. The first group is composed of *The Americans*—white Protestants with no distinguishable ancestry of foreign origin. They are called "The Americans" here because that is the stereotypic designation for this type of "unadulterated" person.

Not all the non-Americans were treated alike, and the other two groups are composed of subgroups within the minorities, and foreigners. The basic distinction is not that between all American minorities on the one hand and all foreigners on the other; these two groups were approved and disapproved to the same extent. Rather, the important distinction appeared between those American hyphenates and foreigners with Anglo-Saxon and Nordic backgrounds, on the one hand, and the Jews, the Negroes, and the hyphenates and foreigners with other European, Latin-American, and Oriental backgrounds, on the other. On all the important considerations, the former group showed up to better advantage than the latter.

Accordingly, the findings shall be presented as comparisons of these three groups: *The Americans*—84 per cent of the total group of characters; Anglo-Saxon and Nordic minorities and foreigners (abbreviated *The AS&Ns*) —7 per cent of the total; other minorities and foreigners—Jews, Negroes, Italians, Germans, Poles, Orientals, etc. (abbreviated *The Others*)—9 per cent of the total. Since World War II did not serve to increase or otherwise modify the treatment of minority and foreign characters in these stories, the data reported in this study include both the 1937 and the 1943 samples.[9]

THE ROLES OF THE CHARACTERS

The characters in these stories play all sorts of parts, ranging from the central and highly approved figure appearing throughout the action to the marginal and unsympathetic figure appearing only for a few lines. What about the importance to the story of our three basic groups of characters?

The Majors and the Minors: The characters in these stories can be conveniently classified into three groups—major, submajor, minor—in terms of their importance to the story (as measured by the amount of attention given to them). Those playing the most important roles, i.e., given the most space, are the major characters. The characters given a medium amount of space in the stories are the submajor, and those who appear in incidental roles are the minor characters.

The Americans appeared as major characters just over half the time and as minor characters only about a third of the time (Table 2).

But *The AS&Ns* appeared slightly more frequently in minor roles than major, and *The Others* much more frequently. Not only did *The Americans* appear more often than the rest, but they also got more than their share

Table 2—The Americans Appeared More Often in the Major Roles

	The Americans	The AS&Ns	The Others
Major characters	52%	38%	30%
Submajor characters	16	18	14
Minor characters	32	44	56
Total No. of Identifiable Characters (equalling 100%)	745	61	77

of the important roles. When *The AS&Ns* and *The Others* did get into the stories, they were placed in smaller roles.

The heroes and heroines occupy the best roles of all. Again *The Americans* furnished more than their share, and so did *The AS&Ns*. About 35 per cent of all *The Americans* and 31 per cent of *The AS&Ns* were heroes or heroines, as against only 10 per cent of *The Others*. In other words, the heroes and heroines in these stories were almost exclusively either of "pure" American or else of Anglo-Saxon or Nordic stock. *The Others*—Italian-Americans, Jews, Negroes, *et al.,*—rarely reached such lofty positions.

The Approved and the Disapproved: Similarly, the characters can be differentiated on the basis of the approval or disapproval attached to their roles in the stories. The approved characters were likeable, personable, wise, desirable, respectable, honest, upright; the disapproved characters were the opposite. In such "light" fiction as these magazine stories—which are entertaining and pleasant rather than "realistic" or "serious"—the large majority of the characters are approved. This was true, in this sample, for all three groups—but not equally true (Table 3). Here *The Americans* and *The AS&Ns* were approved more often than *The Others*. Incidentally, the heavy appearance of neutral characters among the minority and foreign groups reflects the colorless roles to which they were assigned.

This tendency of the minority and foreign groups to draw minor, less approved roles and seldom to reach the positions of hero or heroine obviously places serious limitations on the extent to which their personalities can be developed. Space limitations, together with the general lack of sophistication of these stories, impose a low level of complexity for all characters, and have a particularly strong impact upon the minority and foreign groups. Since they were more often hand-maidens to the plot, they must more often be one-dimensional in personality. They were usually developed only in

Table 3—The Characters Were Differentiated by Their Approval in the Stories, with The Others the Least Approved of All

	The Americans	The AS&Ns	The Others
Approved characters	80%	78%	62%
Neutral characters	4	14	14
Disapproved characters	16	8	24
Total No. of Identifiable Characters (equalling 100%)	726	60	77

that aspect of their personalities necessary to their dramatic function, namely, the most obvious or stereotypic aspect which made the author's point facilely and quickly.

Indeed, some of the minor non-Americans, falling even lower on a scale of personalities-in-their-own-right, came to serve the function of *things* in the stories. That is, they merely provided atmosphere and mood or dramatized the broad-minded or cosmopolitan nature of *The Americans*. A typical case, for example, was the American heroine who was seen "talking charmingly to the quaint Italian flower vendor," who in that sentence fulfilled his role in the story.

THE STATUS OF THE CHARACTERS

Now let us turn to the characters' position in the socio-economic hierarchy. Did differences appear between *The Americans* and the rest in the possession of man's worldly goods? What kinds of jobs were held by what kinds of people? What sort of social interaction, if any, occurred between different groups of characters?

Status—Possessed and Deserved: The general economic level of characters in these stories was assessed as an interviewer for an opinion survey would assess the economic level of a respondent—by the person's appearance, clothes, home, possessions, etc. The characters were classified on four levels, designated A, B, C, and D. The A people have the most money, influence and prestige, and the D people have the least.

Again, *The Americans* showed to better advantage than *The AS&Ns* or *The Others* (Table 5). Almost three-fourths of the former fell on the upper two levels of this status index as against less than half of the latter. This simple index reflects substantial differences in characters' standards of living. *The Americans* lived better in various ways: they ate better food, wore better clothes, resided in better homes, and generally enjoyed more material conveniences and luxury possessions.

Not only that, they also seemed to *deserve* their higher status; it was usually taken for granted. People can achieve wealth, power and prestige in a variety of ways—through fortunate birth or fortunate marriage or hard work or crooked dealing or luck. In these stories, only infrequently were the sources of *The Americans'* high status positions explicitly mentioned. However, when the representatives of minority and foreign groups appeared in high status positions, *their* paths to power—whatever they were—were more often explicitly mentioned (Table 6). In other words, the claim of *The Americans* on society's rewards was presented much less as a matter for explanation or justification. Their acceptance at the top, without elaboration, subtly suggested that they belonged there. But when the rest appeared at the top, their rise had to be explained more often, because they did not belong there.

Occupational Level—"Positions" and "Jobs": The Americans also engaged in pleasanter and more desirable work than the members of minority

Table 5—The Americans Enjoyed Higher Socio-Economic Status Than the Rest[12]

Socio-Economic Status	The Americans	The AS&Ns	The Others
A	39%	24%	16%
B	33	18	28
C	23	49	37
D	5	9	19
Total No. of Identifiable Characters (equalling 100%)	722	55	76

and foreign groups. For the sake of convenience, the occupations have been grouped in a few major categories. Once more *The Americans* came off best, *The AS&Ns* next, and *The Others* worst (Table 7). Not only did *The Others* contain many more characters in illegal and "suspect" occupations; in addition, they were more likely to be enlisted men rather than officers in the armed forces (two-thirds of *The Others,* one-half of *The AS&Ns,* and one-fourth of *The Americans*). Thus the distinctions among the groups extend even into the military hierarchy.

Table 6—Fewer Explanations Were Forthcoming of The Americans' High Status Positions

	The Americans	The AS&Ns and The Others
Source of high status not explained in the story	78%	43%
Source of high status explained in the story	22	57
Total number of stories with characters in high status positions (equalling 100%)	93	14

Social Interaction: The Upper and the Lower: These stories contain whole networks of personal interactions, some conducted on a basis of equality but others serving to place one character in a lesser position relative to another. Such social interaction varies from the intimate to the incidental; that is, two characters can marry each other or they can have a chance meeting in a restaurant when one serves the other. How did such social interaction take place among our groups of characters?

Table 7—The Americans Had More Desirable Occupations Than the Other Groups[13]

	The Americans	The AS&Ns	The Others
High Occupations	59%	29%	20%
Middle Occupations	19	23	20
Low Occupations	11	27	36
Illegal and "suspect" occupations	1	2	15
Members of the armed forces	10	19	9
Total No. of Identifiable Characters (equalling 100%)	602	52	66

The distribution of occupations suggests the answer. Whenever social interaction in these stories occurred *on the job,* it was the members of minority and foreign groups who were found in the subordinate roles. They were the servants, the dressmakers, the liverymen, the restaurateurs, the peddlers. The "quaint flower vendor" was Italian; Mr. Beilstein was a butcher; Mr. Gasparri ran a restaurant; Silva was a Filipino houseman; Ella was an Irish cook and Hong a Chinese cook; Rosemary and Bessie and Sidonia, and many others, were Negro servants. They worked for, and served, *The Americans.*

In some cases, the minority and foreign representatives appeared subordinate to *The Americans* in nonoccupational roles. For example, an Irish mother pleaded with a wealthy American for her criminal son; an Italian gangster was slavishly devoted to an American heroine who once helped him; Tanya Verriki was an inmate of a home for delinquent girls where all the staff members were Americans. And when social interaction between *The Americans* and rest did occur on a basis of equality, it was usually *The AS&Ns* who participated. The English girl entertained American soldiers; British army officers (aristocrats) were invited to dinner; the Irish-American flyer became his ship's hero; the Scotch-American photographer won the motion-picture actress; the Irish sea captain was fully accepted and admired by his American fellows. Only occasionally did *The Americans* associate with *The Others* on an equal basis, and even in such cases it was usually the former who monopolized the spotlight.

But the acid test for personal relations is courtship and marriage. Who married whom in these stories? What boys won what girls? The distribution of marriages and successful courtships in these stories, closely paralleling the distribution of characters, reveals the slight extent to which *The Americans* courted or married members of minority and foreign groups (Table 8). It also shows the still smaller extent to which either *The Americans* or *The AS&Ns* courted or married *The Others.* Interlove and intermarriage were not sanctioned in magazine fiction.

Table 8—On the Whole, Courtship and Marriage Were Intragroup

Love or Marriage Partners	Frequency
The Americans—The Americans	85%
The Americans—The AS&Ns	5
The Americans—The Others	4
The AS&Ns—The AS&Ns	3
The AS&Ns—The Others	2
The Others—The Others	1
Total identifiable courtships and marriages (equalling 100%)	153

In sum, then, not only did *The Americans* play the leading roles in the stories. In addition, they were also represented as getting more of the world's material values and they occupied the superordinate roles in most of the human relationships. They made more money, lived more comfortably, had better occupations, gave more orders. In these stories, the world belonged to them, and they ran it.

THE GOALS OF THE CHARACTERS

Finally, what were the different groups of characters striving for in these stories? What did they want from life? People in magazine fiction pursue a variety of goals—romantic love, settled marriages, money, power, prestige, idealism, and a few more. These goals were classified into two broad categories—"heart" goals, which are emotional and affective, and "head" goals, which are rational and calculating. These specific goals subsumed under each category, and the frequency with which they appeared, are these:

"HEART" GOALS	"HEAD" GOALS
Romantic love (231)	Solution of an immediate concrete
Settled marriage state (190)	problem (94)
Idealism (74)	Self-advancement (92)
Affection and emotional security (62)	Money and material goods (58)
Patriotism (57)	Economic and social security (51)
Adventure (20)	Power and dominance (22)
Justice (9)	
Independence (8)	

The "heart" goals are "in the clouds" and the "head" goals are "down to earth." In these stories, *The Americans* were less encumbered with such down-to-earth goals (Table 9). Their goals were more frequently pleasant and idealistic and "pure." Particularly *The Others* were bound to mundane and calculating aims.

Table 9—The Americans Pursue "Heart" Goals More Than the Other Two Groups

	The Americans	The AS&Ns	The Others
"Heart" goals	69%	61%	49%
"Head" goals	31	39	51
Total Number of Identifiable Goals (equalling 100%)	793	57	53

SUMMING UP

This concludes the analysis of the differential treatment of characters in magazine fiction. On the whole, life in the United States as reflected in these stories was lived differently by our three basic groups. On almost every index—frequency, role, delineation, status, goals—*The Americans* received better treatment, both qualitatively and quantitatively, than the minority and foreign groups. And within the latter, a preference operated in behalf of *The AS&Ns*. The rules seem to be that the character receives better treatment the closer he is to the norm of *The Americans*, i.e., white, Protestant,

English-speaking, Anglo-Saxon. Common ancestry and common characteristics are decisive.

And even within *The Others* some kinds of people came off better than others. The minority and foreign groups from the other European and Oriental countries, deprived as they were, received preferential treatment in these stories over two critical American minorities—The Negroes and the Jews. On several characteristics this distinction held up. The Negroes and Jews never appeared as heroes and heroines. No Negroes or Jews were depicted as members of the armed forces. They had the lowest occupational rating. They constituted the only group with more disapproved than approved traits. In short, of all the distinguishable groups of characters in magazine fiction, the Negroes and the Jews were depicted least favorably.

INTENT AND EFFECT

Such a description of magazine fiction (or of any other communication content) supports two sets of interpretations. One set deals with the *intent* behind the communication; how did it get that way? The second set deals with the *effects* of the communication; what difference does it make in the readers' attitudes? The communication itself—in this case short stories in popular magazines—occupies a midway position between the writers and the readers.

Presumable Intents: How do these stories happen to be written in this way? We can undoubtedly discount at once any malice on the part of the writers and editors responsible for these stories.

First, it is a convenient method of writing. Such short stories call for brief, compact plots in which the action begins immediately and moves rapidly, and any techniques which facilitate "getting the character across" easily and immediately are at a premium. Thus, many stock roles must be filled by stock characters, and they are often conveniently found in minority groups. For example, whenever the plot requires a gangster it is the simple and "natural" thing to cast an Italian in the role and put it up to the readers to fill in the overtones for himself on the basis of the familiar sterotypes. Although this practice makes for shallow and cliché-filled writing, it does save time and space in the development of the story.

Secondly, the standard pattern for such short stories demands, and gets, conformity. Inertia on the one hand and fear of changing a "successful" formula on the other, combine to keep the stories within designated bounds. Just as certain language is proscribed, so are certain ("controversial") topics and certain uses of fictional characters. An editor or publisher who would eagerly accept another variant of the typical boy-meets-girl story starring Julie Britton and Bill Davis would not consider printing the same story if the leading figures in it were called Sadie Horowitz and Abe Goldstein, or Lorenzina Sereno and Sebastian de Grazia.

Further, the heterogeneity of the audience to whom such stories are directed may necessitate the use of the broadest symbols of identification.

As the types of readers in an audience increase in diversity, both the variety and the complexity of communicable ideas decrease. Heterogeneity breeds generality, and thus the leading characters become members of the dominant and presumably the best-recognized group.

Finally, insofar as the leading roles are taken by members of probably the most respected and certainly the most envied group in the community, these stories correspond to the historical bias of literature in centering upon the economic, prestige, and power elites of every age. On the one hand they have traditionally been considered the people most worth writing about, and on the other hand, as the people most deferred to, they present a convenient focus of attention for large groups of readers who seek to identify themselves with the rich and the powerful.

Presumable Effects: These stories are probably offered and accepted purely as entertainment. Their typical effect upon readers is a respite effect; that is, they normally provide a satisfying and enjoyable vacation from daily routines and daily cares. That may be the typical effect, but it is certainly not the only one. Many communications have other than their intended effects upon readers or listeners and this is probably such a case. In all likelihood, the consistent deprivation of *The AS&Ns* and especially *The Others* in these stories, over a long period of time, serves to activate the predispositions of a hostile or even an indifferent audience. Readers with latent tendencies to assign the usual stereotypic descriptions to groups whom they do not know, or toward whom they are unsympathetic, or with whom they do not come in personal contact, can find support for their convenient tags, labels, and aggressions in such magazine fiction. And this all the more striking as a result of the implicit comparison with *The Americans*. Thus the condition and behavior of fictional characters can readily be used to "prove" that the Negroes are lazy or ignorant, the Jews sly, the Irish superstitious, the Italians criminal, and so on.

THE IMPLICIT YES AND THE IMPLICIT NO

The nature of these stories, then, tends to perpetuate the myth of the "100 per cent American" by differentiating, subtly and consistently, between *The Americans* and the representatives of other groups. Such differentiation in itself constitutes an implicit recognition of a "minority problem" in this country. What about the explicit handling of the problem in these stories? Was the direct relationship between various ethnic groups overtly discussed in these stories, and if so, how?

One of this country's favorite ideologies claims equality for the diverse national, racial, and religious strains which make up the United States. In one sense, it is "immoral" to suggest that inequality actually exists, or, if it is acknowledged, that it cannot be attributed to biological factors or individual inadequacies. This ideology is not challenged in these stories. Minority differences are regularly recognized but the minorities are not overtly depreciated.

Of our sample of 185 stories, only four contained a direct reference of any kind to this problem area in American life. Only four brought the issue into the open:

An Indian girl is subject to conflict between loyalty to and marriage into her own people and assimilation into the American culture. Her ambivalence is resolved by acceptance of Indian social life (marriage to an Indian) and by acceptance of material conditions characteristic of American life (clothes, household appliances, etc.). Caste lines are maintained.

A Polish girl rebels against the traditional life of the American-Polish community, notably by dating an outsider. She is shamed by her people, almost loses her fiancé, acknowledges her mistake, and ends by accepting the traditional life of her community.

An upper-class American girl tries to evade jury duty and is chastised: "This country would get into a pretty mess if a girl of the more intelligent class, why, she just checked aside and the foreign element administrate justice in our courts."

An "American-born" man protests against being identified with French-Canadians living in New England: "But I'm an American." A character refers to such French-Canadians as "kind of Americans—but ain't."

The latter two references were only incidental comments on the problem. Only the first two—involving the adjustment problems of the Indian and Polish girls—contained "serious" and extended considerations of the problem itself. And in each case, the "out-group" heroine solved her problem by remaining within her own group. In each case, social assimilation was unsuccessful—although in each case the material trappings of American civilization, such as washing machines and radios were secured. The moral for these stories was sounded by an Indian character: "We want to win a place among the white people by our efforts and our determination, but we can never hope to be accepted socially."

Thus the consistent deprivation of the minority groups is indirect; it is present in the stories, but only seldom is it directly acknowledged or its implications discussed. The readers of short stories in popular magazines are constantly exposed, implicitly, to the prejudices and stereotypes attached to minority problems in the United States. But they are almost never exposed to serious and direct presentation of the problems themselves. Minority representatives are consistently deprived within an atmosphere which acknowledges no basis for such deprivation.

Minority problems in the United States are serious and deep-rooted. They will not be solved by symbols alone, but symbols will help. So will recognition of the pervasiveness of the problems. Even here, in ephemeral fiction fashioned of sweetness and light and designed purely for entertainment and divertissement, a subtle discrimination against minorities and foreigners has found its way. Even here, there are different classes of citizenship for different classes of people.

Notes

1. Number A-75.

2. The results reported in this paper are substantially the same for each magazine, so they are presented for the group as a whole.

3. This procedure calls for a total of 192 stories but it could not be fulfilled in seven instances, leaving a total of 185 stories actually analyzed.

4. The distribution of the population in magazine fiction and the actual population of the country is as follows:

	United States	Magazine fiction
New York City	5%	34%
East Coast	24	30
Middle West	30	17
West Coast	11	12
South	30	7

5. A set of the initial hypotheses, the code sheets, and the analysts' instructions for the study are available on request.

6. In the 185 stories, a total of 889 characters and groups were identifiable by racial, religious, or national origins. Of these, only 25, or less than 3 per cent, were groups.

7. Since relatively few of the characters were explicitly identified by national origin, it was necessary to classify them by other indicators. The following sources of identification were used (the total is more than 100% because some characters were identified in more than one way):

Explicit Identification	21%
Identified by: Name	58
Language	21
Appearance	17
Position	8
Other indicators	2

Examples of names used for purposes of identification:
American: Julie Britton, Eleanor Madison, Doris Baldwin, Martha Langford, Dorothy Green, Dick Ferris, Steve Kennedy, Perry West, Bill Davis, Joe Blake. *Italian:* Mr. Casparri, Marty Spinelli, Louis di Paolo. *Jewish:* Max Betterman, Chick Bernstein. *Scandinavian:* Sven Borsen, Fred Gorse. *Irish:* Marty Flanagan, Officer Flaherty. *German:* Adolph Hertz. *Polish:* Anna Krupek. The assumption here is that such names would be similarly identified by typical readers. In both the American minority and the foreign groups the following classification is used: *Anglo-Saxon and Nordic:* English, Irish, Scotch, Canadian, Scandinavian (Nor wegian, Swedish, Finish, Danish).

Other: German, Polish, Italian, Russian, Austrian, Czech, Portuguese, Spanish, Latin-American, Oriental.

8. The foreigners in the stories are omitted here. The data are not strictly comparable, but provide the best comparison which could be secured from available information. The population data, taken from the World's Almanac for 1944, are from the 1940 census (except for the figures for Jews, which come from the Jewish Statistical Bureau). The data on hyphenates represent the foreign-born and the native-born of foreign and mixed parentage. (In this respect, there is a bias against the distribution of minority characters in the stories, who are of any generation.) The figures for the Americans were secured by subtracting the total for the other groups from the total population.

9. Only about 5 per cent of the stories in these magazines were laid in foreign countries. In such stories, too, The Americans and the Anglo-Saxons received preferential treatment. If anything, the descriptions of the foreigners were even more stereotyped in these stories than in those laid in the United States.

10. These figures are not exactly alike from table to table because of varying numbers of indeterminate characters for the different catgeories.

11. A character delineation was accepted as a stereotype when a sizeable proportion of the American public would have identified it as such, according to our assumption based upon knowledge of the experimental studies. The examples cited in the text are typical illustrations.

12. These status differences are not simply a reflection of the differences in role among our three basic groups of characters. The status differences remain even when role is held constant. The data:

Role	The Americans		The AS&Ns and The Others	
Major	71%	(387)	58%	(46)
Submajor and Minor	68%	(353)	32%	(94)

There was thus a stronger association between *The Americans* and high status than between major role and high status. Similarly, it can be shown that *The AS&Ns* and *The Others* were approved less than *The Americans* when status is held roughly constant; thus, the fact that they were approved less is not simply the result of their lower status. (Although similar control tables do not appear in the text in connection with other tables, the differences have all been tested in this way.)

13. *The high occupations:* Business executives; the "idle rich"; parent-supported college students; lawyers, doctors, professors, ministers, architects, artists, musicians, and other professions; entertainers; major government officials; "luxury" housewives.

The middle occupations: White-collar workers, minor government officials, small business-men, farmers, housewives who do their own housework.

The low occupations: Fishermen, skilled laborers, servants, building maintenance workers, unskilled laborers.

The illegal and "suspect" occupations: Racketeers, thieves, gamblers, night club proprietors (suspect in these stories).

FURTHER READING

Allen, Frederick Lewis. "The American Magazine Grows Up," *Atlantic,* Vol. 180, November, 1947, pp. 77-83.
Bainbridge, John. *Little Wonder and How It Grew.* New York: Reynal and Hitchcock, 1946.
Brustein, Robert S. "The New Faith of the Saturday Evening Post," *Commentary,* Vol. 16, 1953, pp. 367-69.
Butterfield, Roger. "What Pocket Magazines Feed On," *Saturday Review,* Vol. 29, March 9, 1946, pp. 5-6.
Ellison, Jerome. "Selling Dreams in Marble Halls," *New Republic,* Vol. 117, October 13, 1947, pp. 20-24.
Gibbs, Wolcott. "Time, Fortune, Life, Luce," *New Yorker,* November 28, 1936.
Kerr, W. A., and Remmers, H. H. "Cultural Value of 100 Representative American Magazines," *School and Society,* Vol. 54, 1941, pp. 476-80.
Mott, Frank L. *A History of American Magazines, 1741-1885.* (3 vols.) New York: Appleton-Century-Crofts, 1930; and Cambridge, Mass.: Harvard University Press, 1938-1939.
Noel, Mary. *Villains Galore—the Heyday of the Popular Story Weekly.* New York: Macmillan, 1954.
Reynolds, Quentin. *The Fiction Factory: 100 Years of Publishing at Street and Smith.* New York: Random House, 1956.
Sisk, J. P. "Exposé Magazines," *Commonweal,* Vol. 64, 1956, pp. 223-25.
Tebbel, John. *George Horace Lorimer and the Saturday Evening Post.* Garden City: Doubleday, 1948.
Wolseley, Roland E. *The Magazine World.* New York: Prentice-Hall, 1951.
Wood, James Playsted. *Magazines in the United States: Their Social and Economic Influence.* New York: Ronald Press, 1956.

4
Motion Pictures

MOTION PICTURES

If there were ever any doubt of the influence the movies exert on the phantasies of the American people, it should have been dispelled when Grace Kelly married Prince Rainier and more correspondents covered the wedding than reported the D-day landings in France. True, this minor version of a Graustarkian romance had all the elements of the American social-mobility comedy, wherein the beautiful and talented daughter of a bricklayer-to-millionaire father marries a prince and lives happily ever after.

It is probably true that the "average" American's knowledge about the lives, loves and neuroses of the demi-gods and goddesses who live in the Olympian heights of Beverly Hills far surpasses his knowledge of civic affairs (local, state and national combined). That such a mass entertainment colossus should have begun at the penny arcades around Koster and Bial's Music Hall in New York City and within a few decades moved into so important a position in the reveries of a nation is one of the remarkable facts of life of the twentieth century. Yet the success of the movies, as indeed of the huge-circulation magazines, the comic strips and their ill-bred cousins, the comic books, are all representations of essentially the same phenomenon, which Gilbert Seldes has named the "public arts."

In his analysis of national types as Hollywood sees them, Siegfried Kracauer shows how the movie industry helps to perpetuate stereotypes of foreigners. Kracauer points out that in dealing with an "in-group" such as the English, Hollywood emphasizes only the obvious and often misleading personality traits.

In her severely honest book on Hollywood (the dream factory), Hortense Powdermaker concludes that Hollywood is more of a caricature than a reflection of certain contemporary tendencies in American culture. She views it as a three-way circular interaction between Hollywood, the U. S. A. and the movies.

Drs. Wolfenstein and Leites provide a psychological study of the movies. A detailed analysis of what they have termed the "good-bad" girl is an important aspect of their findings. By giving the audience a heroine who appears to be "bad" but in the last reel proves to be "good," Hollywood allows us to eat our cake and have it. If our Puritan morality forbids the overtly sexual enticement of a Gilda *(who evokes "bad" thoughts in us), it is clear at the end that Gilda was only pretending to be promiscuous but at heart is as good a* hausfrau *as any Middletown matron.*

Following our examination of Hollywood through the eyes of an anthropologist (Powdermaker) and psychologists (Wolfenstein and Leites), a sociologist, Frederick Elkin, joins the symposium. In his study of the movie

The Next Voice You Hear, *he shows how Hollywood deals with the problem of portraying God, religion and the American Way of Life.*

The complexities of the audience image as a feedback element in the making of movies is investigated by Herbert J. Gans. He indicates that the role of the audience extends beyond the creation and the content of the movie per se *to the structure and the culture of the movie industry itself.*

A thorough analysis by Eric Larrabee and David Riesman of the movie Executive Suite, *reveals that this portrayal of Big Business has Veblenian and populist overtones. This company-town pastoral romance, as they call it, needs to be understood not only in terms of its surface "meanings" but of the dreams that lie behind them.*

National Types as Hollywood Presents Them

By SIEGFRIED KRACAUER

UNESCO HAS BEGUN to inquire into the nature of tensions inimical to mutual understanding between the peoples of the world. Part of this "Tensions Project" is an analysis of "the conceptions which the people of one nation entertain of their own and of other nations."

It seems likely indeed that international understanding depends to some extent on the character of such conceptions—particularly if they assert themselves within the media of mass communication. Among these media the film is perhaps the most impressive.

If we are to study national images as presented in films, two broad areas for research immediately confront us. How do the films of any nation represent their own nation? And how do they represent others? The first of these two problems, increasingly dealt with in current writings, can be dismissed here in favor of the second which seems to me more important for UNESCO's quest. It is a new problem, not yet posed in a general way. Along with a whole family of similar problems, it has come into focus only now that world government is a possibility and world domination a threat. Only now, in fact, has the goal of mutual understanding through knowledge changed from an intellectual pleasure to a vital concern of the democracies.

The following study is by no means intended to provide a comprehensive analysis of the various screen images which the peoples of the world have formed, and continue to form, of each other. It is a pilot study, and merely attempts to prepare the ground for such an investigation by examining a small sector of the total subject: the appearance of English and Russian characters in American fiction films since about 1933.[1]

In the universe of fiction films two types are of lesser importance— films about the past of the English and Russians, and screen adaptations of literary masterworks from the two countries. This is not to say that such films are rare. On the contrary, Hollywood finds Victorian England endearing and Catherine the Great amusing. Also, it often feels compelled to exchange entertainment for what it believes to be a culture, and thus it eagerly exploits Shakespeare's plays and Tolstoy's novels, trying to make of them entertainment.[2] No doubt both these historical and literary films are well-established genres. And of course I do not deny that they help build up the screen images of the foreign peoples to which they refer. Yet since they deal with remote events, they are decidedly less relevant to this study than films that have a direct bearing on present-day reality.

Reprinted from the *Public Opinion Quarterly*, Vol. 13 (1949), pp. 53-72, by permission of the author and the publisher. (Copyright, 1949, by Princeton University Press.)

It is these latter films on which I am concentrating here—films, that is, which involve contemporary Russian and British characters in real-life situations. There has been no lack of them since 1933. I am thinking, for instance, of *Ninotchka* (1939), with its pleasantries at the expense of Soviet mentality, and of *Cavalcade* (1933), which follows the destinies of a well-to-do English family through two generations. What concepts the American screen entertains of the English and Russians can best be elicited from such more or less realistically handled comedies and dramas.

OBJECTIVE AND SUBJECTIVE FACTORS IN NATIONAL IMAGES

In the cases of individuals and peoples alike, knowledge of each other may progress from a state of ignorance to fair understanding. It is, for instance, a far cry from what the average American knows about the Japanese to Ruth Benedict's recent disclosure of the set of motives that determine Japanese attitudes and actions. Her study, *The Chrysanthemum and the Sword,* marks progress in objectivity; it challenges us to dispose of the familiar notions and common prejudices which help fashion our standard images of that people. Generally speaking, any such increase of knowledge is identical with a closer approach to the object we seek to penetrate.

This approach, however, is bound to remain asymptotic for two reasons, one of which lies in the object itself. An individual or a people is not so much a fixed entity as a living organism that develops along unforeseeable lines. Hence the difficulty of self-identification. It is true that the successive images a people creates of its own character are as a rule more reliable than those it forms of a foreign people's; but they are not complete and definite either.

The other obstacle to perfect knowledge, alone important in this context, lies in ourselves. We perceive all objects in a perspective imposed upon us by our environment as well as by certain inalienable traditions. Our concepts of a foreigner necessarily reflect native habits of thought. Much as we try to curtail this subjective factor, as we are indeed forced to do in the interest of increased objectivity, we still view the other individual from a position which is once and for all ours. It is just as impossible for us to settle down in a vacuum as it would be to fuse with him.

Any image we draw up of an individual or a people is the resultant of an objective and a subjective factor. The former cannot grow indefinitely; nor can the latter be completely eliminated. What counts is the ratio between these two factors. Whether our image of a foreign people comes close to true likeness or merely serves as a vehicle of self-expression—that is, whether it is more of a portrait or more of a projection—depends upon the degree to which our urge for objectivity gets the better of naïve subjectivity.

MEDIA INFLUENCES ON OBJECTIVITY-SUBJECTIVITY RATIO

The ratio between the objective and the subjective factor varies with the medium of communication. It is evident that within the medium of the printed word objectivity may go the limit. In the radio, also, objective information plays a considerable role, even though it is hampered by various restrictions, most of them inherent in the nature of this mass medium. Yet for all its limitations the radio registers any signal increase of knowledge. I do not doubt, for instance, that the evolution of modern anthropology—resulting from the necessities of psychological warfare and this country's engagements in international affairs—has been instrumental in bringing about recent radio programs which surveyed living conditions in other countries, and in particular focused on "the character and ideals of the Russian people."[3]

And what about the film? Hollywood's fiction films are commercial products designed for mass consumption at home and, if possible, abroad. The implications of this overall principle are obvious: Hollywood must try to captivate the masses without endangering its affiliations with vested interests. In view of high production costs it must try to avoid controversial issues lest box office receipts fall off. What the latter "must" means for the representation of foreigners is classically illustrated by the setback which the Remarque film, *All Quiet on the Western Front* (1930), suffered in Germany after a few Berlin performances, in December, 1930. This film, with its emphasis on the antiwar mood of German soldiers in the years of trench warfare, stirred the Nazis to violent demonstrations which in turn caused the German government to suspend its further screening.[4] Similar experiences, made with vaguely anti-Fascist films in neutral countries shortly before World War II, have corroborated the sad truth that foreign peoples are as touchy as domestic groups, professional or otherwise. The film industry therefore "remains afraid of portraying characters or situations in a way which will offend its existing foreign market: why jeopardize a source of revenues?"[5]

Hollywood, then, is faced with the task of producing films that draw the masses, in particular the American masses. The problem of how it measures up to this task has long since been a subject of discussion. Many hold that Hollywood, with the support of its affiliated chains of movie houses, manages to sell films which do not give the masses what they really want. From this viewpoint it would seem that Hollywood films more often than not stultify and misdirect a public persuaded into accepting them by its own indolence and by overwhelming publicity. I do not believe that such a viewpoint is tenable. Experience has taught us that even totalitarian regimes cannot manipulate public opinion forever; and what holds true for them applies all the more to an industry which, despite its monopolistic tendencies, still functions within the framework of a competitive society. The film industry is forced by its profit interest to divine the nature of actually existing mass trends and to adjust its products to them. That this necessity leaves a margin for cultural initiative on the part of the industry does not alter the situation. To be sure, American audiences receive what Hollywood wants them to want; but in the long run audience desires, acute or dormant, determine the character of Hollywood films.[6]

The audiences also determine the way these films picture foreigners. The subjective factor in any such image is more or less identical with the notions American public opinion entertains of the people portrayed. It is therefore highly improbable that a nation popular with the average American will be presented unfavorably; nor should we expect currently unpopular nations to be treated with condoning benevolence. Similarly, screen campaigns for or against a nation are not likely to be launched unless they can feed on strong environmental moods in their favor.

Yet its surrender to such moods need not prevent Hollywood from volunteering information about foreign people. It is true that we usually want to understand other nations because of our concern with mutual understanding; but fear and distrust of a people may no less urgently compel us to inquire into the motives behind its aspirations. The desire for knowledge, an essentially independent inner drive, thrives on both antipathy and sympathy. To what extent do Hollywood films satisfy this desire? Or, more specifically: what is the ratio between the subjective and the objective factor in American screen images of foreigners? And has this ratio been stable so far, or are we justified in assuming, for instance, that the images of 1948 surpass those of 1933 in objectivity?

HOLLYWOOD'S ESTIMATE OF ITS AUDIENCE

Without anticipating answers, I wish to formulate a principle derived from the all-powerful profit motive. Hollywood's attitude toward the presentation of any given piece of information ultimately depends on its estimate of how the masses of moviegoers respond to the spread of that information through fiction films. It seems to me important in this connection that the film industry calls itself an entertainment industry—a term which, whatever it connotes, does not precisely make one think of films as carriers of knowledge (nor as works of art, for that matter). There has indeed been a widespread tendency not only to equate screen entertainment and relaxation, but to consider anything informative an undesirable admixture. This entertainment formula, championed as late as 1941 in the sophisticated Preston Sturges film *Sullivan's Travels,* rests upon the conviction that people want to relax when they go to the movies; and it further implies that the need for relaxation and the quest for knowledge oppose rather than attract each other. Of course, as always with such formulas, they characterize the mental climate without being strictly binding. Many a prewar film has defied the usual Hollywood pattern and has deepened our understanding of the world.

Only since the end of the war have ideological conventions undergone a change; and again this change must be traced to mass moods. Obviously inspired by the general desire for enlightenment in the wake of the war, spokesmen of the industry now advocate films that combine entertainment with information. "Motion pictures," says Jack L. Warner, "are entertainment—but they go far beyond that." And he coins the term *"honest* entertainment" to convey the impression of a Hollywood fighting for truth,

democracy, international understanding, etc.[7] Eric Johnston, President of
the Motion Picture Association, lends his authority to this view. In his statement, *The Right To Know*—which is none the less pertinent for referring
to fiction films and factual films alike—he contends that "the motion picture,
as an instrument for the promotion of knowledge and understanding among
peoples, stands on the threshold of a tremendous era of expansion."[8]

Whether the American motion picture has already trespassed this threshold remains to be seen. On the purely domestic scene it has done so—at
least up to a point and temporarily. Attacking social abuses, such films as
The Best Years of our Lives (1946), *Boomerang* (1947), and *Gentleman's
Agreement* (1947) reveal a progressive attitude which undoubtedly owes
much to wartime experiences.[9] They still play to full houses, even though
political pressures have meanwhile caused the industry to discontinue this
trend. Will Hollywood revert to its old entertainment formula? For the time
being, we must remain in suspense.

THE TIME ELEMENT

Such foreign peoples as one does see on the American screen do not
appear consecutively in films about present-day life.

The English were featured in a number of prewar films succeeding each
other closely—among them were the above-mentioned *Cavalcade* (1933),
Of Human Bondage (1934), *Ruggles of Red Gap* (1935), *The Lives of a
Bengal Lancer* (1935), *Angel* (1937), *Lost Horizon* (1937), *A Yank at
Oxford* (1938), *The Citadel* (1938), *The Sun Never Sets* (1939), *We Are
Not Alone* (1939), *Rebecca* (1940), *Foreign Correspondent* (1940), and
How Green Was My Valley (1941). No sooner did the United States enter
the war than the frequency of topical films about Great Britain and her
people increased, as is instanced by *Mrs. Miniver* (1942), *The Pied Piper*
(1942), *Journey for Margaret* (1942), *The White Cliffs of Dover* (1944),
etc.

This vogue broke off immediately after the war. To the best of my
knowledge, the British postwar generation would be nonexistent in the
cinematic medium, were it not for *The Paradine Case* (1948), a murder
story without any bearing on current issues, and the international-minded
melodrama *Berlin Express,* released as late as May, 1948. Between 1945
and 1948, there was a gap spanned only by a few films that focused exclusively on the past—Lubitsch's *Cluny Brown* (1946) which satirized prewar
attitudes, fashionable or otherwise; *So Well Remembered* (1947), a social-
minded chronicle of small-town life between the two wars; *Ivy* (1947);
Moss Rose (1947); and *So Evil My Love* (1948). The last three were
mystery thrillers playing in turn-of-the-century Britain, if not earlier. Though
three years may not be a long period, this sustained unconcern for the
present still seems a bit strange.

During the thirties, contemporary Russians were less in view than the
English, without, however, being wholly neglected. I have already mentioned

Ninotchka (1939). Other films of the period were *Tovarich* (1937), and *Comrade X* (December, 1940). In the war, when Stalin joined the Allies, Hollywood permitted no one to outdo it in glowing accounts of Russian heroism. *Mission to Moscow, Miss V. from Moscow, The North Star, Three Russian Girls, Song of Russia*—a veritable springtide of pro-Russian films —flooded the movie houses in 1943 and 1944.

Then, exactly as in the case of the English, the Russians disappeared for three years. They disappeared even more completely than the English, for I do not know of a single, halfway important film since Lubitsch's resurrection of Catherine the Great (*A Royal Scandal*, 1945) which has dealt with their literature or past. Of course, I discount the "mad Russian," who re-emerged in *The Specter of the Rose* (1946); this stereotyped favorite of American audiences—usually a Russian-born artist having sought shelter in the West—is on the whole too estranged from the country of his origin to be identified as a Soviet citizen. It is true that Russians were also rare on the prewar screen, but in those days they were not featured in other media either. What makes one wonder at the absence of Soviet Russia on the postwar screen is just the fact of her omnipresence in speech and print at this time. Between 1945 and 1948, the films alone seemed unaware of a mass obsession.

That Hollywood behaved true to pattern in thus ignoring the Russians is proven by its equally conspicuous silence about the Nazis in the years preceding 1939. It is not as if Gemany had played any noticeable role in American films prior to 1933. Yet precisely in the critical years 1930-1934, two grade-A films turned the spotlight on her—*All Quiet on the Western Front* and *Little Man, What Now?* (1934), a screen adaptation of Hans Fallada's pre-Hitler novel about unemployment in Germany. Hollywood, it appears, had become mildly interested in things German. And what came out of it? During the subsequent year Hitler was a topic everywhere but on the screen. If I am not mistaken, only two films with Germans in them appeared in this interval: *The Road Back* (1937) and *Three Comrades* (1938). Both were adapted from novels by Remarque, whose name meant business, and both were laid in the early Weimar Republic, which was dead and buried at the time of their release.

TIMES WHEN SILENCE SEEMS WISE

This temporary withdrawal from certain peoples at certain times can be explained only by factors affecting commercial film production. Significantly, prewar Germany as well as postwar Russia provoked impassioned controversy in the United States. Before the war the country was divided into isolationists and interventionists; immediately after the war it heatedly debated the problem of whether the United States should be tough or soft in her dealings with the Kremlin. I believe it is this split of public opinion which accounts for Hollywood's evasiveness in both cases. Hollywood, as I have pointed out earlier, is so sensitive to economic risks that it all but automatically shrinks from touching on anything controversial. Germany and Russia were tabooed as "hot stuff"; and they were hot stuff as long as everybody argued about them and a decisive settlement of this nation-wide strife was not yet in sight. They disappeared, that is, not in spite of their hold on the American mind, but because of it.

There has been no such controversy with regard to Anglo-American relations. Why, then, the scarcity of postwar Britons in Hollywood films? Considering the impact of mass attitudes on film content, this scarcity may well result from the uneasiness with which Americans react to Labor rule in Britain. Their disquiet is understandable, for what is now going on in Britain means a challenge to American belief in free enterprise and its particular virtues. In the United States any discussion of British affairs is therefore likely to touch off an argument about the advantages and disadvantages of the American way of life. But once this kind of argument gets started you never know where it will lead. The whole matter is extremely delicate and involved, and it is for such reasons, I submit, that Hollywood producers currently neglect, perhaps without consciously intending it, the living English in favor of their less problematic ancestors.[10]

. . . AND TIMES TO SPEAK OUT

These periods of silence may suddenly come to a close, with mimosa-like shyness yielding to uninhibited outspokenness. In the prewar era, the years 1938-39 marked a turning of the tide. At the very moment when the European crisis reached its height, the American screen first took notice of the Axis powers and their creeds. *Blockade* (1938), a Walter Wanger production, initiated this trend. It denounced the ruthless bombing of cities during the Spanish civil war, clearly sympathizing with the Loyalist cause —which, however, was left unmentioned, as was France, the villain in the piece. Hollywood soon overcame these hesitations. *The Confessions of a Nazi Spy* (1939), a realistic rendering of Nazi activities in the United States, overtly stigmatized Hitler Germany and all that it stood for. Then came the war, and anti-Nazi films, less realistic than well-intentioned, grew rampant.

During those fateful years 1938-39, other national film industries began to speak up also. The French released *Grand Illusion* (1938), which resurrected World War I in a pacifistic spirit, and *Double Crime in the Maginot Line* (1939) whose German characters were indistinct. Even though both these films shirked any direct mention of Nazi Germany, they effectively conjured up her giant shadow. A similar device was used by Eisenstein in his *Alexander Nevsky,* shown in the United States in 1939. In picturing the defeat which thirteenth-century Russia inflicted upon the Teutonic Knights, Eisenstein—and through him Stalin—warned Hitler not to try the old game again.

Shortly after the release of *Blockade,* John C. Flinn, a *Variety* correspondent, emphasized Hollywood's vital interest in its career: "Upon its success financially revolve the plans of several of the major studios heretofore hesitant about tackling stories which treat with subjects of international economic and political controversy."[11] This expert statement sheds light on the motives that prompted the film industry into action. Despite the protests of certain Catholic groups, *Blockade* was a success financially; and though Hollywood might have felt tempted to produce anti-Nazi films even before *Blockade,* it did so only after having made fairly sure that they would be accepted on a nation-wide scale. The appearance of Nazis on the screen was connected with the evolution of public opinion in the United States. They appeared when, after the debacle in Spain and Austria's fall, the time of wavering controversy was practically over. Isolationism, to be sure, persisted; but the whole country bristled with indignation against the Nazis, and there was no longer any doubt that some day the world would have to stop Hitler and his associates. Since this conviction also prevailed in Britain, France, and elsewhere, Hollywood did not risk much in expressing sentiments so universally popular.

What happened in 1939, repeats itself in 1948: after a lull of three to four years, Russians now begin to reappear on the American screen as abruptly as did the Germans. The parallels between *The Iron Curtain* of May, 1948 and *The Confessions of a Nazi Spy* are striking. Like the latter film, this new one is a spy thriller—a pictorial account of the events that led to the discovery, in 1946, of a Russian-controlled spy ring in Canada. Both films are based on scripts by the same author; and both are narrated in documentary fashion. Should these similarities be symptomatic of analogous situations, as I believe they are, then *The Iron Curtain,* with its avowed hostility toward the Soviet regime, would indicate that American public opinion has come out of the controversial stage in favor of a tough stand on Russia.

TREATMENT OF ENGLISH CHARACTERS

For a long time Great Britain and the United States have been entertaining an alliance founded upon the community of race, language, historical experience, and political outlook. Interchange has been frequent; processes of symbiosis have been going on. To Americans the English are an "in-group" people; they belong, so to speak, to the family, while other peoples—"out-group" peoples—do not. Where such intimate bonds exist, knowledge of each other seems a matter of course. American screen images of Britons might therefore be expected to be true likenesses.

Hollywood has tried hard to justify such expectations. Many American films about the English are drawn from their own novels or stage plays; and the bulk of these films are shot on location, involving genuine mansions, lawns, and London streets. In addition, there is rarely an important English part in an American film that is not assigned to a native Briton.

This insistence on authenticity and local color benefits films which cover a diversity of subjects: middle-class patriotism (*Cavalcade, Mrs. Miniver*); empire glorification (*The Lives of a Bengal Lancer, The Sun Never Sets,* etc.); Anglo-American relations (*Ruggles of Red Gap*); upper-class ideology (again *Ruggles of Red Gap,* then *Angel, The White Cliffs of Dover,* etc.); sports (*A Yank at Oxford*); social issues, such as the status of physicians (*The Citadel*) and of coal miners (*How Green Was My Valley*), and so on. Strictly personal conflicts prevail in *Of Human Bondage* and *Rebecca*; public school life is featured in *Goodbye, Mr. Chips* (1939), a retrospective film.

The wealth of themes engenders a wide range of types. I dare say that, taken together, American films offer a more complete cross-section of the English than they do of any other people. From night club musicians to Kiplingese colonels and from workers to diplomats, nearly all strata of the population are presented on some occasion and somehow. Frequent among these types are well-to-do gentlemen and their manservants—a couple of figures forever illustrating the Lord-Butler relationship, which has been so delightfully patterned in *Ruggles of Red Gap.* (Incidentally, in any film about foreigners the minor characters tend to be more true to type than the protagonists, because they are less deliberately constructed.)

In short, the English are rendered substantially as befits the prominent place they hold in American traditions. The result is a fairly inclusive image of their national traits, an image which for all its emphasis on snobbish caste spirit permits the audience to catch glimpses of British imperturbability, doggedness, and sportsmanship. *The Lives of a Bengal Lancer,* which initiated a trend of cloak-and-dagger melodramas—films playing in an India or Africa faintly reminiscent of the Wild West—points up the frontier bravura of English empire-builders and their soldiery;[12] *The Pied Piper* in a highly amusing sequence shows members of a London club indulging in the native penchant for understatement, while German bombers noisily drop their loads.

This many-sided approach further testifies to Hollywood's concern with the British way of life. Small wonder that several prewar films succeeded in reflecting it faithfully. A model case of objectivity is *Cavalcade,* the well-known screen version of Noel Coward's play. Before this film with its English cast went into production, its original director filmed the whole London stage performance of the play so as not to miss any of those minutiae upon which the impression of genuineness depends. Such efforts paid: *Cavalcade,* according to a report from London, "convinced the most skeptical Englishmen that the American film capital can on occasion produce a much better British picture than any English studio has yet managed to achieve."[13]

At this point the problem of the ratio between the objective and the subjective factor arises. Can the latter be neglected in the case of the English? Or, rather, does experience show that in the long run subjective influences—influences exerted by American mass attitudes—win out over that urge for objectivity of which *Cavalcade* is so impressive an instance? I wish to make it clear from the outset that all the measures Hollywood has taken in the interest of authenticity do not suffice to eliminate distortions. A script may be one hundred per cent British and yet materialize in a film imbued with Hollywood spirit. Nor do views of the Tower or a Tudor castle warrant accuracy; documentary shots, as is proven by many propaganda films and newsreels, can be juxtaposed in such a way that they falsify the very reality which they candidly capture. But are not English actors a guarantee for the truthful representation of English life? They are not, for two reasons. First, the screen appearance of any actor results not only from his own acting, but from the various cinematic devices using in building up his image on the screen, and because of their share in its establishment this image may well express other meanings than those conveyed by the actor himself. Secondly, even though an English actor is under all circumstances an Englishman, he may have to appear in a film so little suggestive of typically English behavior and thought patterns that he finds no opportunity of substantiating them. He will be neutralized within such contexts. In other words, whether or not screen portrayals of a foreign people are convincing does not solely depend upon their being enacted by native actors. What counts most is the whole film's susceptibility to the characteristics of that people.

THE SNOB

The influence of American preconceptions shows in the selection of English character traits. Hollywood films establish a hierarchy among these traits in which snobbishness, as I have indicated, figures foremost. Inseparable from class-mindedness, snobbishness pervades the servant's quarters in numerous films, confers upon screen aristocrats an air of inimitable superiority, surrounds as a palpable halo all those Englishmen who by provision of the plots defend advanced colonial outposts or mingle with Americans and Frenchmen, and makes itself felt everywhere not only in the manner of speaking but at decisive turning-points of dialogue. It is the one British characteristic which American movies never tire of acknowledging, ridiculing, condoning, or repudiating, according to the views expressed in them.

No doubt this trait actually exists. The English writer Margaret Cole, who is all against snobbishness, neveretheless admits that much in her recent *Harper's* article: "The British have a pretty lively sense of birth and upbringing: they like titles and honors, and they like to know people who have titles and honors . . . they are, most of them, pretty good snobs."[14] Yet this does not mean that the English are primarily snobs. Like any other people, they have a complex character structure; snobbishness therefore need not appear as their main trait. As a matter of fact, it could easily be shown that the films of different nations have conceived of Englishmen in quite different ways.[15] Take the German cinema: for all their surface similarities, the German and the American screen Britons are by no mean counterparts. Such German peacetime films as dealt with the English at all paid tribute grudgingly to their way of life. Among the traits featured, however, correctness and decency (e.g., of British navy officers) were more conspicuous than snobbishness—a trait whose social implications eluded a people which had never had a society in the Western sense. And when war came the Germans expressed their pentup resentments against the British Empire in films which made no bones about the ruthlessness of the English and about their alleged hypocrisy. The latter characteristic, passed off as an English cardinal vice by the Germans, is practically nonexistent in American films.

Any nation, it appears, sees other peoples in a perspective determined by its experience of them; and, of course, its cinema features those character traits of theirs which are an integral part of this experience. Hence the emphasis on English caste spirit in Hollywood films. To Americans this trait stands out among others because it affected them deeply under British rule. And since nations, like individuals, tend to build on their early impressions, the mass of Americans, among them swarms of Irish immigrants, took it for granted that the typical Briton is essentially a caste-proud snob. They reacted to him in two opposite ways—a further symptom of the imprint which his conduct, or, rather, their conception of it, had left on them. On the one side, they condemned British snobbishness for offending their sense of equality; on the other, they admired and imitated it. American snobbery contributes much to stabilizing the English snob on the screen; his recurrent image is both a reflection of and a protest against native cravings for nobility, Oxford, and authentic manners. This is confirmed by *Ruggles of Red Gap,* which mingles gentle gibes at the foreign idol with a solid satire of its Middle-West worshippers. Another case in point is Preston Sturges' brilliant comedy *Lady Eve* (1941). Even though this film does not include any Britons, it does show a cute American girl who reconquers her lover by posing as Lady Eve, the daughter of an English aristocrat.

The American screen image of the English is more or less standardized. True as this image is to reality, as a stereotype it has also a life of its own, a life independent of that reality. The English snob, as he appears in Hollywood films, is a figure which has in some degree drifted away from its original to join those mythological figures that people the world of American imagination. Whether angry at him or fond of him, Americans consider this kind of Briton one of theirs. He "belongs"; like Huckleberry Finn or Mickey Mouse, he is part of their universe.

This permanent preoccupation with British snobbishness is not the only subjective element in Hollywood's portrayal of the English. Other influences, equally instrumental in its composition, arise from changes on the domestic scene. In prewar days, when relations between the United States and Great Britain developed along traditional lines, there was no reason why these changes should interfere with an objective rendering of Britons. Domestic mass desires asserted themselves merely in the preference given to such film subjects as were likely to draw American audiences at a specific moment. *Cavalcade* was particularly well-timed. This film, with its unflinching belief in Britain's greatness, appeared at the depths of the Depression, a comfort to all those Americans who despaired of the predicament they were in. Many wept when seeing the film, and more than one reviewer declared it to be a tribute to what is best in all national spirits. Two years later, *Ruggles of Red Gap,* a comedy about the molding of a class-conscious English butler into a free American, struck that tone of self-confidence which by then filled the air. And so it goes. It would, by the way, be tempting to inquire into the causes of the enormous popularity which films about British imperialism enjoyed for a stretch of years. That they had a definite bearing on domestic issues is evident even in their casting: the elder colonels in *The Lives of a Bengal Lancer* and *Gunga Din* fell to the charge of English actors, while the young protagonists, heroes or cowards, were played by stars genuinely American.

BRITISH CHARACTERS IN WARTIME

Once the war was on, national exigencies encroached on the tendency toward objectivity. American public opinion endorsed the war effort, and Britain was now an Ally. For these reasons Hollywood could no longer afford to approach the English in that spirit of impartiality which is indispensable for an understanding of others. Rather, it was faced with the task of endearing everything British to the American masses. The task was not simply to represent the English, but to make them seem acceptable even to the population whose pro-British feelings were doubtful.

Significantly, most Hollywood films about Britain at war attempt to weaken the existing antipathies against English snobbishness, thus reaffirming American obsession with this trait. *Mrs. Miniver,* representative of the whole trend, shows wartime Britain undergo processes of democratization tending to transform her national character. In this film, as a reviewer judiciously points out, "even Lady Beldon, the aged, local autocrat, finally realizes that her class-conscious, if gracious, civilization has been forged into the practical democracy of an entire country united against the enemy."[16] *The Pied Piper* features an old English gentleman whose noble impulses increasingly get the better of his outward standoffishness; *The White Cliffs of Dover,* a sentimental retrospect which tries to enlist audience sympathies for British upper-class people, ends with hints of their readiness to conform to more democratic standards. It is not that such motifs had been entirely omitted in prewar films; but during the war they grew into leitmotifs, coloring all films of the period and serving as their very justification.

Produced in response to powerful domestic urges, these films, I assume, would have misrepresented English reality even if they had been shot on location. To what extent they actually distorted it can be inferred from the criticism with which they were received in Britain itself. *Mrs. Miniver,* though recognized as a laudable American tribute to English war heroism, was nevertheless blamed for "its faults and frequent air of English unreality."[17]

Of *The White Cliffs of Dover* the London *Times* said that it "misses the tones and accents of the country in which the action passes."[18] And with regard to *Random Harvest,* another Hollywood wartime production, a polite reviewer remarked that "Greer Garson and Ronald Colman act away the frequent obtrusion of error in English detail and behavior."[19]

ABSENCE OF THE POSTWAR BRITAIN

The war over, one might have expected Hollywood to resume its relatively objective approach to contemporary Britons. Yet it preferred, and still prefers, to ignore their existence. Nothing proves more conclusively the overpowering effect of domestic influences in the field of screen entertainment. Now that the English in some respects really live up to the image drawn up of them in all American war films—class-mindedness is on the decline and snobbery less domineering—it would seem natural for Hollywood to acknowledge what it praised only yesterday. Instead, it resolutely turns its back on Britain, for reasons at which I have made a guess in earlier contexts. During the war, folks at home took delight in a Lady Beldon who proved herself a convinced democrat; at present, the peculiar flavor of English democracy so little pleases many Americans that the Lady Beldons are being held incommunicado until further notice.

The meaning of this temporary blackout—all the more striking in view of the influx into America of English films about postwar life in Britain—is enhanced by those Hollywood productions which introduce British characters of the past. They not only re-establish the stereotype of the English snob (*Cluny Brown*), but draw on other familiar prewar patterns as well. All of them could have been made before 1941. In thus combining disregard of the present with uninhibited rendering of the past, Hollywood follows a rule of conduct which it has already practiced before. Nor is this treatment of foreign peoples unknown to other national film industries: at a time when the German pre-Hitler cinema was completely oblivious of Soviet Russia, it elaborated profusely on the blessings of the Czarist regime. I have reason to believe that in all such cases the emergence of films about the past of a people betrays discontent with its present state of affairs. What makes these films into vehicles of indirect criticism is the fact of their appearance at a moment when any direct mention of that people is strictly avoided. They manifest apprehensions not so much through their content as their sheer existence. Only occasionally do they come into the open, picturing past events for the thinly veiled purpose of dealing with present ones. In *Alexander Nevsky* the eyes that gleam through visors of the Teutonic Knights are unmistakably the eyes of contemporary Nazis.

In sum, the objective factor in American screen images of the English is extremely vulnerable. Much as the age-old intimacy of Anglo-American relations favors its growth, the impact of subjective influences invariably tends to stunt it. Domestic needs and mass desire have on more than one occasion caused Hollywood to portray the English inadequately or not to portray them at all, which amounts to the same thing. There is no progress of knowledge noticeable as these portrayals succeed each other—in fact, *Cavalcade,* released as early as 1933, has probably never been surpassed in objectivity. Everything, it appears, hinges on market necessities which may or may not permit Hollywood to reflect the English closely.

RUSSIAN CHARACTERS

In their *America in Midpassage* the Beards mention the success of the first Russian Five-Year Plan among those foreign events which augmented American anxieties in the spring of 1933. "Still Russia was far off," they remark before turning to the more stirring repercussions of Hitler's rise to power, "and could be discounted as a bit oriental in its ways and values."[20]

To Americans the Russians are an "out-group" people indeed. There is a pronounced lack of traditions common to both countries, and there has never been an intermingling of their nationals as in the case of the English. The chasm separating the two countries is deepened by the antagonism between their regimes—an antagonism so laden with dynamite that it pre-determines all popular notions Americans and Russians hold of each other. Unsustained by experience and inevitably biased, these notions are outright clichés. The average American has incorporated the figure of the "mad Russian" into the collection of his pet stereotypes; he knows that Russians are fond of music, ballet, and vodka. And, of course, innumerable editorials and the like have impressed upon him fixed concepts of Bolshevism as something with collective farms, secret police, and purges. Most of it is sheer hearsay, however true.

Hollywood, always inclined to capitalize on existing clichés, is not in the best of positions to breathe life into them. For obvious reasons American films about Russia are studio-made; and because of the scarcity of Russian actors in this country their native characters are as a rule assigned to Hollywood stars—or to German actors, who seem to have a knack for portraying Russians. In *The Last Command* (1928) Emil Jannings was a very convincing Czarist general. I have pointed out that even films with English actors in the cast may misrepresent the English; conversely, actors in the roles of foreigners need not, under all circumstances, miss the essentials. Nevertheless it remains true that the reliance on outside portrayals in imitation settings thwarts, rather than facilitates, an objective rendering of other peoples.

Such scattered Hollywood films about contemporary Russia as did appear between 1927 and 1934 frowned upon the Soviet Union with an air of grave concern. Most of them were laid in, or referred to, the early days of the Russian Revolution when everything was still fluid. Even though they did not pass over the disastrous abuses of Czarist rule—how could they?—yet they managed to make you feel gloomy about the victory of a cause so obviously barbarian. I am thinking of *Mockery* (1927), *The Tempest* (1928), *The Last Command,* and *British Agent* (1934). Except for Sternberg's *Last Command,* each of these films culminated in a romance between a Russian Red and his, or her, class enemy, which drove home the humanly destructive effects of Bolshevist class hatred. *Forgotten Commandment* (1932), "a sermon on the evils of Soviet Land,"[21] accused Russia of having forsaken Christianity. Of these productions only the Sternberg film and perhaps *British Agent* had some merits. The Beards are right: "Russia was far off . . ."

She did not come nearer after her recognition by President Roosevelt late in 1933. Yet American attitudes changed. After a period of silence filled in by several films which involved Catherine the Great, Tolstoy's *Anna Karenina,* and Dostoievsky's *Crime and Punshment* (like the current films about the English past, these may have conveyed polite discontent with the stubborn survival of Russian Communism), this change showed in Hollywood's transition from serious criticism to critical comedy. *Tovarich,* I believe, was the first film to endorse the fact of political recognition by substituting light skirmishes for heavy attacks. Hostilities continued, but they adjusted themselves to the improved relations with the Soviet Union which after all was here to stay. Lubitsch's *Ninotchka,* with Garbo in the title role, also marked a precarious rapprochement. This amusing piece of raillery which showed Marxist-trained Russians succumbing to the frivolous attractions of the West, viewed Soviet life with the condescension of an adult who watches fledglings romp. It was a sort of shoulder-patting; why not finally grow up, the film seemed to ask. Its success bred other films in this vein: *He Stayed for Breakfast,* "a gay spoof of the Communistic camaraderie that flourished in Paris before the war,"[22] and *Comrade X* which, laid in Moscow, equally jeered at the conversion of rabid Communist. Released in 1940, both films not only lacked Lubitsch's finesse, but struck a tone of poignant aggressiveness absent in his *Ninotchka.* Of *Comrade X,* Bosley Crowther says: ". . . seldom has a film . . . satirized a nation and its political system with such grim and malicious delight as does this . . . comedy."[23]

THE WARTIME RUSSIAN

The English characters in American war films about Britain still resembled their predecessors of a few years before, but no such resemblances connected the intrepid Russian woman fighter glorified by Hollywood between 1942 and 1944 with the yielding Ninotchka so popular shortly before. This was not simply a shift of emphasis as in the case of the English, but a radical change of scene, with Stalin becoming Uncle Joe and collective farming a source of happiness. I scarcely need elaborate on characters and situations in *Mission to Moscow, The North Star,* and so on. All these films sprang from the overwhelming desire, on the part of the home front, to keep Russia in the war. The surprising thing is their unconcern for continuity: they idolized what had been condemned in times of peace, or winked at it unshamedly. It was a complete turnabout.

In thus wooing Russia for reasons of domestic self-interest, Hollywood ignored its otherwise guiding rule of leaving controversial issues untouched. Opposition against the Soviet regime was too stable a factor of American public opinion to be eliminated by the necessities of the war. Subdued as it was, it continued to smolder. This accounts for the criticism which in particular *Mission to Moscow,* with its indulgent references to the Moscow trials, met from diverse quarters. And about *The North Star,* which in its opening scenes extolled the insouciant life of Russian villagers before 1941, the *Daily News* wrote that this film is more Communistic "than the Russians themselves who have never pretended that pre-war Russia was a musical-comedy paradise."[24]

. . . AND THE RUSSIAN OF TODAY

Now that the spell of amnesia from which Hollywood suffered in the postwar years is over, we are witnessing another turnabout. Gone are the brave Russian women fighters, the happy villagers, and the democratic allures of the rulers. In their places somber bureaucrats, counterparts of the Nazis, spread an atmosphere of oppression. This at least is the way *The Iron Curtain* pictures Soviet officials—they appear as ruthless totalitarians obeyed by devout slaves. And the only "good" Russian is a man who so firmly believes in the superior value of Western civilization that he deserts Communism and betrays his country. Similar types were also advertised in American prewar comedies; but unlike *Ninotchka, The Iron Curtain* avoids any satirical overtones that might weaken the impact of its accusations. Other current films draw no less determinedly on the anti-Communist sentiments of American audiences. In *The Fugitive* (late 1947)—a deliberately fantastic film with exotic settings—humble priests are wantonly persecuted by all-powerful authorities which everybody is free to identify as Communists. The Russian black-market racketeer in *To the Victor* (April 1948) is no endearing figure either. And we may soon see more anti-Soviet films; two or three have already been scheduled for production. This general insistence on toughness, however, seems to be slightly mitigated by the fearful prospect of another war: *Berlin Express* and *A Foreign Affair* (June 1948), both laid in Germany, indulge in a relatively amiable approach to their Russian characters, thus intimating that we should not give up hope for an understanding after all.

DOMINANCE OF THE SUBJECTIVE FACTOR

All this illustrates Hollywood's unconcern for Russian reality. Unlike the English characters in Hollywood films which at least give one a taste, however faint, of genuine life, American screen portrayals of Russians conform to what Americans imagine far-away Russians to be like. Even Russian-born actors are strangely colorless in plots based upon such subjective concepts; and, of course, Garbo in *Ninotchka* always remains Garbo in the guise of Ninotchka. The objective factor in these portrayals is negligible—they are not experienced, but constructed. Hence their remoteness from the originals they pretend to portray. Commenting on *The North Star*, Archer Winston, one of the most observant New York film critics, states that its characters are "single-plane cutouts rather than those deeply modelled characterizations of the best Russian films . . ."[25] He might have added that the many Russian films shown in the United States have not in the slightest degree stimulated Hollywood to relinquish its home-bred notions of Russia.

These notions are of a political nature. All Hollywood films about Russia raise topical issues, and many of them, I presume, would have never been produced were it not for the purpose of externalizing American attitudes toward the Soviet regime. This explains why the characters in them are so poorly instrumented. As compared with English screen figures, Hollywood-made Russians are sheer abstractions. Instead of being introduced for their own sake as are the English in many cases, they merely serve to personify pros and cons in the ever-fluctuating debate on Russian Communism. It is as if they were drawn from editorials. They resemble marionettes, and you cannot help seeing the strings by which they are pulled.

And finally these marionettes lack the relative stability of English characters. The English snob has survived the war, while Ninotchka was popular only for a transient moment. Her ephemeral vogue is symptomatic of the frequent, occasionally hectic changes which Russian characters undergo in American films. They succeed each other with a disregard for psychological consistency which again testifies to their function of conveying domestic views of Russia. In 1941, when these views changed so abruptly that films in keeping with the latest developments were not yet available, Hollywood tried to adjust an existing film to the new situation. Under the heading: "Whitewashing Reds," *Variety*, of October 22, 1941, published the following notice: "Reflecting the changed public opinion in this country towards Russia, Metro has added an explanatory foreword on the film *Comrade X* to make clear that any spoofing of Russians in the picture was entirely intended as good clean fun." Metro simply was loath to shelve *Comrade X,* a film released only a few months before Hitler's invasion of Russia; yet this grim satire of Soviet life could not be kept in circulation unless it was made to appear as a meek banter among friends.

Russian characters in American films are projections rather than portraits. Chimerical figures, they unhesitatingly change with the political exigencies of the moment. Russia is far off.

CONCLUSIONS

The film industries of other democracies, I assume, behave in much the same way as Hollywood. Fiction films are mass entertainment everywhere, and what information they include is more or less a by-product. Any national cinema yields to the impact of subjective influences in portraying foreigners; these portrayals, that is, are strongly determined by such audience desires and political exigencies as currently prevail on the domestic scene. There are different degrees of subjectivity, though: peoples intimately connected by common experiences can be expected to form more objective screen images of each other than they do of peoples with whom they have little or nothing in common.

In other words, images of "in-group" peoples surpass those of "out-group" peoples in reliability. But even they are halfway reliable only as long as public opinion in the country of their origin does not interfere with their relatively unbiased approach. And under the pressure of alienating developments this may happen at any moment, as is instanced by Hollywood's conspicuous neglect of postwar Britons. On the whole, screen portrayals of foreigners are rarely true likenesses; more often than not they grow out of the urge for self-assertion rather than the thirst for knowledge, so that the resultant images reflect not so much the mentality of the other people as the state of mind of their own. International understanding is in its infancy.

Or, rather, does it begin to show signs of growing up? I have not yet mentioned a new international film trend which seems to justify Mr. Johnston's contention quoted above that the motion picture is on the point of becoming "an instrument for the promotion of knowledge and understanding among peoples." This trend, a spontaneous reaction to the effects of the war, originates in Europe. Representative of it are the somewhat sentimental Swiss pictures *Marie Louise* and *The Last Chance,* and the two Rossellini films, *Open City* and *Paisan*—wartime and postwar semi-documentaries much acclaimed by American audiences. In a similar vein is *The Search* (1948), a Metro-sponsored film about European war orphans which has been made by the producer of *The Last Chance* and his associates in collaboration with a Hollywood director. Hollywood seems to be interested in this genre.

It is by no means a new genre. D. W. Griffith, great innovator as he was, developed some of its inherent potentialities, and his ideas were followed up by Eisenstein and Pudovkin in their classic screen epics—masterful blends of reportage and fiction, matter-of-fact statements and emotional appeals. What is new in the most recent semi-documentaries is their content: a changed outlook on the world which, of course, entails changes of cinematic approach. All these films denounce Fascist lust for power and race hatred; and whatever they picture—Nazis torturing their enemies, scenes of heroic resistance, abandoned children, indescribable misery in bombed-out cities—is rendered with profound compassion for the tortured, the killed, the despondent. They are films with a message. They not only record the frightful encounters of persecutors and victims, masters and slaves, but glorify the bonds of love and sympathy that even now amidst lies, ruins, and horrors connect people of different nations. Their goal is mutual understanding between the peoples of the world.

I do not know a single prewar film which is so deliberately international as is any of these semi-documentaries. All of them reflect, in loosely knit episodes, the vicissitudes of the war, featuring chance meetings between soldiers and civilians of diverse countries. German refugees join company with a British officer; an Amercan G.I. makes love to an Italian girl; under-nourished French children regain health in Switzerland. And most of these figures are fashioned with a minimum of subjectivity on the part of the film makers. Instead of serving as outlets for domestic needs, they seem to be elicited from reality for no purpose other than of mirroring it. They tend to increase our knowledge of other nations out of an overwhelming nostalgia for international co-operation.

CAN HOLLYWOOD AFFORD THE INTERNATIONAL TREND?

The whole trend, provided it is one, proves that screen portrayals of foreigners need not under all circumstances degenerate into stereotypes and projections. At this point the problem arises of what can be done to improve these images. It is a vital problem in view of the influence which entertainment films exert on the masses. There is no doubt that the screen images of other peoples help to weaken or strengthen popular interest in mutual understanding.

This does not contradict the fact, emphasized throughout my study, that entertainment films on their part are strongly influenced by actually prevailing mass desires, latent tendencies of public opinion. Such desires and tendencies are more or less inarticulate, and do not materialize unless they are forced out of ther pupa state; they must be identified and formulated to come into their own. Film industries everywhere, as I have mentioned earlier, are therefore faced with the task of divining audience expectations at any particular moment. Sometimes they miss their opportunities. The response which the Swiss and Italian semi-documentaries have found in the United States, for thematic rather than for aesthetic reasons, reveals a disposition in their favor on the part of American audiences which Hollywood has hitherto failed to recognize. On the other hand, Hollywood films occasionally react to well-nigh intangible emotional and social constellations with such a promptness that they seem to create desires out of nothing, especially in the dimension of taste. Characteristically, the trade has coined the term "sleeper" for films which are believed to be flops and, once released, prove themselves as hits. Film making involves constant experimenting—and many surprises.

What matters most in this context, then, is the essential ambiguity of mass dispositions. Because of their vagueness they usually admit of diverse interpretations. People are quick to reject things that they do not agree with, while they feel much less sure about the true objects of their leanings and longings. There is, accordingly, a margin left for film producers who aim at satisfying existing mass desires. Pent-up escapist needs, for instance, may be relieved in many different ways. Hence the permanent interaction between mass dispositions and film content. Each popular film conforms to certain popular wants; yet in conforming to them it inevitably does away with their inherent ambiguity. Any such film evolves these wants in a specific direction, confronts them with one among several possible meanings. Through their very definiteness films thus determine the nature of the inarticulate from which they emerge.

Once again, how can screen images of other peoples be improved? Since film producers, for all their dependence on current main trends of opinion and sentiment, retain some freedom of action, it may well be that they will find a more objective approach to foreign characters to be in their own interest. Hollywood is presently undergoing a crisis which challenges producers to probe into the minds of weary moviegoers, and documentary techniques, much-favored in Hollywood since *Boomerang,* lend themselves perfectly to objective portrayals. And has not *The Search* been a success? There is no reason why Hollywood should not explore this success and try its hand at films, semi-documentaries or not, which in however indirect a manner serve the cause of one world. U.S. audiences may even welcome a comprehensive rendering of Russian problems, or of life in Labor-governed Britain.

Or, of course, they may not. And Hollywood (any national film industry, for that matter) has some reason to believe that in the long run it knows best what spectators look out for in the movie houses. I doubt whether it will follow suggestions inconsistent with its estimate of audience reactions. Therefore a campaign for better screen portrayals of foreigners—portrayals which are portraits rather than projections—carries weight only if the motion picture industry is made to realize that the broad masses care about such portrayals. This accounts for the primary importance of mass education. Unless organizations such as UNESCO can stir up a mass desire for international understanding, prospects for the co-operation of film producers are slim. *The Last Chance* and *Paisan* came from countries where this desire was overwhelmingly strong. Can it be spread and sustained? Films help change mass attitudes on condition that these attitudes have already begun to change.

Notes

1. Films of fact—documentaries and newsreels—will not be considered here, even though they frequently picture foreigners and events abroad. To exclude them is not to belittle their significance as a means of conveying information, but is simply acknowledgment of the fact that they all but disappear in the mass of fiction films. Except perhaps for their transitory wartime vogue, films of fact still belong among the sideshows, at least in the United States.

2. Professor Robert H. Ball, of Queens College, is presently preparing a survey of the innumerable American and European screen versions of Shakespearean plays. In it he plans to comment on the national differences between these versions as well as on the changes they have undergone in each country with the passing of time.

3. *You and the Russians: A series of five programs presented on the Columbia Broadcasting System* . . . A pamphlet issued by CBS. The programs were broadcast in November 1947.

4. Siegfried Kracauer, *From Caligari to Hitler: A Psychological History of the German Film,* Princeton, 1947, p. 206.

5. Leonard W. Doob, *Public Opinion and Propaganda*, New York: Henry Holt, 1948, p. 507.

6. For the whole argument, see Kracauer, *op. cit.*, pp. 5-6.

7. Jack L. Warner, "What Hollywood Isn't," publicity sheet issued by *Hollywood Citizen News and Advertiser*, 1946.

8. *Motion Picture Letter*, issued by the Public Information Committee of the Motion Picture Industry, June 1946, Vol. 5, No. 6.

9. See Kracauer, "Those Movies With a Message," *Harper's Magazine*, June, 1948, pp. 657-72.

10. More immediate reasons for Hollywood's conduct may be found in the "cold war" between the American and British film industries and also in the gloomy aspect of life in Britain, hardly attractive to a screen infatuated with glamor. But what weight these reasons carry accrues to them from the atmospheric pressures on the political scene.

11. John C. Flinn, "Film Industry Watching 'Blockade' as B.O. Cue on Provocative Themes," *Variety*, June 22, 1938.

12. Other films in this vein: *The Charge of the Light Brigade* (1936), *Gunga Din* (1939), *The Sun Never Sets*, etc.

13. Ernest Marshall, "Featured Players and Costly Set . . . ," *New York Times*, April 9, 1933. (Quoted from a clipping which does not include the rest of the title.)

14. Margaret Cole, "How Democratic Is Britain?," *Harper's Magazine*, July, 1948, Vol. 197, No. 1178:106.

15. It even seems that the images which one and the same nation forms of a foreign people in different media of mass communication are far from concurring with each other. In American radio comedies, as Mr. Oscar Katz of Columbia Broadcasting System has informed me, the English are typecast as dull-witted fellows unable to understand a joke.

16. "Mrs. Miniver's War," *Newsweek*, June 15, 1942.

17. Evelyn Russel, "The Quarter's Films," *Sight and Sound*, Winter 1942, Vol. 11, No. 43:69.

18. Quoted from Lewis Gannett, "British Critics' Storm Lashes 'White Cliffs,' " *New York Herald Tribune*, August 20, 1944.

19. Evelyn Russel, "The Quarter's Films," *Sight and Sound*, Summer 1943, Vol. 12, No. 45:17.

20. Charles A. Beard and Mary R. Beard, *America in Midpassage*, vol. III: The Rise of American Civilization, New York: The Macmillan Company, 1941, p. 201.

21. "It Isn't the Screen; It's the Story," *New York World Telegram*, June 4, 1932.

22. Quoted from Kate Cameron's review of this film in the *New York Daily News*, August 31, 1940.

23. Quoted from Bosley Crowther's review of this film in *New York Times*, December 26, 1940.

24. Quoted from Kate Cameron's review of this film in *New York Daily News*, November 5, 1943.

25. Quoted from Archer Winsten's review of this film, *New York Post*, November 5, 1943.

Hollywood and the U.S.A.

By HORTENSE POWDERMAKER

THE ANTHROPOLOGIST sees any segment of society as part of a whole; he views Hollywood as a section of the United States of America, and both in the larger frame of Western civilization. The problems of the movie industry are not unique to it. But some characteristics of the modern world have been greatly exaggerated in Hollywood while others are underplayed. Hollywood is therefore not a reflection, but a caricature of selected contemporary tendencies, which, in turn, leave their imprint on the movies. It is a three-way circular interaction between Hollywood, U.S.A. and movies.

Many people would agree with the characterization of our society by the poet W. H. Auden as "The Age of Anxiety." The present generation has known two world wars and is worried about the possibility of a third, even more devastating. We won the last war and are probably the strongest nation, and yet we are insecure in our relations with former enemies and allies. Our country is prosperous and we have demonstrated an enormous capacity for production, but we are worried about a possible recession and unemployment. We live in a fast changing world but have lost faith in our belief that change is always for the better, and that progress is inevitable. We are not so sure of the happy ending.

Man has become increasingly lonely. Although people live in close physical contact, their relationships have become more and more depersonalized. We have a sense of being with people, and yet do not feel in any way related to them. In cities we are accustomed to having strange people beside us in street car, bus, or uncomfortably close in the subway. The technique of business and many other organizations, in trying to personalize their selling relationships, such as by announcing the name of employees to customers, really fools no one. The fact that the name of the post office clerk, the bank teller or the person who handles complaints in the department store, is posted, does not really influence their relationship with customers. The market place is still basically impersonal. Over the radio, we listen to the voices of strangers relating intimate domestic stories or giving us their opinions about the latest national or world event. All these factors give an illusion of companionship which, however, only increases the feeling of being alone. This loneliness is particularly striking when we compare modern to primitive man with his web of personal relationships within his clan. From birth to death he was tied through reciprocal duties and responsibilities to his clan kindred. Clan membership could not be lost and was as fixed for

Reprinted from *Hollywood, the Dream Factory* (1951), pp. 307-32, by permission of the author and the publisher. (Copyright, 1950, by Hortense Powdermaker.)

the individual as was his sex. He belonged to his group through basic biological ties and isolation was rare.

Many other factors contribute to modern man's anxiety. The traditional American belief that anyone, by working hard and industriously, may rise in the social hierarchy and become rich and successful is being questioned. There is considerable evidence that the American worker realizes that social mobility is decreasing. Workers increasingly believe that hard work no longer counts for as much as it did and that opportunities for advancement are restricted.[1] Many employees do not even understand the immediate aspects of their work situation. A study made at an electric company, which had an unusually good relationship with its employees, showed that there was much that the worker did not understand about his job, even including the method of payment. The author thought that this lack of understanding caused a feeling of exasperation and sense of personal futility on the part of the workers.[2] Modern man lives in a world which is difficult to comprehend. He is prosperous or unemployed in recurring economic cycles about which economists talk in learned words of cause and effect. But the average man sees only the effect, and is confused as to the causes.

In Hollywood there is far more confusion and anxiety than in the society which surrounds it. Even in its most prosperous periods when net profits were enormous, far surpassing those of other businesses, everyone was scared. Now, when diminishing foreign markets, increasing costs of production, competition with European pictures, and changing box-office tastes threaten the swollen profits of past prosperity, fear rises to panic. Anxiety grips everyone from executive to third assistant director. The happy endings of at least 100 per cent net profit for the studio and a relatively long period of employment at high salaries for employees, are becoming less common. Yet, although this is well known, many individuals still cherish the fantasy for themselves. In the movies the happy ending is still almost universal. Perhaps the people who make the movies cannot afford to admit that there can be another kind of ending, and many of those who sit in the audience prefer this fantasy, too. But an increasing number are becoming dissatisfied with the so obviously contrived nature of these endings. The neat and unrealistic movie solution to all problems is neither satisfying nor entertaining.

Attitudes stem from the past and change slowly. In a rapidly changing society such as ours, some attitudes born out of a past situation continue under new conditions, even when inappropriate. Today there are people who will still believe in the *laissez-faire* economy of the frontier days and are hostile to planning designed for a country which no longer has a frontier. But many who stubbornly cling to the old *laissez-faire* thinking are uneasy lest they fight a losing battle, while many of those who plan are afraid that the planning may go too far. Neither side is really very sure of itself. In Hollywood the lack of planning and extemporizing has been carried to extremes probably not known even on the frontier, and greater certainly than in any contemporary industry. Even more important, extemporizing without a plan has long been regarded by many as a necessary and inherent part of movie making. However, the proper accompaniment, the frontier self-confidence and courage in taking chances, is very rare in Hollywood. The distinguished director-producer William Wyler appeals for

". . . 'men of courage' in Hollywood to reach out for a wealth of picture material which the industry has shunned so far. . . . We need men of courage in high places who will not be intimidated or coerced into making only 'safe' pictures—pictures devoid of any ideas whatsoever." Too often he has bunked up against a situation where the top men were forced to decide between two stories and asked the question, "Which is the safest?" Mediocrity in films is the direct result of playing it safe.[3]

The men who make these decisions do not trust the public to like a picture which has ideas in it, Mr. Wyler says, in the same interview. It might be added that the men who do not trust the public usually do not trust themselves.

From the frontier past comes also the tradition of individual aggressive behavior. This persists although industry has become increasingly regimented and co-operation more essential. In the movie industry which depends on the collaborative effort of many people, the aggression is more ruthless than any described on the frontier, although, due to the insecurities of most people, it is masked under "Darlings" and "Sweethearts" and costly presents and parties. In the movies, however, the hatred and aggression comes through with a bang. Here is undiluted violence. This may meet the needs of the makers of our daydreams, as well as of those who consume them. Many people in our society experience a high level of frustration but are unable, either because of social pressures or inner fear, to express their resentment. In the movies they may find comfort and encouragement for their fantasies.

We have also inherited a Puritan tradition, stressing the sinfulness of human nature and giving us taboos to curb it. Today the doctrine of the innate evilness of man has lost much of its force and is far less a part of the conscious beliefs of many people. There is a growing awareness that babies are born neither sinful nor virtuous, but with potentialities for many different kinds of behavior, and even the definitions of sin and virtue continue to change. Hollywood, however, even more than the rest of society, feels the weight of Puritan traditions. The industry has imposed on itself a set of taboos derived in part from seventeenth-century New England Protestanism, in order to appease the Catholic Legion of Decency and other would-be censors. No one in Hollywood, and very few outside of it, believe in the Code, nor are the censors appeased or pleased. For while the taboos are applied in the production of each movie, they fail completely to achieve the Puritan concepts on which they are based. They serve merely to make movies more dishonest, which is the natural result of any hypocrisy.

An important focus for much of the anxiety in our modern world is in our changing values and goals. The anthropologist knows that the important differences between groups of men are not biological, but lie in their goals. Among the same people the goals may change from one historical period to another, such as from Elizabethan to Victorian England, and they obviously vary from one society to another. In the early Middle Ages religion provided the sanctions for most behavior. Since then the church, while still a functioning institution, has continued to lose much of its vitality. As Kluckhohn writes:

> The anthropologist must characterize our cultures as profoundly irreligious. More than half of our people still occasionally go through the forms, and there are rural and ethnic islands in our population where religion is still a vital force. But very few of our leaders are still religious in the sense that they are convinced that prayer or the observance of church codes will affect the course of human events. . . . Belief in God's judgments and punishments as a motive for behavior is limited to a decreasing minority.[4]

Even more importantly, relatively few people today, as compared to a couple of hundred years ago, have the kind of relationship with God to bring them security or comfort. Our society stresses the search for a good time rather than the quest for salvation.

Traditions, however, have a habit of living on in the deeper levels of our consciousness, even when they are overtly denied. Comparatively few people give the impression of really enjoying their wealth or their good times. Many of them appear to be consumed with an obsession to merely fill up time with more and more activity, and space with more and more costly objects. The frenzied and compulsive activity in the studios and outside of them is one of Hollywood's most striking characteristics. Another is the evaluation of not only objects, but people too, in terms of how much they cost. In making movies, this is reflected in the idea that the more a picture costs the better it must be. The tendency towards lavish sets, costumes, and other extravagances is now being curtailed because of the need for economy and the trend to shooting on location. But, with a few exceptions, the correlation of the value of pictures with their budgets is still the prevalent type of thinking in Hollywood. The greater the cost the more sure the studio feels of success, and hence high costs become one way of reducing anxiety. Actually, money can no more guarantee dramatic values than it can insure accuracy or significance in research.

The U.S.A. has been labeled by many students as a business civilization as contrasted to a religious one. This is obviously true, but not the whole truth. Roger Butterfield has described the dominant themes of American life as "the desire to see all men free and equal, and the desire to be richer and stronger than anyone else."[5] This conflict between human and property rights has, as this author points out, generated much of the drama of American life. The political idealism and humanitarianism of the eighteenth and nineteenth centuries, as well as the earlier Puritanism, still influence our business civilization. In our Declaration of Independence is the quintessence of idealism, expressing for the first time the idea that all men have a right to happiness. If the anthropologist interested in our contemporary society digs under the top layers of people's beliefs, he will find still surviving the archaic concepts that money is not the road to happiness, or, at least, not the main one. If he is historically minded, he will note that when private capitalism was developing, the man who accumulated wealth through his own hard work was respected and admired; but that later when private capitalism changed to a corporate form, the corporation was regarded as an enemy of the people. Theodore Roosevelt became famous as a "trust-buster." No man in the U.S.A. becomes a national hero just through making a lot of money. He must have made some contribution to the welfare of his fellow men; most of the nation's heroes have been humanitarians.

In Hollywood the concept of a business civilization has been carried to an extreme. Property is far more important than man, and human values have to struggle hard to exist at all. But, while the heroes in Hollywood are those with the most money, in the movies we find the opposite extreme. The wealthy tycoon is almost always the villain and the hero is the man of good will. The hero or heroine may be rich, but wealth does not give them their status. Often we are asked to admire the poor little rich girl who breaks away from her luxurious environment to marry the poor hero whom she loves. Hollywood leans over backward to sentimentalize love, which in the movies is always more important than wealth. Earning a living is never shown with any sense of reality and making a fortune is rarely portrayed sympathetically. True, most of the characters in the movies are better dressed and live more luxuriously than do their counterparts in real life. The secretary dresses like a wealthy debutante and the female psychoanalyst like the popular concept of a Hollywood star. But neither they nor any other heroine or hero are shown as fundamentally interested in or concerned about the problem of making a living or becoming rich. It is only possible to speculate on the reasons for this almost complete negation of economic motives which are so prevalent in our society. The very extremes to which most movies go in the negation may mean that the executives who control the contents of the movies have themselves some hidden ambivalence about their goals. After all, the executives, as well as the actors, do belong to the human species and are not completely unaffected by the conflicting values of our society. Or, they may think that this underplaying of economic motives in the movies is desired by the audience. Neither reason precludes the other, and both could be true, as well as other unknown ones. Whatever the reasons, Hollywood represents a caricature and overelaboration of the business motives and goals of our society, while the movies consistently underplay the same characteristics.

Art and aesthetic goals have always been less important in our society than either business or humanitarian ones.

So in the actual production of movies in Hollywood, the American concept of the unimportance of the artist is magnified. Those who know most about storytelling, who are gifted with imagination, and who have a knowledge of human beings, all raw materials which the camera transforms into a movie, do not have sufficient status to use their abilities. As one director expressed it, "the environment is hostile to them." The environment favors the latest developments in sound and color, but discourages new ideas from its artists. These men, who traditionally have known considerable freedom in expressing themselves, work under the direction of businessmen.

The movies have to earn their living. Unlike some of the fine arts, they are not privately endowed nor are they an esoteric medium for the enjoyment of the few. The goals of business and art are each justifiable and not necessarily irreconcilable. When art meets the needs of a large number of people in our society, it inevitably makes a profit. Some of our most creative popular artists, such as Chaplin, Gershwin, Walt Disney and Irving Berlin, have made fortunes. The problem is not the simple one of art versus business. The artist can contribute to business. But his stock-in-trade is not only his technical know-how: it includes the ability to interpret man to himself. This is true in folk art, popular art and fine art. But it makes little difference to the businessman whether he assuages man's anxieties by interpretation, or whether he exploits them; but the latter is easier. Or, if phoniness brings in money easily, why bother about the details of honesty? The front-office executives are not completely blind to humanitarian issues, but they seem far more interested in profits than in man. Most of them are not conditioned to be otherwise. Artists have a different kind of conditioning. While they are concerned about money, they must also, in order to be reasonably contented, use their gifts to give their interpretations. It has already been indicated that while only relatively few of the Hollywood writers, directors and actors are artists in this sense, they are far more important than the host of mediocre people.

The social organization of Hollywood has, however, permitted the businessman to take over the functions of the artists and to substitute his values for theirs. The movies are the first art form of any kind, popular, folk or fine, to become a trust. Quite early the major companies combined in their efforts to restrain competition and to blacklist those who would not do their bidding. The struggle between the Independents and the organization of the major studios still continues. At the same time movies increasingly make use of a developing technology and of the heritage from theater and literature. Under any circumstances such a combination would create complex problems. In this particular situation, the men with power have known how to exploit the advantages of a trust better than they could utilize the assets of literature and drama. They have not seemed to realize that the efficiency of the factory is possible because it turns out identical products, whether automobiles or coffeepots, and that this principle cannot be applied to the making of movies. Since these businessmen have neither understanding nor respect for the artist's ability, they attempt to negate or destroy it, partly out of ignorance and partly from a desire to satisfy their urge to dominate men. It is only an exceptional executive who does not give the impression that he would have been equally satisfied as a tycoon in any other industry.

Another trait of our civilization is its high level of ingenuity and inventiveness in the mechanical skills. Our heroes include men such as Thomas Edison, Alexander Graham Bell, Eli Whitney and Henry Ford as well as the humanitarian, political figures. We are justly famous for the enormous number of additions to material culture which make life more comfortable. Movies are themselves a remarkable invention in their integration of electricity, photography, color, sound and acting. The history of inventions from the first stone ax is a fascinating story and one peculiar to our species. For only man is a tool-making and tool-using animal. Each succeeding example of his ingenuity and cleverness has brought, however, its own problems. This has always been true, but only recently has atomic energy forced a public recognition of the serious social consequences of technological developments.

The control of machines and of all our inventions for the benefit of man is one of the most pressing problems of our time. Machines can enslave people or free them. The Industrial Revolution brought young children into sweatshops and kept them and their parents for long hours at machines. Gradually changes in the social and economic organization reduced the hours of work, set age limits for workers, and enabled them, as well as other people, to enjoy the higher standard of living which machines made possible. But even the most casual observer of our society today recognizes its machinelike character. Not only do machines increasingly replace human labor, but what is left of it grows more mechanical. The role of the individual worker on the assembly line tends to be more and more automatic and he has less and less understanding of its relationship or his own to the whole. The ironic climax is his attempt to escape into fantasies and daydreams, themselves manufactured on an assembly line, far more concerned with technology than with meaning.

The problem of power has been important since the beginning of mankind's existence. Its history follows no straight line, but lunges forward and backward, always correlated with the concept of what is human nature and with the meaning of freedom. In the very beginning of his history, man was more at one with the natural world than he is today. He might think he was descended from a totemic animal and there was a close tie with other animals and to the world of nature. Primitive man was also more closely linked with his kindred than is modern man. Much of life in Stone Age societies consisted of a series of reciprocal duties and responsibilities between members of an extended family, clan or other social group, which continued even after death. In this system of close relationships there was little room for emphasis on individuality. Differences between people might be noted, but were not considered particularly important. Rebels from traditional customs were few. If head-hunting was a way of proving manhood and becoming eligible for marriage, it would be unusual to find one of the young men of the tribe staying behind, murmuring "I'm not the type," as the others went off on a head-hunting expedition. Some primitive societies do have institutionalized modes of behavior for people who do not fit into the norm, such as homosexuals; but on the whole little attention is paid to the less striking individual differences. Traditions are followed, and power to implement them lies with the elders.

The process of the emergence of the individual from these primary ties Erich Fromm calls "individuation." He points out that the same process occurs in the life history of an individual.[6] Birth involves a biological separation from the mother and the beginning of an individual existence, even though the child is functionally dependent on his mother for a considerable time. Mankind as well as the individual struggles through the ages to free himself from primary ties. Familiar landmarks in this history are Christianity, with its emphasis on the importance and value of each individual's soul to God, the end of Feudalism, the Reformation, the Industrial Revolution, political revolutions with their overthrow of monarchies, and the development of political and economic democracy. During this process power has gone through many re-allocations, from the tribal elders to feudal lords, popes, kings and emperors. Gradually it was diffused from the hands of a few to the many, who include elected political representatives, owners of industry, leaders of labor and others. This century has seen revolutions which reversed the process and concentrated power again in the hands of a few dictators. Man, as Fromm says, both wants and fears freedom; he struggles to gain it and he gives it up.

The meaning of the word "freedom," of course, is not the same to all men, or at all times. There are many freedoms and none is absolute. Most of them connote freedom from some form of constraint, either in society or within man's personality. But, underlying all freedoms, as Ralph Barton Perry writes, is the freedom of thought. This implies choice and an awareness of alternatives, based on both imagination and knowledge.[7] The *exercise* of the freedom of choice may be restricted, by institutions and customs, or by psychological forces within man, due to ignorance and fear. The degree to which freedom of choice is permitted is always linked with society's particular concept of the nature of man. Today, at one end of the power scale is the idea of man as a passive creature without ability to choose for himself, manipulated by a powerful few who claim omniscience. Men are puppets pulled by strings, seen and hidden. They are told what to think politically, scientifically, morally, and aesthetically. Spontaneity in thinking is discouraged and conformity is the goal. Choice of an alternative which involves different values is not presented in this concept. When all the manipulation is done by the state and when the strings are pulled by a dictator, it is called totalitarianism.

The democratic concept of the nature of man is in continuous conflict with the totalitarian one, but the struggle is not confined to the political level, or to international relationships. It is part of the texture of our daily lives, in the family, in school and college, in courts, in Congressional and State legislative committees, and in every other area which has responsibility in human relations. There appears to be an increasing tendency in some of these areas to stifle, overtly and subtly, the expression of opinions which are not those of the majority, to overstress conformity, and to so prevent freedom of thought and of choice.

Family life, education, and political organizations have always been conditioning forces molding the lives of people; but mass communications are new. Certainly they have enriched our culture. Without the invention of printing, literacy for masses of people would be impossible. Radio gives a speed and ease of communication undreamed of by our ancestors. Movies can bring drama to millions of people who otherwise would never enter a theater. But the mass communications, like every other advance, bring problems as well as advantages. Among the most serious is the capacity of these communications to manipulate the ideas, opinions and emotions of vast audiences. More and more do people depend on what they read in their daily newspaper or what their radio commentator says, for their opinions. This means that man functions passively, taking over opinions, ideas, and prejudices ready-made from others, rather than actively examining a number of choices and making up his own mind. In a totalitarian society all the mass communications are controlled by a ruling clique, and no choice is permitted the citizen. In the United States there is a choice, but relatively few people avail themselves of it. They do not all seem to realize that almost every newspaper has its own line, whether it be the [New York] *Daily News* or the *Daily Worker,* as has each radio commentator; and many do not bother to examine different lines. Albert Schweitzer thinks that our whole society is geared to what he calls "the renunciation of thinking," and he labels our age one of spiritual bankruptcy. He writes:

The organized political, social and religious associations of our time are at work to induce individual man not to arrive at his convictions by his own thinking but to take as his own, such convictions as they keep ready-made for him. Any man who thinks for himself and at the same time is spiritually free is to the associations something inconvenient and even uncanny. He does not offer sufficient guarantee that he will merge himself in their organizations in the way they wish. All corporate bodies look today for their strength not so much to the spiritual worth of the ideas they represent and to that of the people who belong to them, as to the attainment of the highest possible degree of unity and exclusiveness. It is here that they expect to find their strongest power for offense and defense.[8]

The tendency of our age is not only to take over our thoughts ready-made and to lazily conform, but to continue the same pattern with our emotions. This is to be expected, since the dichotomy between thought and feeling is, of course, artificial. In manipulating and defining our emotions and ideas about human relations, mass communications are among the most powerful agents. For instance, the pulp literature, advertising and movies all hammer home a similar concept of love. Advertising both uses and abuses man's basic need for love to sell its ware. The young woman who rides the subway or bus to work, daily reads that holding a husband is dependent on using certain soap flakes which will keep the color of her underwear fresh; and in the past, there was the negative campaign of "Always a bridesmaid and never a bride" unless a certain mouthwash was used. Not only does advertising sell its products, but it also sells a concept of love and human relations. The pulps and movies sell their concept of love, too, with the movies being probably far the more powerful, since in them, love objects are dramatically portrayed by glamorous or highly attractive men and women. Love, in most movies, is limited to instant biological attraction without any other elements. The hero sees a girl waiting for a bus; one look at her well-shaped legs, strutting bosom, and golden hair is sufficient to tell him that this is his mate for life, and the pursuit begins. In actual life in Hollywood, and elsewhere, the end of such a pursuit would usually be only the bed, quickly reached. Censorship, of course, forbids this portrayal, and so the ending is transformed into the romantic one of happiness ever after. This confusion between love and infatuation or an adolescent "crush" is repeated over and over again. Another recurring theme in movies is the loss, or threatened loss, of a love object; the solution is usually suicide, murder, or insanity. Finding another love object rarely occurs, although our divorce and remarriage rate indicate this is a fairly frequent modern solution. Love is also supposed to be the mainspring for all creative work, whether in science or the arts. In the lives of great artists and scientists which have been filmed, the hero is usually dependent for his accomplishment not on his own genius, intelligence, or hard work, but on the loving devotion of his mate, or more colloquially, "the little woman."

The other emotional behavior most frequently emphasized in the movies, besides love, is violence. Radio, comics and headlines are vibrant with it. Like love, violence has long been a part of all drama. But, as John Houseman writes:

What is significant about our contemporary "tough" films (critics and ladies' organizations to the contrary) is *not* their surface violence but the neurotic reaction that accompanies it. It is not the act of brutality that is repellent, but the indifference with which it is regarded by those who commit it and those whom it affects.[9]

As Houseman points out in his discussion of the characters in *The Big Sleep,* "It is these people—spiritless zombies, utterly lacking in moral or tragic sense—that are really frightening, not their forays with blackjack and pistol."

The problem of aggression in our society is not an easy one. The ordinary frictions of life generate an aggressive attitude and it is a necessary ingredient underlying much success. Yet aggressive behavior in general is not approved. Rarely is an outlet permitted in the family. If an adolescent or person in his late teens is angry with his father or mother, instead of letting his anger out on them, he is more apt to rush out of the house and go to a movie. Here, he can find an outlet for his feelings. But his relationship with parents and the situation which caused his aggression remains unchanged. Many other older people are afraid of showing their aggressive feelings, because they fear loss of love or affection. Movies provide a vicarious outlet, but the basic insecurities of the individual are left untouched.

The heightening of suspense is part of most pictures in which violence is a part. These movies aim to increase tensions and their advertisements feature the breathless suspense, excitement and horror. An element of suspense is part of all drama. But never has it been so intense and so exaggerated as in most current thrilling movies. A possible hypothesis is that people cannot permit themselves to be fully aware of all the suspense and fear involved in the atomic bomb, a possible third war, and the future in general for themselves and the world. Although they try to evade the problem, the anxiety remains. The suspense of finding out "who done it" in the movie or detective story may be one way of relieving the greater suspense of what is going to happen to them and their children in the future. The suspense gags of a man dangling on a clothesline between two high buildings and wild hysterical automobile chases, in all of which no one gets hurt, may offer some relief. In a typical Abbott and Costello comedy, *The Buck Private Comes Home,* Costello drives a midget car in a race and through all kinds of fantastic obstacles. He does not know how to drive, is unable to control the car, and throughout the whole race is scared stiff. Through a series of miraculous escapes he comes out safely and wins the race. An audience who feels helpless to control an equally fantastic social situation, would like nothing better than a Costello victory through a miracle.

The manipulation of behavior as well as emotions is common to our society. Salesmen are important in our business civilization, and success in selling is attained primarily through the manipulation of people. *How to Win Friends and Influence People,* and all the books similar to this best seller, attempt to give the techniques. Knowing the right people is regarded as more important to success in many jobs than knowledge, experience, or integrity. Many young men go to prestige universities in the East in order to make "contacts," which will help them in Wall Street or business careers after commencement. There is hardly a profession, even those in which skill and knowledge count, that does not number among its successes a goodly number who have come to the top primarily through the slap-on-the-back and similar techniques. Of course, knowing influential people and getting their help is part of human relations in every society. But our society exaggerates the pattern.

While these are some of the totalitarian elements which exist in democratic societies, there are basic differences between them and totalitarian ones. In the latter, the manipulation of people is carried to the greatest extremes and, even more important, is always done by a few powerful men at the head of the state. In democracies, the manipulation is done by many different forces with diverse goals and often in conflict. The differences between the totalitarian philosophy of man as an obedient robot and the traditional democratic concept of man's freedom and independence are very significant. These differences in social organization and in philosophy should not be underestimated. Totalitarian elements in our society, whether in school, home, politics, are only one of a number of alternatives. For, while democratic ideas and behavior are not always implemented or used, there are opportunities for freedom of thought and behavior. It is true that sometimes the citizen merely repeats opinions he hears over the radio or reads in the newspaper. But there are other times when he bursts through all these synthetic ideas and thinks for himself, as he has demonstrated in several presidential elections. The election of President Roosevelt in 1944 and of President Truman in 1948 ran counter to the majority of editorial opinions and radio propaganda. As far as is known, the citizen of the totalitarian state is not given this opportunity to choose or the family and educational conditioning to utilize it. In American society, as in many of the Western European ones, there are present conflicting trends of totalitarianism and democracy.

Hollywood represents totalitarianism. Its basis is economic rather than political but its philosophy is similar to that of the totalitarian state. In Hollywood, the concept of man as a passive creature to be manipulated extends to those who work for the studios, to personal and social relationships, to the audiences in the theaters and to the characters in the movies. The basic freedom of being able to choose between alternatives is absent. The gifted people who have the capacity for choice cannot exercise it; the executives who technically have the freedom of choice do not actually have it, because they usually lack the knowledge and imagination necessary for making such a choice. Much behavior is compulsive, springing from fears, hidden and open. The careful planning and good judgment of the exceptional people have been already described and are in dramatic contrast to the hysterial behavior of the others.

The Hollywood atmosphere of crises and continuous anxiety is a kind of hysteria which prevents people from thinking, and is not too different from the way dictators use wars and continuous threats of war as an emotional basis for maintaining their power. As the late Dr. Harry Stack Sullivan pointed out, there is considerable difference between fear and anxiety. Fear, he said, is often provoked by a new or novel situation and wears off as one becomes accustomed to it. Anxiety, however, arises out of relationships with other people which are disturbed, and "from its mildest to its most extreme manifestations interferes with effective alertness to the factors in the current situation that are immediately relevant to its occurrence, and thus with the refinement and precision of action related to its relief or reduction."[10] Put more colloquially and applied to Hollywood, this means that a stage director who directs a movie for the first time might have some fear which would disappear as he became more accustomed to the new situation. In the meantime, the fear would not inhibit his learning as much as possible about the new situation and applying his knowledge to it. But the anxiety of the average producer who has been in movies all his adult life springs out of his character and interpersonal relations, and the Hollywood situation calls forth and increases what is already there. Nor is it possible to become accustomed to anxiety-provoking situations. The very anxiety prevents an awareness of the factors which call it forth and of realistically doing something about them. These anxiety-ridden producers and executives of Hollywood try to reduce anxiety by spending more money, buying a best seller whether or not it is appropriate for a movie, using ten writers instead of one, having three "big name" stars in a movie, and so on. But none of these formulas rids him of his anxiety. Even where a picture is a big success, he knows the same anxiety on the next one.

In *Mein Kampf,* Hitler wrote about Fate as sometimes cruel and other times loving. Whether it is called Fate, destiny, or breaks, the underlying concept is the same: man gives up the attempt to exercise some control over his life through his own intelligence, because he thinks forces beyond his domain completely direct it.

The totalitarian concept of man is not limited to human relationships in Hollywood, but is reflected in many movies. Life, success or misfortune is usually portrayed as caused by luck or an accident. Only rarely does a movie show the process of becoming successful or the process of disintegration. Either one is treated as a *fait accompli* in the beginning of the picture or as caused by accidents during the course of the movie. Most movie characters, whether hero or villain, heroine or jade, are passive beings to whom things happen accidentally. Rarely do they even try to think through the situation in which they find themselves. They are buffeted about and defeated; or Fate smiles on them and almost magically they are successful. A few pictures have freed themselves from this formula. In *Home of the Brave* the Negro hero is shown as suffering realistically from prejudice. His escape is not on a magic carpet into a never-never world but through a painful psychological process, which the movie plainly says is kaleidoscoped. The Negro problem is seen as part of a larger human one. Nor is the problem over at the end of the picture. The hero merely understands it better and has a way of handling it.

The totalitarian concept likewise extends toward the audiences, often regarded as suckers whose emotional needs and anxieties can be exploited for profit. Hollywood producers are, of course, not the only people with undue anxieties and many of the movies cater to the same kind of anxieties in their audiences, strengthening rather than reducing them, and contributing nothing to understanding. Only men who are not completely ridden with anxieties and who have some understanding of their own, as well as mankind's problems, can make other kinds of pictures. "The people," however, are always used as a rationalization—by dictators who say they rule for the good of the people, and by Hollywood producers who say they give the people what they want.

Until recently Hollywood offered very little more choice to audiences than it did to its artist employees. Today, because of competition from both exceptional Hollywood movies and foreign films, there is more choice.

The ultimate in totalitarian power is power for its own sake, although dictators offer various rationalizations for propaganda purposes. Some of the men with power in Hollywood present the same picture. These men have made millions, and more money means very little to them; but they cannot get enough of power: power over human beings in the studio and power over the daydreams of men and women who sit in the darkened theater.

For men of this type there is often enjoyment also in the power to humiliate, which they exercise in their relationships with their employees.

Of course Hollywood is no more completely totalitarian than it is completely primitive. The genesis of Hollywood is different from that of any totalitarian state. In the latter the dictators either seize power through revolution, or attain it by making promises to relieve the misery and anxieties from which people suffer, or they do both. In Hollywood most of the men who enjoy power have it simply because they got there first and were able to form the social structure of movie-making as they desired, rather than in the interests of movie-making. The Hollywood dictators have not been able to make converts, in the way of any successful political dictator. He gets his subjects when young, and conversion begins in the kindergarten. The subjects in Hollywood arrive there as adults with fairly well-formulated ideas about how they can best work and live. They accept the dictatorship only nominally, because of the high salaries. They rarely accept it emotionally and, instead, are filled with resentment and bitterness toward it.

The rebels, in this case the artists, do not struggle in underground movements to outmaneuver the studio executives. They fight openly to gain power, that is, to get into positions in which they can make important decisions and influence the movies. A sufficient number of gifted writers, directors and actors are succeeding to indicate at least a trend which offers a variation and may, eventually, modify or change the system.

These exceptional individuals receive little help in their struggles. The Federal Government tries to reduce the monopolistic power of the industry and to regulate its buying and selling practices. Censorship groups attempt to regulate the morality of the pictures and succeed only in making them dishonest. Guilds fight for more money for their members, but do nothing about a contract, which allows the employer almost literally to own his employees for its duration. The exceptional individuals, with great strength of character and drive, with high talent, and with a true morality, work on their own as they try to dent the power situation in Hollywood, alter the human relationships, and give meaning to their movies.

Totalitarianism, whether in a foreign nation or in Hollywood, represents one of the backward swings in history. But primitive societies seldom know the degradation that modern man can suffer under a dictator. Although primitive cultures have a similar lack of emphasis on the individual, there are wide differences between them and modern totalitarian states. The two situations differ widely in origin and effect. In primitive societies man has not yet emerged sufficiently from his primary ties to his family and clan kindred to emphasize his own individuality. But totalitarianism attempts to negate the individuality of men who *have* broken these primary ties, who *have* known, and valued, freedom. The force of tradition offers very little choice to primitive man. The force of the modern police state also offers very little choice. Primitive cultures lack the knowledge and awareness of man's potentialities. Modern totalitarian societies fear and distrust them. Evolutionary thinking is not in style in the social sciences, but it is possible to view the history of man as a gradual freeing of himself from primary ties and becoming freer to utilize and develop his uniquely human characteristics.

Hollywood has the elaborated totalitarian elements we have described: the concept of people as property and as objects to be manipulated, highly concentrated and personalized power for power's sake, an amorality, and an atmosphere of breaks, continuous anxiety and crises. The result of this over-elaboration is business inefficiency, deep frustration in human relations, and a high number of unentertaining second- and third-rate movies.

There are, of course, other patterns in the U.S.A. which Hollywood could elaborate. They are the democratic ones of the dignity of man, the concept of freedom, a belief in man's capacity to think, create, and to exercise some control over his life—a belief that man is more important than property—all part of our cultural heritage. How far will Hollywood utilize them? It is not a matter of more brains and talent or of money, but of generating new modes of behavior and a system in which collaboration is more important than domination. Any changes that will occur will not come out of magical thinking or waiting for breaks. Nor is it possible to be sure of a "happy ending." No anthropologist exer expects a complete break from the past. But he does know that societies assume different forms through contact with others, through technological inventions, and through changes in values and goals. He can predict that Hollywood will not go back to its isolated position and that there will be new technological developments. The really difficult question to answer is, Can Hollywood change its way of thinking and its values, so that the democratic concept of man becomes more important than a totalitarian one?

Notes

1. William Lloyd Warner and J. O. Low, *The Social System of the Modern Factory*, p. 182. New Haven: Yale University Press.

2. Elton Mayo, *The Human Problems of an Industrial Civilization*, 2nd ed., pp. 119-120. New York: The Macmillan Co.

3. *Variety*, October 12, 1949.

4. Clyde Kluckhohn, *Mirror for Man*, pp. 247-248. New York: McGraw-Hill.

5. The American Past: *A History of the United States from Concord to Hiroshima*, p. 5. New York: Simon and Schuster.

6. Erich Fromm, *Escape from Freedom*, New York: Rinehart. Fromm discusses this whole problem and its relation to freedom in detail. ,

7. Ralph Barton Perry, *Characteristically American*, pp. 148-149. New York: Knopf.

8. Albert Schweitzer, *Out of My Life and Thought*, p. 255. New York: Henry Holt.

9. John Houseman, "What Makes American Movies Tough?," in *Vogue*, January, 1947.

10. Harry Stack Sullivan, "Multidisciplined Co-ordination of Interpersonal Data," in *Culture and Personality*, p. 179. Proceeding of an Interdisciplinary Conference held under the auspices of the Viking Fund. Published by the Viking Fund, New York.

The Good-Bad Girl

By MARTHA WOLFENSTEIN AND NATHAN LEITES

THE DIFFICULTY of choosing between a good and a bad girl is one of the major problems of love-life in western culture. The problem is to fuse two feelings which men have found it hard to have in relation to the same woman. On the one hand, there are sexual impulses, which a man may feel to be bad, and which he may find it hard to associate with a woman whom he considers admirable. The image, and the actuality, of the "bad" woman arises to satisfy sexual impulses which men feel to be degrading. On the other hand, there are affectionate impulses evoked by women who resemble the man's mother or sister, "good" women. A good girl is the sort that a man should marry, but she has the disadvantage of not being sexually stimulating.

There are various possible solutions to this conflict. The attempt may be made to satisfy one of these impulses at the expense of the other, to satisfy them both but in different directions, or to combine the two impulses in a single relationship. Exclusive devotion to a good woman constituted the stock image of Victorian marriage. Oppressed by the sway of the Angel in the House, rebels might go to the opposite extreme of seeking only prostitutes. In the supposedly frequent pattern of various continental European cultures, a man might keep both a wife and a mistress. Satisfaction was thus sought for both sexual and affectionate feelings, but it was not supposed that one woman could satisfy both. Another presumably frequent arrangement has been for a young man to have relations with bad women up to marriage, after which there is a substantial shift of attachment towards the good woman. In the reverse possibility the established husband and father of a family breaks away, or is diverted by wicked seductress.

Efforts to combine the two components produce a variety of real or imagined feminine types. The image of the bad woman may be transformed so that she becomes the object of more ideal feelings. The prostitute may be redeemed by love, as in the case of Camille. Her prostitution may be compensated for by a saintly character, as in the case of Sonia, in Dostoievsky's *Crime and Punishment,* who walked the streets only to save her family from starvation. Her involvement in low life may seem irrelevant to the essential nature of the beautiful woman who passes through it detached and unaffected. Or the attempt may be made to glorify the bad woman, to see her as a priestess of a pleasure unspoiled by scruples (Swinburne's Dolores). Proceeding in the other direction, an effort may be made to

Reprinted from *Movies: A Psychological Study* (1950), pp. 25-46, by permission of the author and the publisher. (Copyright, 1950, by the Free Press.)

infuse the image of the good woman with some qualities of her opposite. The good woman may appear for a time to be bad, so that she acquires an exciting aura which is not entirely dissipated when her goodness becomes established. Or the good woman may become transformed—the business-like career girl takes off her glasses. The dull wife may learn a lesson from a lover and return to her husband more pleasurable.

The man may see the beloved woman in different ways. He may mis-takenly form an idealized picture of a bad woman, and suffer disillusion-ment. The good girl may appear to him as bad, and the eventual revelation may be in her favor. The woman also may present herself in various ways. The bad woman may conceal her badness; the good woman may pretend to be bad, or make no effort to conceal what, misleadingly, looks bad. A variety of dramatic possibilities results from combinations of the different feminine types, the way they present themselves, and the sequence of im-pressions that the man gets. While Camille was being transformed by love, she deceived her lover into believing that she was still bad. His image of her declined at the same time that her character became ennobled.

Current American films have produced the image of the good-bad girl. She is a good girl who appears to be bad. She does not conceal her apparent badness, and uncertainty about her character may persist through the greater part of the film. The hero suspects that she is bad, but finally discovers this was a mistaken impression. Thus he has a girl who has attracted him by an appearance of wickedness, and whom in the end he can take home and introduce to Mother.

Usually the good-bad girl appears to be promiscuous, or to be involved with a bad man. Occasionally she appears guilty of theft or murder. The title character in *Gilda* (after whom a Bikini bomb was named) appears quite promiscuous through the greater part of the film; in the end she turns out to be a faithful and devoted woman who has never loved anyone but the hero. Gilda and the hero had been lovers before the action of the film begins and had separated because of his jealousy. When they meet again the hero has become the right-hand man of a big gambler and international schemer; Gilda has become the gambler's wife. The hero is tortured not only by seeing Gilda as his boss's wife, but also by her strenuous flirtations with other men. Eventually the boss disappears and is considered dead. Gilda has tried to persuade the hero of her continued love for him and he now agrees to marry her. But he does not believe in her. To punish her for her apparent infidelities to the boss and to himself, he holds her a virtual prisoner. His strong-arm men follow her wherever she goes and forcibly dissuade her admirers. One night Gilda appears at the swank night club adjoining the gambling casino which the hero now runs. She sings and dances seductively and begins stripping off her clothes (she doesn't get much farther than her long black gloves) while men from the audience rush for-ward to assist her. The hero, who enters just in time to get a glimpse of the climax of the performance, sends his men to carry her out.

While episodes of this sort present the image of the beautiful promiscuous woman, they are interspersed with occasions when Gilda pleads with the hero to believe that she has never loved anyone but him. In the end it turns out that what the hero saw was a deceptive appearance, and what Gilda told him was quite true. An understanding police official, who interests himself in their affairs, persuades the hero of this. All the carryings-on of Gilda with other men have been motivated by her love for the hero, whom she wished to hold by making him jealous. Once this has been explained to the hero by an impartial observer, everything is cleared up.

The hero's distress when he believed in Gilda's promiscuity did not impel him to look for a more quiet domestic type. In the end he finds that he can eat his cake and have it. He gets the girl with the aura of innumerable men in her life, and the guarantee that she is a good girl and belongs to him alone.

In *Till the End of Time,* the hero has several occasions for suspecting the heroine of promiscuousness, but each time this is successfully explained away. While the image of Gilda seemed intensely bad till the final explanation, the image of this heroine fluctuates back and forth between apparent lapses and virtuous explanations. The figure of the beloved woman who continually allays doubts about her fidelity with plausible explanations is familiar. Only in other versions this woman was deceiving her man. His suspicions were well-founded, and her explanations were false. In the case of the good-bad girl this is reversed. What the man sees turns out to be illusory; what the woman tells him is true. Deceptive circumstances have been substituted for the deceiving woman. And the denouement in which the trusting man realizes that his beloved is false has been replaced by the happy outcome in which the suspicious hero learns that the seemingly bad girl is really good.

In *The Big Sleep,* the heroine appears involved with a shady night club owner, who turns out to be a gangster and murderer. The hero, a private detective, who has been hired by the heroine's father, finds the girl trying to block his investigations. Her efforts seem related to her connection with the night club owner. The hero appears unexpectedly at the night club and finds the heroine there singing with the band and apparently very much in her element. Later she wins a lot of money at roulette. The night club owner seems reluctant to let her leave when she is so much ahead. Under pressure from the hero she leaves, but is immediately held up by the night club owner's thugs. The hero is convinced that this is all an act put on to conceal from him some guilty partnership between the girl and the night club owner, to fool him into thinking that their relations are unfriendly. After more confusion of this sort, it finally comes out that it is not the night club owner whom the heroine is trying to shield, but her unfortunate sister who has committed a murder. Since the night club owner knows about this killing he is able to blackmail the heroine. It was to pay the blackmail that she had to come to the night club so often.

In *The Strange Love of Martha Ivers,* the combination of badness, seeming badness, and goodness in the heroine is quite complicated. The girl has just come out of jail, to which she had been sent for stealing a fur coat. She explains to the hero that the coat was given to her by a boy friend who later disappeared. Thus she did not steal the coat, but wasn't she rather friendly with the thief? In another episode she is forced by the wicked district attorney, who is still pursuing her for the crime she didn't commit, to play a rather mean trick on the hero. She gets the hero to go with her to a cafe where, by pre-arrangement, a man appears who claims to be her husband and demands that the hero come outside and fight. The hero is then forced into a waiting automobile in which several thugs beat him up. The heroine later has a chance to explain the whole thing to the hero; she really has no husband, and so on. In this series of bad appearances and explanatory denials, one or two bad things remain that are not explained. However, since the girl repeatedly turns out to be so much better than she seemed, there is probably the feeling that with a few more explanations, for which the film perhaps didn't have time, she could be shown to be completely good.

The good-bad girl has supplemented the vamp of earlier American films. The vamp created the illusion of exclusive passionate attachment to the hero, but was in the end found out to be untrue. The hero at first believed in her, later became disillusioned. The picture was the reverse of that of the good-bad girl, whose apparent badness rouses the hero's suspicions but is later explained away. In a Greta Garbo film of the twenties, *Flesh and the Devil,* the hero fell in love with a seductive woman who responded passionately to the advances she provoked. He was forced to go away and, during his absence, she married his best friend. On the hero's return a bitter quarrel arose between the two men. They were about to shoot each other in a duel, but, suddenly remembering their old friendship, fell into each other's arms. The wicked woman was, by an appropriate accident, drowned. The dangerousness of the vamp was associated with the man's intolerance for sharing her with other men. Her seductive appearance and readiness for love carried a strong suggestion that there had been and might be other men in her life. But while the hero loved her, he excluded this possibility from his thoughts. When the proof of her infidelity was established, he renounced her. The good-bad girl is associated with a greater tolerance for sharing the woman, although this sharing remains subject to limitations. The hero believes that the woman he loves is involved with other men. While this disturbs him, it does not drive him away. In effect, the woman's attraction is enhanced by her association with other men. All that is needed to eliminate unpleasantness is the assurance that these relations were not serious (only apparent).

The good-bad girl is perhaps a melodramatic reflection of the American popular girl, whose attractiveness is directly proportional to the number of men she goes out with. The American attitude is in contrast to that of cultures where attractive women are secluded, where men feel that the attractiveness of a beautiful woman for other men is a liability. The man who guards the beautiful woman whom he loves from the eyes of others believes that if they only look at her they will start making plans to go to bed with her. American courtship patterns are based on a series of breaks between looking and going to bed. It is possible to look and go no further, to kiss and go no further, to pet and go no further. The attractiveness of the popular girl derives from her association with many men, combined with the assurance that she has not gone "too far" with them. In the case of her movie counterpart, the good-bad girl, the hero's doubts express uneasy fantasies about the possibly more serious involvement of the girl with these other men. The films express the man's uncertainty about whether the girl has only gone so far and no further, and the difficulty of holding in check his own fantasies about her relations with other men. The happy outcome reassures us that the system works. The girl's relations with other men were only apparent (did not go too far sexually). Her attractiveness for other men then ceases to arouse anxiety and becomes positive. Where the vamp evoked a complete sexual response, and so could not be shared without intense jealousy, the good-bad girl is sexy in a different sense. Her attractiveness is not in her inducement to passion, but in her (harmless) association with other men.

In comedies it may be manifest that the girl's associations with other men are harmless. She may, to the knowledge of the audience, construct a pretense of such relations in order to interest the man she wants. The desired man may see through the pretense, and nevertheless be favorably influenced by the appearance of the girl with other men. In *Every Girl Should Be Married,* the hero is mostly aware that the heroine has contrived the semblance of a relationship with a rich playboy in order to make herself attractive to him. Eventually she draws a third man into her scheme, a hillybilly radio comedian who poses as her old sweetheart from back home. Although the hero also recognizes the comedian, he is moved to oust these pseudo-rivals and claim the girl. Her desperate efforts to make herself appear to be associated with other men achieve the desired result. (The hero's positive reaction despite his awareness of what goes on behind the scenes appears related to a larger trend. There seems to be a fairly widespread American tendency not to devalue an effect though one sees how it is achieved—whether it is the technique of a movie trick shot, or the beautiful complexion derived from assiduous application of a certain soap.)

Another film reflection of the popular girl with her many escorts is a frequent dance pattern in musicals where a girl dancer appears with a chorus of men. Her relation to them is stylized and superficial as she dances with each in rapid succession, not favoring one more than another. The male chorus alternate their attentions to the girl with routines in which they dance together in amicable accord. This parallels a frequent comedy theme of playful woman-sharing which has no negative effect on the friendly relations between the men. The girl's potentiality for bestowing true love on one man alone may be expressed by her singing, while she dances with several dozen men, a song whose sentiment is that of exclusive love: "You do something to me that nobody else can do" (*Night and Day*). Thus in her dance the girl gratifies the wish of the man who will eventually win her to see her associated with other men, while in her song she satisfies his demand for assurance that she is not emotionally involved in these other relations.

The good-bad girl is an American product; the vamp was an import. As sex is no longer associated with the strange woman, it ceases to be admittedly mysterious and dangerous. What was formerly dangerous, but no longer appears so, frequently becomes comic. The foreign vamp now appears mainly as a comic figure. Her charms are revealed as a set of obvious tricks, as we see her dimming the lights and spraying perfume around the room. She seems to be trying too hard, the more so as her tricks prove ineffective. In *She Wouldn't Say Yes,* the heroine, who wants to get rid of the hero, arranges for him to have dinner alone in her apartment with a foreign woman called Allura, who has conceived a passion for him. Allura appears at their rendezvous in a tight satin gown, half-closes her eyes in apparent love-sickness, and expresses her warm feelings with an exuberant foreign accent. Her efforts to envelop the hero lead to his running away from her while she chases him around the table. In *The Sailor Takes a Wife,* the hero similarly finds it easy to resist a too obviously alluring Rumanian with a heavy accent and an exotically furnished apartment.

The degeneration of sexual dangers into comedy is expressed in the changed use of the symbolism of falling. In an early vamp movie, *A Fool There Was,* the hero has been lured away from his family and respectable life by a wicked, seductive woman. As he becomes increasingly debauched, a symbolic passage shows him falling down a flight of stairs. In current films, a fairly frequent comic episode shows the hero and heroine, in an early stage of their courtship, falling together, while skiing or at a dance. This is a favorable portent for the future of their relationship. The man was being made to fall by the dangerous woman. The wholesome young couple are falling for each other.

The disappearance of the vamp, except in the comic version, is illustrated in the change of movie spy types from World War I to World War II. The earlier spy, like Mata Hari, was an irresistible woman who lured men from the opposite side to betray their secrets to her. She was cold and ruthless until the day when she fell in love with one of her victims. At this point her employers had to kill her; she was no longer useful. In contrast to this version of the prostitute ennobled by love, World War II women spies tend to be clean-cut American girls doing a patriotic job. They do not have to be redeemed by love since they are good all along; and they are in love with men on their own side. The enterprising girl from home is thus substituted for the alluring foreign woman. A foreign woman spy may be a forbidding person who goes around most of the time in men's clothes (*The House on 92nd Street*).

In *OSS,* the recruiting agent tries to kiss the future woman spy at their first meeting. When she slaps his face he hires her. In the course of her work, she gradually falls in love with a fellow-worker. She is also called upon to dupe a Nazi officer, but a minimum of amorousness is required for this. She chiefly spends her time with him modeling his bust in explosive clay. The Nazi takes the bust on a train with him and it blows up, together with an important tunnel.

While *Notorious* retains the most vestiges of the spy who uses sex as a lure, its heroine, unlike Mata Hari, is not a professional bad woman. At the beginning of the movie she is temporarily leading a wild life as a reaction to a personal disillusionment. The hero succeeds in recruiting her as a spy because of her patriotism. She immediately concludes her interlude of debauchery and conceives a deep and lasting love for the hero. They would proceed happily as lovers and comrades if she did not get the assignment to marry an important elderly Nazi in order to spy on him. The hero for a while cannot realize that her heart is not in her work. When he finally becomes aware of it, they are happily reunited. The heroine of *Mata Hari* was a professional vamp without any convictions, who seduced the hero and robbed him of secret documents, discovering too late that she loved him. The betrayal of the man by the old type of vamp was symbolized by the scene in which Mata Hari forced her lover to blow out the lamp in front of the ikon his mother gave him; she wanted the apartment in complete darkness so that her accomplices could steal the papers while she was distracting her victim with kisses. Greta Garbo, as Mata Hari, first appeared to the man she was going to betray as she was performing an allegedly Hindu dance before an idol. Ingrid Bergman, the round-cheeked spy in *Notorious,* pursues her acquaintance with her Nazi victim during brisk canters before breakfast.

In the place of the vamp there now appears a new type of bad girl who exactly resembles the good-bad girl, except that she really is all the things the good-bad girl seems to be. (The same actress may play either interchangeably; for instance, Lizbeth Scott in *The Strange Love of Martha Ivers* and *Dead Reckoning.*) The bad girl has no appeal which the good-bad girl does not also have, but she has a considerable disadvantage. The good-bad girl has demonstrated that it is possible to get sex and a square deal at the same time. The man no longer has to pay the current bad girl's price. In the majority of films where the issue about the goodness and badness of women is raised, the good-bad girl is the main female character. Sometimes she has no other woman to compete with. More often she is opposed by a bad girl, over whom she regularly wins out. The cards are stacked. The vamp offered excitement and passion not otherwise available. The man was tempted away from the less stimulating good woman, and concealed from himself the indications of the vamp's wickedness. His progress was from idealization to disillusionment. The current bad girl does not start with any advantage. She looks suspicious, just as the good-bad girl does. In the end, the suspicions about her are confirmed. It is only where the bad girl is opposed to a good girl that she has a chance to win. In *The Killers,* the hero drops his colorless and loyal girl friend when he meets the glamorous gangster's moll. The bad girl's loss of power over men is frequently indicated by the fact that, while she is unable to get the man she wants, she is pursued by others whom she detests.

Among the bad girls who come to no good is the hero's wife in *The Blue Dahlia.* The hero returns from the war to find her drunk in the midst of a wild party, and on terms of obvious intimacy with an older man who later turns out to be a gangster. After the party has dispersed she tells her husband that their baby was killed in an auto accident caused by her drunken driving. In *The Big Sleep,* the sister of the heroine is a nymphomaniac and has killed a man who repulsed her advances. The title character in *The Strange Love of Martha Ivers* has a long list of crimes to her credit. She has murdered her aunt and let someone else hang for it; she has taken possession of the vast fortune of the murdered aunt; she has married a man she loathes in order to cover up her crimes and has driven him to drink by her contempt. When the hero appears she immediately wants to make love to him, a gesture which, according to an unchecked statement of her husband's, is habitual with her. And she attempts alternately to kill the hero and to get the hero to murder her husband. In each of these cases, the bad girl loses out to a good-bad girl who is equally attractive and less harrowing to have around.

The most forbidding feature of the bad girl, even more than promiscuity or crime, is that she coldly uses men, or at least is willing to sacrifice them for her own advantage. The bad woman in *Johnny Angel* has married a rich shipowner whom she despises, and forces him to board a ship and kill the whole crew to steal a cargo of gold for her. She shows no regard for his protest that being on a ship makes him sick. In *The Killers,* the bad woman allows the hero to go to jail for a theft she committed, and then dupes him into taking the blame for a grand larceny from which she and her husband get all the benefit.

For the current bad girl love comes second. More brutal than the old-style roué who cast aside the women of whom he tired, she is ready, at any moment, to kill the man she loves if he becomes a threat to the security of her criminal career. The murderess in *Framed* is making coffee for the hero, whom she loves. As he seems to be making some objection to helping her cover up her crimes, she is about to put poison in his coffee. The conversation takes a more reassuring turn and she puts the poison back on the shelf. They proceed to an affectionate breakfast. In *Dead Reckoning,* the girl who has committed murder and grand larceny is secretly married to her partner in crime. She falls in love with the incorruptible hero, but tries to kill him when he uncovers the truth about her. These girls justify

their actions by stories of early deprivations. They had to work as waitresses
or model beautiful clothes for other women to wear. They have felt these
hardships as so cruel and unusual that anything is justified which insures
escape from such a life. Where the vamp was a kept woman, the current
bad girl uses her lovers as witting or unwitting partners in crime. Coldly
self-centered and controlled, she does not run the risk, as the vamp did,
that unanticipated feelings of love will disrupt her exploitative way of life.
She is not subject to any conflict; it is quite clear what comes first. However,
she is not a woman with only one interest. As long as her man is useful to
her income and safety, or at least not dangerous to them, the pleasure she
gets from her relation with him occupies a major place in her life. The hero,
on his side, suffers no conflict in relation to her. The lover of the vamp
tended to be drawn into a guilty abandonment of honor for her sake. The
hero who loves the current bad girl turns her over to the police as soon as
he learns about her crimes. In *Framed,* the hero turns up with the police
just as the girl is taking out of a safety deposit box her long-dreamed-of
fortune, which she had offered to share with him. In *Dead Reckoning,* the
girl tries to persuade the hero to go away with her instead of turning her
over to the police. He refuses and she tries to shoot him. They struggle,
the car in which they are driving is wrecked, and she is fatally injured. In
the hospital, he holds her hand while she dies. The hero may resist the bad
girl even though there is no one to take her place, as in the two films just
mentioned. In a world where the good-bad girl is an ever-present possibility,
he presumably feels no need to accept the unfavorable terms proposed by
the bad girl.

These bad girls, however, are not entirely unsympathizable. The world
threatened to withhold from them the luxury which they felt was their due,
and they look very beautiful in the furs and jewels which they had to commit
murder to obtain. While the hero brings love into their lives for the first
time, and this really matters, they cannot abandon their previous interests.
In this they are unlike the vamp or prostitute redeemed by love, who aban-
dons all her previous aims. The bad girl tries to satisfy two sets of values,
and does not lose sight of the first for the sake of the second. The inadequacy of love without the material comforts that one must murder to obtain
is demonstrated by the bad girl in *The Postman Always Rings Twice.* She
and the hero, having fallen in love, run away together, leaving behind her
aging husband and his promising lunchroom business. As they trudge along
the highway where fast cars pass them by, the girl, an ex-waitress, is overwhelmed by the meagerness of their prospects, and insists they turn back.
It thus becomes necessary for them to kill her husband in order to take over
the business. The financial gain is somewhat more modest than in the case
of the previous bad girls, and requires only a single crime, rather than a
series of crimes. Having solved her economic problem in this way, the girl
would have been content to settle down with the man she loved. This is an
exceptional case in which the hero succumbs to the bad girl's efforts to lead

him into crime. In contrast to the man lured by the vamp, who exploited and then abandoned him, this hero, but for an accident, might have lived happily ever after with his partner in crime.

A type related to the bad girl is the home-digger. This is an intensely attractive and emotionally cold girl, suffering from humble circumstances, who is ready to marry any man who will give her the comforts she requires. The beautiful waitress in *The Fallen Angel* encourages the hero, whom she does not love, to join in the competition for her. She differs from the previous girls in that her financial aims are quite modest, and do not lead to crime. Instead of taking care of herself, she demands, in the face of a world that seems grudging and untrustworthy, that she be taken care of. While equally free from conscience, she lacks the boldness of the bad girls, and their capacity for love.

American ways of fusing goodness and badness in women start with a good woman and spice her up. The major result of this procedure is the good-bad girl whom we have described, whose goodness is concealed behind a facade of badness. An alternative procedure is to take a girl who appears too good and make her more sexy. In older films such as *She Married Her Boss,* the tailored, bespectabled and efficient secretary raged and suffered while her boss carried on with fluffy blondes. Eventually she took off her glasses, put on a décolleté evening gown which made the boss look at her for the first time, got drunk, flirted, and ended up in his arms. Current comedies on this theme tend to avoid having the woman unattractive to begin with. Rather they present a girl who seems attractive, but who temporarily alienates her man by sexual unreadiness. She must then demonstrate added charms to win him back.

In *The Sailor Takes a Wife,* the hero falls in love at first meeting with the heroine, a popular hostess in a servicemen's canteen. They are married almost immediately. On the wedding night she appears in "jamies" with her hair in pigtails. When the sailor laughs at her outfit, she indignantly locks the bedroom door. The next night she wears herself out dancing at the canteen, and falls asleep on the couch the moment she comes home. In this more literal presentation of the popular girl, exuberant dancing with dozens of men is an antidote to lovemaking. The third night the hero gets innocently involved with a comic Rumanian vamp who lives in the same house. As he leaves her apartment drunk, she finally succeeds in planting an imprint of lipstick on his cheek. The bride gives a serious interpretation to this, and the couple are about to break up. The following day the vamp comes to their aid. While they are out, she prepares the apartment for a reunion. She provides soft music, perfume-drenched air, and a black lace nightgown which she lays out on the bed. (She is the proprietress of a lingerie shop and the hero had ordered the nightgown from her as a surprise for the heroine.) The heroine assumes that these arrangements are for a rendezvous with the Rumanian. There are further explanations. In the happy ending, the bride appears in the black lace nightgown. In this parody of the once serious issues between a good and a bad woman, the hero is not tempted by the vamp. But he requires that the good girl assume at least superficially some of the vamp's effects.

In *Without Reservations,* the hero is at once attracted to the heroine. But when he tries to make love to her, he is warded off by a forbidding talk about spiritual understanding, and he leaves her. The heroine then goes to Hollywood, where she frequently goes out with film actors, and changes the plot of her novel (which is to be filmed) so that love replaces politics as the major motivation of her characters. It is only then that the hero comes back. The sexualization of the good woman is generally confined to comedy and appears much less frequently than the good-bad girl. Infusing sex into the girl who is not sexy enough seems a less stimulating undertaking than toning down the one who has too much.

French films tend to concentrate on the bad girl. Where a conflict between a good girl and a bad girl arises, the man tends to prefer the bad one. However, a variety of devices are used to etherealize or ennoble her. The prostitute transformed by love still appears. The bad woman is sometimes presented as a superior being, unaffected by the more sordid aspects of her life. Her career of seducing men may be invested with a metaphysical significance. The bad woman may at first appear good, and thus subject the man to deep disappointment. The sequence of the man's impressions of her is then the reverse of that associated with the good-bad girl. The French hero idealizes the woman who he later learns is bad.

In *Macadam,* a prostitute triumphs over a nice girl, but is then transformed by love. A rather severely good girl has met a young sailor, and a promising relation develops between them. The sailor is accidentally implicated in some underworld affair, and, to check up on him, a prostitute is instructed by her pimp to seduce him. The sailor falls in love with her and immediately loses interest in the good girl, whom he then treats quite rudely. The prostitute, on her side, falls in love with the sailor, breaks off with her pimp, and moves toward respectability.

In *Les Visiteurs du Soir,* the beautiful bad woman is a supernatural creature sent by the devil to corrupt and destroy. The prostitute and pimp are here invested with a higher significance, and adorned with medieval trappings. In *Les Enfants du Paradis,* the beautiful bad woman moves through her shady life with an air of untouched remoteness. She appears in the sideshow of a fair as a naked Venus, associates with underworld characters, and has evidently lived a promiscuous life. The hero at first sight sees her as an ideal creature. His penetration of her dubious façade is expressed in an episode at their first meeting where he proves that she is not guilty of a theft of which she is suspected. His idealization of her is further expressed in his hesitation to make love to her on short acquaintance, despite her readiness. This has unfortunate consequences, as it results in her becoming the mistress of his friend. However, she loves the hero, and suffers from the series of accidents which keep them apart. She is like the prostitute redeemed by love, except that her love leads to no change in her mode of life. But this love is a sufficiently redeeming feature in the image of her life and character. In comparison with this woman, the devoted good girl, whom the hero marries but never loves, is pale.

In *La Passionelle,* the hero worsips from a distance a beautiful young girl far above him in station. When one day she invites him to her room, he learns that she has had a lover whom she has murdered. She wants the hero to dispose of the body for her, and offers herself to him in exchange for this service. Unable to forgive her for destroying his dream, he refuses her offer.

American films, in the effort to fuse goodness and badness, take a good girl as the base and try to disguise her as bad, or otherwise to enliven her. French films, concerned with the same problem, proceed in the opposite direction. The point of departure is a bad girl, who may appear to be good, or be redeemed, or carry on an aura of idealization. The bad woman may deceive the man as to her character. The woman sent by the devil in *Les Visiteurs du Soir* confides a fictitious story of her unhappy life to engage the sympathy of the man she intends to seduce. However, this wilfull deception is not usual. The double aspect of the woman derives more often from the man's tendency to idealize her, his difficulty in seeing her as she is.

British films seem to be less concerned than American and French with goodness and badness in women. Possibly this issue is replaced by that of men's destructive impulses toward women. In *Madonna of the Seven Moons,* a rare film dealing with the mixture of goodness and badness in a woman, the heroine is a dual personality. Most of the time she is a rather prim and stately wife and mother, devoted to her family and to good works. Periodically her other personality takes possession of her. She forgets her usual life, assumes a gypsy-like costume and abandon, and runs away to join her lover, a dark and passionate underworld character. All this is attributed to a girlhood seduction by a dark vagabond. Thus it is the fault of a bad man that the sexy potentialities of a good woman are brought to the surface There is a much sharper dissociation of the two aspects of this heroine than in the American good-bad girl or in the French mixed types. Her husband knows her only as good, her lover, only in her gypsy role. She herself, when she assumes one character, loses all memory of the other. American and French heroes, though with differing feelings, see the women they love as both good and bad. In the British film, the bad aspect of the woman is evoked by a dark foreigner, the seducer and later the lover, and appears in an alien gypsy guise. Her husband is completely satisfied with her without knowing anything of this other side of her nature. It is only by an unfortunate accident that the good woman develops a sexy character. She is then insane, and eventually destroyed by this abnormal component.

A few observations may be added about the types of men who accompany, or correspond to, various types of women. In early American films, the good girl was attacked by a wicked seducer and rescued by the hero.

As heroines have become more worldly-wise and able to take care of themselves, there has been a tendency for both the seducer and the rescuer to
degenerate into comic figures. The fatal man, particularly the foreign one,
has suffered the same fate as the vamp. In a transitional stage, *Hold Back
the Dawn* exposed the tricks of the foreign lover. As an emigré, hoping to
gain entrance into the United States, he wants to marry an American schoolteacher. He uses in a calculating way the seductive tones and looks which
in previous films seemed to be inspired by passion. The girl is naïve enough
to be taken in. However, in an eventual reversal of their relationship, the
man falls in love with her. Her patriotic lectures also take effect; a wish to
become a good American is substituted for his originally cynical motives.
In *Lover Come Back,* the foreign charmer is a comic character. He pursues
the heroine with flattering speeches in a heavy accent, with bows, hand-
kissings, and self-congratulations on his irresistible technique. The heroine
has no difficulty in resisting him. A less comic, but still far from menacing
derivative of the seducer, is the wolf. He is easily converted into a monoga-
mist when he meets the right girl. In *Those Endearing Young Charms,* the
hero is an Air Force officer who is in the habit of making easy conquests
and not taking them seriously. When the heroine, whom he has taken away
from his less exciting buddy, confides that she has fallen in love with him,
he is at first annoyed that she does not share his frivolous attitude. She
breaks with him, and he is soon hanging around pleading with her mother
to put in a good word for him. In the end, persuaded of his conversion, the
girl throws herself into his arms.

The rescuer of women is now apt to appear as a case of arrested development. He is sexually unawakened, a male sleeping beauty, and over-
estimates the value of his heroics for the woman who is usually more competent than he. The hero in *Ball of Fire* is an unworldly, middle-aged
scholar. While compiling a slang dictionary, he interrogates a gangster's
moll. To explain a term, she gives him what is evidently his first kiss. He
resolves to free her from her underworld involvements and eventually succeeds, although both the girl and the gangsters take advantage of his naiveté
for some time. In the remake of this film (under the title *A Song is Born*)
the comic Danny Kaye replaces the romantically serious Gary Cooper in the
hero's role. In *Hold That Blonde,* the rescuer is a completely comic figure.
The girl whom he is rescuing from involvement with a gang of thieves
watches over his blundering efforts and knocks him out when his zeal
threatens to get him into real danger. The incompetent hero of *The Paleface*
is misled into believing that he has saved the life of the heroine by killing
a horde of attacking Indians, while it is really her more accurate shots which
achieved this.

Another derivative of the rescuer is what we may call the standing-offer
man. He is always devotedly waiting for the heroine, ready to help, and
undeterred by her failure to respond. He regularly loses the girl to a more
enterprising and demanding suitor. The help which he offers is reduced to
routine services which the heroine permits him to render in the interests of

her relation with the other man. In *Young Widow,* the heroine's boss is a suitor of long standing. When she repulses his rare efforts at lovemaking, he assures her that he will always be there if she needs him. In the end she takes advantage of this offer by calling him to drive her to the airport so that she can wave goodbye to the man she has fallen in love with. In *The Sailor Takes a Wife,* the heroine uses her long-term suitor to help her move into the apartment where she is going to live with the sailor who has won her in an overnight courtship. Such are the current forms of the devotion of a good man which might once have saved a woman from ruin.

In British films, the standing-offer man has a better chance of being accepted. His restraint does not need to be attributed, as in the American case, to a lack of strong impulses. He is the more acceptable as his opposite, the seducer, remains a danger. In *The Years Between,* the heroine, after the presumed death of her husband, falls in love with a man who has loved her for years. Despite his long quiescence, he manifests sufficient intensity when he finally gets his chance. In *This Happy Breed,* the girl is glad to return to the devoted boy from next door after she has been deserted by the lover with whom she ran away to Paris. The picture of a good and a bad man who make conflicting claims on a good woman persists in British films, as we have seen in *Madonna of the Seven Moons.* The bad man degrades the woman rather than yielding to her ennobling influence, as he is apt to do in American films. In *Love on the Dole,* the heroine is continually importuned by a vulgar, affluent gambler, and finally gives in to him after the death of the good man she loved. The gambler, untouched by the fact that she comes to him only because she needs money for her sweetheart's funeral, proceeds to install her as his mistress just as he had long intended.

The partner of the good-bad girl in American films is a good-bad man. However, the double aspect of his character is connected with violence rather than with sex. As we shall see later, he is frequently suspected of crimes which he did not commit. He tends to be absorbed in crime investigation and in warding off attacks by male assailants. As a result of this preoccupation, he cannot be as immersed in love as the earlier great lover or the devoted rescuer. The suspicious appearance of the girl further tends to evoke a certain wariness. At the same time, the hero's manner with women is sure and easy, and suggests experience. He talks in a tough bantering style, and without polite preliminaries. The hero of *Nocturne,* a detective, first meets the heroine, a murder suspect, as she is climbing out of a swimming pool. His first words to her are, "Why did you kill him?" Moderated by this tough scepticism, the hero's feelings are not likely to become urgent or overpowering. There is little chance of his being deceived or swept off his feet like the victim of the vamp. While assuming a quick though casual tone of intimacy, he makes it quite clear to the woman that he can take her or leave her; and that he will take his time to find out about her. He is carrying on two investigations: one to clear himself, the other to clear the heroine. In the first case he is the suspect, in the second the one whose suspicions are aroused.

God, Radio, and the Movies

By FREDERICK ELKIN

In AUGUST, 1948, *Cosmopolitan* magazine published "The Next Voice You Hear," a short story by George Summer Albee, which, said the editor, "we believe, sincerely, will be the most discussed short story of the year." The story never received this predicted acclaim, but Dore Schary, production executive at MGM, saw in it a powerful spiritual idea which, considering the troubled conditions of the present-day world, should have a deep appeal for the general public. Schary himself wrote a screenplay treatment and then produced a movie of intense religious and spiritual power.

The picture, also entitled *The Next Voice You Hear,* and first released in New York's Radio City Music Hall theater, is not one that "just entertains," not one that is forgotten immediately upon leaving the theater. Few who see the picture can remain unaffected by it. Some have been sharply annoyed by the treatment of God and religion, and in England the picture was temporarily banned. But there are tens of thousands who are acclaiming the film as one of the greatest achievements of Hollywood. Many in the audience have felt pangs of conscience and wept; others have been inspired to support their churches with a new vigor; still others, with a somewhat more objective outlook, have suggested that Hollywood has atoned for some of its sins. It behooves us, therefore, to analyze the picture, to indicate what it suggests about God, religion, and the American way of life, and to discuss why it should have been produced.

The basic story is as follows: A Voice is heard over the radio one evening which says, "This is God. I will be with you the next few days." The Voice is heard throughout the entire world, each country hearing it in its native language. At first everyone is incredulous and the Voice is thought to be an advertising stunt or a malicious hoax. But when science cannot account for the Voice and it is heard again the following evening, the mass of people realize that it really is God who is speaking to them. God tells them not to be afraid; He tells them they have forgotten their lessons and must create for themselves the miracles of kindness, goodness, and peace. After six days, a miracle has truly been wrought. The people have taken to heart these words of God, have tempered their feelings of bitterness and hate, and lead more kindly and understanding lives.

Dramatically, the movie version is much more effective than the original story. The movie, first of all, has eliminated the theatrical, almost "cheap" miracles of the original. In the *Cosmopolitan* story, God proves His existence

Reprinted from *Hollywood Quarterly,* Vol. 5 (1952), pp. 108-11, by permission of the author and the publisher. (Copyright, 1952, by the University of California Press.)

by being spectacular. A woman attempts suicide by jumping off a bridge and hangs suspended in mid-air for forty-five minutes; all the metal weapons and equipment belonging to our armed forces are found cut into scrap and piled alongside the furnaces of the steel mills; the continent of Australia is sunk under water for one minute. The movie, much more effectively, does not suggest that God has to *prove* his power; rather, it quite clearly indicates that God has such power but does not choose to use it.

In the original story, God seems aggressive and vengeful. He greatly embarrasses a group of atheists at a mass meeting by having them suddenly sprout wings and halos; He pulls Russia's United Nations representatives back by the seat of their pants when they try to stalk out of a U.N. meeting; He turns Russia's military equipment into manure carts. In the movie version, God remains always, to everyone, the all-loving and sympathetic Father.

The movie is also much more effective in that it suggests a modern parable. The picture is full of simple symbols—the good of the home and the evil of the barroom; the good of work and the evil of sloth; the good of humility and the evil of conceit; the good of restraint and the evil of anger; the good of the housewife and the evil of the cheap woman; the good of the protecting policeman and the implied evil of a domineering authority.

Contributing to the parable-like effect is the fact that the picture focuses on a supposedly typical American family and shows how this family responds to the shock of hearing God's Voice. The husband is Joe Smith, typical factory employee; the wife is Mary, typical housewife and mother; the son is Johnny, typical ten-year-old schoolboy. They live in an ordinary house and lead ordinary lives. They eat crunchy breakfast cereals, save box tops, listen to the radio, follow a regular work routine, and go to church together. The husband is annoyed by starter trouble in his old car, carries a lunch box to work, gripes about his foreman, and goes bowling with his fellow-workers. The wife takes care of the house, prepares sandwich lunches for the husband and son, helps the boy with his homework, and experiences the pains of pregnancy. The boy goes to school, likes to listen to the radio, has a newspaper route, is reluctant to do his homework, and calls his friends "drips."

Such suggestions of reality apply as well to other aspects of the picture. There are references to the FCC, to the Nielsen rating, to scientists, to radio commentators, and to specific foreign countries. The residential area in which the Smith family lives is like thousands of others in the country and the minor characters are ordinary people, very much like those we all meet in our daily lives.

The simple symbolism, the parable-like aspects, and the suggestions of reality combine to make this picture a powerful production and one with which the audience feels a deep sense of identification.

It has often been noted that neither American movies nor American religion can be understood apart from the rest of our culture. That Bruce

Barton's book, *The Man Nobody Knows,* which pictured Jesus as a "go-getter" who could "sell" an idea to hundreds of millions of people, should become a best seller; That Russell Janney's *Miracle of the Bells,* which describes how religious values are promoted by the publicity methods of a press agent, should be read by millions of people and then be made into a successful movie—these are expressions of a religion that only we in business-conscious America could accept so readily and without question.

In *The Next Voice You Hear* is revealed another characteristic of the link between our religion and our American culture—the link of sentiment, sociability, and the American middle-class family. This is a picture about religion, but it is not the religion of a crusading St. Paul or of a stern and serious Puritan or of a deeply emotional orthodox Jew or of an ascetic monastery monk. Rather, the religion of this picture suggests a friendly, sociable relationship with God and one's neighbors. Man is not inherently evil; he is good and has infinite possibilities. It is not necessary, or even advisable, to bemoan one's sins, to feel deep pangs of conscience, to proselytize, to worry about salvation and redemption, or to be concerned with tragic aspects of life. Here, in this picture, we have a religion in which improvement comes from within ourselves; a religion of friendliness and tolerance for one's neighbors, even if they do not believe as we do; a religion of dressing up for Sunday churchgoing, of a sweet sentimentality of mother-son love. It is the religion that is part of our American middle-class way of life—a religion that sings hymns and popular songs like "Good Hearts and Gentle People" or "Let's Go to Church Next Sunday Morning," rather than spirituals and masses; a religion which is concerned with the Easter parade and the Easter bunny as well as the resurrection; a religion which decorates the Christmas tree and sings "I'm Dreaming of a White Christmas" as well as that which expresses wonder and gratitude at the Nativity.

In this picture the major themes are rather evident. They suggest that God exists and watches over us; that we should have faith in Him and not be afraid. They suggest that in our everyday lives and personal relationships we have forgotten God's message and should lead better and more understanding lives; that the world is full of miracles—the sun, the moon, a blade of grass, and the birth of a baby. We should recognize and appreciate these gifts of our God.

However, in such a picture, there are also numerous, more subtle themes and implications that are worthy of particular mention. One such theme is that if you have faith in God and live according to His word, all will be well in the world. There will be no bitterness between an employer and an employee, between a husband and his in-laws, between a policeman and a citizen, and presumably, between one nation and another. With such faith and a good life, a son will try not to worry his mother, a pregnant woman will bear her child without difficulty, and perhaps even a defective automobile starter will begin to work properly.

It is also implied that our God is a God of all the world and of all the peoples. He does not demand that we follow specific rituals or that we believe in specific religious doctrines. There are truths in all religions and it seems of minor importance whether we believe in the Trinity, in Buddha, or in the teachings of Mohammed. Rather, God judges us on the way we live, on the goodness of our works. Even an avowed atheist, as suggested in this picture, may be a worthy person.

It is further suggested that we should look upon God as fatherly and paternal, as a God who loves His children. Of course, God has the power to do whatever He wishes—and we should not tempt Him too far—but He is not a God of anger and vengeance. Rather, He is a God who talks soothingly to His children. He asks only that we count our blessings and do our "homework," and create for ourselves such miracles as understanding, peace, and loving kindness. "You are like children going to school," He says, "you have forgotten some of your lessons. I ask you to do your homework." We must do these good deeds, it is suggested, not because of fear, but because of trust and of love.

Worthy of note also are the numerous implications about family life. The type of family life presented is not uncommon in America—it is the ordinary middle-class family so often met in movies, radio dramas, and magazine stories. However, in this picture, as typified by the Joe Smith family, it is of particular importance because of the suggestion that it has religious sanction, that it is approved by God.

There is the implication, first of all, that a family relationship is the normal relationship in our society, that it is proper for men and women to have children and homes. The men and women who live alone, who have no family responsibilities and possibly hang around bars, are condemned as unworthy.

Secondly, it is suggested that the woman, as housewife and mother, has the most important role in the family. For example, in this picture, she is wiser than the husband and helps the son with his arithmetic, the husband preferring to wash the dishes. It is she, too, who holds the family together. Her husband and her aunt are always fighting, but the wife loves and appreciates the virtues of both. Should anything ever happen to the husband, we could be sure the rest of the family would stay together; but should anything ever happen to the wife, it is quite possible that the family would soon fall apart.

The husband, according to this recurrent pattern, evident in such good films as *The Best Years of Our Lives* and *Apartment for Peggy,* as well as in numerous soap operas and stories, has an adequate job and is respected by other men and women. But when faced with emotional problems, and in this case religious problems, he becomes troubled and loses his self-control. Under the confusion and strain—resulting from the shock of hearing God's Voice, the anxiety about his wife's pregnancy, the tension with his foreman and aunt—husband Joe Smith becomes so upset that he begins drinking in a bar and soon becomes woefully drunk. After a thick-voiced denunciation of the irresponsible man and loose woman at the table with him, he staggers back, like a guilty puppy, to his sympathetic, understanding wife. The wife, too, in this picture breaks down under stress, but, because of her inner strength, her recovery is almost immediate.

It is the mother also who has the prime responsibility of training the son in American middle-class virtues. Primarily because of her influence, the boy will be polite and dutiful; he may fight if attacked by another boy, but he will never strike a girl; he will see goodness in all people; he will never seriously violate any of our conventional standards. He has learned, like his mother, to affirm morality. When the father arrives home drunk, it is not the understanding wife who expresses shock (although, unconsciously, she may well feel it), but the ten-year-old boy. The boy, in fact, is so shocked and so disillusioned that he cannot look his father in the face and runs away from home.

The role of the wife is further enhanced in the picture by the fact that she is pregnant. Not only does this become the basis for some touching sentimentality between mother and son, but also, it is suggested, this pregnancy is quite heroic and miraculous.

There are a few other important implications about our way of life that are also, by suggestion, sanctioned by God. One such implication is that our American economic and political system is a good system. The factory foreman may continually urge the men on to work with the phrase, "An honest day's work for an honest dollar," and a policeman may give our hero two traffic tickets in one day, but these representatives of authority are basically fine people and it is wrong to think badly of them. If we hate and fear them, it is because we do not have faith in God and do not live as He wants us to live.

It is also suggested that the ideal person is one who leads, who accepts a generally simple, steady, and responsible life. While on his binge, Joe Smith bemoans the fact that he has been plodding along for years, barely making ends meet. "To what purpose?" he asks. But it is clearly indicated here that Joe Smith is expressing a wrong, if not immoral, outlook. He should accept and appreciate his life; he should not be so concerned with a factory hot water faucet that doesn't work or other such trivialities; rather, he should be appreciating the simple miracles of nature and the simple life he leads.

Psychologically, this picture is very reassuring. We are told, first of all, that God is our all-powerful, all-loving Father who looks upon us as His children. Life is not so complex, we are advised; our problems aren't so difficult. If things aren't going well, it is only because we have forgotten some of our lessons. And it is sympathetically suggested that all we need do is lead our ordinary lives, have faith in Him, and be good and kind, and our problems will be simply and magically resolved. We need only become like children again and obey our Father, and we shall be protected forevermore.

Also very reassuring is the suggestion that God sanctions our way of life and our middle-class virtues, especially those which emphasize the role of the housewife. We are told, for example, that the ordinary "common-man" family is the basic unit in American life; that people are to be judged not by income or social background but by character and personality; that the good wife is more worthy than the bad woman, and the dependable husband more worthy than the sluggard; that, if we are conventional and moral, and show a bit of self-restraint, we shall succeed and be happy; that our world of the factory, the radio, the school, the bowling team, the front lawn, and the nickname is right and proper. The picture will not be so psychologically reassuring to any socioeconomic groups that have hostile attitudes toward conventional demands, or to the upper-level groups who feel socially superior; but it will be tremendously satisfying to the great majority of ordinary Americans, especially women, who want to feel that what they believe is right, that what they have learned from their parents, teachers, and ministers is proper.

Every picture which emphasizes certain ideas inevitably de-emphasizes the opposites of these ideas. Thus, for example, if this picture stresses the important role of the housewife, it devalues the role of the career woman; if it emphasizes the crucial role of the mother in solving emotional problems, it suggests the inability of the father to do so; if it stresses the child-centered family, it plays down the family in which the child must make concessions to the personality demands of others; if it emphasizes that an individual should be judged by his character, it de-emphasizes a judgment based on intelligence or social position.

However, what is most noticeably devalued in this picture, and what seems to be of particular importance in this present world of ours, is the demand for positive action in the face of our problems. The picture suggests that, if we love God and become good and kind, life will almost automatically go on without tension or friction. All our problems will be magically resolved and relationships with everyone will be pleasant. Nothing in the picture suggests how we should act in a world where not everyone has heard the Voice of God. Suppose a stronger nation attacks a weaker one; suppose there is discrimination against a minority group; suppose local politicians accept graft from gamblers; suppose a foreman *is* arbitrary and demanding; suppose a mother dies in childbirth. What of any problem that requires intelligent thought, or a firm hand, or an adjustment to tragedy? This picture, in its emphasis on passive dependency, in its implication that it is so easy for this world to become a Garden of Eden, ignores the fact that there are serious and difficult problems in our contemporary world which must be squarely faced.

If this picture were an isolated expression of wishful passivity, it would be only of passing significance. However, it seems that such expressions of dependency, with such magical solutions of our problems, may be signs of a growing tendency within our society and within ourselves and, if so, we should be aware of it.

Such a tendency, of course, is understandable amidst all the tensions of our contemporary world. Our material and scientific strides forward have certainly not lessened our personal anxieties. We know that we live in a precariously balanced world that may suddenly explode into a devastating world war. It is little wonder that many feel weak and powerless and are frightened.

Where are we to turn? Neither retreat nor standing our ground has decreased the danger or reduced the tension. What better course then, than to return to our all-loving sympathetic God, the God we prayed to when we were children, to ask Him to look down upon us once more, to reassure us that we need not worry and all will be well. It is this which seems to be a strong, unexpressed wish of many who have resumed their churchgoing, of the Wheaton College students who fervently confessed their sins, of the tens of thousands who have been flocking to hear evangelist Billy Graham, and of many who are acclaiming the motion picture, *The Next Voice You Hear.*

The Creator-Audience Relationship in the Mass Media:
An Analysis of Movie Making

By HERBERT J. GANS

ONE OF THE ELEMENTS in the process by which movies (as well as other mass-media products) are created is the feedback that takes place between the audiences of that product and its creators. The creators referred to here are the movie-makers, i.e., the producers, directors, writers, actors and others whose decisions and actions create the movie. These creators get some feedback from the box office and from audience research. However, this paper argues that there is another, prior feedback which operates within the movie-making process itself.

The general feedback hypothesis suggests that there is active, although indirect interaction between the audience and the creators, and that both affect the makeup of the final product. This is in contrast to earlier models of the relationship, in which one or the other of the participants were pictured as passive. Thus some critics have suggested that Hollywood products are so similar that the audience has no real choice, but must passively accept what is offered. Others have argued the opposite, that the movie makers are virtually passive, and give the people "what they want." Neither statement is accurate, but each has some truth. The audience is obviously limited by what is offered, but what is offered to it depends a good deal on what it has accepted previously. The movie-makers try to create pictures good enough to attract the audience, but at the same time they try to make sure that people will be satisfied with the movie they have chosen, by guessing and anticipating what will please them. Here, they use audience research to find out what people want, and make inferences from the choices people have previously expressed at the box office.

However, such inferences are complicated by two factors—the wants of the individual movie-goers and the nature of the total audience. Whether the movie-goers have specific and manifest wants is a moot question. Most likely they do not, and are satisfied to select from what movies are available, but *then* they expect to be entertained by the choices they have made. Being entertained means, on the one hand, that people want to satisfy various latent needs or predispositions, and on the other hand, that they want to be surprised with something new or different. Because people have these pre-

Published for the first time in this volume, this is a revised version of a paper read at the 1956 meetings of the American Association for Public Opinion Research. I am indebted for helpful criticism especially to Samuel Bloom, Fred Elkin, Elliott Freidson, Eric Larrabee, and Rolf Meyersohn.

dispositions, their choices follow some analyzable pattern. But while there may be enough of a pattern to encourage the movie makers to inferences about future choices, there is never enough to provide reliable predictions.

The process of prediction is further complicated by the composition of the audience. The movie audience can be described in many ways. From the box office it may look like a mass. To the sociologist,[1] it appears as an aggregate of youthful clique members who have followed the advice of their opinion leaders.[2] The creator sees the audience in its reaction to his product. For him, it is important to recognize that the members of an audience who have made the same choice at the box office may have done so with different predispositions. The audience for each movie can be classified into a large number of publics, each public being an aggregate of people who have made a choice with the same predisposition, or set of related predispositions. Every ticket-buyer will respond to several themes in a single movie, and thus "belongs" to a number of publics.[3] Moreover, since he will look for different gratifications in a musical than in a western, he will "belong" to a different set of publics for every type of movie. The total potential movie audience is thus composed of innumerable publics, and every movie attracts a distinctive combination of them.[4]

There are so many publics that market research can never do more than skim the surface in providing information about the present audience, or inferences about future ones. Yet the movie-makers continue to make successful pictures. One reason for this is the existence of a further feedback mechanism which exists within the creative process itself, and literally permits the audience to follow the creators into the studio. Let us see how this takes place, and how it seems to shape the final product.

Every creator is engaged to some extent in a process of communication between himself and an audience, that is, he is creating *something* for *somebody*. This somebody may be the creator himself, other people, or even a nonexistent stereotype, but it becomes an *image* of an audience which the creator develops as part of every creative process. For analytical purposes this *audience image* can be isolated from the creative process as a whole.

This image, though projected by the creator, functions as an external observer-judge against which he unconsciously tests his product even while he is creating it.[5] As a result, the creation of any product may be described as a series of steps in which the creator selects one solution out of several possible ones, partly on the basis of the supposed judgment of this audience image. Obviously, the literary and other requirements of the product to be communicated are also involved in the selection between alternatives, but in the mass media product, these are often less important than the expectations of the audience image.[6]

The audience image is not a unified concept, but a set of numerous impressions, many of which are latent and contradictory. These impressions

deal primarily with how people live, and how they look at, and respond to
the roles, personalities, relationships, institutions and objects that movies
portray. These impressions develop and accumulate in the mind of the
creator in his contacts with potential audiences. The experienced movie-
maker must have some image of the audience response to all of the innumerable situations and characters that he is apt to work into different movies.
As he begins to work on a specific picture, what probably happens is that
he pulls together a group of more or less consistent impressions which will
evolve into his audience image for *that* movie. This image is broad enough
to permit him to communicate with many of the publics who will come to
see the picture, although only rarely can he reach all publics. Also, his
image changes somewhat from movie to movie, but it can do so only within
limits which are imposed on his sensitivity and skill by the familiarity he
has with the social, cultural and psychological experiences of the total
audience.

It must be emphasized that the creator not only anticipates his audience,
but tries to create or attract one for his product. In order to do this, the
movie-maker concentrates on the product itself, and tries to make a "good"
movie. He may succeed if his work on the product (and his audience image)
are sensitive to the predispositions of any part of the total movie audience.
The "great" movie-maker may be able to create a loyal audience precisely
because he knows or feels something, perhaps within himself, that is shared
by a large number of publics, but has not been sensed by other creators
who are perhaps equally bold or adept in other aspects of movie-making.

Every creator has a somewhat different life history and consequently a
distinctive image of the audience. Sometimes, he shares enough of the
characteristic of an actual audience so that by creating for himself, that is,
for his self-image, he is also communicating to a larger audience. This
perhaps describes the folk artist in pre-urban societies, whose audiences
were relatively homogeneous. The mass media creator, however, works for
a large number of publics. Many of these publics have tastes and predispositions that vary from his own, and in many cases, these are evaluated socially
as inferior, or "lower" than his. As a result, the creator may feel somewhat
intolerant of his audience.[7] Much of our popular culture is produced by
creators whose personal tastes are "higher" than those of their audiences.
Although this relationship breeds problems of role, morale, and product
quality, it may also provide the creator with enough emotional distance
between himself and the audience to permit him to create for an audience
of so many different publics.

In summary, the audience image thus functions to bring the movie-
maker in contact with one of his major reference groups. Other reference
groups affect the creator's total image, e.g., colleagues, superiors, critics,
and respected creators in other fields. Their demands may sometimes conflict with those of the imagined ticket-buyers, and will remind the creator
of his role conflicts, although they may also broaden and diversify his own

audience image. In addition, pressure groups are able, through their clamor, to win a place in the creator's audience image, and may also limit his communications with other publics, or force it into devious channels. Empirical research would undoubtedly permit refinement of the audience-image concept, especially of its latent aspects.[8]

The audience participates in the making of a movie through the audience image held by the individual creator. Since a movie needs a large audience to be commercially successful, it must be made as attractive to as many publics as possible, within the literary elasticity of the screen play. Consequently, its creation involves several different audience images.[9]

The making of the picture itself can be viewed as a decision-making process. As each creator applies his audience image in the decisions that have to be made, he is "representing" some of the publics who will eventually see the movie. The completed picture is a combination of the decisions made by its creators, and also a compromise or perhaps more correctly, a "negotiated synthesis" of their individual audience images. However, this synthesis takes place within a power structure, and the final decisions are often made by studio executives who point the compromise in a direction that seems to assure the largest box office. Thus, the final product has some of the characteristics of a political party platform, seeking to please as many as possible. The making of a movie can be studied much like any other political decision-making process (such as a party caucus, or a labor-management conference), and it is possible to observe how each creator makes decisions in terms of his position in the power structure, his audience image and his other reference groups, all of which have implications for the makeup of the actual audience.

The portion of each creator's audience image that is most important in the making of the movie depends partially on the role he plays in the production process. The studio executives work intimately with financing, and their images are likely to seek out the largest number of people. They are perhaps especially conscious of the audience as a mass with a lowest common denominator of interest. The director and writer are probably able to give fullest rein to their audience images, and have served as models for much of the foregoing discussion of the mass media creator. The producer occupies the ambivalent position of the foreman, and his audience images must take into account the studio as profit-making institution, and his own image as creator.[10] The actors may not develop audience images, for their work is frequently dependent on the director, or, if they are stars, they have a ready-made audience in their fans.[11]

Descriptions of the movie-making process suggests the multiplicity of potential audience images involved.[12] The process may begin with a product created for another audience entirely, such as readers or theater-goers. The studio's readers may see it as suitable for movie audiences. If the executive producer agrees, he may assign it to a producer, director and writer. Presumably his choice of specific persons is related to his feeling that they will agree with his audience image for the eventual movie. Quite often several writers are employed before a satisfactory screenplay is achieved. Perhaps they function to assure the movie's appeal to more publics by adding their own audience images. When stars are chosen, the picture may be rewritten further to strengthen their parts, in order to attract the audiences that they bring with them.[13] The cameramen and technicians may also play roles beyond their technical ones.[14]

When the shooting itself is completed, the cutter will edit in his or her image. After the sneak previews, when the movie has been tested against a sample ritually presumed to represent all future publics, the picture may be reworked to add appeal for publics left unconvinced by the preview. Even before completion of the picture the advertising department has begun to build expectations among what it considers to be the potential audience and its opinion leaders. Their various ads are calculated to reach as large a number of specific publics as possible. This process may continue even after the picture is released, for if a movie proves to be weak at the box office, the studio suddenly rewrites its ads in the hope of seeking other publics that will make the picture profitable.[15]

Many of these hypotheses can be illustrated from a study Lillian Ross made some years ago of the production of the movie, *The Red Badge of Courage.*[16] Her account first appeared in the *New Yorker,* and combined reporting with many personal (and satirical) interpretations. However, on the assumption that the main facts can be abstracted from her report with some reliability, the data can be re-analyzed to show how the creators of the picture sought to affect it in terms of their audience images, and how the picture changed when different images were applied during its making. The description will be quite brief, and will therefore rely, for summary, on the highbrow, middlebrow, lowbrow terminology. These terms will be used as oversimplified but objective categories of audience preferences, without any value connotations attached to them.[17]

The Red Badge of Courage had three main creators: John Huston, the writer-director, Gottfried Reinhardt, the producer, and Dore Schary, the studio production head.

John Huston is a successful and many-faceted director. In this picture he was trying to bring a famous novel, and the novelist's conception, to the screen with maximum fidelity to both media.[18] His aims suggest that he was making the movie primarily for his colleagues, critics, and himself— and with a highbrow audience image. However, while working on this picture, he was already planning his next one, *The African Queen,* for a much larger audience.

Schary, the studio head, wanted to have "a wonderful picture and a commercial success,"[19] and his audience image was somewhat larger than Huston's and more middlebrow. At the time, Schary was involved in a struggle over control of production in the studio with Louis B. Mayer. Mayer was bitterly opposed to making *The Red Badge of Courage* because he felt that its lack of plot and romance would mean box-office failure, at least in terms of the audience for whom he had been creating. For many decades, he had been identified in the studio with gay musicals and sentimental family trade pictures, such as the *Andy Hardy* series.

Reinhardt, the producer, came from a well-known German theatrical family. He was caught between Huston's image of the highbrow publics, which he seemed to share, and Schary's desire for an audience large enough to make the movie profitable.

Huston shot the picture much as he wanted it. However, Reinhardt felt that the first version lacked both the kind of story and the element of surprise that he felt necessary for *his* image of the audience, and just before the first sneak preview, he persuaded Huston to make the necessary changes.

However, this review and a second one made it clear that the two movie-makers were not communicating to a considerable portion of the publics represented at the preview. Then the transformation of the picture began. Schary wanted it made into more of a battle picture, with an eye on the publics who liked a war story. Reinhardt, trying to hold on to Huston's audience, and his own, persuaded him not to touch the picture itself. Instead, he added a narrated introduction that urged people to enjoy the movie because it was based on a literary classic. This appeal to cultural duty was perhaps intended for what Russell Lynes would call an upper middlebrow audience.

However, the third sneak preview showed that the actual audience was not persuaded. Huston had meanwhile left for Africa, and Schary now took over production. He proceeded to simplify the movie by taking out several of Huston's favorite scenes, in which the director had tried to portray the novelist's conceptions of men's emotions in war. He also changed the order of events to allow the plot to move more directly and toward a single and final climax.

Reinhardt described the process in a letter to Huston:

. . . Dore had secretly higher hopes for the picture box office wise than I . . . [he] . . . wanted to conquer the resistance of the audience which he clearly, and we both, felt. . . . I seriously questioned our ability to win the hearts of those who objected to the picture basically; those who hated it. On the other hand, we might easily, in trying to win them, lose those who were already our friends, those who loved the very things the others hated.[20]

He also described the new version of the movie:

. . . The picture had lost some of its complexities and colors. It was now a straighter, simpler picture. The consensus was, you can follow it now, you can understand it. . . . It is probably a very fine picture. Everybody tells me it is. But I would have to lie if I said it was the picture I had hoped for. . . .[21]

After these changes were made, a fourth preview was held, and this time 70 per cent of the people present were willing to recommend the movie to their friends.[22] It was finally released, and was well received by the critics, but the box-office results were disappointing.

Afterwards, Nicholas Schenck, then the president of the studio, explained to Miss Ross that he had questioned the commercial potential of the movie from the start, but had given his approval to the film in order to support Schary in his struggle with Mayer. Schary he seemed to consider a young, promising executive whose audience images were likely to mean profits for the studio in the future. Mayer, on the other hand, appeared to represent a set of lowbrow publics who were either decreasing in number or were finding satisfactory entertainment on television.

For the purpose of our analysis, it must be noted that *The Red Badge of Courage* was in many respects an atypical movie, and the differences in audience images among the participating creators were unusually extreme. Nevertheless, it is likely that the processes described here take place in the making of every movie, though in different ways. In a more representative picture, other kinds and combinations of audience images are likely to be involved. Differences of opinion between creators might focus on such topics as the characteristics and social roles of hero and heroine, the actors to interpret them, the portrayal of complex social relationships and issues, the depiction of emotional and moral conflicts in the story, and the solution of these in the ending. However, what a sociological study of movie-making ought to investigate is precisely what audience images are represented, and what major issues have to be resolved in the more representative kinds of Hollywood movies.

The ideas illustrated here by the movies could, of course, be tested in other mass media as well—for example, by a study of the staging of a TV spectacular, or of the editing of any magazine emphasizing features rather than news. One could even investigate the writing of a popular novel, although many of the audience-image struggles take place within the mind of a single person.

The preceding analysis can be placed in a broader context by suggesting that it has dealt with the role of the audience (through the audience image) in the *creation* of the mass-media product. One implication of this role is that the audience also affects the *content* of the product. This can be observed most clearly when the content of a product changes as it is communicated to new audiences. For example, it is possible to observe the changes made in a novel when it is brought to the screen, and to relate these to the creators' desire to appeal to different publics.[23] Similar alterations in content take place in a stage play as it prepares on hinterland try-outs for the larger set of publics it will meet on Broadway, or when scientific data are popularized in the Sunday supplements. An important problem for study is the extent to which audience characteristics affect the content that is being communicated, and the amount and kind of deviation from the creator's original intent that takes place.

An understanding of the role of the audience in affecting content can also contribute to the clarification of mass-media criticism. The critic addresses himself to the content of a product, but in this process he makes assumptions and judgments about the audience. For example, the critic who condemns the changes made in a novel by the producer of the screen version is assuming that the book which appealed to a smaller reading audience ought to be made into a movie for the same kind of audience. What is offered as criticism of the content is really in part—though only in part —a value statement about the proper audience to be sought. Further analysis of this example would show the extent to which the standards used to judge the mass media today are based on single audience assumptions more applicable to a past European leisure class than to contemporary America.[24] Research on the relationship between content and audience might contribto the reformulation of the critic's role, and the development of standards appropriate to the heterogeneous set of publics served by the mass media.

It can be shown that the role of the audience extends beyond the creation and the content of the mass-media product, but affects the structure and the culture of the mass media industries themselves. For example, note the indirect part the audience has in the oft-mentioned insecurity of the mass-media creators, and the apparently irrational decision-making patterns that have sometimes been observed. Every mass-media creator, whatever his skill, is to some degree dependent on the validity of his audience image for his status and standing in the industry. However, publics are so numerous and so fickle in their infinite combinations that it is impossible to tell in advance whether a once successful image is still accurate. Every new product is thus a gamble, and each time the problem of what the audience is like, and which publics are to be sought, must be determined and negotiated again. In this process, the creator who was successful the last time has the most status, and his ideas are influential until he guesses incorrectly.[25] Often the decision-making process can become a struggle between creators with various audience images, none of which can be tested before the release of the product. Consequently decisions may be made on the basis of irrelevant, but enforceable criteria. In the movies, only the top creators, the big stars, and a few formulas and stereotypes seem to be able to escape this insecurity, and to achieve a somewhat more permanent and more stable level of acceptance. The stars do it by typing themselves, and by establishing quasi-personal relationships with fans. At the same time, the turnover of creators probably also reflects the role of the audience and the turnover of publics within it.

No attempt has been made to list all the roles played by the audience in the relationship with the mass media. In summary, it can only be suggested that the explanation of various media phenomena by looking for possible audience roles might be a promising one for future research. Such research might also provide insights useful for the evaluation and perhaps even the creation of mass-media fare.

Notes

1. For an exhaustive critique of the concept of mass, and an analysis of the audience in terms of sociological data, see Eliot Freidson, "Communications Research and the Concept of the Mass," *American Sociological Review*, 18:313-317, June, 1953.

2. See Elihu Katz and Paul Lazarsfeld, *Personal Influence*, Glencoe: The Free Press, 1956.

3. For example, from the audience for a Western movie, one might be able to isolate a public that has come to see a conflict between good and evil, another that has come primarily to see a heroic individualist, and a third that wants to commute for a few hours to the wide open spaces. Undoubtedly there are many other such publics. In addition, each theme is probably interpreted somewhat differently by different people, so that publics are further stratified by age, sex, socio-economic characteristics, education and taste level.

4. In addition, there is that sizeable but probably decreasing band of people who go to the movies regardless of what is playing, or who come with limited expectations. They provide a "cushion" for predictions, and soften the effects of wrong guesses by the movie-makers.

5. The relation between creating and judging aspects of the creator might be compared to the "I"-"me" relationship of George Herbert Mead. See Anselm Strauss, ed., *The Social Psychology of George Herbert Mead*, Chicago: University of Chicago Press, 1956, esp. pp. 242 ff.

6. The similarities and differences between mass-media creator and artist here remain to be explored.

7. He may even consider that he is prostituting himself. This is so partly because the artist, whose norms he still follows, traditionally created for himself, or for a like-minded audience. Many observers have called attention to the desire of mass-media creators to gain the approval and respect of critics, intellectuals and others who follow the norms of "high culture." The fact that the mass-media creators are wedded to the demands of their audiences while retaining the norms of the artist might explain the intensity of their desire for approval, as well as their dilemma.

8. These might be studied in four ways. First, through the creator's cultural background, his education, work and leisure history, his various reference groups, and the audiences and cultures he knows. Second, through his aspirations, the kinds of things he would like to create, the audiences he would want to create for, and the career goals he has generally. Third, through his personal tastes and preferences, both as a creator and as a member of audiences. And finally, through his role in the making of the product, and the decisions he makes in those situations that have implications for the eventual audience.

9. The exception might be the "great" producer or director, whose audience image is so multifaceted that he is able, by himself, to command a large number of publics.

10. Rosten's study of a sample of 144 producers indicated that 52 had held jobs as movie writers and 21 as directors. See Leo Rosten, *Hollywood*, New York: Harcourt, Brace, 1941, p. 270.

11. Many actors undoubtedly have audience images, and those who do are probably considered to be the better actors.

12. See for example Dore Schary (as told to Charles Palmer), *Case History of a Movie*, New York: Random House, 1950, and Rosten, Ch. 11.

13. Leo Handel advises producers "to increase the potential audience for a film by combining, in one picture, players appealing to different audience sectors." See Leo Handel, *Hollywood Looks At Its Audience*, Urbana: University of Illinois Press, 1950, p. 150.

14. David Riesman suggests the role of the camera crew as a "near audience" (personal communication). Since these people are involved in the instrumental, rather than the substantive aspects of movie-making, and in their own leisure choices are more like the rest of the audience than others involved in the production, they may provide the creators with the earliest preview of the validity of their audience images.

15. For example, according to a story in *Variety*, " 'The Harder They Fall' is being given a campaign overhaul as the result of a reportedly spotty box office . . . ads focussing on prizefighting seem to have discouraged femme ticket-buyers. As a consequence, a switch will be made to emphasis on the racket angles. While 'Fall' does deal with boxing, a criminal element associated with that sport forms the basis of the story." *Variety*, April 18, 1956, p. 4.

16. Lillian Ross, *Picture*, New York: Harcourt, Brace, 1952.

17. The best recent description of these terms is by Russell Lynes, although he mixes analysis and evaluation freely. See his *The Tastemakers*, New York: Harper's, 1954, Ch. 13.

18. ". . . Like Stephen Crane, he wanted to show something of the emotions of men in war, and the ironically thin line between cowardice and heroism." Ross, p. 8.

19. *Ibid.*, p. 21.

20. *Ibid.*, p. 222.

21. *Ibid.*

22. These were presumably opinion leaders, scouting for the publics they represented.

23. This is in addition to changes required by the technical differences in the media. See Lester Asheim, "From Book to Film," in B. Berelson and M. Janowitz, eds., *Reader in Public Opinion and Communication*, Glencoe: The Free Press, 1953, pp. 299-308.

24. Paul Lazarsfeld and Robert K. Merton, "Communication, Taste and Public Action," in Lyman Bryson, ed. *Communication of Ideas,* New York: Harper's, 1948, p. 111.

25. When a group of movie-makers is successful in creating an audience for a new product, the product is soon copied by others pursuing what they imagine to be an empirically verifiable set of publics. In Hollywood, this initiates the phenomenon known as the cycle.

Company-Town Pastoral:
The Role of Business in "Executive Suite"

By ERIC LARRABEE AND DAVID RIESMAN

THE TEMPER OF THE TIMES toward business can be read on numerous
barometers, but few of them are as legible as the fictional and dramatic
arts—where popular images are projected twice life-size, and public attitudes
and assumptions are converted into "stories." Business is not always shown
here at its best; thus the demands of Allan Nevins, Edward N. Saveth, John
Chamberlain, and others for a more favorable treatment of business life in
history and in novels. Yet of all the media the most massive and the most
revealing are not books but the movies, and recently it is to them that observers who look for a rapprochement between the world of business and
the world of the arts and intellect have turned. If the images of business
have been changing, it is on the screen that their new shapes will soon
appear.

Of the several current movies with a business background, the most
conspicuous and the most informative by far is *Executive Suite*—the film
produced by John Houseman of M-G-M from Cameron Hawley's novel
about the office warfare within a furniture company over the picking of a
new president. It was generously reviewed and attended, and eventually, if
somewhat grudgingly, the fifteenth International Film Festival at Venice
gave it a special award. Moreover, it is a wholly "business" story, with
few of the fancy frills that are sometimes used to glamorize business by
misrepresenting it. The narrative is uncompromisingly held to the simple
and the reasonable: the head of a company dies, his subordinates jockey
for his place, there is a board meeting, and one of them is elected. That's
all there is to it. No wonder it has been used to prove that a new era of
interest in the commonplace facts of commercial and industrial life is at hand.

But is *Executive Suite* really so favorable to business? We greatly doubt
it. The film has a surplus of admirable qualities; it reflects to an extraordinary
degree—perhaps more sharply than the book does—the shadings of manner
and atmosphere that make contemporary business recognizable to businessmen. Some of these effects, on the other hand, may be semiconscious; some
are certainly at odds with the film's declared message: that even in the
"sky-reaching towers of big business" people remain human and presumably
lovable. The skill of actors, director, writers, and producer is all the more
reason for examining what they are saying, in contrast to what they say

Expanded version of an article which originally appeared in *Fortune*, Vol. 51, 1955, pp.
108-09. Reprinted by permission of the authors and the publisher. (Original article copyright, 1955, by Time, Inc.)

they are saying. For *Executive Suite* is in many respects a pastoral romance, peopled with twentieth-century equivalents of nymphs and shepherds, and it needs to be understood therefore not in terms of its surface "meanings" but of the dreams that lie behind them.

True, the movie does conclude in a series of humane reconciliations— between home and office, between good design and good sales, between individualism and teamwork. It has much that is straightforward and approving to say about the ethics of enterprise, the function of managers, the operation of offices, and the nature of success. Yet in each instance it has much also to say that is subtly ambiguous; or, if not ambiguous, antipathetic. *Executive Suite* draws far more heavily than may first appear on the anti-business sentiments of a half-century ago; on half-forgotten longings for a vanished world of rural, craftsmanlike virtues; and hence on assumptions that—far from being "capitalistic" or contemporary—are actually populist and Veblenian. If this is what "business" means to an audience large enough to interest the movies, then business still has something to be uneasy about in its artistic and intellectual reputation.

The dominant mood of *Executive Suite* is nostalgic reverie for the company town—the home of paternalistic order, domestic virtue, and productive work. A contrast established early in the picture shows us life in Millburgh, Pennsylvania (the imaginary seat of the imaginary Tredway Corporation) as personal, vulnerable, and arduous, while the Big City (evidently New York, and not at all imaginary) is anonymous, all-powerful, and indifferent. We see the unscrupulous stockbrocker, George Caswell (Louis Calhern), looking down into Wall Street as the president of Tredway, of which Caswell is a director, collapses of a heart attack at the curb. By implication the city is a place where a man of such achievement—Avery Bullard, who has "made" Tredway—can have his pocket picked when he dies, becoming a nameless corpse to the hospital and police, while a villain like Caswell sells the company short by telephone as the body is carried away.

We first encounter Caswell in a small-talk conversation with a wise "Jewish" banker who is shrewd, humorous, relaxed—far too self-assured to feel the ambitions we later find to drive the main characters at Millburgh (his accent is several times made "German," to obscure any ethnic implications, though a type-cast movie German would not be so cosmopolitan and worldly-wise, even if so benign; his function in the film is to suggest that big-city bankers, if no longer powerful enough to be villains, may nonetheless err in being soft on villainy). The city can afford a denatured toleration of Caswell's chicanery, just as it affords the anonymous refuge of the showy night club to which Caswell shortly retreats, to wait for his obvious plans to mature. This is baldly identified as the Stork Club, though one wonders why any establishment (even for the publicity) would want itself so vividly portrayed as a place where people engaged in something a little bit shady bring their dissatisfied and dissatisfying women, at once cold and expensive. (It is characteristic of the film, however, to employ brand-name touches, for "realism.")

In contrast with these brittle and heartless doings, the first appearance of the Executive Suite itself in the Tredway Tower at Millburgh sets a tone of fortified worthiness, almost of American feudalism. The Tower is taller —and the plant around it, larger—than a furniture company would conceivably need or support (let alone support an entire Pennsylvania town). The decoration of the Suite, on the highest floor, is mournfully dark and Gothic: heavy oak chairs and cabinets, stone floors, mullioned windows. It is unclear whether this is permissible ostentation for a community which centers around its lords of the manor, or whether it is meant to convey a slight odor of decay, of stuffiness, of sliding behind the times; in either case we know immediately that we are now miles from Rockefeller Center.

The lesser inhabitants of the Tower, conforming to its atmosphere, reflect the manorial style in their first confusion over Bullard's unexplained absence and their subsequent consternation over his demise. There is Luigi, the elevator man, the stock butler of the run-down aristocratic family. There is the boss's secretary, Erica Martin (Nina Foch), the housekeeper who holds the place together and broods through the halls, remembering the Old Days. As Bullard's handmaiden, she inherits the function of reminding others of his ghost, appearing on the screen with monotonous regularity and with a facial expression that rarely changes, or shows any other emotion than Doom. As manorial custodian, she is logically the one to introduce us to the important tenants, the vice-presidents of Tredway who will dramatize among themselves the contrasts between various business values: those of the administrator, the accountant, the salesman, the designer, and the production man.

We meet Evil first. Miss Martin eavesdrops on the firm's grimly ambitious comptroller, Loren Shaw (Fredric March), as he eavesdrops on himself, listening to a playback of his own astringent dictation on what is obviously a Dictaphone—like the Stork Club, a brand identification. His motto—the label on a chart over his desk which reads, in heavy black letters, "Materials Rejection"—implies that he cares less for the substance of the Company's production than for its shadow, the figures in his ledger.

Then we discover another vice-president, Fred Alderson (Walter Pidgeon), whom we gather to be the most senior. He *looks* more like an executive than his colleagues and clearly thinks himself in line for Bullard's job. Yet he has both a comfy office and a comfy personality, a faint suggestion that he —like the New York banker in the opening scene—could be disqualified simply by his old-shoe decencies.

Walter Dudley, the sales manager (Paul Douglas), is found at the telephone, a prisoner of his inability to hang up on his wife. (The Salesman must be Good-Natured and Listen to Everyone.) In this, as in so many movies on contemporary subjects, the telephone is an important symbol of communication—from Caswell's jittering over his calls from the night club to the phoned message the hero's wife deliberately fails to put through later on. Dudley's intermediary at the phone, his secretary, Eva Bardeman (Shelley Winters), is both protective and unhelpful—the characteristic attitude of the wives and quasi-wives of the film, all of whom are purposeful and have goals for their husbands or protectors, but none of whom are able to influence the attainment of those goals or even, in any significant way, to understand them. Indeed, part of *Executive Suite's* implicit savagery about business lies in the picture it presents of the uncoordinated Wives of Management who can do nothing but hurt their men, even when they try to help them. (Sales Manager Dudley is the only one who has contact with the Company information network through his secretary-mistress, but she is as helpless as all the others and ends merely as a vehicle for his blackmail by Loren Shaw.)

We do not meet the Designer, however, in his office—a fact which tells us he is not an "executive" in the pejorative sense.[1] MacDonald Walling (William Holden) does possess an office, of which we catch a glimpse, but its exaggerated tidiness proves that he is rarely in it; naturally we expect him to be down at the Plant, tinkering and being obstructed there by managerial interference from the Tower. We find him surrounded by reverently eager-beaver subordinates, whose work (they immediately say) could not go forward without him. Yet he wears white coveralls and is therefore something of a Scientist, not a "production" man in the Knudsen or Sorensen mold. Appropriately, he is not actually making something, but experimenting with how to make it. Though later he assures his wife that certain machines he had unsuccessfully requested would have made his presence unnecessary, the minute he is called to the Board Room and left to his own devices he grabs a phone (again the essential prop) and barks browbeating instructions into it. This, plainly, is intended to be Veblen's technocratic man, committed to craftsmanship and materials against the "nonsense" of accounting and finance, who resents the predominance of the higher echelons where pecuniary arts replace—or at least supersede—his industrial ones. Who can doubt that this young Ford deserves to Go Far?

From these scenes of work, the camera shifts to the management men coming out to their cars after five o'clock—a poignant hour: time of unwinding, meeting of wives, reassurances, and idling bonhomie (observe how this procession differs from a later exodus of the factory workers, who seem to fear the possible release from work through unemployment as much as their bosses anticipate it through retirement). Here we are chiefly introduced to Mrs. Walling (June Allyson), very much the companionable modern wife, interested in her husband's work—more interested, in fact, than he is. Her full-throttle curiosity is one of the pressures on him, as for that matter is her very presence with its tense conviviality, its athletic sympathies, its suggestion of laboriously faked breeding. She can hardly wait to reproach Walling for being insufficiently idealistic, for not admitting that "the dream is dead" and that his hopes in Tredway have not been realized. With passionate jealousy, she picks and tears away at his attachment to the Company and his remnants of personal devotion to Bullard.

There is a suggestion here that the couple spats this way fairly often—we are told this, as Walling jumps out of the car in fury and strides off into the dark, by the production vice-president, Jesse Grimm (Dean Jagger), who happens to be driving past. Grimm remarks to his wife that Walling has lost his temper "earlier than usual," and looks on with scorn at the "college-boy" theorist who has tried to tell him how to run "his" production lines. Grimm's wife, however, is sympathetic—the only woman in the film who wants her husband to retire totally from business. She is thus the opposite of Alderson's wife, who is an unadulteratedly detestable character with a grasping stridency unalloyed by warmth or competence (possibly she *has* to be this mean in order to explain why so nice a man as Alderson is not going to get the job, and why seniority—a current American substitute for competence—will not prevail; by putting in her mouth the film's only argument for seniority, "You've waited for it," the argument is undercut).

The split in Walling's allegiance suggested by his violent response to his wife's needling—between his love of power and of "pure" design, between conventionality and unconventionality—is further emphasized by his house: junior-executive suburban on the outside and Mixed Moderne on the inside. Yet even a would-be sophisticate's interior does not represent Walling's "true" self; this appears only in his study, an upper-middlebrow version of Charles Eames' studio (Eames, an architect and furniture designer, was technical adviser to the film) with its collection of little contemporary-chic bibelots like Chinese kites or notion-counter odds and ends. Here Walling doodles; his wife says that without this room—and presumably without these *objets de vertu*—he would have gone crazy. She tells him that what he is drawing looks good to her; as though she knew, or as though such a comment (in the light of their previous argument) were not aggressive. In fact she makes the aggression explicit by still another pep-talk about how Walling should "design what you want, build what you want"—meaning quit the Company and go out on his own, since obviously he cannot have his way within the Company.

With what must be accumulated hatred, though it masquerades as fond reasonableness, she goes on to reproach him for having liked Avery Bullard for bringing him to Tredway in the first place.[2] Walling apparently had kept hoping, as so many subordinates do hope, that the Old Man would "reform" and come around to the idealism-cum-modernity of his young designer; and necessarily he goes on hoping that the Company will reform, very likely that he can reform it himself by stirring others to emulate his ardor. And while Mrs. Walling has the good sense of the bystander, who sees that reform is unlikely, she has also the solipsism of the wife who thinks that everything impossible to her husband when he must work with others would be easy if he worked alone. She urges him therefore to unspecific and largely unreal goals, while being terrified of—and eventually seeking to defeat—the one goal within realistic reach: succession to Bullard, and with it a chance to salvage the withered hopes.

Verbally, Walling rejects either possibility—saying, of the presidency, "I'm a designer, not a politician"—but not with convincing finality; perhaps he realizes that he is kidding himself, and that to care too deeply about the Company's designs means that he must ultimately dirty his hands in something else besides his nice clean chemicals. As it turns out, all the "political" machinations (in the sense that clean-cut Americans like Walling must reject politics) are eventually laid at the door of Loren Shaw, and Walling wins office through a series of temper tantrums which make his bid for authority seem less calculating, therefore less "political."

Just as the Walling house dramatizes the divided counsels and discussion-group intensities of their daily life, so does the subplot revolving around their son Mike. Unlike the gewgaws in the study, he is not a solace to his father but a further drain on the family reservoir of chumminess. Twice the seriousness of Walling's own conflict is accentuated by his shattering the bonds of camaraderie with his son—once when they are playing catch, and again at the Little League baseball game where Mike is pitching against heavy batting and psychological odds. In the American idiom, where baseball is the area for father-son conciliation and reconciliation—much as going to bed together is in husband-wife relations—this is strong stuff; we would expect broken hearts, tears, recriminations. But strangely none result; Mike is undisturbed, in part because he is not surprised by his father and in part because his mother takes up the slack, making enough noise for both parents.

Mike's Big Game comes up at the same time his father's does, so that at the close the latter's renewal of interest in his son's concerns can round out the picture with a double-Walling victory. Yet it is striking how unambiguous the movie is about the Little League, in view of its strictures on the Big one. There is no hint of the possibility that a child's strenuous competition may exhaust and victimize him emotionally, for the benefit of parents' zeal and equipment manufacturers' sales (*Life* recently acknowledged such misgivings by arguing that they were unfounded). In fact Mike himself, though greatly worried about the game in a kind of tongue-biting way, shows none of his father's perplexities—even about his father's problems (note his early question: "When are you going to be president?"). He not only remains calm in the face of his mother's chattering away at him over the catchers' mitt but also takes for granted his father's drive to power, which he understands in Little League terms.

And it is a childlike vision of the company town, as somehow an American norm, that gives *Executive Suite* its most romantic qualities. Millburgh is not a place, but Hometown, U.S.A.—where so much that is problematic in the national life can be dissolved in a golden glow of recaptured youth, whether real or synthetic. American pastoral, in its purest form, has this extraordinary ability to draw the sting of both competition and paternalism. What would be an anxiety-ridden crisis to Walling becomes "character building" to his son; for self-seeking is all right when it is innocent and juvenile, when it does not involve Wall Street, women, stocks, and other imponderables. To the Millburgh in heart, all things are Millburgh—just so long as the Tredway Company is there to pay the bills. Doubtless the stadium in which the Little League plays, before a shouting crowd of local patriots (and a prominent Coca-Cola sign), is one of the many blessings for which the town is indebted to the distant occupants of the Executive Suite.

Having seen the Company brass home to their villas, we move to the Plant and the people in it. Scenes involving workers are photographed in a gray-day "documentary" half-light, fittingly proletarian; the labor force we see is somber, querulous, pathetic, aureoled in 1930's melancholy. They do not leave work with the mellow fatigue of the executives rejoining wives and cars, but make for the trolley in a nervous, abstracted, robot-like crowd. They are oppressed. They remember; "You weren't here in 1933," a little old lady wails to Walling. They cling around him, helpless; he must save them. They are worried and unhappy because they don't make furniture the way they used to—i.e., the image of the craftsmanlike Past versus the commercial Present.

Thus the way is prepared for one of Walling's clinching arguments in the closing scene: that some of the workers have taken a transfer and a loss of wages rather than work on the crude "new line" Comptroller Shaw has encouraged. They see the change precisely as Walling does, in terms of managerial decay; they share with him the idol of the Old Man, who brought them up from the Slump, and hence they respond with as little awareness as anyone but Shaw and the Sales Manager of the part that markets and profits play in manufacture. Though the profit-minded Shaw would seem to have their interests more closely at heart, the supervisory workers would rather talk to Walling about Good Design. "Four years since we've made anything like that," a foreman says to him as they inspect his trophies—two awards for pieces of furniture we briefly see, the only time the quality and direction of Walling's aspirations are actually revealed.[3]

The assumption shared by Walling, the foreman, and nearly everyone else is that Avery Bullard was corrupted when Loren Shaw (nothing but a night-school CPA, as Caswell nastily reminds him) came to the upper levels of the Company. This disintegration is attributed both to aging might and the changing times, which raise needs, not for the sort of robber baron we are told that Bullard was (that this should have helped him or his business in the 1930's seems anachronistic), but for a different type. We can understand how Bullard, who encompassed in his own character not only Walling's lust for idealism but Shaw's aptitude for shadiness, could only delay decision by pitting one man against the other. And yet, since Walling seems less of a master than Bullard, and Shaw much more of a menace, it is another of the romantic attributes of the film to suggest that business generally, with the decline in cantankerous individualism, now faces such a choice among the fragments of its once-unified power—or that at the end, when Walling wins, he can resolve the split not by firing (or even demoting) Shaw but by retaining him as a member of a new "team," which will try to replace the monolithic Bullard by subdividing the labor of imitating him. Ah, there were giants in the earth in those days.

This magnanimity of Walling's seems all the more surprising as Shaw, long before the final scenes, begins to fall apart and parody himself. We find him keeping a box of clean handkerchiefs in his desk drawer—a Lady Macbeth touch; we find him blackmailing Sales Manager Dudley to vote for him with a snarling vindictiveness quite out of tune with the restrained clarity he has demonstrated on other occasions; we find him nonplussed at the Board meeting by Caswell's maneuver over the first ballot, when one would have expected such jackals to have negotiated from their respective strengths long before this formality[4] (unless we are meant to believe that Caswell was only pretending to have cast the abstention, and that it really was Miss Julia Tredway's [Barbara Stanwyck], as at first implied). And we find Shaw attempting to block Walling's flood of rhetoric in the final encounter by describing a sly tax dodge by which he has saved the Company more money than it makes on furniture. This, for so clever a man, merely highlights his venality and further antagonizes his fellow-executives—and Miss Tredway, the heiress of Company stock, Company memories, and her long-term affair with Bullard himself.

By this time, Walling should be able to see at least as clearly as the audience does that Shaw has overreached himself. In a way, Shaw's sense for relevance has been self-defeating in its excess, as though the film were saying that relevance and lust for power are the same thing. Shaw, of course, is the only one who speaks up in specific terms for the stockholders or for the good of the Company. But what he does is defend "security"—that is, the "highest and safest return on investment"—only to have "efficiency" hurled back in his teeth: engineer's efficiency à la Veblen rather than financier's. Poor Shaw is caught up in the involuntary honesty with which he admits that he thinks people like himself, self-made by education, are going to have to run things from now on; inevitably he offends the others by this lack of guile. He has already shown—in a sharp little scene with Alderson, over the suitability of a one-day work-stoppage for Bullard's funeral—that he has a "modern" indifference to sentiment and appetite for details, and is thus the only one who can "run" the Company. His failure is an inability to run his colleagues, each of whom in his own way is just as insistently and "lovably" irrational as Miss Tredway (a Tennessee Williams character transplanted to the Alleghenies). Walling wins by showing that he *can* run these people; he would never make Shaw's mistake, least of all with Shaw.

As in the symbolically and stylistically influential movies of Frank Capra

—such as *Mr. Smith Goes to Washington*—the amateur always proves to be a better politician than the pro. Capra's moral was often that the vanished America of reliable rewards for rural naïveté is still there, if only you know how to plug in connections with it, but where *Executive Suite* tries to continue the tradition it suffers from the increased sophistication of America itself. The role of MacDonald Walling is not sufficiently naïve to be played by Jimmie Stewart, nor is Walling—being half-scientist, with one foot in the future—anywhere near helpless enough to crystallize sympathy for himself as an underdog, or to make common cause with the ethic of fair play. Perhaps, with business becoming increasingly refined and complex, it will increasingly be natural to dramatize business conflicts in terms of the Shaws and the Wallings, these two types of hard-driving men, while the other vice-presidents—the safe-and-sane (and stuffy) Alderson, the piddling production man, the philandering salesman—never get a look-in at the Ultimate Job.

All these currents swirl through the Board Room of the Executive Suite, where the directors meet to pick Bullard's successor. (After the fashion of modern professional management, the directors are all active executives except for the broker Caswell and the hold-over Miss Tredway, neither of whom could affect the decision were the others to agree.) For males in the audience (including the authors) the scenes in the Board Room apparently had tension and suspense even though the outcome was foretold; but for women and children—to judge by our informally collected impressions—the sequence was nearly meaningless and certainly boring, a lot of talking and voting that was badly if at all understood. It must have taken courage to make a movie on an "A" budget as sex-differentiated as this; and one wonders, too, what working-class people were expected to make of events that called for a grasp of short-selling, proxies, and the like, to comprehend. Few courageous European films, surely, would run such risks of being misconstrued as this one does during the long moments of the tactical preliminaries through which only Miss Martin, approaching her big moment with a radiantly stony face—she hates Shaw, wants Walling to win, and will in any event be the recording angel—moves with slow solemnity, dispensing pencils and compiling the transcript.

Yet despite a skillful conception, and the effectiveness with which it is carried out, the Board Room scenes in retrospect have an unreal quality; we are not convinced we are watching an operating and powerful group, on whose decisions others depend, in action at the nexus of control, but rather a role-playing drama, scenic and stage-managed—as when Luigi carefully carries in a table which we later discover is there only for Walling, in his frenzy, to bust to pieces. The directors reveal no functional relationships to one another nor, save for Caswell, to the outside world one would expect to converge on them at this point: banks, suppliers, minority stockholders, lawyers, reporters (the Company, after all, is listed on the Stock Exchange). The inference—in spite of the point repeatedly made that the town depends on them—is that these men are managers chiefly in the sense that they manage plane reservations, telephones, and one another; only Caswell, the irresponsible outsider, is self-controlled enough to inject any humor—which in him is made to seem simply despicable—to relieve the onerous burden of decision.

The inability of the managers to manage is ironically, if unintentionally, underlined by a parenthetical shot of Alderson out at a highway control booth, trying to get hold of Jesse Grimm by locating his car in traffic (Miss Martin had earlier suggested this device to Miss Bardeman, an example of the crucial role of the secretary in controlling information and of the intuitive insight of film-makers where questions of communication are concerned). Here the individual has been released from the Company net—that is, telephone and squawk box—just as Grimm really wanted to be liberated from his job, so that he must be sought personally rather than by number (even license number) in the anonymous, mechanical flow of the open road. The search for Grimm gives a movie-chase quality to the otherwise room-bound Board meetings, though in fact Grimm is unco-operative when found, and eventually easy to sway.

Walling's real victory, however, is over the salesman, Walter Dudley. (He had begun his conquest of Julia Tredway earlier, in an adjoining room, by a vicious display of temperament which almost drives her to jump out the window; the shock of this onslaught is represented as so therapeutic that she later thanks him for "saving her life.") Dudley has promised to vote for Shaw, on whose graphs and figures he depends for success at his sales conventions and who can threaten to expose his liaison with his secretary; of course he too hates Shaw, and everything Shaw stands for, with what appears to be a kind of Irish geniality and fecklessness. If a good salesman is someone who can be sold, then Dudley proves himself in being won over by Walling's last-ditch sales-pitch. For not only is Dudley vulnerable to the argument that Shaw compels him to handle cheap goods, but Walling's ultimate reliance on "personality" accords with Dudley's own; by turning inspirational, Walling can reassure Dudley that the vocation of selling is worthwhile—depend though he may on a secretary's favors, whiskey, and the comptroller's charts. The turning point is reached when Dudley rises to the bait, risks exposure, and shifts the balance of power.

In a related sense, what Walling does at the meeting is throw another temper tantrum—like his jumping out of the car and walking home alone, or his sudden assertiveness at the airport which lets Alderson give in and coyly say, "Is that an order?" His tone, as distinguished from what he says, is one of petulance; he is upping the price to be placed on his own co-operation, demonstrating that he will be harder to get on with than the others if *not* made president (and with Grimm quitting, who else knows anything of design and production?). His case is unanswerable both in terms of personalities and of the sentimental indifference to fiscal evaluations that all but Shaw display. Walling begins gently, reasonably, drawing

Shaw out at the point where Shaw's own integrity is vulnerable—security, yes, but to what end? What do you really want in life? In playing them off against one another—in somehow linking Julia Tredway's family pride with Grimm's in workmanship and Dudley's in having good goods to sell— he is never offensive, much as he may dominate them all by a threat of latent temperament. One by one he rings in the sacred symbols, both of Past and Future, in terms of the team and of his ability to focus and interpret the symbols (as who else can?) to hold the team together. Though one of his clinchers is the boast that he has never appeared in *Fortune,* he may well want nothing more, and will not be long in making the grade.

It is perhaps no accident that William Holden, though a fine performer, comes through indistinctly in the part of Walling, compared to the other stars; he is conceived as a personality boy while they are "characters." In passing we discover his reasoning about Avery Bullard: that Bullard's sin was individual pride, not so much in the Company as in himself, so that he drew apart from the people he worked with and they became bitter (as Miss Tredway was bitter and broken) at being kept at arm's length, at being so evidently not communicated with. Prior to the last scenes, Miss Tredway had been burning papers in the fireplace next door; we never find out what they are—bonds, a will, stock powers?—though it is clear they are important; perhaps this echoes the meaning of Walling's triumph, which is that "personality"—still better, manipulation, considering that Miss Tredway had gone back on her promise to Shaw in voting for Walling— counts for more than paperwork. Walling will not be remote; he will play ball with everyone—keep Bullard's dream alive, make the Company aesthetically respectable, and (a sop to Shaw) use scientific methods. There are no divisive gaps, at home or in the office, that the chummy democratic personality cannot bridge.

Yet one uncertainty remains for Walling: will not his career success still further alienate him from a home life which depends on companionship, from a new-model wife who so prefers a husband uncommitted to his office that she fails to put through a phone call that might have made the difference between his success and failure? In the general emotional glow which follows Walling's display of virtuosity and schmaltz, Julia Tredway tosses away her life's bitterly won lesson to assure Mrs. Walling that the spare-time attentions of a man headed for the heights are prizes beyond compare. It is enough that he should sometime remember to ask who won the Little League game, and the fact that he *does* remember is the formal happy ending of the film (perhaps Miss Martin will in the future mark his son's birthday on his desk calendar). Otherwise we are left with the impression—as in *Point of No Return,* a far subtler and more experienced statement of the same theme—that Walling has made a great sacrifice, that there will be no more pitch-and-catch with Mike, and that the substance of glory will be an anticlimax, even though Mrs. Walling will be barred by the memory of her abortive sabotage from ever saying so.

It is a sociologist's vice to take as literal myth a book-and-movie combination which had to run a variety of more or less happenstance gauntlets (what will we do about Barbara Stanwyck?) before achieving final form. Yet what is so striking about *Executive Suite* is the matching of the film's snobberies to those of so many contemporary intellectuals: good design is highbrow; baseball is highbrow-lowbrow; cities are inhuman; there is something a little déclassé about too great an interest in profits and balance sheets, about Shaw's night-schooling, and by inference about his bad-formal manners, and so on. Dudley's lower-middle-class vulgarities are sufficiently picturesque to be treated charitably, but the middle-class virtues of thrift, precision, and foresight (represented by Shaw) are denigrated, while Caswell's *arriviste* nervousness is contrasted unfavorably with both the New York banker's solidity and with Walling's high-powered "idealism." It is to Walling, the egghead with the Madison Avenue veneer, that both workers and vice-presidents in their massed anxieties look for salvation; he will restore the company's dignity and style, sooth all its ruffled feathers, and guard it, too, against Depression. *Executive Suite* is an intellectual's dream of business life made manifest, a Walter Mitty fantasy of what might happen to him if *he* were MacDonald Walling.

In this *Executive Suite* is once again anachronistic. While its imagery of business has a homespun, nineteenth-century quality, emphasizing the divorce between New York money-juggling and small-town reliability, the conflict between the Tredway Tower and "outside" is resolved only by the morale-building qualities of a typically twentieth-century man. Walling is the end-product of that most modern process, the institutionalization of institutional advertising—the methods of conscious myth-making through which a company (or, through psychological warfare, a country) can concoct a new personality for itself in order to make malleable its previous conflicts. Ordinarily, to be sure, these conflicts are "real," in the sense that they exist between management and labor, or between both together and the consumer, or between the U.S. and the U.S.S.R. But the conflicts of *Executive Suite* exist mainly in fantasy, for they are conflicts between the desire for glamor—whether in the Stork Club or an Eames design—and the nostalgia for pre-glamor days when men were men, wives stayed home, and workers depended on their bosses.

Walling himself is "real"; we all know many Wallings. The prototype has been skillfully up-dated, leaving his populist and Veblenian forebears far behind. This is no longer the hard, insensitive, neutral engineer with an austere professionalism as his shield and device. He has been both corrupted and transfigured by power. Somewhere along the road to the managerial summit the fumbling hero of pure design and no politics has lost his innocence, and gained the Executive Suite only at the cost of that boyish, sand-lot opacity which first endeared him to our sympathies. Transparently unprotected by the defenses that would serve an intractable Bullard or a tractable Shaw, he faces alone those total claims for attention his seeming success will now make on him—workers, managers, wife, and child, all equally demanding on his universally accessible affections.

Yet if this is a fate many of us would willingly call tragic, it is not so in terms of the film but of what the film leaves unsaid. We are led to the threshold of a future in which Walling is to Live Happily Ever After, with the premonitions of his "failure of success" damped down to a faint suggestion of the lofty distance which now separates him from his erstwhile peers. We are left with the feeling that the story has just begun, and that so far it has revealed rather than healed the breach between business and literature. With its many deft touches and not a few moments of drama, *Executive Suite* has done well to show how many motivations besides production-mindedness can eddy about in a corporation, how many varieties of temperament a blanket term such as "business" can conceal, and how many opportunities for individual good and evil lie in the most ordinary events. But it suffers by leaving behind it the sense that business is more interesting than it has managed to say, deserves a still more attentive scrutiny, and has the makings of more movies than this. If business were less interesting, after all, the wives in *Executive Suite* would not seem so bereft or all the men but Grimm so torn.

Notes

1. The modern office is frequently designed to minimize the baronial element and accentuate the executive's right to pose as "ecologically" mobile and group-conscious, ejecting files and incunabula so as to set the scene less for giving orders than for holding conferences. Cf. Eric Larrabee, "The Cult of Work: What is Happening to the Office?," *Industrial Design*, 1, 2; April, 1954; pp. 22-3.

2. The names hardly seem accidental: "Tredway" with its echo of "treadmill" and of a distinguished chain of New York and New England country inns, "Bullard" with its combination of "bully" and "dullard."

3. The examples are a cabinet and a bench, the first a watered down version of an Eames design with touches of George Nelson, the second a Shaker-like imitation in the style that George Nakashima calls Cocktail Shaker, neither especially distinguished nor drawn or framed with any kind of Museum of Modern Art éclat.

4. One of the many revealing, if inevitable, differences between the movie of *Executive Suite* and the book, where there is no Board meeting as such and—as in "real" life—more of the important dickering is done covertly, informally, and ahead of time.

5. Cf. Russell Lynes, "What Has Succeeded Success?," *Mademoiselle*, September, 1954, for the aspirations of recent women's college graduates, who fear ulcers for their husbands and crave for themselves—once the income plateau which sustains the suburban life-style has been reached—a companionate marriage in which home looms far larger than office.

FURTHER READING

Alpert, Hollis. "Sexual Behavior in the American Movies," *Saturday Review*, Vol. 39, 1956, pp. 9-10.

Blumer, Herbert. *Movies and Conduct.* (Motion Pictures and Youth: Payne Fund Studies.) New York: Macmillan, 1933.

Blumer, Herbert, and Hauser, Phillip M. *Movies, Delinquency, and Crime.* New York: Macmillan, 1933.

Capp, Al. "The Comedy of Charlie Chaplin," *Atlantic*, Vol. 185, 1950, pp. 25-30.

Charters, W. W. *Motion Pictures and Youth.* New York: Macmillan, 1933.

Cohen, Elliot. "The Film Drama as a Social Force," *Commentary*, Vol. 4, 1947, pp. 110-18.

Coughlan, Robert. "Television's Effects on Moving Picture Business," *Life*, Vol. 31, 1951, pp. 102-08.

Crowther, Bosley. "The Strange Case of the 'The Miracle,'" *Atlantic*, Vol. 187, 1951, pp. 35-39.

Denney, Reuel. "Joe Friday—the Plainest Plain-Clothesman," *New Republic*, Vol. 132, 1955, pp. 14-17.

Dale, Edgar. *The Content of Motion Pictures.* New York: Macmillan, 1935.

Elkin, Frederick. "The Value Implications of Popular Films," *Sociology and Social Research*, Vol. 38, 1954, pp. 320-22.

Elkin, Frederick. "The Psychological Appeal of the Hollywood Western," *Journal of Educational Sociology*, Vol. 24, 1950, pp. 72-86.

Fadiman, William J. "The Sources of Movies," *Annals of the American Academy of Political and Social Science*, Vol. 254, 1947, pp. 37-40.

Farber, Manny. "Movies Aren't Movies Any More," *Commentary*, Vol. 13, 1952, pp. 560-66.

Fearing, Franklin. "Influence of the Movies on Attitudes and Behavior," *Annals of the American Academy of Political and Social Science*, Vol. 254, 1947, pp. 70-79.

Fenin, George N. "Motion Pictures and the Public," *Film Culture*, January-February, 1955, pp. 15-18.

Fenin, George N. "The Western—Old and New," *Film Culture*, May-June, 1956, pp. 7-11.

Funk, A. *The Film and Youth: An investigation of the psychological effects of films on the life of the young.* Munich: Reinhardt, 1934.

Fülöp-Miller, René. *The Motion Picture in America.* New York: Dial Press, 1938.

Gladstone, Gabriel. "Hollywood, Killer of the Dream," *Dissent*, Vol. 2, 1955, p. 166.

Goodman, Walter. "How Not to Produce a Film," *New Republic*, Vol. 133, 1955, pp. 12-13.

Gundlach, Ralph. "The Movies: Stereotypes or Realities?" *Journal of Social Issues*, Vol. 3, 1947, pp. 26-32.

Hafeez, M. A. "Psychology of Films," *Journal of Education and Psychology*, Vol. 8, 1950, pp. 14-22.

Halsey, Edwin. "The Defective as Movie Hero," *Commonweal*, Vol. 55, 1951, pp. 445-46.

Handel, Leo A. *Hollywood Looks at Its Audience.* Urbana: University of Illinois Press, 1950.

Handel, Leo A. "The Social Obligations of Motion Pictures," *International Journal of Opinion and Attitude Research*, Vol. 1, 1947, pp. 93-98.

Handel, Leo A. " Study to Determine the Drawing Power of Male and Female Stars upon Movie-Goers of Their Own Sex," *International Journal of Opinion and Attitude Research,* Summer 1948, pp. 215-20.

Harley, John E. *World-Wide Influences of the Cinema.* Los Angeles: University of Southern California Press, 1940.

Hauseman, J. "Today's Hero: A Review," *Hollywood Quarterly,* Vol. 2, 1947, p. 161.

Hauser, Arnold. "Can Movies Be Profound?" *Partisan Review,* Vol. 15, 1948, pp. 69-73.

Inglis, Ruth A. *Freedom of the Movies.* Chicago: University of Chicago Press, 1947.

Irvine, Keith. "The Film You Won't See: Unofficial Censors at Work," *Nation,* Vol. 181, 1955, pp. 109-10.

Jacobs, Lewis. *The Rise of the American Film: A Critical History.* New York: Harcourt, Brace, 1939.

Johnston, Eric. "The Motion Picture as a Stimulus to Culture," *Annals of the American Academy of Political and Social Science,* Vol. 254, 1947, pp. 98-102.

Jones, Dorothy B. "Quantitative Analysis of Motion Picture Content," *Public Opinion Quarterly,* Vol. 14, 1950, pp. 554-58.

Kracauer, Siegfried. "Hollywood's Terror Films," *Commentary,* Vol. 2, 1946, pp. 132-36.

Kracauer, Siegfried. "Those Movies With a Message," *Harper's,* June 1948, pp. 657-72.

Lawson, John Howard. "Hollywood—Illusion and Reality," *Hollywood Quarterly,* Vol. 1, 1946, p. 233.

Lazarsfeld, Paul F. "Audience Research in the Movie Field," *Annals of the American Academy of Political and Social Science,* Vol. 254, November, 1947.

Lehman, Milton. "Who Censors Our Movies?" *Look,* March 9, 1954, pp. 86-92.

Manvell, Roger. *The Film and Its Public.* New York: Penguin Books, Ltd., 1955.

Mayer, Arthur. "Myths, Movies and Maturity," *Saturday Review,* Vol. 39, 1956, pp. 7-8.

Mayer, J. P. *Sociology of Film.* London: Faber and Faber, 1945.

Mercey, A. A. "Social Uses of the Motion Pictures," *Annals of the American Academy of Political and Social Science,* Vol. 250, 1947, pp. 89-97.

Metzger, Charles R. "Pressure Groups and the Motion Picture Industry," *Annals of the American Academy of Political and Social Science,* Vol. 254, 1947, pp. 110-15.

Mirams, Gordon. "Drop That Gun!," *Quarterly of Film, Radio and Television,* Vol. 6, 1951, pp. 1-20.

Moellenhoff, F. "Remarks on the Popularity of Mickey Mouse," *American Imago,* Vol. 3, 1940, pp. 19-32.

Montani, A., and Pietranera, G. "First Contribution to the Psychoanalysis and Aesthetics of Motion Pictures," *Psychoanalysis Review,* Vol. 33, 1946, pp. 177-96.

Panofsky, Erwin. "Style and Medium in the Motion Pictures," *Critique* (New York), Vol. 1, No. 3, Jan.-Feb. 1947, pp. 5-18, 27-28.

Peterson, Ruth C., and Thurstone, L. L. *Motion Pictures and the Social Attitudes of Children.* New York: Macmillan, 1933.

Powdermaker, Hortense. "An Anthropologist Looks at the Movies," *Annals of the American Academy of Political and Social Science,* Vol. 254, 1947, pp. 80-85.

Quigley, Martin. "Public Opinion and the Motion Picture," *Public Opinion Quarterly,* Vol. 1, 1937, p. 129.

Ramsaye, Terry. "The Rise and Place of the Motion Picture," *Annals of the American Academy of Political and Social Science,* Vol. 254, 1947, pp. 1-11.

Riesman, David, and Riesman, Evelyn T. "Movies and Audiences," *American Quarterly,* Vol. 4, 1952, pp. 195-202.

Rosenthal, S. P. "Changes of Socio-Economic Attitudes Under Radical Motion Picture Propaganda," *Archives of Psychology,* No. 166, 1934.

Ross, Lillian. *Picture.* New York: Harcourt, Brace, 1952.

Rosten, Leo C. *Hollywood.* New York: Harcourt, Brace, 1941.

Rosten, Leo C. "Hollywood Revisited," *Look,* Vol. 20, 1956, pp. 17-28.

Rosten, Leo C. "Movies and Propaganda," *Annals of the American Academy of Political and Social Science,* Vol. 254, pp. 116-24.

Rule, John T. "Movies and TV: Murder or Merger," *Atlantic,* Vol. 192, 1953, pp. 55-59.

Schwartz, Delmore. "Mary Pickford: the Little Girl in Curls," *New Republic,* Vol. 132, 1955, pp. 17-20.

Sisk, John P. "Life in the Movie Magazines," *Commonweal,* Vol. 61, 1955, pp. 634-35.

Sprager, Harva K. "Hollywood Foreign Correspondents," *Quarterly of Film, Radio and Television,* Vol. 6, 1952.

Suckow, Ruth. "Hollywood Gods and Goddesses," *Harper's,* July, 1936.

Thorp, Margaret F. *America at the Movies.* New Haven: Yale University Press, 1939.

Warshow, Robert. "A Feeling of Sad Dignity," *Partisan Review,* Vol. 21, 1954, pp. 664-75.

Warshow, Robert. "The Movie Camera and the American," *Commentary,* Vol. 13, 1952, pp. 275-82.

Warshow, Robert. "The Westerner," *Partisan Review,* Vol. 21, 1954, pp. 190-203.

Weinberg, Herman A. "Hollywood, O Hollywood!" *Film Culture,* May-June, 1955, pp. 7-10.

Wilner, Daniel M. "Attitude as a Determinant of Perception in the Mass Media of Communication: Reactions in the Motion Picture, 'Home of the Brave.' " Doctoral dissertation, University of California, Los Angeles, 1951.

Woelfel, Norman. "The American Mind and the Motion Picture," *Annals of the American Academy of Political and Social Science,* Vol. 254, 1947, pp. 89-94.

Wolfenstein, Martha, and Leites, Nathan. "The Unconscious vs. the 'Message' in an Anti-Bias Film," *Commentary,* Vol. 10, 1950, pp. 388-91.

Wolfenstein, Martha, and Leites, Nathan. "An Analysis of Themes and Plots," *Annals of the American Academy of Political and Social Sciences,* Vol. 254, 1947, pp. 41-48.

5

Television and Radio

Does wide acceptance of one mass-culture medium condition society to receive a newer medium more quickly? The fact that television takes up more American leisure time than any other activity seems to answer the question affirmatively. For where it took the movie industry three decades to reach its peak in audiences, radio reached its summit in half that time. Then came television and in scarcely more than six years it had surpassed the biggest audiences of the competing media. During its first few years, critics of the new medium wishfully believed that people soon would become surfeited with TV's constant fare. However, whatever it was that television gave them, from wrestling to Omnibus, *from Shakespeare to the $64,000* Question, *people continued to glue their eyes on an aluminumized cathode tube. While television throve to the point where in 1955 seven out of every ten American homes had at least one set, the movies came upon hard days. Where the movies had played host to more than 82 million customers in 1946 (their peak year), by 1953 the number had dwindled to little more than half that.*

Even though a large proportion of the programs are banal, repetitious and replete with stereotyped situations, television continues to grow as a colossus in the mass entertainment field.

Whether the effect of television on American life will be beneficial when assessed over a substantial range of years or the opposite, is the subject of much controversy. Those who say yes point to the growing number of educational TV stations which indicate that the medium can and is being used for more than mass entertainment. Harvard recently announced that two of its best-known professors, Edwin G. Boring and Zechariah Chafee, would give courses over Boston's educational Channel 2. Even Variety, *the weekly chronicleer of the popular arts, found this interesting, and distinctively headlined the story:*

HARVARD GIVES 2 PROFS
THE ELECTRONIC CHAIR

Introducing this section, Rolf B. Meyersohn surveys research done on the alleged effects of television, and points out the difficulties involved in discerning and measuring effects due solely to this medium.

Gunther Anders believes that television will hasten the transformation of autonomous individuals into mass man. *With genuine anxiety, Anders sees radio and television robbing Americans of their ability to speak, since the machines make all the conversation that is necessary.*

So severe an indictment of television inevitably drew a counter argument. The next issue of the magazine which published Anders' essay carried a forceful rebuttal by Henri Rabassiere. Beyond the immediate task of chal-

lenging Anders' underlying ideas on television, Rabassiere extends his remarks to a defense of mass culture in general.

Another critic of television, Murray Hausknecht, sees the medium as devoid of power to "spread culture" when its primary purpose is entertainment and the use of individual talent as a come-on for the "hard sell." Moreover, television is another step in the invasion of privacy. For Hausknecht, the symbolic figure of mass-cultured society is the technician who places the mike in the bosom on the television show Person to Person.

Kurt Lang shows that popular taste for radio and television programs is erroneously considered as merely a conglomeration of polyglot tastes. He sees "mass appeal" rather as based on a group of distinct tastes held by a majority of the audience. The conventions which influence audience preferences for programs should be differentiated from program content, format and tone of the offerings.

Social Research in Television[1]

By ROLF B. MEYERSOHN

"IF TELEVISION IS A FAD, so is breathing," at least according to one network vice-president.[2] (This may be why he is only a vice-president.) True enough, television's expansion in the first ten years of its life has been relentless. By now almost three-quarters of all the homes in this country are equipped with a TV set[3] and approximately 75 million adults watch it for an average of over eighteen hours a week.[4]

But what does it all mean? Sociologists as well as most other people have been unable to understand the statistics. Despite numerous studies of television and its "effects" conducted in both the academic and commercial worlds (summaries of most of these works may be found in Coffin,[5] Meyersohn,[6] and Finn[7]), it must be said that only little has emerged that touches on the really important problems created by television. As a result no systematic confirmation or denial can yet be made of the numerous charges against the medium.

The criticism itself, however, has assumed a systematic content. It centers around two charges; the more serious one that television viewing leads to passivity and/or that the act of television watching is itself passive. Here social research has contributed little, in part because it is more difficult to study people than it is to study television—and easy to overlook that passivity is a human trait, not a characteristic of television.

The other charge is against television's purported massive poor taste and/or its taste-debasing effects. Studies here have also been ineffectual, and for similar reasons: the complex interaction between people and their television sets, the entertainment alternatives that exist, and the norms for good taste by which television as well as people might be judged—these things are virgin research material. And it must be remembered that most critics and research people are more educated and sophisticated than the general TV viewer.

It may some day be possible to design a study good enough to analyze and predict long-term consequences of television, a study that deals with the problems of passivity and taste levels. For the present it seems we must be satisfied with limited knowledge about limited areas. As it is, research findings that do exist have been neglected in most discussions about television. For our purposes some of these findings will be used to focus on television as a medium of entertainment and as a mass medium.

Published for the first time in this volume. This is a publication of the Center for the Study of Leisure, The University of Chicago. The Center is supported by a grant from the Behavioral Sciences Division of the Ford Foundation.

TELEVISION AS ENTERTAINMENT

TV has been called everything from baby-sitter to time-trap, been cursed for ruining eyesight and corrupting youth. But nobody has charged it for being "entertainment" even though this is all that television *per se* is. Any examination of the content of television provides evidence enough that the largest proportion of programs is clearly designed for entertainment purposes. In various carefully administered "monitoring studies" it was found that at least 75 per cent of all programs fall into the "entertainment" classification (as opposed to "information" or "orientation").[8] If such a trichotomy seems absurd to those who believe that entertainment might also inform or educate, or that "educational" programs could conceivably be entertaining (even without being "watered-down" high brow)—remember that no other classificatory schemes have been presented. Worse, there has been almost no serious research dealing with the meaning of entertainment.

Precisely how high or low the level of this entertainment is or "ought" to be is hard to say even if one assumes that television fare is at best mediocre. Research has actually been undertaken to find out just how mediocre it is—and of course discovered the expected. Only 32 per cent of the programs were rated as excellent or good, 29 per cent fair or poor, and 39 per cent objectionable or worse.[9] While these statistics were gathered only for children's programs, there is no reason to believe that adult entertainment would have been rated any more highly.

Most viewers, however, apparently consider such questions of levels and standards unimportant and have far clearer ideas on the "function" of TV than do critics. If one asks people why they bought a television set, the most common reply is "for entertainment."[10] Raymond Stewart, who studied these matters in Atlanta, Georgia, makes the point as follows:

> The Atlanta family purchased television to be entertained. And, when asked what television had done for them and their families, the great majority answered that it had entertained them.[11]

Certainly there were other motives as well. It is no longer relevant what kinds of people were the most eager to acquire a TV set, since almost everybody has one. But prior to saturation, it is evident from the data that television's audiences were not a "class" group. The greatest eagerness to purchase was found among middle and lower income groups, with higher ones "catching up" only as late as 1954.[12]

Bernard Fine considers this differential development as greater "dependency on television" on the part of lower income groups, accounting for it in the following way:

> People of limited income cannot secure very much entertainment outside of the home due to financial considerations. Television satisfies to a degree a need for entertainment, be it good or bad.[13]

Particularly interesting is the evidence that early television purchasers were likely to be those whose educational level was relatively lower than their income level.[14] For such people the new entertainment medium perhaps served as a way to make up in one respect for the gaps suffered in others. It is impossible to determine whether television ownership as such—and the pride of being, temporarily at least, the first owners in the neighborhood— did in fact help some to achieve prestige, or whether the kind of "au cour- antism" that television provides was successfully passed off as genuine sophistication. Undoubtedly television operated both as a "status-conferring device"[15] and as a modern version of adult education.

Less complicated motives for buying the new entertainment have also been established. Early TV buyers were primarily families with children[16] —a condition which requires among other things the accumulation of toys, diversions, and reliefs. If people bought television for entertainment, to some extent this meant entertainment for the children. There has yet to be discovered a more dependable distraction service. Eleanor Maccoby, who has carried out one of the few incisive investigations on children and tele- vision, finds parents highly uncritical of TV:

Although many educators and social scientists are concerned over the long range effects of television on children, the large majority of parents are *not* con- cerned. Most parents who own television, and even a large number of those who do not yet own it, consider television an unmixed blessing for themselves and and their children.[17]

The absence of criticism on the part of viewers is almost universal. Even television commercials are swallowed without objection.[18] When asked point-blank, "Does any of the advertising on television annoy or irritate you?" nearly three-fourths of the respondents in one survey replied with an unqualified *no*.[19]

As Gilbert Seldes has pointed out, lack of criticism does not necessarily mean enthusiasm.[20] It has been difficult to get viewers to criticize, and truly impossible to obtain meaningful answers to the question "Is there anything not now on television that you would like to see?" But this absence of verbal- ization is not enthusiastic endorsement. Whether the actual programs seen year in and year out have been ideal or even more enjoyable than any others remains an open question. Seldes warns:

Even if all the rest are "satisfied," we still have to watch out for the moment of hocus-pocus when "satisfied" is translated into "wouldn't care for anything else" and becomes virtually equivalent to "enthusiastic."[21]

Perhaps the best way to account for the silence is to call it an expression of the unspecific. The entertainment that is television is not simply an accretion of entertaining programs; it is the television set' and the watch- ing experience that entertains. Viewers seem to be entertained by the glow and the flow, regardless of whether it presents a commercial, a second-rate comic or an ancient Western. Television succeeds "because it is there."

TELEVISION AND ITS COLLEAGUES

At the beginning of the great romance between the American people and television, much was heard about TV's novelty effect. Hopefully (or sadly), it was predicted that the first careless rapture would settle down into an orderly relationship, with television becoming simply another member of the mass media family. Surveys have shown otherwise. The length of time spent viewing television has hardly decreased at all as new owners age.[22] The habit has become habit-forming.

Clearly something has had to give. Even if the American work week has been decreasing coincidentally, the resulting leisure doesn't add up to the weekly eighteen hours that have been allocated to television. How time has been redistributed cannot be stated precisely, but it is eminently clear that as television became a habit, others were broken.

The main victim has been night-time network radio. Very much as radio itself had in its beginnings cut heavily into the prevailing—and at that time, largely unorganized—evening activities, especially weekend evenings, so television has attracted America's attention. Except for the unhappy few —temporarily homeless, travelers, music-lovers, or the weak-stomached— who constitute TV's minority group problem, telecasters can count on a full house. Radio generally has changed noticeably in the past few years. Aside from the disappearance of the famous Sunday night radio comedians, there has been a general shift from network mass radio to local independent station broadcasting. As other parts of American culture become "nationalized," the sources of radio programming are seemingly more regional than ever. (It so happens, of course, that the output on most stations is virtually identical, namely, popular music, occasional newscasts and some sports announcing.)

The radio industry is not the only one affected. Hollywood, general magazines, and to some extent even newspapers have been made very much aware of television.[23] In the case of magazines, publishing houses generally have sustained enormous financial and circulation losses in the past ten years.[24] A number of them have folded (e.g., *Bluebook, Better Living, Today's Woman, American*); others have had to switch from weekly to bi-weekly (*Collier's* and *Look*). Ironically, one of the most successful publishing ventures in recent years has been a magazine devoted exclusively to television, *TV Guide*. Of the mass media, newspapers have been least affected, in part perhaps because they too provide television schedules.

Out of this very rough picture of what has happened to TV's colleagues, one generalization might be made. A rather neat pattern of displacement emerges, wherein it appears that whatever can be done effectively on television has ceased being as effective on any other medium. Put in more theoretical terms, television has become a functional substitute for certain contents of the other media.

The kinds of programs which are presented more effectively on television have to date been general entertainment forms, and as a provider of entertainment TV has displaced parts of the older media. Thus the principal casualties for radio have been drama and comedy (which had been the mainstay of radio network broadcasting) and magazines have had to sacrifice a number of "fiction and feature" titles; both are forms of entertainment more effectively viewed than heard or read.

The survivals are found in those areas which television cannot or will not subsume. Radio music is undoubtedly safe for a while—at least so long as music is only heard and not seen. Magazines which offer "interpretive" rather than instantaneous news coverage, such as *Time,* are also notable exceptions; along with newspapers they provide services which television cannot perform economically. But most media have had to accommodate in order to survive. This process of accommodation amounts to expanding their more basic and "unique" functions. Radio, as broadcasting studies have pointed out,[25] has had to give up trying to entertain families in their living rooms, concentrating instead on trying to be everywhere else and counting on individual, irregular, and inattentive listening. Essentially radio is now designed to fill in those areas—temporal, spatial and perhaps even intellectual—which television can't reach (N.B.C.'s "Monitor" is an example of a program which has taken such new demands fairly seriously.) And as television extends its coverage, radio will undoubtedly retreat still further or find other areas.

These retreats are equally clear in the other media. Cinemascope, all-night radio or magazines that list TV programs are all admissions of defeat.

In some ways the media too small to be swallowed by television have been far more successful. Thus in the wake of this vast trend there have been notable upsurges in particular and potentially "elevating" realms, e.g., highbrow paperbacked books and FM.

As for the "mass" mass media, the effect of television may be, as Hans Zeisel hopes, limited merely to an exchange of one kind of diversion for another equivalent one, with little gained or lost by society in the process:

> Whether America gets from now on some of its news, or its light entertainment, or its trash from television instead of from magazines, radio or newspapers is important only to these media and their advertisers.[26]

THE QUESTION OF PASSIVITY

Despite reassurances that television may have displaced only the expendable, few exchanges fail to have further consequences. As long as they are confined to media-swapping, perhaps they are negligible; the intrinsic differences between reading a comic book, attending a movie, and watching television may be unimportant. (While reading, which permits individual symbolization, is more creative than "viewing," there is some doubt that comic books provide this kind of autism.) But each of these activities carries with it social meaning.

A small study by Eliot Freidson, for example, reported that among children each activity occurred in a different social context: comic-book reading was carried on alone, television watching was likely to go on in the bosom of the family, and movie-going (particularly among adolescents) was a peer group activity.[27]

But *do* the different media force certain social contexts? Perhaps it is that each medium is accompanied by a distinct social form. The movie situation, for example, cannot be duplicated—a large anonymous audience, dim lights, an uninterrupted flow of screen "play." One can never "disappear" into TV as satisfactorily. Movies are equally conducive to individual or group attendance and facilitate dating, even mating. (Adolescents, incidentally, who form so large a part of the movie audience, are among the less enthusiastic television fans.)

TV, on the other hand, is living room entertainment (though it does form a new and essential ingredient for taverns) and restricts its viewers to shared but interrupted pleasure.[28]

One early claim for television was that it united the family. That family life was necessarily made more harmonious is something else again. If one observes a family watching television, he is likely to notice little interaction. Eleanor Maccoby found, for instance, that in only about one in ten families does any substantial amount of talking take place. She explains the matter as follows:

It appears that the increased family contact brought about by television is not social except in the most limited sense: that of being in the same room with other people. Whether the shared experience of television programs gives family members a similar perceptual framework with which to view the world, so that there are fewer differences in point of view among family members and fewer grounds for conflict is a matter which cannot be appraised with the data on hand.[29]

Bernard Fine calls it "unity without conversation."[30]

The social context of television must be considered from another viewpoint as well. Current addiction to TV means equally stimulant or narcosis. Presumably TV stimulates people to go out and buy, buy, buy, to attend the World Series, performances of Shakespeare, even to play baseball or play-read Shakespeare at home. At the same time, it is accused of turning its fans into wall-eyed vegetables hypnotizing so thoroughly that stimulation has become an end in itself.[31] Which is it?

At the simplest level this controversy is illustrated by the quarrel between TV manufacturers and sports entrepreneurs who can't agree on whether television has damaged sports. The former claim that TV has created a greater interest in sports, which ultimately results in greater attendance at ball games.[32] The other side, represented by a series of carefully designed studies carried out by the National Opinion Research Center, has demonstrated that football attendance, at least, has suffered considerably when its games were televised. The N.O.R.C. report concludes that the advantages of home viewing more than outweigh the excitement of being there.

It is difficult to see why a fan who has reduced his attendance because of television should later resume his old habits. he may spend fewer hours watching his set as the "novelty" wears off, or he may spend less time viewing events which he would not attend in any case. But if he has the opportunity, on his set at home without any charge, to watch a football game which interests him and which he could not otherwise see without buying a ticket, it would certainly appear to be less incentive for him to go out to the stadium—no matter how long he has owned the set.[33]

Whether watching a game on TV is any more "passive" than watching it in a stadium is not discussed, although in the more simplistic classifications of leisure activities the former is termed passive, the latter active.[34] *Where* it happens is apparently considered more important than *how,* even though it is quite possible to be extremely involved watching an event on television and, conversely, indifferent in the bleachers. It is of little use to brand different leisure activities with an immutable involvement label; far better to discover what in fact people do and feel as they pursue different activities.

In other words, stimulant *vs.* narcotic is a question that cannot yield an answer, even if we are able to establish that activities seen on TV are any more attractive than physical attendance.

When one moves from the sports controversy to problems such as the effect of TV on children's play there is much more at stake. In part the complexity of the issue itself has made social research much more difficult to conduct. The anxiety felt by some social critics and educators that children might stop reading altogether led to research that concentrated on correlating reading rates with television viewing rates. Similarly, concern that TV might affect school grades, homework or sleep led to the attempt to answer these questions *directly*—a true "fallacy of misplaced concreteness." While looking for immediate connections—and failing usually to locate any—many of the social scientists who studied the problem fell into the trap of making general statements based on concrete effects. Rather than organize experimentally or empirically matched groups—and attempt to count the reading, sleeping or productivity effects of watching television over a short period of time—one must deal with broader variables. Rather than positing as a model "what would children do and think if they didn't have a television set?"—an absurd question, impossible to answer scientifically since television is almost inseparable from its owners—better to ask "what *do* they do and think, given television and all the other possessions and objects that help to provide a way of life."[35]

So considered, television can be studied as an intervening variable—not taken as a purely independent element—subject to the same conditions as any other element in man's make-up. With such an approach, the problem of passivity is no longer a point of departure but becomes a possible conclusion.[36]

For example, in a recent study by the British psychologist William Belson,[37] interest in a number of leisure activities is studied according to strength of identification or involvement as well as according to the level of participation. At the same time, Belson has measured the degree of initiative. Cutting through the business of labeling particular activities passive or active, Belson was able to determine the general pattern of leisure participation.

Still more to the point is the work of the Rileys and of Eleanor Maccoby, who have stopped worrying about direct effects altogether. Mrs. Maccoby found that television is most frequently viewed by those children whose "real life satisfactions" are lacking and who utilize television as a fantasy outlet.[38] Similarly the Rileys discovered that children who are well integrated into peer groups often use television themes as the basis for group play, while for isolated children television programs are incorporated into private fantasy much more frequently.[39]

It is interesting to note that just as TV displaces other *media* activities, it is also capable of routing less structured preoccupations as well. Far from losing its entertainment function television is transformed into any number of complex entertainment roles. For certain types of people it provides fantasy stimulation, but for others it may reduce fantasy life considerably. Implied in both the Maccoby and the Rileys' studies is the question of whether such fantasy stimulation has further deleterious effects. This is of course the aspect on which certain educators, psychologists and even legislators have fastened, blaming television as they do comic books for all indignities. In neither case can anything be proved against the accused, and it is studies such as Mrs. Maccoby's that help remove the argument from the naiveté of "passivity" or the trap of trying to measure television's *direct* effects on psychological, social and even literary habits.

TELEVISION AS A MASS MEDIUM

Georg Simmel has pointed out that a conversation between two people may touch on a number of highly differentiated and intimate subjects; as soon as a third person is added, the conversation must be altered and compromised. As the group grows, the compromises become greater and the conversation more restricted. Subjects tend to center more and more around areas of common interest.[40] By the time the group reaches the size of a mass audience, it can be expected that absolutely nothing would be of common interest, or what is of common interest would never suit those who happen to have more than superficial concern with it.

To a large extent all forms of mass communications have operated along such lines—and are quite correctly charged with appealing to the lowest common denominator. Furthermore, since the model of a mass medium is never perfect and can never, except in some totalitarian dream, hope to engage 100 per cent of the population, how then can it work? Precisely by *not* engaging 100 per cent but, let us say, 40 per cent and making that 40 per cent endlessly receptive to whatever it chooses to introduce, experiment with or reject.[41] This is how it operates, first by following traditional lines of entertainment, that is, employing every play form culturally available until it has brought its audience to a peak, and then by creating new forms which are incorporated by the audience into the framework of the medium and beyond it.

Each mass medium resigned itself long ago to losing some segment of the total audience with any particular program. No matter how generalized the program might be, it is—luckily—impossible to interest everyone. Recognizing that a percentage of the audience is always missing, manipulators of the mass media concentrated on pleasing all of the people some of the time by presenting a variety of programs. Radio and television thus provide drama, comedy, sports, news, movies, music—everything. General magazines contain dozens of different sections or departments, each one designed to catch someone's attention, and newspapers regularly carry women's pages, comics, astrological forecasts, bridge games, and crossword puzzles. By offering something for everybody the medium succeeds in its first step, and can advance to the stage of creating tradition and taste as well as obeying it. Even if most people were neither interested in nor accustomed to crossword puzzles, comedy teams, or serial dramas, mass media developed their own world in which such features became of interest. In this sense the mass media not only appeal to the lowest common denominators, they make them.[42]

In television this process has reached a maximum. Because the percentage of the total audience needed to "break even" is so high, the medium has been forced to create as many lowest common denominators as possible. Getting perhaps as much as a half or a third of the total audience, television programs have created more "universal" interests than any pre-existing medium. By developing its own rhetoric, its own heroes, villains and struggles, television has developed interests that never existed before. The family conflict drama, for instance, never terribly popular with the movies, has been brought to a fine art by television which features almost nightly the same ineffectual father, tormented youngster, and self-willed mother. Paddy Chayefsky is now available in movie theaters, but the voice is the voice of TV.

The fact that such a large segment of the total audience is needed for each program has imposed a frightening restriction of choices on television producers, who must attempt to keep as low as possible the number of people who might be affronted, antagonized or uninterested in any particular program.

The results are clearly visible. Most television programs appear to have succeeded in antagonizing a minimum, at the same time reducing the number that can be truly enthusiastic or interested. This in essence is the meaning of the low taste levels of TV.

The actual operations of the system are complicated. Since the demands for audiences are monstrously large (and the supply *is* finite), the only measure of success is "The Rating." In a kind of satire of the democratic process, the "people" determine what their programs will be, how much they will cost advertisers, when they will be put on the air, and how much the entertainers will be paid. And since the "people" are a great beast, it is not possible simply to present the same kind of program over and over again. Thus the creation of new forms which quickly become what everyone really wanted anyway.

In its simplest form, a television program contains enough ingredients to appeal to a highly heterogeneous audience. It may explicitly cut across a number of economic and class lines by featuring, for example, essentially "deviant" types in the sociological sense—priests who know all about jazz, soldiers who can cook, or still cruder, little Negro girls who are champion spellers. This mix-up in stereotypes is one reason for the success of the "$64,000 Question."[43] (It must be remembered that there is no guaranteed formula for successful TV programs and the above discussion is in no way intended to suggest that this is the secret of success. Hundreds of programs using similar class jumbling have failed miserably.)

Or TV programming may bring together viewers and viewees by matching situational or psychological similarities. Instead of relying on common characteristics of background, universal *situations,* e.g., "boy-meets girl," "the boss is coming to dinner," "my wife doesn't understand me," etc., constitute the essential appeal. It is of course hard to know once again to what extent such situations have been *made* universal by the mass media and how much feeling existed about these matters before they became stock plots.

Another alternative, a riskier one, removes direct identification or matching by providing scenes or contests in which viewers are manifestly uninvolved and have "nothing to gain." Sports contests are perhaps the best illustration, and here it is clear that the mass media have done more to create than to reflect common interests. Far more Americans hunt and fish than play baseball or box; yet the latter are the most popular sports programs. Its spectators learn nothing "useful"—as they claim to do from soap operas.[44] What they get out of it is this: a common interest is developed and perpetuated which enables virtually any American male to carry on intense conversations with any other. It is the illustration par excellence of a truly common denominator.

These are the success forms of television. The medium takes up what is most common, creates other forms and *defines* them as common, and in the process amasses the vast audiences it needs.

Social research has not yet been able to dissect the complex relationship that exists between producers and audiences.[45] Until we understand the system, we must be satisfied with describing the reflections and shadows of the real (if invisible) mass interaction and "feedback" that changes and, at the same time, makes permanent what is produced and consumed in television. The dynamics may reveal why television is the way it is.

We hope that TV is not taken too seriously as a thing in itself. As an entertainment force its impact has been felt by the other media perhaps even more than by its audience; for they have suffered visible losses, while the viewers feel that television has been their gain. What latent losses we may suffer, what effects on taste and temperament—these things are hard to observe, harder still to measure. Indeed, passivity might be the end result. We know it is not the symptom. We also know that in the ratings, their theory and their use, lies one essential ingredient of audience-telecaster abuse.

Notes

1. I am grateful to the Bureau of Applied Social Research at Columbia University and the Implementation Committee on Television for sponsoring the bibliography on which this paper is based; I should like to express particular thanks to William N. McPhee of the Bureau of Applied Social Research and to Marjorie Fiske, presently at the University of California, for the assistance rendered at the time of the preparation of that bibliography.

2. Cited in Geoffrey Wagner, *The Parade of Pleasure*. London: Derek Verschoyle, 1954, p. 157.

3. According to a survey conducted through the Advertising Research Foundation, 35,495,330 out of a total of 48,784,000 households in the U.S. are equipped with television (as of March 1956). Reported in *Broadcasting-Telecasting*, October 1, 1956, p. 40.

4. One research report indicates that for the week ending September 15, 1956, 74,885,000 was the average daily number of adults who watched television, spending 18 hours and 36 minutes per capita per week (1,392.9 million hours total). *Activity*. [Ridley Park, Pa.: Sindlinger & Company.] 1:3, September 28, 1956.

5. Thomas E. Coffin, "Television's Impact on Society." *The American Psychologist*, 10:10, October 1955, pp. 630-41.

6. Rolf B. Meyersohn, *Television Research: an Annotated Bibliography*. New York: Bureau of Applied Social Research, Columbia University, 1953. (Mimeographed.)

7. James D. Finn, "Television and Education: a Review of Research." *Audio-Visual Communication Review*, 1:3, Spring 1953, pp. 106-26.

8. The National Association of Educational Broadcasters has sponsored at least seven monitoring studies. The most recent one available to me, used for the data presented here, is H. H. Remmers *et al., Four Years of New York Television, 1951-1954*. Urbana, Illinois: National Association of Educational Broadcasters. June 1954.

9. National Association for Better Radio and Television. *Children's Radio and Television Programs*. Third Annual Report. Los Angeles, July 28, 1953. The ratings were based on standards developed by the United States Office of Education and reported in the booklet *Your Child and Radio, TV, Comics and Movies* by Paul Witty and Harry Bricker. (Chicago, Illinois: Science Research Associates, 1952.)

10. See for example, Bernard J. Fine, *Television and Family Life. A Survey of Two New England Communities*. Boston, Massachusetts: School of Public Relations and Communications, Boston University, July 1952.

11. Raymond Stewart, *Social Impact of Television on Atlanta Households*. Emory University, Georgia: Division of Journalism, Emory University, 1952.

12. In surveys conducted annually since 1948 in New Brunswick, New Jersey, the following distribution has been found:

TV OWNERS PER 100 FAMILIES, BY INCOME GROUPS

Income Group	1948	1949	1950	1951	YEAR 1952	1953	1954	1955
Upper	2.7	12.4	24.4	40.2	55.5	68.1	80.2	90.1
Middle	1.3	7.8	21.5	48.1	63.7	73.7	79.5	90.6
Lower	0.7	5.6	16.1	33.8	43.4	49.7	59.6	62.7
TOTAL	1.4	8.0	20.9	44.2	58.3	68.1	76.0	85.5

Videotown 1948-1955. New York: Cunningham & Walsh Inc. Advertising, 1955, p. 22.

13. Bernard J. Fine, *op. cit.*

14. The discrepancy between income and education levels was noted by a number of investigators, including the following: Charles E. Swanson and R. D. Jones, "Television Owning and Its Correlates." *Journal of Applied Psychology*, 35, October 1951, pp. 352-7;

John W. Riley, Frank Cantwell and Katherine Ruttiger, "Some Observations on the Social Effects of Television." *Public Opinion Quarterly*, 15:2, Summer 1949, pp. 223-34; Everett C. Parker, David Barry and Dallas Smythe, *The Television-Radio Audience and Religion*. New York: Harper & Brothers, 1955.

15. A phrase used by Chapman to account for the mass consumption of virtually all appliances. Dennis Chapman, *The Home and Social Status*. London: Routledge and Kegan Paul, 1955, p. 23.

16. Thomas E. Coffin, *op. cit.*, makes reference to eight separate studies bearing on this finding.

17. Eleanor E. Maccoby, "Television: Its Impact on School Children." *Public Opinion Quarterly*, 15:3, Fall 1951, pp. 421-44.

18. Bernard J. Fine, *op. cit.* See also, *Survey on Public Attitudes toward Commercials over Television*. Chicago, Illinois: The Philip Lesly Company, 1951; this study reports discrepancy between high and low income families in their criticisms. Among the former, 25 per cent reported "objectionable changes in family life (meal-time and homework difficulties for children being most prevalent), as against 3.7 per cent among low income groups.

19. Forest L. Whan, *The 1952 Iowa Radio-Television Survey*. Des Moines, Iowa: Central Broadcasting Company, 1952.

20. Gilbert Seldes, *The Public Arts*. New York: Simon & Schuster, 1956, ch. 23.

21. *Ibid.*, p. 206.

22. Thomas E. Coffin, *op. cit.*

23. The changes in time allocation to the different mass media that occur when television is introduced are quite remarkable. A panel study conducted in Ft. Wayne obtained such before and after figures.

CHANGES IN TIMES SPENT ON EACH MEDIUM AFTER PURCHASE OF TV SET

	Minutes per Person "Yesterday"	
Medium	*Before TV*	*After TV*
Magazines	17	10
Newspapers	39	32
Radio	122	52
Television	12*	173
Total Time	190	267
* From "guest-viewing"		

This table originally appeared in Thomas E. Coffin, Jack Landis and Marvin Baiman, *Strangers into Customers*. New York: National Broadcasting Company, 1955. It was reproduced in Thomas E. Coffin, *op. cit.*

24. For a recent summary of the state of consumer magazine publishing, see *Tide*, October 12, 1956, pp. 38-9.

25. William N. McPhee and Rolf B. Meyersohn, *Futures for Radio*. A Report Submitted to the National Broadcasting Company. Bureau of Applied Social Research Columbia University, 1955. (Mimeographed.) Parts reprinted in *Broadcasting-Telecasting*, January 16 and 23, 1956.

26. Hans Zeisel, "The Effect of Television on Other Media." Talk given before the New York Chapter, American Marketing Association. Press release dated December 13, 1951.

27. Eliot Freidson, "The Relation of the Social Situation of Contact to the Media of Mass Communication." *Public Opinion Quarterly*, 17:2, Summer 1953, pp. 230-8.

28. Raymond Stewart, in a study of 333 television owners in Atlanta, Georgia (*op. cit.*), reported that more than half preferred to watch television with someone; as a matter of fact, over 15 per cent went so far as to say that they would not watch television at all if they were alone.

29. Eleanor E. Maccoby, "Television: Its Impact on School Children," *loc. cit.* The same finding appeared in Bernard Fine's study (*op. cit.*) among television owners in two suburbs near Boston; here 70 per cent of the respondents (ranging from 83 per cent in the lowest socio-economic level to 65 per cent in the highest) stated that "during the time that television is watched no concurrent activity goes on."

30. Bernard J. Fine, *op. cit.*

31. For a general discussion of the "narcotizing dysfunction" of the mass media, see Paul F. Lazarsfeld and Robert K. Merton, "Mass Communication, Popular Taste and Organized Social Action," in Wilbur Schramm, ed., *Mass Communications*, Urbana, Illinois: University of Illinois Press, 1949, pp. 468-9. [Reprinted in this volume.]

32. The evidence was provided by three reports: Jerry N. Jordan, *The Long Range Effect of Television and Other Factors on Sports Attendance*. Washington, D.C.: Radio-Television Manufacturers Association, 1950; Jerry N. Jordan, *Analysis of 1950 Baseball Attendance*. Washington, D.C.: Radio-Television Manufacturers Association, undated; Radio-Television

Manufacturers Association, *Just What Has Television Done to Recreation-Communications?* Washington, D.C., 1952.

33. Paul B. Sheatsley and Paul N. Borsky, *The Effects of Television on College Football Attendance.* Chicago, Illinois: National Opinion Research Center.

34. One of the many pieces of research which equates spectatorship with passivity is the interesting study recently reported by Alfred C. Clarke, entitled "Leisure and Levels of Occupational Prestige," *American Sociological Review,* 21:3, June 1956, pp. 301-7.

35. While literally hundreds of studies have attempted to study the relationship between television and children, few have succeeded in providing much of consequence. Listed here are some of the more rigorous attempts: Walter J. Clark, *Of Children and Television.* Cincinnati, Ohio: Xavier University, 1951; Hilde Himmelweit (Work in progress under the auspices of the Nuffield Foundation at the London School of Economics.); Frank L. Sweetser, *Grade School Families Meet Television.* Boston, Massachusetts: Department of Sociology and Anthropology, Boston University Research Report No. 1, Preliminary Edition, April 1953; Paul A. Witty, "Children's Reaction to TV—a Third Report." *Elementary English,* December 1952, pp. 469-73.

36. For an excellent appeal to research on what people have done with the mass media instead of what mass media have done to people, see Elihu Katz and Paul Lazarsfeld, *Personal Influence.* Glencoe, Illinois: The Free Press, 1956.

37. William A. Belson, "The Effects of Television upon the Interests and the Initiative of Adult Viewers." Paper read at the Annual Meeting of the British Association for the Advancement of Science, August 1956.

38. Eleanor E. Maccoby, "Why Do Children Watch Television?," *Public Opinion Quarterly.* Fall 1954, pp. 239-44.

39. Matilda W. and John W. Riley, "A Sociological Approach to Communication Research." *Public Opinion Quarterly,* Fall 1951, pp. 445-60.

40. Georg Simmel, "The Quantitative Determination of Group Divisions and of Certain Groups." In Kurt Wolff (ed.), *The Sociology of Georg Simmel.* Glencoe, Illinois: The Free Press, 1950, esp. pp. 112-13. I am indebted to William McPhee for this formulation.

41. Forty per cent is the figure given by Sylvester L. Weaver, Jr., former president and board chairman of the National Broadcasting Company, as cited in *Broadcasting-Telecasting,* October 8, 1956, p. 102.

42. An excellent discussion of the functions of the mass media as linking heterogeneous groups appears in Gerhart Wiebe, "Mass Communications." In E. L. and R. E. Hartley, eds., *Fundamentals in Social Psychology.* New York: Alfred A. Knopf, 1952, chapter 7.

43. An ingenious and comprehensive analysis of this program is presented by Gilbert Seldes, *op. cit.*

44. Herta Herzog, "On Borrowed Experience." *Studies in Philosophy and Social Science,* 1941.

45. Plans are being made by William McPhee at the Bureau of Applied Social Research, Columbia University and James Coleman of the Department of Sociology, The University of Chicago, to engage in long-term studies of this problem.

The Phantom World of TV

By GUNTHER ANDERS

I

Modern mass consumption is a sum of solo performances; each consumer, an unpaid homeworker employed in the production of the mass man.

IN THE DAYS before the cultural faucets of radio and television had become standard equipment in each home, the Smiths and Millers used to throng the motion picture theaters where they collectively consumed the stereotyped mass products manufactured for them. One might be tempted to regard it as peculiarly appropriate that the mass product should be thus consumed by a compact mass. Such a view, however, would be mistaken. Nothing contradicts the essential purpose of mass production more completely than a situation in which a single specimen of a commodity is simultaneously enjoyed by several, let alone by numerous, consumers. Whether this consumption is a "genuine communal experience" or merely the sum of many individual experiences, is a matter of indifference to the mass producer. What he needs is not the compact mass as such, but a mass broken up or atomized into the largest possible number of customers; he does not want all of his customers to consume one and the same product, he wants all of his customers to buy identical products on the basis of an identical demand which has also to be produced.

In countless industries this ideal has more or less been achieved. Whether the motion picture industry can ever achieve it seems doubtful, because this industry continues the tradition of the theater: the commodity it produces is a spectacle designed for simultaneous consumption by a large number of spectators. Such a situation is obsolete. No wonder that the radio and television industries could enter into competition with the motion picture despite the latter's tremendous development: for the two newer industries benefited from the possibility of marketing, in addition to the commodity to be consumed, the devices required for its consumption, devices that, unlike the motion pictures, could be sold to almost everyone. And so it came about that many of the evenings the Smith and Millers had formerly spent together in motion picture theaters, they began to spend at home. The situation that is taken for granted in the motion picture theater—the consumption of the mass product by a mass of people—was thus done away with. Needless to say, this did not mean a slowing-up of mass production; rather, mass production for the mass man, indeed mass production of the mass

Reprinted from *Dissent*, Vol. 3, 1956, pp. 14-24, by permission of the author and the publisher. (Copyright, 1956, by Dissent Publishing Association.) This article is a slightly condensed version of the first of three articles on television which appeared in the distinguished German review, *Der Merkur*.

man himself, was speeded up daily. Millions of listeners were served the identical product; each of these was treated as a mass man, "an indefinite article"; each was confirmed in his character—or absence of character—as a mass man. But with this difference, that collective consumption became superfluous through the mass production of receiving sets. The Smiths consumed the mass products *en famille* or even singly; the more isolated they became, the more profits they yielded. The mass-produced hermit came into being as a new human type, and now millions of them, cut off from each other, yet identical with each other, remain in the seclusion of their homes. Their purpose, however, is not to renounce the world, but to be sure they won't miss the slightest crumb of the world as image on a screen.

It is well known that the principle of industrial centralization, which ruled unchallenged only a generation ago, has now been dropped, mainly for strategic reasons, in favor of the principle of dispersal. It is less known that this principle of dispersal is also applied in the production of the mass man. Although we have so far spoken only of dispersed consumption, we are justified in speaking of production because in this case both coincide in a peculiar way. As the German proverb has it, *Mensch ist was er isst,* "man is what he eats" (in a nonmaterialistic sense): it is through the consumption of mass commodities that mass men are produced. This implies that the consumer of the mass commodity becomes, through his consumption, one of the workers contributing to his own transformation into a mass man. In other words, consumption and production coincide. If consumption is "dispersed," so is the production of the mass man. And this production takes place wherever consumption takes place—in front of each radio, in front of each television set.

Everyone is, so to speak, employed as a homeworker—a homeworker of a most unusual kind: for he performs his work—which consists in transforming himself into a mass man—through his consumption of the mass product offered him, i.e., through leisure. Whereas the classical homeworker manufactured his wares in order to secure a minimum of consumer goods and leisure, the modern homeworker consumes a maximum of leisure products in order to help produce the mass man. To complete the paradox, the homeworker, instead of receiving wages for his work, must pay for it by buying the means of production (the receiving sets and, in many countries, also the broadcasts) by the use of which he becomes transformed into mass man. In other words, he pays for selling himself: he must purchase the very unfreedom he himself helps to produce.

This conclusion may seem far-fetched. But no one will deny that for the production of the kind of mass man that is desired today, the formation of actual mass gatherings is no longer required. Le Bon's observations on the psychology of crowds have become obsolete, for each person's individuality can be erased and his rationality leveled down in his own home. The stage-managing of masses in the Hitler style has become superfluous:

to transform a man into a nobody (and one who is proud of being a nobody) it is no longer necessary to drown him in the mass or to enlist him as an actual member of a mass organization. No method of depersonalizing man, of depriving him of his human powers, is more effective than one which seems to preserve the freedom of the person and the rights of individuality. And when the conditioning is carried out separately for each individual, in the solitude of his home, in millions of secluded homes, it is incomparably more successful. For this conditioning is disguised as "fun"; the victim is not told that he is asked to sacrifice anything; and since the procedure leaves him with the delusion of his privacy or at least of his private home, it remains perfectly discreet. The old saying "a man's own home is as precious as gold" has again become true, though in an entirely new sense. For today, the home is valuable not only to its owner, but also to the owners of the home-owners—the caterers of radio and television who serve the home-owner his daily fare.

II

Radio set and telescreen become transformed into a negative family table; the family into a miniature audience.

Needless to say, this mass consumption is not usually called by its true name. On the contrary, it is represented as favoring the rebirth of the family and of privacy—an understandable hypocrisy.

In actual fact, the type of mass consumption discussed here threatens to dissolve the family under the guise of fostering the intimacy of family life. For what now dominates in the home, thanks to television, is the outside world—real or fictional; and this outside world is so unrestrictedly dominant that the reality of the home—not only the four walls and furniture, but precisely the shared family life—becomes inoperative and phantom-like. When that which is remote becomes familiar, that which is familiar becomes remote. When the phantom becomes real, reality becomes a phantom. The home tends to become a container, its function to be reduced to containing a video screen for the outside world. The realm of the phantoms is victorious over the realm of the home without even the chance of a contest between the two; it triumphs the moment the television set enters the home: it comes, it is seen, it conquers. At once the ceiling is full of leaks, the walls become transparent, the cement uniting the members of the family crumbles away, the shared privacy disintegrates.

Decades ago it was possible to observe that the social hallmark of the family—the massive table in the center of the living room, which served as the gathering point of the family—had begun to lose its force of attraction, had become obsolete. Eventually the living room table was eliminated from the modern home. Now it has found its authentic successor, the television set, a piece of furniture whose social symbolism and persuasive power can measure against those of the former table. This does not mean, however, that the television set has become the family center; on the contrary, what the set embodies is rather the decentralization of the family, its ex-centricity: it is, so to speak, the *negative* family table. It does not provide a common *center,* but rather a common avenue of escape. Whereas the table was a centripetal force; its existence encouraged the members of the family seated around it to continue weaving the cloth of family life as the shuttles of interest, glances and conversations ran back and forth. The influence exerted by the television screen is centrifugal. The seats in front of the screen are so arranged that the members of the family no longer face each other; they can see or look at each other only at the price of missing something on the screen; they converse (if they still can or want to talk with each other) only by accident. They are no longer together, they are merely placed one beside the other, as mere spectators. There can no longer be any question of a world formed or shared by them. The only thing the members of the family do together—though never as an integrated family group—is to take excursions into a realm of unreality, a world they actually share with no one (for they themselves do not really share in it); or if they do share it, it is only with all those millions of "soloists" of mass consumption who, like them and simultaneously with them, stare at their television screens. The family has been re-structured into a miniature audience, and the home into a miniature theater modeled on the movie house.

III

Because the receiving sets speak in our place, they gradually deprive us of the power of speech, thus transforming us into passive dependents.

Television viewers, we have said, converse with each other only by accident—in so far as they still retain the will or the ability to speak.

This is true even of radio listeners. They too speak only by mistake. Their will and ability to speak decrease from day to day—and this does not mean that they become silent in the literal sense, but that their garrulousness has assumed a purely passive form. Since the receiving sets speak in our place, they progressively rob us of our ability to speak, of our opportunities for speaking, and finally even of our pleasure in expressing ourselves, just as the phonograph and radio have robbed us of live music performed in our homes.

The pairs of lovers sauntering along the shores of the Hudson, the Thames or the Danube with a portable radio do not talk to each other but listen to a third person—the public, usually anonymous, voice of the program which they walk like a dog, or, more accurately, which walks them like a pair of dogs. Since they are an audience in miniature which follows the voice of the broadcast, they take their walk not alone, but in company of a third person. Intimate conversation is eliminated in advance; and whatever intimate contacts take place between the lovers are introduced and even stimulated not by them, but by that third party—the husky or crowing voice of the program which (for is that not the very meaning of "program"?) tells both lovers what and how to feel or do. Since they do what they are told to do in the presence of a third party, they do it in an acoustically indiscreet situation. However entertaining their obedience may seem to the lovers, it is certain that they do not entertain *each other;* rather both are entertained by that third party which alone has a voice; and this voice does not entertain them only in the sense of keeping them occupied and diverting them, but also in the sense of providing them with support: as the third party in the alliance, this voice gives them that support which they, in their ignorance of what they can do with themselves, cannot give each other. Indeed, there is reason to throw the cloak of silence over the fact that today even love-making often takes place to the accompaniment of the radio. The radio set that is admitted or desired in every possible situation is reminiscent of the torch-bearing female guide whom the ancients tolerated or invited as witness to their amorous pleasures; the difference between the two consists in this, that the modern guide is a mechanized public utility, that her torch serves to provide not only illumination but also warmth, and that under no circumstances must she keep her mouth shut, but on the contrary, is expected to talk her head off; she has to supply a background of noise in the form of songs or words and to silence that *horror vacui* which does not loosen its grip on the pair of lovers *in actu*.

But the situation of love-making is only an example, the most blatant. People keep themselves similarly "entertained" in every situation, even while they work; and if by some mistake they talk to each other, the radio voice speaks in the background as the main protagonist, giving them the comforting and reassuring feeling that it will continue to speak even after they themselves have had their say—even after they are dead.

For them words are no longer something one speaks, but something one merely hears; speaking is no longer something that one does, but something that one receives. No matter in what cultural or political milieu this development toward an existence without speech takes place, its end result must be everywhere the same—a type of man who, because he no longer speaks himself, has nothing more to say; and who, because he only listens, will do no more than listen. The initial effects of this development are manifest even today: the languages of all advanced countries have become cruder, poorer; and there is a growing disinclination to use language. But that is not all: human experience, and hence man himself, also becomes progressively cruder and poorer. For man's inward life, its richness and subtlety, cannot endure without the richness and subtlety of language; man not only expresses himself through his speech, he is also the product of his language.

IV

We see the world only when we are inside our homes. The events come to us, not we to them.

The consumer goods by means of which such a transformation of human nature is achieved are brought into our homes, just as is gas or electricity. The deliveries are not confined to artistic products, such as music or radio dramas; they also include actual events, at least those events which are selected and processed to represent "reality" or to serve as substitutes for it. A man who wants to be "in the swim," to know what is going on outside, must go to his home, where the events are waiting for him, like water ready to flow from the faucet. For if he stayed outside, in the chaos of reality, how could he pick out anything "real" of more than local significance? Only after he has closed the door behind him, does the outside world become visible to him; only after we have been transformed into windowless monads, does the universe reflect itself in us.

This brings us to the heart of our subject. For the fact that the events of the day—the events themselves, not reports of events—that football matches, church services, atomic explosions, *visit us at home;* that the mountain comes to the prophet, the world to man, that fact, next to the mass production of hermits and the transformation of the family into a miniature audience, is the revolutionary change brought about by radio and television.

The truly philosophic implications of this change will become apparent from the following tentative list of some of its consequences:

1. When the world comes to us, instead of our going to it, we are no longer "in the world," but only listless, passive consumers of the world.
2. Since the world comes to us only as an image, it is half-present and half-absent, in other words, phantom-like; and we too are like phantoms.
3. When the world speaks to us, without our being able to speak to it, we are deprived of speech, and hence condemned to be unfree.
4. When the world is perceivable, but no more than that, i.e., not subject to our action, we are transformed into eavesdroppers and Peeping Toms.
5. When an event that occurs at a definite place is broadcast, and when it can be made to appear at any other place as a "broadcast," it becomes a movable, indeed, almost ubiquitous object, and has forfeited its spatial location, its *principium individuationis.*
6. When the event is no longer attached to a specific location and can be reproduced virtually any number of times, it acquires the characteristics of an assembly-line product; and when we pay for having it delivered to our homes, it is a commodity.
7. When the actual event is socially important only in its reproduced form, i.e., as a spectacle, the difference between being and appearance, between reality and image of reality, is abolished.
8. When the event in its reproduced form is socially more important than the original event, this original must be shaped with a view to being reproduced: in other words, the event becomes merely a master matrix, or a mold for casting its own reproductions.
9. When the dominant experience of the world thrives on such assembly-line products, the concept "the world" is abolished in so far as it denotes that *in which* we live. The real world is forfeited; the broadcasts, in other words, further an idealistic orientation.

V

Because the world is brought into our homes, we do not have to explore it; as a result, we do not acquire experience. Modern man travels only as a last resort.

In a world that comes to man, man has no need to go to the world in order to explore or experience it; that which was once called "experience" has become superfluous.

Up until recently, expressions such "to go into the world," or "to experience" have denoted important anthropological concepts. Since man is being relatively little endowed with instincts, he has been compelled to experience and know the world *a posteriori* in order to find his place in it; only in this way could he reach his goal and become "experienced." Life used to consist in a voyage of exploration; that is why the great *Erziehungsromane* ("educational novels") dealt with the ways man—although always in the world—had to travel in order to get to know the world. Today, because the world comes to him—as an image—he need not bother to explore it; such explorations and experiences are superfluous, and since all superfluous functions become atrophied, he can no longer engage in explorations and become experienced. It is indeed evident that the type of "experienced man" is becoming increasingly rare, and that age and experience tend to be regarded as less and less valuable. Like pedestrians who have taken to flying we no longer need roads; in consequence, our knowledge of the ways of the world, which we formerly used to explore, and which made us experienced, is declining. Simultaneously with this, the world itself becomes a pathless wilderness. Whereas formerly we stored up experience by means of traveling, today the world is "stored up" for us like a commodity put aside for future use; we do not have to go to the events, the events are paraded before us.

Such a portrait of our contemporaries may at first sight appear distorted. For it has become customary to look upon the automobile and the airplane as symbols of modern man, a being whose essence is travel. What is in question is precisely the correctness of this definition. For modern man does not attach value to his traveling because of any interest in the regions he visits, actually or vicariously; he does not travel to become experienced but to still his hunger for omnipresence and for rapid change as such. Moreover, the speed of his movement deprives him of the opportunity for experience (to the extent that speed itself has now become his sole and ultimate experience)—not to mention the fact that the number of objects worthy of being experienced and capable of adding to his experience is continually decreased by his successful efforts to make the world uniform, and that even today he feels at home, in need of no experience, wherever he may land. A publicity poster of a well-known airline, utterly confusing provincialism and globalism, appeals to its customers with these words: "When you use our services, you are everywhere at home." Everywhere at home: there is indeed good reason to assume that today any trip (even though the man who takes it may sleep comfortably in his electrically heated cabin while flying over the North Pole) is felt to be an antiquated, uncomfortable and inadequate method of achieving omnipresence. Modern man still resorts to this method precisely because, despite all his efforts, he has not yet succeeded in having everything delivered to his home—something he has come to regard as his inherent right.

Such a situation points to a mode of existence, a relation to the world so extraordinarily perverse that even Descartes' malicious demon would be incapable of devising a comparable deception. Such a mode of existence may be described as "idealistic" in two ways:

1. Although we actually live in an alienated world, this world is presented to us in such a manner that it seems to exist for us, as though it were our own and like ourselves.

2. We "take" (i.e., regard and accept) it as such, although we stay at home in our chairs. We do not actually "take" it, in the manner of a devouring beast or a conqueror, and we do not actually make it our own; but the average radio listener or television viewer looks upon the world that is served him in the form of reproduced sounds and pictures as his own. As a result he develops into a kind of Peeping Tom ruling over a phantom world.

VI

The world brought into our homes by radio and television is a debased, philistinized world; pseudo-familiarity is an aspect of alienation.

This is not the place to discuss the origin and symptomatology of alienation. The literature of the subject is enormous, and we must take this phenomenon for granted. The particular deception in question here consists in this, that the radio listener or television viewer, although living in an alienated world, is made to believe that he is on a footing of the greatest intimacy with everything and everybody. He is not invited to become acquainted with an unfamiliar world; instead, people, countries, situations, events, particularly the least familiar of them, are presented to him as though he had always known them; they are thoroughly philistinized in advance.

Whereas our next-door neighbors usually do not know us, and the distance between them and us remains unbridged for years on end, film stars, girls whom we never meet personally but whom we have seen countless times and whose spiritual and physical characteristics are known to us more completely than those of our co-workers, appear to us in the guise of old friends, of "chums." We are automatically on a footing of intimacy, we refer to them by their first names.

To bring about such a state of affairs, to enable the program consumer to treat the world as something familiar, the televised image must address him as an old chum. In fact, every broadcast has this chummy quality. When I tune in on the President, he suddenly sits next to me at the fireplace, chatting with me, although he may be thousands of miles away. (I am only marginally aware of the fact that this intimacy exists in millions of copies). When the girl announcer appears on the screen, she speaks to me in a tone of complete frankness, as though I were her bosom friend. (That she is also the bosom friend of all men is again only a marginal realization.)

All of them come to me as intimate or indiscreet visitors, all of them find me ready to be chummy with them. Not one of these people who are transported into my house retains even an atom of unfamiliarity. And this is true not only of persons, but of everything else, of the world as a whole. Things, places, events, situations—everything reaches us with a chummy smile on its lips. We have now achieved a footing of intimacy not only with film stars but also with the stars of the firmament; we speak of "good old Cassiopeia" just as readily as of Marilyn or Rita. And this is not meant as a joke. The fact that laymen and scientists regard it as possible and even probable that the inhabitants of other planets who allegedly operate the flying saucers have, like us and precisely in our time, no other worry but to undertake interplanetary voyages, proves that we look upon everything in the universe as "one of our sort." This is a sign of an anthropomorphism against which the anthropomorphism of so-called primitive civilizations strikes one as timid. The purveyors of the vulgarized universe realize that unless they bring nature down to our level they will not sell it—which would be to miss a profitable opportunity. But we, the consumers, are systematically transformed into boon companions of everything on our planet and in the universe—no more than boon companions, for of course there can be no question of genuine fraternization or identification.

What we have said of things and persons distant in space, also applies to things and persons distant in time. The past too is philistinized. I shall not speak of the historical motion pictures in which such a treatment is the rule. But even in a serious, vividly written American academic book, Socrates is described as "quite a guy"—in other words he is put in a category that brings the distant great man seemingly close to the reader; for, needless to say, the reader too is "quite a guy." This label gives the reader the unconsciously gratifying feeling that Socrates, if he had not happened to live in that remote past, would be essentially like us, would not have anything to say that is essentially different from what we have to say, and in no case could claim greater authority than we do.

Others perceive historical figures as comical by definition (e.g., their reactions to historical films); this is so because such figures strike them as provincials in the realm of time, as creatures that have not grown up in the capital—the Now—and for that reason behave like village idiots of history or superstitious backwoodsmen; every electrical invention made since their time is looked upon as an eloquent proof of their inferiority. Finally, to many of our contemporaries historical figures appear as nonconformists, as suspiciously queer fellows, for it is obvious that they regard themselves as something quite special—namely, unlike every decent man who chooses to live in the present, they prefer to take up residence in a cavern of the past. (This is the source of comic effects in several pieces by Mark Twain.) But whether a great man of the past is regarded as "quite a guy," a queer fellow, or a provincial, these categories denote proximity, and hence are variations of the chum.

As for the typical case of "Socrates, the guy," the epithet here is obviously based on the great political principle formulated in the Declaration of the Rights of Man, "All men are born equal," which has now been extended into the assertion of the equality of all citizens of the commonwealth of times past and present. Needless to say, such an extension of the principle of equality suggests not only a false historical proximity, but also a misconception of the common denominator of all mankind—for after all the essence of Socrates consists in the very thing that "our sort" is lacking. The method allegedly intended to bring the object close to us, actually serves to veil the object, to alienate it, or simply to do away with it altogether. For once you project history on a single plane of boon companionship, it has actually ceased to exist *qua* history—and this is perhaps even more plausible than our general thesis, that when all the various and variously distant regions of the world are brought equally close to us, the world as such vanishes.

Translated from the German by Norbert Guterman

In Defense of Television

By HENRY RABASSIERE

CASTING AN INDULGENT EYE on the merry-making of Flemish peasants, Breughel found it brutish, vulgar, lusty, guttonous, bibulous and, possibly, dulling. Yet, nothing in his canvases suggests the suspicion that the feudal lords might have devised the popular culture of their time the better to keep the peasantry in submission. Pious monks might have believed that the Devil was to blame, but no serious historian would credit such views today. We condone superstition with reference only to our own culture. According to Gunther Anders (in *Dissent,* Winter 1956), e.g., a dark conspiracy has foisted television on us for the purposes of profit, deception and subjection:

1) "The mass producer . . . needs a mass broken up into the largest possible number of customers; he does not want all of his customers to consume one and the same product (as in looking at a movie together); he wants all to buy identical products" (as in watching television separately).

2) "The method allegedly intended to bring the object close to us, actually serves to veil the object, to alientate it or slowly to do away with it"; the implication is that capitalism needs unrealistic subjects who live in a "phantom world," as the title of the essay says.

3) "Mass production of the mass man himself was speeded up," meaning that by watching TV we acquire, without being aware of what is being done to us, the character of the crowd.

Assertion No. 1 obviously means to inform us of a more shattering discovery than the fact that the electronics industry is interested in the sale of television sets; after all, automobiles and refrigerators are sold without any "phantom" assisting. The real phantom which bothers our author is the little man behind the grey screen; isn't it difficult to realize how he got there, economically speaking? Someone paid to put him there, so he must be a "commodity"; and, reasoning further, one such commodity seen by a thousand people in a movie theatre must bring less profit, hence be less capitalistic than the same picture appearing a thousand times on a thousand little screens.

This is poor economics based on misunderstood technology, and primitive sociology too. A TV program supplies one identical product to a large mass, just as the movies; in both cases the admission price is calculated on the basis of cost and profit. Like any other enterprise, the entertainment industry does not count its customers, but the sales value of its product, no matter whether it is divided into many or few lumps. But worse: How did "the mass producer" convert his "need" into a desire of his customers? It is one thing to say that some modern inventions came as a boon to industry; Mr. Anders implies quite another thing—that these inventions were so conceived, and we consumers were so conditioned, that the greatest number of goods can be sold at the highest profit. He still believes in the omnipotence of the overlords; his new version of the Iron Heel even gives them credit for a far more ambitious scheme: mass production, Mr. Anders says, has been so devised that "mass consumption produces mass man." As a witticism the *aperçu* might be superb; as a theory, expounded at nauseating leisure, it is misleading.

Consider this sentence: "The classical homeworker manufactures his wares in order to secure a minimum of consumer goods and leisure; the modern homeworker consumes a maximum of leisure products in order to help produce the mass man." The first "in order to" refers to the worker's intentions; the second "in order to," however, expresses the mystical power of the Iron Heel. An honest parallel to the latter statement would have been: "The classical homeworker manufactured goods in order to reproduce the social conditions which force him to manufacture more goods." Thus stated, we still have the primitive sociology, but at least the evil cycle of the producer society would be compared with the evil cycle of the consumer society.

Moreover, throughout his essay, as in the last quotation, Mr. Anders consistently idealizes and even idyllicizes the past. That noble worker in the Lord's vineyard seems never to have been conditioned by the ideologies of his terrestrial and spiritual overlords! That touching picture of the happy family, gathered around the big oaken table, seems never to have been marred by the tragedies which constitute up to 90 per cent of the thematic material in nineteenth century literature. Those lovers, before radio, must all have been highly articulate Cyranos, and no Christian ever needed the voice of a poet or the song of a musician to conquer first his shyness and thereafter the bride. Those heroes of yesterday never saw politics as a spectacle but went in there to fight it out for themselves; they never went to a circus, never read novels, penny dreadfuls and Radcliffe, never relied on newspapers for their knowledge of the world, never believed a Napoleon or a Mussolini before radio. Finally, these intellectual giants had no occasion to look at the world in an "idealistic" way, but were always aware of the reality behind the pictures that supplied their limited opportunities of information. What nonsense! All the indictments against "mass culture" are at least as old as Gutenberg—not to speak of Ovid. Ortega y Gasset added elegance and Anders adds brilliant confusion, punning happily along Heidegger alley where all lights are fueled by free association.

Granted that the new inventions may create opportunities for manipulation or tend to cripple our sensorial experience of the world; it still does not follow that mass communication methods doom our intelligence to misorientation. The truth is that at all times most public events are experienced vicariously and that each society has its special means of communicating to its citizens the preferred picture of reality; at all times did people rely on teachers, travelers, pictures and other second-hand information to form their view of the world. Today's mass media and extreme mobility potentially increase our sources of information to the point of universality, where cross-checking has become easy and wilful distortion has become difficult. The walls of the city and the walls of the home have been laid down; the idols of the market and the idols of the cave have been blown to pieces—Mr. Anders claims that these old and wholesome walls, the protectors of the *penates,* have been replaced by a wide screen where the idols of the theatre simulate an unreal world.

I do not wish to belittle the difference between reading and viewing. Certainly the latter opens more opportunity to suggestion. Yet, not so long ago, the printed word was held almost sacred by the masses; from escapist literature to tabloids, peoples at all times preferred to read and believe what reassured them, rather than what might shake their complacency. Of their own volition they gave the manipulators a monopoly of information. Today nobody thinks that the picture on the little screen represents the real world; everybody knows that the President uses make-up and tele-prompter; even the children who used to believe in Santa Claus know that Hopalong Cassidy is an actor. The television camera constantly prompts the experienced viewer to cheer the editor who switches to promising angles and selects the most interesting viewpoints. Mr. Anders is blind to the immense widening of our perceptive capacities through the camera.

While the possibility of deception is ever-present, the danger of deliberate manipulation and of "conditioning" through unconscious suggestion might even be declining. The ideals of our society may be less admirable than the virtues of ancient Rome; but if we live by them, not TV is to blame but the erosion of virtue that preceded popular culture. The loss of substance and certainty which characterizes the age began to be noticed eighty years ago by a generation of artists which did not call itself avant-garde but in relation to which our critics of TV are a sorry rear-guard. They first revealed the surface character of our experience, but now we have run full circle: in popular experience, manipulation is visible or suspected everywhere. We know that our environment is being manufactured for us, and after some more years, TV-experienced people may tend to believe nothing, just as they have become fairly immune to propaganda of other sorts. The illusions which we buy—a perfume, a movie, a popular song, a comedian on TV—do not fool us; they are consciously presented and accepted as illusions, not as truth. Far from living in a world of phantoms, we are facing the danger of complete disillusionment.

Another facet of this development is our loss of values. I deplore it as much as Mr. Anders does. But again—is the display of profligacy on big and small screens a cause or a symptom of the decline in the stature of our heroes? What had Hitler or Stalin that Cromwell or Cortez did not have? Is Gary Cooper less real than Robin Hood?

In this connection, Mr. Anders makes the shrewd remark that Socrates is being made over into a pal on TV and in popular science literature. The great men, he says, no longer are revered for their greatness but inserted into a world of appearances; they are known not for their unique substance but for that which the community of pals can understand. He might have addressed his reproach to Aristophanes, and he might have quoted in support of his own views any number of antique writers, beginning with Plato. They all complained that the *profanum vulgus* was taking over; they all hated themselves and others, begrudging the people their daily pleasures. I should have liked to meet Socrates; I understand he used to dine and wine with friends. He might not be less great for that. Plato's Socrates, whom Mr. Anders wishes to raise on a pedestal, is a completely phoney picture—a phantom, to use Mr. Anders's words. The mere fact that so many millions now can become familiar with him, makes Socrates a base commodity: "When the event can be . . . reproduced virtually any number of times, it acquires the characteristics of an assembly-line product; and when we pay for having it delivered to our homes, it is a commodity." Only professional philosophers turned theologians make such elementary mistakes in elementary logic. If I buy the print of a Rembrandt etching, not the meeting of Christ with the disciples at Emmaus is reproduced but its likeness; and neither the event nor Rembrandt's conception of it has become a commodity. What Mr. Anders means to say is much less mystical than the transubstantiation of an event into a commodity. Certain experiences—enjoying a work of art, meeting a great personality, reading a profound book—cannot be duplicated. The reproduction which pretends to be the original merely reminds us of it; the exciting moment of a live concert is not recorded along with the sound track; an "art appreciation course" substitutes learning for spontaneous perception. Manufacturers of such ersatz satisfaction surely would have us accept their wares for the real thing; clever producers even may exploit the real love affairs of a movie star or create suitable stories from the whole cloth to provide vicarious experiences for an audience that increasingly likes to have the proper feelings pre-assembled and delivered along with the "event." Not multiplication of the event, but vulgarization of its stand-in, not communication of an experience but pre-digestion of experience results in the stunted sensibility of mass culture.

In similar ways, totalitarian governments may create events for political exploitation; their policies often are designed to confirm the dream world where they keep their subjects. Occasionally they fall for their own phantasmagoria and walk into an abyss where they had seen a road to glory. Strangely enough, the totalitarian implications are not discussed by Mr. Anders, though everywhere else he insists on the modern-age nature of his phantom world. In the German version of his essay, which is more complete, however, he speaks of important mimesis phenomena which belong here. "In the beginning, there was broadcasting," he says ironically, "and the world was made to suit it." He concludes: "Were one of us to try and go forth in quest of the real world . . . he soon would be disappointed. For out there he would find nothing but models modeled after the pictures of which they are supposed to be the originals." It may be unfair to polemicize against something that was not published; yet I feel that the published fragment does not do justice to Mr. Anders. He has developed an interesting theory of cognition which may apply to human nature. His may be a great discovery, occasioned by certain outstanding traits of perception which now are more visible than before. He is wrong, I submit, in trying to make a double discovery—namely, that these features are characteristic of the present society. A sociological analysis of knowledge must start out from sound sociology and careful use of history. Certainly, Orson Welles's famous radio invasion from Mars says something about the United States in the thirties—but have there not been panicky flights to the hills before, when a comet seemed to announce a new Flood? Certainly we pity the old ladies who start knitting baby clothes when their favorite soap opera heroine is pregnant; but did not Goethe get hundreds of letters from imaginary Lottes and did not would-be Werthers actually commit suicide?

Neither the economics nor the technical facilities of mass communication are to blame for the use which their owners make of them. We, on the other hand, are not helpless, powerless and hopeless in front of inexorable forces unleashed by industry's ingenuity or the Iron Heel's clever scheming. These phantoms were built up by the pseudo-radicalism of the snobs to justify their flight into the cultural preserve, a Messianic religion, political or other nihilisms. Not popular culture but their own craving for "alienation" keeps their eyes away from the realistic, "materialistic," Mr. Anders might say, conditions which must be changed. Mass entertainment can be debased by commercial or by political interests, but only if and while these interests retain their monopoly of communication. The ultra-left culture snobs from the start concede this monopoly to the interests. They have no real quarrel with the world as it is, except that they pretend not to like it that way. The hypocrites! They like it exactly in such a desperate state that they can lament about their impotence in facing it.

For the newest fashion in mass culture is to scorn mass culture. Everybody does, nowadays; those who don't either are writing a book on mass culture or collect early jazz records. Conformism has come around full circle; one dares no longer be "conformist," enjoy any product of the entertainment industry, see differences between the two major parties, admit opinions which might be shared by the multitude. Those who cannot possibly be radicals on the left develop at least a radical or "new" conservatism; these nonconformists in reverse usually get along with the older variety of nonconformists in forward gear. In friendly competition, the two élites are trying to outdo each other at deriding the "mass." Members of their bi-partisan club display in their home a copy of *Partisan Review* together with a painting conceived in an advanced style (as to records, progressives favor Bach while new-conservatives may boast a Shostakovitch concerto played by Oistrakh), and are conversant with words such as alienation, popular culture, pseudo-whatever-fashion-is, anxiety, crowd, absurd and a few others, judicious use of which will silence the un-initiated and bring recognition from those who belong; many will grant you such recognition to be recognized themselves.

Nonconformist tolerance leaves a choice of many peculiar ways to exquisiteness. One may be an existentialist, a Marxist, a surrealist, a fascist— the crowd of frightened snobs will be so discriminating as not to discriminate against him. They may differentiate, though; through marginal differentiation between various crowds, each of them very distinctive, the crowd of the anti-crowds constitutes itself as an effective instrument of terror. No one ever dares to defy its edicts. To be amused by Groucho, to be excited by Armstrong, to be moved to tears by Molly Goldberg (or Werther, for that matter), amounts to backwardness, lack of sensitivity, vulgarity and cultural treason. One has to be alienated to be counted. For here is art, there is entertainment.

In their dread of being caught in a profane mood, would-be intellectuals alienate themselves from the sources of national experience and risk forfeiting their share in forming it. They refuse to see any transmission belt between popular and higher culture, or between popular ideologies and true ideals. Yet, popular culture may be a watered-down, vulgarized version of yesterday's class culture; it also may contain groping, unconscious adumbrations of tomorrow's means of expression. Contemporary indictments of jazz often are literal repetitions of similar pronouncements on the waltz 130 years ago. "Baroque" once had a meaning similar to our "kitsch," and already the suggestion has been made that the first half of this century may be known to, and admired by, posterity as the "Age of Kitsch." Kitsch, by the way, is most children's avenue to artistic expression—some never get beyond that stage, and much of the so-called folk culture, which often is favorably compared with our "mass culture," really is or was the mass culture of civilizations which knew few fashion changes. Though this difference may be decisive, it is precisely one where our mass culture and our nonconformists stand on the same side. Both fear nothing so much as yesterday's conformity. The mad chase for newness in "original creations" is fittingly aped on the assembly line of popular fashion. Mass production processes in the entertainment industries make its content repetitious, self-perpetuating, inflexible. It produces no original material but, on the contrary, transforms its consumer into a passive recipient of sense stimuli. There is no cross-fertilization, no participation in a creative process, but only the surrender to the narcotic effects of a merchandise. Popular culture no longer is entertainment which we provide for ourselves, but has become the supply of entertainment which we buy. All this is true, and serious, too. Our spectator sports, the Roman *circenses,* are opium for the crowds. Unable to escape the insanity of their existence, they purchase escape by the hour; incapable of facing their own feelings, they have sentimentality expressed for them; too sluggish to rebel against their impotence, they watch Superman conquer space and time.

Yet, these vicarious gratifications also express a yearning for a different world and reflect a search for a different humanity. The material content of some escape literature even points to pre-conscious states of rebellion. Sometimes in curiously inverted forms Al Capp, through his "Li'l Abner" cartoon, projects the immolated image of humanity into crudely ironical utopias. It is a gross overstatement that the alienation process in popular culture has gone too far for remedy and return. There is no conformistic material that cannot be turned into nonconformist outcries. Kung Fu changed a few words in a simple calendar to express his political criticism and everybody can think of many superb works of art issued from the new media. The technical characteristics of printing, photographing, filming, broadcasting, television, recording do not restrict, but enlarge the range of our experience and the possibilities of expression.

The Mike in the Bosom

By MURRAY HAUSKNECHT

THE TELEVISION SHOW *Person to Person* employs a technician whose job is to hide a small microphone in the bosoms of women who appear on the show so that they may be heard without the technical apparatus being visible to the audience. This tactful technician—he is reported to do his job with a craftsmanlike efficiency, courtesy, and discretion—is a symbol of the main drift of contemporary society. In the dim world of mass communication and mass culture he stands out as a startlingly clear figure.

Consider *Person to Person* as we see it after the tactful technician and his colleagues have prepared the way. With Edward R. Murrow we look at a picture of one of the homes we are going to "drop in on" that night. Then, as Mr. Murrow turns his attention from us to our "host," we are plunged into the interior of the home. After a few minutes of conversation in which we are introduced to the "host," his family and pets—the inevitable bit of whimsy—we are taken on a tour of the home. Along with the ubiquitous camera and the hidden mike we poke and pry nearly everything which is exposed to us—the magic of television makes *voyeurs* of us all.

All this must be understood within the context of the persistent cliché that television brings the world into our living room. Obviously, Mr. Murrow has hit upon the most intriguing variation of this theme: he brings other living rooms into ours. And with the help of his tactful technician he allows us to snuggle up close in this other living room. It is also clear that Mr. Murrow, like the rest of his fraternity, has a positive answer to the question, Do we want the world continually pouring into our living room? Another question, Does it make a difference how the world comes into the home? has apparently never been considered at all.

I pick on Mr. Murrow and his show because more often than not it is conducted with an intelligence and urbanity which distracts our attention from its inherent vulgarity. Mr. Murrow, in short, seduces us while his competitors attempt to rape us. For what we are often tempted to forget is that *Person to Person* is merely the sugar-coated end of a continuum at the other end of which is *This Is Your Life* and *Strike It Rich*. These two shows are notable for the exquisite refinement of the process of alienation. The industrial worker sells his labor power and relinquishes control over his tools and product. But on *This Is Your Life* and *Strike It Rich* what the sponsor buys are the feelings, emotions, and intimate relationships of the participant which define him as a *person,* as a distinct and unique human being. Mr. Murrow's show is not that crude, but differs only in degree. At

---

Published for the first time in this volume.

both ends of the continuum the boundaries between the public and the private sphere have disappeared.

To be sure, the process of breaking down the private sphere of life has been going on for a long time; television is only the latest instrument. But it is, perhaps, the most important if for no other reason than the fact that the printed page is less powerful than "audio-visual" means of mass communication. As a Madison Avenue philosopher might put it, a mike in the bosom is worth a thousand words. This same philosopher could also point out that the people appearing on these shows are usually "celebrities," people who live their private lives publicly. But this argument misses the point.

Not all celebrities have equal value and the same symbolic status. This simple fact is the basis for one of Mr. Murrow's most fascinating wiles: *Person to Person* consists of two "visits" on the same night, and he strives for incongruity rather than harmony. An early program epitomized this strategy—Krishna Menon and one of the Gabor sisters within the same half hour. Such a juxtaposition, while it tickles our fancy, also manages to blur the distinction between the meaning of a Krishna Menon and a Gabor; by giving both equal value it trivializes the significance of one. Such a trivialization of symbolic figures is the obverse of the transformation of emotions and intimate relationships into commodities. Insofar as it touches the private life of a celebrity who is a political and social symbol it distracts attention from his symbolic significance.

Since privacy is an end in itself, the destruction of privacy is to be condemned. But the significance of the mingling of living rooms must be seen in terms of a broader context.

Every society and every group has the persistent problem of getting people to behave in a manner which supports and maintains the existent social structure. The norms which prescribe the approved behavior may be conceived of as the "discipline" of a society or group; they represent the standard of conformity. But disciplines vary in the degree of conformity demanded. On the one extreme there is the discipline of an army, which is tight and narrow: the goal is as much uniformity of behavior as possible; the degree of variation permitted in role performance is small. Toward the other extreme is the discipline of science: the norms of the "scientific method," unlike military norms, prescribe behavior and thought only within very wide limits. In a word, the discipline defines the degree of individual freedom permitted.

The main drift of contemporary societies is toward tight and narrow discplines. When we talk of the pressures for conformity we are saying in effect that it is increasingly difficult for individuals to bring their own distinctive styles to social roles. We are saying that it is becoming harder to seize upon the ambiguities which pervade all spheres of action and use them to explore other alternatives, because the disciplines are being narrowed so as to eliminate these ambiguities. To deal with this drift we must pay attention to the ways in which disciplines become imposed and accepted.

Control of the environment, as exemplified by a military organization, facilitates the acceptance of a discipline. The members are insulated from the rest of the society, and the authoritarian power structure allows the exercise of brute coercion against any breaches of discipline which are generated by internal forces. But the control and locus of power is only one element. Equally critical is the acceptance of the legitimacy of a social structure in which it is virtually impossible *to resist the internalization* of its discipline. The tight discipline of an army is not so much the result of brute coercion as the fact that it has been able to socialize individuals in its own terms.

This brings us back to the Peeping Toms of television. First, and most obviously, the penetration of the home by camera and microphone and the support given to the sale of emotions and intimate relationships creates a frame of reference for accepting this as expected and conventional behavior. "Life in a goldfish bowl" is transformed from metaphor into accepted reality. Admittedly, television represents merely a culmination of something which has been going on for a long time; nonetheless, its powerful appeal allows it to give the strongest impetus to the notion that there is nothing inherently illegitimate in a living room becoming public domain. The strength of television as a promoter of discipline does not derive solely from its intrinsic appeal; it is also congruent with other forces pushing in exactly the same direction. *Fortune* reports that in the "new-middle class" communities it is virtually impossible to keep the neighbors from invading one's living room at the slightest pretext or without any pretext at all. This, combined with the uncritical acceptance of the *Person to Person* show, indicates how far we have come from the innocence of the nineteenth century when "A man's home is his castle" was practically an inviolable rule.

The broader the limits of a discipline, the easier it is for any individual to shape his role in a manner most congruent with his own personality. Of course, the chances of resisting or escaping from a narrow discipline are largely determined by the nature of the social structure of society. On the other hand, the strength of resistance to the acceptance of an alienated life is greatly lowered when there is no high valuation of those aspects of life which define the individual as a person.

This allows us a perspective from which to view the social consequences of the trivialization of emotions and intimate relationships. As soon as these aspects of personality become commodities and means of titillating the sado-masochistic impulses of an audience they become alien characteristics, and, as such, cannot serve as bases for a defense against the pressures for a tight discipline. We must not be deluded into thinking that this is the participants' problem and not ours. For, as in the case with the invasion of privacy, this continual exposure to the denigration of others' identities creates an environment in which it is difficult to maintain a high valuation of the elements which define our own identity.

There is another relation between the invasion of privacy and the trivialization of sentiments. Broad and rather loose disciplines are maintained by a constant exploration of their limits and by attempts to extend those limits. But such efforts require social support and approval which, at the present time, do not come from the community as a whole. Increasingly, the sources of social support for behavior and thought which deviate from the ever tightening norms comes from solitary primary groups, family, friends, etc. The invasion of privacy is, in effect, a subversion of these groups.

When any group has control of the environment it is comparatively easy to socialize the members in terms of a given discipline through the classical methods of censorship, etc. But there are other means as well. One such method involves the distortion of the meanings or significance of certain symbols and actions which represent other possible alternatives of belief and behavior. That is, if you throw a Krishna Menon in with a Gabor, bill the entire "package" as entertainment, and sell it by way of television, you have gone a long way toward creating an image of an unambiguous world.

What I am getting at here may become clearer by mention of Norman Vincent Peale. His success in converting the New Testament into a gospel of Positive Thought is, in part, due to his ability to destroy his own symbolic status. Will Herberg points out that a biblical faith is a declaration of resistance against the claims of society. The minister is a symbol of that resistance; but if one uses the mass media and its techniques as a vehicle of communication it is impossible to be perceived as a figure of "resistance," since they are not structured for the expression of resistance. Nor is resistance the only thing which cannot be expressed. A medium which is predominantly devoted to the production of entertainment and use of individual talent as a come-on for the "hard sell" cannot simultaneously be used for "education" and the "spread of culture." Each requires its own setting; to put them into the same medium is to invoke a kind of Gresham's Law of Communication. Again, television is not the only medium which destroys the meaning and significance of symbolic figures. *Person to Person* is, after all, a lineal descendant of the covers of *Time* which within a month may feature anyone from Howdy Doody to David Riesman. What is crucial is the fact that the mass media function to present the world in such a manner that the inherent complexities and ambiguities which represent challenges to existing disciplines cannot emerge saliently.

In the *lingua franca* of contemporary sociology there is the term, "anticipatory socialization," which means, roughly, behaving now in a way which will make adjustment in some future situation easier. It adequately describes, I think, one meaning of mass culture. When the man slips the mike in the bosom he helps train us for the time when we shall willingly do the job for ourselves; he is preparing us for adjustment to a future nightmare.

Mass Appeal and Minority Tastes

By KURT LANG

WHAT PEOPLE GENERALLY have in mind when they allude to "popular" taste is that which somehow has mass appeal. Further, if any radio or TV show or comic strip, any offering typical of the popular culture, has mass appeal, this is supposed to be because it holds some attraction for almost everyone, a sort of lowest-common-denominator appeal, and not because of its ability to satisfy a distinct and definable taste, one which happens to be shared by a vast number of people. According to such a concept, it matters little whether the success of mass appeal is a sort of negative one, achieved by omitting all that may possibly offend, as charged by some critics of popular culture, or whether it is chalked up to an ability to satisfy a con-glomeration, a polyglot of tastes. A study of the findings of a recent inquiry into audience preferences for radio programs suggests that, on the contrary, mass appeal stems from a distinctive "majority" taste rather than widespread satisfaction of a polyglot of tastes.

Most attempts to study the appeal of the mass-media fare, or to assay, more or less empirically, the popular taste, assume some kind of continuum along which audience tastes can be graded. In terms of such a continuum, it is thought possible to divide off and speak of a "lowbrow" fare, appealing to a mass audience of "lowbrows," and a "highbrow" fare, attracting a small but sophisticated and selective group of "highbrows." In the accom-panying diagram, the narrow stratum at one end of the continuum repre-sents the sophisticated audience with its discreet tastes. All else falls within the category of lowbrow fare, some of which is supposed to command a mass audience by managing to have some appeal for everyone. This notion of a mass audience, as opposed to select and selective audiences, is widely held among program planners. To qualify as a popular attraction, according to this view, the radio program, for instance, must satisfy tastes as far down toward the lowbrow end of the continuum as possible, while the program appealing to selective and discriminatory taste is aimed at the small audience at the "high" end of the continuum. The selective audience is assumed to be small, even if not every small audience qualifies as selective.

Actually, selectivity exists at every level, and the mass communicator's concern for audience ratings attests to how vividly he is aware of this. Yet the very fact that the people who have so much to do with creating a popular culture think of the mass or popular taste as a polyglot, rather than distinctive taste, deflects their attention from the real problem of determin-ing how popular selections of mass-media fare are actually governed. Plan-

Published for the first time in this volume.

ning on the basis of *how many* people can be expected to like a particular
type of program (i.e., opera for the few highbrows, quiz shows to satisfy
mass demand) can and does interfere with fresh scrutiny of who actually
likes what. Such stereotypy also keeps us from tackling the more tricky
problem of determining which likes go together, that is, what forms the
basis for the diverse enthusiasms evidenced by consumers of the public arts.

Audiences, for the mass communicator, are people to be "delivered,"
and he "makes a play" for his audiences in accordance with workaday
assumptions about listener or viewer preferences. The varying abilities of
programs to attract and hold given-size audiences are pretty much estimated
from the format, the particular subject matter, and general "tone" of a
program. Format, subject matter, and tone are adapted to the presumed
tastes of the age, educational or occupational makeup of audiences available
at any given time or in given areas. That use of these production categories
has a certain pragmatic justification cannot be doubted. For example, heterogeneity in the age and educational makeup of audiences which consistently
turn up for shows having particular formats or dealing with certain subject
matter indicates that these formats and subjects may have a distinct and
uniform appeal.

Nevertheless, information on audience composition reveals only general
tendencies. We appear justified in supposing that *addicts* of lowbrow soap
operas will regularly tune in to evening programs, such as wrestling, whose
format, subject matter, and style of presentation are usually pitched at the
level of the "mass audience." Fans of the Metropolitan Opera broadcasts,
however great their resistance to video as a part of modern life, may be
expected to patronize an offering such as *Omnibus,* which seeks to elevate
the level of television content. Reasoning along this line, groups and individuals who worry about the low cultural quotient of the airwaves often
talk of rectifying this by educating the critical or selective taste of the

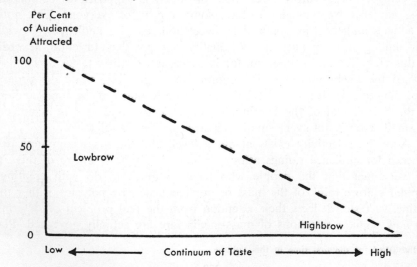

lowbrows. They argue that fewer programs should be designed to satisfy the polyglot tastes of the Great Audience while more attention should be paid to elevating their taste through continued exposure to highbrow fare.[1]

The pitfalls of labelling (whether or not in these specific terms) particular offerings lowbrow and others highbrow has been illustrated by Russell Lynes.[2] In a series of effective pictures he demonstrates how the commonplace artifacts of one generation often become sought after by the highbrows of the next, while the esthetic discoveries of one decade's cultural élite become vulgarities for their successors. Lynes disputes the existence of an intrinsic quality, apart from public appreciation, which is said to mark a given *product* as inherently or lastingly of one level or the other. These vagaries of taste greatly confuse any attempts to decide, at any specific time, what is highbrow or lowbrow, and make it difficult to shape highbrow programs to suit highbrow tastes, etc. Such efforts at labelling are further complicated by the technological production of mass culture, which, by drawing on entire industries, places mass culture—of all levels of sophistication—within the horizons of practically everyone. Not only does this wide availability of popular culture speed up the process by which mass acceptance changes into mass rejection, and vice versa, but various members of an audience may simultaneously classify identical material in a broadcast as highbrow or lowbrow, or middlebrow for that matter. Can the producer assume that classical ballet presented on an Ed Sullivan show with its high audience rating will have mass appeal, while, put on as a cultural offering, the ballet will attract only a select audience?

In delineating areas of taste, we need not rely entirely on *a priori* classifications of radio or TV programs, but should also examine audience preferences as such. In the study of audience preferences for radio offerings,[3] mentioned earlier, a sample of 500 residents of a medium-sized city, not yet exposed to television, were asked to name their favorite radio programs. The answers were spontaneous, that is, respondents were not asked to choose from among a list of programs nor were they in any way limited in their replies. As the result of our analysis of their responses, we defined taste empirically as the tendency for two or more preferences to exist in one and the same person. The process by which people come to decide on certain favorite programs is by no means random. A listener does not haphazardly become a fan of all types of programs, but is inclined to favor those which especially suit his dispositions and to reject those which are incompatible with them. Therefore whenever a respondent, asked about his favorites, mentioned two programs together, this fact was considered as testimony supporting the compatibility in appeal of the two offerings. We may say that two or more radio programs which are the joint favorites of one and the same person reflect an area of taste. Likewise, a convergence of preferences for a fairly limited group of programs, revealed by the responses of a number of listeners, becomes for us the expression of an underlying mass disposition.

On the basis of this kind of examination, what can we say about popular tastes? The existence of a definite and distinguishable "majority" taste is indicated by the frequency with which the most widely liked programs are paired with each other as preferences by listeners. If people cite among their own favorites the program mentioned most often by the group as a whole, they are more likely than not to cite also certain other programs very widely liked by the group.

But let us look at this compatibility among programs a little more closely. Seven programs most often cited as favorites happened also to be among those which were constantly paired with each other as favorites on individual lists. The obvious question which arose was: Were we dealing with a real instance of compatibility and a legitimate area of taste, or did this pairing merely reflect the simple fact that the more popular a program, the greater the chance that it would be found on the same list with other programs? Thus, the recurrence of pairs formed by the most popular offerings may have indicated a distinct area of taste. On the other hand, their ubiquity may have resulted simply from the fact that the appeal of a "majority" program was so broad as to encompass practically all discrete and specialized areas. The appeal of such a program might be randomly scattered among persons with all sorts of tastes, though frequent pairing would have arisen just because of the number of times the program was mentioned. Actually, the statistical "overlap" analysis of favorites—not to be detailed here—gave assurance that the association between these majority programs divulged areas of taste and did not merely prove their obvious popularity.

The underlying taste reflected by the clustering of the seven most popular programs was shared by a large number of listeners. These mass appeal programs did not *all* have the same format nor did they deal with comparable subject matter. To be sure, all were designed for entertainment and not as serious intellectual fare; they included the *Lux Radio Theater,* featuring Broadway plays, as well as comic sketches such as *Our Miss Brooks* and such completely diversionary banter programs as *People Are Funny*.[4] But how clearly was this cluster of preferences made up of the "majority shows" separated from clusters of other programs which were cited as favorites somewhat less often? Before we could be certain that what we had located was a clearly defined majority taste, as distinct from a "universal" taste (i.e., a mass taste shared by almost everyone), we had to show that there were discernable boundaries beyond which this area of preferences did not extend. In our statistical language, this meant that the positive valences (the mutual attractiveness among these programs) were supplemented by negative valences according to which other programs were repelled and thus were rarely found listed as favorites along with the majority shows.

Indeed, boundaries were set by areas of taste foreign to fans of the mass-appeal shows. Thus, another clearly defined cluster was revealed by the four-way overlap among a symphonic program, the Metropolitan Opera broadcasts, another weekly drama series, and a fifteen-minute daily show which featured satirical impersonations and records.[5] Clearly, we were dealing with a group of persons whose favorites involved, though not exclusively, serious musical fare. Also involved were programs with formats and subject matter—comedy and plot—strongly represented in the mass-appeal cluster. But when persons with serious musical interests turned to drama and comedy, they did not turn to the majority taste. The dramatic and comedy programs they cited were not those with the widest popularity, and the seven most popular programs were mentioned definitely less often by this minority group than by the remainder of listeners.

The relation between subject matter and taste may be illustrated by reference to two clusters of favorites in the survey. On the basis of expressed preferences for sportcasts no discrete area of appeal could be mapped out, though an interest in boxing seemed related to an interest in hockey and so forth. Though there was a cluster of favorites, comprising sports news and the broadcasts of various sports events, it could not be *separated* out as an area of taste *distinct* from the majority taste or from any of the minority clusters. Apparently the interest in *radio* broadcasts of sports events had more to do with interest in sports than with interest in radio, and so preferences for sportcasts were evenly distributed among listeners regardless of taste as here defined. At the same time, we found clusters of programs dissimilar in content—such as the linkage of religious programs with an amateur singing program. The singing program was not paired with any other musical program. This seemed to point to some basic similarity between the amateur program and religious fare which transcended their subject matter. Subject matter was dissimilar, but the same people were nonetheless attracted.

It should be added, however, that there were instances in which the clustering of favorites followed common program format. Those who liked one soap opera were likely to laud at least one other. Also, they were more apt to express a liking for soap operas in general—that is, to state that they favored the "type" of program—than were music fans to say they preferred music, drama fans to say they liked drama, etc. A taste for soap opera was clearly distinguishable from the majority taste. Moreover, program testing by broadcasters themselves has confirmed that women could be divided into those who would never listen to a daytime serial and those who were real fans.

This affinity among "soaps" may have revolved not so much around the format as around the similarity of values revealed in the stereotyped solutions which leading characters applied to the moral dilemmas confronting them. In addition, the common appeal may have hinged on the personal image of leading *dramatis personae*.

A similar fascination with the public images of radio performers seemed to characterize another area of taste. A high degree of overlap among preferences for three women's commentators could be isolated. Each one had a distinctive style and talked of different subjects. Yet the three shared with each other a studied awareness of housewives' problems, and they identified themselves with housewives as a group. We can speculate that a certain authenticity about what these women's commentators said and did was derived from this identification. They were viewed by their followers as genuinely anxious to serve, and, moreover, as enjoying themselves in rendering service. The parallel to the public images of popular entertainers could easily be found.

Mass appeal, it can be concluded, does not simply reflect an "average" taste of the general public devoid of a particular slant. It is better visualized as a "modal" taste. The Great Audience seems characterized by a specifiable taste, which is distinguishable from the tastes of other not-so-great audiences. Moreover, what differentiates this majority from the rest, and what appears also to distinguish one minority audience from another, is not so much its choice of subject matter (e.g., drama, music, comedy, sports, information, etc.) as its attraction to something that underlies the manner of presenting very similar subject matter. Evidently there are certain conventions, hardly as readily identifiable as format and subject matter, which demarcate various areas of taste, and these conventional elements, too, are indicated by the readiness with which people are led to name as *a* favorite a whole program series.

On the whole, what seem to demarcate one area of taste from another are certain common conventions which admittedly are not easy to identify. However, the evidence of a discrete majority taste which is linked to a disaffinity for other areas of taste indicates that the conventions employed in the mass appeal programs may not be true universals. Their meaning is time-bound, but the formulas they contain become popular because at a given time they happen to be enjoying reinforcement among the plurality of the available audience. However these formulas arise—and they certainly must change along with other fashions—the notion advanced here is that mass appeal does not depend on nonselective, polyglot tastes, but on a distinct and definable Great Audience as an aggregate of listeners with an identifiable taste, and, we can suppose, particularly sensitive to suggestions from without. The lowest common denominator is far from common to all.

Notes

1. Gilbert Seldes, *The Great Audience.* New York: Viking Press, 1950.
2. Russell Lynes, *The Taste-makers.* New York: Harper and Brothers, 1954.
3. The data were collected as part of a survey in Halifax, Nova Scotia, conducted by the Canadian Broadcasting Corporation's Bureau of Audience Research. The author wishes to acknowledge permission to exploit the data for the present analysis.
4. In addition to the ones mentioned, these shows were: *Amos and Andy, Boston Blackie, Fibber McGee and Molly,* and *The Great Gildersleeve.*
5. These featured the Toronto Symphony Orchestra, the CBC Stage series, and *Rawhide.*

FURTHER READING

Archer, Gleason L. *Big Business and Radio*. New York: American Historical Society, 1939.

Arnheim, Rudolph. "The World of the Daytime Serial," *Radio Research, 1942-43*, Lazarsfeld, Paul F., and Stanton, Frank K. (eds.). New York: Duell, Sloan and Pearce, 1943, pp. 507-48.

Baker, K. H. "Radio Listening and Social Economic Status," *Psychological Record*, Vol. 1, 1937, pp. 99-144.

Bartlett, Kenneth G. "Social Impact of the Radio," *Annals of the American Academy of Political and Social Science*, Vol. 250, 1947, pp. 89-97.

Bernays, Edward L. "The Public Fights TV Commercials," *New Leader*, June 7, 1954, pp. 3-6.

Beville, Hugh M., Jr. *The True Dimensions of the Radio and TV Audience*. New York: National Broadcasting Company, 1949.

Cantril, Hadley; Gaudet, Hazel; and Herzog, Herta. *Invasion of Mars*. Princeton: Princeton University Press, 1940.

Carson, Saul (ed.). "Television and Education," *New Republic*, Vol. 124, 1951, pp. 18-27.

Coffin, Thomas. "Television's Effect on Leisure-Time Activities," *Journal of Applied Psychology*, Vol. 32, 1948, pp. 550-58.

Coffin, Thomas. "Television's Impact on Society," *American Psychologist*, Vol. 10, 1955, pp. 630-41.

Crosby, John. *Out of the Blue*. New York: Simon and Schuster, 1952.

Goodman, Walter. "Bang-Bang! You're Dead!" *New Republic*, Vol. 131, 1954, pp. 12-15.

Head, Sydney W. "Television and Social Norms: An Analysis of the Social Content of a Sample of Television Dramas," *Quarterly of Film, Radio and Television*, Vol. 9, 1954, pp. 175-94.

Herzog, Herta. "What Do We Really Know About Day-Time Serial Listeners?" *Radio Research, 1942-43*, Lazarsfeld, Paul F., and Stanton, Frank K. (eds.). New York: Duell, Sloan and Pearce, 1943, pp. 3-23.

Hileman, Donald G. "The Young Radio Audience: A Study of Listening Habits," *Journalism Quarterly*, Vol. 30, 1953, pp. 37-43.

Lasswell, Harold. "Radio as an Instrument of Reducing Personal Insecurity," *Studies in Philosophy and Social Science*, Vol. 9.

Lazarsfeld, Paul F., and Field, Harry. *The People Look at Radio*. Chapel Hill: University of North Carolina Press, 1946.

Lazarsfeld, Paul F. *Radio and the Printed Page*. New York: Duell, Sloan and Pearce, 1940.

McDonagh, Edward C., and associates. "Television and the Family," *Sociology and Social Research*, Vol. 35, 1950, pp. 113-22.

McKellar, Peter, and Harris, Ralph. "Radio Preferences of Adolescents and Children," *British Journal of Educational Psychology*, Vol. 22, 1952, pp. 101-13.

Maccoby, Eleanor E. "Television: Its Impact on School Children," *Public Opinion Quarterly*, Vol. 15, 1951, pp. 421-44.

Marx, H. L. (ed.) *Television and Radio in American Life*. New York: H. W. Wilson, 1953.

Meerloo, J. A. M. "Television Addiction and Reactive Apathy," *Journal of Nervous and Mental Disorders,* Vol. 120, 1954, pp. 290-91.

Merton, Robert. *Mass Persuasion.* New York: Harper, 1946.

Minear, Verna. "An Initial Venture in the Use of Television as a Medium for Psychodrama," *Group Psychotherapy,* Vol. 6, 1953, pp. 115-17.

Muhlen, Norbert. "Radio: the Networks' Influence on the Public Mind," *Commentary,* Vol. 3, 1947, pp. 201-09.

O'Brien, Mae. *Children's Reactions to Radio Adaptations of Juvenile Books.* New York: King's Crown Press, Columbia University, 1950.

Parker, Everett C.; Barry, D. W.; and Smythe, D. W. *The Television-Radio Audience and Religion.* New York: Harper, 1955.

Podhoretz, Norman. "Our Changing Ideals, as Seen on TV," *Commentary,* Vol. 16, 1953, pp. 534-40.

Ricciuti, Edward A. "Children and Radio: A Study of Listeners and Non-Listeners to Various Types of Radio Programs in Terms of Selected Ability, Attitude and Behavior Measures," *Genetic Psychology Monographs,* Vol. 44, 1951, pp. 69-140.

Saxon, Graham. "Cultural Compatibility in the Adoption of Television," *Social Forces,* Vol. 33, 1954, pp. 166-70.

Schramm, Wilbur. "What Radio Means to Middleville," *Journalism Quarterly,* Vol. 23, 1946, pp. 173-81.

Seagoe, May V. "Children's Television Habits and Preferences," *Quarterly of Film, Radio and Television,* Vol. 6, 1951, pp. 143-53.

Seldes, Gilbert. "A Clinical Analysis of TV," *New York Times Magazine,* Nov. 28, 1954, pp. 13, 55-56, and 59.

Seldes, Gilbert. "The News on Television," *New Republic,* Vol. 130, 1954, pp. 7-10.

Seldes, Gilbert. "Sir Lawrence and the Bard: Presentation of Richard III," *Saturday Review,* Vol. 39, 1956, p. 28.

Seldin, Joseph J. "Selling the Kiddies: TV Admen's Master Stroke," *Nation,* Vol. 181, 1955, p. 305.

Shayon, Robert Lewis. *Television and Our Children.* New York: Longmans, Green, 1951.

Siepmann, Charles A. *Radio, Television and Society.* New York: Oxford University Press, 1950.

Smith, Jeanette S. "Broadcasting for Marginal Americans," *Public Opinion Quarterly,* Vol. 6, 1942, pp. 594-95.

Smythe, Dallas W. "An Analysis of Television Programs," *Scientific American,* Vol. 184, 1951, pp. 15-17.

Smythe, Dallas W. "The Content and Effects of Broadcasting," *Mass Media and Education.* Chicago: University of Chicago Press, 1954.

Smythe, Dallas W. *Three Years of New York Television,* National Association of Educational Broadcasters. Urbana: University of Illinois Press, 1953.

Steinbeck, John. "How to Tell Good Guys from Bad Guys," *Reporter,* Vol. 12, March 10, 1955, pp. 42-44.

Sterner, Alice P. *Radio, Motion Picture and Reading Interests: A Study of High School Pupils.* New York: Columbia University Press, 1947.

Stocks, Mary. "Television and the Young Viewer," *Political Quarterly,* October, 1953, pp. 349-56.

Swanson, Charles E., and Jones, R. L. "Television Owning and its Correlates," *Journal of Applied Psychology,* Vol. 35, 1951, pp. 352-57.

Toffler, Al. "Crime in Your Parlor: TV Programs Under Fire," *Nation,* Vol. 181, 1955, pp. 323-24.

Warner, W. Lloyd, and Henry, William E. "The Radio Day-Time Serial: A

Symbolic Analysis," *Genetic Psychology Monographs,* Vol. 37, 1948, pp. 7-13, 55-64.

Weaver, S. L., Jr.; Kintner, R. E.; and Van Volkenburg, J. L. "Outlook for Serious Music on Television and Radio," *Musical America,* Vol. 16, 1956, pp. 25-27.

Wharton, D. "Let's Get Rid of Tele-Violence," *Parents Magazine,* Vol. 31, 1956, pp. 54-56.

Wiebe, G. D. "Responses to the Televised Kefauver Hearings: Some Social Psychological Implications," *Public Opinion Quarterly,* Vol. 15, 1951, pp. 179-200.

Whiteside, Thomas. *The Relaxed Sell.* New York: Oxford University Press, 1954.

Wylie, Evan M. "Violence on TV—Entertainment or Menace?" *Cosmopolitan,* February, 1953, pp. 34-39.

Wylie, Max, *Clear Channels: Television and the American People.* New York: Funk and Wagnalls, 1954.

Zinsser, W. K. "Out Where the Tall Antennas Grow," *Harper's,* Vol. 212, April, 1956, pp. 36-37.

6
Divertissement

DIVERTISSEMENT

There is some debate whether the word "jazz" derives from an old Creole verb meaning "to speed up" or is a euphemism for the activity that took place in the New Orleans brothels in which it originated. Whatever the source of its name, jazz is a truly American art form. The pure jazz afficionado has no use for so-called popular songs as such. By the same token, when the special jargon of the jazz devotee (a great deal of which originates in New York's Harlem section) is adopted by the public at large, it loses much of its "cool" flavor. While the study and appreciation of jazz as a serious art form is flourishing, the Hit Parade (the apotheosis of "commercial" music) is far more widely known. The intricate rhythms of a Dave Brubeck quartet may draw an attentive and appreciative crowd into Carnegie Hall, but Lawrence Welk's gurgling arpeggios attract an infinitely greater audience.

The eminent musicologist, Sigmund Spaeth, has listed what he believes are the ten most popular songs since 1900. They include "Down By the Old Mill Stream," "God Bless America," "I Want a Girl Just Like the Girl that Married Dear Old Dad," "Let Me Call You Sweetheart," "St. Louis Blues," "School Days," "Shine On, Harvest Moon," "Smiles," "Stardust" and "Sweet Adeline." Only two of the ten are likely to be acceptable to jazz purist and general public alike.

The distinction between popular songs and jazz is made clearly by S. I. Hayakawa, in the first essay in this section. Hayakawa believes that the words of true jazz songs (especially the Negro blues) tend to be unsentimental and realistic about life. The words of most popular songs, on the other hand, tend towards wishful thinking, unrealistic phantasy and sentimental clichés masquerading as emotion.

Morroe Berger writes of the new popularity of jazz. Whatever the reason for its acceptance, he points out, jazz has continually belied the critics who predicted its decline.

David Riesman distinguishes two opposing attitudes toward popular music, a majority *one which accepts the adult picture of youth somewhat uncritically, and a* minority *one in which there are certain socially rebellious themes. The majority group form the audience for the disc jockeys, Hit Parade, etc. The minority group are the real jazz devotees, readers of* Downbeat *and* Metronome, *and the beraters of sentimental "commercial" music.*

Another form of mass divertissement is card playing. In a pioneering study, Irving Crespi shows that card playing is a prevalent leisure-time activity in the United States today despite the dominance of the mass media. He examines the appeal of card playing and suggests reasons for its widespread acceptance.

In the final essay in this section, Henry Popkin discusses certain trends in American drama which suggest "a pattern of wholesale flight from the reality of our lives." That this is not restricted to the 1952 Broadway season, may be discerned in subsequent plays by Miller, Inge and Williams, to name three of the most prominent American playwrights. The flight from reality, Popkin says, is common to all the popular arts, and it is interesting that virtually all of the plays to which he refers were subsequently made into motion pictures.

Popular Songs vs. The Facts of Life[1]

By S. I. HAYAKAWA

BECAUSE I have long been interested in jazz—its history, its implications, its present developments—I also listen to some extent to popular songs, which are, of course, far from being the same thing. My present subject is an attempt to examine, from a semantic point of view, the words of popular songs and jazz songs in order to discover their underlying assumptions, orientations, and implied attitudes.

First, let me clarify the distinction between popular songs and jazz. In "true" jazz, as the jazz connoisseur understands the term, the basic interest on the part of both musician and listener is in the music as music. Originality and inventiveness in improvisation are highly prized, as are the qualities of instrumentation and of rhythm. Popular music, on the other hand, stands in about the same relationship to jazz as the so-called "semi-classics" stand in relation to Bach, Beethoven, and Brahms. Just as the musical ideas of the classics are diluted, often to a point of insanity, in the "semi-classics," so are the ideas of jazz (and of semi-classics) diluted in popular music— diluted, sweetened, sentimentalized, and trivialized.

Now the contrast between the musical sincerity of jazz and the musical slop of much of popular music is interestingly paralleled in the contrast between the literary sincerity of the words of blues songs (and the blues are the basic source of jazz inspiration) and the literary slop in the majority of popular songs. The words of true jazz songs, especially the Negro blues, tend to be unsentimental and realistic in their statements about life. (In saying "Negro blues," I should add that most of these are written by Negroes, but some have been written by whites under Negro inspiration.) The words of popular songs, on the other hand, largely (but not altogether) the product of white song-writers for predominantly white audiences, tend towards wishful thinking, dreamy and ineffectual nostalgia, unrealistic fantasy, self-pity, and sentimental clichés masquerading as emotion.

We have been taught—and rightly— to be more than cautious about making racial distinctions. Hence let me hasten to explain that the differences between (predominantly Negro) blues and (predominantly white) popular songs can, in my opinion, be satisfactorily accounted for without "racial" explanations. The blues arise from the experiences of a largely agricultural and working-class Negro minority with a social and cultural history different from that of the white majority. Furthermore, the blues— a folk music which underwent urbanization (in New Orleans, Chicago, New

Reprinted from *Etc.*, Vol. 12 (1955), pp. 83-95, by permission of the author and the publisher. (Copyright, 1955, by the International Society for General Semantics.)

York, Memphis, Kansas City, and elsewhere)—developed in an economic or market situation different from that in which popular songs, aimed at mass markets through mass entertainment media, developed.[2] With these cultural and economic conditions in mind, let me restate the thesis of this paper, using this time the terminology of general semantics: The blues tend to be *extensionally* oriented, while popular songs tend to exhibit grave, even pathological, *intensional* orientations.

Perhaps I can make my thesis come to life by discussing a specific area of emotion about which songs are written, namely, love in the light of what Wendell Johnson calls the IFD disease—the triple-threat semantic disorder of Idealization (the making of impossible and ideal demands upon life), which leads to Frustration(as the result of the demands not being met), which in turn leads to Demoralization (or Disorganization, or Despair).[3] What Johnson says in *People in Quandaries* is repeatedly illustrated in the attitudes toward love expressed in popular songs.

First, in looking forward to love, there is an enormous amount of unrealistic idealization—the creation in one's mind, as the object of love's search, a dream girl (or dream boy) the fleshly counterpart of which never existed on earth:

> Will I ever find the girl in my mind,
> The girl who is my ideal?[4]

> Every night I dream a little dream,
> And of course Prince Charming is the theme,
> The he for me . . .[5]

Next, of course, one meets a not-altogether-unattractive person of the other sex, and the psychological process called *projection* begins, in which one attributes to a real individual the sum-total of the imaginary perfections one has dreamed about:

> I took one look at you,
> That's all I meant to do,
> And then my heart stood still . . .[6]

> You were meant for me, and I was meant for you.
> Nature fashioned you and when she was done,
> You were all the sweet things rolled up in one . . .
> I confess, the angels must have sent you,
> And they meant you just for me.[7]

Wendell Johnson has commented frequently on what he calls a prevalent belief in magic.[8] Some of his clients in his speech clinic at the University of Iowa, he says, will do no drills, perform no exercises, read no books, carry out no recommendations; they simply seem to expect that now that they have come to THE right speech clinic their stuttering will somehow magically go away. The essence of magic is the belief that you don't have to do anything—the right magic makes all effort unnecessary.

Love is depicted in most popular songs as just this kind of magic. There is rarely an indication in the accounts of love-euphoria commonly to be found in these songs that, having found the dream-girl or dream-man, one's problems are just beginning. Rather it is explicity stated that, having found one's ideal, all problems are solved:

> We'll have a blue room, a new room, for two room,
> Where every day's a holiday, because you're married
>   to me . . .[9]

The "Blue Room" song hints at what other songs often state, namely, that not only are emotional problems (and apparently economic problems) automatically solved by finding "the sweetheart of all my dreams"; the housing problem is also solved:

> You'll find a smiling face, a fireplace, a cozy room,
> A little nest that's nestled where the roses bloom . . .[10]

> In a bungalow all covered with roses,
> I will settle down I vow,
> I'm looking at the world thru rose-colored glasses,
> And everything is rosy now.[11]

That, then, is the idealization. And students of general semantics know from reading Wendell Johnson what that leads to. The unrealistic expectations—for love is never expected to last for any shorter a period than "forever"—result inevitably in disappointment, disenchantment, frustration, and, most importantly, self-pity. Hence:

> I'm all alone every evening,
> All alone, feeling blue,
> Wondering where you are, and how you are,
> And if you are all alone too.[12]

What if it turns out that he wasn't all alone at all, but two-timing her? She complains bitterly:

> You were only fooling,
> While I was falling in love.[13]

> Little you care for the vows that you made,
> Little you care how much I have paid . . .[14]

But in spite of the disappointments he has caused, she still loves him:

> Yesterday's kisses are bringing me pain,
> Yesterday's sunshine has turned into rain,
> I'm alone because I love you,
> Love you with all my heart.[15]

> Am I blue, am I blue,
> Ain't these tears in these eyes telling you?[16]

> How can I go on living, now that we're apart?[17]

She admits vociferously, "I'm a fool to care," but she wallows nevertheless in self-commiseration:

> No day or night goes by,
> That I don't have my cry . . .[10]

The next stage in the progress from disenchantment to demoralization and despair is, of course, another popular song theme, "I'm through with love, I'll never love again"—a theme which has such variants as these:

> I'll never love again,
> I'm so in love with you.
> I'll never thrill again
> To somebody new . . . [19]

> And if I never fall in love again,
> That's soon enough for me,
> I'm gonna lock my heart and throw away the key.[20]

And what is the final stage? Students of general semantics are familiar enough with psychiatric concepts to know that when the world of reality proves unmanageable, a common practice is to retreat into a symbolic world, since symbols are more manageable and predictable than the extensional realities for which they stand. The psychiatric profession classifies this retreat as schizophrenia, but that does not prevent it from being the theme of a popular song:

> I'm going to buy myself a paper doll to call my own,
> A doll that other fellows cannot steal. . . .
> When I come home at night she will be waiting,
> She'll be the truest doll in all the world.
> I'd rather have a paper doll to call my own
> Than a fickle-minded real live girl.[21]

This, then, is the picture of love's unhappy progress, as presented by the song writers of the commercial song-publishing world. The unrealistic emotions and the bathos of popular songs have, of course, long been notorious. It may well be asked if songs can be otherwise and yet be popular.

In answer to this question, let me next present the problems of love as seen by the writers of blues songs, such as are the basis of jazz. The first thing to be noticed is that the object of love is not idealized, but is looked at fairly realistically. It is one thing to call a pretty girl an angel, but quite another to look at angels as they are seen in "Harlem Blues":

> Now you can have your Broadway, give me Lenox Avenue,
> Angels from the skies stroll Seventh, and for that thanks are due
> To Madam Walker's Beauty Shops and the Poro System too,
> That made them angels without any doubt.[22]

Shortcomings of character or appearance in the object of one's love are candidly acknowledged:

> The man I love's got lowdown ways for true,
> Well, I am hinkty and I'm lowdown too.[23]

> You're so mean and evil, you do things you ought not to do,
> But you've got my brand of honey, so I guess I'll have
>   to put up with you.[24]

In other words, there is no to-do made about looking and looking for an ideal girl or man—one adjusts oneself to the kind of women and men that actually exist. Refraining from "always chasing rainbows," the people depicted in the blues appear to save themselves a vast amount of emotional energy.

The loved one's imperfections, however, do not appear to stand in the way either of the intensity or durability of one's affections, as is indicated in this lament over a woman's death:

> I went down to St. James Infirmary,
> Heard my baby groan,
> I felt so broken-hearted,
> She used to be my own.

> I tried to keep from cryin'
> My heart felt just like lead,
> She was all I had to live for,
> I wish that it was me instead . . .

> Though she treated me mean and lowdown,
> Somehow I didn't care.
> My soul is sick and weary,
> I hope we'll meet again up there.[25]

Furthermore, there is no magical attitude toward love indicated in the blues. Love means a mutual human relationship, and therefore there are duties and responsibilities, no less than there are rewards. In its crudest and most elementary statement, the duty is financial:

> You want to be my man you got to give me $40 down,
> If you don't be my man, your baby's gonna shake
>   this town.[26]

> You sittin' down wonderin' what it's all about,
> If you ain't got no money, they will put you out,
> Why don't you do right, like other men do?
> Get out of here, and get me some money too.[27]

In general the duties described are those of living up to one's obligations as a mate, of providing that minimum of dependability that makes, as they say, a house a home:

> Kind treatment make me love you, be mean and you'll drive me away,
> You're gonna long for me baby, one of these old rainy days.
> Yes, I love you, baby, but you don't treat me right,
> Walk the streets all day, baby, and never come home at night.[28]

And the famous blues singer, Bessie Smith, gives the following advice to girls—advice which is full of the sense of one's own responsibility in a love situation:

> So if your man is nice, take my advice,
> Hug him in the morning, kiss him every night,
> Give him plenty loving, treat him right,
> For a good man nowadays is hard to find.[29]

The physical basis of love is more candidly acknowledged in the blues than in most popular songs. I am indebted to Dr. Russell Meyers of the University of Iowa Hospitals for the following observation about Jelly Roll Morton's "Winin' Boy Blues," in which there occurs the line, "Pick it up and shake it, life's sweet stavin' chain."[30] Dr. Meyers equates this line to Herrick's "Gather ye rosebuds while ye may," translating thus: "A stavin' chain is the heavy chain used by loggers to bind together logs to be floated down river, so that it is metaphorically that which binds together, i.e., sexuality; the idea is, as in Herrick, that you shake it now, while you are still able."

Popular songs, to be sure, also refer to the physical basis of love, but usually in extremely abstract periphrasis, as in "All of me, why not take all of me?" In the blues, however, as in the Elizabethan lyric, the subject is treated metaphorically. The following is from a song made famous by Bessie Smith:

> You better get yourself to a blacksmith shop to get yourself overhauled,
> There ain't nothing about you to make a good woman bawl.
> Nobody wants a baby when a real man can be found,
> You been a good ol' wagon, but you done broke down.[31]

So there are disappointments in love in the blues, no less than in popular songs. But the quality of disappoinment is different. The inevitability of change in a changing world appears to be accepted. Conditions change, people change, and in spite of all one can do to preserve a valued relationship, failure may result:

> Folks I love my man, I kiss him morning, noon and night,
> I wash his clothes and keep him dry and try to treat him right.

> Now he's gone and left me, after all I've tried to do,
> The way he treat me, girls, he'll do the same thing to you.
> That's the reason I got those weeping willow blues.[32]
>
> I've got a hard-working man,
> The way he treats me I can't understand,
> He works hard every day,
> And on Sat'day he throws away his pay.
> Now I don't want that man,
> Because he's done gone cold in hand.
>
> Now I've tried hard to treat him kind,
> But it seems to me his love has gone blind,
> The man I've got must have lost his mind,
> The way he treats me I can't understand.
> I'm gonna get myself another man,
> Because the one I've got done gone cold in hand.[33]

The most vivid statement of a sudden change of situation, involving desertion and heartbreak, is made in "Young Woman's Blues," by Bessie Smith:

> Woke up this morning when the chickens were crowin' for day,
> Looked on the right side of my pillow, my man had gone away.
> By the pillow he left a note,
> Reading, "I'm sorry, Jane, you got my goat" . . .

Her reaction to this blow, however, is not, as in popular songs, any giving away to self-pity. The song continues:

> I'm a young woman, and I ain't done running round.[34]

In other words, she may be hurt, but she is far from demoralized. This refusal to be demoralized under conditions which in popular songs call for the utmost in wailing and self-commiseration is repeatedly to be found in the blues. Instead of the self-abasement that we find in the "kick-me-in-the-face-again-because-I-love-you" school of thought, the heartbroken men and women of the blues songs regroup their emotional forces and carry on without breakdown of morale. The end of a love relationship is by no means the end of life. As Pearl Bailey has sung:

> Gonna truck downtown and spend my moo,
> Get some short-vamp shoes and a new guy too . . .
> Cause I'm tired, mighty tired, of you.[35]

There is then, considerable tough-mindedness in the blues—a willingness, often absent in popular songs, to acknowledge the facts of life. Consequently, one finds in the blues comments of many problems other than those of love, for example, the problem of urban congestion, as in "I'm going to move to the outskirts of town," or of alcoholism, as in the song,

"Ignorant Oil." There is also much folk wisdom in the blues, as in "Nobody knows you when you're down and out," or in such observations as:

> Now if a woman gets the blues, Lawd, she hangs her head and cries,
> But if a man gets the blues, Lawd, he grabs a train and rides.[36]

I am often reminded by the words of blues songs of Kenneth Burke's famous description of poetry as "equipment for living." In the form in which they developed in Negro communities, the blues are equipment for living humble, laborious, and precarious lives of low social status or no status at all—nevertheless, they are valid equipment, in the sense that they are the opposite of escape literature. "Rock Pile Blues" states explicitly what the blues are for:

> My hammer's heavy, feels just like a ton of lead,
> If they keeps me slaving someone's gonna find me dead.
> Don't mind the rock pile, but the days are oh so long,
> Ain't no end of misery, that is why I sing this song.[37]

As a student of general semantics, I am concerned here with two functions which literary and poetic symbols perform with respect to our emotional life. First, by means of literary symbols we may be introduced vicariously to the emotions and situations which we have not yet had occasion to experience; in this sense, literature is preparation. Secondly, symbols enable us to organize the experiences we have had, make us aware of them, and therefore help us to come to terms with them; in this sense, literature is learning.

If our symbolic representations give a false or misleading impression of what life is likely to be, we are worse prepared for life than we would have been had we not been exposed to them at all. The frustration and demoralization of which Wendell Johnson writes are of necessity preceded by the expectations created by unrealistic idealizations. This is not to say, of course, that idealizations are in themselves unhealthy; they are a necessary and inescapable product of the human processes of abstraction and symbolization, and without idealizations we should be swine indeed. But there is a world of difference in the semantogenic effects of possible and impossible ideals. The ideals of love, as depicted in popular songs, are usually impossible ideals.

Hence the question arises: do popular songs, listened to, often memorized and sung in the course of adolescent and youthful courtship, make the attainment of emotional maturity more difficult than it need be? It is almost impossible to resist having an opinion on this question, although it would be hard to substantiate one's opinion except on the basis of considerable experience in contact with the emotional problems of young people. Mr. Roy E. Dickerson, executive secretary of the Cincinnati Social Hygiene Society, who has had this experience, has offered the following comment on the thesis of this paper:

In my judgment there is no doubt about the unfortunate influence of IFD upon the younger generation today. I detected it, I think, in even such a highly selected group as the delegates to the Seventh National Hi-Y-Tri-Hi-Y Congress held under the auspices of the National Council of YMCA's at Miami University recently. I had the pleasure of handling the group of the section of the Congress which gave attention to courtship and marriage. It was still necessary to debunk some super-romantic concepts.

I am up to my eyes in marriage counseling. I feel that I am consulted again and again about ill-considered marriages based upon very superficial and inadequate ideas regarding the nature of love and how it is recognized.[38]

The existence of the blues, like the existence of occasional popular songs with love themes which do not exhibit the IFD pattern, demonstrates that it is at least possible for songs to be both reasonably healthy in psychological content and widely sung and enjoyed. But the blues cannot, of course, take over the entire domain of popular song because, as widely known as some of them have been, their chief appeal, for cultural reasons has been to Negro audiences—and even these audiences have been diminishing with the progressive advancement of Negroes and their assimilation of values and tastes in common with the white, middle-class majority. Furthermore, while there is lyricism to be found in blues tunes and their musical treatment, the words of blues songs are notoriously lacking in either lyricism or delicacy of sentiment—and it would seem that popular songs must, to some degree, supply the need for lyrical expression, especially about matters of love.

With all their limitations, however, the blues demonstrate that a popular art can function as "equipment for living." Cannot our poets and our song-writers try to do at least as much for our young people as Bessie Smith did for her audiences, namely, provide them with symbolic experiences which will help them understand, organize, and better cope with their problems? Or, if that is too much to ask (and perhaps it is, since Bessie Smith, was, in her own way, an authentic genius), can they not at least cease and desist from further spreading the all-too-prevalent IFD disease?

Notes

1. Originally presented at the Second Conference on General Semantics, held under the auspices of Washington University and the St. Louis Chapter of the International Society for General Semantics, at St. Louis, Missouri, June 12, 1954.

This paper was also presented before the Associated Students of San Francisco State College at Nourse Auditorium, San Francisco, July 8, 1954. On this occasion the lecture was illustrated by music performed by the Bob Scobey Frisco Jazz Band and Claire Austin. I wish to thank again, for their excellent and spirited contribution to the program, the performers of that evening: Bob Scobey (trumpet), Fred Higuera (drums), Dick Lammi (bass), Bill Napier (clarinet), Wally Rose (piano), Jack Buck (trombone), and Clancey Hayes (banjo and voice). Whatever was left unclear in the speech was made more than clear by the skilful interpretive singing of Mr. Hayes and the deeply felt blues-singing of Mrs. Austin.

The materials of this paper were again presented at the Folk and Jazz Festival at Music Inn, Lenox, Massachusetts, September 5, 1954. Music on this occasion was supplied by the Sammy Price Trio, with blues-singing by Jimmy Rushing and Myra Johnson. I am deeply indebted to these gifted performers for their help, and for their sympathetic understanding of the argument of this paper.

2. I might add that I do not know enough about folk music among the whites (hillbilly music, cowboy songs, etc.) to be able to include these in my discussion. Hence in comparing folk blues with commercial popular songs, I am comparing two genres which are not strictly comparable.

3. Wendell Johnson, *People in Quandaries:* (New York: Harper, 1946), pp. 14-20.

4. "My Ideal," by Leo Robin, Richard Whiting, and Newell Chase. Copyright, 1930, by Famous Music Co.

5. "The Man I Love," by George and Ira Gershwin. Copyright, 1924, by Harms, Inc.

6. "My Heart Stood Still," by Lorenz Hart and Richard Rodgers. Copyright, 1927, by Harms, Inc.

7. "You Were Meant for Me," with lyrics by Arthur Freed, melody by Nacio Herb Brown. Copyright, 1929, by Robbins Music Corp.

8. For example, at a lecture at University College, University of Chicago, May 14, 1954, under the auspices of the Chicago Chapter of the International Society for General Semantics.

9. "Blue Room," by Lorenz Hart and Richard Rodgers. Copyright, 1926, by Harms, Inc.

10. "My Blue Heaven," by George Whiting and Walter Donaldson. Copyright, 1927, by Leo Feist, Inc.

11. "Looking at the World Thru Rose Colored Glasses," by Tommy Malie and Jimmy Steiger. Copyright, 1926, by Pickwick Music Corp.

12. "All Alone," by Irving Berlin. Copyright, 1924, by Irving Berlin.

13. "You Were Only Fooling," with words by Billy Faber and Fred Meadows, music by Larry Fotine. Copyright, 1948, by Shapiro, Bernstein & Co.

14. "Somebody Else Is Taking My Place," by Dick Howard, Bob Ellsworth, and Russ Morgan. Copyright, 1937, by the Back Bay Music Co.—assigned to Shapiro, Bernstein & Co. Copyright, 1941, by Shapiro, Bernstein & Co.

15. "I'm Alone Because I Love You," words and music by Joe Young. Copyright, 1930, by M. Witmark & Sons.

16. "Am I Blue," by Grant Clarke and Harry Akst. Copyright, 1929, by M. Witmark & Sons.

17. "Have You Ever Been Lonely?" with words by George Brown (Billy Hill) and music by Peter de Rose. Copyright, 1933, by Shapiro, Bernstein & Co., Inc.

18. "I Need You Now," by Jimmy Crane and Al Jacobs. Copyright, 1953, by Miller Music Corp.

19. "I'll Never Smile Again," with words and music by Ruth Lowe. Copyright, 1939, by Pickwick Music Corp.

20. "I'm Gonna Lock My Heart," by Jimmy Eaton and Terry Shand. Copyright, 1938, by Shapiro, Bernstein & Co., Inc.

21. "Paper Doll," by Johnny Black. Copyright, 1915, by E. B. Marks.

22. "Harlem Blues," by W. C. Handy. Copyright, 1922, by W. C. Handy; copyright renewed. Included in *A Treasury of the Blues,* ed. W. C. Handy (New York: Simon and Schuster, 1949).

23. "The Basement Blues," by W. C. Handy. Copyright, 1924, by Handy Bros. Music Co., Inc.

24. "Goin' to Chicago Blues," by Jimmy Rushing and Count Basie. Copyright, 1941, by Bregman, Vocco and Conn, Inc.

25. "St. James Infirmary," by Joe Primrose. Copyright, 1930, by Gotham Music Co.

26. "The Memphis Blues," by W. C. Handy. Copyright, 1912, by W. C. Handy. (Included in *A Treasury of the Blues.*) When the lecture on which this paper was based was delivered in San Francisco, it was extensively reported in the San Francisco *News.* In the correspondence columns of the *News* a few days later, there appeared a protest from a reader who remarked regarding my quotation of these lines, "It is good to know that our future teachers (at San Francisco State College) are acquiring moral and spiritual values by getting the good honest feel of the brothel." Mr. Ralph Gleason, writing in the musicians' magazine, *Downbeat,* and taking his interpretation of my lecture from the letter-writer in the *News,* worked himself up into quite a moralistic lather against what he imagined to be my recommendation of love on a cash-down basis over white middle-class morality. I trust it is not necessary to explain to readers of *Etc.* that what I am doing here is attempting to draw a humorous contrast between love regarded as magic and love (including facsimiles thereof) regarded as involving mutual obligations. The statement that love involves obligations is not entirely absent, of course, from popular songs. A recent example is "Little Things Mean a Lot," by Edith Lindeman and Carl Stutz (New York: Leo Feist, 1954), which, as sung by Kitty Kallen, has recently enjoyed vast popularity.

27. "Why Don't You Do Right?" by Joe McCoy. Copyright, 1942, by Mayfair Music Corp.
28. "Blues in the Dark," by Jimmy Rushing and Count Basie. Copyright, 1943, by Bregman, Vocco and Conn, Inc.
29. "A Good Man Is Hard to Find," by Eddie Green. Copyright, 1917, by Mayfair Music Corp. This song is not of Negro composition and is not, strictly speaking, a blues. However, ever since its famous rendition by Bessie Smith (Columbia 14250-D), it has been part of the blues repertory.
30. See General 4004-A, in the album *New Orleans Memories,* by Jelly Roll Morton.
31. "You've Been a Good Ole Wagon" (Smith-Balcom), sung by Bessie Smith (Columbia 14079-D; re-issue, Columbia 35672).
32. For this and several other quotations from blues songs in this paper, I am indebted to Professor John Ball of the Department of English, Miami University, Oxford, Ohio, who, as a student of jazz, has transcribed from his record collection the words of many blues songs, including many which have never appeared in print.
33. "Cold in Hand Blues" (Gee-Longshaw), sung by Bessie Smith (Columbia 14064-D; re-issue, Columbia 35672).
34. "Young Woman's Blues" (Bessie Smith), sung by Bessie Smith (Columbia 14179-D; re-issue, Columbia 35673).
35. "Tired" (Roberts and Fisher), sung by Pearl Bailey (Columbia 36837).
36. See note 32. Memo to Professor Ball: Where on earth did you find this, John?
37. "Rock Pile Blues," by Spencer Williams. Copyright, 1925, by Lincoln Music Co. (Included in *A Treasury of the Blues.*)
38. From a personal letter dated July 13, 1954.

The New Popularity of Jazz

By MORROE BERGER

IN SPITE OF its having been frequently pronounced dead or dying, jazz is now enjoying another period of relative popularity. Music lovers of all previous affiliations, including ex-jitterbugs and devotees of the classics, flock to concerts at Carnegie Hall and Town Hall in New York, and similar halls in other cities, as well as to the night clubs in New York's Greenwich Village and Fifty-Second Street. These places have become the main auditoriums for jazz.

The character of its audience reveals the long journey jazz has made from its early days in New Orleans at the turn of the century. During its birth and early life jazz appealed chiefly to poor and often illiterate Negroes, who heard it in their saloons, dance halls and sporting houses. Today it has entered our most hallowed concert halls, where it attracts mainly middle class intellectual whites who do not find this kind of music in their traditional places of enjoyment, but have to seek it out. In forty years jazz has travelled from the Red Light district to the concert hall.

This odyssey was not made without setbacks and difficulties of many kinds.[1] Until quite recently the city of New Orleans was one of the most ardent disparagers of the jazz music which, one day, scholars may agree is that city's most lasting contribution to American culture. When, for example, the name Basin Street acquired scandalous connotations the New Orleans civic leaders, with true semantic blindness, changed its name to North Saratoga Street. The situation is quite reversed today. In 1944 jazz lovers of New Orleans organized a National Jazz Foundation which stated that one of its aims was to bring back to that city much of the jazz music that was born and flourished there. Semantic sanity apparently returned, too, for the name Basin Street was restored. (Art conspired with business, no doubt, to attract the tourist.) Finally plans were made to elevate jazz to a new status by the construction of a jazz museum in a warehouse building on Basin Street near Canal, formerly known as Lulu White's Mahogany Hall, one of the city's wickedest sporting houses.

The kind of jazz that we have been discussing has been the subject of innumerable debates concerning its character and definition. To avoid another one, let us merely say that jazz is the music originated around 1890 by Negroes of New Orleans, developed and spread from its birthplace by both Negroes and whites, and still played in our day generally by small bands of musicians who are not very familiar to the public, whose musical tastes

---

are satisfied by the derivatives of jazz. "Genuine" jazz is distinguished from popular or "commercial" music, which is composed in Hollywood and on Broadway, and played by "name bands" (and by aspirants to that status) on the radio and in the movies.

Considering its origin, how can we account for the appeal of jazz among urban, middle-class, intellectual whites? There have been a variety of answers to this question. Some writers claim that jazz has a rhythmic vitality and tunefulness that is superior to that of commercial music, and hence attracts the more intelligent person who has listened to popular dance music. Others go further and see in jazz the expression of our turbulent, quick-paced twentieth-century life, and say that consequently jazz has a natural appeal for us. It has been argued, also, that urban sophisticates find a new kind of musical thrill in jazz because its folk origin answers some deep need in ourselves for an identification with the folk in an age of complexity and thoroughgoing social change. Finally, some students insist that the conditions of insecurity and oppression which characterized the lives of the Negroes who developed jazz is now characteristic of the lives of most of us, and the intelligent person is the first to recognize this feeling and to react to it in the form of appreciation of jazz music.

Whatever the reason, jazz has continually belied the critics who predicted its decline. The first of these predictions came from writers who considered jazz to be nothing more than a "child" of the "roaring twenties," which in turn they believed was but a transitory period in our national development. Yet jazz enjoyed renewed popularity during the 1930's and again in the present decade. Between revivals, too, jazz was never dead, for it thrived in New Orleans, Chicago and New York, as well as in isolated spots and in recordings.

In connection with recordings and the interest in jazz, mention must be made of the "collectors," those jazz lovers who devote much time and energy to the collection, exchange and cataloging of records, and whose concern with the music never flags. They are its unfailing supporters in good times and bad. The practice of collecting has developed into a "science" of discography, and has also assumed many aspects characteristic of religious and political cults, with special rules of conduct, esoteric interests, special literature hardly comprehensible to outsiders, and a good measure of evangelism.

The common belief, still prevalent, that jazz is a child of the twenties ignores two or three decades of jazz playing before that.[2] Nevertheless, it is true that while jazz was born long before the twenties, it was given a powerful impetus during those years by the emergence of some great Negro and white musicians. The considerable migrations of Negroes from the South to the North, just after World War I, transplanted both the jazz musicians and a substantial part of their audience to new areas. At the same time, two external conditions conducive to jazz were present in many places during that decade.

First, as Frederick Ramsey, Jr., aptly put it in the February, 1944, issue of *The Jazz Record,* "Jazz . . . needs the intimacy of small halls." It is not merely the size that is meant, but chiefly the informal atmosphere. The players of jazz are unceremonious men, not encrusted with tradition in manner of performance. Jazz is not customarily played by men in boiled shirts and white ties, with the accumulated precedent of centuries of the concert stage and music chamber. It grew up in a very informal atmosphere, the small saloons and sporting houses where people went to relax and throw off convention and dignity. In the speakeasies and dives of the post-World War I era, then, jazz found the same informality and intimacy in which it had originally flourished

The second external aspect of the growth of jazz was the community of interest between players and listeners in a familiar atmosphere which, too, was characteristic of the small clubs of the twenties. In New Orleans most of the early jazzmen, great and small, did not live apart from the people who heard their music. Many players had other jobs that brought them into the life of the community. They lived with their neighbors, played and drank with them; they were not a class apart, seen only when performing. During the twenties, too, there was relatively little separation between the performer and the listener, especially when compared with the gap that is apparent today in the contempt many "name" band leaders and musicians have for the teen-agers and moon-struck older people who idolize them.

In the relations between jazz and commercial music in the twenties and the thirties we can see an interesting example of the interaction between original and imitative types of culture. Commercial "jazz" owes its extreme popularity to a simple characteristic: it combines the features of easily comprehended music with something of the vitality of genuine jazz. It is a medley of light classical, chamber, ragtime and jazz music. Requiring little concentration and evoking no deep emotional reaction (except on the part of jitterbugs, in whose case the reaction is the product at least as much of the advertising and publicity work as of the music itself), it appeals to a wider audience that is not stirred by it but accepts the music mainly as background for dancing, reading, parties and vaudeville acts.

The claim that jazz has passed a Golden Era and is in a period of decline simultaneously exaggerates its popularity in the past and belittles its place in the music of the present. Actually, jazz was never very widespread. In a period when musical taste was varied, however, and not yet forced into certain patterns by the radio and recordings, jazz was able to live alongside its predecessors and imitators.

Until the radio and sound movies standardized all popular music, jazz could be found in many places. But the wide distribution of radios, recordings and juke boxes led to the monopolization of the field by commercial music—the palatable simple music in which most people could find something they liked, since there were so many styles and techniques blended in it. Other types of music suffered. Jazz could be heard in fewer places during the thirties, while commercial music was dinned into the ears of radio listeners and moviegoers. When, in the mid-thirties, commercial music reached another dead end in its standardized and lifeless arrangements, it recahed again into the jazz tradition and tried to capture the lilt and freedom it saw there. This was the birth of "swing" music, in which the bands led by the late Glen Miller, Benny Goodman and Tommy Dorsey excelled. It is noteworthy that all these three most popular swing band leaders got their early training in jazz.

The gradual but almost total elimination of other kinds of music by the growth of commercial jazz was chiefly a matter of indoctrination and custom, not of any natural or instinctive traits of the people who liked it. Since it requires little concentration by the listener, it achieved a measure of popularity which grew as the dispensers and financiers of entertainment found it profitable, through radio and the movies, to reach the lowest common cultural denominator.

Our discussion of the notion that jazz is a child of the twenties, and its relation to commercial music, has revealed that jazz is a product of the cultural impetus of an earlier era. For many years, in fact, it looked as though jazz could attract no young musicians, but during the last five years the situation has improved. Jazz has also made an initial penetration of the academic world, not (as might have been expected) through the universities, but through the secondary schools, which are apparently much less tradition-bound. If the popularity of jazz continues to grow, it will be able to compete with commercial music from the standpoint of remuneration for the musician, and will certainly accord him more prestige at the same time.

It is difficult to see, nevertheless, how the two external conditions conducive to jazz (informal atmosphere and close community of feeling between players and audience), which we discussed above, can even be approximated today. Undoubtedly some new adjustment and balance will be made. The mere presence of these two conditions will not, of course, insure the continuation of jazz. There are too many other factors involved in the growth of an art, including the incalculable one of personal genius, to be expressed in neat formulas.

Notes

1. On the opposition to jazz in various quarters, see the author's article, "Jazz: Resistance to the Diffusion of a Culture-Pattern," *The Journal of Negro History,* Vol. 32, No. 4, October 1947, pp. 461-494.

2. For a sociological discussion of this earlier era of jazz see the author's chapter, "Jazz Pre-History—and Bunk Johnson," in Ralph de Toledano, editor, *Frontiers of Jazz,* Durrell, New York, 1947, pp. 91-103.

Listening to Popular Music

By DAVID RIESMAN

THE STUDY OF POPULAR CULTURE—radio, movies, comics, popular music, and fiction—is a relatively new field in American social science. Much of the pioneering in this field has been done by or on behalf of the communications industry to prove to advertisers that it can influence buying habits, and to pretest its more expensive productions, such as potential best sellers and movies. At a more theoretical level, a good deal of current interest in popular culture springs from the motives, seldom negligible in scientific investigation, of dismay and dislike. Gifted Europeans, horrified at the alleged vulgarization of taste brought about by industrialization of left-wing critics in the traditions of Marx or Veblen who see popular culture as an anti-revolutionary narcotic, highbrows who fear poaching on their preserves by middlebrow "culture diffusionists"—all these have contributed approaches, and sometimes methods as well, to the present state of research in this field.

In using Harold Lasswell's formula—"who says what to whom with what effect"—the question of effects has proved most intractable to study, being at the same time in my opinion the most important and rewarding area. By its very nature, popular culture impinges on people unceasingly; it is part of their environment, part of the background noise, color, and verbal imagery of their lives from the age at which they can first listen to the radio, watch television, or "read" comics. The researcher has two courses open to him. He can either question listeners and readers to see what uses they make of popular culture materials, or he can study the materials themselves and make guesses about the uses made of them. He is usually pushed by the difficulties of interviewing toward the latter procedure, that is, toward some form of content analysis. This is especially the case where he wants to discover the effects of nonverbal materials such as music and paintings. For he will find that, on the whole, people can talk more readily about their responses to words than about their responses, say to a tune. Yet this very readiness to talk, this availability of a critical vocabulary, may hinder as well as help the researcher; words about words may screen rather than reveal underlying meanings. The current preference for the Rorschach test or the Thematic Apperception test ("inkblot" or pictorial stimuli) as a way of getting at underlying character is evidence that verbal responses to verbal cues are likely to be stereotyped and conventionalized.

I do not mean to deprecate content analysis where this is used to suggest

Reprinted from the *American Quarterly*, Vol. 2, 1950, pp. 359-71, by permission of the author and the publisher. (Copyright, 1950, by the University of Pennsylvania Press.)

possible audience effects. T. W. Adorno's essays on radio music[1] and recently the Wolfenstein-Leites' book on the movies[2] indicate how suggestive such work can be, where it is informed by a grasp of the social structure into which and out of which the content comes. We must be on guard against a tendency to sniff at library or arm-chair research as against field work; certainly the quickest short cut to understanding what popular culture does for people—and hence to understanding a great deal about American culture as a whole—is to make oneself the relevant audience and to look imaginatively at one's own reactions. But the danger exists then of assuming that the *other* audience, the audience one does not converse with, is more passive, more manipulated, more vulgar in taste, than may be the case. One can easily forget that things that strike the sophisticated person as trash may open new vistas for the unsophisticated; moreover, the very judgment of what is trash may be biased by one's own unsuspected limitations, for instance, by one's class position or academic vested interest.

While field work may not cure this attitude, it may chasten and modify it, provided that we can find the vocabulary to talk to people about experiences which are not particularly self-conscious ones. My judgment is that the same or virtually the same popular culture materials are used by audiences in radically different ways and for radically different purposes; for example, a movie theater may be used to get warm, to sleep, to neck, to learn new styles, to expand one's imaginative understanding of people and places—these merely begin an indefinitely expansible list. What these various ways and purposes are, we can scarcely imagine all by ourselves; we must go out and talk to various sorts of people in various moods to get at them. It may then appear that it is the audience which manipulates the product (and hence the producer), no less than the other way around.

This is a particularly important consideration in the field of popular music, where the music industry, with its song pluggers, its jukebox outlets, its radio grip, seems to be able to mold popular taste and to eliminate free choice by consumers. The industry itself may like to think it can control matters, even at the price of feeling a good deal of guilt over trashy output or dubious monopolistic practices. Nevertheless, there seems to me no way of explaining by reference to the industry controllers the great swings of musical taste, say, from jazz to sweet in the last decade; actually the industry ignores these swings in consumer taste only at its peril. Even in the field of popular music, there is always a minority channel over which less popular tastes get a hearing, eventually perhaps to become majority tastes.

These, then are some of the very general assumptions which guided me in setting down the following hypotheses about a majority and a minority audience for popular music among teen-age groups. These hypotheses were directed to the Committee on Communication of the University of Chicago as a tentative basis for research, and in the period since their drafting several students have been working in this area. They have, as was to be anticipated, come up against the great methodological obstacles already indicated:

how to isolate music from the influences of other media; how to understand the relations between musical conventions and the conventions of the peer-groups (the groups of age-mates); how, in the case of popular tunes, to separate the mélange of words and music, performer and piece, song and setting.

It has proved easy enough, through *Billboard, Variety,* and other trade sources, to establish popularity ratings for hits; through a study of juke-box preferences in particular neighborhoods to get an indication of class and ethnic, sex and age differences; through an analysis of chord progressions or arrangements to get clues to what musical patterns and conventions might be common to a group of hit tunes. But to move from there to the more basic problems of the use of music for purposes of social adjustment and social protest, or the role of music in socializing the young, teasing the adolescent, and quieting the old—such things as these loom on the far horizon as unsolved problems.

Bearing the difficulty of these problems in mind, I venture to suggest, nevertheless, that one role of popular music in socializing the young may be to create, in combination with other mass media, a picture of childhood and adolescence in America as a happy-go-lucky time of haphazard clothes and haphazard behavior, jitterbug parlance, coke-bar sprees, and "blues" that are not really blue. Thus the very problems of being young are evaded —the mass media also furnish comparable stereotypes for other deprived groups, such as Negroes, women, GIs, and "the lower classes." I do not mean to suggest that in thus presenting the young with a picture of Youth drawn by adults there is conspiratorial intent—rather there is a complex interplay of forces between the adults who are the producers and the young who are the consumers.

Most teen-agers, though much more "knowing" than the picture gives them credit for being, do not think about this situation at all. Among those who do, some are aware that their group standards are set by outside forces. But their loss of innocence has made them cynical, not rebellious; and they are seldom even interested in the techniques of their exploitation or its extent.

A small minority is, however, not only aware in some fashion of the adult, manipulative pressure but is also resentful of it, in many cases perhaps because its members are unable to fit themselves by any stretch of the imagination into the required images. Such a "youth movement" differs from the youth movements of other countries in having no awareness of itself, as such, no direct political consciousness, and, on the whole, no specialized media of communication.[3] If we study, for instance, the hot rodders, we see a group of young (and pseudo-young) people who, in refusing to accept the Detroit image of the automobile consumer, create a new self-image though one in turn liable to manipulation. Likewise, the lovers of hot jazz, while not explicitly exploring the possibilities of how youth might take a hand in formulating its own self-images, do in fact resist certain conventional stereotypes. But they do so by making a differential selection from what the adult media already provide.

Thus, we may distinguish two polar attitudes toward popular music, a *majority* one which accepts the adult picture of youth somewhat uncritically, and a *minority* one in which certain socially rebellious themes are encapsulated. For the purposes of this analysis, I shall disregard the many shadings in between, and also neglect the audiences of hillbilly and "classical" music.[4]

Most of the teen-agers in the majority category have an undiscriminating taste in popular music; they seldom express articulate preferences. They form the audience for the larger radio stations, the "name" bands, the star singers, the Hit Parade, and so forth. The functions of music for this group are *social*—the music gives them something to talk or kid about with friends; an opportunity for competitiveness in judging which tunes will become hits, coupled with a lack of concern about how hits are actually made; an opportunity for identification with star singers or band leaders as "personalities," with little interest in or understanding of the technologies of performance or of the radio medium itself. Thus I assume that the psychological functions of this medium for most of its audience include those that Herta Herzog has found in the radio daytime serial or the quiz program and that Leo Lowenthal has found in popular biographies.[5]

It is not easy at this stage to state the precise way in which these indiscriminate listening habits serve to help the individual conform to the culturally provided image of himself. To discover this is one of the tasks of research. And to this end some further lines of inquiry suggest themselves.

First, it has often been remarked that modern urban industrial society atomizes experiences, isolating each experience from other experiences. Does this same pattern operate, as T. W. Adorno suggests, in the auditory experience of popular music? Such music is presented disconnectedly, especially over the radio—where it is framed by verbal ballyhoo and atomized into individual "hits"—like the disparate items on a quiz program. Can it be established that this mode of presentation reinforces the disconnectedness often associated with modern urban life?

Second, by giving millions of young people the opportunity to share in admiration for hits, hit performers, and the hit-making process, are identifications subtly built up which serve to lessen the effects of social conflicts and to sustain an ideology of social equality?[6]

Third, does the music tell these people, almost without their awareness, how to feel about their problems in much the same way that the daytime serials package their social lessons?

Fourth, since this music is often dance music, does it help to create and confirm postural and behavioral attitudes toward the other sex? Does the facial expression assume the "look" the music is interpreted as dictating? Is the music felt as inculcating the socially right combination of "smoothness" with stylized "spontaneity," of pseudosexuality with reserve? Do these psychic and gestural manifestations then carry over from the dancing situation to other spheres of life? We should not be surprised to find that such molding of the body-image and body responses affects girls more powerfully than boys; as the subordinate group, with fewer other outlets, girls can less afford even a conventionalized resistance.

It is not unlikely that we will discover that the majority role represents in many of its aspects a pattern of "restriction by partial incorporation."[7] That is, the majority is continuously engaged in the process of adapting elements of the minority's musical outlook, while overtly ignoring or denigrating minority patterns. Jazz itself,[8] many of the dance steps, and lyrical images are almost entirely minority products to begin with. But they undergo significant changes in being incorporated into the majority style, just as radical intellectual and ideological developments are modified by academic acceptance.

The minority group is small. It comprises the more active listeners, who are less interested in melody or tune than in arrangement or technical virtuosity. It has developed elaborate, even overelaborate, standards of music listening; hence its music listening is combined with much animated discussion of technical points and perhaps occasional reference to trade journals such as *Metronome* and *Downbeat*. The group tends to dislike name bands, most vocalists (except Negro blues singers), and radio commercials.

The rebelliousness of this minority group might be indicated in some of the following attitudes toward popular music: an insistence on rigorous standards of judgment and taste in a relativist culture; a preference for the uncommercialized, unadvertised small bands rather than name bands; the development of a private language and then a flight from it when the private language (the same is true of other aspects of private style) is taken over by the majority group; a profound resentment of the commercialization of radio and musicians. Dissident attitudes toward competition and cooperation in our culture might be represented in feelings about improvisation and small "combos"; an appreciation for idiosyncrasy of performance goes together with a dislike of "star" performers and an insistence that the improvisation be a group-generated phenomenon.[9]

There are still other ways in which the minority may use popular music to polarize itself from the majority group, and thereby from American popular culture generally: a sympathetic attitude or even preference for Negro musicians; an equalitarian attitude toward the roles, in love and work, of the two sexes; a more international outlook, with or without awareness, for example, of French interest in American jazz; an identification with disadvantaged groups, not only Negroes, from which jazz springs, with or without a romantic cult of proletarianism; a dislike of romantic pseudosexuality in music, even without any articulate awareness of being exploited; similarly a reaction against the stylized body image and limitations of physical self-expression which "sweet" music and its lyrics are felt as conveying; a feeling that music is too important to serve as a backdrop for dancing, small talk, studying, and the like; a diffuse resentment of the image of the teen-ager provided by the mass media.

To carry matters beyond this descriptive suggestion of majority and minority patterns requires an analysis of the social structure in which the teen-ager finds himself. When he listens to music, even if no one else is around, he listens in a context of imaginary "others"—his listening is indeed often an effort to establish connection with them. In general what he perceives in the mass media is framed by his perception of the peer-groups to which he belongs. These groups not only rate the tunes but select for their members in more subtle ways what is to be "heard" in each tune. It is the pressure of conformity with the group that invites and compels the individual to have recourse to the media both in order to learn from them what the group expects and to identify with the group by sharing a common focus for attention and talk.

Moreover, many factors, including the youth orientation of the culture generally, lower the age at which children venture into the "personality markets" to be judged by their success in terms of popularity. As high schools adopt the social customs and listening habits previously postponed until college, so the grammar school tends to ape the high school in dating patterns, proms, and so on. At the same time, the personalities of the popular music industry have every reason to cultivate the child market and are quite willing to "rob the cradle." This convergence of forces means that children are compelled to learn how to respond to music, in a fashion their peer-group will find acceptable, at increasingly earlier ages. Under these pressures, music can hardly help becoming associated with both the excitements and the anxieties of interpersonal relationships.

So far, I have obtained some fifteen long interviews with young people about popular music. Since these interviews were in the nature of a limited pretest, simply part of the long process of developing a questionnaire which could then be used on a selected sample, I made no effort to obtain a sample but engaged in random house and street interviewing in white (and Nisei) South Side Chicago, seeking to vary only sex, age, and economic standing in a very rough way. The respondents ranged from fourteen to twenty-two and from probably upper-lower to middle-middle class. In addition, I sought data on the higher social strata from the always available "sample" of traditional social psychology—namely, my students—and data on the Negro community from a few discussions with Negro students and musicians.

One advantage in interviewing teen-agers about their music listening habits is that as compared, for instance, with interviewing on politics—one meets little resistance (save for an occasional overprotective mother), since all do listen and like to talk about their tastes; if the interviewer had cards with hits listed on them, they would doubtless enjoy ranking the cards and then explaining their rankings. However, the group as a whole—as compared with housewives—tended to be inarticulate, even if not shy; a good deal of direction was needed in some portions of the interview, and this ran the obvious risk of tilting the responses.[10] After introductory questions concerning the respondent's age, schooling, family data (for example, siblings, father's occupation, residential mobility, and, where possible, socio-economic status and mobility strivings), I turned to general questions about radio listening habits: length of time, place (that is, where, and with whom, listening occurs), favorite types of programs, and the like. Then came the questions about music. (Depending on the rapport, the order was sometimes reversed.) The schedule was long and open-ended, pointing toward the problems indicated in the analysis above.[11]

One question which sometimes led to illuminating answers was this: "How do you and they (your friends) decide what is a good or bad piece?" One seventeen-year-old girl, the daughter of a railroad telegrapher, said, "If it's popular we go for it; if it's played on the Hit Parade." Her answer to whether her social life would be affected if she hated music was, "That's all there is to do for kids our age." Yet the time she craved music most was when she was alone; the somewhat sultry love ballads that were her favorites were perhaps vicarious company. Like virtually all the other respondents, she vigorously denied attending broadcasts or having any desire to meet her favorite performers. "I don't swoon over anybody," she said.

I also discovered that respondents generally felt much safer in stating their musical dislikes than their musical likes; the former were volunteered readily, while the latter came out only if approval for the preference seemed in the offing. That is, many would quickly reject a whole area: "I hate hillbilly," or "I can't stand fast music," or "Negroes are too jumpy." More rarely something specific was rejected: "I dislike Tommy Dorsey; he has no rhythm, just blasting of horns." Or, " 'Bubble Gum' is the craziest song." Many said they disliked commercials and several that they would not buy anything that was advertised. As in highbrow circles, so in middlebrow and lowbrow ones, enthusiasm would seem to be a greater social danger than negativism: the fear is to be caught liking what the others have decided not to like.

Among these young people, music seemed to be one of the principal areas for peer-group training in the appropriate expression of consumer preferences; by learning to talk about music, one also learned to talk about other things. Yet the vocabulary used to discuss music, as it turned up in the interviews, was in the majority of cases not a very differentiated one, but rather the "swell," "lousy," "I go for that," and so on which signify preferences for other cultural commodities, tangible and intangible. Indeed, one differentiation, as already indicated, between my hypothetical majority and minority wings lies in the latter's development of strict and often highly articulate standards for judging jazz.

This leads us to a final paradox. The hot jazz lovers are protesters. They are individualists who reject contemporary majority conformities. In the very process, however, do they not in many, perhaps most, cases simply move into another peer-group which holds them fast, and adopt a new conformity under the banner of nonconformity? While my handful of interviews in white South Side Chicago brought to light only a single hot-jazz fan, there have been a number of such fans among the students at the University of Chicago. Sometimes these are young men—strikingly enough there are very few hot-jazz girls, save in an occasional "symbiotic" relation to a hot-jazz boy—who grew up as somewhat rebellious individuals in a small high school group where they stood almost alone in their musical orientation. Then, when they came to the university, they found many other such people and for the first time experienced the security and also the threat of peers who shared their outlook.

What happens then, when this discovery is made, is something we are far from understanding; obviously, the problem touches on the whole congeries of issues connected with social and intellectual mobility, the American *rites de passage,* the role of big cities and intellectual centers. We may perhaps assume that the hot-jazz fan can employ his *musical* deviations (from the standpoint of the great majority) to conceal from himself other surrenders he makes to his peer-group. Or, he may find within the field of jazz further possibilities of protest by taking a still more esoteric stance, for example in favor of "pure" Dixieland or of some similar now-frozen cult. But what if his peer-group, conceivably as the result of his own initiative, moves with him there also? Does popular music itself offer him enough variety to permit him to use it alternatingly to establish prestigeful social distance from others and needed ties to them? And how does it compare in this respect with other cultural products, such as books, movies, art, and modern furniture?

Difficult as these questions are, it seems to be easier to understand the uses of music in this sociological sense than it is to understand the variations in what people of different psychological types actually hear when they listen to music. Is it foreground noise for them or background noise? What is it, precisely, that they "perceive?" Ernest Schachtel has made a brilliant beginning on the question of what meaning physical forms have for people, through seeing what they make of Rorschach inkblots. Experts in auditory perception have not succeeded, so far as I know, in finding an auditory stimulus as useful as the Rorschach test in circumventing cultural stereotypes. Our problem is to reach the people for whom music or plastic art or the movies are appealing in part just because they are more comfortable with sounds and images than with print and words. We are brought back to our problem of how to communicate with them.

While the interview guide I developed on the basis of these research

suggestions covered movies, magazines, and favorite radio programs as well
as music, it did not explore the whole range of popular culture activities (and
inactivities such as just sitting), or pay sufficient attention—though it did
pay some attention—to hobbies, pets, dating, and other leisure pursuits. I
am convinced that we cannot understand the role of any communication
medium in isolation from the other media and from other leisure activities,
any more than we can understand individual manipulation of the materials
in the media without understanding the group which the individual belongs
to, wants to belong to, or wants to be set apart from.

This truism led me to the further conclusion that one cannot hope to
understand the influence of any one medium, say music, without an understanding of the total character structure of a person. In turn, an understanding of his musical tastes, and his use of them for purposes of social conformity, advance, or rebellion, provides revealing clues to his character, to
be confirmed and modified by a knowledge of his behavior and outlook in
many other spheres of life. . . . Plainly, we cannot simply ask "who listens
to what?" before we find out who "who" is and what "what" is by means
of a psychological and content analysis which will give us a better appreciation of the manifold uses, the plasticity of music for its variegated audiences.

Notes

1. T. W. Adorno, "On Radio Music," in *Studies in Philosophy and Social Science* (New
York: Institute of Social Research, 1941), vol. 9, and "A Social Critique of Radio Music,"
Kenyon Revew, vol. 7, p. 208 (1944).
2. Martha Wolfenstein and Nathan Leites, *Movies: A Psychological Study.*
3. This is of course not intended to deny that there are certain very small groups in the
United States who follow the patterns of European youth movements. Many teen-age fol-
owers of Henry Wallace and young left-wing Zionists preparing for emigration to Palestine
seem to have all the emotional paraphernalia of European movements, whether nominally
"right" or "left."
4. Actually, both these areas are very important ones. It would be interesting to study
urban fanciers of hillbilly music as possible exemplars of the many city folk who, though
they depend on the city for income, friends, and entertainment, despise or pretend to despise
it and long nostalgically for the very rural life from which they or their parents may have
fled; perhaps for such people to define themselves as country folk in their musical and
other leisure tastes is the only way they can accept the city. As for "classical" music, it
is worth observing that people who tell the interviewer that they like, or "don't mind,"
classical (or "symphonic") music almost invariably in my own experience mean Tchaikovsky,
sometimes Chopin, and occasionally Brahms. People of serious musical taste almost never
describe their interests by means of a rubric, but rather by reference to specific composers
or, perhaps, distinctive musical epochs. It is striking that some of the new, big, hundred-
selection jukeboxes will have a "classical" section, which is apt to include some Tchaikovsky
(in an André Kostelanetz version). Indeed, "classical," for this sizable audience, might be
defined as whatever music Kostelanetz will arrange and play.
5. Herta Herzog, "Professor Quiz—A Gratification Study," *Radio and the Printed Page*,
Paul F. Lazarsfeld, ed., and "On Borrowed Experience," *Studies in Philosophy and Social
Science*, vol. 9 (1941). Leo Lowenthal, "Biographies in Popular Magazines," *Radio Research
1942-43*, Paul F. Lazarsfeld and Frank Stanton, eds.
6. Cf. my article "Equality and Social Structure," *Journal of Political and Legal Sociology*, vol. 1, p. 72 (1942).

7. See Harold D. Lasswell, *World Politics and Personal Insecurity*.

8. Cf. Kurt List, "Jerome Kern and American Operetta," *Commentary*, vol. 3, p. 433 (1947).

9. This combination of respect for group co-operation along with individual spontaneity can be found here in both unconscious preference and explicit formulas. Sometimes hot jazz constitutes a satire on sweet or corny music, hence of the attitudes that go with them.

10. I have also found that dual interviewing, in which my colleague Reuel Denney participated, can help to establish easier rapport and deeper probing and can allow much closer analysis of the interviewing process itself. Here one of the pair of interviewers can take notes—or fend off the baby—while the other chats with the respondent; of course, the two interviewers have to be sensitive to each other's cues if they are not to get in the way.

11. A few sample questions: favorite tunes (and how far back these, and the lyrics, can be recalled); favorite bands; perhaps a discussion about the shift from swing to sweet and the reasons for it; what the hit-making process is and what effect a disclosure of such information has on the respondent; questions about the function of popular music in the peer-group, e.g., for dancing, kidding around, appearing sophisticated, and what would be the effect on his popularity—or on his more general feelings of "belonging" to the community —if the respondent could no longer listen (where I went into this, and the respondent was willing to make the experiment of thought, he said, in effect, "I would be isolated," or "I would be lost," or sometimes, "It would make no difference"); attitudes toward Negro musicians; favorite movie stars and fan attitudes generally; feelings about people with different musical tastes (often revealing within a family constellation, either vis-à-vis adults or vis-à-vis siblings); attendance at radio broadcasts; possible relations between mood and amount and type of music listening. Of course it often turned out that a whole congeries of questions was irrelevant for the participating respondent, or he was incapable of answering them; further interviewing should sharpen the questions that can be asked and shed further light on those that provoke anxiety, sudden awareness, sudden rapport, and so forth.

Card Playing as Mass Culture

By IRVING CRESPI

THE PHRASE "CARD PLAYING" conjures up the image of a silent group vying with each other for stakes heaped on the center of a table. This image is a manifestation of the common tendency to identify card playing with gambling. Consequently it may seem rather startling to discover that in a representative American community, card playing is most typically an activity of families and friendship groups, meeting in their own homes, and playing either for no stakes or for only trivial sums.[1] Furthermore, it is also the case in this community that few card-playing groups are formed for the purpose of playing the game.

Typically, the pattern is for groups already in existence to play cards in lieu of other forms of entertainment. A small minority of card players exists who can, with justification, be typed as "Card Players" in the sense that they play for the sake of the game itself or in the fond, if futile, hope of winning a fortune. For the greatest number of card players in this community, however, the desire to play cards is not based on an interest in the intrinsic qualities of card playing; rather, it is founded on the fact that card playing for them is a highly diverting and exciting form of personal entertainment that simultaneously acts to transform group gatherings into pleasurably cohesive units.

It is this simultaneity of individual entertainment and group integration that differentiates card playing from entertainment through the mass media. Even when one attends a movie with friends, wife, or date, or, while one watches television in the comfort of the family living room with the entire family gathered after the evening meal, pleasure—or at least titillation— derives not from the group but from stimulation external to it. The individual may enjoy himself, but not as a group member. Furthermore, because of the passivity inherent in being a member of a mass audience, the individual's isolation is further increased because he does not experience the socializing effect of active participation and involvement in a group endeavor. No matter how effectively the mass media entertain the individual, they are hardly capable of deepening and extending group ties, let alone establishing new relationships. Only through direct participation in group action, and not by vicarious identification with a distant and impersonal entertainer, can the need for grouping be satisfied.

The fact that card playing, a small-group game, competes successfully with mass diversions appears to suggest that it may be a counterforce which neutralizes the debilitating effects of mass entertainment upon group life.

Published for the first time in this volume.

It is our contention that, in fact, widespread participation in card playing is an index of the extent to which the forms of small-group living have been conditioned by the impact of mass society. Before we can establish this, however, we must first demonstrate that card playing is a prevalent leisure-time activity in the United States today despite the dominance of the mass media.

The competitive strength of card playing in the leisure market can be measured by the extent of participation and by its persistence. For example, 56 per cent of a national sample reported that they play cards either regularly or occasionally.[2] Another national survey revealed that cards are played in 87 per cent of American homes and that 83 per cent of American families play cards.[3] Thus, while not everybody plays cards, it is so widespread an activity that we can without exaggeration conclude that there is mass participation in this leisure-time activity.

As a more precise measure of participation in card playing vis-à-vis mass-media activities, we can examine its place in the total pattern of leisure time. A few observations will suffice for our purposes. In reply to a poll which asked how the respondent had spent the previous night, 5 per cent of a national sample mentioned card playing.[4] Twenty-two per cent named listening to the radio, 16 per cent reading (most likely a newspaper or magazine, but not a book), 19 per cent entertaining or being entertained, and 7 per cent the theater. Card playing and the ambiguous "entertaining" are the only two group activities mentioned frequently enough to be classified separately.

The findings of other polls are consistent. For example, the Fortune Poll asked "Which two or three of the things on this list do you really enjoy doing most during your spare time?"[5] Twenty per cent of the men and 18 per cent of the women chose playing cards. Listening to the radio was named by 51 per cent of the men and 54 per cent of the women. Other frequently named activities were: watching sports (by men), doing outdoor sports (by men), doing needlework (by women), visiting with friends, reading books, and going to the movies. In both of these polls, mass-media activities are the major category.[6] If we exclude sports, whose appeal tends to be restricted to men, and the vaguely defined categories of "entertaining" and "visiting," card playing is the *only* group activity that has been able to maintain a sizeable following in the face of competition from the mass media.

The sales figures on decks of playing cards not only establish this fact conclusively, but also testify to the staying power of the game. In 1900, approximately sixteen and a half million decks of playing cards were sold.[7] After a peak of over eighty million decks sold in 1950—a consequence of the canasta fad—sales have levelled off to over fifty million decks sold annually.[8] The ratio of sales to population, on the basis of the above sales data, has increased during the past half century from twenty-two per hundred to over thirty per hundred. Since 1930, the ratio has not dropped below thirty per hundred, *not even as a result of the introduction of television.* Card playing has maintained and perhaps even increased its popularity precisely during the period in which the mass media and commercial activities have undergone their peak expansion.

We can conclude from these statistics that card playing, in competition with these other pastimes, has managed to establish for itself a definite niche in the total pattern of leisure-time life in the United States. But we may go beyond mere description to an analysis that answers the question, "Why card playing?" Only by answering this question can we determine the significance of these findings.

A sociological analysis of card playing in terms of its effects upon group integration indicates what role card playing has in modern society.[9] In playing, attention is focused on the exciting and depersonalized competition of actively seeking to attain the most powerful combination of cards. In this competitive struggle, the process of playing in itself is challenging and stimulating. In addition, the outcome of the game is tantalizing. No communication other than that specifically required to play the game is permissible. Furthermore, all those playing must be physically members of the group, seated around a common table, with attention focused on the cards—and in some cases stakes bet on the outcome of the game. Each player has a clearly defined relationship to all the others, a relationship impersonally defined by the rules governing play.

With involvement in the game, therefore, regardless of what specific motives impelled the group members to play in the first place, there develops a small group characterized by an intense concentration on a common but highly impersonal activity. Personal animosity and hostility, it should be noted, stem not from the innate qualities of the game but from the lack of skill of some players or, more characteristically, the pretensions to skill superiority on the part of would-be experts.[10]

Card playing physically brings a group into face-to-face contact, in order to participate in an intriguing form of competition. Every member of a card-playing group is caught up in a highly structured interactional process. Since each specific card game requires different types and levels of skill, there are few who are incapable of playing at least one game with an acceptable degree of competence. In a society such as ours, which has made a fetish out of performance in competitive action, the opportunity that card playing affords for competing on an equal basis has the effect of rendering it particularly appropriate for intimate and friendly groups.

The fact that card playing is a highly entertaining activity gives it further value. Friends and families who have no specific reason to meet, but who feel that they would like to spend time with each other, can make card playing the ostensible purpose of visiting. Without the excuse of wanting to play cards, these groups feel the lack of some specific justification for meeting. Card playing is to many an enjoyable substitute for, or addition to, traditional communal festivities and periodic ritual gatherings. Either as a basis for inviting friends and relatives or as a means of occupying groups that have somehow met, card playing mitigates boredom through structured group action.

The game also functions to create and discharge feelings of group obligation. "Sociability" makes it difficult for anyone to refuse to play, since refusal entails both rejection and hindrance of the group in its search for entertainment. Not agreeing to play when the suggestion is made means not living up to one's obligations as a friend or relative. Passive mass activities cannot impose such constraint upon behavior. Neither can they impose a feeling of obligation such as results from prior commitment to attend a card party. Having once agreed to be present, the individual owes it to the group to attend; he must not make any last-minute changes in his plans since his absence would mean too few players. The acceptance of an invitation to play results in the reinforcement of group obligations.

A final, apparently paradoxical, but extremely significant characteristic of card playing that enables it to bind small groups is its impersonality. Since card playing makes minimal demands upon the personal capabilities and characteristics of the players, it is possible for groups to meet for the purpose of playing cards frequently over extended periods of time without having any other basis for acting together. In a highly mobile society such as ours, in which the individual continually finds himself forced to associate with total or near-strangers, the card game provides a semblance of group identification based on involvement in an impersonal process.

This analysis makes clear the fact that the prevalence and persistence of card playing in the United States today results from the crisis of the small group in our segmented, mobile, mass society. The inner resources of groups, deriving from the socialization of individuals into groups with a rich traditional basis of group identification, have been dissipated. As the small group becomes merely one of a mass of indistinguishable, interchangeable units, it seeks entertainment from without. Group enjoyment—a transitory, titillating involvement rather than the persistence of deep-seated satisfactions based upon the fulfillment of personality—is sought after. Comparable excitation is characteristically provided by the mass media to the detriment of group cohesion. In contrast, card playing, *because of its triviality,* can create the conditions for group integration while it diverts and entertains. The fact that card playing is competing successfully with the mass media is not indicative of its countervailing effect; rather, it is symptomatic of the intrusion of the mass even into the small group.

Notes

1. The conclusions summarized in this report are based on a field investigation conducted in Endicott, New York. A complete documentation of the findings is to be found in Irving Crespi, *A Functional Analysis of Card Playing As A Leisure Time Activity*, unpublished dissertation, New School for Social Research, June 1955. Consult especially Chapters 3, 4 and 8.

2. AIPO poll, December 13, 1947, *Public Opinion Quarterly*, Spring, 1948, p. 148.

3. "Playing Cards—A National Survey," *Hobbies*, December, 1942, p. 12.

4. AIPO poll, March 20, 1948, *Public Opinion Quarterly*, Summer, 1948, p. 357.

5. The Fortune Poll, March 1949, *Public Opinion Quarterly*, Summer, 1949, p. 354.

6. The lack of mention of television is due to the fact that these polls were conducted prior to its introduction to the mass market.

7. Jesse Steiner, *Americans at Play*, New York, McGraw-Hill, 1933, p. 138.

8. Based on tax receipts reported in *The Budget of the U. S. Government for the Fiscal Year Ending June 30, 1953*, U. S. Government Printing Office, Washington, D. C., 1955, p. 1149.

9. This analysis deals only with the group *consequences* of playing cards, not with individual motivations. Individual motivations range from sheer conformity to group pressures to an intense preoccupation with the content of playing.

10. Crespi, *op. cit.,* Chap. 7.

Broadway and the Flight from American Reality

By HENRY POPKIN

WE ARE ON THE THRESHOLD of a new Broadway season, but there seems
little reason to expect that it will depart in any fundamental way from the
pattern of the past season: a pattern of wholesale flight from the reality of
our lives. Several times during the past season it was possible to look at the
full list of current plays and observe that not one of them pretended to give
any kind of recognizable portrait of American life. To make this observation is not necessarily to enthrone the realistic or naturalistic plays that
excel in reproducing the surfaces of contemporary life; but the absence of
such plays, which have for decades been the staple of our dramatic fare, is
unquestionably a curious phenomenon.

And even more curious is the rigid consistency of the themes of most
of last season's plays. Almost without exception, they have shown the necessity of escaping from stultifying, imprisoning circumstances by some bold,
if unlikely, act. Usually there is one central character who is capable of
sincere feeling, or of emotional depths that no one around him can appreciate. He is chained to a psychic incompleteness, to childishness, by circumstances or by the apathy of those around him. And he cannot solve his
problems; he can only go away or commit suicide or commit murder or
retreat into dreams or memories of the past.

In most of the plays this childish dreamer is the character we are asked
to admire: that is quite clear, for instance, in such "serious" plays as Tennessee Williams' *Camino Real* and William Inge's *Picnic*. Here the "big
kids" are the play's heroes. Only a "trivial" play like Frederick Knott's
Dial M for Murder can afford to put forth a traditional, common-sense
attitude by making its overgrown, childlike man a villain, a murderer. Only
an unpretentious mystery-writer would be so cruel to childhood: in other
circles there seems to be an intellectual obligation to burrow deep into the
recollections of childhood and of the past, to live sentimentally, emotionally,
and nostalgically.

Perhaps the most striking manifestation of this back-to-the-cradle movement is the fiction of Truman Capote; it is no accident that Capote has
lately discovered in the New York theater a new audience for his nostalgia.
After an unsuccessful run on Broadway, his dramatized novel, *The Grass
Harp,* has been well received at the Circle in the Square in Greenwich Village. Malcolm Cowley has recently written that childhood nostalgia of the
sort Capote retails is all the rage in the huge stacks of novels that editors
are daily and hourly rejecting. And childishness is the rage, too, in the plays
that Broadway producers accept.

Reprinted from *Commentary*, Vol. 15, 1953, pp. 241-46, by permission of the author and
the publisher. (Copyright, 1953, by The American Jewish Committee.)

To be sure, many of Broadway's principal theatrical events belong to another category entirely, the musical production—"play" is getting to be an inexact word for them. The musicals do not pretend to be imitations of life; they improve on life by stylizing it. But perhaps one can build a bridge to the main theme of this essay by suggesting that this stylization bears some resemblance to the play-acting of children: in the child's conception of an actable character, only the salient traits, the most easily parroted ones, are retained. The same is true of our musical-comedy stylization, which is as fixed and almost as amusing as the Jonsonian comedy of "humours."

If our musical plays have not given us a whole gallery of "humorous" characters, at least they have perfected one archetype, a comic character who seems available for use in any kind of play. He is the tough-talking New Yorker who strains for a gentility of phrase that he can never quite attain. He seems to come equally from Arthur Kober's would-be-genteel Bronx maidens and from Damon Runyon's excessively polite roughnecks, who never speak in the past tense and never use contractions. His rise has been unmarked and unheralded, but this comic character has caught the popular imagination as has no other in our generation. He has even found his way into "serious" plays: Tennessee Williams, in *A Streetcar Named Desire* and *The Rose Tattoo,* has created roughnecks who aspire to a more elegant speech. More recently, we have found the Runyon-Kober archetype in *Guys and Dolls* (based on Runyon's stories), *Wish You Were Here* (based on Kober's earlier play), and John O'Hara's *Pal Joey.*

What characterizes Runyon's and O'Hara's tough guys most of all is an improbable air of aspiration. Joey pretends to an education at "Dartmouth University," and Runyon's gamblers are in constant danger of being reformed by their women or by the Salvation Army. But the loftiest aspiration—the aspiration toward a colorful syntax—is reserved for the toughest characters of all. In *Pay Joey* the fanciest line of talk is put out by the blackmailer, Ludlow Lowell, and in *Guys and Dolls* the glibbest "guys" are the Chicago killer Big Jule and his flunkey. The effect is one of incongruity: the ugliest characters use the prettiest words and get the most disarmingly comic effect. This intention succeeds here as elsewhere, for the incongruity of the New York roughneck's glib words and his base intentions has captured the national fancy. But the extraordinary popularity of this characterization should remind us that it really is a type. It amuses, it delights, it deserves all the praise it gets, but it has no genuine relation to reality.

The stylization of *Porgy and Bess* is equally obvious and much more familiar. Everyone knows and no one (well, practically no one) believes DuBose Heyward's myth of the shiftless, happy-go-lucky, pious, superstitious, razor-wielding Negroes of the Old South. To the audience that received *Native Son, On Whitman Avenue,* and *Deep Are the Roots, Porgy and Bess* is a harmless fiction and not a slander on the Negro, since to be a slander it would have to be taken for truth. Once more, stylization provides a holiday from real life and real people.

Stylized characterization is one refuge from reality; costume drama is another, especially if it is costume drama pretending to be something else. Arthur Miller's *The Crucible* is nominally about the Salem witch trials, but it is a matter of general agreement that this play is actually concerned with the trials and Congressional investigations of our own day. For most men of good will, the public issues of our time are sadly mixed. Neither the professional martyrs nor the professional Communist-hunters have consistently remained heroic figures. Occasionally, there is an innocent victim and sometimes a scrupulous accuser, but the real scene-stealers inspire no great warmth or sympathy. What Arthur Miller has done is to indulge a wish for clarity by simplification, creating a world in which the McCarthys are still McCarthys yet the Rosenbergs are no longer accused of espionage but rather of the unlikely crime of witchcraft. No longer need we entertain any embarrassing fears as to whether the accused actually dealt with some real Prince of Darkness. And if we need some symbolic parallel to their real twentieth-century guilt, we can have that, too: Miller's John Proctor has committed the irrelevant sin of adultery, and he is being accused by a jealous woman; this furnishes the shadow of a morally complicated situation without the substance. Thus *The Crucible,* widely hailed as the most "timely" play of the season, must also be classified as a dream-play. It is a great feeling, this luxuriating in simple black-and-white issues, but it is purchased only at the price of flight into the seventeenth century.

The Spewacks' *My Three Angels* offers an equally fanciful solution. Here we observe a family that faces a perplexing difficulty—how to forestall merciless creditors who insist on having a look at the books. The answer is simple—have some good angels appear to assassinate the creditors. The angels are as unreal and as incongruous as Ludlow Lowell and Big Jule; they are pleasant, reasonable men who happen, quite inconceivably, to be convicts on Devil's Island. Indeed, everything that happens here is only further evidence of the pure impossibility of the proceedings. The angelic identifications are supplied in full abundance, and they have the effect of suggesting that such a solution as this—or, in fact, any solution—to the real troubles of the world is as unlikely as an angelic visitation. In true angelic fashion, these three Devil's Island angels make their first entrance from above, where they have been repairing the roof. (This was a great season for entrances through the ceiling.) Their ministrations on behalf of their troubled friends invariably inspire analogies with divine interventions: "Praise the Lord from whom all blessings flow," we are told, and "The Lord giveth and the Lord taketh away," when one of the villains is hastened to his grave.

Such plays as these merely reject reality or thumb a nose at it. Other plays of the season made bolder recommendations of flight into an unknown, quixotic fantasy. William Inge and Tennessee Williams, who share with Arthur Miller the distinction of being regarded as our most promising playwrights, both enlisted themselves on the side of sentiment—for Williams this is one of several re-enlistments—in a world of conventionality and cynicism.

Hal Carter of Mr. Inge's *Picnic* comes out of nowhere to preach the gospel of love, of glory, of impractical individualism, footloose and footless, and he wins the prettiest girl in town away from the richest boy in town. All that seems substantial and real about Hal Carter is just what we can see—his physique, unveiled through most of the play; everything else is no more than a loud noise—his boasts of sexual adventures, of diving championships, of ventures in the oil business. But Hal's greatest asset is precisely his matchless unreliability. The girl must choose Hal because he is unknown and, so far as he is known, unstable. Curiously, it was reported that the ending of the play was changed out of town, that originally Inge ended *Picnic* without permitting the girl to follow Hal to Tulsa; I take it that the dramatist found out the iron strength of our stage conventions. This is predestination with a vengeance; a stage heroine is doomed, inevitably, to marry the poor boy whom she has just met. This heroine's mother did it in her time, and surely the daughter of the next generation will do it in time to come, if she happens to be a character in a Broadway play.

Exactly the same sort of decision was exhibited in another of the season's plays, Viña Delmar's *Midsummer*. Here the chief character is torn between being a high-school teacher or a vaudeville comedian. Miss Delmar tries out both endings (as Inge did by altering his ending on the road) by having her heroine prepare first for one life and then for another, but no one who has seen *Picnic* will have any trouble predicting the outcome of *Midsummer*: the little white house and the placid domesticity of the teacher's life must be rejected in favor of the romantic, uncertain, happy-go-lucky way of the actor.

In *Camino Real*, Tennessee Williams transmits his sentiments about sentiment more abstractly but no less doggedly. Here we follow one Kilroy who has arrived in a cruel, nameless country where the word "brother" is forbidden, where he must discard his mementoes of past pugilistic glory and become a "patsy," a professional victim, fully aware of the nightmare of present reality. Kilroy loses his golden gloves and his championship belt, and he learns the folly of responding to that sweetest of all words, "champ." But he ends up victoriously by joining the futile pilgrimage of Don Quixote, and we are told that the violets in the mountains have broken through the rocks. Williams' violets have a way of pulverizing their rocks—but why should they not? They are his violets and his rocks.

The rocks are rugged enough in *Camino Real*: the meaningless cruelty of this (evidently) Latin American community, the unspeakable indignities visited upon our Everyman Kilroy, the arbitrary violence of the burst of gunfire, the sinister threat of the ubiquitous street-cleaners who wait to cart away the dead. Who can hope or dream in such a world? But it is precisely because it is so arbitrary, so violent, so brutal that this world has been created, and the brave, sentimental souls of Casanova, Camille, Byron,

Don Quixote, and Kilroy have been created, or resurrected, to inhabit it. The authors of *Picnic* and *Midsummer* may measure out their unfriendly circumstances with coffee spoons, but Williams uses a ladle. And the moral is all the more strident: "Be Quixote; be quixotic."

Other plays of the season call for a collective treatment. They provide variations on the same theme. All seem to examine a real problem—the plight of the emotionally maladjusted person, particularly the person whose sexual drives are too strong or too weak for him to be at ease in society. The plays are uniformly on the side of love, but they can offer no solution except suicide, murder, escape into dreams, or flight to another country. Hester Collyer of Terence Rattigan's *The Deep Blue Sea* can find no male counterpart capable of her emotional depths; neither her affectionate but shallow husband nor her even shallower playboy-lover can give her the love she needs. In contrast with this pathetic picture, George Axelrod, in *The Seven Year Itch,* offers a comic portrait of a man whose emotional ambitions are limitless but whom society has kept in check for the duration of a seven-year marriage. Similarly, Leona Samish of Arthur Laurents' *The Time of the Cuckoo* has, in her career as a super-efficient secretary, neglected her career as a woman. Her recourse is to seek romance in Italy, for a large measure of her difficulty rests in the fact that she has the misfortune to be an American. On the other hand, Geoffrey Hawke's trouble, in Moss Hart's *The Climate of Eden,* is that he is a European, the product of a tradition-ridden civilization. Another play presents the complete emotional cripple who is completely satisfied with his emotional atrophy and strives only to make it permanent: Tony Wendice, the would-be killer of *Dial M for Murder*. Each of these people is restricted, inhibited, practically imprisoned; each play but the last records a desperate attempt to escape.

What these emotional deficients have in common is their childishness. They want to be children, and they show it, for one thing, by a somewhat nostalgic preoccupation with games and sports. We have remarked that Williams' Kilroy lives in the aura of his boxing championship and Inge's Hal Carter in the glory of his achievements as a football player. The murderous husband of *Dial M for Murder* is a retired tennis player whose triumphs are continually called to our attention by the silver cups that line his shelves. He, too, prefers to live in the past with his tennis victories. His addiction to stag parties seems intended as one of several symptoms of an aversion to facing his adult role as a husband. Similarly, the shallow lover of *The Deep Blue Sea* makes golf his full-time activity and dreams of his past glory as an RAF flier and a test pilot, two typical goals of childish aspiration. Childish in other matters as well, he continues to use RAF slang and to favor his male companions. On the other hand, the comic hero of *The Seven Year Itch* has childishness thrust upon him. We find him living in an enforced bachelorhood while his wife is away; he does not play tennis or golf, but, as the curtain rises, he makes his obeisance to the world of sports by listening to a baseball game on the radio. His wife has enjoined upon him a distinctive stigma of childhood by forbidding him to smoke or drink; he is reduced to sipping raspberry soda through a straw.

Occasionally the playwright employs adult children to set off the juvenility of his childish adults. *The Climate of Eden* provides one instance, but *The Time of the Cuckoo* is more emphatic: Leona Samish is forever being shocked by the sophistication of her ten-year-old guide, who swears, arranges romantic rendezvous in gondolas, and generally takes theft and adultery in his stride. Appropriately, the principal American characters, who are often referred to as "greedy children," are younger than the Europeans; the European head-start of centuries seems in a sense symbolized by this specific seniority in years. And, in addition, although both Americans and Italians might be expected to have language difficulties, it is always the Americans' linguistic troubles we are reminded of: like children, they are once more learning to speak, making mistakes, showing joy at the mastery of new words.

Such are the problems. As for solutions—you can always kill yourself or your tormentors. In *The Deep Blue Sea,* Hester is trying to commit suicide as the play begins, and she is dissuaded from a second attempt only by a very hasty and unconvincing compromise with life. The tennis-playing husband of *Dial M for Murder* plots his wife's death, ostensibly because he wants her money, but we may suspect that he is motivated also by an awareness of his inadequacy as a man. *The Seven Year Itch* toys with the possibility of murder. The subject is first broached by a psychiatrist, Dr. Brubaker, who describes his own "strong unconscious desire to murder my wife," adding that he has no actual wish "to do the good woman any bodily harm." Later, the play's principal character dreams that his wife shoots him upon learning of his infidelity. One way or another, a gun looks like a fairly satisfactory aid in escaping from a dilemma.

If there is nobody to kill, go away. This advice is especially suited to those who suffer from spiritual emptiness and long to be filled. Emotional hungers, loneliness, instability are taken to be merely features of the local scene; fulfillment lies beyond the sea. Leona Samish seeks it in Italy but she finds she is hopelessly childish before the warm-hearted, warm-blooded natives; she cannot accommodate herself to this freer, coarser world. Like two other recent plays, *The Grand Tour* and *In Any Language, The Time of the Cuckoo* seems to be asking, "If Ingrid Bergman could do it, why can't we?" And the same answer is heard in all three plays: "I don't know why, but you can't."

The great example of "going away" is Moss Hart's *The Climate of Eden.* In the Reverend Gerald Harmston's little settlement in British Guiana, everyone goes about his private quest for the Kingdom of Heaven, destroying every European "taboo" in sight and yet doing it almost perfunctorily, with a disarming tranquillity. To Geoffrey Hawke, a harried refugee from

European neuroses, this haven is at first as frightening as Italy to Leona Samish. Still, Hawke manages to adjust, to find an alternative to the real world in this free-wheeling Utopia. He is evidently plagued, however, by the original sin of belonging to the civilized world, for the parson tells his daughter: "This is not a way of life for him, my dear. Not forever. He thinks so now—but it isn't. . . . Our way of living is not life, Olivia—it's just a way of looking at life." But everything possible has been done to make "civilized" life look pallid and restrictive in comparison to Reverend Harmston's green paradise. These last qualifying words do not alter the picture. The climate of never-never land is much more pleasant than ours.

Even if you cannot take passage, no one can stop you from dreaming. *The Seven Year Itch* offers a series of wish-fulfillment dreams, taken from the troubled imagination of a man who lives in dread of what "People" will say. At work, he plans bosomy covers and sexy titles for pocket books; at home, he has been a model of fidelity for seven years. What is more natural than for his dreams to embody all the sexual cravings he had denied? He dreams out both his hopes and fears, and at last, after imagining a romance with the pretty girl upstairs, he actually has one—or does he? He tries to kiss her, takes her to dinner, and is finally bidden good night. And that would seem to conclude this abortive affair. Then the girl re-enters by a sort of trap-door, like the Spewacks' three angels, and, as the conventional phrase has it, she gives herself to him. Now, the existence of the trap-door has been "planted" well in advance, and yet the very fact of its use makes the events that follow a little less than real. I am reminded of a conversation I overheard many years ago when I was seeing a movie version of *A Christmas Carol*. The couple behind me were speculating as to the reality of one of the Christmas Spirits, who had just left by the window. My neighbor remarked: "If the window closes, it's only a dream; the ghost isn't real." Whereupon the window slammed shut. The same principle applies in *The Seven Year Itch*. If on this occasion the girl had come through the door, as she does in all her undeniably real appearances, it would have been possible to believe in the events that followed, but her coming through the ceiling lends an unmistakable touch of fantasy. What would you think if a pretty girl came through *your* ceiling? Precisely! Surely this is no more than one dream following another. The play's hero first has some less spectacular, less convincing dreams of romance; then, so to speak, he turns over and dreams on the other side, this time producing a vision that is much more exciting and even more convincing. This is enough to solve his problem; he is able even to face the prospect of seeing his wife again.[1]

All that remains is to wonder *why* this motif of flight so dominates the recent theater and the rest of our popular arts. Why are we always in flight for the solace of sentiment, childhood, and the world of dreams? One likely answer could be found on the front page of any newspaper. I don't mean to say, with Arthur Miller, that the trouble is the shadow of McCarthy over the land. No, the trouble is McCarthy and everything else. We live with the atomic bomb and under a permanent threat of war. Who wouldn't rather be eight years old?

This answer may be far too easy. There are always advantages in being eight years old. The point is that the desire to be eight years old is no advantage to a dramatist if he wants to write adult drama.

Note

1. Two years after these words were written, the film version of *The Seven Year Itch* turned the seduction scene into a dream. This change was made in deference to the Hollywood Production Code, but I find it a striking justification of my comment.

FURTHER READING

Adorno, T. W. "A Social Critique of Radio Music," *Kenyon Review,* Vol 7, 1945, pp. 208-17.

Balliett, Whitney. "Jazz Today," *Atlantic,* Vol. 192, 1953, pp. 76-81.

Barzun, Jacques. "Kind Word for Pop, Bop and Folk," *Reporter,* Vol. 14, 1956, pp. 36-39.

Borneman, Ernest. *The Critic Looks at Jazz.* London: Jazz Music Books, 1946. (Originally published serially in the U.S. magazine *Record Changer,* under the title "The Anthropologist Looks at Jazz.")

Feather, Leonard. "What is Jazz: A Musical Analysis," *The Encyclopedia of Jazz.* New York: Horizon Press, 1953.

Handy, W. C. *Father of the Blues.* New York: Macmillan, 1941.

Harris, Rex. *Jazz.* New York: Penguin, 1952.

Hentoff, Nat, and Shapiro, Nat. *Hear Me Talkin' to Ya—the Story of Jazz by the Men Who Made It.* New York: Rinehart, 1955.

Hobson, Wilder. *American Jazz Music.* New York: W. W. Norton, 1937.

Hoffman, David G. "Jazz: the Survival of a Folk Art," *Perspectives: USA,* Vol. 15, 1956, pp. 29-42.

Levy, Hal. "A Lyric is a Sometime Thing," *New Republic,* Vol. 131, 1954, pp. 16-17.

Merriam, Alan P. (ed.) *A Bibliography of Jazz.* Philadelphia: American Folklore Society, Bennett Hall, University of Pennsylvania, 1953.

Riesman, David, and Denney, Reuel. "Football in America: A Study in Culture Diffusion," *American Quarterly,* Vol. 4, 1951, pp. 309-25.

Shaw, Artie. *The Trouble With Cinderella.* New York: Farrar, Straus and Young, 1952.

Spaeth, Sigmund. *A History of Popular Music in America.* New York: Random House, 1948.

Stearns, Marshall W. "Is Jazz Good Propaganda? The Dizzy Gillespie Tour," *Saturday Review,* Vol. 39, 1956, pp. 28-31.

Swados, Harvey. "Popular Music and the New Man of Skill," *Dissent,* Vol. 1, 1954, p. 269.

Ulanov, Barry. *A History of Jazz in America.* New York: Viking, 1952.

7
Advertising

ADVERTISING

In the kingdom of mass culture, advertising is the prime minister. Critics and defenders of popular art alike recognize advertising as a powerful economic and social force in modern society. During his waking hours, an American is exposed to a wide variety of persuasive techniques whose aim is to make him desire and ultimately buy something.

There are few Americans who would fail to identify the advertising slogans of the great corporations. Even those who don't smoke have LSMFT indelibly imbedded in their consciousness. Radio jingles, television commercials, the cards on the walls of the subways, busses, and streetcars in which he rides to and from his work, all practice the Big Sell. Whereas an ancient queen needed four handmaidens to anoint her with frankincense and myrrh, any number of modern advertising modalities assure us that the magic qualities of a bar of Vanisheen will make our womenfolk beautiful, free from blemishes, and desirable.

The urge to advertise goes back to antiquity, where one would have found the walls in Herculaneum and Pompeii covered with announcements of the "spectaculars" of the day, gladiatorial shows. Modern advertising, however, was given its greatest impetus with the advent of the printing press. Nowhere has it found a more receptive climate than in the United States, where advertising revenue exceeds five billion dollars annually. Of this figure, newspaper advertising accounts for about one-third and magazines about one-tenth. The new media are making themselves felt, year by year, in the competition for the advertising dollar. Television, for example, increased tenfold in advertising revenue from 1949 to 1953. In 1955, it exceeded a billion dollars.

To Marshall McLuhan, American advertising has developed a jungle of folklore "beside which the tales from the Schwartzwald belong with Winnie-the-Pooh." In the realm of the "dramatic" advertisement, he says, Americans have paced the field.

Messrs. White, Albert and Seeger have analyzed newspaper advertisements for approximately 1000 movies from the period of 1935-1955. The advertisements for the most part appear to be directed toward a public with a "teen-age mind." Content analysis of the ads indicates that next to the build-up of the stars in terms of glamour, the most widely used elements are sex and violence. Even films that contain little emphasis on either sex or violence are often advertised in such a misleading way as to allow the public to infer that sex and violence are main themes in the films.

American Advertising

By MARSHALL McLUHAN

A FEW MONTHS AGO an American army officer wrote for *Printer's Ink* from Italy. He noted with misgiving that Italians could tell you the names of cabinet ministers but not the names of commodities preferred by Italian celebrities. Furthermore, the wall space of Italian cities was given over to political rather than commercial slogans. Finally, he predicted that there was small hope that Italians would ever achieve any sort of domestic prosperity or calm until they began to worry about the rival claims of cornflakes or cigarettes rather than the capacities of public men. In fact, he went so far as to say that democratic freedom very largely consists in ignoring politics and worrying about the means of defeating underarm odour, scaly scalp, hairy legs, dull complexion, unruly hair, borderline anaemia, athlete's foot, and sluggish bowels, not to mention ferro-nutritional deficiency of the blood, wash-day blues, saggy breasts, receding gums, shiny pants, greying hair, and excess weight. Here we are perhaps in the presence of an excluded middle rather than a *non sequitur,* because American advertising has developed into a jungle of folklore beside which the tales from the Schwartzwald belong with Winnie-the-Pooh.

It is, therefore, quite possible that there is a core of political reality and even health in the wildly proliferating forms of American advertising. The hyperaesthesia of the ad-men's rhetoric has knocked the public into a kind of groggy, slap-happy condition in which perhaps are cushioned a good many of the brutal shocks felt more keenly by the realistic European. Viewed merely as an interim strategy for maintaining hope, tolerance, and good humour in an irrational world, this orgy of irrationalism may not be without its cathartic function. At any rate, the multi-billion dollar, nationwide educational programmes of the ad-men (dwarfing the outlay on formal education) provide a world of symbols, witticism, and behavior patterns which may or may not be a fatal solvent for the basic political traditions of America, but which certainly do comprise a common experience and a common language for a country whose sectional differences and technological specialisms might easily develop into anarchy. The comedian at the microphone or the professor in the classroom can always be sure of an effective gibe or illustration based on the ads. And both community and communication, in so far as they are managed at all at the popular level, are in the same debt. Moreover, by various means, the whole technique and hallucination of Hollywood has been assimilated to the ads *via* pic-

Reprinted from *Horizon*, No. 93-4, October, 1947, pp. 132-41, by permission of the author and the publisher. (Copyright, 1947, by Horizon.)

torial glamour, so that the two are inseparable. They constitute one world.

It is just as well to preface a glance at American ads with a consideration of the imponderables, because the ads themselves are deceptively
easy to assess. A similar abeyance of judgement about the social effects of
the sadism purveyed, for example, by thriller and detective literature is
indicated. For the extent to which armchair sadism, so fostered, acts as
a preservative of good humour in a lethal and chaotic world it is impossible
to say. But anybody can check for himself the fact that persons with a
penchant for strong-arm political methods are not given to this form of
fantasy life. It is, of course, true that the thriller and sleuth fans, from Poe
to Ellery Queen, are the willing victims of a psychological trick. By identifying their mental processes with those of the manhunter, the readers
achieve a sort of megalomaniac thrill. At the same time they enjoy the illusion of sharing in the scientific techniques of the society which permits them
almost no other kind of congenial adjustment or direct participation. "Happiness," said Swift, "is the possession of being perpetually well-deceived."
And in a merely political regard we cannot any longer dispense with any
source of happiness which will win us a bit of time while we consult the
means of survival.

The intellectual claims to perceive and enjoy an order and symmetry
in the world and in his own life denied to other men. He arms himself today
against the impact of the stereotypes of commercialized culture by keen-
ness of recognition and analysis and engages in a perpetual guerrilla activity.
He is a sort of noble savage free-lancing amidst a zombie horde. The dangers
attending this mode of existence are obvious. Should he find his energies
suddenly depleted or his patience exasperated, he may be tempted to revive
them by adopting some lethal myth-mechanism. And at all times he finds
it hard to remember the common human nature which persists intact beneath
all the modes of mental hysteria rampant from Machiavelli and Calvin until
our own day. Yet it is only in the degree to which he is motivated by the
benevolence imposed by the perception of the rational form rather than
the psychological condition of all men, that he is justified or that he is tolerable. Benda was right. When the intellectual sells out to any brand of social
or political neurosis, when fear or loneliness beckon him into some party,
he is worse than useless. *Corruptio optimi pessima.*

American "market research," which has developed very rapidly in the
past ten years, has a strong totalitarian squint—that of the social engineer.
Two recent items will illustrate this. *Time* magazine for 22 July 1946, described a new gadget:

The finished—but still uncut—picture [movie] is given the works with an
electrical contraption called the Hopkins Televoting System. Each member of
A.R.I.'s [Audience Research Inc.] hand-picked, cross-section audience sits in a
wired section of a preview theater. With his eyes on the screen, he clutches a
gadget that resembles a flashlight. On the gadget's round face is an indicator
that can easily be turned with the fingers. A turn to the right means "Like,"
further right "Like Very Much." A left twist registers as "Dull" or "Very Dull."

The emotional reactions of A.R.I.'s watchers flow into a central machine which combines them all into one big wavy line. This chart, picturing the audience's peaks of ecstasy and valleys of apathy, shows the manufacturer where to trim out dull spots in his picture. It is known as a Preview Profile.

Moviemakers used to throw good advertising money after bad to promote an expensive flop. A.R.I. advises just the opposite. If the Preview Profile looks bad, the ad budget might just as well be slashed. If the preview pans out better than expected, the picture is given special treatment and bigger ballyhoo.

Criteria of cinema art aside, this kind of action for direct social control is politics. It aims not only at providing more and more sensation, but at the exploitation of all emotional sets and preferences as just so much raw material to be worked up by centralized control for purposes of super-profits. Clearly the manipulators of such controls are irresponsible and will probably so continue as long as the flow of merchandise and profits remains unchecked.

Meantime, these appetites for private power are inventing the means of possible political power for the future. And even these private activities are obviously political, indirectly. Perhaps, however, the relevant observation here is simply that appetite is essentially insatiable, and where it operates as the criterion of both action and enjoyment (that is, everywhere in the western world since the sixteenth century) it will infallibly discover congenial agencies (mechanical and political) of expression. Almost any political steps taken to curb the A.R.I. type of mind would inevitably transfer this private anarchy into a public tyranny, because that "mind" is not an exceptional one—it is universal. Actually, the A.R.I. type of activity provides our world with a spectacular externalized paradigm of its own inner drives. Creative political activity today, therefore, consists in rational contemplation of these paradigms. Carried out as an educational programme directed towards self-knowledge and self-criticism, the study of these sprightly fantasies of unrestricted appetitive life would constitute precisely that step toward moral and intellectual regeneration which we have always known must precede any sort of genuine improvement. To contemplate the products of our own appetites rather than to anathematize the people who are keen enough to exploit them—that is surely no programme which must await the setting up of committees or social machinery. It is the only form of adult education which could be called realistic and it is instantaneously practicable. That the highbrows have been content merely to cock a snook at the fauna and flora of popular commercial culture is sufficient testimony to the superficiality with which they have envisaged the nature of politics.

In this respect, the American is in a much happier position than the Englishman whose advertisements are such half-hearted and apologetic attempts to externalize his hopes and fears and appetites. American advertising is Cartesian. The English is Baconian. The American responds to showmanship, clarity of layout and distinctness of formulation. The Englishman, to judge by his ads (and I have some scores by me, collected in England over a period of three years), in his timid concern for demure good form falls into the empirical bog of self-defensive puns, archness, and snob-appeal. The American ad-men put on a decisively superior show and provide the analyst with a much greater variety of lively game. But to establish a national pre-eminence in this province is not to make more general claims.

The second item illustrating the totalitarian techniques of American market research occurs in a paper called "New Facts about Radio Research," by Arthur C. Nielsen, president of the A. C. Nielsen Company, "the world's largest marketing research organization." The paper appeared in 1946. It begins:

A. C. Nielsen Company, founded in 1923, provides an example of outstanding success based on long, unswerving and intelligent devotion to a difficult but worthy task. Educated in various branches of engineering and science, and accustomed to dealing with tangible facts, the early leaders of this company were convinced that some means could be found to substitute facts for much of the guesswork then used in guiding corporate marketing operations.

Despite the commercial failure of all methods developed during the first ten years of operation, despite staggering operating losses which twice brought them to the brink of disaster, this group of pioneers persevered—because the great importance of the goal was very clear, and because some of the experiments seemed to show promise.

The tone of austere scientific dedication to a noble task is not phoney in any simple sense. The language of "human service" is rooted in the respectable neurotic formula of Adam Smith—public good through private greed—a face-saving device which developed a complex face of its own in the nineteenth century. In other words, the kind of self-deception in the language of "public service" is no longer private, but is vertically and horizontally effective, in the English-speaking world at least. The Rousseauistic formula to get the good Society by liquidating "civilization," or the Marxian formula to get the classless society by liquidating the "middle class," are psychologically analogous—massive mechanisms of evasion and irresponsibility.

Well, the Nielsen Company have now lifted the problem of estimating audience character from the level of conjecture to that of certitude. The advertiser sponsoring any given programme wants to know precisely:

(a) Average duration of listening; i.e., "holding power" of the programme.

(b) Variations in audience size at each minute during the broadcast —to permit detection of programme elements which cause audience gains or losses, to locate commercials at moments when the audience is high, etc.

(c) Whether the programme reaches homes that *already* use the product, or homes that offer opportunities for *conversion* of new users.

For this purpose the Nielsen Audimeter has been devised, "the graphic recording instrument installed in a radio receiver in a scientifically selected radio home. By recording every twist of the dial, every minute of the day or night, the Audimeter obtains precious radio data not available through any other means." The Audimeter's data are then tabulated by "The Nielsen Decoder," which is only "one of the many mechanized operations which are producing high values for NIELSEN RADIO INDEX clients." And the installation of audimeters is determined "with utmost care to insure precise proportioning in accordance with a long list of marketing characteristics, including: 1, City size; 2, Family size; 3, Number of rooms; 4, Education; 5, Occupation; 6, Income; 7, Type of dwelling; 8, Number of radio receivers. The characteristics of each N.R.I. home are rechecked monthly, and replacement homes are chosen in a manner which keeps the sample accurately balanced at all times." Moreover, "relations with N.R.I. homes are maintained on such a sound basis that home turnover is limited largely to unavoidable and normal occurrences (e.g., deaths, divorces, fires, removals)."

The direction, as well as the appetitive drive, in this sort of research (the Gallup Polls of public opinion are a more obvious but less impressive instance of the same thing) is to be noted in a recent book on *Reaching Juvenile Markets*. Like most American texts on advertising, it was written by a professional psychologist—in this case a child-psychologist. The book points to the enormous proportion of American income which is expended by and for children and analyses a variety of means for bringing child-pressure on the parents to increase and to control such expenditures. Children are more snobbish than adults, more concerned to conform to the tastes of the community in the use of well-known commercial brands, and so on. The schools offer a means for the subtle subsidization of various products. Special Lone Ranger and Superman radio features for children can do much, but the potentialities of this market are only beginning to be appreciated, etc.

A more common type of advertising manual, however, is that represented by *Psychology in Advertising* by A. T. Poffenberger, Ph.D., Sc.D., Professor of Psychology at Columbia University. This sort of book makes available to the copywriter the results of psychiatric research: "The psychoanalysts have made popular the conception of a kind of behavior which is a sort of compromise between the behavior growing out of desire and thinking behavior" (p. 15). To exploit the irrational and, at all times, to avoid the pitfalls of rational "sales resistance" aroused by the inept ad is the first law of advertising dynamics. Forty-four kinds of "attention-getting power" are graded (p. 90) in accordance with their statistically tested potency in an average community. At the top of the list are: Appetite-hunger 9.2; Love of offspring 9.1; Health 9.0; Sex attraction 8.9. And at the end of the list: Amusement 5.8; Shyness 4.2; Teasing 2.6. "Announcing the birth of a Petunia," said an ad in which a man and woman were bent over a flowerpot: "It takes emotion to move merchandise. *Better Homes and Gardens* [a magazine] is perpetual emotion."

Recently, with much public irritation being expressed at the blatancy, duration and frequency of radio commercials, careful tests have been made to determine the effect on the market. The result has been the discovery that irritation has great "attention-getting power" and that those irritated in this respect are reliable customers. Nausea has, therefore, become a new principle of commercial dynamics as of esthetics. It is not likely, however, to supplant but to reinforce the more familiar techniques, the most important of which is noted many times by Professor Poffenberger: "An appeal through the visual representation of motion will almost invariably find the nerve paths for that motion open, and is thus bound to get the attention of the reader and to induce in him some form of action" (p. 297). It is in their imaginative grasp of this dramatic principle that the American ad.-men are first and the rest nowhere.

"Have you the courage to look ready for Romance: Want to look like a dream walking? . . . Well, you can, so easily! *Just by changing your powder shade!* . . . A delightful 'come hither' look that's so young and feminine— so very inviting!" (A bride in wedding-dress is joyfully whispering this to a thoughtful lady.)

A rugged and determined man with a cigar glints at the reader of a full-page ad of a clothing shop: "I'm TOUGH. Panty-waist stuff burns me. Work ten hours a day. Been at it since I was a kid. Gang at the plant call me 'Chief.' Own the place, now. Sure I've made money. Not a million —but enough to buy steak . . . And good clothes. Been getting my duds at Bond's ever since I shed knee pants . . . No big promises. No arty labels dangling high-hat prices. Just good clothes with plenty of guts."

Obviously the dramatic ad. is a maker of "patterns of living" as much as the speech and gestures of movie idols. The peculiar idiom of a dead-end kid or a psychological freak may thus be sent up to the firing line of a nation-wide advertising campaign to provide temporary emotional strategies for millions of adolescents: A wishful but futile gent beside a self-possessed girl on a love-seat: "I love you! said Pete. 'I like you, too!' said Ann. 'Tell me more,' said Pete. 'You look *so* nice, especially around the neck.' 'Ah,' said Pete. 'That is my Arrow Collar.' . . . P.S. Tough, Pete. But remember —where there's an Arrow, can a girl be far behind?" The ads help old and young to "get hep."

An extremely popular technique is the dramatic sequence presented in four or five separate scenes: Tommy comes home from school with a black eye and is questioned by his lovely young mother. He reluctantly tells her that the kids have been taunting him about how his father is going out with other women. He has had to defend his mother's sex-appeal. Mortified, she hastens to get the appropriate toothpaste. Next morning, Mom, radiant in panties and bra', brushing her teeth in the bathroom, tells Tommy "it works." Later, Tommy and his friends peek round the corner into the living-room where Dad is waltzing Mom around to radio music. "Gee," says one of the kids, "looks like he's going to haul off and kiss her." "Yep," says Tommy, "you can't say my Dad hangs around with other girls now."

This sort of Ad appears in the Sunday Comic Section. Reaching the Juvenile Market.

"Success story of a man in a high position." Picture of blithesome business man seated aloft in the petals of a huge daffodil: "Sitting pretty? You bet . . . this fellow knows how to win and influence customers! He keeps track of their important business events and honors each occasion by sending wonderful fresh flowers by Wire." The wit of the pictorial feature includes an allusion to Jack's bean-stalk.

A nearly nude debutante with zestful abandon applying perfume and sparkling at the reader: "I'm using 'Unconditional Surrender' since he got 6NX Appeal!" "How can *you* get 6NX Appeal? . . . by using the only blades created by the scientific, secret 6NX process. . . . 'Single' men can reach for a star, too!" This is typical of the indirect approach to the American male. Psychological tests prove that he is shy of direct efforts to interest him in glamorizing himself. As social catalysts the ads help also to overcome boy-girl shyness. The girl spots 6NX or some other approved mark of compliance with nationally accredited goods. The boys smells "Unconditional Surrender," and the first thing you know they're able to converse. College courses in "charm" and "gallantry" may soon be unnecessary.

A beautiful girl seated by the telephone while Mom, troubled, hovers in doorway: "Borderline Anaemia deprives a girl of glamor . . . and dates! Medical science says: Thousands who have pale faces—whose strength is at low ebb—may have a blood deficiency. So many girls are 'too tired' to keep up with the crowd—watch romance pass them by because they haven't the energy to make them attractive!"

These ads console and encourage the forlorn by picturing the solitude and neglect suffered by the most ravishing chicks. They analyse the causes of every type of human failure and indicate the scientifically certified formula for "instantaneous or money-back results." The fault is not in our stars but our jars that we are underlings. They display the most ordinary persons surrounded by luxury and old-world charm, suggesting that "a prince and a castle are given away free with every package." The most trashy types of food, crockery, or furniture are exhibited in palatial circumstances. And this "law of association" leads the larger business monopolies to sponsor "the arts" by presenting their product always in conjunction with some aroma of the old masters of paint, pen or music. But just how far these billionaire campaigns of systematic sophistry and hallucination contribute to worsening any given state of affairs would be hard to say. Because there is really nothing in these richly efflorescent ads which has not been deeply wished by the population for a long time. They aren't so much phenomena of a Machiavellian tyranny as the poor man's orchids—both a compensation and a promise for beauty denied. Now, moreover, that the luxuriant and prurient chaos of human passions is thrust forward and gyrated in this way for our daily contemplation, there is the increasing possibility of the recovery of rational detachment. The authors of the Declaration of Independence and the American Constitution were not obsessed with some compulsive psychological strategy for disguising their own irrational wishes or intentions like a Rousseau or a Nietzsche. And their wisdom is far from extinct in the U.S.A. So that, should the energy which activates the ad-men (and the industrial stalks on which they are the passion-flowers) be transferred to the world of political speculation and creation, America could still fulfill many of its broken Utopian promises, because its Jeffersonian tradition is still intact, and likewise its psychological vigour. The two things aren't flowing in the same channels, however, and that is precisely the thing which could be brought about by a frank educational programme based on the curriculum provided by the ad-men.

Hollywood's Newspaper Advertising: Stereotype of a Nation's Taste

by DAVID M. WHITE AND ROBERT S. ALBERT,
WITH THE ASSISTANCE OF R. ALLAN SEEGER

HISTORICAL ANALYSIS SHOWS that most newspaper advertisements for motion pictures, until approximately 1935, were straightforward, simple announcements of the picture's title and its actors. Then, for reasons beyond the purview of this paper, the motion picture industry changed its approach and methods in its newspaper ads. Perhaps this came about because the Depression necessitated a "big sell," perhaps because intensive competition was coming from radio with its widely-listened-to "soap operas" for the women who attended matinee performances. Conceivably, Hollywood took a cue from the way in which daytime serials kept up their listeners' interests about Young Doctor Trent day after day. ("Will young Dr. Trent perform the operation of Milly Sandstone, knowing that her real name is Karen Slogg and that she is really the long-lost daughter of his mother by her long-lost second marriage?") But where the radio had only to sell detergents, tooth paste and depilatories, and the entertainment was "free," Hollywood still had a disadvantage to overcome, i.e., it had to charge admission for its product. Depression, competition, whatever the cause for the change, there emerged a "new look" in Hollywood's ads.

This new type of advertising used a technique similar to the movie's "trailer," that is, it selected a situation purportedly from the movie and dramatized it in the ad. At first, it was only a sentence or two, which might describe the star of the picture, such as, "Tempestuous Clara Bow puts on her charms for the timid professor."

Later, text and pictures of the actors were used. This became the prevalent device. In most cases, a theme was utilized which it was supposed —and hoped—would create a mixture of curiosity ("Why did Helen Greg shoot her lover?") and desire to know how the drama is resolved.

The purpose of the present study is to examine the specific thematic appeals which the motion picture industry thought would be successful in bringing patrons into the theaters.

Nearly 1,000 movie advertisements were analyzed, covering the period from 1935 through 1955.[1] Our raw material was collected and coded by students in the School of Public Relations and Communications, Boston University, under the supervision of the authors. The material was gathered from advertisements appearing each Thursday (the day when new movies are first shown). The main motion picture advertisement appearing on that day in each of three newspapers (the Boston *Globe,* the Boston *Record-Amer-*

ican and the New York *Times*) was studied. Each coder was responsible for a single year, with more than one student taking the same year to allow a check on coder reliability. The Boston *Globe* was selected because it is avowedly a "family" newspaper, the Boston *Record-American* is a tabloid whose content consists mainly of "sensational" material. The New York *Times* was chosen as representative of a conservative, "highbrow" newspaper of highest quality. We were interested in ascertaining whether the ads were directed at different class audiences hypothetically represented by the three different newspapers. Actually, we found that in most cases the same advertisement, i.e., the identical themes, appeared in all three publications.

The study was to test our hypotheses. First, we hypothesized that the main emphasis of movie advertising from 1935 to 1955 has been on sex and violence. The results did not bear this out precisely, since the main focus of the advertising appears to be on the film's stars. However, in another sense, sex *is* the dominant theme of the advertisements, for the stars are not exempt from being explicitly described in terms of their physical attributes. One star, for example, was always referred to throughout her screen career as Marie "The Body" McDonald.

Another good example of a case in which the stars and their physical proportions together make up the major theme of the ads may be seen in the campaign for the recent movie *Trapeze*. Both in billboard and newspaper ads the emphasis was on certain predominant proportions of the anatomy of its feminine star, Gina Lollobrigida. The color of her circus costume (a fleshy pink—more fleshy than pink) accentuated the obviously desired effect of the ad. Not missing a trick, the ad depicted Miss Lollobrigida in a passionate embrace with Burt Lancaster while both were doing a turn on the flying trapeze—an inaccurate, if no less astounding, tour de force on the part of stars and admen alike. Whether or not all red-blooded male Americans are thrown into an erotic stupefaction by contemplating Miss Lollobrigida's upper torso development and envision themselves flying through space so conjoined, obviously Hollywood's advertising and publicity moguls think so.[2]

Next to selling motion pictures by focusing on the personality of the stars, sex and violence do appear to be the most conspicuous element in movie advertisements. Approximately 76 per cent of the 970 films in our sample contained an element of either sex or violence, or both. Moreover, the number of ads containing sex or violence seems to be increasing. About 84 per cent of our postwar sample contains one or both of these elements. (We shall examine this aspect of the study in detail later.)

The second hypothesis investigated was that, because of various factors (such as the intense competition from television which mandated the "Movies Are Better Than Ever" campaign), Hollywood has recently been turning from stressing sex and violence toward a larger emphasis on the quality of the film. Our findings did not bear this out; but rather it appears that the reverse may be happening.

The third hypothesis was that the stars, being an important part of the Hollywood system, are an important part of movie advertising and that their importance has remained fairly constant during the period of our study. This seems to be true; moreover, the emphasis on stars (previously pointed out) appears to be growing. The median number of stars shown per ad in the prewar period was two; for the war and postwar periods it has risen to three.

The last of our primary hypotheses was that there has been a marked change in the emphasis, techniques and "gimmicks" used in movie advertising during the period of the study. There does not seem to be much of a change in emphasis other than the increase in the number of ads containing sex and violence. However, certain techniques and "gimmicks" seem to find favor with the publicity departments of the studios during certain periods of time. During the early 1950's, for example, a high percentage of ads emphasized the process of the film (i.e., 3-D, wide screen, Cinemascope 55, *et al.*).

One important conclusion from this study is that motion picture newspaper advertising is highly ambiguous. Most of the time it is virtually impossible to tell *anything* about the quality of the film from its advertisement. This is true even for the legitimately high quality films, e.g., such as *Cyrano de Bergerac,* which won at least one Academy Award, and which was advertised in the New York *Times* with the following text:

> In all history—no lover as daring as Cyrano—who loved the girl he loved so his rival could love her! See! Only a woman who valued love above everything could dare such a wild dash for freedom—for her man!

Possibly the publicity rationale behind such an ad was that one did not have to worry about serious moviegoers (that small segment of students of cinema art, "longhairs," who go to very few but highly selected movies, etc.) for they, knowing something about the story, would attend this picture anyway; therefore, the advertising campaign should be directed at the millions who had never read *Cyrano* or heard of Edmund Rostand. The overt appeal of this advertisement is that it conjures up the image of a Great Lover, which, considering the drama itself, is patently ludicrous as well as somewhat misleading.

If one is to understand more about Hollywood's own stereotype of Americans' well-concealed dreams and deep-held desires, it seems necessary to examine more closely the themes of sex and violence which abound in motion picture advertising. We observed and coded certain elements of the ads that seemed to come under the category of sex. These elements included: cheesecake, i.e., women in various forms of undress so as to display portions of their anatomy; positive indications of sexual aggression on the part of any of the characters shown in the advertisements; pictures or text indicating moral or immoral sexual experiences, including indications of unmarried parenthood, premarital sexual relations and unfaithfulness; crimes involving sex as a motive or as the nature of the crime, such as rape, etc.; indications of love or desire on the part of the characters; and embracing shown or mentioned in the ad. The number of ads containing one or more of these factors has *always* been high (during our sample periods) and shows an increase over the years, with most years having frequencies of more than 50 per cent of the sample. It can be said that if the leading film characters are the lodestars, sex is definitely used as the lodestone, of motion picture advertisements.

The frequency of ads containing some sex element did not reach as high as 50 per cent in the prewar period. After a very low number of frequencies in 1941 the total per sample year made a big jump to approximately 69 per cent in 1942 and, although it fell off a bit during the next two years, stayed at a high plateau until it reached its peak in 1951 of 70 per cent. After 1951 the frequency began to decline and in 1955 fell below the 50 per cent mark for the first time since 1941.

The most frequent form of sex in the newspaper ads is of the *cheesecake* variety. Cheesecake takes many forms in newspaper advertising; it can be the star in an overtight sweater, skimpy bathing suit or low-cut gown, or it can be a showgirl in tights standing in the background of the ad. The number of ads that displayed cheesecake during the prewar period was very low. Slightly over 9 per cent of the sample of that period contained cheesecake photos. During the war period, however, the frequency of cheesecake rose to 27 per cent of the sample, and in the postwar period it has risen to more than 30 per cent.

Next to cheesecake, the most common form of sex in motion picture advertising is some sort of embracing, either hugging or kissing. The prewar period showed a very small percentage of the ads using this appeal, but during the war years ads showing embraces rose to 19 per cent of the total sample for that period and the postwar period showed an increase to 27 per cent of all ads.

Those ads which state or imply that some form of sexual relationship exists between the characters in the movie also usually suggest immorality. Whether this is because of some unwritten code similar to the "crime does not pay" axiom, or whether there is a stereotype that sexual relations are always immoral, is a moot question. Drs. Wolfenstein and Leites in their psychological study of movies have described the "good-bad girl" gambit of the postwar films, exemplified by such films as *Gilda*. The ads for this Rita Hayworth film exploited the "immoral" aspect of the protagonist. Although only 6 per cent of the ads in the prewar sample contained some indication of immorality on the part of the characters shown or mentioned, the postwar sample shows an increase of this type of appeal to 15 per cent of the sample.

Though *love* is an often-used (and much abused) word in movie ads, marriage, interestingly enough, is seldom mentioned one way or another.

Out of the total sample of 970 ads only twenty-six mentioned marriage. And, of these, only three indicate that marriage is desirable for the female but do not mention the male's point of view, while ten indicate explicitly that marriage is desirable for the *female* but *not* for the male; just five indicate that it is desirable for *both* male and female, and four say that it is undesirable for either. Of the twenty-six ads only one shows that marriage is desirable for the male. It would appear that here, as in other phases of its advertising, Hollywood reinforces—deliberately or not—the anxious "jokes" of the great American middle class. One gets the unhappy feeling that the advertising executives of the studios have their fingers heavy upon the pulse of the Lynds' "Middletown," or do their homework by reading Max Weber's *The Protestant Ethic*—translated into Basic English.

So much for the lively art of marriage, Hollywood-style. When one looks again at the ads one finds sex still there. In fact, it never leaves. Many of the characters shown in motion picture advertisements are definitely implied to be sexually aggressive. More often this is the female character rather than the male. Not only is this state of events a preoccupation of the ads, but there also has been a substantial increase in this category since the end of the war. At times this aggression is self-directed, as in the choice bit of masochism described in the advertisement for *To Please A Lady*:[3]

Hot News! This girl said "No!" to Gable (but not for long). When it comes to taming a haughty lady Gable knows what to do. The rougher he treated her, the better she liked it. When he slapped her on the face, she knew she was madly in love.

Allied to this approach is the type of advertisement that might be termed the "sex in neurosis" school. This variation on *the* theme was well typified by the ad for the movie, *The Cobweb*.[4]

They told everything about shame—the neglected wife who sought love—the girl who feared to be kissed—the boy who couldn't face life—the psychoanalyst's couch held their most intimate secrets in the mansion on the hill.

Although sex is often advertised in a manner as to suggest trauma, psychoanalysis as a means of therapy rarely appears either in the movies or in their ads. The ad implies that the analyst is a mysterious, perhaps Svengali-like character, if not himself the villain. This approach to psycho-analysis by Hollywood is consistent with "Middletown's" ambivalent view of "head-shrinkers."

Whatever one might think, Hollywood knows the varieties of Id as well as William James understood the varieties of religious experience. Sex is not the only powerful emotion used as bait in ads. Crime and violence, too, play an important part in motion picture advertising, though seemingly not so great a role as that played by sex. Violence was the major element of action in only a little more than 8 per cent of the prewar sample, 11 per cent of the war period sample, and has risen to 17 per cent of the postwar sample.

The two most frequent themes of violence depicted were those in which males fought males, and (with only a slightly lower frequency) those in which violence occurred between male and female. In both cases we noted a marked increase in the postwar period.

One out of every five advertisements during the twenty-year period had illustrations or text (or both) which implied some sort of crime. These various crimes were coded into seventeen different categories, such as murder, sex crimes, organized gangs, crimes of intrigue, manslaughter, etc. Of these crimes, not only was the number of ads dealing with murder the greatest, but it also seems to be increasing. While ads which deal with murder account for 15 per cent of all the ads in the crime category, in the postwar period they constitute 20 per cent of the sample.

Another frequently shown type of crime was one coded as "crime involving morals." Although not specifically sex crime, this type usually had a close connection or involvement with sex. Thus, while rape was coded as a sex crime, prostitution, seduction, adultery and other classical sins were coded as crimes against morals. Typical of such ads was the one for *Abandoned*:[5]

No name for her baby . . . only a price!

Or this ad for the picture *Detective Story*:[6]

Yesterday in a moment of weakness, an affair she wanted to forget! Today a threat of exposure by an unlicensed doctor whose business was girls in trouble! Should she sacrifice her future happiness by confessing all to the man she now loves?

The frequency of ads showing crimes of one kind or another appears to be on the increase. During the prewar period only 7 per cent of the sample contained *any* mention of crime. The postwar ads with this appeal have risen to 24 per cent. This follows quite closely the pattern set by items of sex and violence, which also increased substantially since the end of the war.

While Hollywood does appear dedicated to presenting human life in all its more violent aspects, once in a while, but rarely, animals are shown in acts of aggression. One such ad repeated the old balderdash about gorillas taking human females for their mates. The illustration showed a gorilla holding a girl, and the text read:

What do gorilla kidnappers do with their women prey? Do they become slaves? Do they remain captives?

The film's title, appropriately, was *The Love Life of a Gorilla*. Happily, this appeared back in 1940; and seldom have the movies resorted to so crude or ridiculous an appeal.

In summary, we know that newspaper advertising of the movies has a high reader exposure. According to Leo Handel,[7] 86 per cent of the patrons of one film said they had seen the newspaper advertisement for it. Whether newspaper advertising induced them to go to the film, or whether other variables such as reviews in the paper or their favorite magazines, outdoor advertising, or the "personal influence" that Lazarsfeld and Katz feel is the key factor, we cannot say. Nevertheless, it is evident that Hollywood, the distributors and the exhibitors of the films, believe that newspaper advertising is their best medium for bringing people into the theaters. How else to explain the fact that they invest more than $50 million a year in this type of promotion? On this basis, we feel justified in hypothesizing that the newspaper ads represent a projection of Hollywood's concept of the most effective appeals to use on the Great Audience. We have seen an increasing proportion of the advertisements dwell heavily (and heavy-handedly) on themes of sex, violence and crime (even when the movies they advertised did not themselves focus on these aspects). This all leads us to believe that Hollywood's stereotype of its audience consists of people who, for the most part, can be promised *anything,* so long as it smacks a little of the things which both frighten and titillate the great American middle-class mentality. In Hollywood's mind these are especially sex, violence and crime.

The movies, as well as the other mass media, appear to have gone along uncritically with the notion that they must cater to these supposed "needs" of the Great Audience. Frequently, one fears, the promotional heads of the studios have had their stereotypes reinforced by reading certain snobbish critics of popular culture. For when they read that the movies are playing a major role in creating "mass man," the semi-literate who desires nothing more than an anodyne for the boredom of his job and the frustrations of his everyday existence, what should Hollywood do? Beat their breasts and cry *"mea culpa,"* or say, "Yes, but even the learned professors tell us that the Great Audience are just what our hunches have told us they were— slobs."? So the vicious circle is perpetuated; Hollywood accentuates, if anything, the shopworn, banal appeals. Even when television came along to carve the national movie-going audience nearly in half from 1947 to 1951, the worried promotion men continued the time-tested patterns. And when business showed a rising trend because "Movies are [allegedly] Better Than Ever," undoubtedly these self-same advertising executives believed it was due to their persistence in keeping faith with the old appeals.

Would it not be better for the movie industry (and other media could surely take the cue) to re-examine its audience, to conduct some valid research beyond the two-dimensional market research it has sometimes employed, and not take for granted that modern American society has *ipso facto* created a majority who must be appealed to like so many "emotionally starved" children? In fact, Hollywood sees its audience as more emotionally starved than do many professional therapists. The time may someday come when we will see a movie ad in which sex is portrayed neither as some magical power exuding from often falsified Aphrodites, nor as a shocking, evil (but secretly delightful) phenomenon. We may hope for, and even see, the day when a movie ad tells the reader expressly what the picture is really about instead of casuistically trying to entice him into the theater, or appeal to him in the way a child might be appealed to with a stick of peppermint candy. But that day seems remote, if the movie ads of the past two decades are any criterion for prediction. For such a change would demand that Hollywood take a fresh, not a superficial, look at the structure of American society.

Notes

1. For the purpose of comparison we divided our work into three periods: prewar (including years 1935, 1936 and 1937), war (including years 1940, 1941, 1942, 1943, 1944 and 1945), and postwar (the years 1948, 1949, 1950, 1951, 1952, 1953, 1954 and 1955). Throughout the study, when we speak of the periods, e.g., prewar, we mean to include the years mentioned here. The total number of advertisements analyzed for the prewar period was 217, for the war period 326, and for the postwar period 427.

2. This phenomenon of breast adulation, which provides the psychoanalysts with such knowing smiles, is not unique with the movies. The covers of the majority of twenty-five-cent paperbacks also emphasize what is euphemistically termed "chest art," not to mention pin-up pictures, and a host of squalid magazines, one of which goes by the name of *Titter*. The pun is not lost, apparently, even on semi-literates who keep such publications alive.

3. Film advertisement for *To Please A Lady*, Boston *Globe*, October 26, 1950.

4. Film advertisement for *The Cobweb*, Boston *Globe*, August 4, 1955.

5. Film advertisement for *Abandoned*, Boston *Globe*, November 3, 1949.

6. Film advertisement for *Detective Story*, Boston *Record-American*, November 8, 1951.

7. Handel, Leo A., *Hollywood Looks At Its Audience*, Urbana: University of Illinois Press, 1950, p. 74.

FURTHER READING

Dudley, Drew. "Moulding Public Opinion Through Advertising," *Annals of the American Academy of Political and Social Science,* Vol. 250, 1947, pp. 105-12.

Goodman, Ralph. "Freud and the Hucksters," *Nation,* Vol. 176, 1953, pp. 143-45.

McLuhan, Marshall. "The Age of Advertising," *Commonweal,* Vol. 58, 1953, pp. 555-57.

Pearlin, L. I., and Rosenberg, M. "Propaganda Techniques in Institutional Advertising," *Public Opinion Quarterly,* Vol. 16, 1952, pp. 5-26.

Seldin, Joseph. "Selling to the Id: Freud Writes the Ads," *Nation,* Vol. 180, 1955, pp. 442-43.

Turner, E. S. *The Shocking History of Advertising.* New York: E. P. Dutton, 1953.

Warren, Dale. "Aunt Lizzie's Lexicon," *Saturday Review,* Vol. 36, 1953, pp. 21-22.

Whiteside, Thomas. "Ogilvy, the Ineffable Ad Man," *Harper's,* Vol. 210, May, 1955, pp. 51-56.

8
The Overview

THE OVERVIEW

In his Mirror for Man, *Clyde Kluckhohn speculates that if archaeologists excavate the ruins of America 500 years from now they will properly conclude that "American culture was a variant of a culture of world-wide occurrence, distinguished by elaboration of gadgets and especially by the extent to which these were available to all sorts and conditions of men." The aim of this Reader has been to examine the social implications of some of the "gadgets," particularly those which are used to disseminate mass culture.*

This final section does not deal with any particular mass-cultural medium, but rather takes up certain basic questions raised by a general consideration of mass culture. In the initial essay, Drs. Lazarsfeld and Merton discuss the social functions of the mass media. They view the media as conferring status and enforcing social norms, but, on the negative side, also performing a narcotizing dysfunction. They conclude that the present role of the mass media is largely confined to peripheral social concerns and that the media do not exhibit the degree of social power commonly attributed to them.

T. W. Adorno scrutinizes the conventions of mass culture, with special emphasis on television. He sees this medium following the rigid institutionalization that "transforms modern mass culture into a medium of undreamed-of psychological control." To Dr. Adorno the curse of modern mass culture is its adherence to the almost unchanged ideology of middle-class society.

Marshall McLuhan points out that although Americans associate culture mainly with books, paradoxically it is in this country that the new media of sight and sound have had the greatest popularity. He questions whether we have not been hypnotized by book culture to the extent that we cannot regard the new media as serious. His is an earnest plea to see that the revolutions in communications have opened "magic casements" on which few have yet ventured in thought, art or living.

To Irving Howe, mass culture appeals to mass man's unconscious urge toward self-obliteration. Mass culture, he says, tries to cage the unconscious as it strives to disassociate personality. If it allows Americans the illusion "of vicariously rejecting their own adulthood and of safely breaking the laws of social life," mass culture ultimately reinforces real-life adherence to social law.

In what is, perhaps, the definitive statement of the critical view on mass culture, Ernest van den Haag undertakes to analyze the subject as a whole. He traces the eclipse of folk culture and the inroads made upon high culture, against a background of economic and technological change. Without tears of rage, van den Haag describes the exclusion of art in mass media, the corruption of newly produced high culture, the adulteration of past culture, and the feebleness of several countercurrents. He confronts every major objection to his analysis and, in the process, illumines many hitherto obscure areas.

Utilizing the comic books as his touchstone, Leslie Fiedler asks what the "righteous" really have against mass culture. To him the answer involves the problem of class distinction in a democratic society. The middlebrow reacts with equal fury to an art that baffles his understanding (Joyce, Kafka, et al.) and to one which refuses to aspire to his level (Superman, et al.). So he plays the middle against both ends, since "the fear of the vulgar is the obverse of the fear of excellence, and both are aspects of the fear of difference."

Melvin Tumin believes that economic prosperity in America has gone far ahead of cultural growth. He analyzes five areas dangerous to the continuance of an open society in which free inquiry and fair competition between opposing value systems and standards of taste can be maintained.

To conclude the section, Gilbert Seldes discusses the qualities of what he has termed "the public arts." Seldes questions whether degradation is inevitable (as claimed by Greenberg, van den Haag, et al.) when the public arts popularize the classic arts. Although Seldes has been as critical of the performance of the seven lively arts as any American critic (and wears no rose-colored glasses in this essay), he refuses to wishfully think them out of existence. He states his case succinctly when he says: "The fundamental values of our lives and those of our children will be affected by the revolutionary change in entertainment and communications; we have an obligation to control the speed and direction of this change."

Mass Communication, Popular Taste and Organized Social Action

By PAUL F. LAZARSFELD AND ROBERT K. MERTON

PROBLEMS ENGAGING THE ATTENTION of men change, and they change not at random but largely in accord with the altering demands of society and economy. . . . As a host of recent conferences, books and articles indicate, the role of radio, print and film in society has become a problem of interest to many and a source of concern to some. This shift in public interest appears to be the product of several social trends.

SOCIAL CONCERN WITH THE MASS MEDIA

Many are alarmed by the ubiquity and potential power of the mass media. It is widely felt that the mass media comprise a powerful instrument which may be used for good or for ill and that, in the absence of adequate controls, the latter possibility is on the whole more likely. For these are the media of propaganda, and Americans stand in peculiar dread of the power of propaganda. As the British observer, William Empson, recently remarked of us: "They believe in machinery more passionately than we do; and modern propaganda is a scientific machine; so it seems to them obvious that a mere reasoning man can't stand up against it. All this produces a curiously girlish attitude toward anyone who might be doing propaganda. 'Don't let that man come near. Don't let him tempt me, because if he does I'm sure to fall.' "

The ubiquity of the mass media promptly leads many to an almost magical belief in their enormous power. But there is another and, probably, a more realistic basis for widespread concern with the social role of the mass media; a basis which has to do with the changing types of social control exercised by powerful interest groups in society. Increasingly, the chief power groups, among which organized business occupies the most spectacular place, have come to adopt techniques for manipulating mass publics through propaganda in place of more direct means of control. Industrial organizations no longer compel eight-year-old children to attend the machine for fourteen hours a day; they engage in elaborate programs of "public relations." They place large and impressive advertisements in the newspapers of the nation; they sponsor numerous radio programs; on the advice of public relations counsellors they organize prize contests, establish welfare foundations, and support worthy causes. Economic power seems to have reduced direct exploitation and turned to a subtler type of psychological

Reprinted from *The Communication of Ideas* (1948), edited by Lyman Bryson, pp. 95-118, by permission of the authors and the publisher. (Copyright, 1948, by Harper & Brothers.)

exploitation, achieved largely by disseminating propaganda through the mass media of communication.

This change in the structure of social control merits thorough examination. Complex societies are subject to many different forms of organized control. Hitler, for example, seized upon the most visible and direct of these: organized violence and mass coercion. In this country, direct coercion has become minimized. If people do not adopt the beliefs and attitudes advocated by some power group—say, the National Association of Manufacturers—they can neither be liquidated nor placed in concentration camps. Those who would control the opinions and beliefs of our society resort less to physical force and more to mass persuasion. The radio program and the institutional advertisement serve in place of intimidation and coercion. The manifest concern over the functions of the mass media is in part based upon the valid observation that these media have taken on the job of rendering mass publics conformative to the social and economic *status quo*.

A third source of widespread concern with the social role of mass media is found in their assumed effects upon popular culture and the esthetic tastes of their audiences. In the measure that the size of these audiences has increased, it is argued, the level of esthetic taste has deteriorated. And it is feared that the mass media deliberately cater to these vulgarized tastes, thus contributing to further deterioration.

It seems probable that these constitute the three organically related elements of our great concern with the mass media of communication. Many are, first of all, fearful of the ubiquity and potential power of these media. We have suggested that this is something of an indiscriminate fear of an abstract bogey stemming from insecurity of social position and tenuously held values. Propaganda seems threatening.

There is, secondly: concern with the present effects of the mass media upon their enormous audiences, particularly the possibility that the continuing assault of these media may lead to the unconditional surrender of critical faculties and an unthinking conformism.

Finally, there is the danger that these technically advanced instruments of mass communication constitute a major avenue for the deterioration of esthetic tastes and popular cultural standards. And we have suggested that there is substantial ground for concern over these immediate social effects of the mass media of communication.

A review of the current state of actual knowledge concerning the social role of the mass media of communication and their effects upon the contemporary American community is an ungrateful task, for certified knowledge of this kind is impressively slight. Little more can be done than to explore the nature of the problems by methods which, in the course of many decades, will ultimately provide the knowledge we seek. Although this is anything but an encouraging preamble, it provides a necessary context for assessing the research and tentative conclusions of those of us professionally concerned with the study of mass media. A reconnaissance will suggest what we know, what we need to know, and will locate the strategic points requiring further inquiry.

To search out "the effects" of mass media upon society is to set upon an ill-defined problem. It is helpful to distinguish three facets of the problem and to consider each in turn. Let us, then, first inquire into what we know about the effects of the existence of these media in our society. Secondly, we must look into the effects of the particular structure of ownership and operation of the mass media in this country, a structure which differs appreciably from that found elsewhere. And, finally, we must consider that aspect of the problem which bears most directly upon policies and tactics governing the use of these media for definite social ends: our knowledge concerning the effects of the particular contents disseminated through the mass media.

THE SOCIAL ROLE OF THE MACHINERY OF MASS MEDIA

What role can be assigned to the mass media by virtue of the fact that they exist? What are the implications of a Hollywood, a Radio City, and a Time-Life-Fortune enterprise for our society? These questions can, of course, be discussed only in grossly speculative terms, since no experimentation or rigorous comparative study is possible. Comparisons with other societies lacking these mass media would be too crude to yield decisive results, and comparisons with an earlier day in American society would still involve gross assertions rather than precise demonstrations. In such an instance, brevity is clearly indicated. And opinions should be leavened with caution. It is our tentative judgment that the social role played by the very existence of the mass media has been commonly overestimated. What are the grounds for this judgment?

It is clear that the mass media reach enormous audiences. Approximately seventy million Americans attend the movies every week; our daily newspaper circulation is about forty-six million, and some thirty-four million American homes are equipped with radio, and in these homes the average American listens to the radio for about three hours a day. These are formidable figures. But these are merely supply and consumption figures, not figures registering the effect of mass media. They bear only upon what people do, not upon the social and psychological impact of the media. To know the number of hours people keep the radio turned on gives no indication of the effect upon them of what they hear. Knowledge of consumption data in the field of mass media remains far from a demonstration of their net effect upon behavior and attitude and outlook.

As was indicated a moment ago, we cannot resort to experiment by comparing contemporary American society with and without mass media. But, however tentatively, we can compare their social effect with, say, that of the automobile. It is not unlikely that the invention of the automobile and its development into a mass-owned commodity has had a significantly greater effect upon society than the invention of the radio and its development into a medium of mass communication. Consider the social complexes into which the automobile has entered. Its sheer existence has exerted pressure for vastly improved roads, and, with these, mobility has increased enormously. The shape of metropolitan agglomerations has been significantly affected by the automobile. And, it may be submitted, the inventions which enlarge the radius of movement and action exert a greater influence upon social outlook and daily routines than inventions which provide avenues for ideas—ideas which can be avoided by withdrawal, deflected by resistance and transformed by assimilation.

Granted, for a moment, that the mass media play a comparatively minor role in shaping our society, why are they the object of so much popular concern and criticism? Why do so many become exercised by the "problems" of the radio and film and press and so few by the problems of, say, the automobile and the airplane? In addition to the sources of this concern which we have noted previously, there is an unwitting psychological basis for concern which derives from a socio-historical context.

Many make the mass media targets for hostile criticism because they feel themselves duped by the turn of events.

The social changes ascribable to "reform movements" may be slow and slight, but they do cumulate. The surface facts are familiar enough. The sixty-hour week has given way to the forty-hour week; child labor has been progressively curtailed; with all its deficiencies, free universal education has become progressively institutionalized. These and other gains register a series of reform victories. And now, people have more leisure time. They have, ostensibly, greater access to the cultural heritage. And what use do they make of this unmortgaged time so painfully acquired for them? They listen to the radio and go to the movies. These mass media seem somehow to have cheated reformers of the fruits of their victories. The struggle for freedom, leisure, popular education, and social security was carried on in the hope that, once freed of cramping shackles, people would avail themselves of major cultural products of our society—Shakespeare or Beethoven, or perhaps Kant. Instead, they turn to Faith Baldwin or Johnny Mercer or Edgar Guest.

Many feel cheated of their prize. It is not unlike a young man's first experience in the difficult realm of puppy love. Deeply smitten with the charms of his lady love, he saves his allowance for weeks on end and finally manages to give her a beautiful bracelet. She finds it "simply divine"—so much so, that then and there she makes a date with another boy in order to display her new trinket. Our social struggles have met with a similar denouement. For generations, men fought to give people more leisure time, and now they spend it with the Columbia Broadcasting System rather than with Columbia University.

However little this sense of betrayal may account for prevailing attitudes toward the mass media, it may again be noted that the sheer presence of these media may not affect our society so profoundly as is widely supposed.

SOME SOCIAL FUNCTIONS OF THE MASS MEDIA

In continuing our examination of the social role which can be ascribed to the mass media by virtue of their "sheer existence," we temporarily abstract from the social structure in which the media find their place. We do not, for example, consider the diverse effects of the mass media under varying systems of ownership and control, an important structural factor which will be discussed subsequently.

The mass media undoubtedly serve many social functions which might well become the object of sustained research. Of these functions, we have occasion to notice only three.

The Status-Conferral Function. The mass media confer status on public issues, persons, organizations and social movements.

Common experience as well as research testifies that the social standings of persons or social policies are raised when these command favorable attention in the mass media. In many quarters, for example, the support of a political candidate or a public policy by the *Times* is taken as significant; this support is regarded as a distinct asset for the candidate or the policy. Why?

For some, the editorial views of the *Times* represent the considered judgment of a group of experts, thus calling for the respect of laymen. But this is only one element in the status-conferral function of the mass media, for enhanced status accrues to those who merely receive attention in the media, quite apart from any editorial support.

The mass media bestow prestige and enhance the authority of individuals and groups by *legitimizing their status*. Recognition by the press or radio or magazines or newsreels testifies that one has arrived, that one is important enough to have been singled out from the large, anonymous masses, that one's behavior and opinions are significant enough to require public notice. The operation of this status-conferral function may be witnessed most vividly in the advertising pattern of testimonials to a product by "prominent people." Within wide circles of the population (though not within certain selected social strata), such testimonials not only enhance the prestige of the product but also reflect prestige on the person who provides the testimonials. They give public notice that the large and powerful world of commerce regards him as possessing sufficiently high status for his opinion to count with many people. In a word, his testimonial is a testimonial to his own status.

The ideal, if homely, embodiment of this circular prestige pattern is to be found in the Lord Calvert series of advertisements centered on "Men of Distinction." The commercial firm and the commercialized witness to the merit of the product engage in an unending series of reciprocal pats on the back. In effect, a distinguished man congratulates a distinguished whisky, which, through the manufacturer, congratulates the man of distinction on his being so distinguished as to be sought out for a testimonial to the distinction of the product. The workings of this mutual admiration society may be as nonlogical as they are effective. The audiences of mass media apparently subscribe to the circular belief: "If you really matter, you will be at the focus of mass attention and, if you *are* at the focus of mass attention, then surely you must really matter."

This status-conferral function thus enters into organized social action by legitimizing selected policies, persons and groups which receive the support of mass media. We shall have occasion to note the detailed operation of this function in connection with the conditions making for the maximal utilization of mass media for designated social ends. At the moment, having considered the status-conferral function, we shall consider a second: the enforced application of social norms through the mass media.

The Enforcement of Social Norms. Such catch phrases as "the power of the press" (and other mass media) or "the bright glare of publicity" presumably refer to this function. The mass media may initiate organized social action by "exposing" conditions which are at variance with public moralities. But it need not be prematurely assumed that this pattern consists *simply* in making these deviations widely known. We have something to learn in this connection from Malinowski's observations among his beloved Trobriand Islanders. There, he reports, no organized action is taken with respect to behavior deviant from a social norm unless there is *public* announcement of the deviation. This is not merely a matter of acquainting the individuals in the group with the facts of the case. Many may have known privately of these deviations—e.g., incest among the Trobrianders, as with political or business corruption, prostitution, gambling among ourselves—but they will not have pressed for public action. But once the behavioral deviations are made simultaneously public for all, this sets in train tensions between the "privately tolerable" and the "publicly acknowledgeable."

The mechanism of public exposure would seem to operate somewhat as follows. Many social norms prove inconvenient for individuals in the society. They militate against the gratification of wants and impulses. Since many find the norms burdensome, there is some measure of leniency in applying them, both to oneself and to others. Hence, the emergence of deviant behavior and private toleration of these deviations. But this can continue only so long as one is not in a situation where one must take a public stand for or against the norms. Publicity, the enforced acknowledgment by members of the group that these deviations have occurred, requires each individual to take such a stand. He must either range himself with the nonconformists, thus proclaiming his repudiation of the group norms, and thus asserting that he, too, is outside the moral framework, or, regardless of his private predilections, he must fall into line by supporting the norm. *Publicity closes the gap between "private attitudes" and "public morality."* Publicity exerts pressure for a single rather than a dual morality by preventing continued evasion of the issue. It calls forth public reaffirmation and (however sporadic) application of the social norm.

In a mass society, this function of public exposure is institutionalized in the mass media of communication. Press, radio and journals expose fairly well known deviations to public view, and as a rule, this exposure forces some degree of public action against what has been privately tolerated. The mass media may, for example, introduce severe strains upon "polite ethnic discrimination" by calling public attention to these practices which are at odds with the norms of nondiscrimination. At times, the media may organize exposure activities into a "crusade."

The study of crusades by mass media would go far toward answering basic questions about the relation of mass media to organized social action. It is essential to know, for example, the extent to which the crusade provides an organizational center for otherwise unorganized individuals. The crusade may operate diversely among the several sectors of the population. In some instances, its major effect may not be so much to arouse an indifferent citizenry as to alarm the culprits, leading them to extreme measures which in turn alienate the electorate. Publicity may so embarrass the malefactor as to send him into flight—as was the case, for example, with some of the chief henchmen of the Tweed Ring following exposure by the *New York Times*. Or the directors of corruption may fear the crusade only because of the effect they anticipate it will have upon the electorate. Thus, with a startlingly realistic appraisal of the communications behavior of his constituency, Boss Tweed peevishly remarked of the biting cartoons of Thomas Nast in *Harper's Weekly*: "I don't care a straw for your newspaper articles: my constituents don't know how to read, but they can't help seeing them damned pictures."[1]

The crusade may affect the public directly. It may focus the attention of a hitherto lethargic citizenry, grown indifferent through familiarity to prevailing corruption, upon a few, dramatically simplified, issues. As Lawrence Lowell once observed in this general connection, complexities generally inhibit mass action. Public issues must be defined in simple alternatives, in terms of black and white, to permit of organized public action. And the presentation of simple alternatives is one of the chief functions of the crusade. The crusade may involve still other mechanisms. If a municipal government is not altogether pure of heart, it is seldom wholly corrupt. Some scrupulous members of the administration and judiciary are generally intermingled with their unprincipled colleagues. The crusade may strengthen the hand of the upright elements in the government, force the hand of the indifferent and weaken the hand of the corrupt. Finally, it may well be that a successful crusade exemplifies a circular, self-sustaining process, in which the concern of the mass medium with the public interest coincides with its self-interest. The triumphant crusade may enhance the power and prestige of the mass medium, thus making it, in turn, more formidable in later crusades, which, if successful, may further advance its power and prestige.

Whatever the answer to these questions, mass media clearly serve to reaffirm social norms by exposing deviations from these norms to public view. Study of the particular range of norms thus reaffirmed would provide a clear index of the extent to which these media deal with peripheral or central problems of the structure of our society.

The Narcotizing Dysfunction. The functions of status conferral and of reaffirmation of social norms are evidently well recognized by the operators of mass media. Like other social and psychological mechanisms, these functions lend themselves to diverse forms of application. Knowledge of these functions is power, and power may be used for special interests or for the general interest.

A third social consequence of the mass media has gone largely unnoticed. At least, it has received little explicit comment and, apparently, has not been systematically put to use for furthering planned objectives. This may be called the narcotizing dysfunction of the mass media. It is termed *dys*functional rather than functional on the assumption that it is not in the interest of modern complex society to have large masses of the population politically apathetic and inert. How does this unplanned mechanism operate?

Scattered studies have shown that an increasing proportion of the time of Americans is devoted to the products of the mass media. With distinct variations in different regions and among different social strata, the outpourings of the media presumably enable the twentieth-century American to "keep abreast of the world." Yet, it is suggested, this vast supply of communications may elicit only a superficial concern with the problems of society, and this superficiality often cloaks mass apathy.

Exposure to this flood of information may serve to narcotize rather than to energize the average reader or listener. As an increasing amount of time is devoted to reading and listening, a decreasing share is available for organized action. The individual reads accounts of issues and problems and may even discuss alternative lines of action. But this rather intellectualized, rather remote connection with organized social action is not activated. The interested and informed citizen can congratulate himself on his lofty state of interest and information, and neglect to see that he has abstained from decision and action. In short, he takes his secondary contact with the world of political reality, his reading and listening and thinking, as a vicarious performance. He comes to mistake *knowing* about problems of the day for *doing* something about them. His social conscience remains spotlessly clean. He *is* concerned. He *is* informed. And he has all sorts of ideas as to what should be done. But, after he has gotten through his dinner and after he has listened to his favored radio programs and after he has read his second newspaper of the day, it is really time for bed.

In this peculiar respect, mass communications may be included among the most respectable and efficient of social narcotics. They may be so fully effective as to keep the addict from recognizing his own malady.

That the mass media have lifted the level of information of large populations is evident. Yet, quite apart from intent, increasing dosages of mass communications may be inadvertently transforming the energies of men from active participation into passive knowledge.

The occurrence of this narcotizing dysfunction can scarcely be doubted, but the extent to which it operates has yet to be determined. Research on this problem remains one of the many tasks still confronting the student of mass communications.

THE STRUCTURE OF OWNERSHIP AND OPERATION

To this point we have considered the mass media quite apart from their incorporation within a particular social and economic structure. But clearly, the social effects of the media will vary as the system of ownership and control varies. Thus, to consider the social effects of American mass media is to deal only with the effects of these media as privately owned enterprises under profit-oriented management. It is general knowledge that this circumstance is not inherent in the technological nature of the mass media. In England, for example, to say nothing of Russia, the radio is to all intents and purposes owned, controlled and operated by government.

The structure of control is altogether different in this country. Its salient characteristic stems from the fact that, except for movies and books, it is not the magazine reader nor the radio listener nor, in large part, the reader of newspapers who supports the enterprise, but the advertiser. Big business finances the production and distribution of mass media. And, all intent aside, he who pays the piper generally calls the tune.

SOCIAL CONFORMISM

Since the mass media are supported by great business concerns geared into the current social and economic system, the media contribute to the maintenance of that system. This contribution is not found merely in the effective advertisement of the sponsor's product. It arises, rather, from the typical presence in magazine stories, radio programs and newspaper columns of some element of confirmation, some element of approval of the present structure of society. And this continuing reaffirmation underscores the duty to accept.

To the extent that the media of mass communication have had an influence upon their audiences, it has stemmed not only from what is said, but more significantly from what is not said. For these media not only continue to affirm the *status quo* but, in the same measure, they fail to raise essential questions about the structure of society. Hence, by leading toward conformism and by providing little basis for a critical appraisal of society, the commercially sponsored mass media indirectly but effectively restrain the cogent development of a genuinely critical outlook.

This is not to ignore the occasionally critical journal article or radio program. But these exceptions are so few that they are lost in the overwhelming flood of conformist materials. Dr. Lyman Bryson, for example, has been broadcasting a weekly program in which he critically and rationally appraises social problems in general and the institution of radio in particular. But these fifteen minutes in which Mr. Bryson addresses himself to such questions over one network constitute an infinitesimally small drop in the weekly flood of materials from four major networks, from five hundred and seventy or so unaffiliated stations, from hundreds of magazines and from Hollywood.

Since our commercially sponsored mass media promote a largely unthinking allegiance to our social structure, they cannot be relied upon to work for changes, even minor changes, in that structure. It is possible to list some developments to the contrary, but upon close inspection they prove illusory. A community group, such as the PTA, may request the producer of a radio serial to inject the theme of tolerant race attitudes into the program. Should the producer feel that this theme is safe, that it will not antagonize any substantial part of his audience, he may agree, but at the first indication that it is a dangerous theme may alienate potential consumers, he will refuse, or will soon abandon the experiment. Social objectives are consistently surrendered by commercialized media when they clash with economic gains. Minor tokens of "progressive" views are of slight importance, since they are included only by grace of the sponsors and only on the condition that they be sufficiently acceptable as not to alienate any appreciable part of the audience. Economic pressure makes for conformism by omission of sensitive issues.

IMPACT UPON POPULAR TASTE

Since the largest part of our radio, movies, magazines and a considerable part of our books and newspapers are devoted to "entertainment," this clearly requires us to consider the impact of the mass media upon popular taste.

Were we to ask the average American with some pretension to literary or esthetic cultivation if mass communications have had any effect upon popular taste, he would doubtlessly answer with a resounding affirmative. And more, citing abundant instances, he would insist that esthetic and intellectual tastes have been depraved by the flow of trivial formula products from printing presses, radio stations and movie studios. The columns of criticism abound with these complaints.

In one sense, this requires no further discussion. There can be no doubt that the women who are daily entranced for three or four hours by some twelve consecutive "soap operas," all cut to the same dismal pattern, exhibit an appalling lack of esthetic judgment. Nor is this impression altered by the contents of pulp and slick magazines, or by the depressing abundance of formula motion pictures replete with hero, heroine and villain moving through a contrived atmosphere of sex, sin and success.

Yet unless we locate these patterns in historical and sociological terms, we may find ourselves confusedly engaged in condemning without understanding, in criticism which is sound but largely irrelevant. What is the historical status of this notoriously low level of popular taste? Is it the poor remains of standards which were once significantly higher, a relatively new birth in the world of values, largely unrelated to the higher standards from which it has allegedly fallen, or a poor substitute blocking the way to the development of superior standards and the expression of high esthetic purpose?

If esthetic tastes are to be considered in their social setting, we must recognize that the effective audience for the arts has become historically transformed. Some centuries back, this audience was largely confined to a selected aristocratic élite. Relatively few were literate. And very few possessed the means to buy books, attend theaters and travel to the urban centers of the arts. Not more than a slight fraction, possibly not more than one or two per cent, of the population composed the effective audience for the arts. These happy few cultivated their esthetic tastes, and their selective demand left its mark in the form of relatively high artistic standards.

With the wide-sweeping spread of popular education and with the emergence of the new technologies of mass communication, there developed an enormously enlarged market for the arts. Some forms of music, drama and literature now reach virtually everyone in our society. This is why, of course, we speak of *mass* media and of *mass* art. And the great audiences for the mass media, though in the main literate, are not highly cultivated. About half the population, in fact, have halted their formal education upon leaving grammar school.

With the rise of popular education, there has occurred a seeming decline of popular taste. Large numbers of people have acquired what might be termed "formal literacy," that is to say, a capacity to read, to grasp crude and superficial meanings, and a correlative incapacity for full understanding of what they read.[2] There has developed, in short, a marked gap between literacy and comprehension. People read more but understand less. More people read but proportionately fewer critically assimilate what they read.

Our formulation of the problem should now be plain. It is misleading to speak simply of the decline of esthetic tastes. Mass audiences probably include a larger number of persons with cultivated esthetic standards, but these are swallowed up by the large masses who constitute the new and untutored audience for the arts. Whereas yesterday the elite constituted virtually the whole of the audience, they are today a minute fraction of the whole. In consequence, the *average* level of esthetic standards and tastes of audiences has been depressed, although the tastes of some sectors of the population have undoubtedly been raised and the total number of people exposed to communication contents have been vastly increased.

But this analysis does not directly answer the question of the effects of the mass media upon public taste, a question which is as complex as it is unexplored. The answer can come only from disciplined research. One would want to know, for example, whether mass media have robbed the intellectual and artistic elite of the art forms which might otherwise have been accessible to them. And this involves inquiry into the pressure exerted by the mass audience upon creative individuals to cater to mass tastes. Literary hacks have existed in every age. But it would be important to learn if the electrification of the arts supplies power for a significantly greater proportion of dim literary lights. And, above all, it would be essential to determine if mass media and mass tastes are necessarily linked in a vicious circle of deteriorating standards, or if appropriate action on the part of the directors of mass media could initiate a virtuous circle of cumulatively improving tastes among their audiences. More concretely, are the operators of commercialized mass media caught up in a situation in which they cannot, whatever their private preferences, radically raise the esthetic standards of their products?

In passing, it should be noted that much remains to be learned concerning standards appropriate for mass art. It is possible that standards for art forms produced by a small band of creative talents for a small and selective audience are not applicable to art forms produced by a gigantic industry for the population at large. The beginnings of investigation on this problem are sufficiently suggestive to warrant further study.[3]

Sporadic and consequently inconclusive experiments in the raising of standards have met with profound resistance from mass audiences. On occasion, radio stations and networks have attempted to supplant a soap opera with a program of art music, or formula comedy skits with discussions of public issues. In general, the people supposed to benefit by this reformation of program have simply refused to be benefited. They cease listening. The audience dwindles. Researches have shown, for example, that radio programs of art music tend to preserve rather than to create interest in such music and that newly emerging interests are typically superficial. Most listeners to these programs have previously acquired an interest in art music; the few whose interest is initiated by the programs are caught up by melodic compositions and come to think of art music exclusively in terms of Tschaikowsky or Rimsky-Korsakov or Dvorák.

Proposed solutions to these problems are more likely to be born of faith than knowledge. The improvement of mass tastes through the improvement of mass art products is not as simple a matter as we should like to believe. It is possible, of course, that a conclusive effort has not been made. By a triumph of imagination over the current organization of mass media, one can conceive a rigorous censorship over all media, such that nothing was allowed in print or on the air or in the films save "the best that has been thought and said in the world." Whether a radical change in the supply of mass art would in due course reshape the tastes of mass audiences must remain a matter of speculation. Decades of experimentation and research are needed. At present, we know conspicuously little about the methods of improving esthetic tastes and we know that some of the suggested methods are ineffectual. We have a rich knowledge of failures. Should this discussion be reopened in 1976, we may, perhaps, report with equal confidence our knowledge of positive achievements.

At this point, we may pause to glance at the road we have traveled. By way of introduction, we considered the seeming sources of widespread concern with the place of mass media in our society. Thereafter, we first examined the social role ascribable to the sheer existence of the mass media: their status-conferral function, their function in inducing the application of social norms and their narcotizing dysfunction. Secondly, we indicated the constraints placed by a structure of commercialized ownership and control upon the mass media as agencies of social criticism and as carriers of high esthetic standards.

We turn now to the third and last aspect of the social role of the mass media: the possibilities of utilizing them for moving toward designated types of social objectives.

PROPAGANDA FOR SOCIAL OBJECTIVES

This final question is perhaps of more direct interest than the other questions we have discussed. It represents something of a challenge to us since it provides the means of resolving the apparent paradox to which we referred previously: the seeming paradox arising from the assertion that the significance of the sheer existence of the mass media has been exaggerated and the multiple indications that the media do exert influences upon their audiences.

What are the conditions for the effective use of mass media for what might be called "propaganda for social objectives"—the promotion, let us say, of nondiscriminatory race relations, or of educational reforms, or of positive attitudes toward organized labor? Research indicates that at least one or more of three conditions must be satisfied if this propaganda is to prove effective. These conditions may be briefly designated as: (1) monopolization, (2) canalization rather than change of basic values, and (3) supplementary face-to-face contact. Each of these conditions merits some discussion.

Monopolization. This situation obtains when there is little or no opposition in the mass media to the diffusion of values, policies or public images. That is to say, monopolization of the mass media occurs in the absence of counterpropaganda.

In this restricted sense, monopolization of the mass media is found in diverse circumstances. It is, of course, indigenous to the political structure of authoritarian society, where access to the media of communication is wholly closed to those who oppose the official ideology. The evidence suggests that this monopoly played some part in enabling the Nazis to maintain their control of the German people.

But this same situation is approximated in other social systems. During the war, for example, our government utilized the radio, with some success, to promote and to maintain identification with the war effort. The effectiveness of these morale-building efforts was in large measure due to the virtually complete absence of counterpropaganda.

Similar situations arise in the world of commercialized propaganda. The mass media create popular idols. The public images of the radio performer,

Kate Smith, for example, picture her as a woman with unparalleled understanding of other American women, deeply sympathetic with ordinary men and women, a spiritual guide and mentor, a patriot whose views on public affairs should be taken seriously. Linked with the cardinal American virtues, the public images of Kate Smith are at no point subject to a counterpropaganda. Not that she has no competitors in the market of radio advertising, but there are none who set themselves systematically to question what she has said. In consequence, an unmarried radio entertainer with an annual income in six figures may be visualized by millions of American women as a hard-working mother who knows the recipe for managing life on fifteen hundred a year.

This image of a popular idol would have far less currency were it subjected to counterpropaganda. Such neutralization occurs, for example, as a result of pre-election campaigns by Republicans and Democrats. By and large, as a recent study has shown, the propaganda issued by each of these parties neutralizes the effect of the other's propaganda. Were both parties to forego their campaigning through the mass media entirely, it is altogether likely that the net effect would be to reproduce the present distribution of votes.

This general pattern has been described by Kenneth Burke in his *Attitudes Toward History*: ". . . businessmen compete with one another by trying to *praise their own commodity* more persuasively than their rivals, whereas politicians compete by slandering the *opposition*. When you add it all up, you get a grand total of absolute praise for business and grand total of absolute slander for politics."

To the extent that opposing political propagandas in the mass media are balanced, the net effect is negligible. The virtual monopolization of the media for given social objectives, however, will produce discernible effects upon audiences.

Canalization. Prevailing beliefs in the enormous power of mass communications appear to stem from successful cases of monopolistic propaganda or from advertising. But the leap from the efficacy of advertising to the assumed efficacy of propaganda aimed at deep-rooted attitudes and ego-involved behavior is as unwarranted as it is dangerous. Advertising is typically directed toward the canalizing of pre-existing behavior patterns or attitudes. It seldom seeks to instill new attitudes or to create significantly new behavior patterns. "Advertising pays" because it generally deals with a simple psychological situation. For Americans who have been socialized in the use of a toothbrush, it makes relatively little difference which brand of toothbrush they use. Once the gross pattern of behavior or the generic attitude has been established, it can be canalized in one direction or another. Resistance is slight. But mass propaganda typically meets a more complex situation. It may seek objectives which are at odds with deep-lying attitudes. It may seek to reshape rather than to canalize current systems of values. And the successes of advertising may only highlight the failures of propaganda. Much of the current propaganda which is aimed at abolishing deep-seated ethnic and racial prejudices, for example, seems to have had little effectiveness.

Media of mass communication, then, have been effectively used to canalize basic attitudes, but there is little evidence of their having served to change these attitudes.

Supplementation. Mass propaganda which is neither monopolistic nor canalizing in character may, nonetheless, prove effective if it meets a third condition: supplementation through face-to-face contacts.

A case in point will illustrate the interplay between mass media and face-to-face influences. The seeming propagandistic success achieved some years ago by Father Coughlin doesn't appear, upon inspection, to have resulted primarily from the propaganda content of his radio talks. It was, rather, the product of these centralized propaganda talks *and* widespread local organizations which arranged for their members to listen to him, followed by discussions among themselves concerning the social views he had expressed. This combination of a central supply of propaganda (Coughlin's addresses on a nationwide network), the co-ordinated distribution of newspapers and pamphlets, and locally organized face-to-face discussions among relatively small groups—this complex of reciprocal reinforcement by mass media and personal relations proved spectacularly successful.

Students of mass movements have come to repudiate the view that mass propaganda in and of itself creates or maintains the movement. Nazism did not attain its brief moment of hegemony by capturing the mass media of communication. The media played an ancillary role, supplementing the use of organized violence, organized distribution of rewards for conformity and organized centers of local indoctrination. The Soviet Union has also made large and impressive use of mass media for indoctrinating enormous populations with appropriate ideologies. But the organizers of indoctrination saw to it that the mass media did not operate alone. "Red corners," "reading huts" and "listening stations" comprised meeting places in which groups of citizens were exposed to the mass media in common. The fifty-five thousand reading rooms and clubs which had come into being by 1933 enabled the local ideological élite to talk over with rank-and-file readers the content of what they read. The relative scarcity of radios in private homes again made for group listening and group discussions of what had been heard.

In these instances, the machinery of mass persuasion included face-to-face contact in local organizations as an adjunct to the mass media. The privatized individual response to the materials presented through the channels of mass communication was considered inadequate for transforming exposure to propaganda into effectiveness of propaganda. In a society such as our own, where the pattern of bureaucratization has not yet become so pervasive or, at least, not so clearly crystallized, it has likewise been found that mass media prove most effective in conjunction with local centers of organized face-to-face contact.

Several factors contribute to the enhanced effectiveness of this joining of mass media and direct personal contact. Most clearly, the local discussions serve to reinforce the content of mass propaganda. Such mutual confirmation produces a "clinching effect." Secondly, the central media lessen the task of the local organizer, and the personnel requirements for such subalterns need not be as rigorous in a popular movement. The subalterns need not set forth the propaganda content for themselves, but need only pilot potential converts to the radio where the doctrine is being expounded. Thirdly, the appearance of a representative of the movement on a nationwide network, or his mention in the national press, serves to symbolize the legitimacy and significance of the movement. It is no powerless, inconsequential enterprise. The mass media, as we have seen, confer status. And the status of the national movement reflects back on the status of the local cells, thus consolidating the tentative decisions of its members. In this interlocking arrangement, the local organizer ensures an audience for the national speaker and the national speaker validates the status of the local organizer.

This brief summary of the situations in which the mass media achieve their maximum propaganda effect may resolve the seeming contradiction which arose at the outset of our discussion. The mass media prove most effective when they operate in a situation of virtual "psychological monopoly," or when the objective is one of canalizing rather than modifying basic attitudes, or when they operate in conjunction with face-to-face contacts.

But these three conditions are rarely satisfied conjointly in propaganda for social objectives. To the degree that monopolization of attention is rare, opposing propagandas have free play in a democracy. And, by and large, basic social issues involve more than a mere canalizing of pre-existent basic attitudes; they call, rather, for substantial changes in attitude and behavior. Finally, for the most obvious of reasons, the close collaboration of mass media and locally organized centers for face-to-face contact has seldom been achieved by groups striving for planned social change. Such programs are expensive. And it is precisely these groups which seldom have the large resources needed for these expensive programs. The forward-looking groups at the edges of the power structure do not ordinarily have the large financial means of the contented groups at the center.

As a result of this threefold situation, the present role of mass media is largely confined to peripheral social concerns and the media do not exhibit the degree of social power commonly attributed to them.

By the same token, and in view of the present organization of business ownership and control of the mass media, they have served to cement the structure of our society. Organized business does approach a virtual "psychological monopoly" of the mass media. Radio commercials and newspaper advertisements are, of course, premised on a system which has been termed free enterprise. Moreover, the world of commerce is primarily concerned with canalizing rather than radically changing basic attitudes; it seeks only to create preferences for one rather than another brand of product. Face-to-face contacts with those who have been socialized in our culture serve primarily to reinforce the prevailing culture patterns.

Thus, the very conditions which make for the maximum effectiveness of the mass media of communication operate toward the maintenance of the going social and cultural structure rather than toward its change.

Notes

1. James Bryce, *The American Commonwealth,* Volume 2. Copyright 1898 by Macmillan and Company; 1910, 1914 by The Macmillan Company; 1920 by The Right Honorable Viscount Bryce.

2. *Ibid.,* Part IV, Chapter LXXX, James Bryce perceived this with characteristic clarity: "That the education of the masses is nevertheless a superficial education goes without saying. It is sufficient to enable them to think they know something about the great problems of politics: insufficient to show them how little they know. The public elementary school gives everybody the key to knowledge in making reading and writing familiar, but it has not time to teach him how to use the key, whose use is in fact, by the pressure of daily work, almost confined to the newspaper and the magazine. So we may say that if the political education of the average American voter be compared with that of the average voter in Europe, it stands high; but if it be compared with the functions which the theory of the American government lays on him, which its spirit implies, which the methods of its party organization assume, its inadequacy is manifest." *Mutatis mutandis,* the same may be said of the gap between the theory of "superior" cultural content in the mass media and the current levels of popular education.

3. *Cf.* Chapter XVI of *The Communication of Ideas.*

Television and the Patterns of Mass Culture

By T. W. ADORNO

THE EFFECT OF TELEVISION cannot be adequately expressed in terms of success or failure, likes or dislikes, approval or disapproval. Rather, an attempt should be made, with the aid of depth-psychological categories and previous knowledge of mass media, to crystallize a number of theoretical concepts by which the potential effect of television—its impact upon various layers of the spectator's personality—could be studied. It seems timely to investigate systematically socio-psychological stimuli typical of televised material both on a descriptive and psychodynamic level, to analyze their presuppositions as well as their total pattern, and to evaluate the effect they are likely to produce. This procedure may ultimately bring forth a number of recommendations on how to deal with these stimuli to produce the most desirable effect of television. By exposing the socio-psychological implications and mechanisms of television, which often operate under the guise of fake realism, not only may the shows be improved, but, more important possibly, the public at large may be sensitized to the nefarious effect of some of these mechanisms.

We are not concerned with the effectiveness of any particular show or program; but we are concerned with the nature of present-day television and its imagery. Yet, our approach is practical. The findings should be so close to the material, should rest on such a solid foundation of experience, that they can be translated into precise recommendations and be made convincingly clear to large audiences.

Improvement of television is not conceived primarily on an artistic, purely aesthetic level, extraneous to present customs. This does not mean that we naïvely take for granted the dichotomy between autonomous art and mass media. We all know that their relationship is highly complex. Today's rigid division between what is called "long-haired" and "short-haired" art is the product of a long historical development. It would be romanticizing to assume that formerly art was entirely pure, that the creative artist thought only in terms of the inner consistency of the artifact and not also of its effect upon the spectators. Theatrical art, in particular, cannot be separated from audience reaction. Conversely, vestiges of the aesthetic claim to be something autonomous, a world unto itself, remain even within the most trivial product of mass culture. In fact, the present rigid division of art into autonomous and commercial aspects is itself largely a function of commercialization. It was hardly accidental that the slogan *l'art pour l'art*

Reprinted from the *Quarterly of Film, Radio and Television*, Vol. 8, 1954, pp. 213-35, by permission of the author and the publisher. (Copyright, 1954, by the University of California Press.)

was coined polemically in the Paris of the first half of the nineteenth century, when literature really became large-scale business for the first time. Many of the cultural products bearing the anticommercial trademark "art for art's sake" show traces of commercialism in their appeal to the sensational or in the conspicuous display of material wealth and sensuous stimuli at the expense of the meaningfulness of the work. This trend was pronounced in the neo-Romantic theater of the first decades of our century.

OLDER AND RECENT POPULAR CULTURE

In order to do justice to all such complexities, much closer scrutiny of the background and development of modern mass media is required than communications research, generally limited to present conditions, is aware of. One would have to establish what the output of contemporary cultural industry has in common with older "low" or popular forms of art as well as with autonomous art, and where the differences lie. Suffice it here to state that the archetypes of present popular culture were set comparatively early in the development of middle-class society—at about the turn of the seventeenth and the beginning of the eighteenth centuries in England. According to the studies of the English sociologist Ian Watt, the English novels of that period, particularly the works of Defoe and Richardson, marked the beginning of an approach to literary production that consciously created, served, and finally controlled a "market." Today the commercial production of cultural goods has become streamlined, and the impact of popular culture upon the individual has concomitantly increased. This process has not been confined to quantity, but has resulted in new qualities. While recent popular culture has absorbed all the elements and particularly all the "don'ts" of its predecessor, it differs decisively inasmuch as it has developed into a system. Thus, popular culture is no longer confined to certain forms such as novels or dance music, but has seized all media of artistic expression. The structure and meaning of these forms show an amazing parallelism, even when they appear to have little in common on the surface (such as jazz and the detective novel). Their output has increased to such an extent that it is almost impossible for anyone to dodge them; and even those formerly aloof from popular culture—the rural population on one hand and the highly educated on the other—are somehow affected. The more the system of "merchandising" culture is expanded, the more it tends also to assimilate the "serious" art of the past by adapting this art to the system's own requirements. The control is so extensive that any infraction of its rules is *a priori* stigmatized as "highbrow" and has but little chance to reach the population at large. The system's concerted effort results in what might be called the prevailing ideology of our time.

Certainly, there are many typical changes within today's pattern; e.g., men were formerly presented as erotically aggressive and women on the defensive, whereas this has been largely reversed in modern mass culture, as pointed out particularly by Wolfenstein and Leites. More important, however, is that the pattern itself, dimly perceptible in the early novels and basically preserved today, has by now become congealed and standardized. Above all, this rigid institutionalization transforms modern mass culture into a medium of undreamed of psychological control. The repetitiveness, the selfsameness, and the ubiquity of modern mass culture tend to make for automatized reactions and to weaken the forces of individual resistance.

When the journalist Defoe and the printer Richardson calculated the effect of their wares upon the audience, they had to speculate, to follow hunches; and therewith, a certain latitude to develop deviations remained. Such deviations have nowadays been reduced to a kind of multiple choice between very few alternatives. The following may serve as an illustration. The popular or semipopular novels of the first half of the nineteenth century, published in large quantities and serving mass consumption, were supposed to arouse tension in the reader. Although the victory of the good over the bad was generally provided for, the meandering and endless plots and subplots hardly allowed the readers of Sue and Dumas to be continuously aware of the moral. Readers could expect anything to happen. This no longer holds true. Every spectator of a television mystery knows with absolute certainty how it is going to end. Tension is but superficially maintained and is unlikely to have a serious effect any more. On the contrary, the spectator feels on safe ground all the time. This longing for "feeling on safe ground"—reflecting an infantile need for protection, rather than his desire for a thrill—is catered to. The element of excitement is preserved only with tongue in cheek. Such changes fall in line with the potential change from a freely competitive to a virtually "closed" society into which one wants to be admitted or from which one fears to be rejected. Everything somehow appears "predestined."

The increasing strength of modern mass culture is further enhanced by changes in the sociological structure of the audience. The old cultured elite does not exist any more; the modern intelligentsia only partially corresponds to it. At the same time, huge strata of the population formerly unacquainted with art have become cultural "consumers." Modern audiences, although probably less capable of the artistic sublimation bred by tradition, have become shrewder in their demands for perfection of technique and for reliability of information, as well as in their desire for "services"; and they have become more convinced of the consumers' potential power over the producer, no matter whether this power is actually wielded.

How changes within the audience have affected the meaning of popular culture may also be illustrated. The element of internalization played a decisive role in early Puritan popular novels of the Richardson type. This element no longer prevails, for it was based on the essential role of "inwardness" in both original Protestantism and earlier middle-class society. As the profound influence of the basic tenets of Protestantism has gradually receded, the cultural pattern has become more and more opposed to the "introvert." As Riesman puts it,

. . . the conformity of earlier generations of Americans of the type I term "inner-directed" was mainly assured by their internalization of adult authority. The middle-class urban American of today, the "other-directed," is, by contrast, in a characterological sense more the product of his peers—that is, in socio-logical terms, his "peer-groups," the other kids at school or in the block.[1]

This is reflected by popular culture. The accents on inwardness, inner conflicts, and psychological ambivalence (which play so large a role in earlier popular novels and on which their originality rests) have given way to unproblematic, cliché-like characterization. Yet the code of decency that governed the inner conflicts of the Pamelas, Clarissas, and Lovelaces remains almost literally intact.[2] The middle-class "ontology" is preserved in an almost fossilized way, but is severed from the mentality of the middle classes. By being superimposed on people with whose living conditions and mental make-up it is no longer in accord, this middle-class "ontology" assumes an increasingly authoritarian and at the same time hollow character.

The overt "naïveté" of older popular culture is avoided. Mass culture, if not sophisticated, must at least be up to date—that is to say, "realistic," or posing as realistic—in order to meet the expectations of a supposedly disillusioned, alert, and hard-boiled audience. Middle-class requirements bound up with internalization—such as concentration, intellectual effort, and erudition—have to be continuously lowered. This does not hold only for the United States, where historical memories are scarcer than in Europe; but it is universal, applying to England and Continental Europe as well.[3]

However, this apparent progress of enlightenment is more than counterbalanced by retrogressive traits. The earlier popular culture maintained a certain equilibrium between its social ideology and the actual social conditions under which its consumers lived. This probably helped to keep the border line between popular and serious art during the eighteenth century more fluid than it is today. Abbé Prévost was one of the founding fathers of French popular literature; but his *Manon Lescaut* is completely free from clichés, artistic vulgarisms, and calculated effects. Similarly, later in the eighteenth century, Mozart's *Zauberfloete* struck a balance between the "high" and the popular style which is almost unthinkable today.

The curse of modern mass culture seems to be its adherence to the almost unchanged ideology of early middle-class society, whereas the lives of its consumers are completely out of phase with this ideology. This is probably the reason for the gap between the overt and the hidden "message" of modern popular art. Although on an overt level the traditional values of English Puritan middle-class society are promulgated, the hidden message aims at a frame of mind which is no longer bound by these values. Rather, today's frame of mind transforms the traditional values into the norms of an increasingly hierarchical and authoritarian social structure. Even here it has to be admitted that authoritarian elements were also present in the older ideology which, of course, never fully expressed the truth. But the "message" of adjustment and unreflecting obedience seems to be dominant and all-pervasive today. Whether maintained values derived from religious ideas obtain a different meaning when severed from their root should be carefully examined. For example, the concept of the "purity" of women is one of the invariables of popular culture. In the earlier phase this concept is treated in terms of an inner conflict between concupiscence and the internalized Christian ideal of chastity, whereas in today's popular culture it is dogmatically posited as a value *per se*. Again, even the rudiments of this pattern are visible in productions such as *Pamela*. There, however, it seems a by-product; whereas in today's popular culture the idea that only the "nice girl" gets married and that she must get married at any price has come to be accepted before Richardson's conflicts even start.[4]

The more inarticulate and diffuse the audience of modern mass media seems to be, the more mass media tend to achieve their "integration." The ideals of conformity and conventionalism were inherent in popular novels from the very beginning. Now, however, these ideals have been translated into rather clear-cut prescriptions of what to do and what not to do. The outcome of conflicts is pre-established, and all conflicts are mere sham. Society is always the winner, and the individual is only a puppet manipulated through social rules. True, conflicts of the nineteenth-century type—such as women running away from their husbands, the drabness of provincial life, and daily chores—occur frequently in today's magazine stories. However, with a regularity which challenges quantitative treatment, these conflicts are decided in favor of the very same conditions from which these women want to break away. The stories teach their readers that one has to be "realistic," that one has to give up romantic ideas, that one has to adjust oneself at any price, and that nothing more can be expected of any individual. The perennial middle-class conflict between individuality and society has been reduced to a dim memory, and the message is invariably that of identification with the *status quo*. This theme too is not new, but its unfailing universality invests it with an entirely different meaning. The constant plugging of conventional values seems to mean that these values have lost their substance, and that it is feared that people would really follow their instinctual urges and conscious insights unless continuously reassured from outside that they must not do so. The less the message is really believed and the less it is in harmony with the actual existence of the spectators, the more categorically it is maintained in modern culture. One may speculate whether its inevitable hypocrisy is concomitant with punitiveness and sadistic sternness.

MULTILAYERED STRUCTURE

A depth-psychological approach to television has to be focused on its multilayered structure. Mass media are not simply the sum total of the actions they portray or of the messages that radiate from these actions. Mass media also consist of various layers of meanings superimposed on one another, all of which contribute to the effect. True, due to their calculative nature, these rationalized products seem to be more clear-cut in their meaning than authentic works of art, which can never be boiled down to some unmistakable "message." But the heritage of polymorphic meaning has been taken over by cultural industry inasmuch as what it conveys becomes itself organized in order to enthrall the spectators on various psychological levels simultaneously. As a matter of fact, the hidden message may be more important than the overt, since this hidden message will escape the controls of consciousness, will not be "looked through," will not be warded off by sales resistance, but is likely to sink into the spectator's mind.

Probably all the various levels in mass media involve *all* the mechanisms of consciousness and unconsciousness stressed by psychoanalysis. The difference between the surface content, the overt message of televised material, and its hidden meaning is generally marked and rather clear-cut. The rigid superimposition of various layers probably is one of the features by which mass media are distinguishable from the integrated products of autonomous art, where the various layers are much more thoroughly fused. The full effect of the material on the spectator cannot be studied without consideration of the hidden meaning in conjunction with the overt one, and it is precisely this interplay of various layers which has hitherto been neglected and which will be our focus. This is in accordance with the assumption shared by numerous social scientists that certain political and social trends of our time, particularly those of a totalitarian nature, feed to a considerable extent on irrational and frequently unconscious motivations. Whether the conscious or the unconscious message of our material is more important is hard to predict and can be evaluated only after careful analysis. We do appreciate, however, that the overt message can be interpreted much more adequately in the light of psychodynamics—i.e., in its relation to instinctual urges as well as control—than by looking at the overt in a naïve way and by ignoring its implications and presuppositions.

The relation between overt and hidden message will prove highly complex in practice. Thus, the hidden message frequently aims at reinforcing conventionally rigid and "pseudo-realistic" attitudes similar to the accepted ideas more rationalistically propagated by the surface message. Conversely, a number of repressed gratifications which play a large role on the hidden level are somehow allowed to manifest themselves on the surface in jests, off-color remarks, suggestive situations, and similar devices. All this interaction of various levels, however, points in some definite direction: the tendency to channelize audience reaction. This falls in line with the suspicion widely shared, though hard to corroborate by exact data, that the majority of television shows today aim at producing, or at least reproducing, the very smugness, intellectual passivity, and gullibility that seem to fit in with totalitarian creeds even if the explicit surface message of the shows may be antitotalitarian.

With the means of modern psychology, we will try to determine the primary prerequisites of shows eliciting mature, adult, and responsible reactions—implying not only in content but in the very way things are being looked at, the idea of autonomous individuals in a free democratic society. We perfectly realize that any definition of such an individual will be hazardous; but we know quite well what a human being deserving of the appellation "autonomous individual" should *not* be, and this "not" is actually the focal point of our consideration.

When we speak of the multilayered structure of television shows, we are thinking of various superimposed layers of different degrees of manifestness or hiddenness that are utilized by mass culture as a technological means of "handling" the audience. This was expressed felicitously by Leo Lowenthal when he coined the term "psychoanalysis in reverse." The implication is that somehow the psychoanalytic concept of a multilayered personality has been taken up by cultural industry, and that the concept is used in order to ensnare the consumer as completely as possible and in order to engage him psychodynamically in the service of premeditated effects. A clear-cut division into allowed gratifications, forbidden gratifications, and recurrence of the forbidden gratifications in a somewhat modified and deflected form is carried through.

To illustrate the concept of the multilayered structure: the heroine of an extremely light comedy of pranks is a young schoolteacher who is not only underpaid but is incessantly fined by the caricature of a pompous and authoritarian school principal. Thus, she has no money for her meals and is actually starving. The supposedly funny situations consist mostly of her trying to hustle a meal from various acquaintances, but regularly without success. The mention of food and eating seems to induce laughter—an observation that can frequently be made and invites a study of its own.[5] Overtly, the play is just slight amusement mainly provided by the painful situations into which the heroine and her arch-opponent constantly run. The script does not try to "sell" any idea. The "hidden meaning" emerges simply by the way the story looks at human beings; thus the audience is invited to look at the characters in the same way without being made aware that indoctrination is present. The character of the underpaid, maltreated schoolteacher is an attempt to reach a compromise between prevailing scorn for the intellectual and the equally conventionalized respect for "culture." The heroine shows such an intellectual superiority and high-spiritedness that identification with her is invited, and compensation is offered for the inferiority of her position and that of her ilk in the social setup. Not only is the central character supposed to be very charming, but she wisecracks constantly. In terms of a set pattern of identification, the script implies: "If you are as humorous, good-natured, quick-witted, and charming as she is, do not worry about being paid a starvation wage. You can cope with your frustration in a humorous way; and your superior wit and cleverness put you not only above material privations, but also above the rest of mankind." In other words, the script is a shrewd method of promoting adjustment to humiliating conditions by presenting them as objectively comical and by giving a picture of a person who experiences even her own inadequate position as an object of fun apparently free of any resentment.

Of course, this latent message cannot be considered as unconscious in the strict psychological sense, but rather as "inobtrusive"; this message is hidden only by a style which does not pretend to touch anything serious and expects to be regarded as featherweight. Nevertheless, even such amusement tends to set patterns for the members of the audience without their being aware of it.

Another comedy of the same thesis is reminiscent of the funnies. A cranky old woman sets up the will of her cat (Mr. Casey) and makes as heirs some of the schoolteachers in the permanent cast. Later the actual inheritance is found to consist of the cat's valueless toys. The plot is so constructed that each heir, at the reading of the will, is tempted to act as if he had known this person (Mr. Casey). The ultimate point is that the cat's owner had placed a hundred-dollar bill inside each of the toys; and the heirs run to the incinerator in order to recover their inheritance. The audience is given to understand: "Don't expect the impossible, don't daydream, but be realistic." The denunciation of that archetypical daydream is enhanced by the association of the wish for unexpected and irrational blessings with dishonesty, hypocrisy, and a generally undignified attitude. The spectator is given to understand: "Those who dare daydream, who expect that money will fall to them from heaven, and who forget any caution about accepting an absurd will are at the same time those whom you might expect to be capable of cheating."

Here, an objection may be raised: Is such a sinister effect of the hidden message of television known to those who control, plan, write, and direct shows? Or it may even be asked: Are those traits possible projections of the unconscious of the decision-makers' own minds according to the widespread assumption that works of art can be properly understood in terms of psychological projections of their authors? As a matter of fact, it is this kind of reasoning that has led to the suggestion that a special sociopsychological study of decision-makers in the field of television be made. We do not think that such a study would lead us very far. Even in the sphere of autonomous art, the idea of projection has been largely overrated. Although the authors' motivations certainly enter the artifact, they are by no means so all-determining as is often assumed. As soon as an artist has set himself his problem, it obtains some kind of impact of its own; and, in most cases, he has to follow the objective requirements of his product much more than his own urges of expression when he translates his primary conception into artistic reality. To be sure, these objective requirements do not play a decisive role in mass media, which stress the effect on the spectator far beyond any artistic problem. However, the total setup here tends to limit the chances of the artists' projections utterly. Those who produce the material follow, often grumblingly, innumerable requirements, rules of thumb, set patterns, and mechanisms of controls which by necessity reduce to a minimum the range of any kind of artistic self-expression. The fact that most products of mass media are not produced by one individual but by collective collaboration—as happens to be true with most of the illustrations so far discussed—is only one contributing factor to this generally prevailing condition. To study television shows in terms of the psychology of the authors would almost be tantamount to studying Ford cars in terms of the psychoanalysis of the late Mr. Ford.

PRESUMPTUOUSNESS

The typical psychological mechanisms utilized by television shows and the devices by which they are automatized function only within a small number of given frames of reference operative in television communication, and the socio-psychological effect largely depends on them. We are all familiar with the division of television content into various classes, such as light comedy, westerns, mysteries, so-called sophisticated plays, and others. These types have developed into formulas which, to a certain degree, pre-established the attitudinal pattern of the spectator before he is confronted with any specific content and which largely determine the way in which any specific content is being perceived.

In order to understand television, it is, therefore, not enough to bring out the implications of various shows and types of shows; but an examination must be made of the presuppositions within which the implications function before a single word is spoken. Most important is that the typing of shows has gone so far that the spectator approaches each one with a set pattern of expectations before he faces the show itself—just as the radio listener who catches the beginning of Tschaikowsky's Piano Concerto as a theme song, knows automatically, "Aha, serious music!" or, when he hears organ music, responds equally automatically, "Aha, religion!" These halo effects of previous experiences may be psychologically as important as the implications of the phenomena themselves for which they have set the stage; and these presuppositions should, therefore, be treated with equal care.

When a television show bears the title "Dante's Inferno," when the first shot is that of a night club by the same name, and when we find sitting at the bar a man with his hat on and at some distance from him a sad-looking, heavily made-up woman ordering another drink, we are almost certain that some murder will shortly be committed. The apparently individualized situation actually works only as a signal that moves our expectations into a definite direction. If we had never seen anything but "Dante's Inferno," we probably would not be sure about what was going to happen; but, as it is, we are actually given to understand by both subtle and not so subtle devices that this is a crime play, that we are entitled to to expect some sinister and probably hideous and sadistic deeds of violence, that the hero will be saved from a situation from which he can hardly be expected to be saved, that the woman on the barstool is probably not the main criminal but is likely to lose her life as a gangster's moll, and so on. This conditioning to such universal patterns, however, scarcely stops at the television set.

The way the spectator is made to look at apparently everyday items, such as a night club, and to take as hints of possible crime common settings of his daily life, induces him to look at life itself as though it and its conflicts could generally be understood in such terms.[6] This, convincingly enough, may be the nucleus of truth in the old-fashioned arguments against all kinds of mass media for inciting criminality in the audience. The decisive thing is that this atmosphere of the normality of crime, its presentation in terms of an average expectation based on life situations, is never expressed in so many words but is established by the overwhelming wealth of material. It may affect certain spectator groups more deeply than the overt moral of crime and punishment regularly derived from such shows. What matters is not the importance of crime as a symbolic expression of otherwise controlled sexual or aggressive impulses, but the confusion of this symbolism with a pedantically maintained realism in all matters of direct sense perception. Thus, empirical life becomes infused with a kind of meaning that virtually excludes adequate experience no matter how obstinately the veneer of such "realism" is built up. This affects the social and psychological function of drama.

It is hard to establish whether the spectators of Greek tragedy really experienced the catharsis Aristotle described—in fact this theory, evolved after the age of tragedy was over, seems to have been a rationalization itself, an attempt to state the purpose of tragedy in pragmatic, quasi-scientific terms. Whatever the case, it seems pretty certain that those who saw the *Oresteia* of Aeschylus or Sophocles' *Oedipus* were not likely to translate these tragedies (the subject matter of which was known to everyone, and the interest in which was centered in artistic treatment) directly into everyday terms. This audience did not expect that on the next corner of Athens similar things would go on. Actually, pseudo-realism allows for the direct and extremely primitive identification achieved by popular culture; and it presents a façade of trivial buildings, rooms, dresses, and faces as though they were the promise of something thrilling and exciting taking place at any moment.

In order to establish this socio-psychological frame of reference, one would have to follow up systematically categories—such as the normality of crime or pseudo-realism and many others—to determine their structural unity and to interpret the specific devices, symbols, and stereotypes in relation to this frame of reference. We hypothesize at this phase that the frames of reference and the individual devices will tend in the same direction.

Only against psychological backdrops such as pseudo-realism and against implicit assumptions such as the normality of crime can the specific stereotypes of television plays be interpreted. The very standardization indicated by set frames of reference automatically produces a number of stereotypes. Also, the technology of television production makes stereotypy almost inevitable. The short time available for the preparation of scripts and the vast material continuously to be produced call for certain formulas. Moreover, in plays lasting only a quarter to half an hour each, it appears inevitable that the kind of person the audience faces each time should be indicated drastically through red and green lights. We are not dealing with the problem of the existence of stereotypes as such. Since stereotypes are an indispensable element of the organization and anticipation of experience, preventing us from falling into mental disorganization and chaos, no art can entirely dispense with them. Again, the functional change is what concerns us. The more stereotypes become reified and rigid in the present setup of cultural industry, the less people are likely to change their preconceived ideas with the progress of their experience. The more opaque and complicated modern life becomes, the more people are tempted to cling desperately to clichés which seem to bring some order into the otherwise ununderstandable. Thus, people may not only lose true insight into reality, but ultimately their very capacity for life experience may be dulled by the constant wearing of blue and pink spectacles.

STEREOTYPING

In coping with this danger, we may not do full justice to the meaning of some of the stereotypes which are to be dealt with. We should never forget that there are two sides to every psychodynamic phenomenon, the unconscious or id element and the rationalization. Although the latter is psychologically defined as a defense mechanism, it may very well contain some nonpsychological, objective truth which cannot simply be pushed aside on account of the psychological function of the rationalization. Thus some of the stereotypical messages, directed toward particularly weak spots in the mentality of large sectors of the population, may prove to be quite legitimate. However, it may be said with fairness that the questionable blessings of morals, such as "one should not chase after rainbows," are largely overshadowed by the threat of inducing people to mechanical simplifications by ways of distorting the world in such a way that it seems to fit into preestablished pigeonholes.

The example here selected, however, should indicate rather drastically the danger of stereotypy. A television play concerning a fascist dictator, a kind of hybrid between Mussolini and Peron, shows the dictator in a moment of crisis; and the content of the play is his inner and outer collapse. Whether the cause of his collapse is a popular upheaval or a military revolt is never made clear. But neither this issue nor any other of a social or political nature enters the plot itself. The course of events takes place exclusively on a private level. The dictator is just a heel who treats sadistically both his secretary and his "lovely and warmhearted" wife. His antagonist, a general, was formerly in love with the wife; and they both still love each other, although the wife sticks loyally to her husband. Forced by her husband's brutality, she attempts flight, and is intercepted by the general who wants to save her. The turning point occurs when the guards surround the palace to defend the dictator's popular wife. As soon as they learn that she has departed, the guards quit; and the dictator, whose "inflated ego" explodes at the same time, gives up. The dictator is nothing but a bad, pompous, and cowardly man. He seems to act with extreme stupidity; nothing of the objective dynamics of dictatorship comes out. The impression is created that totalitarianism grows out of character disorders of ambitious politicians, and is overthrown by the honesty, courage, and warmth of those figures with whom the audience is supposed to identify. The standard device employed is that of the spurious personalization of objective issues. The representatives of ideas under attack, as in the case of the fascists here, are presented as villains in a ludicrous cloak-and-dagger fashion, whereas those who fight for the "right cause" are personally idealized. This not only distracts from any real social issues but also enforces the psychologically extremely dangerous division of the world into black (the outgroup) and white (we, the ingroup). Certainly, no artistic production can deal with ideas or political creeds *in abstracto* but has to present them in terms of their concrete impact upon human beings; yet it would be utterly futile to present individuals as mere specimens of an abstraction, as puppets expressive of an idea. In order to deal with the concrete impact of totalitarian systems, it would be more commendable to show how the life of ordinary people is affected by terror and impotence than to cope with the phony psychology of the big-shots, whose heroic role is silently endorsed by such a treatment even if they are pictured as villains. There seems to be hardly any question of the importance of an analysis of pseudo-personalization and its effect, by no means limited to television.

Although pseudo-personalization denotes the stereotyped way of "looking at things" in television, we should also point out certain stereotypes in the narrower sense. Many television plays could be characterized by the sobriquet "a pretty girl can do no wrong." The heroine of a light comedy is, to use George Legman's term, "a bitch heroine." She behaves toward her father in an incredibly inhuman and cruel manner only slightly rationalized as "merry pranks." But she is punished very slightly, if at all. True, in real life bad deeds are rarely punished at all, but this cannot be applied to television. Here, those who have developed the production code for the movies seem right: what matters in mass media is not what happens in real life, but rather the positive and negative "messages," prescriptions, and taboos that the spectator absorbs by means of identification with the material he is looking at. The punishment given to the pretty heroine only nominally fulfills the conventional requirements of the conscience for a second. But the spectator is given to understand that the pretty heroine really gets away with everything just because she is pretty.

The attitude in question seems to be indicative of a universal penchant. In another sketch that belongs to a series dealing with the confidence racket, the attractive girl who is an active participant in the racket not only is paroled after having been sentenced to a long term, but also seems to have a good chance of marrying her victim. Her sex morality, of course, is unimpeachable. The spectator is supposed to like her at first sight as a modest and self-effacing character, and he must not be disappointed. Although it is discovered that she is a crook, the original identification must be restored, or rather maintained. The stereotype of the nice girl is so strong that not even the proof of her delinquency can destroy it; and, by hook or by crook, she must be what she appears to be. It goes without saying that such psychological models tend to confirm exploitative, demanding, and aggressive attitudes on the part of young girls—a character structure which has come to be known in psychoanalysis under the name of oral aggressiveness.

Sometimes such stereotypes are disguised as national American traits, a part of the American scene where the image of the haughty, egoistic, yet irresistible girl who plays havoc with poor dad has come to be a public institution. This way of reasoning is an insult to the American spirit. High-pressure publicity and continuous plugging to institutionalize some obnoxious type does not make the type a sacred symbol of folklore. Many considerations of an apparently anthropological nature today tend only to veil objectionable trends, as though they were of an ethnological, quasi-natural character. Incidentally, it is amazing to what degree television material even on superficial examination brings to mind psychoanalytic concepts with the qualification of being a psychoanalysis in reverse. Psychoanalysis has described the oral syndrome combining the antagonistic trends of aggressive and dependent traits. This character syndrome is closely indicated by the pretty girl that can do no wrong, who, while being aggressive against her father exploits him at the same time, depending on him as much as, on the surface level, she is set against him. The difference between the sketch and psychoanalysis is simply that the sketch exalts the very same syndrome which is treated by psychoanalysis as a reversion to infantile developmental phases and which the psychoanalyst tries to dissolve. It remains to be seen whether something similar applies as well to some types of male heroes, particularly the super-he-man. It may well be that he too can do no wrong.

Finally, we should deal with a rather widespread stereotype which, inasmuch as it is taken for granted by television, is further enhanced. At the same time, the example may serve to show that certain psychoanalytic interpretations of cultural stereotypes are not really too far-fetched; the latent ideas that psychoanalysis attributes to certain stereotypes come to the surface. There is the extremely popular idea that the artist is not only maladjusted, introverted, and *a priori* somewhat funny; but that he is really an "aesthete," a weakling, and a "sissy." In other words, modern synthetic folklore tends to identify the artist with the homosexual and to respect only the "man of action" as a real, strong man. This idea is expressed in a surprisingly direct manner in one of the comedy scripts at our disposal. It portrays a young man who is not only the "dope" who appears so often on television but is also a shy, retiring, and accordingly untalented poet, whose moronic poems are ridiculed.[7] He is in love with a girl but is too weak and insecure to indulge in the necking practices she rather crudely suggests; the girl, on her part, is caricatured as a boy-chaser. As happens frequently in mass culture, the roles of the sexes are reversed—the girl is utterly aggressive, and the boy, utterly afraid of her, describes himself as "woman-handled" when she manages to kiss him. There are vulgar innuendos of homosexuality of which one may be quoted: the heroine tells her boy friend that another boy is in love with someone, and the boy friend asks, "What's he in love with?" She answers, "A girl, of course," and her boy friend replies, "Why, of course? Once before it was a neighbor's turtle, and what's more its name was Sam." This interpretation of the artist as innately incompetent and a social outcast (by the innuendo of sexual inversion) is worthy of examination.

We do not pretend that the individual illustrations and examples, or the theories by which they are interpreted, are basically new. But in view of the cultural and pedagogical problem presented by television, we do not think that the novelty of the specific findings should be a primary concern. We know from psychoanalysis that the reasoning, "But we know all this!" is often a defense. This defense is made in order to dismiss insights as irrelevant because they are actually uncomfortable and make life more difficult for us than it already is by shaking our conscience when we are supposed to enjoy the "simple pleasures of life." The investigation of the television problems we have here indicated and illustrated by a few examples selected at random demands, most of all, taking seriously notions dimly familiar to most of us by putting them into their proper context and perspective and by checking them by pertinent material. We propose to concentrate on issues of which we are vaguely but uncomfortably aware, even at the expense of our discomfort's mounting, the further and the more systematically our studies proceed. The effort here required is of a moral nature itself: knowingly to face psychological mechanisms operating on various levels in order not to become blind and passive victims. We can change this medium of far-reaching potentialities only if we look at it in the same spirit which we hope will one day be expressed by its imagery.

Notes

1. David Riesman, *The Lonely Crowd* (New Haven, 1950), p. v.
2. The evolution of the ideology of the extrovert has probably also its long history, particularly in the lower types of popular literature during the nineteenth century when the code of decency became divorced from its religious roots and therewith attained more and more the character of an opaque taboo. It seems likely, however, that in this respect the triumph of the films marked the decisive step. Reading as an act of perception and apperception probably carries with itself a certain kind of internalization; the act of reading a novel fairly close to a *monologue interieur*. Visualization in modern mass media makes for externalization. The idea of inwardness, still maintained in older portrait painting through the expressiveness of the face, gives way to unmistakable optical signals that can be grasped

at a glance. Even if a character in a movie or television show is not what he appears to be, his appearance is treated in such a way as to leave no doubt about his true nature. Thus a villain who is not presented as a brute must at least be "suave," and his repulsive slickness and mild manner unambiguously indicate what we are to think of him.

3. It should be noted that the tendency against "erudition" was already present at the very beginning of popular culture, particularly in Defoe who was consciously opposed to the learned literature of his day, and has become famous for having scorned every refinement of style and artistic construction in favor of an apparent faithfulness to "life."

4. One of the significant differences seems to be that in the eighteenth century the concept of popular culture itself moving toward an emancipation from the absolutistic and semifeudal tradition had a progressive meaning, stressing autonomy of the individual as being capable of making his own decisions. This means, among other things, that the early popular literature left space for authors who violently disagreed with the pattern set by Richardson and, nevertheless, obtained popularity of their own. The most prominent case in question is that of Fielding, whose first novel started as a parody of Richardson. It would be interesting to compare the popularity of Richardson and Fielding at that time. Fielding hardly achieved the same success as Richardson. Yet it would be absurd to assume that today's popular culture would allow the equivalent of a *Tom Jones*. This may illustrate the contention of the "rigidity" of today's popular culture. A crucial experiment would be to make an attempt to base a movie on a novel such as Evelyn Waugh's *The Loved One*. It is almost certain that the script would be rewritten and edited so often that nothing remotely similar to the idea of the original would be left.

5. The more rationality (the reality principle) is carried to extremes, the more its ultimate aim (actual gratification) tends, paradoxically, to appear as "immature" and ridiculous. Not only eating, but also uncontrolled manifestations of sexual impulses tend to provoke laughter in audiences—kisses in motion pictures have generally to be led up to, the stage has to be set for them, in order to avoid laughter. Yet mass culture never completely succeeds in wiping out potential laughter. Induced, of course, by the supposed infantilism of sensual pleasures, laughter can largely be accounted for by the mechanism of repression. Laughter is a defense against the forbidden fruit.

6. This relationship again should not be oversimplified. No matter to what extent modern mass media tend to blur the difference between reality and the aesthetic, our realistic spectators are still aware that all is "in fun." It cannot be assumed that the direct primary perception of reality takes place within the television frame of reference, although many movie-goers recall the alienation of familiar sights when leaving the theater: everything still has the appearance of being part of the movie plot. What is more important is the interpretation of reality in terms of psychological carry-overs, the preparedness to see ordinary objects as though some threatening mystery were hidden behind them. Such an attitude seems to be syntonic with mass delusions such as suspicion of omnipresent graft, corruption, and conspiracy.

7. It could be argued that this very ridicule expresses that this boy is not meant to represent the artist but just the "dope." But this is probably too rationalistic. Again, as in the case of the schoolteacher, official respect for culture prevents caricaturing the artist as such. However, by characterizing the boy, among other things by his writing poetry, it is indirectly achieved that the artistic activities and silliness are associated with each other. In many respects mass culture is organized much more by way of such associations than in strictly logical terms. It may be added that quite frequently attacks on any social type seek protection by apparently presenting the object of the attack as an exception, while it is understood by innuendo that he is considered as a specimen of the whole concept.

Sight, Sound, and the Fury

By MARSHALL McLUHAN

ON HIS RECENT VISIT to America, Roy Campbell mentioned that when Dylan Thomas had discovered he could read poetry on the radio, this discovery transformed his later poetry for the better. Thomas discovered a new dimension in his language when he established a new relation with the public.

Until Gutenberg, poetic publication meant the reading or singing of one's poems to a small audience. When poetry began to exist primarily on the printed page, in the seventeenth century, there occurred that strange mixture of sight and sound later known as "metaphysical poetry" which has so much in common with modern poetry.

American colonization began when the only culture available to most men was that of the printed book. European culture was then, as now, as much an affair of music, painting, sculpture, and communication as it was of literature. So that to this day North Americans associate culture mainly with books. But, paradoxically, it is in North America that the new media of sight and sound have had the greatest popular sway. Is it precisely because we make the widest separation between culture and our new media that we are unable to see the new media as serious culture? Have four centuries of book-culture hypnotized us into such concentration on the content of books and the new media that we cannot see that the very form of any medium of communication is as important as anything that it conveys?

Ireland is perhaps the only part of the English-speaking world where the oral tradition of culture has strongly persisted in spite of the printed page. And Ireland has given us Wilde, Shaw, Yeats, Synge, and Joyce in recent years—all of them masters of the magic of the spoken word. A Ballynooley farmer who returned to Ireland from America said to his neighbor: "In three years I didn't meet a man who could sing a ballad, let alone compose one on his feet."

The printed page was itself a highly specialized (and spatialized) form of communication. In 1500 A.D. it was revolutionary. And Erasmus was perhaps the first to grasp the fact that the revolution was going to occur above all in the classroom. He devoted himself to the production of textbooks and to the setting up of grammar schools. The printed book soon liquidated two thousand years of manuscript culture. It created the solitary student. It set up the rule of private interpretation against public disputation. It established the divorce between "literature and life." It created a new

Reprinted from the *Commonweal*, Vol. 60 (1954), pp. 168-97, by permission of the author and the publisher. (Copyright, 1954, by The Commonweal Publishing Co., Inc.)

and highly abstract culture because it was itself a mechanized form of culture. Today, when the textbook has yielded to the classroom project and the classroom as social workshop and discussion group, it is easier for us to notice what was going on in 1500. Today we know that the turn to the visual on one hand, that is, to photography, and to the auditory media of radio and public address systems on the other hand, has created a totally new environment for the educational process.

André Malraux has recently popularized the notion of the art revolution of our time in his *Museum without Walls*. His theme is that the picture book today can embrace a greater range of art than any museum. By bringing such a range of art within portable compass, however, it has changed even the painter's approach to painting. Again, it is not just a question of message, image, or content. The picture-book as a museum without walls has for the artist a new technical meaning, just as for the spectator, pictorial communication means a large but unconscious shift in his ways of thought and feeling.

We have long been accustomed to the notion that a person's beliefs shape and color his existence. They provide the windows which frame, and through which he views, all events. We are less accustomed to the notion that the shapes of a technological environment are also idea-windows. Every shape (gimmick or metropolis), every situation planned and realized by man's factive intelligence, is a window which reveals or distorts reality. Today, when power technology has taken over the entire global environment to be manipulated as the material of art, nature has disappeared with nature-poetry. And the effectiveness of the classroom has diminished with the decline of the monopoly of book-culture. If Erasmus saw the classroom as the new stage for the drama of the printing press, we can see today that the new situation for young and old alike is classrooms without walls. The entire urban environment has become aggressively pedagogic. Everybody and everything has a message to declare, a line to plug.

This is the time of transition from the commercial age, when it was the production and distribution of commodities which occupied the ingenuity of men. Today we have moved from the production of packaged goods to the packaging of information. Formerly we invaded foreign markets with goods. Today we invade whole cultures with packaged information, entertainment, and ideas. In view of the instantaneous global scope of the new media of sight and sound, even the newspaper is slow. But the press ousted the book in the nineteenth century because the book arrived too late. The newspaper page was not a mere enlargement of the book page. It was, like the movie, a new collective art form.

To retrace some of this ground, it will help to recall that in the *Phaedrus,* Plato argued that the new arrival of writing would revolutionize culture for the worse. He suggested that it would substitute reminiscence for thought and mechanical learning for the true dialectic of the living quest for truth by discourse and conversation. It was as if he foresaw the library of Alexandria and the unending exegesis upon previous exegesis of the scholiasts and grammarians.

It would seem that the great virtue of writing is its power to arrest the swift process of thought for steady contemplation and analysis. Writing is the translation of the audible into the visual. In large measure it is the spatialization of thought. Yet writing on papyrus and parchment fostered a very different set of mental habits from those who associate with print and books. In the first place, silent reading was unknown until the macadamized, streamlined surfaces of the printed page arrived to permit swift traverse of the eye alone. In the second place, difficulty of access to manuscripts impelled students to memorize so far as possible everything they read. This led to encyclopedism, but also to having on tap in oral discourse one's entire erudition.

The child at school in the Middle Ages had first to make his own copies of texts from dictation. He had next to compile his own grammar and lexicon and commonplace book. The arrival of plenty of cheap, uniform, printed texts changed all this. The mechanization of writing by means of the assembly line of movable type speedily expanded the range of available reading and just as quickly reduced the habit of oral discourse as a way of learning. During the sixteenth century, however, a degree of equilibrium persisted between oral and written learning which we associate with the special excellence of Elizabethan drama, sermon, and poetry.

In the reverse direction, much of the vivid energy of American speech and writing in the twentieth century is the result of the movement away from book-culture toward oral communication. This nonliterary direction of speech has been felt to a much smaller degree in England and in Europe during the same period. Radio in particular has encouraged the return to the panel discussion and the round table. But the spontaneous move toward the seminar and class discussion as learning process has been helped by press and photography too, in so far as these have challenged the monopoly of the book.

Above all, the habits of the business community in demanding conference and discussion as the swift way of establishing insight into method and procedure in various specialized branches of business—these have prompted the new reliance on speech as a means of discovery. It is significant, for example, that the atomic physicists found that only by daily, face-to-face association could they get on with their tasks during the past war.

It has long been a truism that changes in material culture cause shifts in the patterns of the entire culutre. The ancient road made possible armies and empires and destroyed the isolated city states of Greece. But the road depended in the first place on writing. Behind the imperial command of great land areas stood the written word in easily transportable form. In the nineteenth century, the newspapers, especially after the telegraph, paid for new roads and faster transport by land and sea. The press altered the forms of government, and the telegraph brought secret diplomacy to an end. When events in Egypt or Russia, London, Paris, or New York were known everywhere at once, the time for secret negotiation was reduced to hours and minutes. And the great national populations of the world, alerted and emotionalized by the press, could confront one another immediately for a showdown.

Printing had from the first fostered nationalism because the vernaculars with their large reading publics were more profitable to commercial publishers than Latin. The press has pushed this nationalism to its ultimate point. There it remains. But photography and movies, like music and painting, are international in their power of appeal. The power of pictures to leap over national frontiers and prejudices is well-known, for good and ill.

One aspect of the press deserves special comment in this same respect. The contents of newspapers, their messages and information, have steadily promoted nationalism. But the form of the newspaper page is powerfully intercultural and international. The unformulated message of an assembly of news items from every quarter of the globe is that the world today is one city. All war is civil war. All suffering is our own. So that regardless of the political line, or the time or the place, the mere format of the press exerts a single pressure. Basic acceptance of this fact is recorded in the steady weakening of interest in political parties everywhere.

From the point of view of its format, the press as a daily cross-section of the globe is a mirror of the technological instruments of communication. It is the popular daily book, the great collective poem, the universal entertainment of our age. As such it has modified poetic techniques and in turn has already been modified by the newer media of movie, radio, and television. These represent revolutions in communication as radical as printing itself. In fact, they are "magic casements opening on the foam of perilous seas," on which few of us have yet ventured in thought, art or living. If Erasmus was the first to size up and exploit the printing press as a new force in art and education, James Joyce was the first to seize upon newspaper, radio, movie, and television to set up his "verbivocovisual" drama in *Finnegans Wake*. Pound and Eliot are, in comparison with Joyce, timid devotees of the book as art form. But most of the difficulties which the ordinary person encounters with the poetry of Pound and Eliot disappear if it is viewed as a historical newsreel of persons, myths, ideas, and events with thematic musical score built in. Joyce had a much greater trust of language and reality than Pound or Eliot. By contrast they give their language and reality the Hollywood glamor treatment. Joyce is closer to a De Sica film with its awareness of the intimate riches of the most ordinary scenes and situations.

But the reader who approaches Pound, Eliot, and Joyce alike as exploiters of the cinematic aspects of language will arrive at appreciation more quickly than the one who unconsciously tries to make sense of them by reducing their use of the new media of communication to the abstract linear forms of the book page.

The basic fact to keep in mind about the movie camera and projector is their resemblance to the process of human cognition. That is the real source of their magical, transforming power. The camera rolls up the external world on a spool. It does this by rapid still shots. The projector unwinds this spool as a kind of magic carpet which conveys the enchanted spectator anywhere in the world in an instant. The camera records and analyzes the daylight world with more than human intensity because of the forty-five degree angle of the camera eye. The projector reveals this daylight world on a dark screen where it becomes a dream world.

The wonderful resemblance in all this to human cognition extends at least this far: in cognition we have to interiorize the exterior world. We have to recreate in the medium of our senses and inner faculties the drama of existence. This is the work of the *logos poietikos,* the agent intellect. In speech we utter that drama which we have analogously recreated within us. In speech we make or *poet* the world even as we may say that the movie parrots the world. Languages themselves are thus the greatest of all works of art. They are the collective hymns to existence. For in cognition itself is the whole of the poetic process. But the artist differs from most men in his power to arrest and then reverse the stages of human apprehension. He learns how to embody the stages of cognition (Aristotle's "plot") in an exterior work which can be held up for contemplation.

Even in this respect the movie resembles the cognitive process since the daylight world which the camera rolls up on the spool is reversed and projected to become the magical dream world of the audience. But all media of communication share something of this cognitive character which only a Thomist vision of existence and cognition dare do justice to.

Television, for example, differs from the movie in the immediacy with which it picks up and renders back the visible. The TV camera is like the microphone in relation to the voice. The movie has no such immediacy of pickup and feedback. As we begin to look into the inevitably cognitive character of the various media we soon get over the jitters that come from exclusive concern with any one form of communication.

In his *Theory of the Film,* Bela Balazs notes how "the discovery of printing gradually rendered illegible the faces of men. So much could be read from paper that the method of conveying meaning by facial expression fell into desuetude. Victor Hugo wrote once that the printed book took over the part played by the cathedral in the Middle Ages and became the carrier of the spirit of the people. But the thousands of books tore the one spirit . . . into thousands of opinions . . . tore the church into a thousand books. The visible spirit was thus turned into a legible spirit and visual culture into a culture of concepts."

Before printing, a reader was one who discerned and probed riddles. After printing, it meant one who scanned, who skipped along the macadamized surfaces of print. Today at the end of that process we have come to equate reading skill with speed and distraction rather than wisdom. But print, the mechanization of writing, was succeeded in the nineteenth century by photography and then by the mechanization of human gesture in the movie. This was followed by the mechanization of speech in telephone, phonograph and radio. In the talkies, and finally with TV, came the mechanization of the totality of human expression, of voice, gesture, and human figure in action.

Each of these steps in the mechanization of human expression was comparable in its scope to the revolution brought about by the mechanization of writing itself. The changes in the ways of human association, social and political, were telescoped in time and so hidden from casual observers.

If there is a truism in the history of human communication it is that any innovation in the external means of communication brings in its train shock on shock of social change. One effect of writing was to make possible cities, roads, armies, and empires. The letters of the alphabet were indeed the dragon's teeth. The printed book not only fostered nationalism but made it possible to bring the world of the past into every study. The newspaper is a daily book which brings a slice of all the cultures of the world under our eyes every day. To this extent it reverses the tendency of the printing press to accentuate merely national culture. Pictorial journalism and reportage tend strongly in the same international direction. But is this true of radio? Radio has strengthened the oral habit of communication and extended it, via the panel and round table, to serious learning. Yet radio seems to be a form which also strengthens the national culture. Merely oral societies, for example, are the ultimate in national exclusiveness.

A group of us recently performed an experiment with a large group of students. We divided them into four sections and assigned each section to a separate communication channel. Each section got the identical lecture simultaneously, but one read it, one heard it as a regular lecture in a studio, one heard it on radio and one heard and saw it as a TV broadcast. Immediately afterwards we administered a quiz to determine apprehension and understanding of this new and difficult material. The TV section came out on top, then the radio section, then the studio, and reading sections at the bottom. This was a totally unexpected result and it is too soon to generalize; but it is quite certain that the so-called mass media are not necessarily ordained to be channels of popular entertainment only.

It is "desirable" in thinking about the new media that we should recall that buildings are mass communications and that the first mechanical medium was print from movable type. In fact, the discovery of movable type was the ancestor of all assembly lines, and it would be foolish to overlook the impact of the technological form involved in print on the psychological life of readers. To overlook this would be as unrealistic as to ignore rhythm and tempo in music. Likewise it is only common sense to recognize that the general situation created by a communicative channel and its audience is a large part of that in which and by which the individuals commune. The encoded message cannot be regarded as a mere capsule or pellet produced at one point and consumed at another. Communication is communication all along the line.

One might illustrate from sports. The best brand of football played before fifty people would lack something of the power to communicate. The large, enthusiastic crowd is necessary to represent the community at large, just as the players enact a drama which externalizes certain motivations and tensions in the communal life which would not otherwise be visible or available for audience participation. In India huge crowds assemble to experience *darshan,* which they consider to occur when they are massed in the presence of a visible manifestation of their collective life.

The new media do something similar for us in the West. Movies, radio, and TV establish certain personalities on a new plane of existence. They exist not so much in themselves but as types of collective life felt and perceived through a mass medium. L'il Abner, Bob Hope, Donald Duck, and Marilyn Monroe become points of collective awareness and communication for an entire society. And as technology increasingly undertakes to submit the entire planet as well as the contents of consciousness to the purposes of man's factive intelligence, it behooves us to consider the whole process of magical transformation involved in the media acutely and extensively.

From this point of view it should be obvious, for example, that the framers of the Hollywood morality code were operating with a very inadequate set of perceptions and concepts about the nature of the movie medium. Modern discussions of censorship, in the same way, are helplessly tied to conceptions borrowed from book-culture alone. And the defenders of book-culture have seldom given any thought to any of the media as art forms, the book least of all. The result is that their "defense" might as well be staged on an abandoned movie lot for all the effect it has on the actual situation.

When I wrote *The Mechanical Bride* some years ago I did not realize that I was attempting a defense of book-culture against the new media. I can now see that I was trying to bring some of the critical awareness fostered by literary training to bear on the new media of sight and sound. My strategy was wrong, because my obsession with literary values blinded me to much that was actually happening for good and ill. What we have to defend today is not the values developed in any particular culture or by any one mode of communication. Modern technology presumes to attempt a total transformation of man and his environment. This calls in turn for an inspection and defense of all human values. And so far as merely human aid goes, the citadel of this defense must be located in analytical awareness of the nature of the creative process involved in human cognition. For it is in this citadel that science and technology have already established themselves in their manipulation of the new media.

Notes on Mass Culture

By IRVING HOWE

WHEN WE GLANCE at the pseudo-cultural amusements that occupy the American people's leisure time, we soon wonder: what happens to the anonymous audience while it consumes the products of mass culture?[1] It is a question that can hardly be answered systematically or definitively, for there is no way of knowing precisely what the subterranean reactions of an audience are—and it will certainly not do merely to ask it. We can only speculate, and the answer to our question, if one is to be had at all, can be found only within ourselves.

Here we meet our first difficulty: the only people who can analyze the effects of mass culture on an audience are those who reject its uncritical acceptance of mass culture. "Contaminated" by art standards, the intellectual must necessarily hesitate when he tries to decide which of his reactions to mass culture are similar to those of the audience and which are the product of his private cultivation. He may overcome this difficulty by frankly admitting to himself that, like it or not, he is part of the mass audience and is influenced by mass culture. If he is to speculate fruitfully, he must reach that precarious condition where he can identify himself with the audience's reactions while yet retaining his critical distance.

To some extent the intellectual can dispense with mass culture, though far less than he knows or is willing to admit. So long as we live in a class society, mass culture will remain indispensable even to those who have learned to scorn it; we cannot escape what is so much a part of the atmosphere in which we live. Nor would such an attempted escape be particularly desirable: the price of public experience may be a kind of contamination, but in view of the alternative it is not too high a price to pay.

THE UNCONSCIOUS URGE TO SELF-OBLITERATION

Mass culture is an urban product. Confined to the close spaces of a city, members of an industrial society must always face the disturbing problem of what to do with their leisure time, how to organize it in relation to their work day.

One thing seems certain: except during brief revolutionary intervals, the quality of leisure-time activity cannot vary too sharply from that of the work day. If it did, the office or factory worker would be exposed to those terrible dualities of feeling that make it so difficult for the intellectual to adjust his job to himself. But the worker wants no part of such difficulties, he has enough already. Following the dictum of industrial society that

Reprinted from *Politics*, Vol. 5, Spring, 1948, pp. 120-23, by permission of the author and the publisher. (Copyright, 1948, by Dwight Macdonald.)

anonymity is a key to safety, he seeks the least troublesome solution: mass culture.

Whatever its manifest content, mass culture must therefore not subvert the basic patterns of industrial life. Leisure time must be so organized as to bear a factitious relationship to working time: apparently different, actually the same. It must provide relief from work monotony without making the return to work too unbearable; it must provide amusement without insight and pleasure without disturbance—as distinct from art which gives pleasure through disturbance.

Mass culture is thus orientated toward a central aspect of industrial society: the depersonalization of the individual. On the one hand, it diverts the worker from his disturbing reduction to semi-robot status by arranging "relaxing" amusements for him. The need for such amusements explains the ceaseless and hectic quest for novelty in the mass-culture industries (e.g., the "twist" in popular songs, the melodic phrase the audience remembers.) On the other hand, mass culture reinforces those emotional attitudes that seem inseparable from existence in modern society—passivity and boredom. Precisely the frenetic chase after novelty, after something new that might rise above routine experience, becomes the means of molding leisure-time activity according to work-time patterns. What is supposed to deflect us from the reduction of our personalities actually reinforces it.

In a fascinating study, "On Popular Music,"[2] T. W. Adorno makes some remarks on the standardization of popular music that seem a specific working-out of the views expressed here:

> . . . the harmonic cornerstone of each hit—the beginning and the end of each part—must beat out the standard scheme. . . . Complications have no consequences . . . regardless of what aberrations occur, the hit will lead back to the familiar experience, and nothing fundamentally novel will be introduced. . . . The composition hears for the listener. This is how popular music divests the listener of his spontaneity.
>
> Boredom has become so great that only the brightest colors have any chance of being lifted out of the general drabness. Yet it is just those violent colors which bear witness to the omnipotence of mechanical, industrial production . . . the means used to overcome reality are more humdrum than reality itself.
>
> To escape boredom and avoid effort is incompatible. . . . They seek novelty but the strain and boredom associated with actual work lead to avoidance of effort in leisure time. . . . That means boredom again. . . .

What is true for popular music is also true for the movies. The movie theatre is like a dark cavern, a neutral womb, into whose soothing and dissolving blackness we can escape from our frayed selves. In a nonreligious age, the movie theatre is one of the few places that provides a poor man with a kind of retreat, a place where he can throw off the shackles of his social responsibility, relationships and personality. Here, at least, he does not have to acknowledge his irritating self.

It is interesting to compare the movie theatre with the baseball park. In the theatre one ceases, in a sense, to exist. One seldom talks, one is

seldom brought to those heights of consciousness that a genuine work of
dramatic art can arouse. (Even the adolescents necking in the back row do
so with a kind of grim anonymity.) The movie house is a psychological
cloakroom where one checks one's personality. But baseball, one of the
few mass urban activities that seems to retain some folk spontaneity, is
different. The game is so paced that one usually has enough time to return
to oneself, and the entire atmosphere of the ball park allows for some spontaneity: the audience argues, eats, shouts, participates as an independent
group that is reacting to the events on the field. As a result, one encounters
a kind of rough and pleasing wit in the ball park, as well as an easy-going
camaraderie. The ball park, I find, is one of the few public places where
one can converse uninhibitedly with total strangers.

If only because it must conform to the psychological patterns of industrial society, mass culture is inseparably related to common experience.
The notion that it concocts a never-never world of irrelevant fantasy is
nonsense spread by the kind of people whose only complaint about Hollywood is that it isn't "realistic" enough. In actuality, the audience accepts
both mass culture and daily experience precisely to the degree that the two
blend. By now neither can be maintained without the other, which is one
reason why there prevails in this country such a blurred notion of what
human experience is and such an inadequate notion of what it should be.

But, it may be objected, don't the movies create atmospheres and situations totally removed from the experience of the audience? How many
people are in a position to lead the kind of lives that Van Johnson and
Bette Davis, Ronald Colman and Ingrid Bergman portray on the screen?
Precious few, of course; and if the comparison between the life of an
audience and that portrayed on the screen is made simply in such formal
terms, it will yield us nothing. Furthermore, there are obviously many films
whose major purpose is to construct an atmosphere or environment characterized precisely by its complete irrelevance to the audience's life. But I
think that the majority of films do have strong psychological contact with
our lives. From the tough-guy films we find so exciting because they rouse
our unexpended sadism to the sophisticated comedies that play on our
yearning for charm and grace, from the musical comedies that make taffy
of our tensions to the socially conscious films that seek to exorcise our guilts
—more movies than we know are comments on our experience and help
us to "adjust" to it, that is, to acquiesce in it. They may not be truthful or
authentic or profound comments, but they do touch on essential aspects of
our relationship both to society and ourselves. The movies help us remain
at peace with ourselves by helping us to suppress ourselves.

By now daily experience and mass culture are so interlaced that it
would be futile to seek causal relationships between them. Does Gregory
Peck model himself after the American Lover or does the American Lover
model himself after Gregory Peck? It would be hard, and unnecessary, to
say. All we need know is that the relationship between mass culture and

daily experience is so intimate that millions of people seem hardly able or willing to distinguish between the two. They send letters of advice to comic-strip and radio characters. Little Orphan Annie has for years been receiving letters from readers that tell her how to get out of her endless difficulties. (She never seems to follow the advice.) Some years ago when the creator of "Terry and the Pirates" was rash enough to kill a favorite character, the New York *Daily News* was besieged with letters of complaint. And the movie magazines establish relationships between millions of American women and idealized versions of movie stars in which it is impossible to distinguish between reality and fantasy, so closely are they interwoven.

Mass culture elicits the most conservative responses from the audience. So long as the audience feels that it must continue to live as it does, it has little desire to see its passivity and deep-seated though hardly conscious boredom upset; it wants to be titillated and amused, but not disturbed. For those molded in the image of contemporary society, art has many dangers: its effects are unpredictable and its demands tremendous. Art demands effort, a creative response from the audience. Joyce makes it hard for us, but he offers us the tempting possibility of reaching his heights of sensibility. But mass culture is safe, for its end is already present in its beginning.

A common item of experience tends to confirm these observations. When we feel vaguely upset and dissatisfied with ourselves, we "take in" a movie. If we are somewhat intellectualized, we know the movie will not provide us with the fundamental satisfactions that, say, a Dostoievsky novel might, but because of our attachment to our disturbance we are unable to summon the effort a work of art would demand. In an act of self-destructive bravado we even deliberately look for a "bad" movie; we punish ourselves for "feeling bad" by doing something that must ultimately make us feel worse. The analogy with neurosis, in which the sufferer clings to the source of his disturbance, is obvious.

THE DISSOCIATION OF PERSONALITY

Mass culture seems always to involve a pact between medium and audience to suppress the free play of the unconscious. Where art stirs a free and rich passage of materials from dream to experience and from experience to dream, mass culture tries to cage the unconscious. It cannot, of course, succeed, but it does often manage to dissociate conscious from unconscious life. The audience therefore responds on two unintegrated levels: surface consciousness ("having a good time") and suppressed unconscious (the distorted evocation of experience by popular culture themes). On the surface the Donald Duck and Mickey Mouse cartoons seem merely pleasant little fictions, but they are actually overladen with the most competitive, aggressive and sadistic themes. Often on the verge of hysteria, Donald Duck is a frustrated little monster who has something of the SS man in him and whom we, also having something of the SS man in us, naturally find quite charming. . . .

This discrepancy between conscious and unconscious reactions to mass culture seems inseparable from the audience's need for social approval. Whoever has attended a jam session or gone to the Paramount Theatre when a favorite bandleader is featured, knows how compulsive the seemingly spontaneous audience responses can be. No doubt the audience believes it is "enjoying" itself, but a central component of that enjoyment is the very powerful pressures toward social conformism. How can a bobby-soxer admit to not enjoying Vaughn Monroe?

(In fairness, it should be admitted that there is probably nothing more conformist about the mass audience's feeling that the famous bandleader or the all-star picture must be entertaining, than the intellectual's analagous feeling that the great writer must be profound.)

In the comics, this dissocation of personality is taken for granted. Comic characterization consists of persistent identification of each name with an outstanding personality trait: Tillie is always the toiler, Joe Jinks always worries, Little Orphan Annie always suffers and Maggie always wants to break into society. Dissociation of personality has been institutionalized in the "balanced comic section" of the McCormick-Patterson chain:

> The Gumps [represent] gossip, realistic family life; Harold Teen, youth; Smitty, cute-kid stuff; Winnie Winkle, girl; Moon Mullins, burly laughter; Orphan Annie, sentiment . . . Dick Tracy, adventure and the most up-to-date sophisticated type; Smilin' Jack, flying and sex. [This rather naïve list is taken from a naïve but useful book, *The Comics* by Colton Waugh.]

The comics further dissociate personality by erasing the distinctions between adulthood and childhood. (Popular songs revert to baby-talk to relieve adult tension.) The first comic strip in this country was "The Yellow Kid," a creature half-man and half-child, full of premature and malicious wisdom. Little Orphan Annie and Kayo are both of uncertain age, neither children nor adults, and show no sign of growing older (or younger, for that matter) in the next few decades. Harold Teen is blessed with the secret of eternal adolescence, than which his readers find little more desirable. Such strips allow adults to sink, for the moment, into the uncomplicated ways of childhood. On the other hand, the numerous comics that are little more than schematized abstractions of violence and sadism quickly push children into premature adulthood.[3]

Like comic strips, though seldom so simply, movie stars also tend to become identified in the mass mind with one personality strand. Their status as stars is seldom secure unless they have developed one dominant emotional characteristic which serves the audience as an identifying sign. It is this characteristic that determines the emotional essence of a movie, as distinct from the surface subject. Although *The Hucksters* was presumably a satire on advertising, it was actually about Clark Gable, the irresistible male. Every Gable film has sexual aggression as its dominant inner theme no matter what its ostensible plot. Similarly, no matter which role he plays

Ronald Colman is always the man of the world. In no picture has the divergence between inner theme and apparent subject been so wide as in the film *Crossfire,* which, while ostensibly an attack on anti-Semitism, was actually about a tough guy who violates social convention and in passing accidentally kills a Jew.

At most, Hollywood allows several characters in a movie to represent conflicting emotional strands. Like all mass-culture media, it is neither able nor interested in grouping conflicting emotions within one character. From its point of view, that would be dangerous.

THE UNPUNISHED VIOLATION OF LAW

"Mit dose kids, society iss nix," says the Inspector about his juvenile tormentors, the Katzenjammer Kids. The adult-baiting that is the main theme of this comic strip seems never to weary its audience, since children and adults are always at war and adults often secretly sympathize with children. To children the strip appeals directly and for obvious reasons, and to adults it offers the possibility of vicariously rejecting their own adulthood and of safely breaking the laws of social life. While perpetuating passivity and shredding personality, mass culture yet allows the audience the limited freedom of vicariously breaking social law which, in turn, satisfies "a perpetual latent craving in the American psyche for physical expression, for a type of energy that humdrum factory and office jobs have no way of releasing" (Parker Tyler, *The Hollywood Hallucination*). But even this safe violation of social law in the audience's reactions to mass culture serves ultimately to reinforce real-life adherence to social law.

Krazy Kat, the one comic strip intellectuals have admitted to liking, won wide favor with mass audiences simply because Herriman satisfied this deep craving for safe violations of traditional orders. He obeyed neither the conventions of social life nor the internal requirements of his medium; he simply did what he pleased. To the audience there was something immensely gratifying when for no apparent reason the background of the strip moved while its characters remained still. The knowledge that no matter what else happened Ignatz would for no discernible reason always throw his brick was both reassuring and consoling. For once, when straphangers glanced each evening at Krazy Kat, they could escape from the tyranny of causality. In a world too cluttered with reasons, there seemed no reason for what happened to Offisa Pupp, Ignatz and Krazy—and this very lack of order helped the audience re-establish order in its own life.

What happens when a mass-culture product does not conform to this pattern of safely violating social law, I learned in a rather terrifying incident several years ago. I was then stationed at an army reception center where new recruits were prepared for military life. After they exchanged civilian for army clothes, their behavior often took a sharp turn to a kind of lawlessness, a break from old patterns. Feeling that they had to live up to a new role, they indulged in a fantastic amount of profanity and wild sexual boasting. They had to show they were men.

One evening at a showing of the film *The Ox-Bow Incident* I could not help noticing that most of the new soldiers were volubly identifying themselves with the film's lynch mob as it tracked down and murdered three innocent men. The feelings they had about their new status in life were apparently projected into sympathy for the lynchers, also men of violence. And they assumed that this film would allow them, as might most Hollywood products, to cheat out of the consequences of their vicarious violence.

When, however, at the end of the film the lynching was sharply condemned—not merely in formal terms but in psychic and visual images the audience could not escape—the soldiers openly jeered. They were as perplexed and disoriented as the lynchers in the movie. For once, they discovered, they could not identify themselves with the lawbreakers without suffering emotionally. And they felt that in this way the movie was "cheating" them, as in a sense it was.

The motif of unpunished violation of social law is strongly emphasized in the most important recent development in mass culture—the "tough-guy" movies. When we go to see the old-fashioned detective (Sherlock Holmes, Ellery Queen) and western films, we are hardly involved emotionally; such films are put together along strictly stereotyped patterns that permit us the pleasure of relapsing into passive spectators. Their crimes and their punishments provoke no violent reactions since they concern relationships to law that no longer count. In fact, their major source of pleasure is their frank irrelevance.

But we react both violently and with some complexity to the tough-guy films. (The detective film is concerned with patterns of deduction, the tough-guy film with situations of existence, even if distorted ones.) When we project ourselves into the position of the tough guy who is often not quite clearly on either side of the law, our enjoyment in this identification is deep since it is so close—for does not modern life force all of us to be at least part-time tough guys? And our pleasure in the inevitable denouement is equally deep, since the greater the evil by which we have been tempted the greater our relief at escaping it. Like the Christian who views the Jew as both murderer and murdered, the spectator can gain from the tough guy the symbiotic pleasure of being both hunter and hunted.

I think this can best be illustrated by going back to a movie made several years ago, *Double Indemnity*. In this film an insurance agent named Neff is attracted by a woman, Phyllis, who lures him into a plot to kill her husband and share his insurance. In the end they are trapped by Keyes, the insurance company's claims investigator. As played by Barbara Stanwyck, Phyllis is a remarkably sexual woman: frank, aggressive, bitchy. To the spectator's mind she therefore represents lawlessness, the violation of traditional sex mores. She is what the audience might like to be or like to possess, but she is too much so to allow us readily to identify ourselves with her. Keyes, on the other hand, is a creature of sheer intelligence: the supervisory mind that investigates and punishes us for our hidden transgressions. With neither can we fully identify ourselves.

But Neff, the hapless victim in the middle, is just another little guy, as bumbling as you, I or Fred MacMurray. We could fall for Phyllis and we could be trapped by Keyes. Neff is a passive transmission belt through which runs the conflict between Phyllis and Keyes—lawless instinct versus lawful conduct. Since Neff's feelings about that conflict are as ambiguous as those of the audience itself, he is, in a sense, the audience brought directly into the film, the modern anonymous moviegoer torn between what he takes for lawless sexual desire and intelligent lawful suppression. Further in the violation of social law, mass culture cannot go. And this, too, is the deepest identification we can feel toward a mass-culture hero—an identification that, unlike a genuine work of art which brings into play a variety of emotions and character components, rests largely on the least individualized and most anonymous aspects of ourselves. The identification is ultimately with our role of social anonymity.

But this is as far as mass culture can go in the direction of art—much farther, incidentally, than the more pretentious or "socially significant" products of Hollywood. The next step is the crucial step, and Hollywood, like all other mass-culture industries, cannot take it. Here it has reached the great divide.

Notes

1. As used in recent discussions, "mass culture" refers to the production of synthetic, easily accessible amusements for mass audiences, as well as to the products themselves. In mass culture the materials of art are exploited, although art works, except very rarely and that by accident, are not created. Mass culture allows art neither to thrive nor to perish, since art is at once its most dangerous competitor and its one indispensable source of "ideas."

2. *Studies in Philosophy and Social Science*, Vol. IX, 1941.

3. The idea for this paragraph has been developed from a note on the comics by Dwight Macdonald; *Politics*, April, 1945.

Of Happiness and of Despair
We Have No Measure

By ERNEST VAN DEN HAAG

*"non ridere non lugere, neque destestari;
sed intelligere."* Spinoza

UNLIKE ANY OTHER TYPE OF CULTURE, popular culture— a full fledged style of living with a distinct pattern of feeling, thinking, believing and acting— was made possible and in the end necessary by mass production. Unless the requirements and effects of industrialization are fully grasped, popular culture does not become intelligible.[1]

THE INDUSTRIAL SETTING

In the last two centuries, machinery and specialization have immensely increased economic productivity—the amount of goods produced per man hour—in Europe and America. This process has gone farthest in America where popular culture too has gone farthest. Although enrichment led to a vast population increase, production per head rose stupendously and is still rising. Everybody benefited materially, but the main beneficiaries were the poor. Their income rose most. Besides, if the income gap between poor and rich had not narrowed as it did, an expanded national income distributed in unchanged proportions still would have augmented the welfare of the poor disproportionately. If the income of poor and rich alike increases by 50 per cent, the welfare of the poor is raised far more than that of the rich. Our progressive tax system—which taxes additions to the income of the poor less than additions to the income of the rich—is based entirely on this (roughly)[2] correct view.

Mass production has magnified the power of the poor as well as their income. The establishment of a progressive tax system itself eloquently testifies to the mounting political power of the lower income groups.

Since so much more is produced in less time, more time is left over to

This essay, published for the first time in this volume, is a chapter from an analysis of modern life: *The Fabric of Society* (Ralph Ross, co-author) which Harcourt, Brace & Co. will publish in 1957.

1. Crucial as the differences are in other respects, popular culture is a by-product of industrialization whether under democratic or dictatorial auspices, and regardless of whether the economy is planned or unplanned. Totalitarianism would compel composers to compose in the popular manner. A non-totalitarian system induces them to do so by rewards rather than positive punishment. In human terms, the difference is enormous. But popular culture may be produced either way. (However, in a non-totalitarian industrial society, individuals not sharing popular culture can survive physically. Totalitarian industrialism makes survival even in the interstices of society doubtful.)

2. There is no actual proof of the diminishing "utility" of successive additions to income, particularly when the comparison is interpersonal. The idea becomes doubtful indeed, once the income of the poor is high enough to satisfy the most compelling needs.

spend rather than earn income.[3] This, too, probably has benefited the poor most—the work-time of the rich has scarcely declined. Indeed, partly because of inheritance taxation, partly because of loss of prestige, the leisure class which supported the high culture of the past has dwindled as a separate group. In general, although the material need is less, ideological changes have caused the gainfully employed proportion of the population to grow as technology improved.

The increased productivity which bore these fruits also lessened physical toil during the abridged work-time. But drudgery was intensified. Owing to specialization and mechanization, work for most people is standardized and less varied, its pattern and rhythm inflexibly set by machinery with little scope for individual intelligence or initiative and for spontaneous action.[4] Organized production lines which feed machinery and are fed by it depend on a bureaucratic organization and demand of each worker only a small, endlessly repeated manipulation. Monotony is made more dreary by the vastness of production lines which weakens the relationship of each worker to the end product and indeed to production as a meaningful process. Emotional attachment to production tasks and to products also is loosened as each contribution becomes insignificant and the end products are uniformly bereft of identifying marks of individual skill or imagination. Once the techniques of production are standardized, they require more self-repression than self-expression from workers.

Actually, by helping machines, workers increasingly produce something abstract and shapeless for themselves: money income and time in which to spend it. Life falls into two compartments: work—a means; and play—an end.

The burden of enjoyment and of personal experience falls heavily on the extended proportion of life left over from work. But the longest period of time spent on any one thing is still spent on work. The deadening effect of the meaningless drain on energy carries over and influences the kind of play-experience sought. Though condemned to pleasure, people often find themselves out on parole, craving to be "distracted from distraction by distraction."[5] Monotony depletes people psychologically and makes them weary and restless. The spontaneous imagination needed for recreation seeps out through non-use during working hours.[6] Thus "recreation" often becomes a search for excitement—vicarious or direct—to offset the monotony of work and give a feeling of "living." But excitement pursued for its own sake only exhausts eagerness and impulse without creating anything.

3. Fewer hours per day are spent working than before, and fewer days per week. As a proportion of the lifespan, work-time has shrunk beyond this. People live longer but start work later and retire earlier.

4. Mass production is distinguished in this respect from work on small farms, and in small firms. The farm population has dwindled as has the share of total output produced by small firms and farms. Note further that specialization has reached a high degree in the surviving small units.

5. T. S. Eliot.

6. Though physically fewer, working hours become psychologically longer through the repetitiveness of tasks.

The wish for the creation of personal experience is overwhelmed, perhaps, but it is not satisfied once it has degenerated into greed for sensation.

In addition to shortening work-time and toil, lengthening play-time and increasing fatigue and income, mass production has heightened and spread mobility. Population is concentrated in metropolitan areas to an unprecedented degree. Even where the population is dispersed, ubiquitous, swift and cheap transportation leads to far more frequent and varied contacts outside the home than in former times and to congestion and crowding as well. Airplane or bus rides throw together people from distant areas and groups on their way to distant places. The multiplicity of contacts is compounded by the ubiquity of means of communication. Movies, television programs, newspapers and magazines link vast, heterogeneous publics and establish constant contact among people even if they stay put. They bring about some uniformity of attitude and a blending of customs and beliefs.[7] However, most contacts are casual and transitory, or in the case of mass media of communication, generalized, vicarious and abstract. They do not replace personal relationship to things or people, but make it harder for them to grow. No man is an island—everybody is at sea though, and the electrically amplified bell tolls so deafeningly for all that conversation degenerates into shouting.

Mass production not only makes mobility possible, it also makes it necessary. Changing techniques, markets and products, the expansion and contraction of industries—in short, innovation—cannot proceed unless people can be induced to go from one residence and occupation to another, and therewith to exchange one group of friends for another, and sometimes their status, role and social class.

Industrialization also grinds down the autonomy and intensity, the numerical size, the duration and the functions of primary groups such as the family, and expands the role of fluid secondary groups. The influence of mass media rises correspondingly. The unprecedented spread of formal mass education contributes to the readiness for change. Education brings together the offspring of heterogeneous groups and subjects them to a homogenizing curriculum. The main effect is to weaken any differentiating heritage and to prepare each generation for mobility in pursuit of ambitions such as success or happiness, by means of the newest techniques.

As contacts multiplied and geographical distances shrank, so did social distances. Most of the things produced by modern industry tend to shorten the span between rich and poor. The poor read, travel, wear nylon stockings and see the same television programs in their homes as do the rich. With

---

7. To call popular culture heterogeneous is correct with reference to its origins, but incorrect with reference to the smooth blend that constitutes it and that makes American society remarkably homogeneous. Social distances dividing groups horizontally and vertically are smaller than within any European country. The contrary impression comes about because fluidity is great and contacts frequent. Thus individuals experience differences more intensely and more often, though the differences are fewer and less steep than elsewhere. Hence the illusion shared by many sociologists. (The latter may magnify group differences also because of occupational and ideological bias.)

regard to the kinds of things consumed, the monopoly which distinguished the rich has been broken. To be wealthy means chiefly to have more, rather than different, things—and often only to have more command over things. We can do no better than to quote John Stuart Mill,[8] a prophetic witness, on the whole friendly to the industry which blurred the contours of society by levelling the elevations and filling in the chasms that formerly divided it into remote, noncompeting segments.

The circumstances which surround different classes and individuals, and shape their characters, are daily becoming more assimilated. Formerly, different ranks, different neighborhoods, different trades and professions, lived in what might be called different worlds; at present to a great degree in the same. Comparatively speaking, they now read the same things, listen to the same things, go to the same places, have their hopes and fears directed to the same objects, have the same rights and liberties, and the same means of asserting them. Great as are the differences of position which remain, they are nothing to those which have ceased. And the assimilation is still proceeding. All the political changes of the age promote it, since they all tend to raise the low and to lower the high. Every extension of education promotes it, because education brings people under common influences, and gives them access to the general stock of facts and sentiments. Improvement in the means of communication promotes it, by bringing the inhabitants of distant places into personal contact, and keeping up a rapid flow of changes of residence between one place and another. The increase of commerce and manufactures promotes it, by diffusing more widely the advantages of easy circumstances, and opening all objects of ambition, even the highest, to general competition, whereby the desire of rising becomes no longer the character of a particular class, but of all classes. A more powerful agency than even all these, in bringing about a general similarity among mankind, is the complete establishment, in this and other free countries, of the ascendancy of public opinion in the State. As the various social eminences which enabled persons entrenched on them to disregard the opinion of the multitude gradually become levelled; as the very idea of resisting the will of the public, when it is positively known that they have a will, disappears more and more from the minds of practical politicians; there ceases to be any social support for non-conformity—the substantive power in society which, itself opposed to the ascendance of numbers, is interested in taking under its protection opinions and tendencies at variance with those of the public."

The increased income and power, the shortened work time of the lower income groups; the mechanization of work; the increased mobility, the lessened social distances and the weakened and abridged primary groups; and finally the rise of mass communication—all these things are direct effects of industrialization and direct causes of the erosion of folk and high culture. Cumulatively, they create the attitudes and ambitions, the sensibilities and insensibilities which prepare the market for popular culture.

"Folk" and "high" cultures flowered simultaneously in different strata of many past societies. But popular culture[9] when fully developed penetrates

---

8. *On Liberty*, Ch. III.
9. This threefold classification is meant to be exhaustive. However much cultures differ, they fall into one or several of these types. For instance, all American Indian cultures were folk cultures; and Europe had a combination of folk and high cultures in antiquity and from the Middle Ages to the 19th Century. Note that folk cultures fall in the first half of

all strata about equally and without significant variation of its main qualities. As society becomes fully industrialized, popular culture becomes the most universally shared type of culture and colors most aspects of individual and social life. High and folk culture retain only marginal influence on private and social life. They become islands lapped at and often swamped by popular culture. They are isolated and dry up in institutions or regions cut off from social development. If they are not isolated, high and folk culture tend to become denatured.[10]

THE ECONOMICS OF TASTE

Most of the goods monopolized in the past by the privileged few are now available to the many not only because they have more time and money but also because the goods themselves are mass produced and have become cheap.[11] Quality has changed but not necessarily for the worse. Our dental fillings and eyeglasses are better than those available to George III or Louis XIV. Our food, to judge from the increased lifespan, is not less nourishing and it is more plentiful. Lighting, heating, cooling and transportation are much better. More books are more available to more people, not to speak of television, movies, the radio and records. Even in live entertainment, George III probably could not get as much as our poor can afford. Surely he had nothing like Radio City Music Hall. The variety of entertainment available to any New Yorker should arouse (indeed does arouse) the envy of many a prince.

However, only those things—good things or bad things—are cheap that are demanded by enough people to make mass production feasible. Things that are not mass produced are hard to find and very expensive. Anyone cursed with an unshared taste—be it good or bad taste—must rid himself of it or be prepared to pay an awful price. For the gap between the cost of an article which must be custom-made to supply an unshared taste and that of an article which can be mass produced to supply a widely shared taste is steadily widening.

The real income of a consumer who cleaves to an individual taste has declined precipitously, and is much lower than that of a person who never formed one. Though the material and workmanship of his specially made suits, china, furniture or house are no better than the material and work-

---

the usual dichotomies (Weber's "traditionalistic-rationalistic"; Tonnies' "community-society"; Redfields' "folk-secular"; Becker's "sacred-secular"). The second half of the dichotomies is *one* characteristic of all popular cultures. High cultures, finally, straddle the dichotomies by growing from the first into the second half. But the process affects only a small stratum of society—unless it is spread through industrialization. When this occurs, popular culture replaces both high and folk culture. Finally, note that some elements of each culture type are usually contained in the other. Thus, wherever there was an urban proletariat, or some form of mass production, there also were elements of popular culture. But they did not prevail until the machine age came.

10. Fragments may be conserved, however, and mounted as quaint tourist attractions (for instance, Henry Ford's Greenfield Village and the great English country estates).

11. Remaining differentiation or privilege stimulates resentment the more for it sticks out on an otherwise level plane; yet it does not stick out far enough to remove the privileged from invidious comparison. Envy and the craving for equality feed on their own success.

manship of mass-produced ones, the person who sticks to an idiosyncratic taste has to spend more.[12] If he makes as much money as someone bereft of individual taste, the individualist must buy fewer things. Else he must forego indulging his personal taste by buying mass-produced articles. But since these yield less satisfaction to him than they give the person whose widely shared preferences they meet, the individualist would still have a lower real income. He cannot benefit from the economies of mass production; on the contrary, he must pay for the factors which mass production has made expensive: work-time and overhead. As mass production techniques improve, the gulf between the real income of consumers with shared taste and of consumers with unshared tastes opens wider and wider. The industrial system penalizes individual taste economically regardless of what goods or services are affected. Either your life is styled in conformity with mass tastes or it becomes a series of deprivations, material if you cling to your taste and forego some purchases to pay for it, psychological if you don't. That much can be said without in the least suggesting that individual taste is necessarily more sensitive to aesthetic values than mass taste or that the mass taste is necessarily bad. Only it is not individual.

The social (as distinguished from the economic) repercussions should be obvious: clinging to an individual personality is penalized to an unprecedented degree, for it is likely to be disapproved and resented by all groups. The individualist must choose between isolation and repression—he cannot, as in former times, live in a personal universe. He cannot hope to find a restaurant that caters to his tastes; the owner will soon find it more profitable to cater to more widely shared tastes, possibly by advertising his place as a haunt of individualists—whereupon it becomes a crowded place invaded by great masses. The same is true for a resort, or an idea. The choice is between isolation and the commonplace, gregariousness and solitude with no room for mere sociability.[13]

Of course, mass taste can be subdivided. There is a selection of different mass-produced teacups. But still, each can be mass produced only by appealing to a sizeable group. Hence the selection can fully meet only a few individual preferences. Besides, as techniques improve, the number of simultaneously available types dwindles, though the models are changed each year (in response to changing mass taste, or technology, or to stimulate a change and, therewith, demand). With all this, the actual selection available to a consumer below the middle-income groups has broadened, as we mentioned before. But he must not develop unshared tastes. If he does, his living standard is severely reduced.

The economics of this situation are almost embarrassingly obvious. Nevertheless, the cultural effects have been neglected, or at least not properly

---

12. The idea that the custom-made article is better is based chiefly on the snob appeal of rarity and expensiveness. Often both quality and taste are worse.

13. Sociability may be defined as a wish to enrich, refine, conserve and express individuality by relations with others. Gregariousness is a wish to lose individuation by merging into a crowd. The relationship is like that of poetry and babbling.

linked to the economics of mass production. For instance, the price of books expected to appeal only to a small group has risen, while the price of books sold on the mass market has fallen—even though they both have the same number of pages. The gap widens the more the popular book profits from the economies of mass production and the more the book appealing only to a few suffers the diseconomies of being printed in a small edition. (The size of the edition required to profit from economies also has increased.)[14]

Publishers can count on a mass market for classics or, generally, when authors or works are favorably known; or when the topic or treatment supply an existing mass demand (for instance, *The Power of Positive Thinking* or *New York Confidential*). Mass production must appeal to an already widely shared taste or one so near formation that the book which is to supply it may be expected to call it into being. Books that appeal only to a few because they are original in topic or treatment and therefore cannot supply an already widely shared demand become inordinately expensive (unless the publisher miscalculated and the book is remaindered). Of course, these are the books that in the end might create new taste. But the process is slow and life is short. As the cost of experimentation rises, so, necessarily, does caution. Publishers will still take a gamble on a possible best seller; rewards have increased, too. But they have no reason to publish a book expected to appeal only to a few people unless they can sell the small edition at a high price (and to an assured market; no reason to gamble here).[15]

Still, books that appeal only to a small public are published and sold, though they are comparatively expensive. In this respect the direct impact of the economics of mass production does not seem impressive so far. The impact on writing and reading will be discussed after some of its sources have been examined.

THE FORMATION OF MASS TASTE

How is the mass market formed on which popular culture is sold and perpetuated? In the first place, individual taste has become uneconomic for the purchaser and for the seller, and this effectively stunts its growth. People are prepared accordingly throughout the educational process. Group acceptance, shared taste, takes the place of authority and of individual moral and aesthetic judgment and standards. But as we mentioned, people often move from group to group. Any taste that cannot be sloughed off—an in-dividual taste, not easily divided from the person in whom it dwells—becomes an obstacle to adaptation. Success is hindered by a discriminating personal taste which expresses or continues an individual personality, and success is fostered by an unselective appetite.

Numerous precautions are taken, beginning in nursery school (itself

14. This situation existed as an effect of book clubs long before paperbacks became respectable in America. Paperbacks may indeed alleviate it a little.

15. Periodicals without mass appeal are in a similar situation. Compare the cost of *Kenyon Review* or *Partisan Review* to that of the *Readers' Digest* or of *True Stories*. Yet the latter magazines are profitable (and pay their contributors well) whereas the former are not and do not.

hardly an individualizing institution) to avoid elaboration of personal discernment and to instill fear of separation from the group. Group acceptance is stressed through formal and informal popularity contests, teamwork, and polling. Education altogether stresses group instruction. For instance, the size of his classes and the class average, not the qualities of individual pupils, are often considered the measure of the teacher.[16] The student himself is so much treated as part of a group that, except in higher education (which is only partly immune), he may be automatically promoted with his group regardless of individual achievement or variation. Finally, the surviving individual talent is instructed not to cultivate, but to share, itself. The writer gives a writing course, the scholar lectures and writes popularizations, the beauty models or appears on TV, and the singer deserts the concert hall for the juke box.[17]

ADVERTISING

The aggregate effect of advertising is to bring about wide sharing of tastes. The actual social function of advertising is *not* to mold taste in any particular way, nor to debase it.[18] This goes for manufacturers, publishers and movie-makers too. They are quite content to produce and advertise what people want—be it T. S. Eliot or Edgar Guest, Kierkegaard or Norman Vincent Peale, "September Morn" or mobiles. It does not matter what people want to buy as long as they want to buy enough of the same thing to make mass production possible. Advertising helps to unify taste, to de-individualize it and thus to make mass production possible.

There is no evidence to support conspiracy theories which hold that wicked capitalists, through advertising and mass media, deliberately (or stupidly) debauch the originally good, natural taste of the masses. Mass production—capitalist or socialist—demands unified taste; efficiency (or profitableness) is dependent only on its being shared by sizeable groups.[19]

THE NATURE OF MASS TASTE

Can one say anything about mass tastes beyond saying that they are widely shared? Are they homogenized on the "lowest common denominator?" There seems to be no good reason to assume that the lowest tastes are most widespread. One may say something of the sort about some crowds united temporarily by crude common appetites at the expense of reason, restraint and refinement. But why consider consumers a crowd? Even the

---

16. Santayana recounts, in his *Character and Opinion in the United States,* how he was made aware of this at Harvard University.

17. We shall turn to compromises below.

18. The molding of taste may be among the motivations of individual advertisers—though at least in the long run they are often equally motivated to mold the product to the prevailing taste. At any rate, we are interested in function, not motivation, and in aggregate cumulative effect, not in a particular campaign.

19. In a capitalist system, some men might use their wealth to express a personal taste, even though unprofitable. This is less likely under socialism. Socialist planners would be under moral obligation and political pressure to use public money to satisfy the most widely shared taste. Further, capitalist producers can take risks which managers might not be allowed to take with public money under socialism. (If planners have not been subservient to mass desires in Russia, it is because the Soviet Union is not a democracy.)

fare offered by the entertainment media is usually consumed by people separately or in very small groups. (Except for movies, but movie-goers are isolated from each other though they are together.)

Producers have no interest in lowering taste or in catering to low rather than high taste. They seek to provide for a *modal* average of tastes which through advertising they try to make as congruent with the *mean* average as possible. Neither average can be identical with the "lowest common denominator."[20]

Yet in one sense consumers are treated as a crowd: their individual tastes are not catered to. The mass-produced article need not aim low, but it must aim at an average of tastes. In satisfying all (or at least many) individual tastes in some respects, it violates each in other respects. For there are—so far—no average persons having average tastes. Averages are but statistical composites. A mass-produced article, while reflecting nearly everybody's taste to some extent, is unlikely to embody anybody's taste fully. This is one source of the sense of violation which is rationalized vaguely in theories about deliberate debasement of taste.

The sense of violation springs from the same thwarting of individuality that makes prostitution (or promiscuity) psychologically offensive. The cost of cheap and easy availability, of mass production, is wide appeal; and the cost of wide appeal is de-individualization of the relationship between those who cater and those who are catered to; and of the relationship of both to the object of the transaction. By using each other indiscriminately as impersonal instruments (the seller for profit, the buyer for sensation—or, in promiscuity, both parties for sensation and relief of anxiety) the prostitute and her client sacrifice to seemingly more urgent demands the self which, in order to grow, needs continuity, discrimination and completeness in relationships.[21] Though profit and sensation can be achieved by depersonalization, the satisfaction ultimately sought cannot be, for the very part of personality in which it is felt—the individual self—is stunted and atrophied, at least if de-individualization continues long enough and is comprehensive. Ultimately, the sense of violation too is numbed.

Now, the depersonalizing effects of the mass production of some things —say, electric clocks—may be minor as far as consumers are concerned and more than offset by the advantages of cheapness. The same cannot be said for mass entertainment or education. And though some individuals

---

20. The average taste cannot be easily calculated. It is subject to fashion. Indeed, popular culture is far more fickle and eager for the new than any other type of culture. There would be no risk for song-writers or movie producers if appeal could be calculated mechanically. But there is. Indeed, it takes a special talent to sense what might appeal, the talent the editor of a popular magazine and the advertising man and the "stylist" must possess—and an equally special talent to produce it, the talent of the writer of best sellers and the popular entertainer.

21. Prostitution is not always the greater evil, of course, and may spring from many motives, as do objections to it. There is no doubt, though, that it becomes psychologically injurious, or expresses a psychological injury suffered, when it is the only and permanent form of sexual activity.

may, society cannot have one without the other. The effects of mass production on people as producers and consumers are likely to be cumulative. Besides, even goods that seem purely utilitarian include elements of non-utilitarian, of aesthetic and psychic (e.g., prestige) appeal. Indeed, less than half of consumer expenditure goes for the satisfaction of simple biological needs. (More, perhaps, in the lowest income groups, and much less still in the higher ones.) Distinctions of this kind are necessarily hazy, but if cigarettes, newspapers, television, drinks, shaving lotion or lipstick, the prestige location of one's apartment, the fashionableness of one's clothing, etc., are taken to satisfy nonbiological needs—and we can do without them biologically—than we are motivated by psychic needs in spending most of our money. This, of course, is not in itself objectionable—except that the processes by which many of these needs now arise and are stilled bring to mind the processes by which bread is now mass produced.

In milling and baking, bread is deprived of any taste whatever and of all vitamins. Some of the vitamins are then added again (taste is provided by advertising). Quite similarly with all mass-produced articles. They can no more express the individual taste of producers than that of consumers. They become impersonal objects, however pseudo-personalized. Producers and consumers go through the mass production mill to come out homogenized and de-characterized—only it does not seem possible to reinject the individualities which have been ground out, the way the vitamins are added to enrich bread.[22] The "human relations" industry tries to do just that and it doubtlessly supplies a demand and can be helpful, just as chemical sedatives or stimulants can be. But it seems unlikely that any assembly line—including one manned by human relations counselors—can give more than the illusion of individuality.

To produce more, people work under de-individualizing conditions and are rewarded by high income and leisure. Thus they can and do consume more. But as consumers, they must once more rid themselves of individual tastes. The benefits of mass production are reaped only by matching de-individualizing work with equally de-individualizing consumption. The more discontinuous income earning and spending become physically, the more continuous they seem to become psychologically. Failure to repress individual personality in or after working hours is costly; in the end the production of standardized things by persons demands also the production of standardized persons.

In a material sense, this assembly-line shaping, packaging and distributing of persons, of life, occurs already. Most people perch unsteadily in mass-produced, impermanent dwellings throughout their lives. They are born in hospitals, fed in cafeterias, married in hotels. After terminal care,

---

22. Though books on "How to Become an Individual," "How to Acquire a Personality" —books, in short, that insist that by following a general recipe you will bake an original cake—abound in popular culture as do restaurants advertising "home-cooked meals."

they die in hospitals, are shelved briefly in funeral homes, and are finally incinerated. On each of these occasions—and how many others?—efficiency and economy are obtained and individuality and continuity stripped off. If one lives and dies discontinuously and promiscuously in anonymous surroundings, it becomes hard to identify with anything, even the self, and uneconomic to be attached to anything, even one's own individuality. The rhythm of individual life loses autonomy, spontaneity, and distinction when it is tied into a stream of traffic and carried along according to the speed of the road, as we are, in going to work, or play, or in doing anything. Traffic lights signal when to stop and go, and much as we seem to be driving we are driven. To stop spontaneously, to exclaim, *Verweile doch Du bist so schoen* (Stay, for you are beautiful), may not lose the modern Faust his soul—but it will cause a traffic jam.

One motive for delinquency—a way of getting out of line—is, possibly, a preference for occasional prison terms to imprisonment by routine. Crime, by its ultimate irrationality, may protest against the subordination of individual spontaneity to social efficiency. Three further reactions to anonymity may be noted:

(1) The prestige of histrionics has risen. We long to impersonate, to get a name—better a pseudonym than to remain nameless; better a borrowed character than none; better to impersonate than never to feel like a person. The wish to be oneself does not occur, for the only self known is empty and must be filled from the outside.

(2) The attempt to become "interesting" (no doubt unconsciously to become interested) by buying a ready-made individuality, through "sending for," "enrolling in," or "reading up on" something, or "going places."

(3) Impersonal and abstract things and utilitarian relationships are cozily "personalized" as though to offset the depersonalization of individual life.

De-individualization, however, should not be viewed as a grim, deliberate, or coercive process. It is induced gradually by economic rewards and not experienced as de-individualization at all, though the symptoms are demonstrable. Most of the people who are nourished with homogenized pap never had solid food on which to cut their teeth. They feel vaguely restless and dissatisfied, but do not know what they are pining for and could not masticate or digest it if they had it. The cooks are kept busy ransacking all the recipes the world has ever known to prepare new dishes. But the texture is always the same, always mushy, for the materials are always strained, blended, beaten, heated, and cooled until it is.

MASS MEDIA: THE EXCLUSION OF ART

Let us briefly tour the institutional kitchens where "recreation" is cooked up—movies, radio, television.

Mass media cannot afford to step on anyone's toes, and this implies a number of restrictions which, though less significant than the positive prescriptions, are not negligible. We can forebear rehearsing tiresome minutiae

—forbidden words, topics, situations, actions;[23] but the countless dangerous associations mass media must avoid deserve some scrutiny.

No religious, racial, occupational, national, economic, political, etc., group can be offended. Hence: Can an evil man be Jewish? Left-handed? Pipesmoking? Can he perish in an airplane accident? Can a villain have any qualities shared with non-villains and a hero have disapproved traits? In short, can either be human? The playwright or script writer may not mean to say that Jews are evil or all evil men left-handed, or all pipe-smokers; he may not intend to advocate bigamy or to suggest that airplanes are dangerous or that we ought to be atheists. Joseph Conrad did not intend *The Nigger of the Narcissus* as an anti-Negro tract, any more than Shakes-peare intended *Othello* as a tract against handkerchiefs (in favor of Kleenex?). No matter. There is a danger that the play will be so under-stood. In Shylock and Fagin,[24] Shakespeare and Dickens created individuals, experiences, and ideas and, unlike copywriters or propagandists, did not intend them as instructions on how to act and think. Yet the groups that press restrictions on mass media are not wrong. For the audience tends to react as though such instruction had been received.

The audience of mass media always expects to be sold goods, stereo-types, and recipes for living—a new vitamin for that tired, listless feeling, or a new line for romance. And the audience is usually right: the same actress who just implored a soap-opera husband not to leave her and the kids turns and implores one and all in identically sincere and personal tones to buy insurance or perfume. The small boy's heroes admonish him to get mommy to buy this or that (and even if the heroes didn't, someone will sell Davy Crockett caps to the small boy). In many breakfast and news shows, advertising recommendations are deliberately mixed in with "actual" ex-pressions of opinion. Even nonprofessionals—society leaders, well-known novelists, successful and "average" common men—ringingly declare their profound personal convictions on brands of soap, or beer, or God: "This I believe." The line dividing views and characters presented as fiction and as "real" becomes hazy and the audience necessarily muddled about sep-arating advertisements, pleas, and recipes from art. In such a context, the audience cannot receive art as individual experience and perspective on experience. Art becomes irrelevant. It is not perceived in its own terms, but first reduced to, then accepted or rejected as, a series of rules and opinions on what to expect or do.

The idea that something must be sold is held by the media managers as fervently as it is held by the audience. It transcends the commercial motives which begot it. Thus public or educational stations, which do not accept

---

23. Modesty is spared ritualistically. But in a suggestive, voyeuristic and at times nauseat-ingly coy way, programs can be quite pornographic. It is actually the sentimentality and the clichés of the audience that are spared religiously: "To hell with Christmas" causes more of a television scandal than the sexiest wiggle.

24. Note the controversy when *Oliver Twist* was filmed. And controversies over dialect stories, etc.

commercial advertising, spend nearly as much time on (noncommercial) attempts to sell something as do commercial ones. They sell themselves or
their program, or next week's offering—anything at all, as long as something is sold: "please listen again tomorrow," "please send for our booklet," "please do this or don't do that"—the listener must always be hectored,
sold on or wheedled into something.[25]

How, then, could the audience see that a character such as Shylock
simply is? A character in the audience's experience always exists for a
purpose; a character is invented to sell something, a point of view, or a
product, or himself. It is never an end in itself. Hence the audience always
asks, Should we buy his line?, and it is nearly impossible to present something without suggesting by implication that it be bought. Art, like love, can
be experienced only as a personal, continuous, cumulative relationship. Else
art becomes entertainment—dull entertainment often—just as love is reduced to sex or prestige. Not that art should not be entertaining; but it is
no more deliberately aimed at entertainment than love is. Art (and love)
must be felt; they cannot be manufactured by someone to suit the taste of
someone else. Yet mass-media fare is prepared for consumers devoted to
amusement, not, as art (and love) must be, devoted to the work (or person) itself.

The circumstances which permit the experience of art are rare in our
society anyway and they cannot be expected in the audience of mass media.
That audience is dispersed and heterogeneous, and though it listens often, it
does so incidentally and intermittently and poised to leave if not immediately
enthralled and kept amused. Such an audience is captured by loud, broad, and
easy charms, by advertising posters, by copywriter's prose. And the conditions
and conditioning of the audience demand a mad mixture of important and
trivial matters, atom bombs, hit tunes, symphonies, B.O., sob stories, hotcha
girls, round tables and jokes. It jells into one thing: diversion.[26] Hence what
art is presented is received as entertainment or propaganda. Shylock would
be understood as an anti-Semitic stereotype. The mass media may as well fit
their offerings to the audience which they address and, knowing the limitations of that audience, they would be irresponsible to disregard the kind of
understanding and misunderstanding their offerings will meet. They must omit,
therefore, all human experience likely to be misunderstood—all experience
and expression, the meaning of which is not obvious and approved. Which is
to say that the mass media cannot touch the experiences that art, philosophy
and literature deal with: relevant and significant human experience presented
in relevant and significant form. For if it is such, it is new, doubtful, difficult,
perhaps offensive, at any rate easily misunderstood. Art is not concerned with

---

25. Note further that within institutionally set limits, non-commercial stations try to
enlarge more than to instruct or delight their audiences. Classical music—but whenever possible, the popular classics in popular versions, and with all the advertising techniques, including the "theme" (trademark) stripped from some symphony to introduce all "symphony
hours," including also the outrageous mutilations of works of art, etc.

26. Again, noncommercial stations do the same thing, though more insipidly by mixing
dentistry and Dante.

making the obvious and approved more obvious and approved; it is precisely after this point that art begins and the mass media stop.

When attempting to be serious, the mass media must rig up pseudo-problems and solve them by cliché. They cannot touch real problems or real solutions. Plots are packed with actions which obscure the vagueness and irrelevance of meanings and solutions. Similarly, to replace actual individuality, each character and situation is tricked up with numerous identifying details and mannerisms. The more realistic the characteristics, the less real the character usually, or the situation, and the less revealing. Literal realism cannot replace relevance. Mass media inveigh against sin and against all evils accepted as such. But they cannot question things not acknowledged as evil or appear to support things felt as evil. Even *Rigoletto*, were it a modern work, could not be broadcast since crime and immorality pay and the ending is unhappy for everybody but the villain.[27]

Combating legal censorship, organized group pressures, and advertising agencies is gallantly romantic—and as quixotic as man's rage against his own mirrored image. These agencies are interested only in presenting what is wanted and in preventing what might offend people.[28] They are nuisances perhaps, but things could not be very different without them. Policemen do not create the law, though becoming the target of the few who would defy it.

The very nature of mass media excludes art, and requires surrogation by popular culture. Though the Hays production code applies only to movies, its basic rule states a principle which all mass media must follow: "Correct standards of life, subject only to the requirements of drama and entertainment" must be upheld. Doubtless "correct standards" are those standards most of the audience is likely to believe correct.[29] They authorize whatever does not upset or offend the audience, and nothing else. "Correct standards of life" must exclude art (except occasional classics).[30] For art is bound to differ from the accepted, that is, the customary moral and aesthetic view, at least as it takes shape in the audience's mind. Art is always a fresh vision of the world, a new experience or creation of life. If it does not break, or develop, or renew in significant aspects the traditional, customary, accepted

27. Classics can be presented occasionally since they are sterilized by remoteness. Tolerance is a tribute ignorance pays to reputation.

It is remarkable that the original censor objected to the possibly subversive *political* implications of *Rigoletto*. Victor Hugo's play was suspected of casting aspersions on monarchy or monarchs. It did not occur to the censor to object to the essential content of the play, to its view of the human predicament, of love, crime, violence. The situation has been significantly reversed. We could not wish for a better illustration of our argument.

28. They are not always right in their estimates. But who would be? They have an interest in gauging correctly, apart from fairly small side interests favoring organized opinion. On these we invoke *de minimis non curat scriptor*.

29. Though they do not necessarily observe these standards in practice.

30. Past audiences were fairly homogeneous and accustomed to the artistic traditions being developed, whereas the mass audience comes from many traditions or no tradition. Therefore some segments of it would be shocked by a presentation which, though not actually offering anything new, offers what is new and shocking to them. Hence usually the mass media present even classics in mutilated form, sometimes to the point of disemboweling them or reversing the moral. For instance, Tolstoi's *Anna Karenina* had to be recalled to the studio to make it palatable by a happy ending.

aesthetic and moral standards, if it merely repeats without creating, it is not art.[31] If it does, it is incompatible with the "correct standards of life" which must control mass media.

Mass media thus never can question man's fate where it is questionable; they cannot sow doubt about an accepted style of life, or an approved major principle. To be sure, mass media often feature challenges to this and that, and clashes of opinion. These are part of our accepted style of life, as long as challenges do not defy anything but sin and evil in the accepted places and manner. The mass media must hold up "correct standards of life" whereas art must create, not uphold views. When filmed or broadcast, the visions of the playwright or novelist cannot deviate from the accepted "correct standards" and they must be entertaining. They must conform to the taste of the audience; they cannot form it. Virtue must triumph entertainingly—virtue as the audience sees it.

THE POWER OF CONSUMERS

The poets, Shelley thought, are "the unacknowledged legislators of the world." Shelley's poets wrote for a few who would take the trouble to understand them.[32] They addressed an audience that knew and shared the common traditions they were developing. High culture was cultivated in special institutions—courts, monasteries, churches, universities—by people who devoted their lives to the development of its traditions, and were neither isolated nor surrounded by masses wishing to be entertained. (Besides, there were no means of addressing a mass.) There was no need and no temptation for the artist to do anything but to create in his own terms.[33] Poets, painters, or philosophers lived in and were of the group for whom they produced, as did most people, were they peasants, artisans or artists. The relations between producers of culture and consumers were so personal (as were the relations between producers and consumers generally) that one can hardly speak of an impersonal market in which one sold, the other bought.

In both high and folk culture, each bounded and autonomous universe —court or village—relied on the particular cultivators and inventors of its arts and sciences no less than the latter relied on their patrons. Each region or court depended on its musicians as it depended on its craftsmen, and vice versa. The mutual personal dependence had disadvantages and advantages, as has any close relationship. Michelangelo or Beethoven depended

31. It is not suggested that the new view is better. Only that it is new.
32. The understanding of art has always been troublesome. "Wise beyond doubt, I hold him who divines what each word in my song means" the Provencal troubadour Marcabru wrote. The average Athenian hardly understood the tragic mysteries (any more than the average Roman Catholic fully understands the Mass) or the average Roman Horace, who indeed wrote: *"Odi profanum vulgo et arceo."* No, most modern poetry is not more obscure *per se* than poetry has always been. What has happened is that more people, less well equipped, demand to understand it without wanting to take the necessary trouble. And if they find it hard, why, it's the poet's fault. The evidence is very plain, for instance, in I. A. Richards' *Practical Criticism.*
33. There was censorship at times, and desires of specific patrons had to be considered. But though they restricted expression, they seldom prescribed it. And in particular, they did not insist on things being made easy.

on irksome individual patrons more than they would today. On the other hand, whatever the patrons' tastes or demands, they were individual and not average tastes or demands. Folk culture grew without professional help. High culture was cultivated like an orchard or garden. But both folk and high cultures grew from within the groups they distinguished and remained within them.

High culture was entirely dominated by people with more than average prestige, power and income—by the elite as a group, who also dominated politics and society in general.[34] This group determined what was to be produced, culturally and otherwise; and they took their toll often by oppression and spoliation of the mass of people whom they ruled.

With the development of industry, the elite as a group lost its power. The great mass of consumers now determines what is to be produced. Elite status, leadership in any form, is achieved and kept today by catering to the masses, not by plundering or oppressing them. The nobleman may have become rich by robbing (taking from) his peasants.[35] But the industrialist becomes a millionaire by selling (exchanging with) to farmers. And his business is helped by giving his customers, via television, the entertainers they want. These in turn reach elite status by appealing to the masses. So do politicians.

The elite no longer determines what is produced, any more than it dominates society in other respects. Rather, the elite becomes the elite by producing the goods that sell, the goods that cater to an average of tastes. With respect to culture, the elite neither imposes any taste nor cultivates one of its own. It markets and helps homogenize and distribute popular culture—that which appeals to an average of tastes—through the mass media. The changes in income distribution, mobility and communication, the economics of mass production already discussed, have caused the power of individual consumers to wane. But the power of consumers as a group has risen and that of producers as a group has dwindled.

With the invention of mass media, a mass market for culture became possible. The economies yielded by the mass production of automobiles became available in the mass production of entertainment. Producers of popular culture supply this new mass market. Popular culture does not *grow* within a group. It is manufactured by one group—in Hollywood or in New York—for sale to an anonymous mass market. The product must meet an average of tastes and it loses in spontaneity and individuality what it gains in accessibility and cheapness. The creators of popular culture are not a sovereign group of "unacknowledged legislators." They work for Hooper ratings to give people what they want. Above all, they are salesmen; they sell entertainment and produce with sales in mind. The creators of high culture are no longer insulated from the demands of the mass market by

---

34. The distance between the elite and other groups was greater and the mobility less than today in all major pre-industrial societies.

35. As well as protecting them from other robbers and each other.

an educated elite, as they still were during the nineteenth century (and there are no stable, isolated communities in which folk culture could grow). They do not create for or have personal relationships with patrons whom they can lead as a man may lead in a conversation. A personal tutor is much more dependent on a few persons than a television lecturer. But his influence on his pupil is also much greater than the influence of any one television lecturer on any one pupil.

Today's movie producer, singer, or writer is less dependent on the taste of an individual customer, or village, or court, than was the artist of yore; but he does depend far more on the average of tastes, and he can influence it far less. He need not cater to any individual taste—not even his own. He caters to an impersonal market. He is not involved in a conversation. He is like a speaker addressing a mass meeting and attempting to curry its favor.[36]

THE CORRUPTION OF NEWLY PRODUCED HIGH CULTURE

Why is Brooklyn, so much richer and bigger, so much more literate and educated—and with more leisure—so much less productive culturally than was Florence? Though the absence of demand for high culture from the mass media has a bearing, it does not fully explain why so little of it is produced. After all, high culture existed before mass media were invented. To account for the blight of high and folk cultures, we must consider the positive pull of the mass market on artists. This pull, which was absent in former times, explains why artists are more "market-oriented" and less "taste-oriented," why they create for the sake of anonymous consumers rather than for the sake of creation, why the mass market tends to be internalized and to draw the talent that otherwise might have been devoted to high culture.[37]

By cheapening his product or making it easier, Dante could not have gained success and prestige as today's artist might. Had he renamed the *Divine Comedy, Florence Confidential,* the number of copies sold would not have risen much. The market was restricted; there was no mass market for anything, good or bad. And the techniques that gave mass production advantages had not been invented yet. Had Dante written a best seller, more in demand than his work actually was, it still could not have been sold at a cheaper price. (On the contrary, the price might have risen.) Today, however, the more something appeals, the cheaper it becomes for the consumer and the greater the reward for the producer. The temptation to meet the average of tastes, rather than one's own (or not to develop one's own) grows accordingly.

36. The increased power of consumers noted here is the major point of Ortega y Gasset's *Revolt of the Masses.* De Tocqueville too saw the ascendancy of "public opinion," though focusing on political causes and effects.

37. Similar reasoning helps explain why even in the natural sciences American success has so largely consisted of ingenious application and mass production of major discoveries made elsewhere. This can surely be said up to and including radar, penicillin and atomic fission. Not that Americans have less talent for pure research; but American talent was more drawn to application. The difference in profitability was greater. Now that the pragmatic importance of pure theory has been more fully understood, a change may be expected, but it comes because of basically utilitarian considerations.

Past inducements which might have tempted producers to defile or deflect their talents were small. Dante was not tempted to write for *Sports
Illustrated,* to condense his work for *Readers' Digest* or to adapt it for the
movies. He had no chance to write television scripts or commercial jingles,
Saturday Evening Post stories or newspaper columns. If he was impelled to
write, there were no alternatives to being as good a writer as his talent permitted.[38] There were, of course, political and religious pressures concerning
the philosophical ideas he might express. But there was no mass market to
entice the author to streamline the aesthetic vehicle of these ideas to make
it a common carrier so that the average man could ride along without effort
or understanding. Today the alternatives and temptations are very real. The
rewards of the mass market are immense—and so are the deprivations of
the creator of, one is tempted to say, custom-made literature. The real income of producers who do not cater to mass taste has fallen even more
than that of individualistic consumers. Cole Porter has described the situation (and for him popular appeal was not a matter of sour grapes):

> Why be a great composer with your rent in arrears?
> Why be a major poet and you'll owe it for years!
> When crowds will pay to giggle
> If you wiggle
> Your ears. . . .

Our society may not treat the creator of great works of art much worse
than he was treated in the past. But we treat the creator of popular art so
much better that the inducement becomes almost irresistible. There was no
such temptation in the past. And it was, of course, easier to decide to please
yourself when pleasing others instead was not overwhelmingly rewarded
anyway. Most talent is plastic to some extent.

There are some who doggedly insist on being themselves, but the
temptations are infinite and infinitely disguised and insinuating. Too, the
psychological burden of isolation has drawbacks affecting creation. The
ability and the will to communicate are impaired if there is no public; and
the defense against the temptations of popular culture uses much of the
energy needed for creating. The artist who by refusing to work for the
mass market becomes marginal, cannot create what he might have created
had there been no mass market. One may prefer a monologue to addressing
a mass meeting. But it still is not a conversation.[39]

We need not maintain that the taste of the masses has become worse
than it was. Only that it has become more important to the potential producers of high culture, important enough to isolate them or draw them to

---

38. It is unlikely that the possibility of doing hackwork ever was totally absent. "Grub
Street" came into existence in the 17th Century. Some sort of hackwork probably existed
even in Dante's time. But the difference between then and now remains immense, though like
the difference between being tempted by $1 and $1,000,000, it is quantitative.

39. And a marginal clique is not an elite, whatever its claim. Perhaps it should be. But
as a social fact, it is not unless society gives it that status. We are dealing here with the
recognition, not with the presence, of value.

the mass market. However good or bad, mass taste could not interfere much with the production of high culture until the pull of the mass market became as mighty as it is now.

The mass taste itself probably was debased by the de-individualizing and tradition-destroying developments already discussed. Folk culture developed a set of potentialities which requires the personal and communal relations that industrialism destroyed. But another set of potentialities, now fully developed by mass media, always existed (and has been complained about since Plato's time).[40]

The mass media suffice to bring out these potentialities and overwhelm folk (and high) culture. Full-fledged industrialism is not needed, though it might be required to create (rather than spread) popular culture. When movies are imported into a nonindustrial society, into remote parts of Pakistan, Spain, Burma or the Congo, they easily take the place of native plays and rituals for the upper as well as the lower classes. An industrial product aimed at an average of tastes draws better than the best of folk or high culture in nearly any setting.

Apart from the degree of industrialization, invasion by popular culture is facilitated by two conditions: (1) the absence of strong, native-grown, pre-industrial high and folk culture traditions. In the United States, for instance, these traditions, where they existed, were swamped by the influx of great masses with heterogeneous traditions homogenized through popular culture. Native traditions were not entrenched within these masses. (They included few high culture bearers. And the folk cultures were not adaptable to an urbanized industrial civilization.) (2) The suddenness of industrialization, its fragmentariness and particularly the entrance of mass media before the industrialization of production generally. These two hypotheses —and they are necessarily quite speculative—may help explain why popular culture is so pervasive in the United States and so penetrating in the underdeveloped countries, while at the same time, in England, the oldest industrial country, sizeable islands of folk and high culture, though embattled, have so far survived.

THE ROLE OF UNIVERSITIES AND FOUNDATIONS

No doubt universities and foundations provide some shelter for high

---

40. Industrialism is a prerequisite of popular culture, which erodes high and folk culture. We do not suggest, however, that without industrialism there can be no widespread bad taste. No one who has seen the frescoes at Pompeii or studied Rome in its decadence can fail to be impressed—as were Arnold Toynbee, Guglielmo Ferrero and M. I. Rostovtzeff— with some parallels to our own popular culture. Indeed there were parallel developments with regard to mobility, urbanization and commerce. But lacking machinery to spread it, Rome's "popular culture" was a fairly local affair, though it may have sufficed to dry up the flow of Roman high culture, which never had been copious. Our own popular culture is related to its ancestors as a jet-propelled airplane is to the pony express. Without the marvels of modern technology, there could be crowds and traditions could decay; but thoroughgoing, pervasive and (at least potentially) permanent de-individualization was impossible. Elements of popular culture have existed throughout history. We must leave to the historians evaluation of their strength in each period. What is new is that industrialism has made the prevalence of popular culture unavoidable.

culture, however leaky. They can't quite resist infiltration by popular culture
and they imprison high culture as much as they shelter it. Nevertheless, they
often fight a remarkable rear-guard battle.[41]

There is, however, an unfortunate difference between the largesse of a
foundation and that of a Maecenas or of a Medician Court. The admini-
strators of foundations are keenly aware of spending trust funds. They
feel that they must account for their activities. They try, therefore, to spend
money in accordance with some publicly approved standard, or at least in
a manner they feel is of demonstrable social usefulness. They spend funds
on empirical research and on tangible welfare projects so as to produce
measurable results, data, or activities. If foundations attempt to aid literature and the arts, they help artists sufficiently established to exonerate ad-
ministrators from any suspicion of following personal predilections or individual tastes. In short, foundations help those who cater to already formed
tastes, not those who might form them. (We need not tarry with ineffectual
attempts to form, not new tastes, but tastes appreciative of some genteel
but dead past.) The chances of foundation grants for a budding Proust,
Kafka, or Dostoyevski before he has formed his public are slim; the chances
of followers and imitators afterward are reasonable.[42] Foundations may even
tempt artists and often seduce scholars to write or do what will find support
in foundations—which, though it is not what might appeal to the mass
market, is also not what the writer or scholar might have done had he been
independent.

The situation in universities is a little better partly by reason of tradition,
partly because universities mostly pay their personnel for teaching (though
insisting on publications). Since they do not much scrutinize the quality of
publications, the instructor can maintain some independence—that is, unless
he is very ambitious for promotion and success.[43]

Foundations and universities are more useful in cultivating high culture
created in the past than in helping new developments. But their attempts
to transmit the heritage of the past are severely marred by the prevalent
conception of their educational function. To be educationally effective, that
is, to attract an audience in an age of popular culture, universities and
foundations tend to compete with the alternatives open to that audience.
They end up not by bringing the audience to art or any form of high culture,

41. We note the vulnerability of foundations or universities to the inroads of popular
culture and their basic inability to replace the soil on which high culture grew in former times.
The picture of universities and foundations is necessarily one-sided for we are focusing exclusively on their relation to popular culture. The generosity of motive behind them and
the actual help they are still able sometimes to extend individuals and groups who foster
the growth of high culture are not given their full due here.

42. Note that when an award to Ezra Pound was opposed by much public opinion, the
Library of Congress refused to be involved further in these awards. Never mind the merits
of Ezra Pound. The point is that public opinion, right or wrong, can veto and in the end
determine who is to be helped by public money and ultimately by foundations, too.

43. If he is, "teamwork" or publication in mass media are going to help him. And he
would be ill-advised to spend ten years on a major work which he could spend on minor or
less thought-out publications. (This is less true for the exact sciences with established criteria
of value—and more for those endeavors for which standards are difficult to formulate.)

but by bringing art to the audience—by sufficiently adulterating high culture to make it palatable to the mass market.[44]

Sometimes foundations and universities simply have followed the mass media at a dignified distance. The work of art is jazzed up a little or simplified to "make the unskillful laugh [though it] cannot but make the judicious grieve," even though "the censure of the which one must in your allowance overweigh a whole theatre of others." Hamlet's admonition is not easily heeded by an administrator who does not know who the "which one" would be—whereas he can identify "the whole theatre of others."[45]

THE ADULTERATION OF PAST CULTURE

Corruption of past high culture by popular culture takes numerous forms, starting with direct adulteration.[46] Bach candied by Stokowski, Bizet coarsened by Rodgers and Hammerstein, the Bible discolored and smoothed down into academic prose, Shakespeare spiced and made into a treacly musical comedy, Freud vulgarized into columns of newspaper correspondence advice (how to be happy though well-adjusted)—the listing could be infinitely prolonged.

Corruption also takes the form of mutilation and condensation. Mozart meanders, Tolstoi was tedious, Dostoyevski dawdled.[47] To spare us trouble, to save our time for more important things (such as commercials) their

44. We offer no specific proof but refer the reader to undergraduate and extension catalogues, to textbooks and anthologies used, and to the relevant foundation reports and television productions.

45. Matters would not be helped much if the wealthy spent their money personally. The American rich would not be less sensitive to public opinion than their foundations. Even a hundred years ago, when direct "conspicuous consumption" was still fashionable, money was used to display certified culture—antiques or imitations—rather than to support creation. A wealthy class who became wealthy fairly suddenly and temporarily by catering to mass tastes seems less likely to create or support an autonomous culture of its own than an entrenched upper class with traditions of independence from the masses. (However, the situation a hundred years ago had a few advantages: some wealthy people, e.g., the James family, cultivated themselves. Today, they would be more likely to run a newspaper or something else along popular lines.) With all this, what we note in the present was not absent in the past. Patrons often enforced their tastes and universities at times became hotbeds of conformity. The difference is quantitative. But it remains a significant difference.

46. Mr. Dwight Macdonald is entirely right in asserting that "The connection [between cultural traditions and popular culture] is not that of leaf and branch but rather caterpillar and leaf." (*Diogenes,* Summer 1953). He is wrong, though, in holding with Clement Greenberg (quoted, *ib.*) that "a fully matured cultural tradition" is a "precondition" for popular culture. There is no evidence that popular culture *needs* cultural traditions to exploit. Liberace, Max Lerner, and Herman Wouk indeed do. But does "Rock and Roll"? Or a Hollywood extravaganza?
Popular culture drives out high and folk cultures. But Macdonald's "Gresham's Law in culture" makes it hard to explain this. Gresham's Law states that adulterated money alone circulates because people treasure unadulterated money which is thus withdrawn from circulation. But the inroads of popular culture are due to people preferring adulterated material to the good stuff. (Alas, popular culture clichés can infect even staunch opponents.) We hasten to add that some of the most cogent analyses of popular culture patterns are owed to Dwight Macdonald's lively pen. Indeed, he christened the concept, though he did not father it.

47. Of course, these authors have their vices—necessary to their virtues (or so they felt). In a composition, one part may well be better or more important than another. Shall we then cut the great canvasses to pieces accordingly? What of the composition as such? At any rate, the condenser cuts out the virtues with the vices. He is interested in making it easier, shorter, or simpler, not better.

works are cut, condensed, simplified, and rewritten until all possibilities of unfamiliar or aesthetic experience are strained out and plot and action become meaningless thrills with an obligato of maudlin simperings and grandiose defiances; music is reduced to clatter and tinkle or cloying sentimentalities.

Editors who do not simply pretend that they know better than Tolstoi how to write his novels or better than Beethoven how to compose his symphonies say that half a loaf is better than none. Sometimes they argue that their mutilated or adulterated versions will stimulate appetite for the work of art they ravished. This argument is without merit. Why should a reader, listener or viewer accustomed to have all difficulties, complexities and originalities streamlined out develop an appetite for the undigested work? Will it not be indigestible to him? How could its more subtle, and perhaps slow and cumulative appeal rival the succession of action-packed climaxes he is accustomed to? Mothers who give in to a child's whining and feed him candy, unlike popularizers, are candid: they do not pretend that they are arousing the child's appetite for nourishment to follow.

Even if a predigested version were to lead to the original work, the public would be confronted with ideas and tropes which in their adulterated form have become commonplace. The garish image from *Classic Comics,* the gaudy phrase from *Carmen Jones,* the gloss of the condensation, overlay and spotlight the actual work, altering perception of colors and proportions and reducing it to the familiar clichés. No pin-up girl can surfeit appetite for a real one (though it may influence what satisfies it) just as no picture of a steak dulls our hunger. But the pin-up can spoil the appetite for other *images* of girls, particularly for more subtle, less reductive ones. And, if the calendar girl is a streamlined Goya, it certainly obstructs later experience of the actual painting by an untutored eye. Some people may be able to slough off the tawdriness. But even for them, the surprise and delight of freshness are blunted. Besides, how many people are drawn to actual mountaineering by riding a comfortable funicular? In making mountains more accessible, don't funiculars reduce elevation for the passengers?

DO-IT-YOURSELF CULTURE

The "Hundred Great Books" which Mr. Hutchins wants everybody to read are unadulterated and mostly undigested. The praiseworthy motive of the plan was revolt against corruption and neglect of our cultural heritage. But on closer inspection, the nostrum turns out to be but a more ambitious and pretentious form of digesting.[48]

---

48. According to the advertisements, anyone who reads the 100 books will be educated, entertained and helped in "getting along in business . . . with associates and family." He will also learn to meet whatever problem bothers him "squarely and conquer it." Does the end justify *these* means? May not false claims for great works weaken their real claims to greatness and foster expectations sure to be disappointed? Well, this is for the Better Business Bureau to deal with. And we can merely mention the absurdities of selection and of that odd mail order catalogue of ideas, the "Syntopicon," which have been pointed out by many scholars.

By rewriting and paring the condensers insist they get rid of dross and compress the essentials for us. The contrivers of the "Hundred Great Books" program instead brightly discovered that culture is already concentrated in one hundred specific books which, as it were, naturally contain the essentials of all ages. No rewriting needed. Both, the condensers and Hutchins' followers, believe that there are essentials in the cultural heritage which they know and have isolated—by distillation, the condensers say; by simply picking them, Mr. Hutchins says—and that everybody can understand, enjoy and use these essentials by reading the same selection of works, Aristotle to Einstein, but no systematic expositions of physics or philosophy and no commentaries (Hutchins), or the same selection within works (digesters). They have done the "research" for us, we need not bother. Culture is reduced to capsules we all can take to become healthy, wealthy and wise.

In condensation, the elements indigestible to popular culture are omitted and the whole thing is reduced to pap. In the Hutchins approach, the reader jumps from landmark to landmark without regard, without a view even of the land they are marking.[49] The works burst on the reader as though grown on the same timeless soil. The connecting tissue of history which makes them intelligible is omitted. There is no history of, say, economic ideas, or of the economy; nor is there a systematic exposition of economics. The reader simply is given some famous but unrelated works concerned with the subject matter. But there is no way of understanding a classic except through the tradition of which it is a part. And no way of understanding a subject except through systematic study. Finally, there is no way of becoming educated except by absorbing and critically working through a tradition and a subject matter. After all, even a baseball game is meaningless to a spectator who does not know the rules and the background of the contest. The understanding of ideas warrants even a little more knowledge.

THE POPULARITY OF CLASSICS

The "Hundred Great Books" and the many book, record, or digest clubs do not guide the reader through a landscape. At best, they sell him some cut flowers, often with artificial scents and colors. But what about the many excellent uncut and inexpensive editions of the classics, the fine recordings of musical masterpieces which are not hawked as shortcuts to culture?[50] And the symphony orchestras springing up in small towns? And the museums and clubs devoted to culture? Though Americans spend untold time reading newspapers and watching television, they also spend more money on attending concerts than on attending baseball games. Twelve million people listen to the New York Philharmonic each month. And the paperbound classics sell well—though, of course, there is no comparison with *Readers'*

49. When there are no outstanding landmarks, when ideas and views are not found in particular great books, they are ignored, however influential or important.
50. Many are sold under incongruous titles and with ludicrous covers which make promises sure to disappoint the reader enticed by them. But others are decently dressed. Both, it goes without saying, are a boon to individuals still clinging to high culture.

Digest (*ca.* 10 million copies sold per issue in the United States) or *Confidential* (*ca.* 2 million copies per issue), not to speak of comic books, pulps, slicks, or Norman Vincent Peale.[51] The data suggest that at least a few previously indifferent people buy some classics and go to some concerts. Is popular culture receding, then, or being transformed?

The range of widely shared tastes has become broader. In particular, "middlebrow" tastes are more eclectic and now include material that was formely "highbrow" as well as material formerly reserved to "lowbrows."[52] The borderlines are more blurred than ever. The size of the "middlebrow" group itself has grown and its attitudes are less aggressively crude and ignorant than in Sinclair Lewis' and H. L. Mencken's heyday. In short, a wider range of taste is more widely shared and, as was pointed out, this does not imply reduction to "the lowest common denominator." Yet middlebrow culture remains popular culture, even if the Book of the Month Club sends its subscribers Proust; even if more and more people go to college and the *New Yorker* penetrates to Kansas City. The effect is not less but more homogenization. The high and folk culture works, even when they are not physically altered, change their function when they are absorbed into the stream of popular culture. They cannot change the function or the basic character of popular culture.

Years ago a naked African chief wearing a top hat was among the stock figures of humorous magazines. The incongruous setting for the hat, worn in obvious ignorance of its ceremonial function in our society and without the complements it requires, struck us as funny. When other fragments of our civilization are put to uses quite alien to them—outside the patterns that give them their meaning in our society—we are similarly amused.[53]

American homes are now decorated with African masks and statues of Mexican gods, with Gothic crucifixions and Japanese prints as incongruous in them as the top hat on the tribal chief.[54] Whether they come from past civilizations—including Western high and folk cultures—or from contemporary Africa, whether they are tacked to the wall, worn, read, listened to, viewed or danced, such fragments, however entertaining or even instructive, are no more than frosting on the cake of popular culture; they do not change its nature but intensify its syncretistic stylelessness. The very kaleidoscopic variety of chips from nearly all cultures the world has known helps to devalue and denature each, just as the colors of the spectrum fuse into a

---

51. Circulation data are fairly reliable, but most data on how people spend their time are too unreliable to bother with. (Statistics indicate that only 17 per cent of Americans read any books at all after leaving school.) This, too, should be considered an approximation.

52. This terminology used by Van Wyck Brooks in 1915 was later amplified, coarsened and most systematically expounded by Russell Lynes.

53. Slowly accruing new meanings which become part of a new integrated pattern do not strike us as funny or tasteless. But when in changed circumstances the physical object does not become part of a new pattern nor retain its old meaning, when it is simply used for its exotic charm, as the chief uses the top hat, we rightly ridicule the pretentious ignorance displayed.

54. Evelyn Waugh, in condemning the protagonist of his *Handful of Dust* to spend the rest of his life reading Dickens to an illiterate, entertainment-hungry native in the Brazilian wilds, makes this point sharply. The situation must seem familiar to many a college professor.

monochrome white when they are rotated rapidly before our eyes. Oddly enough, we pride ourselves on mixing a variety of culture patterns. We take to jamborees featuring "folk dances (or songs) of all nations," as though this would not deprive the folk dances of each nation of what meaning they might retain singly and reduce them all to quaint imports.

Why do classics clutter rather than enrich the minds of so many readers? Why do we find the glamorous items assembled indiscriminately like "celebrities" in a night club? Why do they not make a whole that organizes minds and sharpens sensibilities? Besides innate capacity, at least some of the following are needed to tutor intellects and sensibilities so that the aesthetic and intellectual values of high culture are apprehended as meaningful: time (and patience), inclination, discipline, focus, guidance, and an environment in which style can be experienced.[55] These conditions have become rare even in our better institutions of high learning.

Were these prerequisites more available in the past? Perhaps some were. The evidence is anecdotal, though sweeping assertions are not missing. But the relevant thing is not that possibly more people were devoted to high culture in proportion to the total population, nor even that they were better supported (which is likely), but that practically none were devoted to popular culture. The high culture of the past, however limited, formed a style. The absence of popular culture and of industrialism meant that high culture functioned under conditions favorable to its continued influence and development, at least in one social stratum. Today, however widely spread, high culture in every stratum of society is a minor ripple in a great flood.

One can live happily and well without high culture. Socrates' plea that the unexamined life is not worth living, after all came from a professional examiner of life, an intellectual and perhaps platonic lover of it, a man with an ax to grind. For him, perhaps, the unexamined life was not worth living. For most people it is. We need only ask them or observe them. (And a world filled with Socrates' would neither be pleasant nor feasible).

What eagerness for high culture there is in popular culture has abetted the invasion of high culture, with unfortunate effect on the invaded territory. Often the effect on the invaders is unhappy, too. In biting into strange fruits they are not equipped to digest they are in danger of spoiling their appetite for what might actually nourish them. It is not new nor disastrous that few people read classics. It is new that so many people misread them. Doubtless they are eager for intellectual and aesthetic experience. Yet their quest is not likely to succeed. A partial response may sometimes be achieved. But it takes far more than training (and even that is often lacking) and formal preparation fully to experience a work of art as meaningful. It takes an environment and a life experience which do not easily grow on the soil of our society.

---

55. Not all these elements are needed. But where one is lacking, the others have to make up for it.

MORAL ISOLATION AND GREGARIOUSNESS

We have noted the effects of popular culture on high (and folk) culture as well as the limitations of mass media and mass tastes. Let us now return to the impact that the stream of popular culture has on persons.

All mass media in the end alienate people from personal experience and, though appearing to offset it, intensify their moral isolation from each other, from reality and from themselves. One may turn to the mass media when lonely or bored. But mass media, once they become a habit, impair the capacity for meaningful experience. Though more diffuse and not as gripping, the habit feeds on itself, establishing a vicious circle as addictions do.

The mass media do not physically replace individual activities and contacts—excursions, travel, parties, etc. But they impinge on all. The portable radio is taken everywhere—from seashore to mountaintop—and everywhere it isolates the bearer from his surroundings, from other people, and from himself. Most people escape being by themselves at any time by voluntarily tuning in on something or somebody. Anyway, it is nearly beyond the power of individuals to escape broadcasts. Music and public announcements are piped into restaurants, bars, shops, cafes, and lobbies, into public means of transportation, and even taxis. You can turn off your radio but not your neighbors', nor can you silence his portable or the set at the restaurant. Fortunately, most persons do not seem to miss privacy, the cost of which is even more beyond the average income than the cost of individuality.

People are never quite in one place or group without at the same time, singly or collectively, gravitating somewhere else, abstracted, if not transported by the mass media. The incessant announcements, arpeggios, croonings, sobs, bellows, brayings and jingles draw to some faraway world at large and by weakening community with immediate surroundings make people lonely even when in a crowd and crowded even when alone.

We have already stressed that mass media must offer homogenized fare to meet an average of tastes. Further, whatever the quality of the offerings, the very fact that one after the other is absorbed continuously, indiscriminately and casually, trivializes all. Even the most profound of experiences, articulated too often on the same level, is reduced to a cliché. The impact of each of the offerings of mass media is thus weakened by the next one. But the impact of the stream of all mass-media offerings is cumulative and strong. It lessens people's capacity to experience life itself.

Sometimes it is argued that the audience confuses actuality with mass-media fiction and reacts to the characters and situations that appear in soap operas or comic strips as though they were real. For instance, wedding presents are sent to fictional couples. It seems more likely, however, that the audience prefers to invest fiction with reality—as a person might prefer to dream—without actually confusing it with reality. After all, even the kids know that Hopalong Cassidy is an actor and the adults know that "I Love

Lucy" is fiction. Both, however, may attempt to live the fiction because they prefer it to their own lives. The significant effect is not the (quite limited) investment of fiction with reality, but the de-realization of life lived in largely fictitious terms. Art can deepen the perception of reality. But popular culture veils it, diverts from it, and becomes an obstacle to experiencing it. It is not so much an escape from life but an invasion of life first, and ultimately evasion altogether.[56]

CHILDREN AND VIOLENCE

Parents, well knowing that mass media can absorb energy, often lighten the strain that the attempts of their children to reach for activity and direct experience would impose; they allow some energy to be absorbed by the vicarious experience of the television screen. Before television, the cradle was rocked, or poppy juice given, to inhibit the initiative and motility of small children. Television, unlike these physical sedatives, tranquillizes by means of substitute gratifications. Manufactured activities and plots are offered to still the child's hunger for experiencing life. They effectively neutralize initiative and channel imagination. But the early introduction of de-individualized characters and situations and early homogenization of taste on a diet of meaningless activity hardly foster development. Perhaps poppy juice, offering no models in which to cast the imagination, was better.[57]

The homogenizing effect of comic books or television, the fact that they neither express nor appeal to individuality, seems far more injurious to the child's mind and character than the violence they feature, though it is the latter that is often blamed for juvenile delinquency. The blame is misplaced. Violence is not new to life or fiction. It waxed large in ancient fables, fairy tales, and in tragedies from Sophocles to Shakespeare.

Mom always knew that "her boy could not have thought of it," that the other boys must have seduced him. The belief that viewing or reading about violence persuades children to engage in it is Mom's ancient conviction disguised as psychiatry.[58] Children are quite spontaneously bloodthirsty and need both direct and fantasy outlets for violence. What is wrong with the violence of the mass media is not that it is violence, but that it is not art—that it is meaningless violence which thrills but does not gratify. The violence of the desire for life and meaning is displaced and appears as a desire for meaningless violence. But the violence which is ceaselessly

---

56. Escape presumes two separate worlds, a life to be escaped from and dreams to be escaped into. But popular culture characteristically blurs both so that one is conceived in terms of the other.

57. Not that all the amusements offered children in the past were blameless. But few were manufactured and de-individualized and none were so pervasive as television.

58. For instance, in Frederic Wertham's *Seduction of the Innocent*. (Dr. Wertham in dressing Mom up as a psychiatrist also used some para-Marxist clichés from the attic.) Of course, the impact of a comic strip or movie on a particularly susceptible child may be bad. But the impact of any otherwise harmless experience may be injurious to particular persons.

supplied cannot ultimately gratify it because it does not meet the repressed desire.[59]

THE OUTLOOK

We have hinted throughout that the gratifications offered by popular culture are spurious and unsatisfactory. Let us summarize these hints now, and then try to make explicit the psychological effects we implied before.

While immensely augmenting our comforts, our conveniences and our leisure, and disproportionately raising the real income of the poor, industry has also impoverished life. Mass production and consumption, mobility, the homogenization of taste and finally of society were among the costs of higher productivity. They de-individualized life and drained each of our ends of meaning as we achieved it. Pursuit thus became boundless. The increased leisure time would hang heavy on our hands, were it not for the mass media which help us kill it. They inexorably exclude art and anything of significance when it cannot be reduced to mass entertainment, but they divert us from the passage of the time they keep us from filling. They also tend to draw into the mass market talents and works that might otherwise produce new visions and they abstract much of the capacity to experience art or life directly and deeply. What they do, however, is what people demand.

We scrutinized the causes, the effects and the general characteristics of popular culture and found them unavoidable in a mass-production economy. But we have hardly touched on the contents of popular culture. Some work on this subject has been done and much remains.[60] Limitations of scope also restricted us from stressing the many material advantages of industrialism. We do not intend to deny them. Finally, prophecy too is beyond our means.[61] True, extrapolation of present trends makes a dismal picture. But

---

59. The same reasoning applies to pornography. It does not seduce, and though it thrills some, it does not gratify. The harm it would do, if widespread, would lie, as with violence, in the debasement of taste. (If there is a general cause of juvenile delinquency, it is likely to be boredom, which causes both addiction to violent fiction and to violent action.)

60. *Movies* by Wolfenstein and Leites is one model of what can be done in interpreting contents or themes. *The Lonely Crowd* by Riesman, Denney and Glazer is rich in insights, though somewhat marred by the excessive journalistic competence of the authors and their unclear concepts (particularly psychological ones). The odd and unwarranted idea of linking the patterns they describe so tellingly to population changes may have barred the authors from fuller exploration of their concepts. But it did not preclude many fascinating observations. Very useful analyses of the programs of mass media are found in the vast literature dealing with public opinion and mass communication and particularly in the volumes on "Radio Research" and "Communication Research" edited by P. R. Lazarsfeld and F. Stanton.

61. Even in examining the present, we sometimes uneasily feel the mantle of the prophet descending on us. We do not deserve it. We claim to have stated, with reasonable clarity, a number of connected hypotheses—a theory—which fit one series of facts and help to explain them, that is, to connect them with another series of facts. The latter (industrialism, etc.) are well established. But the former—popular culture—though factual enough, are not easily measured and tested. Our conclusions are consistent with what measuring has been done. But most testing so far devised is of little relevance to our actual topic. Many sociologists, therefore, have regarded the topic as though irrelevant to sociology. But this merely reduces the relevance of sociology to contemporary culture. Other sociologists have tested where possible but without venturing on comprehensive hypotheses or concepts. This makes the significance of many factual findings unintelligible. (Some facts tested *ad nauseam* are without relevance to any conceivable theory.) We are satisfied then that only the procedure adopted

there is comfort in the fact that no extrapolation has ever predicted the future correctly. Elements can be forecast, but only prophets can do more (and they are unreliable, or hard to interpret). History has always had surprises up its sleeves—it would be most surprising if it changed its ways. Our ignorance here leaves the rosy as well as the grim possibilities open for the future. But this does not allow us to avert our gaze from the present and from the outlook it affords. Neither is cheerful.

REPRESSION AND DISCONTENT

The gist of any culture is an ethos which gives meaning to the lives of those who dwell in it. If this be the purport of popular culture, it is foiled. We have suggested how it comes to grief in various aspects. What makes popular culture as a whole so disconcerting is best set forth now by exploring the relationship among diversion, art and boredom.

Freud thought of art as a diversion, "an illusion in contrast to reality," a "substitute gratification" like a dream.[62] In this he fully shared what was and still is the popular view of art. It is a correct view—of popular "art," of pseudo-art produced to meet the demand for diversion. But it is a mistaken, reductive definition of art.[63]

Freud finds the "dreamwork" attempting to hide or disguise the dreamer's true wishes and fears so that they may not alarm his consciousness. The "substitute gratification" produced by the dreamwork, mainly by displacements, helps the dreamer continue sleeping.[64] However, one major function of art is precisely to undo this dreamwork, to see through disguises, to reveal to our consciousness the true nature of our wishes and fears. The dreamwork covers, to protect sleep. Art discovers and attempts to awaken the sleeper. Whereas the dreamwork tries to aid repression, the work of art intensifies and deepens perception and experience of the world and of the self. It attempts to pluck the heart of the mystery, to show where "the action lies in its true nature."

Though dreams and art both may disregard literal reality, they do so to answer opposite needs. The dream may ignore reality to keep the sleeper's eyes closed. Art transcends immediate reality to encompass wider views,

can do justice to the subject matter though we must rely for verification on the experience and reason of our readers. *Si monumentum quaeris, circumspice.*

62. In dreams and in art, ideas and feelings of which the dreamer (or artist) may not be aware are condensed, fused, or split and expressed as well as disguised through symbols. The analogy must not be driven too far, however. The artist needs special gifts to select, shape, control and organize his materials. A dream is not art, anymore than art is a dream, even if both were only "substitute gratifications." Freud himself did not think that the analogy (or psychoanalysis as a whole) could shed light on artistic gifts or techniques. He realized that the approach, though it may suffice to analyze artistic motivation, does not explain aesthetic quality. Therefore, it cannot define art. Freud was wrong in writing at times as though it did, by sometimes treating the artist as a patient, sometimes as a fellow-analyst. Art can neither be reduced to dreams nor to analysis of dreams, though it contains elements of both.

63. Freud committed the same reduction with religion. In both cases, he inferred more than is legitimate from genesis. And he did not resist enough the temptation to reduce the aesthetic to those elements of it which he could explain.

64. The dreamwork deals similarly with fears. It displaces and disguises them and attempts to produce illusionary reassurances.

penetrate into deeper experience and lead to a fuller confrontation of man's predicament. The dreamwork even tries to cover upsetting basic impulses with harmless immediate reality. Art, in contrast, ignores the immediate only to uncover the essential.[65] Artistic revelation need not be concerned with outer or with social reality. It may be purely aesthetic. But it can never be an illusion if it is art. Far from distracting from reality, art is a form of reality which strips life of the fortuitous to lay bare its essentials and permit us to experience them.

In popular culture, however, "art" is all that Freud said art is, and no more. Like the dreamwork, popular culture distorts human experience to draw "substitute gratifications" or reassurances from it. Like the dream-work, it presents "an illusion in contrast to reality." For this reason, popular "art" falls short of satisfaction. And all of popular culture leaves one vaguely discontented because, like popular art, it is only a "substitute gratification"; like a dream, it distracts from life and from real gratification.

Substitute gratifications are uneconomic, as Freud often stressed. They do not in the end gratify as much, and they cost more psychologically than the real gratifications which they shut out. This is why sublimation and realistic control are to be preferred to substitution and repression. That is why reality is to be preferred to illusion, full experience to symptomatic displacements and defense mechanisms. Yet substitute gratifications, habitually resorted to, incapacitate the individual for real ones. In part they cause or strengthen internalized hindrances to real and gratifying experience; in part they are longed for because internal barriers have already blocked real gratification of the original impulses.

Though the specific role it plays varies with the influence of other formative factors in the life of each individual, popular culture must be counted among the baffling variety of causes and effects of defense mechanisms and repressions. It may do much damage, or do none at all, or be the only relief possible, however deficient. But whenever popular culture plays a major role in life significant repressions have taken (or are taking) place. Popular culture supplants those gratifications, which are no longer sought because of the repression of the original impulses. But it is a substitute and spurious. It founders and cannot succeed because neither desire nor gratification are true. "Nought's had, all's spent/ where desire is got without content."

It may seem paradoxical to describe popular culture in terms of repression. Far from repressed, it strikes one as uninhibited. Yet the seeming paradox disappears if we assume that the uproarious din, the raucous noise and the shouting are attempts to drown the shriek of unused capacities, of repressed individuality, as it is bent into futility.

---

65. In psychoanalytic terms, art is not symptomatic expression of the repressed but a sublimated and controlled expression, not an escape from or a limitation or distortion of experience, but an attempt to face it with enhanced awareness and to deal with its essence. Art differs from science in methods of searching and testing and because it does reveal rather than predict and focuses on human reactions and values. Above all, art strives to produce subjective experiences whereas science produces objective information.

BOREDOM AND DIVERSION

Repression bars impulses from awareness without satisfying them. This damming up always generates a feeling of futility and apathy or, in defense against it, an agitated need for action. The former may be called listless, the latter restless boredom. They may alternate and they may enter consciousness only through anxiety and a sense of meaninglessness, fatigue and nonfulfillment. Sometimes there is such a general numbing of the eagerness too often turned aside that only a dull feeling of dreariness and emptiness remains. More often, there is an insatiable longing for things to happen. The external world is to supply these events to fill the emptiness.[66] Yet the bored person cannot designate what would satisfy a craving as ceaseless as it is vague. It is not satisfied by any event supplied.

The yearning for diversion to which popular culture caters cannot be sated by diversion "whereof a little more than a little is by much too much," because no displaced craving can be satisfied by catering to it in its displaced form. Only when it becomes possible to experience the desire in its true form and to dispense with the internalized processes that balked and displaced it does actual gratification become possible. Diversion at most, through weariness and fatigue, can numb and distract anxiety.

For instance, in many popular movies the tear ducts are massaged and thrills are produced by mechanized assaults on the centers of sensation. We are diverted temporarily and in the end perhaps drained—but not gratified.[67] Direct manipulation of sensations can produce increases and discharges of tension, as does masturbation, but it is a substitute. It does not involve the whole individual as an individual, it does not involve reality but counterfeits it. Sensations directly stimulated and discharged without being intensified and completed through feelings sifted and acknowledged by the intellect are debasing because they do not involve the whole individual in his relation to reality. When one becomes inured to bypassing reality and individuality in favor of meaningless excitement, ultimate gratification becomes impossible.

WHO IS SLAIN WHEN TIME IS KILLED?

Once fundamental impulses are thwarted beyond retrieving, once they are so deeply repressed that no awareness is left of their aims, once the desire for a meaningful life has been lost as well as the capacity to create it, only a void remains. Life fades into tedium when the barrier between impulses and aims is so high that neither penetrates into consciousness and no sublimation whatever takes place. Diversion, however frantic, can over-

---

66. In persons suffering from symptom neurosis, the pressure of the repressed impulses may cause so much anxiety that boredom becomes faint. But this is hardly a desirable alternative.

67. Movies, which are deliberately produced by a group for the broadest possible market, afford an excellent illustration of popular culture. The fact that only the most successful answer fully the description in the text testifies to the difficulty of providing homogenized fantasies that will appeal—despite the *Nielsen Audiometer* and the *Hopkins Televoter*. Perhaps this fact also testifies to some idealism of producers. Sometimes a compromise is reached and it does not always wholly fail commercially, or in its ideal ambition.

whelm temporarily but not ultimately relieve the boredom which oozes from nonfulfillment.

Though the bored person hungers for things to happen to him, the disheartening fact is that when they do he empties them of the very meaning he unconsciously yearns for by using them as distractions. In popular culture even the second coming would become just another barren "thrill" to be watched on television till Milton Berle comes on. No distraction can cure boredom, just as the company so unceasingly pursued cannot stave off loneliness. The bored person is lonely for himself, not, as he thinks, for others. He misses the individuality, the capacity for experience from which he is debarred. No distraction can restore it. Hence he goes unrelieved and insatiable.

The popular demand for "inside" stories, for vicarious sharing of the private lives of "personalities" rests on the craving for private life—even someone else's—of those who are dimly aware of having none whatever, or at least no life that holds their interest. The attempts to allay boredom are as assiduous as they are unavailing. Countless books pretend to teach by general rules and devices what cannot be learned by devices and rules. Individual personalities cannot be mass produced (with happiness thrown in or your money back). Nevertheless, the message of much popular culture is "you, too, can be happy" if you only buy this car or that hair tonic; you will be thrilled, you will have adventure, romance, popularity—you will no longer be lonely and left out if you follow this formula. And success, happiness or at least freedom from anxiety is also the burden of popular religion, as unchristian in these its aims as it is in its means.[68] From Dale Carnegie to Norman Vincent Peale to Harry and Bonaro Overstreet only the vocabulary changes. The principle remains the same. The formula is well illustrated in the following.

Warm Smile Is an Attribute of Charm

For this, train the upper lip by this method:

1. Stretch the upper lip down over the teeth. Say "Mo-o-o-o."
2. Hold the lip between the teeth and smile.
3. Purse the lips, pull them downward and grin.
4. Let the lower jaw fall and try to touch your nose with your upper lip.

Months of daily practice are necessary to eliminate strain from the new way of smiling, but it, too, can become as natural as all beguiling smiles must be.[69]

Whatever the formula, nothing can be more tiresome than the tireless, cheerless pursuit of pleasure. Days go slowly when they are empty; one cannot tell one from the other. And yet the years go fast. When time is endlessly killed, one lives in an endless present until time ends without ever having passed, leaving a person who never lived to exclaim, "I wasted time and now doth time waste me."

---

68. "Make People Like You—Increase Your Earnings" advertises Dr. Peale. These aims are not found in the Gospels, in Luther or in Calvin and not even in Pelagius and Coelestius.

69. Quoted by the *New Yorker*, January 21, 1956, from the *Indianapolis News*.

HAPPINESS AND DESPAIR

To the Christian, despair is a sin not because there is anything to be hoped for in this life, but because to despair is to lack faith in redemption from it—in the life everlasting. As for the pleasure of this life, they are not worth pursuing. Lancelot Andrewes described them: ". . . though they fade not of themselves yet to us they fade. We are hungry and we eat. Eat we not till that fades and we are as weary of our fulness as we were of our fasting? We are weary and we rest. Rest we not till that fades and we are as weary of our rest as ever we were of our weariness?" Our bodies and minds themselves fade as do their pleasures. The insults of time are spared to none of us. Such is the human predicament.

In *Civilization and Its Discontents,* Freud pointed to the additional burdens that civilization imposes on human beings. They, too, are inevitable, for civilization, despite its cost, eases the total burden we bear.

A little more than a hundred years ago, Henry David Thoreau wrote in *Walden*: "The mass of men lead lives of quiet desperation. . . . A stereotyped but unconscious despair is concealed even under what are called the games and amusements of mankind." Despair, we find, is no longer quiet. Popular culture tries to exorcise it with much clanging and banging. Perhaps it takes more noise to drone it out. Perhaps we are less willing to face it. But whether wrapped in popular culture, we are less happy than our quieter ancestors, or the natives of Bali, must remain an open question despite all romanticizing. (Nor do we have a feasible alternative to popular culture. Besides, a proposal for "the mass of men" would be unlikely to affect the substance of popular culture. And counsel to individuals must be individual.)

There have been periods happier and others more desperate than ours. But we don't know which. And even an assertion as reasonable as this is a conjecture like any comparison of today's bliss with yesterday's. The happiness felt in disparate groups, in disparate periods and places cannot be measured and compared.[70] Our contention is simply that by distracting from the human predicament and blocking individuation and experience, popular culture impoverishes life without leading to contentment. But whether "the mass of men" felt better or worse without the mass-production techniques of which popular culture is an ineluctable part, we shall never know. Of happiness and of despair, we have no measure.

---

70. Even in examining a single life it seems absurd to throw onto the same scale the separate raptures generated by hearing chamber music, eating a peach, loving, or winning a fight; harder still to measure the depth of despair into which one sinks if he fails or suffers positive sorrows. Yet to sum, we must set sorrow off against delight and add the net to that of other persons. (Perhaps desire can be measured. But does desire fulfilled bring happiness?) The whole idea does violence to our actual experience, and creates problems which cannot be solved by any observation. What about intensity versus duration or depth? Or suppose the net "amount" of happiness drawn from a life replete with great joys and sorrows equals the "sum" drawn from a life lacking both? Did the two lives lead to equal happiness?

Perhaps we can order the relish elicited by homogeneous segments of life in terms of "none," "some," "much"; thus we might speak of "more" or "less." But even such ordering can only be undertaken from a given standpoint in time and from a given viewpoint. It would differ from person to person.

The Middle Against Both Ends

By LESLIE A. FIEDLER

I AM SURELY ONE OF THE FEW PEOPLE pretending to intellectual respectability who can boast that he has read more comic books than attacks on comic books. I do not mean that I have consulted or studied the comics—I have read them, often with some pleasure. Nephews and nieces, my own children, and the children of neighbors have brought them to me to share their enjoyment. An old lady on a ferry boat in Puget Sound once dropped two in my lap in wordless sympathy; I was wearing, at the time, a sailor's uniform.

I have somewhat more difficulty in getting through the books that attack them. I am put off, to begin with, by inaccuracies of fact. When Mr. Geoffrey Wagner in his *Parade of Pleasure* calls Superboy "Superman's brother" (he is, of course, Superman himself as a child), I am made suspicious. Actually, Mr. Wagner's book is one of the least painful on the subject; confused, to be sure, but quite lively and not in the least smug; though it propounds the preposterous theory that the whole of "popular literature" is a conspiracy on the part of the "plutos" to corrupt an innocent American people. Such easy melodrama can only satisfy someone prepared to believe, as Mr. Wagner apparently does, that the young girls of Harlem are being led astray by the *double-entendres* of blues records!

Mr. Wagner's notions are at least more varied and subtle than Mr. Gershon Legman's, who cries out in his *Love and Death* that it is simply our sexual frustrations which breeds a popular literature dedicated to violence. But Mr. Legman's theory explains too much: not only comic books but Hemingway, war, Luce, Faulkner, the status of women—and, I should suppose, Mr. Legman's own shrill hyperboles. At that, Mr. Legman seems more to the point in his search for some deeply underlying cause than Frederic Wertham, in *Seduction of the Innocent,* with his contention that the pulps and comics in themselves are schools for murder. That the undefined aggressiveness of disturbed children can be given a shape by comic books, I do not doubt; and one could make a good case for the contention that such literature standardizes crime woefully or inhibits imagination in violence, but I find it hard to consider so obvious a symptom a prime cause of anything. Perhaps I am a little sensitive on this score, having heard the charge this week that the recent suicide of one of our college freshmen was caused by his having read (in a course of which I am in charge) Goethe, Dostoevsky, and *Death of a Salesman*. Damn it, he *had* read them, and he *did* kill himself!

Reprinted from *Encounter*, Vol. 5 (1955), pp. 16-23, by permission of the author and the publisher. (Copyright, 1955, by Martin Secker & Warburg, Ltd.)

In none of the books on comics I have looked into, and in none of the reports of ladies' clubs, protests of legislators, or statements of moral indignation by pastors, have I come on any real attempt to understand comic books: to define the form, midway between icon and story; to distinguish the subtypes—animal, adolescent, crime, western, etc.; or even to separate out, from the deadpan varieties, tongue-in-cheek sports like *Pogo,* frank satire like *Mad,* or semi-surrealist variations like *Plastic Man.* It would not take someone with the talents of an Aristotle, but merely with his method, to ask the rewarding questions about this kind of literature that he asked once about an equally popular and bloody genre: what are its causes and its natural form?

A cursory examination would show that the super-hero comic (*Superman, Captain Marvel, Wonder Woman,* etc.) is the final form; it is statistically the most popular with the most avid readers, as well as providing the only new legendary material invented along with the form rather than adapted to it.

Next, one would have to abstract the most general pattern of the myth of the super-hero and deduce its significance: the urban setting, the threatened universal catastrophe, the hero who never uses arms, who returns to weakness and obscurity, who must keep his identity secret, who is impotent, etc. Not until then could one ask with any hope of an answer: what end do the comics serve? Why have they gained an immense body of readers precisely in the past fifteen or twenty years? Why must they be disguised as children's literature though read by men and women of all ages? And having answered these, one could pose the most dangerous question of all: why the constant virulent attacks on the comics, and, indeed, on the whole of popular culture of which they are especially flagrant examples?

Strategically, if not logically, the last question should be asked first. Why the attacks? Such assaults by scientists and laymen are as characteristic of our age as puritanic diatribes against the stage of the Elizabethan Era, and pious protests against novel reading in the later eighteenth century. I suspect that a study of such conventional reactions reveals at least as much about the nature of a period as an examination of the forms to which they respond. The most fascinating and suspicious aspect of the opposition to popular narrative is its unanimity; everyone from the members of the Montana State Legislature to the ladies of the Parent Teachers Association of Boston, Massachusetts, from British M.P.'s to the wilder post-Freudians of two continents agree on this, though they may agree on nothing else. What they have in common is, I am afraid, the sense that they are all, according to their lights, righteous. And their protests represent only one more example (though an unlikely one) of the notorious failure of righteousness in matters involving art.

Just what is it with which vulgar literature is charged by various guardians of morality or sanity? With everything: encouraging crime, destroying literacy, expressing sexual frustration, unleashing sadism, spreading anti-democratic ideas, and, of course, corrupting youth. To understand the grounds of such charges, their justification and their bias, we must understand something of the nature of the subart with which we are dealing.

Perhaps it is most illuminating to begin by saying that it is a peculiarly American phenomenon, an unexpected by-product of an attempt, not only to extend literacy universally, but to delegate taste to majority suffrage. I do not mean, of course, that it is found only in the United States, but that wherever it is found, it comes first from us, and is still to be discovered in fully developed form only among us. Our experience along these lines is, in this sense, a preview for the rest of the world of what must follow the inevitable dissolution of the older aristocratic cultures.

One has only to examine certain Continental imitations of picture magazines like *Look* or *Life* or Disney-inspired cartoon books to be aware at once of the debt to American examples and of the failure of the imitations. For a true "popular literature" demands a more than ordinary slickness, the sort of high finish possible only to a machine-produced commodity in an economy of maximum prosperity. Contemporary popular culture, which is a function of an industrialized society, is distinguished from older folk art by its refusal to be shabby or second-rate in appearance, by a refusal to know its place. It is a product of the same impulse which has made available the sort of ready-made clothing which aims at destroying the possibility of knowing a lady by her dress.

Yet the articles of popular culture are made, not to be treasured, but to be thrown away; a paperback book is like a disposable diaper or a paper milk-container. For all its competent finish, it cannot be preserved on dusty shelves like the calf-bound volumes of another day; indeed, its very mode of existence challenges the concept of a library, private or public. The sort of conspicuous waste once reserved for an élite is now available to anyone; and this is inconceivable without an absurdly high standard of living, just as it is unimaginable without a degree of mechanical efficiency that permits industry to replace nature, and invents—among other disposable synthetics —one for literature.

Just as the production of popular narrative demands industrial conditions most favorably developed in the United States, its distribution requires the peculiar conditions of our market places: the mass or democratized market. Subbooks and subarts are not distributed primarily through the traditional institutions: museums, libraries, and schools, which remain firmly in the hands of those who deplore mass culture. It is in drugstores and super-markets and airline terminals that this kind of literature mingles without condescension with chocolate bars and soapflakes. We have reached the end of a long process, begun, let us say, with Samuel Richardson, in which the work of art has approached closer and closer to the status of a commodity. Even the comic book is a last descendant of *Pamela,* the final consequence of letting the tastes (or more precisely, the buying power) of

a class unpledged to maintaining the traditional genres determine literary
success or failure.

Those who cry out now that the work of a Mickey Spillane or *The
Adventures of Superman* travesty the novel, forget that the novel was long
accused of travestying literature. What seems to offend us most is not the
further downgrading of literary standards so much as the fact that the
medium, the very notion and shape of a book, is being parodied by the
comics. Jazz or the movies, which are also popular urban arts, depending
for their distribution and acceptance on developments in technology (for
jazz, the phonograph), really upset us much less.

It is the final, though camouflaged, rejection of literacy implicit in these
new forms which is the most legitimate source of distress; but all arts so
universally consumed have been for illiterates, even stained glass windows
and the plays of Shakespeare. What is new in our present situation, and
hence especially upsetting, is that this is the first art for *post*literates, i.e.,
for those who have refused the benefit for which they were presumed to
have sighed in their long exclusion. Besides, modern popular narrative is
disconcertingly not oral; it will not surrender the benefits of the printing press
as a machine, however indifferent it may be to that press as the perpetuator
of techniques devised first for pen or quill. Everything that the press can
provide—except matter to be really read—is demanded: picture, typog-
raphy, even in many cases the illusion of reading along with the relaxed
pleasure of illiteracy. Yet the new popular forms remain somehow prose
narrative or pictographic substitutes for the novel; even the cognate form
of the movies is notoriously more like a novel than a play in its handling of
time, space and narrative progression.

From the folk literature of the past, which ever since the triumph of the
machine we have been trying sentimentally to recapture, popular literature
differs in its rejection of the picturesque. Rooted in prose rather than verse,
secular rather than religious in origin, defining itself against the city rather
than the world of outdoor nature, a by-product of the factory rather than
agriculture, present-day popular literature defeats romantic expectations of
peasants in their embroidered blouses chanting or plucking balalaikas for
the approval of their betters. The haters of our own popular art love to
condescend to the folk; and on records or in fashionable night clubs in recent
years, we have had entertainers who have earned enviable livings producing
commercial imitations of folk songs. But contemporary vulgar culture is
brutal and disturbing: the quasi-spontaneous expression of the uprooted
and culturally dispossessed inhabitants of anonymous cities, contriving my-
thologies which reduce to manageable form the threat of science, the horror
of unlimited war, the general spread of corruption in a world where the
social bases of old loyalties and heroisms have long been destroyed. That
such an art is exploited for profit in a commercial society, mass produced
by nameless collaborators, standardized and debased, is of secondary im-

portance. It is the patented nightmare of us all, a packaged way of coming to terms with one's environment sold for a dime to all those who have rejected the unasked-for gift of literacy.

Thought of in this light, the comic books with their legends of the eternally threatened metropolis eternally protected by immaculate and modest heroes (who shrink back after each exploit into the image of the crippled newsboy, the impotent and cowardly reporter) are seen as inheritors, for all their superficial differences, of the *inner* impulses of traditional folk art. Their gross drawing, their poverty of language cannot disguise their heritage of aboriginal violence, their exploitation of the ancient conflict of black magic and white. Beneath their journalistic commentary on A-bomb and Communism, they touch archetypal material: those shared figures of our lower minds more like the patterns of dream than fact. In a world where men threaten to dissolve into their most superficial and mechanical techniques, to become their borrowed newspaper platitudes, they remain close to the impulsive, subliminal life. They are our not quite machine-subdued Grimm, though the Black Forest has become, as it must, the City; the Wizard, the Scientist; and Simple Hans, Captain Marvel. In a society which thinks of itself as "scientific"—and of the Marvelous as childish—such a literature must seem primarily children's literature, though, of course, it is read by people of all ages.

We are now in a position to begin to answer the question: what do the righteous really have against comic books? In some parts of the world, simply the fact that they are American is sufficient, and certain homegrown self-contemners follow this line even in the United States. But it is really a minor argument, lent a certain temporary importance by passing political exigencies. To declare oneself against "the Americanization of culture" is meaningless unless one is set resolutely against industrialization and mass education.

More to the point is the attack on mass culture for its betrayal of literacy itself. In a very few cases, this charge is made seriously and with full realization of its import; but most often it amounts to nothing but an accusation of "bad grammar" or "slang" on the part of some school marm to whom the spread of "different than" seems to threaten the future of civilized discourse. What should set us on guard in this case is that it is not the fully literate, the intellectuals and serious writers, who lead the attack, but the insecure semiliterate. In America, there is something a little absurd about the indignant delegation from the Parent Teachers Association (themselves clutching the latest issue of *Life*) crying out in defense of literature. Asked for suggestions, such critics are likely to propose the *Readers' Digest* as required reading in high school—or to urge more comic-book versions of the "classics": emasculated Melville, expurgated Hawthorne, or a child's version of something "uplifting" like "The Fall of the House of Usher." In other countries, corresponding counterparts are not hard to find.

As a matter of fact, this charge is scarcely ever urged with much conviction. It is really the portrayal of crime and horror (and less usually sex) that the enlightened censors deplore. It has been charged against vulgar art that it is sadistic, fetishistic, brutal, full of terror; that it pictures women with exaggeratedly full breasts and rumps, portrays death on the printed page, is often covertly homosexual, etc., etc. About these charges, there are two obvious things to say. First, by and large, they are true. Second, they are also true about much of the most serious art of our time, especially that produced in America.

There is no count of sadism and brutality which could not be equally proved against Hemingway or Faulkner or Paul Bowles—or, for that matter, Edgar Allan Poe. There are certain more literate critics who are victims of their own confusion in this regard, and who will condemn a Class B movie for its images of flagellation or bloodshed only to praise in the next breath such an orgy of highminded sadism as *Le Salaire de la Peur*. The politics of the French picture may be preferable, or its photography; but this cannot redeem the scene in which a mud- and oil-soaked truckdriver crawls from a pit of sludge to reveal the protruding white bones of a multiple fracture of the thigh. This is as much horror-pornography as *Scarface* or *Little Caesar*. You cannot condemn *Superman* for the exploitation of violence, and praise the existentialist-homosexual-sadist shockers of Paul Bowles. It is possible to murmur by way of explanation something vague about art or catharsis; but no one is ready to advocate the suppression of anything merely because it is aesthetically bad. In this age of conflicting standards, we would all soon suppress each other.

An occasional Savonarola is, of course, ready to make the total rejection; and secretly or openly, the run-of-the-mill condemner of mass culture does condemn, on precisely the same grounds, most contemporary literature of distinction. Historically, one can make quite a convincing case to prove that our highest and lowest arts come from a common antibourgeois source. Edgar Allan Poe, who lived the image of the dandy that has been haunting high art ever since, also, one remembers, invented the popular detective story; and there is a direct line from Hemingway to O'Hara to Dashiell Hammett to Raymond Chandler to Mickey Spillane.

Of both lines of descent from Poe, one can say that they tell a black and distressing truth (we are creatures of dark impulse in a threatened and guilty world), and that they challenge the more genteel versions of "good taste." Behind the opposition to vulgar literature, there is at work the same fear of the archetypal and the unconscious itself that motivated similar attacks on Elizabethan drama and on the eighteenth-century novel. We always judge Gosson a fool in terms of Shakespeare; but this is not the point—he was just as wrong in his attack on the worst-written, the most outrageously bloody and bawdy plays of his time. I should hate my argument to be understood as a defense of what is banal and mechanical and dull (there is, of course, a great deal!) in mass culture; it is merely a counterattack against those who are aiming through that banality and dullness at what moves all literature of worth. Anyone at all sensitive to the life of the imagination would surely prefer his kids to read the coarsest fables of Black and White contending for the City of Man, rather than have them spell out, "Oh, see, Jane. Funny, funny Jane," or read to themselves hygienic accounts of the operation of supermarkets or manureless farms. Yet most schoolboard members are on the side of mental hygiene; and it is they who lead the charge against mass culture.

Anyone old enough to have seen, say, *Rain* is on guard against those who in the guise of wanting to destroy savagery and ignorance wage war on spontaneity and richness. But we are likely to think of such possibilities purely in sexual terms; the new righteous themselves have been touched lightly by Freud and are firm believers in frankness and "sex education." But in the very midst of their self-congratulation at their emancipation, they have become victims of a new and ferocious prudery. One who would be ashamed to lecture his masturbating son on the dangers of insanity, is quite prepared (especially if he has been reading Wertham) to predict the electric chair for the young scoundrel caught with a bootlegged comic. Superman is our Sadie Thompson. We live in an age when the child who is exposed to the "facts of life" is protected from "the facts of death." In the United States, for instance, a certain Doctor Spock has produced an enlightened guide to childcare for modern mothers—a paperback book which sold, I would guess, millions of copies. Tell the child all about sex, the good doctor advises, but on the subject of death—hush!

By more "advanced" consultants, the taboo is advanced further toward absurdity: no bloodsoaked Grimm, no terrifying Andersen, no childhood verses about cradles that fall—for fear breeds insecurity; insecurity, aggression; aggression, war. There is even a "happy," that is to say, expurgated, Mother Goose in which the three blind mice have become "kind mice"— and the farmer's wife no longer hacks off their tails, but "cuts them some cheese with a carving knife." Everywhere the fear of fear is endemic, the fear of the very names of fear; those who have most ardently desired to end warfare and personal cruelty in the world around them, and are therefore most frustrated by their persistence, conspire to stamp out violence on the nursery bookshelf. This much they can do anyhow. If they can't hold up the weather, at least they can break the bloody glass.

This same fear of the instinctual and the dark, this denial of death and guilt by the enlightened genteel, motivates their distrust of serious literature, too. Faulkner is snubbed and the comic books are banned, not in the interests of the classics or even of Robert Louis Stevenson, as the attackers claim, but in the name of a literature of the middle ground which finds its fictitious vision of a kindly and congenial world attacked from above and below. I speak now not of the few intellectual converts to the cause of censorship, but of the main body of genteel book-banners, whose idol is Lloyd Douglas or even A. J. Cronin. When a critic such as Mr. Wagner is led to applaud what he sees as a "trend" toward making doctors, lawyers, etc., the heroes of certain magazine stories, he has fallen into the trap of regarding middling fiction as a transmission belt from the vulgar to the high. There is no question, however, of a slow climb from the level of literature which celebrates newspaper reporters, newsboys, radio commentators (who are also superheroes in tight-fitting uniforms with insignia), through one which centers around prosperous professionals, to the heights of serious literature, whose protagonists are suicides full of incestuous longings, lady lushes with clipped hair, bootleggers, gangsters, and broken-down pugs. To try to state the progression is to reveal its absurdity.

The conception of such a "trend" is nothing more than the standard attitude of a standard kind of literature, the literature of slick-paper ladies' magazines, which prefers the stereotype to the archetype, loves poetic justice, sentimentality, and gentility, and is peopled by characters who bathe frequently, live in the suburbs, and are professionals. Such literature circles mindlessly inside the trap of its two themes: unconsummated adultery and the consummated pure romance. There can be little doubt about which kind of persons and which sort of fables best typify our plight, which tell the truth—or better, a truth—in the language of those to whom they speak.

In the last phrase, there is a rub. The notion that there is more than one language of art, or rather, that there is something not quite art, which performs art's function for most men in our society, is disquieting enough for anyone, and completely unacceptable to the sentimental egalitarian, who had dreamed of universal literacy leading directly to a universal culture. It is here that we begin to see that there is a politics as well as a pathology involved in the bourgeois hostility to popular culture. I do not refer only to the explicit political ideas embodied in the comics or in the literature of the cultural élite; but certainly each of these arts has a characteristic attitude: populist-authoritarian on the one hand and aristocratic-authoritarian on the other.

It is notorious how few of the eminent novelists or poets of our time have shared the political ideals we would agree are the most noble available to us. The flirtations of Yeats and Lawrence with fascism, Pound's weird amalgam of Confucianism, Jeffersonianism, and social credit, the modified Dixiecrat principles of Faulkner—all make the point with terrible reiteration. Between the best art and poetry of our age and the critical liberal reader there can be no bond of shared belief; at best we have the ironic confrontation of the sceptical mind and the believing imagination. It is this division which has, I suppose, led us to define more and more narrowly the "aesthetic experience," to attempt to isolate a quality of seeing and saying that has a moral value quite independent of *what* is seen or heard.

> *Time that with this strange excuse*
> *Pardoned Kipling and his views,*
> *And will pardon Paul Claudel,*
> *Pardons him for writing well.*

But the genteel middling mind which turns to art for entertainment and uplift, finds this point of view reprehensible; and cries out in rage against those who give Ezra Pound a prize and who claim that "to permit other considerations than that of poetic achievement to sway the decision would . . . deny the validity of that objective perception of value on which any civilized society must rest." We live in the midst of a strange two-front class war: the readers of the slicks battling the subscribers to the "little reviews" and the consumers of pulps; the sentimental-egalitarian conscience against the ironical-aristocratic sensibility on the one hand and the brutal-populist mentality on the other. The joke, of course, is that it is the "democratic" center which calls here and now for suppression of its rivals; while the élite advocate a condescending tolerance, and the vulgar ask only to be let alone.

It is disconcerting to find cultural repression flourishing at the point where middling culture meets a kindly, if not vigorously thought-out, liberalism. The sort of right-thinking citizen who subsidizes trips to America for Japanese girls scarred by the Hiroshima bombing, and deplores McCarthy in the public press, also deplores, and would censor, the comics. In one sense, this is fair enough; for beneath the veneer of slogans that "crime docsn't pay" and the superficial praise of law and order, the comics do reflect that dark populist faith which Senator McCarthy has exploited. There is a kind of "black socialism" of the American masses which underlies formal allegiances to one party or another: the sense that there is always a conspiracy at the centers of political and financial power; the notion that the official defenders of the commonwealth are "bought" more often than not; an impatience with moral scruples and a distrust of intelligence, especially in the expert and scientist; a willingness to identify the enemy, the dark projection of everything most feared in the self, on to some journalistically defined political opponent of the moment.

This is not quite the "fascism" it is sometimes called. There is, for instance, no European anti-Semitism involved, despite the conventional hooked nose of the scientist-villain. (The inventors and chief producers of comic books have been, as it happens, Jews.) There is also no adulation of a dictator-figure on the model of Hitler or Stalin; though one of the archetypes of the Deliverer in the comics is called Superman, he is quite unlike the Nietzschean figure—it is the image of Cincinnatus which persists in him, an archetype that has possessed the American imagination since the time of Washington: the leader who enlists for the duration and retires unrewarded to obscurity.

It would be absurd to ask the consumer of such art to admire in the place of images that project his own impotence and longing for civil peace some hero of middling culture—say, the good boy of Arthur Miller's *Death of a Salesman,* who, because he has studied hard in school, has become a lawyer who argues cases before the Supreme Court and has friends who own their own tennis courts. As absurd as to ask the general populace to worship

Stephen Dedalus or Captain Ahab! But the high-minded petty-bourgeois
cannot understand or forgive the rejection of his own dream, which he
considers as nothing less than the final dream of humanity. The very existence of a kind of art depending on allegiances and values other than his
challenges an article of his political faith; and when such an art is "popular,"
that is, more read, more liked, more bought than his own, he feels his *raison
d'être,* his basic life-defense, imperilled. The failure of the petty-bour-
geoisie to achieve cultural hegemony threatens their dream of a truly classless
society; for they believe, with some justification, that such a society can
afford only a single culture. And they see, in the persistence of a high art
and a low art on either side of their average own, symptoms of the re-emer-
gence of classes in a quarter where no one had troubled to stand guard.

The problem posed by popular culture is finally, then, a problem of class
distinction in a democratic society. What is at stake is the refusal of cultural
equality by a large part of the population. It is misleading to think of popular culture as the product of a conspiracy of profiteers against the rest of
us. This venerable notion of an eternally oppressed and deprived but innocent people is precisely what the rise of mass culture challenges. Much of
what upper-class egalitarians dreamed for him, the ordinary man does not
want—especially literacy. The situation is bewildering and complex, for
the people have not rejected completely the notion of cultural equality;
rather, they desire its symbol but not its fact. At the very moment when
half of the population of the United States reads no *hard-covered* book in
a year, more than half of all high-school graduates are entering universities
and colleges; in twenty-five years almost all Americans will at least begin a
higher education. It is clear that what is demanded is a B.A. for everyone,
with the stipulation that no one be forced to read to get it. And this the
colleges, with "objective tests" and "audio-visual aids," are doing their
reluctant best to satisfy.

One of the more exasperating aspects of the cultural defeat of the egalitarians is that it followed a seeming victory. For a while (in the Anglo-Saxon
world at least) it appeared as if the spread of literacy, the rise of the bourgeoisie, and the emergence of the novel as a reigning form would succeed
in destroying both traditional folk art and an aristocratic literature still
pledged to epic, ode, and verse tragedy. But the novel itself (in the hands
of Lawrence, Proust, Kafka, etc.) soon passed beyond the comprehension
of those for whom it was originally contrived; and the retrograde derivations
from it—various steps in a retreat toward wordless narrative: digests, pulp
fiction, movies, picture magazines—revealed that middling literature was
not in fact the legitimate heir of either folk art or high art, much less the
successor of both, but a *tertium quid* of uncertain status and value.

The middlebrow reacts with equal fury to an art that baffles his understanding and to one which refuses to aspire to his level. The first reminds
him that he has not yet, after all *arrived* (and, indeed, may never make it);

the second suggests to him a condition to which he might easily relapse, one perhaps that might have made him happier with less effort (and here exacerbated puritanism is joined to baffled egalitarianism), even suggests what his state may appear like to those a notch above. Since he cannot, on his own terms, explain to himself why anyone should choose any level but the highest (that is, his own), the failure of the vulgar seems to him the product of mere ignorance and laziness—a crime! And the rejection by the advanced artist of his canons strikes him as a finicking excess, a pointless and unforgivable snobbism. Both, that is, suggest the intolerable notion of a hierarchy of taste, a hierarchy of values, the possibility of cultural classes in a democratic state; and before this, puzzled and enraged, he can only call a cop. The fear of the vulgar is the obverse of the fear of excellence, and both are aspects of the fear of difference: symptoms of a drive for conformity on the level of the timid, sentimental, mindless-bodiless genteel.

Popular Culture and the Open Society

By MELVIN TUMIN

AMERICAN INTELLECTUALS seem to be almost evenly divided today into two warring camps. The main issue at contention is the proper evaluation of the condition of life and culture in the United States.

On the one side stand those who find themselves disconcerted, especially if they have had any Marxist background, by the fact that no people has ever been so free from material want, at the same time that, in the judgment of this group, the wealth is being spent in ways which are aesthetically and morally revolting. The responsibility for this phenomenon is attributed to some aspect of the mass-ness of the society and some dimension of the popular-ness of the culture.

On the other side are arrayed those who find it possible to approve the major trends and patterns visible in the country today. If they are disconcerted by some of the excrescences of bad taste and unwise self-indulgence they see around them, they are nevertheless more than heartened by such things as the number of symphony orchestras, and the sales of books and classical records. If sometimes they are guilty of being enthusiastic about the relative decline in attendance at baseball games (how this could mean anything special either way is hard to tell) this is probably unimportant in the total picture. In any event, a thing like this all depends on how devoted one is to the Brooklyn Dodgers.

From the point of view of the sociology of ideas, it is interesting to note how little difference in social origin and background one can find between the members of these two ideological camps. This is an impression more than a statement based on evidence, but it is probably true that there is an equal spread in both groups of a background of poverty, growing up in the depression, European ethnic origins, and involvement in radical politics in the thirties. Even more important, neither group seems to be less well placed in the positions they occupy today. They appear to be equal in the number of important posts they hold at major universities; they seem to be on as many editorial staffs of little and big magazines; they both can and do get Foundation support for their projects; they have as many public platforms from which to deliver their salvos. Both sides are doing comparably well. And relative to what they both expected to be able to do, at a time when it was fashionable and right to be romantically despondent about the future, today's condition of life is beyond the limits of their former imaginings.

In brief, nothing by way of the ordinary sociological variables will help account for their differences—and this is just as it should be in the world of ideas.

Published for the first time in this volume.

There are differences, to be sure, in the popular receptivity for their contrasting points of view. As is only to be expected, those who approve of the condition of life in God's country today are listened to and read with greater frequency and interest. But then, this welcome for an affirmative point of view is exactly what happens everywhere, everytime—except under conditions of great social stress. After all, one could hardly expect anyone to give warm and cordial reception to a scathing denunciation of his morals and tastes.

It is sometimes charged that the motives behind the endorsements of our culture are somewhat less than noble, and consist primarily of a desire for the public eye and ear. But it is probably just as true, in just as many cases, that the motives behind constant attacks against popular culture and mass society arise from a desire to be unpopular—and this desire is fully gratified. Sometimes the imputation of motives serves a vital purpose in the analysis of ideas. At this point it doesn't seem to do anybody any good at all.

Nor is it of any value at all to declare that there is a mixture of truth and error in both points of view. For this is a true statement about almost any pair of contrasting points of view. We take it for granted.

In brief, it will do no good to deny our perplexities, nor hide them, under the guise of either a total denunciation or total approval of American life today. The simple fact is that today's material conditions of life are fantastically better than we ever thought possible; and the quality of our culture, no matter what fine and splendid events and trends are discernible, leaves far more to be desired on its continuum of possibilities than does the economic situation of the average man.

To put it another way: there would be much less cause for concern if levels of taste, thought and morals had come as far from what they were in 1933 as the average income has moved from what it was at the same time. One *could* argue that we had a surfeit of "high culture" relative to the level of income in 1933; and that income has simply been making up for its previous deficiencies. But why should anyone want to argue such a patently false point of view?

Nor, if we are to avoid the trap of "vulgar Marxism," ought we to evince surprise at the disparity between levels of income and culture. Surely we may insist that poverty makes everything harder, without being obliged also to defend the proposition that prosperity makes everything possible. One *can* buy more books and records if he has more money, if he is interested in books and records in the first place. But it is obvious that there are hordes who have money and don't buy books and records; and equally large numbers of poorer people who do. That is, assuming that buying books and records matters.

The question of whether our high prosperity is built on a solid foundation or is simply another of the temporary ups in the cycle of depression and prosperity is a crucial matter, but not crucially relevant here. Our productivity *may* be importantly dependent on the continuing demand from military needs. But these same military demands may continue indefinitely. Or, as some have argued, there is enough resilience and growth potential in our economy, so that nonmilitary sources of demand can move in fluidly and quickly to fill the gaps in our economic structure which the cessation or diminution of the "cold war" may occasion. The burden of proof is upon those who insist on this possibility. But again that is another matter.

Whichever way we turn or squirm, the fact keeps confronting us that America and Americans have available to them the resources, both of mind and matter, to build and support the finest culture the world has ever known; that up until now many of these resources have been spent in foolish and sometimes ugly ways; that the resources nevertheless keep growing, and the chance remains. How can we take advantage of this opportunity?

Can such a society, under the most favorable material conditions ever experienced, rise to the occasion and prove itself worthy? Can it provide for the continuous free play of opposing systems of values and tastes, within the framework of democratic forms? Can it make room for an expansion of those spiritual, creative impulses in man which meaner conditions of life do not allow to come to the surface? Can it find place in its halls of fame for men of letters and arts and science and ideas, as well as those of commerce and power and arms?

In an equally important sense the same kind of test is set for the intellectuals in America today. For never before have they been so well placed in situations where they can function as intellectuals, as men of ideas, and still profit, along with everyone else, from the ample character of the economy. This is not to say that the chance to seize the popular imagination is equally available to all. Not by any means. But in no society, short of Utopia, is that ever likely to be the case. And in any event, is the capture of the popular mind a reasonable goal for the intellectual? Certainly something far more modest and meaningful is likely to be a truer test of his worth.

The conditions of test are easy enough to specify. It is far more difficult to define a measure of outcome. What shall we say will mark the success or failure of the society—and of its intellectuals? Perhaps nothing more specific can be stated than the following, but at least this much is essential: namely, the preservation of an open society, the maintenance of genuinely free inquiry and of fair competition between opposing value systems and standards of taste. So long as these remain operative, the society manages to sustain a democratic condition of life which uniquely distinguishes it from all other such systems and which commends it on those terms to its most sharp and sympathetic critics—regardless of its "mass-ness" or its popular culture.

If I have seemed to overestimate and overstate the praiseworthiness of the present social conditions, it is out of enthusiasm for the possibilities which seem inherent in the situation and not out of mucky sentimentality about the glorious achievements heretofore. Yet one would be most derelict in his obligations as social analyst if he failed to note that the chance for ideas and the men who promulgate them to play significant roles in society is probably greater today than it has ever been before.

But now the cautions and precautions. For no situation is without its mixture of curse and blessing. And the new prominence which men from all segments of American society have recently come to enjoy carries with it enough of its own power for self-destruction to cause considerable anxiety regarding the maintenance and expansion of the open society.

With these in mind, I wish now to state some of the tendencies and patterns, associated closely with the mobility of the last two generations, which seem to me to spell serious danger if allowed to develop. It will be difficult to avoid phrases and formulations which, when taken out of the context of the preceding discussion, will seem like wholesale and unreflective damnations. It must also be remembered that what is about to be said refers as often to emerging tendencies as to well developed practices, and as frequently to dangers likely to be encountered as to difficulties already faced.

1. THE NEW "POPULAR FRONT"

Certainly at the head of any list of requirements and conditions for maintenance of an open society is the prominence and persistence of a body of persons who remain skeptical, critical, querulous and deeply hesitant about popular imagination and taste. There is nothing inherently wrong or right about popular taste. But when the major standard used by the taste-makers is to create that which will sell, there is every good reason to be initially suspicious of what is being bought. This is all the truer, of course, when consumers have had little chance in the past to indulge their tastes, much less to develop them reflectively and critically, and when, therefore, they look anxiously at the style leaders and pacesetters of the community to see what they are doing and buying. Much depends at this point on who are the leaders in the community, who are those who carry the most prestige. And when, as in our society today, it is frequently the case that wealth above all brings prestige, it is hardly likely that one can confidently expect the prevailing styles to reflect critical, reflective judgment based on sound experience with what is available in the world of possible appreciations.

Some have argued that the only effective way to help improve popular taste is to get inside the mass media of communication, surrendering some standards temporarily, and some others permanently, on the grounds that they are inconsequential, and then slowly to help elevate the taste by elevating the products offered for consumption at every opportunity which presents itself. This is an appealing argument. One goes to the people where they are and works with them. One doesn't sit up on top and contemptuously and condescendingly sneer and hope to have any effect. But what, in fact, does the record show? One has to declare his standards here. It seems to me that the overwhelming evidence favors the judgment that those who have pursued this course have themselves been captured, lock, stock and barrel, by the very agencies and temptations which they said they were going to subvert and alter.

Surely, in any institution or agency, compromises of various kinds are required for sheer survival. One measures his tasks and his values, so that, for instance, if being able to continue to teach at a university means that one has to be clean-shaven instead of sporting a beard, the choice is clear. Only a fanatical notion of what constitutes a "principle" could support the importance of keeping a beard. Surely this process of choice among values has its inherent dangers, as does any system of competing values among which one has to choose. No formula will give a standard answer which defines the point at which one must refuse to compromise further. That all depends on how much of what the chooser wants.

The safeguard against being "taken," as everyone knows, is to prefer standards to "success." Each man has, after all, only two major sets of standards that he must observe: those he will keep with regard to his work, and those he will follow with regard to his relations with other people. Neither of these can he afford to compromise in any substantial way whatsoever and still retain hope that he won't get taken by the system. The issues are, of course, far come complex than this simple version suggests. But these are their essential outlines.

These remarks are relevant to the contention that many, if not most, of those who thought they could capture the institutions were instead captured by them. The evidence seems clear: they have made major compromises in their standards of work and their standards of human relations. And they have achieved success—by the standards of other people, and not by their own. They clearly deserve it.

Nor are such people to be counted on very heavily for the future. Reconversions are always possible after an initial conversion; and there are some doctrinal guides about the worthiness of reclaimed sinners. But this is earthly grace we are talking about, and not some eschatological realm of events. Skepticism lost is not readily regained.

2. THE CULT OF GRATITUDE

A second way in which men get taken by a system, instead of being able to play an independent critical role within it, is to start feeling grateful to the system for the opportunities presented. There seems to have developed among a large number of intellectuals a cult of gratitude based on a romantic yearning for failure in their youth, an incredulity that anything good could happen to them personally or to others in general, and a staggering awareness that today they are on or near the top of the heap. Surely gratitude is a reasonable feeling at selected spots in human relationships. One is grateful for genuine favors and help. But what is the sense of gratitude to a system? And even worse, what is the sense of gratitude to the élite representatives of a system?

It stands to reason that worthy people rarely get more than they deserve, even though unworthy people often get an embarrassing amount more. To be glad that one has had the good fortune to have his talents recognized and to be able to capitalize on them in terms of the rewards available in this life—that is one thing. To be grateful to the system in which this occurs is simply a form of ancestor worship. If from time to time one is privately amused and perhaps slightly bewildered by his good fortune, it is urgent, once one has asked himself, "What am I doing here?," immediately to respond with, "Who better?"

Among intellectuals newly risen to fame and fortune, the cult of gratitude destroys critical powers, and makes men captives of the very system of opportunity which their criticisms previously helped make possible.

All intellectuals aside, one notices the growing prevalence of the attitude of gratitude among other sectors of the population also newly risen to high socio-economic status. In evincing this feeling they deny their own history: a history of hard work, of suffering, of indignities, of sweat and toil. In denying this history, they deny the value of the very things which they, in their own ways, contributed toward making this newer success possible. In so doing, they limit and restrict the range of possibilities for continuing openness in society.

More than that, they deny *themselves* and their own dignity. For they have merited their new-found leisure and luxury as much as anyone in the history of man. They may take pride in their present achievements only in terms of their history of struggle. To deny that history, to attempt to hide it, is to deny and hide their manhood. For surely to base their feelings of worthiness on the fact of possession of equal amounts of capital goods is to rest their evaluations on the flimsiest of all possible bases. Genuine security lies in a sense of one's worthiness that exists regardless of his condition in life. One can come by this sense only by respecting his own character and not his worldly fate.

3. THE CULT OF OPPORTUNITY UNLIMITED

A genuine danger has shown itself in recent years in the attitudes of students born during or after the Depression—in any event, among those who did not experience the Depression as an important fact in their fates. One may call it the development of a cult of Opportunity Unlimited. By that I refer to the view of life which entertains only horizons of success; the possibility of failure is nowhere built into the perspective; there is no felt need to be reserved about life and its possibilities.

Almost unavoidably this attitude becomes intimately linked with an uncritical acceptance of the society and its institutions. There is a corollary disdain for sociological analysis of society, or psychological analysis of self. The patent result of this is sheer lack of understanding of the nature of society and of self. Minor downturns or defeats tend, under these circumstances, to be interpreted as major depressions and failures. Simple, healthy and unavoidable argument and conflict in personal relations get quickly judged as fundamental incompatibilities—because there is no room for argument, conflict, hostility and ambivalence in the cult of Opportunity Unlimited.

Within the same framework, critics of the social system are viewed with a sense of great danger, and personal criticism is taken as a deep affront. For in the world of Opportunity Unlimited one must be universally loved, or not loved at all.

Nor are human powers and strengths easily and finely cultivated in this way of life. There are no inbuilt resources with which to deal with adversity, since adversity is not contemplated as really possible. There is no reserve energy system set up to meet expected obstacles, since none such are expected. Cleverness is celebrated far above intellect, and manners far above morals. I suspect, but cannot now prove, that there is a close tie between this outlook and that which holds that there is such a thing as a "good administrator" who can function well as an "organizational man" without any knowledge regarding the organizational goals, purposes and specific content. For here, too clearly, "technique in manipulation" is valued as the supreme requirement.

4. THE CULT OF HAPPINESS

A society is in real trouble with itself when its people get unthinking and unfeeling enough to consider "happiness" as the prime goal in life. One can easily show that some amount of misery and misfortune is probably a necessary condition for cultural growth. But it isn't necessary to show that, to be able to prove quickly that happiness only means trouble. The fact is simple: happiness is no guide to anything. No roads are indicated; no standards suggested; no thought or creativity demanded. Just peace and quiet. That may be fine for a vacation. But not for life.

Nor are the pseudo-thoughtful substitutes any better. The problem is not avoided by talking about happiness under the disguise of peace of mind, soul, spirit, outlook or freedom from anxiety. Nor will appeals to the greater naturalness of love and altruism, or to the natural superiority of women, come to grips with the problem. If men don't think, worry, wonder and keep themselves in some continuous state of internal uproar, they simply will go nowhere and do nothing.

It is not too much of an exaggeration to say that the mass media seem to be singlemindedly devoted to the double task of keeping the American public in continuous jitters about their social standing, and at the same time providing them with every form of psychological anaesthesia and tranquilization available—not excluding frontal lobotomies for the more severe cases.

Happy endings; cheap rehashes of childhood traumas once suffered, but now wiped away by the soothing hand of modern magic and witchcraft; fantasies galore for minds too tired to contrive their own; sexual rating charts to reassure all of us middle-class impotents; bathos; maudlin sentiment: whatever dirty word comes to mind is applicable to the cult of happiness springing up all over the place.

In more sophisticated quarters one hears about the necessity of adjustment; one is warned not to be intolerant of other ideas and values in front of his children, lest they acquire one's own standards and thus fail to "make an adequate adjustment." It is never quite clear whose standards besides one's own it is preferable for the child to acquire, just so long as the parent doesn't impose his own and make his children misfits. Somehow the common denominator of the trash of peer-groups, anxiety-ridden neighbors, and rigid schoolteachers will be better for the child.

In still more sophisticated quarters, loving the child to death is believed to be the best way to bring him to life. A new biologism has emerged in this school. The child is innately good. And so long as he knows that his parents love him, he will come out ripe and rosy as a freestone peach.

On the adult level—or, one should say, for the adult audience—the mass media treat all problems as though they were soluble by fresh applications of shampoo, extra long filter tips and one magic genie per capita.

Real creativity is viewed with suspicion and distrust because it means, above all, difference, intolerance, an insistence on achieving an individual identity.

Real feeling is viewed with equal distrust and hostility because it almost always means bad manners, spontaneity, unpredictability, lack of realism, failure to observe routines. Above all, there is the question of form. One can't play it cool if he insists on the validity of his feelings. To play it hot is bad form. Bad form is worse than halitosis. Well-rounded, adjusted, happy—these are the things we are told it is important for us to be. No points, no sharp cutting edges, no despairs and elations. Just nice, smooth billiard balls, rolling quietly on soft green cloth to our appointed, webbed pockets, and dropping slowly into the slots under the table, to be used in the same meaningless way in the next game. Chalk one up for mediocrity. For it is the only winner in this game.

The most sophisticated "con" game of this type which is being played today is the way in which the importance of men doing meaningful work is being denied. Muzak and "cow sociology"—these aren't quite up to the job any more. The newest version is the game of hobbies. Let men make up in their newly expanded leisure time for the shortcomings of their relations to work. Somehow a home carpentry kit or a set of golf clubs will compensate for the daily, eight-hour denial of life and self at the job.

But this can be true only if the job is not the place at which the man spends his best hours and energy, from which he gets his primary resources, and in terms of which he is placed in the hierarchy of social rating—not only for purposes of club membership but for a more crucial evaluation of his worth to his society. And these are precisely the major components of a man's occupation in modern American society.

If ever a major break-through in thought was needed, it is precisely here, in the area of problems concerned with how to make the work life of the average man a more meaningful experience,

This, and equally crucial problems, can be avoided by focusing on the values of adjustment and happiness. We are truly betrayed, and we surely lose the major value of our new-found prosperity, if we continue to buy the doctrines now being peddled in every bazaar on the street.

5. THE CULT OF THE CLASSLESS SOCIETY

In spite of all the articles and books produced in the last ten years testifying to the significance of "class" in virtually every aspect of modern society, it has recently become fashionable to decry the application of this term to our social structure, and to substitute such nicer-sounding words as *interest groups, pressure groups,* and other comparable euphemisms. Whatever merit these terms may have as descriptions of the groups to which men refer themselves for comparative purposes, or inside of which they seek membership, they lack the essential capacity to account for the lines along which the opportunity for goods and services are distributed in our society. Income, education and occupation: these are the major hierarchies, and these are the major cross-cuts in our social organization. These are the principal determinants of inequality.

To value the extent to which almost all Americans have come to achieve more of the good things in life is one thing. To say that we are no longer a class-structured society *because* everyone has achieved more is quite another thing—and simply untrue.

Interest groups, reference groups, and associations—these are valuable concepts when we try to understand how men will congregate, and how many separate forces any maker of policy must take into account. But when the problem is to figure out how the resources of the society may be more evenly distributed, what are the major obstacles to further growth of the economy, and in what ways life chances are set, then the major criteria of class position become the proper focus of attention.

The difference is substantial. The manipulation of public opinion is one kind of concern. But the alteration of the structure of society is something quite different. We cannot afford to gloss over our class lines and deny their significance if we are genuinely interested in the maintenance of an open and prosperous society.

These five are the leading contenders for the title of "present and imminent danger" to as much of the open society as we have achieved. The new "popular front" deprives the system of its most talented critics. The cult of gratitude deprives men of their dignity and the fruits of history and weakens their sense of the need for struggle. The cult of Opportunity Unlimited systematically misfits men for the expected ups and downs of life, and deceives them into surrendering both caution and daring. The cult of happiness guarantees the triumph of mediocrity. And, finally, the cult of the classless society gives us a cockeyed view of society just when we need to be most straightforward and acute in our perceptions.

These are the main dangers. These, then, are the challenges.

The Public Arts

By GILBERT SELDES

"THIS COUNTRY, with its institutions, belongs to the people who inhabit it," said Abraham Lincoln, and as he was then facing the possible dissolution of the United States, he added, "Whenever they [the people] shall grow weary of the existing government, they can exercise their Constitutional right of amending it or their revolutionary right to dismember or overthrow it."

I am suggesting that the cultural institutions of a country also belong to its inhabitants, and, not having the courage of Lincoln's radicalism, I do not insist upon the revolutionary right of the people to destroy whatever wearies them. Moderately I propose the idea that the people have valid rights over those cultural institutions which can be properly called "the public arts." I have previously indicated that the quality of being "public" inheres in various degrees in all the arts, that oratory and drama in ancient Greece were more public than the art of history, just as in folk arts ballads were more public than pottery, and, although the lively arts are most affected with the special public quality, the movies are more public than dancing. I now propose to bring together the identifying characteristics of these public arts, knowing that to some degree the identification is shadowy, that by definition no communicative art can be totally private. I am, on the other hand, convinced that in some instances the degree of difference is so great that you can no longer compare the effect of the public and the non-public art, as if quantity—the mass of material offered or the mass of people accepting it—had resulted in a change in essence, a quality change. Also, in one single respect the public arts differ absolutely from all others. The major marks of identification are these:

The public arts are popular to the extent of being almost universally acceptable. They tend to be more and more professionalized, less and less to be practiced privately.
They are often produced by teams rather than by individuals. They are commissioned, the patron-sponsor-executive providing the pattern.
They are by intention ephemeral, paying well initially, but not increasing in value with the passage of time.

These are, I think, entirely self-evident.

The public arts are offered to the public as a whole, not to any segment of it.

This is, I believe, a new thing in the world, because these arts solicit the favor of the entire public (excepting the highly intellectualized fringe that turns its back on whatever is popular). This was not the case when a mural, commissioned by a ruling family, was exposed in a Renaissance church or when Shakespeare's plays were presented in the presence of "the groundlings."

Physically, the public arts have mass or velocity or both, and they tend to outstrip or displace all the other arts.
They touch large numbers of people simultaneously, and their effect is not limited to those whom they directly touch.
They interconnect and support one another, thus causing a sort of reverberation.
They are, to an extent, habit-forming, and their effect is contagious.

The social reverberation produced when millions of people follow the same entertainment or receive the same communication at one time is something different from the imitation of a royal mistress's hairdo—the diffusion is immeasurably greater, the penetration deeper. The physical reduplication of comic books and phonograph records, the velocity of radio and television, the availability of the motion-picture film, and the way the various entertainments support one another create another kind of contagion: the public mind is crammed with details about them, so that the true significance of "the mass media" becomes, not their appeal to the mass audience, but their own dimensions, the size and weight and speed and force that the mass media possess. Among these physical properties is the simple one of occupying a certain space and thus preventing any other body from occupying that space. As the public arts occupy more and more of the public mind over longer and longer periods, they are an obstacle to the extension of the other arts.

The public arts popularize the classic arts.

These classic arts they diffuse without substantial alteration, as in the broadcast of a symphony, or they adapt with respect for the original (Shakespeare, for instance), or they degrade. Whether this degradation is inevitable is a prime question. Are the public arts an illustration of "nature's tendency to degrade the organized and to destroy the meaningful"? I am not sure. In *The Human Use of Human Beings,* Dr. Norbert Wiener notes that in control and communication we always fight this entropic tendency, and he adds: "While the universe as a whole . . . tends to run down, there are local enclaves . . . in which there is a limited and temporary tendency for organization to increase. Life finds its home in some of these enclaves." I am not sure whether the parallel I observe is more than verbal. It appears to me that the degradation of the highly organized corresponds to the observed tendency of the popular arts to go steadily to lower levels of general intelligence and emotional maturity; and the enclaves would correspond to those experiments which oppose the tendency toward routine and try to bring individuality back to the mass media.

The public arts create, refuse to create, or destroy their own audiences.
They are, in varying degrees, governed by public law.
The unique element: broadcasting uses a portion of the public domain.

These social factors are obviously connected with the physical items previously noted. Granted that there are no *wholly* private arts, we still perceive a difference between a poem printed on a page of a mass-circulation magazine and a song presented a dozen times a day by singers of intense popularity. There is a difference in effect between "D'ye Ken John Peel" and the singing commercial for Pepsi-Cola, which uses the same tune and whose diffusion is now so great that the original song has virtually ceased to exist. We will not understand *I Love Lucy* in the terms of Walter Pater on the Mona Lisa, nor Disney's Davy Crockett if we think he is "merely" a contemporary version of Leatherstocking.

The physical properties of the public arts give to their managers certain social powers, but the managers do not generally accept responsibility for the creation of audiences; they say they satisfy public demand. To abridge a long argument, let us say they cannot pretend, as they do, that they create audiences for Shakespeare and symphonic music but do not create an audience for crime serials. Public demand is diffused and generalized: for diversion, for escape, for excitement, for something like an emotional spree; it is not specific. The makers of entertainment satisfy demand in the ways they find most profitable—just as the processors of food satisfy a demand. It is not the only way, and it may not even be the best way. In turn, the demand must be stimulated and made specific: the public must be made to *want* split-pea soup and panel shows if the makers of these commodities are to prosper. It is, moreover, demonstrable that the producers suppress those demands which they cannot advantageously fulfill— as when programs, even popular ones, are dropped or shifted or supplied to one part of the country and not to another, to correspond to the marketing requirements of the sponsor. This power to create audiences and to manipulate demand is the least understood element in the structure of the entertainment business.

That the public arts are subject to law is well understood, but it is hard to discover a fixed principle in the shifts of opinion about censorship in the movies, prepublication licensing of comic books, and programs for children in television. The unproved but suspected link between horror books and delinquency is always available for headlines, and a quick, hysterical reaction can get laws on the books which it may take years to revoke.

The last characteristic of the public arts—that they use part of the public domain—applies to the broadcasting arts only and is without complexities. The Federal government lends part of the air to a corporation—obviously it can impose conditions. If the conditions are too harsh, the broadcasters will return their franchises, as they have done recently—the requirement that they transmit programs on the UHF channels in order to hold their rights, even though receivers for these frequencies do not exist in their area, is too harsh. On the other hand, if the conditions are too easy (as in the case of broadcasting, taken as a whole), the public may be short-changed until competitors (e.g., backers of pay-TV) offer better service when a station applies for a renewal of license. The only hidden factor in this special case is that the public seems totally unaware of its legal rights—and the broadcasters are not in any hurry to enlighten them.

But the concept of the public arts to which, I am confident, we must eventually come is not drawn from this single characteristic of the entertainment-and-communications enterprises. The base of this new concept is that, by their own nature, these arts are matters of public concern, subject to public opinion; that even *outside of law* the public has sovereign rights over them, since these arts, no less than the institutions of government, belong to the people.

They belong to the people and consequently the people have certain rights and duties in respect to them. I have not put this down as one of the prime characteristics of the public arts because it seems to me highly subjective—and a matter of morality. Because the moment we see that a transformation in the way we live is taking place, the right and the duty to direct that change become self-evident. This is not only an appeal to the self-interest of the intelligent, the mature, and the educated—like the appeal the Federalists made to "the rich and wellborn" to support a strong Federal government when the structure of our country was shaped. There is a self-interest, obviously. But in the end I must fall back on the simple moral ground that no good citizen, no good man or woman, has the right to abandon ship while there remains a reasonable hope of steering it into safe harbor if all hands do their work. If we knew that our whole system of free education was being undermined, or the right of every citizen to vote, would any citizen have the moral right to indifference? Would any citizen have the right to remain silent if he knew that a vast power was—inadvertently or not—attempting to destroy that system?

I do not assert that either of these things is happening. I note that either or both may happen without our knowing it, that people using power, often enough unaware of the consequences of their actions, may preserve the *forms* of our educational or political system and nullify its *effects*.

I suggest that, as the fundamental values of our lives and those of our children will be affected by the revolutionary change in entertainment and communications . . . , we have an obligation to control the speed and direction of this change. Our *right* has been a thousand times established in law and custom. What we lack is the will.

In my own mind, the defect of all attempts so far to influence the mass media has been an almost snobbish dislike for them and an exaggerated fear. We have to recognize a possible danger. We have no right to panic in front of an imaginary one. The next step, after a realistic appraisal of the incalculable social values of the public arts and of the ills—avoidable or not —they bring, is to gather together all those whose livelihood, whose freedom, whose peace of mind are threatened if substantially *all* communications are used for a single purpose. Fortunately, some extremely skillful users of mass communications are in this number: the publishers of the Luce and Cowles magazines have a stake in intelligence only slightly less than that of the publishers of *Harper's* and the *Atlantic;* within the broadcasting business are groups and individuals who are more secure if the level of intelligence in the audience rises slowly and steadily. The makers of nonfiction movies require a high degree of intelligent attention in their audiences, but Walt Disney also needs something above the lowest common denominator. Beyond these groups are the educators, the publishers of fiction and nonfiction and textbooks, the producers of plays and the managers of concert tours, the museums and art galleries and the manufacturers of reproductions of works of art. Also, the scientists and the great corporations who need scientifically trained personnel, our diplomatic service, and, finally, our statesmen. In simplest terms, all these need citizens of good habits of mind and emotional maturity, and already the lack of these—of teachers and of scientists in particular—is proof that you cannot devote the great part of our communications systems to trivialities and be secure in a world as complex and divided as our own.

I do not know what form the pooling of interests will take. The natural turn is toward the rich foundations for research, for organization, and for publicity. They are, in many cases, already under suspicion as being too intellectual and not patriotic enough, but they can still fight for intelligence and for the kind of patriotism that protects the fundamentals of our national life. One aspect of our common genius is our capacity to organize for action when the necessity becomes clear. It is clear now because the moment we see that the public arts are bringing about social change, the right and the duty to direct this change is in our hands. Between those who are not aware of the effect these changes can have on their inalienable rights and those who do not know that they have the right to control the changes, the managers of the public arts have had almost unlimited freedom. They are not entitled to it.

I have suggested that awareness can start with the people themselves, in small units, combining into greater. Parallel to this, I now suggest that the managers of all our cultural institutions enter into an open conspiracy to *use* the public arts in order to protect our heritage of national culture. They can command the attention of the public and can bring the discussion of our basic problems to those very channels which now are used to dissipate our intellectual energies. As long as the means of communication are not available for criticism of themselves, as long as we are prevented from thinking about the process by which we are hypnotized into not thinking, we remain at the mercy of our simplest appetites, our immediate and almost childish sensations, and these can be exploited—for the arts most useful to the public are essentially those which can be most effectively turned against the public good.

To know this, to know that we have the right to put them into our service, is the beginning of an intelligent approach to the problems and to the opportunities of the public arts.